Contexts of T[...]
Methods for Middle and High School Instruction

Jesus Garcia
University of Kentucky

Elizabeth Spalding
University of Kentucky

Richard R. Powell
University of Colorado at Denver

Merrill
Prentice Hall

Upper Saddle River, New Jersey
Columbus, Ohio

Library of Congress Cataloging-in-Publication Data

Garcia, Jesus
    Contexts of teaching : methods for middle and high school instruction / Jesus Garcia,
Elizabeth Spalding, Richard R. Powell.
        p. cm.
    Includes bibliographical references and index.
    ISBN 0-13-598111-5 (pbk.)
    1. Education, Secondary. 2. High school teaching. 3. Middle school teaching. I.
Spalding, Elizabeth II. Powell, Richard R. III. Title.

LB1607 .G37 2001
373.1102--dc21

                                                                    00-030561

Vice President and Publisher: Jeffery W. Johnston
Editor: Debra A. Stollenwerk
Development Editor: Gianna Marsella
Editorial Assistant: Penny S. Burleson
Production Editor: Mary Harlan
Design Coordinator: Diane C. Lorenzo
Photo Coordinator: Anthony Magnacca
Cover Design: Jeff Vanik
Cover Art: Super Stock
Text Design and Illustrations: Carlisle Publishers Services
Production Coordination: Mary Jo Graham, Carlisle Publishers Services
Production Manager: Pamela D. Bennett
Director of Marketing: Kevin Flanagan
Marketing Manager: Amy June
Marketing Services Manager: Krista Groshong

This book was set in Palatino by Carlisle Communications, Ltd. It was printed and bound by
R. R. Donnelley & Sons Company. The cover was printed by Phoenix Color Corp.

Photo Credits: KS Studios/Merrill, p. 3; Alan E. Goody, pp. 13, 20, 62, 102, 116, 131, 165, 189, 200, 258, 299,
            318; Robert Vega/Merrill, p. 34; Anne Vega/Merrill, pp. 47, 229, 247, 355; Anthony
            Magnacca/Merrill, pp. 83,153; Scott Cunningham/Merrill, p. 214; Barbara Schwartz/Merrill,
            pp. 341, 361; Anthony Magnacca Stock Photography, p. 366; Tom Watson/Merrill, p. 377;
            National Education Association, photo by Carolyn Salisbury, p. 387.

Merrill
Prentice Hall

10 9 8 7 6 5 4 3 2 1
ISBN 0-13-598111-5

PREFACE

GENERAL DESCRIPTION

Contexts of Teaching: Methods for Middle and High School Instruction represents a break from the majority of general methods books now available for undergraduate and graduate courses in teacher education. In our experiences as teacher educators, we have grown increasingly uncomfortable with texts that describe teaching in abstract terms and in an impersonal voice. We have come to believe that a credible depiction of teaching must include descriptions of the professional daily work of contemporary teachers, and that lists of general principles of teaching followed by recipes on how to implement particular teaching practices are less and less useful in today's diverse middle- and high-school classrooms.

We suspect that the generic, distant style of many educational textbooks contributes to prospective teachers' perceptions of a gulf separating theory from practice and university coursework from the "real life" of schools. As the title suggests, this book provides the reader with a realistic portrayal of public schools, teachers, and learners in context. We address topics traditionally covered in general methods courses (e.g., classroom management, planning for instruction), cover current issues in middle and high schools (e.g., standards, assessment, interdisciplinary teaming), and integrate some topics which, though often dealt with in separate courses in teacher education curricula, are crucial to a discussion of general teaching methods (e.g., cultural diversity, gender, adolescent culture). Whenever possible, we contextualize topics in the experiences of real teachers and students we know and have known.

Contexts of Teaching is also unique because we contextualize ourselves for the reader. Often, textbooks leave readers wondering, "Did a human being actually write this book?" As a team of authors, we agree that it is critical for readers of this book to be able to answer that question. Therefore, throughout this book we tell stories of our own experiences as students, as teachers in public schools, and as teacher educators, and describe how these experiences have shaped our teaching perspectives and philosophies. We begin each chapter with personal narratives that illustrate how our own successes and failures have helped us to grow and become who we are today as teachers and researchers. In sharing our autobiographies, we risk being accused of "tooting our own horns." But that is not our intent. Our goal is to connect with readers on a personal level and to model the process of reflection that is critical to one's development as a teacher.

This book is multicultural, but not in the traditional sense. We do not present a chapter on the disadvantaged or at-risk learner. Rather, we treat human diversity as an intellectual concept—not as a political imperative. We present the reader with an inclusive definition of multicultural education and infuse this concept throughout the text. The examples we use in the text—schools, classrooms, and students—convey to the reader that (1) issues and problems when viewed analytically may be described culturally; (2) learners, teachers, and administrators are culturally diverse; (3) there is a need for instruction that provides students with national and multiple perspectives on issues and problems that impact our lives; and (4) the educational community can better address the needs of minorities and other groups who traditionally have not performed well in schools.

Throughout the book, we fuse theory with practice. We consistently refer to our own experiences: teaching, researching in middle and secondary schools, and working with professional organizations. Our intent is to demonstrate to prospective teachers the value of integrating university learning with field experiences. In reading the chapters and working through the Reader Activities, prospective teachers are introduced to the interrelationship between research and practice and learn to value this partnership. More important, prospective teachers have the opportunity to conduct research themselves and to identify its role in helping teachers become more effective in the classroom.

Finally, we stress the human dimension in teaching. In the first part of the book we describe our teaching perspectives, contemporary teenage life in and out of the classroom, and the lives of teachers. Throughout the text we provide realistic examples that address issues relating to culture, color, gender, and socioeconomic status as essential to understanding human behavior and identity. All too frequently, culture, color, gender, socioeconomic status, and exceptionalities are described as factors that impede student school success—if they are described at all. We examine these characteristics as they play themselves out in schools. We believe strongly that prospective teachers should learn about teaching in context with the players involved in the teaching/learning transaction: teachers, students, administrators, and other members of the educational community.

Rationale

As a team of authors, the three of us have accumulated years of experience with middle- and high-school students and teachers, public schools, and institutions involved in teacher preparation. Each of us has enrolled in and successfully completed one or more methods courses, has been a public school teacher, has taught methods courses, and has reviewed more than a few methods textbooks. Our cultural and educational backgrounds are diverse. Presently, one of us (Jesus) teaches a field-based general methods course; another (Liz) has recently completed a four-year stint at a professional organization creating standards and developing alternative assessments as a means of improving and evaluating student learning; and the third (Richard) is conducting teacher education research in the area of multicultural education. Kevin Leander, the author of Chapter Eight, " Teaching with

Technology," is also an experienced classroom teacher who is now an assistant professor at Vanderbilt University.

At Indiana University, where we met, a common topic of discussion was "finding a good methods textbook." Our experiences at Texas A & M, Indiana, Nevada–Las Vegas, Illinois, Kentucky, and Texas Tech Universities suggest that prospective teachers express less interest in their education textbooks when these texts do not contain discussions of real schools or of schools like those they attended. Not surprisingly, they may jump to the conclusion that there is little relationship between book learning and what is occuring in schools or, worse, come to believe that one becomes a teacher by sheer trial and error.

In summary, we wrote *Contexts of Teaching* because we wished to create a textbook prospective teachers would find engaging, intellectually stimulating, and relevant. At the same time, our intent has been to contextualize and personalize the valuable information presented in many general methods books in order to produce a general methods textbook that equips prospective teachers with the core knowledge they need to succeed in middle and high schools.

Organization

In Part One, "Personal Contexts of Teaching," we begin by describing ourselves to the reader and explaining why we decided to write a methods textbook. We move from our own biographies and teaching perspectives to the more general topic of becoming a teacher in a pluralistic society. We then adopt a wide angle lens to give a broad overview of the movement toward multicultural education that gained momentum in the last half of the twentieth century. Next, we focus on students—the context that matters most to teachers. Most important, in Chapter One we introduce readers to a course-long project of constructing a teaching/learning biography, a personal practical philosophy of teaching, and, ultimately, a portfolio that demonstrates their learning and growth in the class. We conclude this part of the book by suggesting that a working definition of teaching and basic knowledge of the worlds of teachers and adolescents are prerequisites for pursuing a career in middle- and high-school teaching. Part One provides the context for the other topics and issues that follow.

In Part Two, "Classroom Contexts of Teaching," we begin with the topic of classroom management—the overwhelming concern of prospective teachers. After describing traditional models of managing students in middle- and high-school classrooms, we suggest a model that focuses on democratizing learning in multicultural environments. We then address the components of teaching: middle- and high-school curricula, planning, instructional materials, integration of technology in instruction, strategies and methods of implementing instruction, and methods of assessing student learning. Interwoven in each chapter are the authors' own stories of their experiences with the topic(s) and descriptions of the practices of beginning and experienced teachers. Because we believe the manner in which students are instructed and learn in public schools will change in the twenty-first century, we advance the model of democratizing the teaching/learning act. That is, we suggest to prospective teachers that they provide students with opportunities to play a role in what they learn, how they learn, and how they are assessed.

A major theme of this part of the book is that engagement with the content presented in Part One is prerequisite to an explanation of questions relating to curricular materials, the use of technology in the classroom, and evaluation. That is, planning for instruction requires more than a superficial knowledge of students. Moreover, when planning for instruction is described in the context of teaching and learning in a democratic environment, the prospective teacher is able to provide reasoned responses to questions related to the selection of instructional materials and educational assessment/evaluation. Similarly, issues related to classroom management are best described in this same context. We believe the topics covered in the first two parts of this book represent core knowledge for effective middle- and high-school instruction.

In the last part of the text, "Professional Contexts of Teaching," we call on the reader to reflect further on a career in middle- and high-school teaching. The first two parts of the text equip the reader with the essential knowledge to begin a teaching career, but moving beyond readiness is a life-long process requiring further reflection on previously covered topics and an introduction to others. In Part Three, we ask the reader to consider the community as a context for teaching, and to reflect again on the value of teaching, on methodology, on the nature of adolescence, and, finally, on what it means to embark on a career in education. Prospective teachers who have a basic understanding of the information presented in the first two parts of the text are more likely to view their responses to the questions raised in the final part as the first step to becoming outstanding teachers.

Special Features

Our approach personalizes general methods. In Chapter One, "Exploring Biography and Teaching Perspectives: Personal Narratives," we begin by sharing our teaching/learning biographies and educational philosophies. Each succeeding chapter begins with a short narrative by the author that connects to the chapter topic and invites readers to explore their own life histories. We have personalized the content further by including the experiences of student teachers, novice teachers, and experienced teachers. We include vignettes of a variety of teachers in a variety of settings to highlight particular issues and problems in middle- and high-school teaching.

A second special feature of the book is the Reader Activities interspersed throughout all chapters except Chapters One and Thirteen. We suggest four different kinds of activities: "In the Field" (mini-research projects requiring interviews and observations); "Theory into Practice" (practical applications of topics discussed, such as planning a unit and designing assessments); "Consulting Other Sources" (consulting other written and electronic texts to gain multiple perspectives on topics and issues); and "What Would You Do?" (critical incidents and case studies centering upon important topics and issues). These activities provide multiple entry points for readers to engage with the content. Not all four types of activities are offered in every chapter, but in every chapter there are several activities from which readers can choose. By giving readers a choice of activities, we recognize the diversity among our readers and their learning styles.

A third special feature appears at the end of each chapter, "Building Your Biography, Your Personal Practical Philosophy, and Portfolio." Just as we begin with ourselves, we invite readers to begin with themselves and to construct their own biographies, chapter by chapter. Secondly, we invite readers to draft portions of a personal practical philosophy of teaching as they work through the issues discussed and implied in the book. Third, we ask readers to collect the chapter Reader Activities they complete, reflect on their learning from completing these activities, and select some for possible inclusion in a course portfolio. Finally, we suggest that the biography, personal practical philosophy, and selected artifacts form the foundation of a culminating course portfolio.

The sequencing of the chapters allows readers to build on each succeeding chapter and on the Reader Activities. While each of us writes with a distinctive voice and style, we believe that common themes recur throughout the book. We repeatedly cross-reference one another's narratives, examples, and themes. By maintaining our own identities as we have collaborated on the writing of this book, we hope we have presented a unique but coherent and cohesive portrait of teaching middle- and high-school students today.

Acknowledgments

We would like to thank the many individuals who contributed to the successful completion of this project: our families and friends who have listened to us patiently for several years; our students and colleagues who gave us valuable feedback on drafts; and the classroom teachers who agreed to share their stories with us.

We are grateful to the professionals at Merrill/Prentice-Hall whose advice and support have been invaluable: Debbie Stollenwerk, our senior editor; Gianna Marsella, our developmental editor; and others who have been involved along the way in the development of this book. We would also like to thank our project director at Carlisle Publishing, Mary Jo Graham, for her efficient processing of the manuscript and our copy editor, Susan M. Dolter, for her insightful and critical reading of the text.

Finally, we owe a great deal to the reviewers who have contributed so much to this book's final shape. They are: Janet E. Boyle, Indiana University-Purdue University at Indianapolis; Leigh Chiarelott, Bowling Green State University; James Dick, University of Nebraska at Omaha; Fred H. Groves, Northeast Louisiana University; Janet Handler, Mount Mercy College; Barbara Kacer, Western Kentucky University; Cynthia G. Kruger, University of Massachusetts, Dartmouth; and Allen Larson, Indiana Wesleyan University.

DISCOVER THE COMPANION WEBSITE
ACCOMPANYING THIS BOOK

The Prentice Hall Companion Website:
A Virtual Learning Environment

Technology is a constantly growing and changing aspect of our field that is creating a need for content and resources. To address this emerging need, Prentice Hall has developed an online learning environment for students and professors alike — Companion Websites—to support our textbooks.

In creating a Companion Website, our goal is to build on and enhance what the textbook already offers. For this reason, the content for each user-friendly website is organized by topic and provides the professor and student with a variety of meaningful resources. Common features of a Companion Website include:

For the Professor—

Every Companion Website integrates **Syllabus Manager**^{TM}, an online syllabus creation and management utility.

- **Syllabus Manager**^{TM} provides you, the instructor, with an easy, step-by-step process to create and revise syllabi, with direct links into Companion Website and other online content without having to learn HTML.
- Students may log on to your syllabus during any study session. All they need to know is the web address for the Companion Website and the password you've assigned to your syllabus.
- After you have created a syllabus using **Syllabus Manager**^{TM}, students may enter the syllabus for their course section from any point in the Companion Website.
- Clicking on a date, the student is shown the list of activities for the assignment. The activities for each assignment are linked directly to actual content, saving time for students.
- Adding assignments consists of clicking on the desired due date, then filling in the details of the assignment—name of the assignment, instructions, and whether or not it is a one-time or repeating assignment.
- In addition, links to other activities can be created easily. If the activity is online, a URL can be entered in the space provided, and it will be linked automatically in the final syllabus.
- Your completed syllabus is hosted on our servers, allowing convenient updates from any computer on the Internet. Changes you make to your syllabus are immediately available to your students at their next logon.

For the Student—

- **Topic Overviews** — outline key concepts in topic areas
- **Electronic Bluebook** — send homework or essays directly to your instructor's email with this paperless form
- **Message Board** — serves as a virtual bulletin board to post—or respond to—questions or comments to/from a national audience
- **Chat** — real-time chat with anyone who is using the text anywhere in the country—ideal for discussion and study groups, class projects, etc.
- **Web Destinations** — links to www sites that relate to each topic area
- **Professional Organizations** — links to organizations that relate to topic areas
- **Additional Resources** — access to topic-specific content that enhances material found in the text

To take advantage of these and other resources, please visit the *Contexts of Teaching* Companion Website at

www.prenhall.com/garcia

BRIEF CONTENTS

CONTENTS

▌▌PART III *Professional Contexts of Teaching* 339

Chapter 11   Understanding the Role of Community   341

Chapter 12   Making a Difference in Today's Classrooms   361

Personal Contexts of Teaching

1

Exploring Biography and Teaching Perspectives

Personal Narratives

Who are we and what experiences do we have individually and collectively that have prompted us to write a general methods textbook for prospective middle- and high-school teachers? We are three teachers who, combined, have spent over twenty-five years in elementary and secondary classrooms. We enjoyed K-12 teaching, but as you will read in our biographies, we returned to the university for a variety of reasons, earned terminal degrees, and eventually became teacher educators. Collectively, we also have spent over twenty-five years in teacher education. Today, we continue teaching and conducting research in field-based teacher-education programs.

A few years ago, while attending a professional meeting in Chicago, Richard Powell, Liz Spalding, and I (Jesus Garcia) met to discuss efforts at maintaining field-based teacher-education programs that promote the preparation of teachers as reflective practitioners (Schon, 1983). In the course of the evening, we agreed that one difficulty we encountered was locating textbooks that contextualized the principles and practices of general methods in field-based teacher education. We were looking for materials that wove the strands of biography/narrative, reflection, and collaboration into a meaningful message and that began by asking teacher candidates to consider some of the following questions: Who am I? Why do I want to teach? What does it mean to teach at the middle- and high-school levels? What knowledge and skills do prospective teachers need to achieve success as student teachers and to launch a promising career in today's schools? What attitudes and beliefs should teacher-education programs cultivate among prospective teachers? That brainstorming session led to the development of this textbook.

Why do we stress field-based teacher-education programs that prepare teachers as reflective practitioners? We believe this model holds the most promise for preparing teachers who are well-grounded in the realities of contemporary middle- and high-school teaching and, as a result, will experience less difficulty when assuming a teaching position than preservice teachers who have spent a limited time observing and practicing in schools. In addition, we believe this approach creates professionals who are willing to question accepted school practices and who work to bring about change benefiting both themselves and their students (Doyle, 1990; Ziechner, 1983).

Field-based education rearranges the context of teacher education. In a systematic fashion, teacher educators, prospective teachers, and classroom teachers work together in order to connect theory to practice and the ideal to the real. Many colleges and universities embracing educational reform have adopted field-based teacher education and are experimenting with this model by constructing theoretical frameworks that better align theory and practice and by forming professional development school partnerships (McIntyre, Byrd, and Foxx, 1996).

Field-based teacher education is collaborative in nature and provides prospective teachers the opportunity to see first-hand how teachers, administrators, staff, and school-related agencies work together. Many schools characterize themselves as communities of learners and/or inquirers. In these schools, teachers and students see themselves as a community, and individually and collectively help one another grow and become more responsible community members (Corrigan & Udas, 1996; McLaughlin & Oberman, 1996). Prospective teachers should witness and participate in collaborative efforts to gain an appreciation of those efforts in schools. Moreover, they should experience the barriers and challenges to nurturing school collaboration in a society that places a high value on competitiveness.

Narrative and biography are powerful tools in field-based teacher education. *Narrative* in teacher education refers both to the creating of story (knowledge, skill, construction) and the story itself (characters, theme). Through narrative or story, individuals give meaning to experience (Coles, 1989). Biography or personal narrative encourages preservice and inservice teachers to construct meaning by consciously tapping previous personal and professional experiences and reflecting upon how these experiences influence the present (Connelly & Clandinin, 1990). Biography in teacher education helps preservice teachers theorize about self, learning, adolescents, and the role of schools in a democratic society, as well as pedagogy and classroom and school practices. Teacher educators who employ biography or narrative in this manner view learning to teach as a "fundamental process of reconstructing one's narrative of experiences with special reference to classrooms, schools, and the demands of being a teacher" (Carter & Doyle, 1996 p. 125). Narrative and biography tap into pools of experiences that many educators believe play significant roles in shaping teacher candidates' beliefs and attitudes toward teaching.

Much research on teaching converges around the finding that teachers teach as they were taught. Before students even enter teacher-education programs, most have spent at least twelve years in close company with teachers. From simple observation, prospective teachers have already learned classroom routines, styles of teaching content, ways of interacting with students, and other facets of what it means to teach. This "apprenticeship of observation" may be unique to teaching (Lortie, 1975). Many teacher educators feel unable to influence the beliefs and actions of prospective teachers that have been formed through this powerful apprenticeship. But prior educational experience can become a valuable resource for reflecting upon who one is as a teacher, who one wants to become, and why one may hold the beliefs that he or she does about teaching. Reflection upon experience is the first step in the process of change.

In an attempt to model the process of reflection and change, we begin with our own teaching biographies. We hope our stories show how experience has helped us grow as human beings and as teachers. We are three teachers with different backgrounds but shared interests in teacher education. I (Jesus) am a Mexican American who grew up in California and was profoundly influenced by the Civil Rights Movement. Liz was raised in West Virginia, attended Catholic schools, and eventually taught fourteen years in grades seven through twelve. Richard grew up poor in Kansas, overcame numerous obstacles to attend college, and became acquainted with cultural diversity while teaching in Saudi Arabia.

When describing our professional selves, we make reference to events and individuals who have had a significant impact on our lives and in shaping our definitions of teaching. We tell you our stories not out of egocentrism, but because we want to personalize the content of this book, to model the process of autobiographical inquiry, and to offer you insights into our educational philosophies. We realize that, to many of you, our stories may seem like ancient history. Yet, in constructing our stories, we found more similarities than differences between the schools we attended and taught in during the 1950s, 1960s, and 1970s and the schools we work in today and that you will soon enter as professionals.

Are our stories and experiences unique? We hope so. We are also confident that your biography will be unique. While none of us may fit the profile of a "typical" middle- or high-school teacher, we have yet to meet a middle- or high-school teacher who is "typical," once we go beyond superficial demographics. While our experiences may be unique, our views on teacher preparation and middle- and high-school teaching are aligned with contemporary research and with recent innovations in field-based education.

We believe this chapter on biography and teaching perspectives is the nucleus of this text. We begin with our own biographies and teaching perspectives and conclude with an edited transcript of a discussion during which the three of us describe our educational philosophies and reach agreement on what constitutes good teaching in middle or secondary schools and what we mean by *core knowledge* and *skills*. Our definitions represent the opinions of three informed educators; other educators may hold different opinions. Your responsibility is to grasp the ideas, reflect on them, and use them to help formulate your own definition of teaching. Hence, we hope you will take the messages in this textbook in the spirit in which they were intended: a serious attempt to provide you with an understanding of teaching and the identification of knowledge and skills needed to survive and grow in today's schools. Now let us introduce ourselves.

■■JESUS GARCIA: BIOGRAPHY AND TEACHING PERSPECTIVE

I grew up and attended high school in Pittsburg, California: a working-class community whose adults were employed principally in the steel or ship-building industries or the military. My parents had both immigrated from Mexico: my father was a steel-worker and my mother was a homemaker. Not until I entered high school did I encounter a teacher who was Mexican American, like me. Mr. Leo Gloria, a counselor at the high school I attended, was the only Mexican American on the faculty. Many of the minority students, Mexican and African American, gravitated toward him because he was "one of us" and, more importantly, because he showed an interest in us. Mr. Gloria spoke Spanish with the Mexican American students, encouraged us to investigate our cultural heritage, and to do well in high school so we could go on to college and serve as role-models to other Mexican American students.

I vividly remember a field trip Mr. Gloria arranged for a group of students he had befriended. He drove us to see a tennis match between the Mexican American tennis great Richard "Pancho" Gonzalez and the equally great Lew Hoad. The highlight of the trip was having our picture taken with Mr. Gonzalez. Since I was one of the smaller students in the group, I stood next to the great athlete. What an experience! I learned first-hand that Mexican Americans were making significant contributions to the American experience, and I became convinced that I, too, could become someone like a Richard Gonzalez or perhaps a high school counselor.

Mr. Gloria also shared with me and other students his commitment to community life. He was an active political leader; individuals of all walks of life spoke of him in positive terms. My parents, community activists like my cousin Ernie Quintana, and others were proud of his accomplishments and encouraged me to follow in his footsteps.

While Mr. Gloria's ethnicity was important to me, his commitment to students and his community was even more important. He was perceived by the faculty and students as someone who cared about **all** students. Because Mr. Gloria was a Mexican American, I viewed him as a role-model. He piqued my interest in matters relating to the Mexican American experience. While my parents reinforced my ethnic heritage, Mr. Gloria raised my consciousness in the area of cultural diversity.

As a result of my secondary experiences, I became concerned with the status of minorities. I wondered why minorities lived in one part of town, held many of the blue collar jobs, and were only occasionally involved in political decisions affecting the greater community. In high school, I silently questioned why most minorities (myself included) were not in college preparatory classes, why there were few teachers of minority background, and why, as a senior, I was not encouraged to attend a college or university after graduation. I wondered out loud why Mr. Gloria never became a principal or superintendent of a school district.

After graduating from high school, I joined the California National Guard, and after basic training decided the armed forces were not for me. I returned home and enrolled in a local community college where I focused on general education and engineering courses, hoping to become an architect. Within a semester, I learned I had little mathematical ability and shifted my interest to history and the humanities. I graduated in two years and went off to a state college.

At San Francisco State University, Dr. Elizabeth Gleason introduced me to the love of knowledge. Dr. Gleason specialized in European medieval and Renaissance history. She was one of the few professors I encountered at the undergraduate level who exhibited an enthusiasm for knowledge and for her students' ability to appreciate it. She came to class prepared, delivered a stimulating lecture, and did not patronize us with such vague expressions as "for all intents and purposes," as some of my other history professors did when not wishing to explore ideas in great depth. She would use Italian, German, and French terms in an attempt to further describe concepts and to recreate history for the class.

I learned from Dr. Gleason that an understanding of human existence is gained through an examination of complex ideas and issues and that historical individuals and events are open to multiple interpretations. Because of her teaching, I began to reflect and ask questions in my other classes. Dr. Gleason taught me that becoming educated is a personal responsibility. She created the climate that allowed students to pursue their intellectual interests.

Eventually I became a teacher at the elementary and high school levels. The students who walked into my classroom each year had an enduring influence on my thinking, teaching, writing, and research. These students were unique individuals: they came in all sizes, shapes, forms, and colors. They brought their distinct personalities and a natural curiosity to the classroom. In their own way, they asked me to prepare them to live in society. Some found it easy to communicate with me and others did not. I employed the information school officials gave me to identify their strengths and weaknesses and created instructional programs that would be of value to them. These students also shared some attributes. They all desired attention and acceptance; they all wanted to be liked by me, other teachers, and their peers. They continually challenged and surprised me. In the morning, they might tell me how much they disliked me and U.S. history, and by the afternoon they were exceeding my expectations in order to please me. Each year it was a challenge to reach out to them and address their varied needs.

Because I have always enjoyed helping others and being with children and adolescents, I continually strove to become an excellent teacher. I was successful some of the time, but not always. Some students enjoyed me as a teacher and grew as a result of their interactions with me; others did not. I did my best and used my strengths to reach those students who were having a difficult time, using my enthusiasm for history to help students "turn on" to school.

Perhaps because I am of minority background and have been influenced by Mr. Gloria and others, I was very conscious that my classroom behaviors could deny a student the opportunity to learn. And, like Mr. Gloria, I took a special interest in helping minority students and others who had been marginalized in the education system. To this day, I detest the forces of discrimination that deny some students the opportunity to learn. From Mr. Gloria I learned to care for all students and to do my very best for all of them. Mr. Gloria's influence, my personal experiences as a minority, and my professional experiences forced me to look deeply into the responsibilities of the classroom teacher. I remain convinced that a teacher's responsibility is to create learning environments where all students have the opportunity to learn and to grow intellectually.

Eventually I made the decision to leave K-12 teaching. While I was teaching at the elementary level, my principal suggested I pursue a graduate degree in education. When I completed my masters degree, my major professor suggested I enroll in a doctoral program. In graduate school I was advised, more than once, to pursue a career in higher education. While I could have returned to my position as an elementary teacher, the promise of an opportunity to have a greater influence on education and to earn a salary more appropriate to the needs of my growing family lured me to a teaching career at the university level.

During my tenure in the classroom, teacher effectiveness was (and frequently still is) rewarded with promotions and positions outside the classroom. I have been asked on numerous occasions whether I would return to public school teaching. The answer is a most definite "yes." I enjoy people and students who wish to learn and who need help learning how to become independent thinkers. Teaching people does not involve steps up or down, but a commitment.

▌▌ELIZABETH SPALDING: BIOGRAPHY AND TEACHING PERSPECTIVE

I grew up in a middle-class home in Charleston, West Virginia, the small capital city of a small, impoverished state. My parents loved books and reading. The walls of our family room were lined with books to which I was attracted at an early age. I fondly remember Mrs. Kenny, my kindergarten teacher, who identified my precocious interest in reading and nurtured that interest into love. I remember incompetent teachers, caring teachers, teachers who cared passionately about subjects in which I had no interest, and teachers who didn't seem to care much about anything. But the teacher who probably influenced me the most and in whose image I unconsciously shaped myself as a teacher was Sister Judeen.

Sister Judeen was an English teacher in the small, Catholic high school I attended. Even though Sister Judeen had acquired the reputation of being a "hard" teacher, about twenty-five of us enrolled in her senior-level World Literature class. Today, I'm astonished at the quantity and the quality of the works we read for this course. Sister Judeen insisted on note-taking and she packed a lot of information into a lecture, which was her preferred mode of instruction. She gave only essay exams.

When I eventually became a teacher in public high schools in Charleston, West Virginia, I taught much as Sister Judeen had. As I reflect back on that fact today, I see its advantages and disadvantages. Today, for example, we know that many students do not learn best from lectures and have difficulty taking notes. I realize now that Sister Judeen was primarily interested in teaching students who were already succeeding in school. She showed little interest in knowing her students personally, much less accommodating their learning-styles or needs. Yet she knew her subject, cared about it passionately, and knew how to teach it (at least to those who were trained to learn from listening). Sister Judeen became a guiding image for me because she wanted her students to share her passion for literature. To that end, she made us believe we were capable of reading, understanding, and discussing sophisticated ideas and works of literature. She treated us as scholars and never lowered her expectations.

In the mid-1980s, after nine years of classroom teaching, I finally encountered a model that was a real alternative to Sister Judeen. At that time, I was teaching English and French in the Department of Defense Dependents Schools (DODDS) system. I lived and worked on a small American army base in Pusan, Korea. Our high school was tiny—graduating classes of twelve to fifteen students. We enrolled not just the children of American military personnel, but the children of Koreans, Norwegians, Dutch, Chinese, and other expatriates who were living in this thriving port city. Because DODDS teachers taught in such far-flung locations and had little or no access to professional development opportunities during the school year, the Department of Defense paid for teachers to attend courses, workshops, and institutes in the United States during summer vacations.

For years I had been frustrated with teaching writing. Despite my assiduous efforts at assigning and grading writing, most students looked at their grades, then crumpled up the papers and deposited them in the trash can or abandoned them on the classroom floor. I jumped at the opportunity to participate in a summer institute—the Bay Area Writing Project at the University of California, Berkeley.

I was quite surprised when I received in the mail information about preparation for the workshop: I was supposed to write a personal narrative and bring it with me. You may find this hard to believe of an English teacher, but I think the last time I had written a personal narrative was in grade school! Completing this assignment was incredibly difficult for me, nevertheless I managed to produce a story. At the institute, we broke into small groups, read our papers aloud, and gave feedback to one another about our writing. Then we revised our papers. In short, I was being introduced to what teachers today know as "writing processes." The Bay Area Writing Project, now part of the National Writing Project with hundreds of sites in the United States and in other countries, revolutionized my teaching. I learned about free writing, brainstorming, webbing, drafting, peer reviewing, revising, editing, and holistic grading. I couldn't wait to get back to my classroom in Korea to try out these new techniques.

The next four years—in Korea and then in the Philippines—were the most satisfying of my career as an English teacher. I discovered that the quality of my students' writing improved measurably when I gave them choices of topics and approaches to writing, responsibility for helping one another through peer review, and an opportunity to revise their writing based on concrete feedback from me and others. These techniques were especially helpful for those students who were still struggling to master written English. My students felt successful and so did I.

After fourteen years, I left classroom teaching but eventually decided to remain in the field of education. I entered a doctoral program at Indiana University in Bloomington with the intent of becoming a teacher of teachers. I saw this as a logical extension of the career to which I had already devoted many years. I wanted to learn more about what it means to be an excellent teacher and then to use my knowledge and experience to help others become outstanding teachers. While at Indiana, I had the good fortune to work in a teacher-education program designed for career-changers and directed by a dedicated teacher educator.

Each summer, a new cohort of aspiring teachers (many of whom were giving up lucrative careers in medicine, engineering, business, or law) entered the program. Their program stressed reflective decision-making, and I saw these beginning teachers grow in knowledge and skill as they learned to think systematically about their practice and to learn from experience through the use of such tools as journal-writing, reflective interviewing, and observation of their videotaped teaching. The director and I also regularly visited graduates in their first, second, and third years of teaching. These visits reinforced my conviction, previously based only on personal experience, of how critical the first few years of teaching are and of how much about teaching can only be learned through experience.

I was diverted from my goal of becoming a university-based teacher educator when I was offered a position at the National Council of Teachers of English (NCTE). As Project Manager for Standards, I became involved in the development of standards and assessments for the teaching and learning of English language arts. The most rewarding aspect of my job was that I had the opportunity to interact with some of the best teachers in the country and discuss their students' work. Working at NCTE expanded my views of the possibilities and challenges of English teaching as I listened to the stories of outstanding teachers from Maine to California. Working with such teachers made me proud to be a member of this profession—even as it made me feel a little guilty that I was neither so skilled nor so thoughtful when I was a classroom teacher.

After a four-and-a-half-year "detour" at NCTE, I am at last becoming a teacher of teachers. I'm now on the faculty at the University of Kentucky, where I work with interdisciplinary cohorts of aspiring middle- and high-school teachers in a graduate level certification program. Over the course of a rigorous academic year combined with intensive field experience and student teaching, the students form strong bonds within their cohorts and across the disciplines. They learn from one another at least as much as from me. All the faculty who work in this program have had to confront the issue of breadth vs. depth: it simply is not possible to "cover" in one year the material that is "covered" in traditional teacher-education programs over the course of two or more years. In writing various chapters of this book, I have kept my own students in mind as an audience.

What does it take to be a good teacher? I think a good teacher, like Sister Judeen, should be knowledgeable and care deeply about the subject he or she teaches. Also, like Sister Judeen, a good teacher cares deeply about student learning, holds high expectations, and treats students as co-inquirers. I have also learned that, unlike Sister Judeen, a good teacher knows how to implement instruction in a variety of ways so that all students have a fair chance to learn and succeed. Sister Judeen's limited repertoire of teaching techniques would not serve her well in today's diverse schools, nor would her apparent indifference to her students' personal and social needs.

From my experiences in the Bay Area Writing Project, at Indiana University, and my work at NCTE, I have learned that good teachers are reflective about their practice, have a "can-do" approach to problem-solving, and seek out opportunities to improve their knowledge and skills. They take pride in working in their disciplines. Perhaps most importantly, they are members of learning communities: their own school faculties, departments, professional organizations, or other professional networks.

Teaching is hard work. The best teachers will attest, however, that it is also exciting, stimulating, challenging, and rewarding work. They will also swear that some days they want to walk out of the classroom, lock the door, and never come back. Fortunately, they don't follow through on that fantasy.

▪▪RICHARD POWELL:
BIOGRAPHY AND TEACHING PERSPECTIVE

As long as I can remember, my mother wanted me to attend college. She believed college would improve my well-being and enhance the quality of my life. She herself had only a high school diploma from a very small rural school in a farming community in western Nebraska. In fact, no one in my immediate family had ever earned a college degree. Farmers, skilled technicians, and beauticians were the cornerstones of my immediate and extended families.

I grew up in southwestern Kansas, in a segregated, mid-size, rural town, living in a mobile home on the fringe of the lower socioeconomic Black community. My initial formal educational experiences were in a poor and working-class, ethnically diverse elementary school. The junior high school I attended was also ethnically diverse and served the working, middle, and upper middle classes in my community.

My first day of junior high school marked my first experience with what I now believe was social class discrimination. When all the students were assembled in the auditorium, the principal began calling out names. The first group of students was the highest academic track in the school. With growing anxiety and much disappointment, I sat waiting for my name to be called, only to watch group after group leave the auditorium. Finally a small number of students remained. Over half of them had attended the same elementary school I had attended. We would comprise the lowest academic track at the school.

As a result of this experience, my public school expectations were determined. The lower-level education I received in junior high school qualified me only for the lower-level classes in high school. Although I tried hard to do well in such courses as geometry and algebra, I was not always successful. Indeed, I had to take geometry twice because I failed it the first time. One day in economics class, the teacher asked each of us what we planned to do after graduation. When I said proudly that I was going to attend college, he replied, "Better try something else, Powell. You'll never make it in college." My high school guidance counselor suggested I attend the local vocational-technical school because my grades and the classes I had taken wouldn't gain me access to a college. Being in the lower academic track, coupled with a very difficult and dysfunctional home life, ultimately led me to graduate in the lower one-third of my senior class. Nevertheless, I continued to think I could make my mother's dream come true.

I ignored the advice of my teacher and counselor and entered a junior college immediately after high school. I did this, however, not because of any family or school role models; I never saw my father read a book, although my mother read as often as she could, given her busy work schedule. And my K-12 experiences suggested I should do almost anything but attend college. I entered college because I had always lived with a parent's dream. When I began my college studies, something inside me clicked, and I began studying like I never had studied before. I wanted to earn straight As and show my mother and the world that I could do well in school.

After two years, I enrolled in a state university that served mostly White middle-class students. While I initially majored in psychology, I ultimately graduated with major studies in biology and English literature. Because my junior high and high school experiences had been so frustrating and discouraging, re-entering public schools as a teacher was something I did not even consider until I was a junior in college.

In my junior year, I enrolled in a class called "Afro-American Literature." The professor was from India, and she was the first instructor that I had in all of my K-12 and undergraduate college classes who was not White. Her class introduced me to literature and poetry dealing with oppression and emancipation. The interest I developed in that class has remained with me to this day. Much of my current reading, research, and writing centers, in various ways, on emancipation.

Perhaps because of the high demand for science teachers, I decided to become a science rather than an English teacher. However, I believe my decision was based more on my interest in botany and my relationship with Dr. Larry Higgins, my biology professor, who became an important role model, perhaps my first positive educational role model. I took all of his classes, and couldn't seem to get enough of his expertise in and enthusiasm for plant taxonomy and morphology.

As I approached the middle of my junior year, the idea of becoming a science teacher began to take shape. I completed the state certification requirements for teaching high school biology during the spring semester of my senior year. In the fall, I secured a job teaching science in a small, rural town in west Texas.

Teaching in a west Texas town was a shock for me. My classes were composed of White, middle- and lower-middle-class students with rural farming and ranching values. I experienced difficulty with this kind of homogeneity; I had been raised in a community and had attended schools that were culturally diverse. I was also rudely introduced to teacher work: I taught Earth Science, physical science, and biology even though I was only licensed to teach biology. With three preparations, I was constantly preparing lessons and laboratories. I also drove a school bus every morning and evening for additional income.

After two years at this school, I secured a high school position in the town where I had earned my baccalaureate degree. The teaching staff was White, and the student population included only a few Blacks and Hispanics. My responsibilities included teaching biology, advanced biology, and human anatomy and Physiology. The school took considerable pride in its academic program, and teaching content by traditional methods was the expectation for all teachers.

I enjoyed secondary teaching, but as my intellectual interests became more global, I began job hunting and secured a junior college position in the area. The students in my science classes were predominately White and middle-class. I taught for one year and concluded that, to remain a faculty member, I would need to earn a doctoral degree. After seeking advice from my mentors about programs in science and science-related fields, I entered a science education program at Texas A & M University. This decision eventually changed my perspective about teaching students whose cultural and ethnic backgrounds differed from my own.

During my first year at Texas A & M, I was offered the opportunity to work in the Kingdom of Saudi Arabia (KSA) for the purpose of writing chemical laboratory training materials. My initial intention was to stay in Saudi Arabia for three months. I ended up staying two years. During that time, I developed close friendships with Saudis and traveled extensively in the Middle East. I became immersed in Saudi culture, learned a small amount of Arabic, and gained a different perspective on American culture.

Writing training materials in Saudi Arabia piqued my interest in training and development, and I decided that when I returned home I would change my area of emphasis to curriculum studies and training and development. Returning to Texas after two years in the Middle East generated quite a culture shock—more profound than my initial experiences in Saudi Arabia. I also deeply missed my Saudi friends, as well as my friends in India, Pakistan, and the Philippines.

In field-based teacher education programs, teacher educators, prospective teachers, and classroom teachers work together to connect theory and practice.

Because of my newfound interests in curriculum and training and development, I transferred to Indiana University at Bloomington. I enjoyed Indiana because I once again experienced rich cultural and ethnic diversity in the student population. My classmates were from all over the United States and the world, including Saudi Arabia. I brought my teaching experiences from rural Texas and my cultural experiences in Saudi Arabia to Indiana. I also encountered still more perspectives—including feminist, gay, and lesbian. Some of my long-held beliefs and values were challenged as a result of these interactions. I met faculty who would serve as mentors and who had a profound influence on my thinking about teaching, views of curriculum development, and beliefs about equity in school.

As I reflect on who I am today as a teacher, I see the cumulative effects of many rich and varied experiences. My sensitivity for how and what to teach is affected as much by the tracking I experienced in junior high school as it is by the faculty in my doctoral programs. There are many things I would do differently if I were teaching in middle or high school today, and I am able to draw upon my previous experiences in education as I work with preservice and inservice teachers now. My biographical factors, then, collectively provide the framework for my beliefs and perspectives about creating teaching environments that encourage students to ask critical questions about the world around them and about forces that bring about social, cultural, and economic oppression.

▮▮ TOWARD CONSENSUS ON A DEFINITION OF TEACHING AND CORE KNOWLEDGE

Following is the edited transcript of a discussion the authors of this text held as we began our work. We include it here because we believe it is important for you, as a prospective teacher, to see that we continue to define and refine our teaching philosophies.

Jesus: Let's bring closure to this chapter by commenting on our narratives. How are we unique? How are we different?

Richard: Several things struck me as I read our biographies. First, we are teachers who are concerned about teaching and that is why we are writing this book. I was intrigued by the biographical factors that ultimately led us to select teaching as a profession. We have different perspectives on teaching, beliefs about teaching, and different methods that we naturally deploy in the classroom. I think it's that individuality of teaching style that makes the biographies so interesting.

Liz: I noticed that we all chose as role models—Sister Judeen, Dr. Gleason, and Dr. Higgins—people who radiated love for their subjects and wanted to pass on that love to students. At the same time, they all taught in a way that none of us today would say is a particularly effective method with diverse learners: transmitting knowledge through lecture. I think many prospective teachers face a similar dilemma—trying to figure out how to teach in ways that they have never really experienced themselves.

Jesus: What struck me was what we have in common. When I began teaching, I focused on providing for minority learners, but as I continued teaching I developed a more inclusive approach. While each of us may view teaching slightly differently, we all are keenly aware of the responsibilities of a good teacher. We value students and subject matter, and strive to strike a balance between the two. Now, as you reflect on your biographies, can you think of a word or phrase that best describes you as a teacher?

Richard: When I see myself as a teacher, whether it is in front of one or a hundred students, I see the sum total of our experiences—mine and theirs. What am I? I am a compilation of all kinds of experiences that over the years have made me the teacher I am and that continue to shape my teaching.

Liz: When I look back on who I was when I was a public school teacher, I would say that I was a very subject-centered—not a student-centered—teacher. I learned more about being student-centered when I left public school teaching and enrolled in graduate school. Today, I still experience the tension between the subject-centered and student-centered parts of my teaching self.

Jesus: I, too, find it difficult to use a word or phrase to describe myself as a teacher. I believe my responsibilities are to provide students with environments where they are able to listen and interact. That is, I want to encourage them to read and discuss with their peers and me the content in such documents as the Seneca Falls Declaration of Sentiments, the Bill of Rights, and the Emancipation Proclamation. I want them to reach educated positions on the ideas put forth in these documents. My goal as a teacher has not changed. I want students to leave my classroom and say to themselves, "I enjoyed Mr. Garcia's class because I learned how to think and to learn on my own."

Let's see if we can define teaching. Reflect on what you do in classrooms or what you have done in classrooms, teaching middle and high school and now college. How would you conceptualize teaching in these settings?

Richard: Initially, I thought teaching was making students aware of science concepts and facts. I didn't see teaching in a cultural framework. Now, when I am asked this question, I respond with more than twenty years of teaching in various settings, observing teachers, and conducting research on teaching. I've learned that teaching is far more complicated than simply putting content in students' heads. A teaching moment is the many different backgrounds, biographical experiences of my students and myself coming together. It is as much a personal experience as an academic one.

Liz: I tell the prospective teachers with whom I work that you don't become an outstanding teacher solely by successfully completing a teacher-education program. Teaching is a lifelong learning process. The best English teachers I know are those with twenty or thirty years' experience who are still coming to NCTE annual conventions and saying, "I just love this convention! I get so many great ideas about teaching here!" They are still learning, still asking questions, passionately interested in their students and their subjects. Another thing I've learned that I didn't understand years ago is that teaching isn't just a teacher in a classroom with students. It occurs in this institution called *school* that subscribes to rules that, in many cases, work against your ability to do what you want to do as a teacher and to help the students in a way that is best. It is also about those social forces—poverty, violence, broken families—that find their way into the classroom. Teaching doesn't take place in a vacuum. It occurs inside an institution and in a society.

Jesus: I majored in history and minored in world literature, and I think early in my career I began to see the connection between students and content. When I taught history, I noticed that some students were interested, others weren't, and some did not possess the knowledge and skills needed to attain the objectives I had set for my lessons. Consequently, I began to think of ways of shaping content to address the particular weaknesses and strengths of my students while remaining committed to meaningful social studies experiences. Like Richard, I also view teaching as a personal act representing the total experiences of teacher and students. Teaching is creating environments where students have an opportunity to pursue their intellectual interests. Finally, I agree with you, Liz. You don't learn to be a teacher by just graduating from a teacher-preparation program.

Now that we have come to a general understanding of what we mean by teaching, let's move to another question. What knowledge and skills do prospective teachers need in order to be effective in their student teaching and their first years of teaching?

Richard: Core knowledge is a very complicated construct because, I imagine, every teacher educator has a different definition of core knowledge. Something else complicates the idea of core knowledge, and that is our own world views. Our world views have a powerful impact on what we believe prospective teachers should know when they exit a teacher-education program. I think prospective teachers should exit a teacher-education program knowing more about themselves and their biographical experiences in and out of school, how they relate to other people, about their perspectives and beliefs, and how these perspectives and beliefs will be transformed into classroom practice. I believe core knowledge will always rest heavily on the personal and, as a result, some element of teacher preparation needs to focus on learning who we are as people relative to other people when we go into classrooms. This, I believe, will ultimately lead to culturally sensitive instruction.

Liz: Our biographies prove the strength of the personal and show how we act on our own experience. On the other hand, if you don't have knowledge of other choices you can make, then you are just going to act out of your own experience. So it's not sufficient just to know about your own biography. Sister Judeen loved literature and lectured about literature. When I became a teacher I wasn't even aware that I had choices to make about teaching literature that were alternatives to standing up in front of the class, giving some background about Shakespeare, and then explaining the symbolism of blood in *Macbeth.* I didn't know about reader response theory or research in writing processes. There is so much to know about teaching that you couldn't possibly cover it all in a teacher-education program. Much will have to be learned **after** exiting a teacher-education program, not just through classroom experience, but also through professional development and personal maturity. You'll see the need to explore areas that were only alluded to or not covered at all in your undergraduate program.

Jesus: I would like to reiterate my concern for the students who did not do well in my classes, many of whom were minorities, students from low socioeconomic backgrounds, or students with exceptional learning needs. In retrospect, I believe there are two reasons these students did not do well. First, I did not know them well enough as individuals to provide for their learning needs. Second, I did not give them sufficient opportunities to master basic knowledge and skills that lead to more complex demonstrations of learning and that provide students with opportunities to function effectively in a variety of settings. Prospective teachers need to spend time learning about themselves and their students. They also need to reflect on their views about children who are "different" and their rationales for why students do not perform well in school. I also know how important it is to learn about organizing for teaching, curriculum, technology, methodology, and assessment. If prospective teachers gain fundamental knowledge in these areas, they are more likely to experience success as student teachers and in their first few years of teaching.

Let's try to end our conversation on a personal level. What would you like a prospective teacher to gain from this book?

Liz: I would like the students not to sell the text back to the bookstore at the end of the semester. I would be extremely pleased if in student teaching or in their first teaching job they actually said, "I need to reread that chapter on classroom management and figure out a good approach to this situation."

Richard: I would like readers to understand how our biographies become central to our teaching. I would also like them to be aware of what we mean by "teaching in context." In addition, I want readers to come away from the book with an awareness of current trends in education and the understanding that their own beliefs and perspectives shape how they view these contemporary trends.

Jesus: I would like prospective teachers to leave our textbook knowing that we value the individual and that a major reason for writing this book was to reinforce a principle that we all agree on: teachers and students should have opportunities to succeed in schools. Achieving success comes from knowing who we are, helping others know who they are, and providing school environments where teachers and learners are able to self-actualize. I also want them to know that knowledge of subject area and pedagogy are fundamental to successful teaching. I hope, through reading our stories and "listening" to our discussions, they have gained some insights into our lives, what we believe, and our perceptions of teaching in today's schools. I hope they keep this information in mind as they read the other chapters in this book, continue their school observations, contemplate student teaching, and continue thinking about teaching careers in a middle or high school.

▌▌▌ASSUMPTIONS UNDERLYING THIS BOOK

Now that you have read our biographies and conversation, you may have wondered about the assumptions we are making about teaching. Let us express some of the assumptions that underlie this book.

1. Teaching is a personal act. To be an effective teacher, you must understand who you are, why you wish to teach, and the many other factors that make up the teaching/learning act. We learn who we are and our role in the teaching/learning act by continually reflecting on our actions and the actions of our colleagues and students.
2. Students are social beings. To understand students we must examine their cultures and draw portraits of them within the context of the many differences that make them unique: gender, socioeconomic status, race, ethnicity, exceptionality. Students come to the classroom with strengths and weaknesses. Effective teachers address the weaknesses and use the strengths to enhance instruction.
3. Teachers need to possess core knowledge as they prepare to reach out to students, introduce them to a subject area, and promote learning. The term *core knowledge* refers to subject-area knowledge, skills, and dispositions, as well as the ability to transform that knowledge into meaningful instruction. We believe teachers should provide students with subject-area knowledge and skills that allow them to pursue independently their own intellectual interests in the discipline.

4. We believe there are many paths to learning and that students can demonstrate learning in a variety of ways. As they gain confidence in the classroom, teachers will develop the pedagogical knowledge and skills to effective design instruction for many different kinds of students.
5. We believe that teachers should strive to help students learn how to live and function productively in a culturally pluralistic society and diverse world.
6. Completing a teacher-education program is only the first step one must take in becoming an effective teacher. Teachers must continue to learn about themselves, their students, and their subject area to remain effective and become outstanding.

▌▌BUILDING YOUR BIOGRAPHY, PERSONAL TEACHING PHILOSOPHY, AND PORTFOLIO

We suggest you undertake four tasks as you read this text. First, we would like you to write your own teaching biography as you work through this book. We begin each chapter with a section entitled "Building On Biography," in which we share some part of our own biographies relevant to the chapter topic. Reflection upon these experiences has helped each of us better understand ourselves as human beings and as teachers. At the end of each chapter, we invite you to go through a similar process by drafting a "chapter" of your own biography. We provide sample questions to set you thinking about relevant life experiences.

Next, as you read each chapter, we would like you to begin building your own educational philosophy. As you reflect on our educational philosophies and others described throughout the book, take a few minutes to react to what we have to say and begin formulating your own philosophy on these topics. At the end of each chapter, we offer several questions to stimulate your thinking on the topics and issues. Retain your writings, and when you reach the last chapter we will ask you to reflect on them again, and then integrate them into a well-written essay in which you articulate your tentative, personal, practical philosophy of teaching.

Third, to assist you in constructing an understanding of the material in each chapter and to give you practice in skills you will need as you begin classroom teaching, we have interwoven Reader Activities throughout each chapter. These activities require you to complete particular tasks, such as observing or interviewing students and teachers in middle- and high-school settings; put educational theory into practice by creating lesson plans, classroom activities, and other applications of the chapter topics; consult a variety of textual, electronic, and other sources in order to gain additional perspectives on a topic; and act on and/or analyze scenarios that ask you to take a position with respect to a particular classroom incident or issue. At the end of each chapter, we ask you to review the activities you have completed and to jot down your reflections on them.

Our hope is that your biography, your personal practical philosophy, selected Reader Activities, and your reflections on them will become core entries in a portfolio of your experiences in this course and while reading this book. A portfolio is compilation of work illustrating learning, growth, and achievement. With respect to this text and class, you should *collect* the artifacts you create over the course of the semester or quarter, *select* the ones that you and your instructor agree best represent you as an aspiring middle- or high-school teacher, and *reflect* upon your understanding of key educational issues and problems at this point in your teacher-preparation program.

In the last chapter of the book, "Reflecting for Professional Renewal," we discuss the growing use of portfolios to document development and mastery in teaching. We guide you through the process of compiling your portfolio and encourage you to continue developing a professional portfolio throughout your teacher-education program and career.

References and Suggestions for Further Reading

Ashton-Warner, S. (1972). *Spearpoint: "Teacher" in America.* New York: Knopf.

Carter, K. & Doyle, W. (1996). Personal narrative and life history in learning to teach. In J. Sikula, T. J. Buttery, & E. Guyton (Eds.) *Handbook of research in teacher education* (Second Edition) (pp. 121–142), New York: Simon & Schuster Macmillan.

Coles, R. (1989). *The call of stories: Teaching and the moral imagination.* Boston: Houghton Mifflin.

Connelly, F. M., & Clandinin, D. J. (1990). Stories of experience and narrative inquiry. *Educational Researcher, 19*(5), 2–14.

Corrigan, D. C. & Udas, K. (1996). Creating collaborative, child- and family-centered education, and health and human service systems. In J. Sikula, T. J. Buttery, & E. Guyton (Eds.) *Handbook of research in teacher education* (Second Edition) (pp. 893–921), New York: Simon & Schuster Macmillan.

Doyle, W. (1990). Themes in teacher education research. In W. R. Houston (Ed.), *Handbook of research on teacher education* (pp. 3–24). New York: Macmillan.

Lortie, D. (1975). *Schoolteacher: A sociological study.* Chicago: University of Chicago Press.

McIntyre, D. J., Byrd, D. M., & Foxx, S. M. (1996), Field laboratory experiences. In J. Sikula, T. J. Buttery, & E. Guyton (Eds.) *Handbook of research in teacher education* (Second Edition) (pp. 171–193), New York: Simon & Schuster Macmillan.

McLaughlin, M. W. & Oberman, I., Eds., (1996). *Teacher learning: New policies, new practices.* New York: Teachers College Press.

Schon, D. (1983). *The reflective practitioner.* New York: Basic Books.

Zeichner, K. M., (1983). Alternative paradigms of teacher education. *Journal of Teacher Education* 34(3), 3–9.

2

Understanding Multiculturalism

BUILDING ON BIOGRAPHY: LEARNING TO "SEE" DIFFERENCES

I (Richard) began my school experiences in Kansas at Washington Elementary School, with a student population predominantly African American, Hispanic, and White, and low socioeconomic status (ses). I was a White student from a low ses family. When I think of my beginning years in public school, teachers who were caring, firm, and compassionate come to mind, but I am not sure I would characterize them as culturally sensitive. The only alternative instruction I recall receiving was from Mrs. Mitchell, my third grade teacher, who observed that I was having difficulty with fractions and asked me to stay a few minutes after school, over a week-long period. To Mrs. Mitchell, providing someone with extra help usually meant revisiting old lessons; but, since she was not having much success teaching me fractions by this method, she tried an alternative approach. One afternoon, after everyone had left the classroom, she brought out a bag of fruit and began cutting each piece into equal parts and asking me questions about "the whole and its parts." After a few of these lessons I began to understand "doing" simple fractions.

When I think of Mrs. Mitchell and my other teachers, I realize now that the instruction they provided was content-driven. By the time I was in the upper elementary grades, it was clear to me that school learning was equated with what was in the textbooks and what the teacher said (which was usually what was in the textbook). Whether my peers and I were performing a teacher-developed exercise, finishing a worksheet, or completing a homework assignment or a test, our activities were all somehow connected to textbooks and to what the teacher had stated in class.

Perhaps because my teachers were so focused on teaching content, they knew little about me. During my years in school, I do not recall a teacher or a school administrator ever inviting me to talk about my interests, home environment, or cultural background. No one ever asked me about my favorite subject area, what I liked to do in class, or how I liked best to express myself. The instruction my teachers provided me and my peers was adequate, but it could have been so much better if my teachers had connected with me as a person.

Unlike Jesus (recall his biography from Chapter One), I never encountered a teacher who was a member of a minority group or who had a physical disability. I do not recall my teachers, who were White and presumably middle class, presenting content that included the experiences of minority groups. Like them, content, for the most part, *was* White. Nor do I recall them making use of cultural background information in an effort to better connect with some of the African American and Hispanic students in my classrooms. In junior high and high school, I learned quickly from my observations who were the "in" and the "out" students. The "in" students—most of whom were White, middle class, and able-bodied—were more accepted by the teachers, received recognition and awards, and went off to colleges and universities. Today I realize that what occurred in the schools I attended reflected the behavior and practice of the community at large; yet, at the time, no one *saw* the inequities or thought of schools as places where these inequities might be corrected.

The teacher-preparation program I completed in the 1970s, like most other teacher-preparation programs of the time, lacked any focus on minorities, pluralism, or the special needs of non-mainstream students. I completed all the required courses and experiences in preparation for the culminating activity student teaching in a large town in western Texas where the student population consisted of White, African American, and Hispanic students. As a student teacher, I would gradually assume responsibility for five periods of introductory biology.

My mentor, Ms. Willis, like my K-12 teachers and university professors, was primarily interested in content. I watched her closely in her classroom before assuming the role of teacher. She seemed to know instinctively which groups of students would be successful, and she gauged the effectiveness of her lessons by those students. When these students did well and others did not, Ms. Willis attributed the former group's success to being attentive in class, doing their homework, and studying for the quizzes and examinations. As a student teacher, I followed Ms. Willis's approach and began putting together learning activities aimed at the "in" students. By the time I completed my student teaching assignment, I had internalized this approach and began to concern myself less and less with the "out" students—those who did not do well in my biology classes. I continued to use this approach as a classroom teacher.

I taught for eight years, in mostly White middle-class communities, and only occasionally encountered minorities or low ses students who were like me when I attended public school. In those eight years, I do not believe I ever considered ses, ethnicity, gender, or exceptionalities such as mental or physical disabilities when identifying content and developing instruction in the life sciences. I focused on content that I loved and directed my energies at attempting to excite students about the life sciences. Was I an effective teacher in the classroom? For the "in" students, yes. But too many "out" students either did not learn the life sciences at all or learned that they weren't skilled in them.

Although I enjoyed teaching in the public schools, I eventually decided to work toward a doctoral degree in science education. Soon after I entered the graduate program, I was invited to work abroad in the Kingdom of Saudi Arabia (KSA). I accepted the invitation and became a technical writer for the Arabian American Oil Company (ARAMCO).

What started as a ninety-day contract turned into a two-year experience that expanded my perspective on cultural pluralism and teaching in diverse classrooms. In addition to writing training manuals, I also taught a few technical classes. At the same time, I became friends with several Saudis and was invited almost daily into their homes. These social occasions opened my eyes to cultural differences. But teaching KSA students put me face to face with the limitations of my White middle-class teaching habits and values.

My responsibility as a teacher in the KSA was to provide students with the content that would allow them to continue their employment with ARAMCO. I packaged this content in such a way that it was transmitted in competitive settings, so as to identify the more gifted students. I used classroom strategies that had been successful for me in the United States. For example, I peppered my lectures with competitive activities such as Teams-Games-Tournament (TGT), a team-centered approach to learning fact-based information. While the lectures were reasonably successful, the Saudi students participated reluctantly in TGT and other competitive games. As my students began to perform poorly academically and to distance themselves from me, I became concerned. Luckily I did not hesitate to seek help from Saudi colleagues and friends.

The Saudis advised me that my difficulties stemmed from not understanding Saudi culture. Saudi students, they explained, were accustomed to working together to solve problems, particularly difficult mental tasks. They were confused and uncomfortable in educational environments that called for activities that pitted one group against another. I had failed to consider how my personal background, ethnicity, and nationality interfaced with the KSA students. Until my extended stay in the KSA, I had never thought much about how teachers' personal and cultural characteristics influence how students learn and understand content.

I returned to the states with a changed perspective. My re-entry into North American culture was almost as difficult as my entry into the KSA culture two years earlier. After I returned, I began *seeing* things that I could not see before—cultural differences, insensitivities, and conflicts—and I began to understand and appreciate the growing emphasis on diversity and pluralism in schools. Perhaps what I learned most from my KSA experience relates to the influence of culture on teaching and learning. This awareness is at the very heart of teaching successfully in a pluralistic society.

Questions to Consider

1. How did Richard's experiences as a student influence who he became as a teacher? How might your own experiences as a student influence who you will become as a teacher?
2. Why didn't Richard's teachers seem to "see" differences and why did his stay in KSA enable him to do so? What experiences have you had that might enable you to "see" differences?
3. The educational experiences Richard describes occurred several decades ago. How have schools and society changed since that time?

PURPOSE

The overall purpose of this chapter is to help you better understand multicultural education and the personal and professional responsibilities of teaching in today's pluralistic society. Ideally, classroom teachers attempt to become familiar with the historical and contemporary experiences of all the students who enter their classrooms. These students come in all colors, shapes, and levels of physical and mental abilities. Their school performance is influenced by a number of forces, including their group membership (historical) and experiences in today's classrooms (contemporary). In this chapter, we provide you with a larger part of the picture by employing the principles of multicultural and inclusive education to help you gain an understanding of the historical and educational experiences of groups who have not been well served by schools. In many cases, this refers to students of color, learners with disabilities, and others we label as "different."

This chapter contextualizes the discussion about those students who have difficulty succeeding in schools by describing teachers, interactions between teachers and minorities and other marginalized groups, and noting policies and practices promoted by schools and administrators that have advantaged some students and disadvantaged others. We also describe important terms, the history of multicultural education, and schools that practice multicultural education. Specifically, this chapter will help you:

- understand the history and broader context of multiculturalism;
- define multiculturalism and related terms;

- examine schools and communities that are meeting the challenges of the increasing diversity of our society;
- gain an overview of the traits that will help you become a successful teacher in today's pluralistic classrooms;
- speculate about the future of multicultural education and diversity.

▌▌▌A BRIEF HISTORY OF MULTICULTURALISM

Multicultural education in the United States did not just emerge as an issue in the 1960s. Politicians and educators have been discussing this issue ever since schooling moved from one-room school houses to public education subsidized by local, state, and federal funds. Multicultural education had its beginnings at the turn of the twentieth century, when public education became a reality and schools were given the responsibility of educating the nation's domestic population and the many immigrants who were coming to America.

The two major educational ideologies at that time were Americanization/Anglo-Saxon conformity and cultural pluralism. These ideologies were in direct conflict.

> Whereas the Americanization process required immigrants to give up their old ways and to assimilate into the dominant Anglo-Saxon culture, the ideal of cultural pluralism denied the supremacy of Anglo-Saxon culture and rejected the demand that immigrant cultures melt and fuse to create an original American (Garcia, 1984, p. 17).

While educators pondered over which ideology would prevail in public education, economic and political forces influenced the debate. Political leaders, acknowledging the pressures of the Nativist Movement, pointed to the "rabble" entering the country, and economic leaders made their concerns known about the need for a compliant work force as the country industrialized. Both forces called for Americanization programs. According to Tozer, Violas, and Senese (1993), "the unprecedented flow of immigrants with different ethnic and religious backgrounds helped turn the nineteenth-century schools into socialization factories where, it was hoped, American values could be instilled into a diverse population" (p. 49). Perhaps to placate the multiculturalists and to gain greater acceptance of the Americanization ideology, educators euphemistically referred to the movement as the "melting pot" process. The term comes from the popular play *The Melting Pot,* which was staged at the turn of the century in New York City.

In the first half of the twentieth century, two trends were evident in the education of minority groups. First, the perception held by educational leaders was that minorities—African, Mexican, and Native Americans—were unassimilable and should not be part of the grand experiment of Americanization programs. Second, many believed that members of these groups were destined to play a subordinate role in society. Restricted from competing with members of the mainstream or European immigrants, they would be provided with a kind of education that would allow them to play out their destined roles in the lower ranks of society. Educational opportunities for women were also limited by society's long-standing perception of the group as subservient.

In the first three decades of the twentieth century, a number of events and trends influenced education in the United States. These included the large influx of European immigrants and the industrialization of America's cities; the Nativist Movement and World War I; the immigration of poverty-stricken Mexicans and the development of the Southwest; the mass migration of African Americans to North American cities; and the Great Depression. With the melting pot ideology holding firm, the academic and personal needs of ethnic and minority groups were not viewed as important factors for discussion in the development of America's public education system. Immigrants would melt into the Great American Pot; minorities would not "melt," but exist outside of the Pot.

In the 1930s, largely as a result of the rise of Nazism, intergroup education was adopted by school boards across the country. Funded by American liberal groups, intergroup educators developed and promoted programs aimed at depicting the cultural contributions of ethnic groups to the United States, highlighting cultural groups near extinction (e.g., Native American tribes), and narrating the horrors of Nazism, particularly the experiences of Jews. In the 1940s, this movement gained greater acceptance when African American soldiers, returning to their communities after serving courageously in World War II, encountered segregation and racial violence and reacted to the status quo by lobbying for change. More and more programs were initiated in schools to stop the violence directed at minorities and to eradicate the intolerance Americans exhibited toward religious, cultural, and racial differences (LaBelle & Ward, 1994). However, major structural changes to schools leading to equity for ethnic and minority groups, females, and the disabled did not appear on the agenda of educational leaders. Those items would surface in the next decade.

The 1960s Civil Rights Movement was the catalyst that ushered in the multicultural movement. Past efforts and programs aimed at addressing the needs of ethnic and minority groups and eradicating intolerance toward ethnic and religious differences had been influential. But events of the late 1950s and 1960s—the publication of Michael Harrington's *The Other America* (a book describing the lives of poor Americans in an affluent society), the *Brown v. the Board of Education* decision, the Montgomery Bus Boycott, the integration of Central High School in Little Rock, Arkansas—were pivotal in prompting community activists, parents, and students to take the initiative in demanding radical change in the education of America's children and youth. These three forces—educational practices prior to the 1960s, Supreme Court decisions in the 1950s and 1960s, and initiatives by minorities and other concerned Americans—along with Civil Rights events, bills that became laws under the administrations of Presidents Kennedy and Johnson, and the infusion of federal monies into the schools brought about changes to the schools.

Initially, educators—state superintendents, teachers, administrators, union leaders—were on the periphery, accepting conditions as they were. The Los Angeles Blowouts in the 1960s (Chicano students walking out of high school to complain about the lack of Mexican American teachers, administrators, and counselors, and a school curriculum that excluded the contributions of the group) and blowouts in other parts of the country embarrassed school officials and sensitized Americans to the plight of minorities. In the 1960s and 1970s, Americans were further embarrassed by demonstrations organized by activists, minority parents, and minority organizations detailing the ill effects of tracking, insensitive teachers and administrators, and funding formulae that discriminated against poor people and minorities. Concomitantly, these same groups called for bilingual education, multicultural education, and structural changes to schools that would insure minority students and others would have access to all educational programs. In the 1970s and beyond, education officials would join others in earnestly pursuing the American dream: quality educational opportunities for all.

Parents and organizations representing the interests of students with disabilities, buoyed by events in the 1960s and court decisions of the early 1970s, pressured Congress in 1975 to pass Public Law 94-142. The law mandated that each state provide a free and appropriate education for people, aged six to twenty-one, with disabilities.

States were to be in full compliance by fall 1980 (Myers & Myers, 1990). In 1990, PL94-142 was renamed the Individuals with Disabilities Education Act (IDEA). IDEA has since been amended and expanded in several ways. In addition, another group of students, while not eligible for special education as outlined in IDEA, is also eligible for accommodations and modifications to instruction. These students are included under Section 504 of the Americans with Disabilities Act (ADA). Students eligible for services under Section 504 may have a range of disabling conditions including HIV infection, heart disease, drug addiction, or alcoholism (Hardman, Drew, & Egan, 1999).

In the area of gender equity, activists and researchers began making educators aware of gender in education by tackling such issues as role expectations, gender issues in the curriculum, and gender-related treatment of students. Efforts at promoting equity for these groups and others continue and are now part of the mainstream of education. There is consensus among Americans that all children and young adults should be provided with quality schools where equal education opportunity is not a dream but a reality.

▌ Reader Activity 2.1

CONSULTING OTHER SOURCES
Researching the Experiences of Groups

In this activity, you will enhance your understanding of the students you will soon teach by gathering information about their historical experiences, particularly information that provides insights into their educational experiences. Form small groups to test the hypothesis given below. (Remember, testing means supporting or rejecting the hypothesis.)

"The treatment of groups in school mirrors their treatment in society."

1. Identify a major group in society (e.g., gays or lesbians, a specific ethnic or minority group, females, gifted individuals, students with disabilities) you wish to study.
2. As a group, assign roles and delegate responsibilities. For example, two people might agree to conduct the historical and educational research, another person might volunteer to explore methods of presenting the information, and a fourth to make the presentation.
3. After the information is collected, examine what your group has found and decide whether your findings support or reject the hypothesis.
4. Develop the presentation.
5. Present your findings to the class.

Below is an example to help you get started on your task. Let us say you identified Americans with mental disabilities as the group you wish to research. One way to begin this process is to ask some of the following questions.

1. Historically, what were some popular perceptions of people with mental disabilities held by Americans?
2. How did the medical community approach the treatment of mental disabilities in the early 1900s? 1950s? 1990s?
3. What perceptions did educators hold of the group?

4. What approach(es) did schools use to educate students with mental disabilities in the early 1900s? 1950s? 1990s?
5. Has it been difficult to provide this group of students with a quality education?

▌▌ DEFINING MULTICULTURAL EDUCATION AND ITS GOALS

Ask a dozen educators to define multicultural education, describe its purpose, and determine whether teachers who teach "multiculturally" are successful, and you will hear a dozen different responses. Why? We believe it is because multicultural education is a relatively new area of study that has not yet matured (Kaltsounis, 1997). To some educators, multicultural education means focusing on the educational experiences of one or more groups for the purpose of highlighting how schools have not served them well; to others it means raising the self-esteem of minorities; to still others it means creating schools that empower students and teachers to work for social justice. Critics, on the other hand, charge that goals and definitions are so expansive they have little meaning and that the movement has become too embroiled in political questions to have any real educational value (Diaz, Massialas, Xanthopoulos, 1999).

Our definition of multicultural education focuses on curriculum and student issues. We have purposely constructed the definition of two components to accentuate the importance of these issues. First multicultural education is a layered concept that includes not only the experiences of particular individuals and groups but also their shared interests and relationships, which, in turn, are embedded in the interconnectedness of all peoples of the world. In its full complexity then, multiculturalism implies the cultivation of a world view of human affairs. Paradoxically, perhaps, this expanded view of multiculturalism places primary emphasis on the individual and on the importance of individual decisions regarding all issues concerning the welfare of humankind (Garcia & Pugh, 1992, p. 218).

Second, multicultural education is education that attempts to provide for the academic needs of children and young adults of groups who historically have not been well served by schools and other children and young adults who experience similar difficulties with schools.

Goals bring meaning to a movement and provide teachers with the opportunity to select one of more areas they would like to address. Various goals of multicultural education have been identified and explained by a number of writers (La Belle & Ward, 1994; Sleeter & Grant, 1993). Our definition focuses on two important and commonly identified goals: expanding multicultural knowledge among students and bringing about equity.

▌▌ UNDERSTANDING THE TERMINOLOGY OF MULTICULTURAL AND INCLUSIVE EDUCATION

Part of being introduced to multicultural education is becoming acquainted with its terms. Because the movement is evolving and addressing issues and problems many consider contentious, agreement on the terms and descriptions here is not unanimous. We provide you with our own definitions (Powell, Zehm, & Garcia, 1996), but also borrow freely from others (e.g., Baruth & Manning, 1992; Banks, 1975, 1994; Campbell, 2000; Davidman & Davidman, 1994; Gollnick & Chinn, 1998).

In the 1950s, under the umbrella of *intercultural education, cultural pluralism,* and *cultural diversity,* programs were developed to reduce prejudice in the schools, highlight the cultural heritage of groups in and beyond the United States, and describe cultures deemed to be on the brink of extinction. In the 1960s, Americans turned their attention to minorities (e.g., African Americans, Mexican Americans, and Native Americans), and educators created what became known as *minority education* (cultural and historical information for and about minorities). Two other terms popular during this time period were *culturally disadvantaged* and *culturally deprived.* These terms surfaced when social scientists and educators keyed on groups' cultural attributes (e.g., the allegation that Mexican Americans do not value formal education) to explain why members did not perform well academically in school. When educators and policy makers broadened their focus and began to look at other factors to explain school performance, the phrase *culturally different* became part of educators' vocabulary. The use of the term "different" rather than "deprived" was important because it suggested that researchers and educators were attempting to be more objective in their examination of groups within the educational process. Educators were beginning to consider schools—teachers, administrators, curriculum, pedagogy—as possible contributors to the poor academic performance of minorities.

The term *race* also became part of the lexicon of multicultural education in the 1960s. According to Campbell (2000), it is a "term used to describe a large group of people with a somewhat similar genetic history. Many observers believe that they can describe a racial group based on hair color and texture, skin color, eye color, and body type" (p. 49). However, Campbell goes on to note that "most biologists and physical anthropologists recognize the futility of previous attempts to 'scientifically' define race and believe that there are no pure races on earth" (p. 49). He concludes his description by noting that "race is more of a social category than a reliable biological classification" (p. 49). Regardless, the term continues to be part of multicultural discussions.

According to Banks (1975), an *ethnic group* (Polish, Jewish, Irish American) "shares a common sense of values, behavior patterns, culture traits, and a sense of peoplehood" (p. 13). A *minority group* also shares a sense of peoplehood, but unlike ethnic groups, it has "unique physical and/or cultural characteristics which enable persons who belong to dominant ethnic groups to easily identify [them and] treat them in a discriminatory fashion" (p. 13). Banks believes the differences between ethnic and minority groups are crucial in gaining an understanding of each and the interactions among the groups:

> While a Polish American immigrant can Anglicize his or her name, acquire Anglo-American cultural traits, and move into almost any White neighborhood without evoking much animosity, no matter how culturally assimilated an [African] American becomes, his or her skin color remains a social stigma of immense importance to most members of White ethnic groups (13).

In the 1960s, African, Mexican, and Native Americans and Puerto Ricans were the major minority groups in the United States. However, as the term *minority* evolved, it was employed to describe other groups, such as White ethnic groups, poor Whites, rural Americans, and children from these groups who did not perform well in school. In the 1970s, the term *minority* came to include Japanese and Chinese Americans and other groups that had experienced prejudice, discrimination, and/or racism. A careful look at the group *Hispanics/Latino(a)s* may illustrate the evolutionary nature of the terminology of multicultural education.

In the 1960s, the term *Mexican Americans* referred to individuals who immigrated to the United States and considered this country their permanent residence, and to individuals who were born in this country of parents (one or both) who were immigrants from Mexico or of Mexican ancestry. *Mexicans* were individuals who had not decided whether they wished to call the United States home or were in this country illegally. On the East Coast, *Puerto Ricans* were the dominant group. As the 1960s Civil Rights Movement gained momentum, some Mexican Americans chose the term *Chicano* as a form of self-identification. According to Nieto (1996):

> Chicano. . . was a decidedly self-affirming and political term reflecting the unique culture and realities of urban, economically oppressed Mexican Americans in U. S. society. Its use in the recent past, however, seems to have been abandoned by many segments of the community. . . (p. 24).

In the 1970s, as immigration from Mexico continued, greater numbers of Puerto Ricans moved to the East Coast, and Cubans immigrated to Florida and other parts of the United States, the term *Hispanic* surfaced and was employed to capture this large Spanish-speaking minority population. According to Baruth and Manning (1992), *Hispanic* was selected because it is "a general title, and included all people of Spanish origin and descent" (p. 8). In the 1980s, as immigration from other Latin American countries to the United States increased, Hispanics looked for a term to better identify more than 20 million people. In the early 1990s, the term *Latino* came into prominence and is used with variations to reflect the influence of the women's movement on this minority group, *Chicano(a), Latino(a)*. Today, the two popular terms are *Latino(a)* and *Hispanic*.

Minorities, in an effort to better define themselves and to build a sense of camaraderie among the groups, offered the multicultural community the phrase *people of color*. Banks (1994), uses "people of color" as a synonym for "minority group." As *minority* evolved into an inclusive term, *at risk, marginalized,* and *disempowered* surfaced as descriptors of the many groups who would be included under the umbrella of multicultural education. Among others, these groups include male, female, gay, lesbian, and bisexual students; people with exceptionalities; recent immigrants; and people living in poverty.

Gender, in the context of multicultural education, refers to the differences between males and females and differences among bisexual, heterosexual, gay and lesbian students and how these differences manifest themselves in the classroom. It also refers to curricular issues, that is, the portrayal of males and females in textbooks and other resources employed by the teacher (Gollnick & Chinn, 1998).

The term *exceptional* is a comprehensive term used to describe "any individual whose physical, mental, or behavioral performance deviates substantially from the norm, either higher or lower. A person with exceptional characteristics is not necessarily a person with a handicap. People with exceptional characteristics may need additional educational, social, or medical services. . . ." (Hardman, Drew, & Egan, 1999, p. 3) Exceptionalities may include learning disorders, behavior disorders, speech and language disorders, sensory disorders, physical disorders, health disorders, or gifts and talents.

Historically, students with exceptionalities have been educated for all or part of the day outside the regular education classroom. In the 1970s, many schools began *mainstreaming* students with exceptionalities. Selected exceptional students were placed into regular classrooms while special education staff provided appropriate support services. Although this term remains in use, *inclusion* is now the preferred term for describing the education of students with exceptionalities in regular education classrooms. Included students are not isolated into special classes or areas of the school. The continuum of inclusion ranges from full to partial.

Another group of terms you will encounter while exploring multicultural education describes what is commonly called the *dominant culture* and by extension, *school culture.* These terms refer to the school and classroom environments culturally different students experience each day. Other terms employed include *Anglo culture* and *mainstream culture.* Campbell (2000) uses the term *macroculture* to define U.S. and school culture:

> The dominant worldview in U.S. society, and therefore, U.S. schools, has been defined by the values, attitudes, beliefs, and folkways of the European American majority. These patterns of communication and life are used as criteria by which to judge right and wrong behavior. In the classroom, this cultural domination is reinforced by the preponderance of middle-class, European American teachers who *unconsciously* [italics added] use their cultural values to judge their students' work and behavior (p. 30).

The focus on the macroculture has led multiculturalists to focus on societal forces seen as limiting the groups' opportunities. With respect to public schools, multiculturalists and inclusionists have pushed for the development of materials that more accurately depict societal groups; inservice programs for teachers aimed at creating multicultural and inclusive classrooms; and activities that provide students with the opportunity to engage in discussions addressing terms like *racism*—the oppression of a group of people based on their perceived race (Campbell, 2000, p. 49); *prejudice*—a set of rigid and unfavorable attitudes toward a particular group or groups that is formed in disregard of facts (Banks, 1975, p. 69); *discrimination*—differential behavior toward a stigmatized group (Banks, 1975, p. 69); *stereotypes*—predispositions and general attitudes and impressions of particular groups; crystallized descriptions of groups allowing for little variability; and *labeling*—the process of describing people who vary significantly from the norm (Hardman, Drew, & Egan, 1999, p. 2).

To conclude this section, we introduce you to the terms employed to describe several curricular manifestations of multicultural education. *Ethnic studies* describes the scientific and humanistic study of the histories, cultures, and experiences of ethnic groups in the United States and other nations (Banks,1994). *Global education* refers to the study of the cultures, institutions, and interconnectedness of nations *outside* [italics added] the United States (Banks 1994): *(centric* (as in *Afrocentric) education* places a particular people's history, knowledge, and values at the center of the curriculum (Asante, 1988). *Multiethnic education* is a broad term used to refer to any reform movement designed to restructure educational institutions so that students from diverse ethnic groups, such as Asian Americans, Native Americans, and Hispanics, will experience equal educational opportunities (Banks, 1994).

For years, the melting pot metaphor described earlier was the predominant way mainstream culture viewed life in the United States and defined the purpose of schools. Today, the salad bowl metaphor depicts newcomers and those who have been marginalized by society as having a right "to maintain their languages and cultures while combining with others to form a 'salad,' which is our uniquely U.S. society" (Nieto, 1996, p. 392). The salad bowl metaphor is inclusive; its supporters aim to increase school success for all students. They view pluralism as a societal condition wherein diverse groups—ethnic, linguistic, cultural, and religious, among others—maintain an autonomous participation in the common culture but do not lose their individual traits.

▮▮▮CULTURAL PLURALISM IN SCHOOLS AND COMMUNITIES

A school or a community is pluralistic when it respects and appreciates multiple forms of diversity, and when it encourages many minority groups to keep their traditions alive (Bennett, 1998). Let's look at one community and two schools in different parts of the country to see examples of contemporary pluralism. The community is Garden City, Kansas—a mid-size, midwestern town attempting to come to terms with a recent major influx of new arrivals. The schools are Mark Keppel High School in Monterey Park, California, and Brown Barge Middle School in Pensacola, Florida.

Garden City, Kansas

When we think of sweeping demographic changes, the midwest rarely comes to mind. But Garden City, a town in western Kansas, experienced considerable change in the 1980s and early 1990s. Garden City is a rural community that depends upon agriculture and meat packing for its economic well-being. The relocation of meat packing plants from Kansas City and Chicago to Garden City have brought about the community's cultural transformation. Stull, Broadway, and Erickson (1992) explain what happened in Garden City:

> In 1980 Garden City's population was 18,256, and in many ways the town typified the so-called heartland. Its citizens were predominantly Anglo (82 percent). Hispanics . . . were the only substantial minority (16 percent). But the 1980s witnessed rapid change. In December 1980, IBP, Inc. (formerly Iowa Beef Processors), opened the world's largest beef-packing plant ten miles west of Garden City, near the hamlet of Holcomb.

In order for IBP to provide a labor force for its large meat packing plant, it recruited personnel from remote parts of the country. This recruitment effort affected the make-up of the other major plant in the area. Stull et al. (1992) report:

> In five short years Garden City was transformed from a bicultural community of established Anglos and Mexican Americans to a multicultural community, as Southeast Asian refugees and Hispanic migrants came to work in the beef plants. By the late 1980s, the minority population had doubled, from 18 percent in 1980 to 36 percent by 1989.

The small western Kansas town was transformed almost overnight from a slow-paced agricultural center to a large multicultural community with established inhabitants making room for the new ones. This change had an immediate impact on the local community and its schools. The community attempted to address its new diversity by recognizing the cultural heritages of both the established and newly arrived inhabitants. Yet, into the mid 1990s, most newly arrived citizens remained separated from the established inhabitants, residing in the poorer sections of the city. Because many of the migrants, refugees, and their children spoke a home language other than English, the schools instituted English as a Second Language Programs and took the initiative in examining the advantages of bilingual programs. The schools also began a program to search for and recruit teachers who were culturally sensitive and knowledgeable of the needs of these new arrivals. Garden City, Kansas is not unique in the changes it is experiencing. Cities, towns, and even rural areas across the country are experiencing demographic changes.

Mark Keppel High School

In a period of three decades, Monterey Park, the Los Angeles suburb that is the site of Mark Keppel High School (MKHS), has undergone two major transformations: from predominantly Anglo American to predominantly Hispanic; and from Hispanic to predominantly Asian (Horton, 1992). As you walk down the streets of Monterey Park, you find yourself looking at advertisements in English, faded business signs in Spanish, and brightly colored signs written in Chinese characters. Driving north out of Monterey Park, you immediately enter Alhambra, an Hispanic suburb. Because MKHS sits on the border of these communities, it draws students from both areas, as well as students from Rosemead, another predominantly Hispanic community. Consequently, MKHS is comprised of Asian, Hispanic, Black, and "Other" students—those who do not fit into the coding schemes for country of origin employed by the school. Students come to school speaking a variety of languages and close to seventy percent are considered limited English-proficient. Approximately thirty first languages other than English are spoken in the school by the students. In addition, many of the students live in poverty and experience disabilities related to learning.

MKHS teachers, administrators, and staff have adjusted to the new realities by viewing diversity as an asset, not a liability. Many of the teachers are bilingual in Spanish, Mandarin, Cantonese, French, German, or Armenian; a few of the school counselors and administrators are also bilingual or have a working knowledge of some of the commonly spoken languages. The teachers and staff at MKHS attempt to develop educational opportunities that are personally meaningful, culturally appropriate, and academically challenging.

In some ways, MKHS is similar to other schools across the nation. The school has a standard high-school curriculum, remains accountable for standardized testing of student achievement, provides athletic opportunities for all students, and has the usual clubs and extracurricular organizations. In addition to this common culture connecting students, MKHS attempts to affirm cultural pluralism by being responsive to individual and group requests. The Spanish bilingual program ranges from college preparatory courses in mathematics and social science to Advanced Placement courses in Spanish language and literature. One of the athletic opportunities for students is badminton, a sport especially prized by Asian students. Many students, Asian and non-Asian alike, participate in the sport and compete for highly coveted positions on the school's badminton teams. MKHS also offers its core classes in Spanish, Cantonese, and Mandarin and sends communications to parents in these and other languages as well as English. MKHS teachers strive continuously to provide students with strong instruction in the major subject areas. Their commitment is to connect with the students and community by offering a curriculum that is culturally responsive, reflective of the needs and interests of students, focused on providing students with the knowledge and skills to compete for worthwhile jobs, and effective in preparing students to become productive members of society and citizens of the world.

Brown Barge Middle School

Later in this chapter, you will meet Linda Fussell, who teaches at Brown Barge Middle School (BBMS) in Pensacola, Florida. BBMS has a school student population that is majority White with a significant number of African Americans and a growing number of immigrants from Central America and Cuba. While the student population has been relatively stable, ethnic tension among the three groups manifests itself in Pensacola and in BBMS, as students from all backgrounds come to this technology magnet school. Aware of what could happen when issues of diversity are not addressed, the teachers at BBMS initiated an integrated curriculum in which teams of teachers develop twelve-week curriculum packets on particular themes called "streams." One stream required of all students is entitled "American Tapestries." In this twelve-week stream, students deal directly with issues of culture, ethnicity, and diversity. The instructional program the teachers develop is based on diversity issues related to the students' experiences at BBMS. "American Tapestries" is an integral part of the education of BBMS students. While issues of diversity are dealt with directly in this packet, it occurs in the context of the overall curriculum. Moreover, issues of diversity are not isolated in this unit but also are dealt with indirectly in the other twelve-week curriculum packets the teachers, students, and parents help to develop.

▌ **Reader Activity 2.2**

CONSULTING OTHER SOURCES
Charting Changes in Demographics

Choose a geographical location—perhaps the town or city in which your college or university is located, your own home town, a community you know or one in which you think you might like to teach. Research the location's population changes over the past twenty years. The purpose of this activity is to help you see for yourself what changes, if any, are occurring in places that affect your own life.

Determine what groups, if any, have influenced the community. For example, has there been an influx of Americans from other parts of the country? An influx of refugees? Immigrants? What percentage of the population would be classified as "minorities"? Is the population growing or decreasing? Is the population aging or getting younger?

After examining for population fluctuations, determine how these changes have influenced the community. What perceptions do established residents hold of these new arrivals? What forces have influenced the development of these perceptions? What perceptions do the new arrivals hold of established residents? How would you characterize the interactions among the groups? What does the future hold for this community?

Next, examine the local school system. Has the school system responded to the needs of the new arrivals? How? Has the overall school system changed (e.g., school board, school staff, core curriculum, policies, rules, and procedures)?

In your opinion, is this community a good home for the new arrivals? Is the school system on the path toward culturally relevant teaching? Does the school system promote a melting pot or a salad bowl ideology? Report your findings to the class.

▍▌ TEACHING IN A PLURALISTIC CLASSROOM

One of the responsibilities of a teacher in the twenty-first century will be to prepare students for a workforce, society, and world that demographers are characterizing as increasingly diverse. That is, whether your students ultimately remain in their home

Culturally relevant teaching treats students as important contributors to classroom discourse.

community or move away, they will become a part of an unprecedented global pluralism. This means that your classroom teaching must reflect local and national concerns and a pluralism that is both local and global.

Recent studies provide insight into what proponents of cultural pluralism characterize as culturally responsive or culturally relevant teaching (Ladson-Billings, 1995; Ladson-Billings, 1994; Powell, 1996). In *Dreamkeepers: Successful Teachers of African American Children* (1994), Gloria Ladson-Billings has described culturally relevant teaching practices of teachers she studied over an extended period of time. While Ladson-Billings focused on successful teachers of African American students, the qualities she identified characterize teachers of students who exhibit many forms of diversity.

Once we acknowledge difference as a fact of contemporary life and begin to view differences as strengths, it is not a great leap to accept the premise that "all persons are equally valued members of this society and that it is worthwhile to do whatever it takes to include everyone" (Stainback, Stainback, & Stefanich, 1996). Just as today's public school classrooms are probably more culturally diverse than at any previous time in our history, so are they more diverse in terms of student abilities. In more and more schools, students with exceptionalities, such as giftedness, learning disabilities, and physical disabilities are being educated in regular classrooms. Teachers who exhibit the culturally relevant characteristics and practices described here are dedicated to the success of all students whatever their differences may be. We will briefly summarize six characteristics and five practices and then see how three successful teachers in diverse school and classroom contexts put them into action.

Personal Characteristics

High Self-Esteem and High Regard for Others

Teachers in the Ladson-Billings study felt positive about the profession of teaching, and they viewed themselves as making an important contribution to society. Moreover, they viewed others, especially their students, as important persons in school and in society.

Self as Part of the Community; Teaching as Giving Back to the Community

A second quality of the teachers is that they sincerely believed they were part of the community in which they taught. They also believed that what they did as teachers—prepare young persons for being successful in the greater society—was giving the community a source of hope and strength for the future.

Teaching as an Art; Teacher as Artist

Teachers sometimes view their professional selves more as technicians than artists. Teachers-as-technicians tend to use the same strategies for teaching, regardless of the diversity of students' backgrounds and of how these backgrounds might enrich their classroom instruction. Teachers who view themselves as artists tend to look for teaching strategies that are more tailored to students' individual backgrounds and cultures.

Believe That All Students Can Succeed

The teachers firmly believed that all students are capable of being successful in school. This meant that they regularly used multiple strategies in the same classroom in order to reach all students and in order to ensure student success.

Help Students Make Connections Among Community, National, and Global Identities

The teachers selected content and implemented instruction so that their students could make connections between what was taught in the classroom and what happens in the local, national, and global communities. Giving students a sense of social responsibility was a foremost concern for all teachers.

Teaching As "Digging Knowledge Out" of Students

Rather than viewing teaching as a process of pouring knowledge into students' minds, the teachers viewed teaching as engaging students' present understandings with the content being taught. This approach to teaching aligns with the constructivist approaches now being espoused across the nation: students are viewed as important contributors to classroom discourse rather than being viewed as commodities to be molded and shaped by the content to be learned and by traditional teaching strategies that help them learn it.

Teaching Practices

Treat Students as Competent Human Beings

In schools where students are organized by ability grouping, teachers can easily fall into the academic trap of treating some students in lower ability groups as incompetent. These teachers believe they have to "water down" the content so that low-ability-grouped students can learn at least something. Successful teachers in diverse classrooms reach into their bag of teaching tricks and try all kinds of things to get their students involved in learning content that is not watered down, but reorganized in such a way to help students be successful in learning the same content as students in other ability groups. These teachers treat all students as competent and capable human beings.

Help Students Move from What They Know to What They Need to Know

In order to do this, of course, teachers must know where students are with the content being taught. An important assumption that goes along with this quality is that teachers do not assume that students know more than they really do know, and do not assume that they know less or nothing at all. Hence, culturally relevant teachers affirm what students now know, and then begin to guide students to what they need to know in order to be successful in school.

Focus Classroom Activities on Instruction

Culturally relevant teachers do not lose sight of the mission of school, namely instruction. Such teachers are aware that some students, perhaps most students, would much rather get by in school doing very little. A continuous focus on instruction, however, ensures student success in school.

Extend Students' Thinking and Abilities

When teachers maintain a focus on extending students' thinking and abilities through careful planning and meaningful teaching, then student performance both in and out of school is enhanced. However, before this can happen, teachers must know students' backgrounds, and they must know how to help students connect subject matter content to their lives outside of school. Then teaching and learning become meaningful activities for students.

Understand Students' Capabilities for Learning Selected Content

In order to do this, teachers first must know who students are, and they must know how students' identities influence what and how they learn. All students do not share the same capabilities for learning a targeted body of content. Many reasons exist for this, including students' cultural backgrounds, aptitude, motivations, and disabilities or talents. Knowing students' readiness for acquiring content is a precursor to understanding students' capabilities. Teachers who lack this understanding run the risk of pushing some students to the margins of their classrooms where they may view learning as irrelevant and meaningless.

Have In-Depth Knowledge of the Subject Matter

Teachers who are successful in diverse classrooms make subject matter to be learned central to all classroom instruction. This does not mean that instructional strategies have to be the same for similar content—teaching strategies must be aligned with students' backgrounds. However, all students must and should be guided in learning subject matter. Consequently, culturally relevant teachers are also learners, continuously upgrading their own knowledge about what they are teaching their students. "Teacher-as-learner" is an important metaphor for any teacher in today's classrooms.

Three Successful Teachers

The case studies presented here focus on Linda Fussell, a Pensacola, Florida middle school teacher; Gissella Castro, an Alhambra, California high school social studies teacher; and Joanie Phillips, a Las Vegas, Nevada high school English teacher. These teachers exhibit both the characteristics and practices described above that enable them to be successful in diverse classrooms. As you will see, it is difficult to tease out and analyze the characteristics and practices that Ladson-Billings has identified. Nevertheless, we will highlight these characteristics as we listen to these skilled teachers. The three teachers described here are very concerned about engaging students in the content areas, and their teaching strategies for doing this extend beyond the mere practice of presenting prescribed information. Their approaches are more reflective of *"digging knowledge out"* of students.

At Brown Barge Middle School (BBMS), Linda Fussell and the teachers on her team developed units of instruction based on students' personal, academic, and cultural needs, as well as school and community values. In order to do this, the teachers used their *in-depth knowledge of subject matter,* their *understanding of students' capabilities for learning selected content,* and their *commitment to helping students make connections among their community, national, and global identities.* Perhaps in part because of her *high self-esteem,* Linda felt comfortable with this nontraditional approach to teaching, but admitted that it can be stressful for teachers who prefer the traditional model of schooling, where teachers view themselves as content specialists and where the content is predetermined. Linda reported,

> This school [BBMS] is a very stressful place for teachers who worry that they're not teaching content because they are most comfortable when they are within the structure of the content. I believe that people who won't work well at this school are just afraid to see themselves from another teacher perspective. They're afraid to give up their traditional roles. But those roles won't work anymore, especially here.

Joanie Phillips, like Linda, distinguished between the purpose of her classroom curriculum, which puts students first, and the purpose of her colleagues' classroom curricula, which put content first. Joanie's metaphor for teaching reveals that she sees *teaching as an art* and herself *as an artist:*

> I love my students like a farmer loves the field, like a musician loves the melody. I don't see the content I teach as the field. You know how a farmer loves the land, and the farmer says, 'I've worked **with** nature to produce something valuable.' I know teachers who feel that way about the subject matter. But I feel that way about the kids. And musicians don't love their instruments as much as the music, as the sound. But some teachers are in love with the instrument and not the music. The music is what happens with the kids. The music is why I teach.

Gissella Castro, viewed herself as a mentor-friend to her students and she grounded this view in her cultural heritage as a Latina. She reported,

> I'm very academic in my classroom. I encourage my students academically. But I also see myself as a mentor-friend to them. And maybe I have this role because I teach in a high school. But I never really accepted the American view of a rebellious [adolescent] that is between adulthood and childhood, and that has to be held in with a tight rein. That's not the Latino view. We don't even have a concept of teenager. And so I'm a mentor-friend from that basis, that my students are more adult than anything else.

Gissella's comments suggest that she *treats students as competent human beings,* that she *believes that all students can succeed,* that she sees herself as *part of the community* and her *teaching as giving back to the community.* Linda, too, exhibited these qualities. She noted:

> Education should be humanistically oriented. That means being teacher as facilitator and empowering kids. What is important, particularly at this school, is that teachers have to learn to be facilitators and share in the learning with kids. Teachers can't be afraid to come down from that authoritarian sphere. They sometimes feel as though they have to be authoritarian because they don't know how to maintain order and control through learning. We need to help guide students. For ourselves as teachers, we just have to quit thinking we're the most important thing around here. And that's what many teachers think.

These teachers demonstrated high self-esteem and treated students as competent human beings in their classroom instruction. For Linda, this meant,

> I like being out in front. I like being on the radical edge. While I've been afraid to take risks from time to time, I've always been glad I did. I think the benefits for students are so much greater when I take risks.

Linda, Joanie, and Gissella were continuously trying new instructional strategies and searching for relevant content, they avoided routine teaching, and they all believed that the prescribed curriculum was unable to meet the needs of their diverse student populations. They were also continuously learning about students' backgrounds and culturally relevant ways to communicate with their students. Joanie, who had a high percentage of Latino students, was learning Spanish; Gissella, who speaks Spanish and English fluently, was learning Chinese phrases.

Joanie, Linda, and Gissella acquired sensitivity for their students' cultural backgrounds. For them, classroom decision-making was based, at least in part, on the students as individuals and members of particular cultural groups. The instructional risks they took affirmed their strong belief that traditional content-centered curriculum (e.g., a prescribed set of knowledge and skills reflective of one cultural value system) was not effective in today's diverse classrooms.

Acquiring sensitivity for students allows teachers to become familiar with their cultural backgrounds, develop an understanding of the many ways culture influences classroom teaching, and gain access to students' first languages and to use these modes of communication to build trust and respect among teachers and students. One way Joanie *helped students make connections among community, national, and global identities* was by having them write about the many aspects of their lives outside school. She admitted that when she started teaching, her sensitivity for students' cultural backgrounds was lacking, but experience helped her to fill in this gap.

Joanie demonstrated a strong disposition to meet students' needs. In her first teaching assignment, she taught English as a second language to limited-English-proficient Latino students. She saw these students as *competent human beings.* At the same time, she recognized that they had many personal and academic needs. She spent many hours thinking about and creating specific kinds of instruction tailored to their needs. She developed a three-prong approach when developing curriculum for her literature classes. First she searched for Latino/a authors who discussed topics relevant to the skeletal literature units she had developed. Second, she developed activities that called for students to connect their lives outside of school to their lives inside of school so she could gain insights into their cultures. Third, she visited students' homes so she could build a fuller and more complete understanding of their home and family cultures.

> The thing that's beautiful about this school is you can hear all different kinds of languages in the hall. That should be affirmed and encouraged. It seems to me that if you're a professional and the place you work is very multicultural then you better make it your business to find out what [your students] are saying, to learn enough of their language.

Like Joanie, Gissella linked cultural sensitivity to knowing her students and becoming more familiar with her own Latino heritage. Gissella reported,

> A big part of what I am as a teacher is being Latina. And I think that's what I try to get across to my kids and how I interact with them. Their culture, their family, their traditions, are just as legitimate, are just as important, as anything else.

Gissella's Latino background has given her insight into how she might best communicate with Latino students.

> For the Spanish speaking kids, the kids that come from a Latino background, the affective level has to be established first. And that means establishing respect with the kids immediately. . . from that you can play your teacher role.

Linda's sensitivity for students' cultural backgrounds is grounded in her experiences with White and Black students. She noted,

> I think that White teachers often think they know what it takes for a Black child to succeed. I think a lot of times they try to make them White, to impress upon them the importance of things they know will make them successful by White standards, like correct grammar and certain behavior qualities. Maybe what these teachers need to be looking at is students' cultural learning styles, then work up lessons around these learning styles.

All three of these teachers demonstrate leadership in diversity issues at their schools. Linda is the instructional leader of the "American Tapestries" stream at BBMS. Joanie sponsors the Hispanic Club; her primary duties include helping students plan Hispanic-oriented events such as dances and field trips. Gissella is one of two teachers who planned, developed, and teaches "Conflict Resolution," a course aimed at helping high school students understand how personal and cultural characteristics may be misunderstood and how to develop and employ conflict mediation skills.

Knowing the cultural and individual backgrounds of their students, Linda, Joanie, and Gissella believed their school districts' prescribed curricula were not always relevant to students' lives, thus disengaging some students from meaningful learning. Joanie's concerns over the literature her department expected her to teach—literature which she characterized as extremely traditional—summarizes this sentiment most clearly. Joanie believed "the great literature that everyone in school always has to read" alienated many of her students. She noted,

> I'm not saying that great literature is irrelevant. It's relevant in that it helps you to see the world in a broader way. But its not relevant if it alienates you. And many of my students

just don't connect with this literature. For my students I try to choose literature that is culturally inclusive.

Joanie believed that to get students to read consistently and regularly, she first had to get them to read literature that was relevant to their lives, that somehow spoke directly to them as persons (Banks, 1993). Later, she could help them build the bridges that would connect them to more traditional authors such as William Shakespeare or Mark Twain.

All three teachers supplemented their districts' established curricula by diversifying theirs. This diversification could be viewed by some as highly subversive, since signing a teacher contract is usually a commitment to teach the established curriculum, even if this means teaching to a standardized test or to an adopted textbook (Dilg, 1999). Linda, Joanie, and Gissella, however, were able to restructure their curricula to fit students' cultural and personal needs without risking their employment security. As a beginning teacher, you might not have this freedom. All teachers have a professional responsibility to help students achieve school district goals. By becoming more knowledgeable and understanding of students' backgrounds, you will be in a more responsive position to connect district goals to these backgrounds.

Linda, Joanie, and Gissella extended their classrooms to the home and family cultures of students in various ways. They acknowledged the profound influence that social and cultural factors outside school have on life in school. By doing this, the teachers and their students were connected not just by their standard roles at school, but by family culture and related values as well.

As you reflect on these brief portraits of Linda Fussell, Joanie Phillips, and Gissella Castro, you will undoubtedly recognize additional ways in which they exhibit the characteristics and practices described by Ladson-Billings. You may also identify characteristics and practices that perhaps we have overlooked.

▌Reader Activity 2.3

WHAT WOULD YOU DO?
A Middle-School Science Exhibition

What does culturally relevant teaching look like in practice? As you read this account of Laura Krich's sixth-grade science exhibition, think about how her classroom illustrates the characteristics and strategies cited above.

In traditional science fairs, students display their original scientific work. Adults judge the competition, and some students are declared the "winners." Laura Krich, a science teacher who teaches a diverse group of sixth-graders in Lexington, Massachusetts, was dissatisfied with this approach and decided to change it. The middle school at which she teaches is located in the greater Boston area. Students come from a range of ethnic and socioeconomic backgrounds: many recent immigrants are settling in the area, and the school practices inclusion of students with special needs. Sensitive to this diversity, as well as the characteristics of young adolescents, she wanted to eliminate the competitive element, place students in the role of evaluators, and to establish high expectations for scientific work that all students could achieve.

Laura's students spent about two weeks preparing for the science exhibition. They began by brainstorming, listing, sorting, and conferencing with peers and family members in order to generate their own experimental questions. Once each student settled on a viable question, he or she received a notebook in which to record the progress of the experiment. Laura gave a brief lecture on the ethical and legal reasons why scientists need to record their work carefully. The school media specialist spent two class periods teaching students how to use printed and electronic reference materials. Students then conducted their research on their own time. In class, Laura frequently modeled experiments and activities in order to teach the students the scientific method, the process they would follow in their own projects. She required regular progress reports from each student, as well as written timelines so that both she and the student would know whether the project was progressing satisfactorily. Several days before the exhibition, her classes brainstormed the criteria by which the work would be judged, e.g., "Did the question make sense?" "Was the work original?" "Was the student able to answer all the interview questions?" From these suggestions, Laura compiled a master list which became the Exhibition Assessment Form.

Because students' work would be evaluated by interviews, Laura trained the students in interviewing techniques and conducted mock interviews before the class. She created a master interview schedule, which students then completed for themselves. Each student was required to conduct five interviews and to be interviewed by five peers.

On the day of the exhibition, the four teachers on Laura's team suspended classes. Students set up their displays during homeroom. They spent the rest of the day interviewing, being interviewed, explaining their projects, and viewing their peers' projects. The teachers circulated through the four exhibition rooms ensuring the process was flowing smoothly. Despite the inevitable "glitches" in any large-scale project, the teachers and students deemed the exhibition a success and plan to continue it annually. The sixth-graders proved that they could take ownership for their work and fairly evaluate their peers. More importantly, they learned that "*everyone* can be a scientist. The secret is to follow a scientific process" (Krich, 1994. p. 33).

Questions to Consider

1. Discuss how Laura Krich exhibits the characteristics of a culturally relevant teacher: high self-esteem, seeing self as part of the community, seeing teaching as an art, belief that all students can succeed, helping students make connections, and teaching as "digging knowledge out" of students.
2. Discuss how Laura's science fair conforms to culturally relevant teaching practices: treat students as competent human beings, help students move from what they know to what they need to know, focus classroom activities on instruction, extend students' thinking and abilities, understand students' capabilities for learning selected content, and have in-depth knowledge of the subject matter.
3. Compare and contrast the benefits and limitations of the traditional science fair model with Laura's exhibition in terms of the following hypothetical students: Tasha, a recent immigrant from Albania and whose English proficiency is limited; Evan, a student with a reading/writing learning disability; Deshonne, a gifted African American student whose parents are doctors; and Tammi, a low-achieving, low ses student from one of the working farms in the community.
4. Some people fear that culturally relevant teaching is equal to "watering down" the curriculum. How would you respond to this criticism?

Classrooms At the Turn of the Century and Beyond

Clearly, classrooms of today are unlike those of only a few decades ago, and if America's prognosticators are correct, classrooms will continue changing and become more and more diverse. What is happening in Garden City, Kansas, Monterey Park, California, and Pensacola, Florida is happening across the nation. Rural, urban, and suburban communities are experiencing change as Americans move from one community to another, immigrants and refugees from the Americas, Europe, Africa, and Asia select the United States as their new home, and schools adopt inclusive policies and practices.

Empirical studies and statistical evidence support our view that progress has been made at enhancing school success for children and young adults of traditional minority groups, as well as for females, students with exceptionalities, and others. Faculties of schools of education, public school teachers, and administrators are more diverse, and all are committed to improving the quality of education for all children. Mark Keppel High School and Brown Barge Middle School are examples of the many public schools providing effective programs for diverse students.

Evidence suggests that schools like BBMS and MKHS are having a positive effect on the targeted populations across the nation: (1) girls' scores on math and science measures have dramatically improved in the past 30 years to narrow the gap between their performance and that of boys (Lawton, 1997); (2) the difference between White and Hispanic reading scores in the National Assessment of Educational Progress (NAEP) has been declining consistently since 1975, as has the gap between White and Hispanic mathematics scores (Bracey, 1994); (3) according to the Department of Education, the number of students with disabilities (aged 6 to 21) receiving educational services in regular classrooms increased significantly from the 1980s to the 1990s (Roach, 1995); (4) the proportion of high school graduates going on to college increased in the 1990s (Finney, 1997); and (5) between 1984-1994, the total enrollment in higher education increased by about two million, or 16 percent, and a significant part of that increase was attributed to minorities. (Menand, 1997).

Nonetheless, multicultural education is not without contemporary critics. Some parents, politicians, and educators oppose multicultural and inclusive education because they believe it emphasizes cultural learning and social skills at the expense of the major important concepts in the curriculum. Critics also argue that multicultural education places too much emphasis on the differences among students and threatens classroom (and, by extension, societal) cohesiveness. Still others aver that it promotes curricular efforts that distort historical interpretations of the American experience. Finally, opponents contend that multicultural education is too expensive (e.g., bilingual programs, courses on minority and ethnic group experiences, provision of support services for students with exceptionalities) and that it is not successful at addressing the academic needs of its targeted population.

Multicultural education is an issue of global importance. As the world "shrinks," more and more countries are facing and meeting the challenges of increasingly diverse populations. The kind of multicultural education a country may pursue is influenced by its history, culture, economic, and political development, immigration and migration patterns, and place in the community of nations. For example, in Japan, its aim is to promote a greater tolerance among the Japanese and nationals from the Philippine Islands and other countries in Southeast Asia who come to Japan on a temporary basis to work in particular areas of the economy. In Australia, the major thrust of the movement is to promote tolerance and to transition into mainstream society the growing number of immigrants who are making Australia their new home. Other countries are developing and practicing their own forms of multicultural education.

Let us use an example to highlight change in the years to come and to underscore the importance of becoming familiar with America's culturally diverse population. You may have heard of Tiger Woods, the outstanding professional golfer, who in 1997 became the youngest person to win the Masters Tournament. Who is Tiger Woods? African American? Thai American? African/Thai American? American? How does Tiger Woods identify himself? How would you identify him? Would you label Tiger Woods a minority? Where does Tiger Woods fit in that list of phrases you read in this chapter?

Partially as a result of the rise in interracial and interethnic marriages, the distinctions among ethnic and minority groups are becoming blurred. Traditional terms and meanings will need to be revised and new terms developed if we are to identify the many students who enter our classrooms. While the increase in relationships and marriages that transcend the traditional boundaries of race and ethnicity may be an indication that positive changes are occurring in society, experience suggests that problems persist. New ones may surface as the diverse peoples of this country attempt to find a place in society. We must continue to address issues relating to identity, color, prejudice, and discrimination. Peoples with blended ethnic backgrounds, as well as those of traditional minority and ethnic groups, and the other groups described in this chapter, will grow in number and continue to challenge the status quo in society and in the schools.

■■ SUMMARY

In this chapter, we sought to heighten your awareness of what becoming a teacher in a pluralistic society entails. We also wanted you to realize that becoming such a teacher will require you to focus not only on the content you teach, but also on how best to connect this content to your students in meaningful ways. Making this connection means knowing who your students are (their weaknesses, strengths, interests), and what kind of home and neighborhood life they live. Knowing these dimensions of your students' lives will help you to meet their educational and personal needs. Becoming sensitive and attuned to your students will not happen magically as you complete your teacher preparation program. It will require a personal, lifelong commitment from you. Key points to remember include:

- Pluralism can be understood through the metaphors of the melting pot and the salad bowl.
- The melting pot metaphor is aligned with the concept of assimilation. The salad bowl metaphor is aligned with the concept of cultural pluralism.
- Although originating from the concerns about the educational needs of minority students, multicultural education is for all students and is synonymous with effective teaching.
- Changes in demographics usually lead to changes in community structure; changes in community structure can lead to changes in schools, and consequently give rise to classrooms that are culturally diverse.

- Multicultural education is still an evolving field. Consequently, terminology changes and continues to change. However, the development of multicultural education in the United States can be traced from its beginnings in turn-of the-century Americanization programs to its present forms, exemplified in schools such as Brown Barge Middle School and Mark Keppel High School. In the twenty-first century, we expect multicultural education to continue to change.
- Culturally relevant teaching includes teachers' personal beliefs and perspectives as well as specific classroom strategies.

This chapter focused on the qualities you will need to become a culturally relevant teacher. In Chapter Three, "Knowing Middle- and High-School Students," you will read in greater depth about the many ways in which students differ and will gain a more specific understanding of why a traditional, "one-size-fits-all" approach to instruction is no longer feasible.

▌▌BUILDING YOUR BIOGRAPHY, YOUR PERSONAL PRACTICAL PHILOSOPHY, AND PORTFOLIO

Building Your Biography

What experiences in your life are relevant to becoming a teacher in a pluralistic society? The following questions are intended to help you generate ideas for writing a chapter of your teaching biography. They are not intended to be answered sequentially or to limit your exploration of the topic.

- How responsive were your teachers to your personal and cultural characteristics as a learner?
- Do you recall one or more teachers who seemed to exhibit the qualities of culturally relevant teachers?
- What experiences have you had that helped you "see" differences?
- Did a particular experience help you gain a global perspective?
- What are your experiences with changing demographics?
- What teaching experiences have you had with diverse students?

Developing Your Personal Practical Philosophy

Draft a section of your personal philosophy that addresses becoming a teacher in a pluralistic society. You might respond to questions such as the following.

- What is meant by a pluralistic society?
- Where do you stand on the melting pot/salad bowl continuum?
- What is/should be the role of school in promoting a common culture?
- What is/should be the role of school in preserving and affirming cultural differences?
- How important is culturally relevant teaching to your subject area? Why?
- Where do you expect to teach eventually? What kinds of diversity can you expect to encounter in this context?

Collecting Artifacts for Your Portfolio

Review the Reader Activities you have completed in this chapter. Identify any that you might eventually select for your portfolio. For each, jot down notes that will help you recall later what you were thinking at the time you completed the activity, what challenges you encountered while completing it, what you learned from doing it, and how this activity reveals something about who you will be as a teacher. Don't worry about style or correctness at this point. The purpose is to begin documenting your thinking as you move through this book and this class.

References

Asante, M. K. (1988). *Afrocentricity.* Trenton, NJ: Africa World Press, Inc.

Banks, J. A. (1975). *Teaching strategies for ethnic studies.* Boston, MA: Allyn & Bacon.

Banks, J. A. (1993). Approaches to multicultural curriculum reform. In J. A. Banks & C. A. McGee Banks (Eds.), *Multicultural education: Issues and perspectives* (pp. 195–214). Boston: Allyn & Bacon.

Banks, J. A. (1994). *An introduction to multicultural education.* Boston, MA: Allyn & Bacon.

Baruth, L. G. & Manning, M. L. (1992). *Multicultural education of children and adolescents.* Needham Heights, MA: Allyn & Bacon.

Bennett, C. (1998). *Comprehensive Multicultural Education: Theory and practice* (4th ed.). Needham Heights, MA: Allyn & Bacon.

Bracey, G. W. (1994). The fourth Bracey report on the condition of public education. *Phi Delta Kappan, 76* (2), pp. 114–127.

Campbell, D. E. (2000). *Choosing democracy: a practical guide to multicultural education.* Upper Saddle River, NJ: Merrill-Prentice Hall.

Davidman, L. & Davidman, P. T. (1994). *Teaching with a multicultural perspective: a practical guide.* New York: Longman Publishing Group.

Diaz, C. F., Massialas, B. G., Xanthopoulos, J. A. (1999). *Global perspectives for educators.* Boston, MA: Allyn & Bacon.

Dilg, M. (1999). *Race and culture in the classroom: Teaching and learning through multicultural education.* New York: Teachers College Press.

Finney, J. E. (1997). Connecting K–12 and college. *Education Week, 16,* (32), p. 52+.

Garcia, J. (1984). Multiethnic education: Past, present, and future. *Texas Tech Journal of Education, 11* (1), 13–29.

Garcia, J. & Pugh, S. L. (1992). Multicultural education in teacher preparation programs: A political or an educational concept? *Phi Delta Kappan, 74*(3), 214–219.

Gollnick, D. M. & Chinn, P. C. (1998). *Multicultural education in a pluralistic society.* Upper Saddle River, NJ: Merrill-Prentice Hall.

Hardman, M. L., Drew, C. J., & Egan, M. W. (1999). *Human exceptionality: Society, school, and family.* Sixth edition. Needham Heights, MA: Allyn and Bacon.

Horton, J. (1992). The politics of diversity in Monterey Park, California. In L. Lamphere (Ed.), *Structuring Diversity: Ethnographic Perspectives on the New Immigration.* Chicago: University of Chicago Press.

Kaltsounis, T. (1977). Multicultural education and citizenship education at a crossroads: Searching for common ground. *The Social Studies, 86* (1), 18–22.

Krich, L. (1994). Everyone can be a scientist. In *Toward inclusive classrooms,* (pp. 25–38). Washington, DC: National Education Association.

La Belle, T. J. & Ward, C. R. (1994). *Multiculturalism and education.* Albany, NY: State University of New York Press.

Ladson-Billings, G. (1994). *The Dreamkeepers: Successful Teachers of African American Children.* San Francisco: Jossey Bass.

Ladson-Billings, G. (1995). But that's just good teaching! The case for culturally relevant pedagogy. *Theory Into Practice, 34*(3), 159–165.

Lawton, M. (1997). ETS disputes charges of gender bias. *Education Week, 16,* (33), p. 1+.

Menand, L. (1997). Everybody else's college education. (The New York Times Magazine p. 49–49). *The New York Times,* April 20, 1997.

Myers, C. B. & Myers, L. K.. (1990). *An introduction to teaching and schools.* Fort Worth, TX: Holt, Rinehart and Winston, Inc.

Nieto, S. (1996). *Affirming Diversity: The Sociopolitical Context of Multicultural Education.* (2nd edition). New York: Longman.

Powell, R. (1996) The music is why I teach: Intuitive strategies of effective teachers in culturally diverse classrooms. *Teaching and Teacher Education, 12*(1), 49–61.

Powell, R., Zehm. S., & Garcia, J. (1996). *Field experience: Strategies for exploring diversity in school.* Englewood Cliffs, NJ: Merrill/Prentice-Hall.

Roach, V. (1995). Supporting inclusion. *Phi Delta Kappan, 77* (4), 295–299.

Sleeter, C. D. & Grant, C. A. (1999). *Making choices for multicultural education: Five approaches to race, class, and gender.* Upper Saddle River, NJ: Merrill/Prentice-Hall.

Stainback, W., Stainback, S. & Stefanich, G. (1996). Learning together in inclusive classrooms. *Teaching Exceptional Children, 28*(3), 14–19.

Stull, D., Broadway, M., & Erickson, K. (1992). The price of a good steak: Beef packing and its consequences for Garden City, Kansas. In L. Lamphere (Ed.), *Structuring Diversity: Ethnographic Perspectives on the New Immigration.* Chicago: University of Chicago Press.

Tozer, S. E., Violas, P. C. , & Senese, G. (1995). *School and society: Educational practice as social expression.* New York: McGraw-Hill.

■■■ ▌▌▐ Websites

http://www.loop.com/~eproud/(Student-maintained website of Mark Keppel High School, Alhambra, CA.)

http://www.escambia.k12.fl.us/schscnts/brobm/home.html (Website of Brown Barge Middle School, Pensacola, FL.)

http://www.gardencity.net/ (Home page of Garden City, Kansas.)
Schools and Towns Mentioned in This Chapter

http://www.ed.gov/offices/OBEMLA/ (Office of Bilingual and Minority Language Affairs. Offers news on language diversity issues and opportunities for grants and professional development.)
Bilingual Education

http://www.pacificnet.net/~sperling/ (The site of Dave's ESL Café where students can learn and practice English.)
English Language Learners

http://www.census.gov/ (United States Census Bureau. Allows user to search by state for demographic and other statistics.)

http://www.state.gov/ (United States State Department. Allows user to search site for agencies such as United States Bureau of Population, Refugees, and Migration and United States Immigration and Naturalization Service.)
Changing Demographics

http://curry.edschool.Virginia.EDU/curry/centers/multicultural/ (Extensive site with many resources for teachers and teaching.)
Multicultural Education

http://www.hood.edu/seri/serihome.htm#inclusion_resources (Extensive site with information on exceptionalities and links to helpful resources of all kinds.)
Special Education

Knowing Middle-and High-School Students

BUILDING ON BIOGRAPHY: FROM BEING SMART TO BEING "COOL"

Thanks in part to my kindergarten teacher's early interest in me and my parents' commitment to nurturing my love of reading and writing, by the end of fifth grade I (Liz) had distinguished myself as an outstanding student at the small Catholic school I attended. I received good grades, participated enthusiastically in class, performed well above my grade level on standardized achievement tests, and pursued a number of interests outside of school, including reading anything I could get my hands on. My parents valued the individual attention I received from my teachers, and so were quite upset to learn that, for budgetary reasons, the sixth-grade class I was entering was going to be combined with the fifth-grade class. They requested that I be tested and, if my score was high enough, be allowed to bypass the combined class and enter seventh grade.

My scores were high, and in September I entered seventh grade. I was at least twenty pounds overweight according to standard height and weight charts, but I was grossly obese according to my own and my peers' standards, gleaned from poring over teen fashion magazines. I was unsophisticated and so "uncool" that I still carried a pink flowered lunch box. It was a miserable year, as I learned all too well that being popular was far more important than being smart. I often came home in tears from being called "fatso," "tub," "brain," or "know-it-all." I studied the popular girls and boys in the class and determined what I needed to do to fit in: I lost weight, got new clothes, ditched the lunch box, learned to dance, and started smoking. In class, I quit volunteering answers and even managed to get punished for whispering and passing notes. By the time I entered high school, I had made the transition to "cool."

In high school, my highest priority was popularity. I did well in my classes, but I carefully avoided being singled out for any academic accomplishments. Toward the end of our high school years, most of my classmates and I took the Scholastic Aptitude Test (SAT) for college entrance. Some weeks later, I was horrified to walk into the main lobby of the high school and see my SAT score posted prominently on the main bulletin board. I had scored 790 out of 800 on the verbal portion of the test. Inwardly, a part of me rejoiced at having done so well, but another part was squirming at the thought of being branded—again—a "brain." As I stood there before the bulletin board, a male classmate came up behind me, looked at the posted scores, and exclaimed, "God, Spalding! I didn't know you were smart!" I took Bobby's remark as both a compliment and a curse: a compliment because it showed that I had truly succeeded in my quest to be "cool," and a curse because it confirmed my fear that I would now be unmasked as a "brain" and therefore "uncool."

Questions to Consider

1. In this story, Liz recalls learning some "lessons" about being female. What other lessons about being female and male are learned in school?
2. What does Liz's story suggest about gender as an issue for adolescents and their teachers?
3. Liz graduated from high school in 1968. How have schools and society changed in regard to gender issues since then?

▪▪ PURPOSE

You already know a lot about students. After all, it probably hasn't been that long since you were a middle-or high-school student yourself. You may already have had some experience working with young people, perhaps as a tutor, counselor, or coach. You may be a parent of an adolescent or have adolescent siblings. You may also have studied theories of adolescent development and learning, and spent time observing and working in middle- or high-school classrooms. Even though you may have already taken a course or may soon take a course that focuses on adolescent learners, we included this chapter because we believe that knowledge of who our students are cannot be separated from knowledge of how to teach them. In this chapter, we want to extend your knowledge by highlighting some individual, social, and cultural characteristics of the students you will someday teach.

The overall purpose of this chapter is to heighten your awareness of middle- and high-school students in general, of some of the attributes and attitudes they share, and of the many dimensions in which they differ. Specifically, this chapter will help you:

- recognize selected characteristics of the present and future middle- and high-school student population;
- acknowledge and reflect upon important features of students' (and teachers') identity—specifically, gender, race, ethnicity, culture, social class, and exceptionalities—that affect how students experience school and how teachers experience students;
- understand how students differ in their preferred learning styles and multiple intelligences;
- think about general issues in classroom organization, curriculum, and instruction that must be addressed if all students are to receive equal opportunities to learn and achieve.

This chapter is intended to serve as a springboard for further study of the most important feature of the context in which you aspire to work: students. As you move into classroom teaching and become more aware of the infinite variety among students and the particular characteristics of the students you teach, you will surely want to expand your exploration of the topics most relevant to your teaching situation.

This chapter is not meant to stereotype any group or to minimize individual differences. Every student, every teacher, every human being is unique. But we also share common characteristics and common experiences as males, females, African Americans, recent immigrants, children of professional parents, children of working-class parents, children of poverty, and so on. The information presented in this chapter can be used as lenses through which you might look at your students and understand how they would be taught.

This chapter is not intended to suggest that teachers are racist, sexist, elitist, or any other "-ist." Yet despite the good intentions of teacher educators and teachers themselves, research continues to document unequal treatment of males and females, of Whites and students of color, of middle- and working-class students, of regular education students and students with special needs—not just in instructional materials but in daily teacher-student interactions (e.g., Klein & Ortman, 1994; Knapp & Wolverton, 1995; Ogbu, 1995; Sadker & Sadker, 1982; Vaughn & Schumm, 1996). Most teachers are not even aware that they treat students differently along some of the lines just mentioned. This makes it all the more important to become aware of factors that may influence our treatment of students and to reflect on how our own experiences may have shaped who we are today.

▪▪ SOCIETAL CHANGES AFFECTING ADOLESCENTS

The adults of every generation, it seems, look at the current crop of future adults and shake their heads in despair. Today, this tendency is especially pronounced as we are inundated with bad news about schools, society, and especially teenagers. Although we do not believe the news is as bad as the media and some public figures would have us believe, a number of facts indicate that many children and youth today are facing serious problems that simply did not affect previous generations in such widespread proportions. Dr. David Hamburg, author of *Today's Children: Creating a Future for a Generation in Crisis* (1994) estimates that

> of the twenty-eight million people between the ages of ten and seventeen in the United States, about seven million are highly vulnerable to the negative consequences of multiple high-risk behaviors such as school failure, substance abuse, and early, unprotected sexual intercourse. So it is reasonable to say that one-quarter of American adolescents fall into a high-risk category. Another seven million are at moderate risk by virtue of lesser involvement in such behavior patterns (p. 197).

The National Longitudinal Study on Adolescent Health (Resnick et al., 1997) examined the risk behaviors of seventh-through twelfth-graders. These behaviors included suicidal thoughts or actions, violence, substance abuse, and sexual activity. Not surprisingly, this study found that parents, family, and home environment play a crucial role in protecting adolescents from such negative behaviors. More relevant to you as a future teacher is the finding that connectedness with school is also an important protective factor for young people. Citing previous research by Steinberg (1996), these researchers report that "school engagement is a critical protective factor against a variety of risky behaviors, influenced in good measure by perceived caring from teachers and high expectations for student performance" (Resnick et al., p. 831).

Of all the risk conditions researchers have identified, poverty is the greatest. While the amount of wealth in the top five percent of the population is increasing, poverty is also on the rise. One quarter of all U. S. children under age six live in poverty. The number of poor children has increased from 10.2 million in 1974 to over fifteen million in 1994. Poor children as a group are more likely to be ill or underweight, fall behind or drop out of school, become teen parents, experience economic troubles as adults, and become victims or perpetrators of crimes. Over seventy percent of prisoners in the U. S. are high school dropouts. The cost of maintaining one prisoner for a year is about $26,000—about equal the cost of sending four students to a state university tuition-free (Hodgkinson, 1997). The reminiscences of former Surgeon General C. Everett Koop might easily be applied to many of the problems besetting school and classrooms today: "When I look back on my years in office, the things I banged my head against were all poverty" (Coontz, 1992, p. 270).

Violence and drugs continue to invade schools. Recent school shootings in disparate parts of the country have shocked the nation and caused everyone to wonder how such seriously disturbed youth can pass through the school system apparently unnoticed. About ten percent of 1992 high school seniors reported that they did not feel safe at school. About twenty-three percent reported that there were often fights between different racial/ethnic groups. While drug and alcohol abuse have actually been declining, about fifty-one percent of high school seniors report using these substances at some time. About thirty percent of high school students surveyed reported having been offered, sold, or given an illegal drug on school property (U. S. Department of Education, 1998).

Not only are people moving into this country, people are moving all over this country. Eighty-five percent of new immigrants come from Latin America, Asia, the Middle East. Muslims are increasing faster than any other religious group. Americans are leaving small towns and rural areas and moving to suburban areas. Half of our public school students live in suburbs; one quarter live in cities; and one quarter live in rural areas (Hodgkinson, 1997). Only thirty percent of Florida residents were born there. Teachers who teach in high mobility areas often end the school year with class rosters that only vaguely resemble the rosters with which they began the year.

Adolescents' Attitudes Toward School

Large scale surveys, ethnographic studies, and journalistic accounts published since the 1980s have confirmed widespread student indifference to academics and enthusiasm for the social aspects of school (e.g., Public Agenda, 1997; French, 1993; Powell, Farrar, and Cohen, 1985; Goodlad, 1984; Sizer, 1984). In fact, Public Agenda's (1997) report on adolescents' attitudes toward school is entitled *Getting By: What American Teenagers Really Think About Their Schools*. While almost two-thirds of the middle- and high-school students surveyed admitted that they could do much better in school if they tried, seventy-nine percent expressed a longing for higher standards. As one student put it, "You can just glide through. You can copy someone's homework at the beginning of a period. I mean you can do whatever you want. . . . They practically hand you a diploma" (Public Agenda, 1997, p. 1). Seventy-eight percent of the public school respondents said that a teacher who tries "to make lessons fun and interesting would help them learn a lot more," but only twenty-four percent think most of their teachers do that now (Public Agenda, 1997, p. 2). In fact, the vast majority of respondents said that a classroom teacher who gives close and careful attention to their learning is even more influential than parents in encouraging them to learn.

Not surprisingly, adolescents hold mixed views of school. It appears that educators continue to consider only minimally students' own views and interests in the design of schools and schooling. Goodlad (1984) termed this "disjuncture between elements of the youth culture on one hand and the orientation of teachers and conduct of schools on the other" potentially explosive (p. 76). Indeed, recent events have borne out this prediction.

Efforts to change the character of teaching and learning in junior high and high schools have been particularly intense over the past decade. Many middle schools now stress active learning, interdisciplinary connections, and exploratory studies for the early adolescent. Many high schools are restructuring the traditional seven-period day into fewer but longer blocks of time so that students can explore topics in depth and teachers can plan more meaningful activities (e.g., Sizer, 1996; Meier, 1995). In many schools, class sizes are being reduced, students are being assigned to "houses" under the guidance of teams of teachers who get to know them well, and time for individualized instruction is built into the school day. Nevertheless, many high schools and even middle schools still resemble massive, impersonal factories or shopping malls.

▌Reader Activity 3.1

In the Field
Surveying Students' Perceptions of School

Work with a partner or small group to develop a brief survey that will help you gain an overview of how adolescents today view school. Some people in the class should survey middle-school students; some should survey high-school students. You might consider asking students what they enjoy most about school, what they enjoy least, what classes they enjoy most and why, what classes they enjoy least and why. You might ask about their career aspirations and which classes are helping them meet their goals. Avoid sensitive questions about personal risk behaviors. Obtain appropriate permissions to administer the survey. Make sure that students understand the purpose of the survey and that you have a procedure for distributing and collecting the surveys. Tabulate and present your findings to the class. Compare your findings with those of other groups. What messages do your findings send to prospective teachers?

Good News About Adolescents

It is rare to read a newspaper headline proclaiming "Another Beautiful Spring Day in Virginia!" or to see a television newscast featuring "Acts of Kindness Committed in Springfield Today." To reverse the cliché: good news is no news, especially in education. One has to do a bit of searching to find good news about adolescents. But it's there if you look for it. For example:

> Nationally, the percentage of students taking algebra and geometry grew from twenty-nine percent in 1982 to fifty percent in 1992. Participation in calculus classes more than doubled over the same period, increasing from four percent to ten percent (Viadero, 1995, p. 1).
>
> In 1983, the report *A Nation at Risk* was published, advocating tougher academic requirements. In 1982, only thirteen percent of high school graduates earned the credits recommended in that report. That number had increased to forty-seven percent by 1992. This increase in course-taking occurred for both male and female students and all racial and ethnic groups (Viadero, 1995, p. 16).

Despite all the negative press, there is plenty of evidence that, in both curricular and extracurricular areas, middle- and high-school students are making a difference in their communities and acting as responsible citizens as the following example suggests:

> On a field trip for their nature-studies class, middle and high school students in LeSueur, Minnesota noticed that at least half of the frogs they saw in the area had deformities. Concerned that the deformities might have been caused by environmental toxins, the students decided to bring their discovery to the attention of state environmental experts and lawmakers. Subsequently, they testified at the state legislature, persuading members of an environment and natural resources committee to approve a $201,000 environmental study of frog deformities and what might be causing them. . . . The students . . . are working with scientists from the state Pollution Control Agency and a University of Minnesota professor to investigate the cause of the deformities . . . [They] have even set up a special site on their school's World Wide Web page about the project (Sommerfeld, 1996, p. 3).

Unless we interact with them daily, we rarely hear the voices of the many adolescents who invest themselves in their school experiences, have faith in their teachers to guide them in their learning, and believe that education will not only help them fulfill their dreams for the future, but also has value in the here and now. Consider the following comments researchers have recently collected from middle- and high-school students.

> I like to work hard and I guess I'll just pound it into myself if I don't understand. If I don't understand something, I make sure that I work at it until I do understand, and I keep it up and I never give up. I'm not a quitter at all (Newmann, 1992, p. 14).

> I sure remember the day I got my first B; I started crying. . . . Most of my friends, you know, get A's and B's, and everything. And it's not to impress them; it's to show them that I'm just as good, you know? It's mostly just for me, to make me know that I'm just as good as anybody else and that I can really do it. . . . I'm ambitious. I always want to get things done. . . . I succeed in everything I do. If I don't get it right the first time, I always go back and try to do it again (Nieto, 1996, p. 130–131).

> When I had to do a report last year in English class, I wanted to do something on David Bowie. But my English teacher wouldn't let me. She said that I was a creative person who was ahead of her time, and that I would like reading about Coco Chanel. Then she gave me the book and I enjoyed it. She just knew, it was weird. . . . After that I became a lot more interested in clothes—fashion design [as a career] never really hit me until then (Csikszentmihalyi, Rathunde, & Whalen, 1993, p. 189).

> I wish I could redo my freshman year. I was hyper, immature, didn't really think school was important. Skipped a lot of classes. I got injured between my freshman and sophomore year over the summer in a soccer game. I was amused by how the trainer wrapped my ankle and what he said was wrong with it. I decided I wanted a career in sports medicine. So I want to get good grades until the end of school to get into a medical program. . . . I just cracked down, kept my eyes in the book, paid attention as best I could in class (Newmann, 1992, p. 24).

> There were times when we [two high school students collaborating on a film project] felt like quitting. And it wasn't until Mr. Stone [their teacher] pushed us . . . . and we were procrastinating. We got so tired looking for the right shots . . . . then Mr. Stone would say, 'It'll work out, I believe in you.' We don't like to do simple work. We like to get into what we're doing. Quality work is what we like—that's what we're all about (Rose, 1995, p. 23).

What do the above quotes suggest about what students want from school and from teachers? What motivates these students?

CONSULTING OTHER SOURCES
Tracking Media Coverage of Adolescents

Collect and/or keep track of newspaper, magazine, radio, or television reports about adolescents for a week. What is the nature of the information being published or broadcast? Does it concern academic achievement? Social issues? Determine the ratio of good news to bad. Report on the frequency and nature of the news you find and create a visual to illustrate your findings. Was it difficult to find good news? If so, how do you explain this?

■■ SOCIOCULTURAL CHARACTERISTICS OF ADOLESCENTS

We have just looked at some ways in which society influences students in school and some ways in which students themselves perceive school. Now we will turn to several major aspects of adolescents' identity that also influence how students perceive and perform in schools. The characteristics discussed in this section—gender, race, ethnicity, culture, and socioeconomic class—are known as *sociocultural* because they are not simply biological features or financial statistics, but are given meanings by the larger society (*socio*-) and mainstream American culture (-*cultural*) in which they exist.[1] Furthermore, consequences result from the meanings given by society. For example, a teacher may view a student who speaks Appalachian dialect as less capable than a student who speaks Standard American English. In turn, this student, viewed as less than competent because of a sociocultural characteristic, may resist being unfairly judged by consciously or unconsciously refusing to learn or use Standard American English. In short, what you as a teacher believe about gender and learning, about ethnicity and learning, about culture and learning, about ability and learning will have a tremendous impact on your students and their learning.

You may be wondering why a discussion of sociocultural characteristics of students is necessary, especially if you aspire to teach in a relatively homogeneous setting. First, you need to keep in mind that as a teacher you will be working with students who may be quite different from the student you were or the students your friends were. Our memories of our own school experiences are framed by the courses we took and the social circles in which we moved. If you were a successful "college-prep" student, chances are most of your friends were, too. As a teacher, however, you will interact daily with students whose academic skills and social interests will be quite different from your own. Secondly, even if you plan to teach in the community in which you grew up in, it may no longer be the same community in which you grew up. As we noted in the preceding chapter, communities are rapidly changing as new residents move in and other residents move on. You need to be prepared to be effective with changing student populations and with the full spectrum of students you will meet in schools.

You need to know as much as you can about students if you expect to engage them with your subject. Yes, you will have many students whose favorite subject is the one you teach. You will also have many students who loathe it. You will have many students who appear to care more about cars, motorcycles, the opposite sex, the pep assembly next period, or the view of the parking lot from your classroom window than they do about your subject. While some of these student reactions may be attributed to individual preferences and differences, some are undoubtedly shaped by the sociocultural characteristics discussed below.

Gender

One salient feature of humans' identity is gender. For middle- and high-school students, gender is one of the most important issues at this stage in life. Girls and boys enter middle school and puberty at approximately the same time. Experienced middle-school teachers often bemoan the impact of "raging hormones" on the behavior and learning of early adolescents. Boys' voices may "break," ranging from a high-pitched squeak to a gruff baritone in a single sentence. Girls with well-developed breasts may be deeply embarrassed by them; girls whose breasts have not yet developed may worry intensely that they never will. Experienced high-school teachers will attest that the "hormones"

---

1. We use the term "race" in this chapter and discuss "race" at some length, because it is a significant feature of students' identity and because we live in a race-conscious society. However, throughout the rest of this book, "race" is subsumed under the term "ethnicity."

continue to "rage" in later adolescence. Although by high school much of the physical transformation of puberty is nearly over, students continue to struggle with questions of what it means to be female or male, heterosexual or homosexual. In short, in order for you to know your students and teach them well, you need to consider how gender influences what goes on in schools and classrooms and how you can create an equitable learning environment for all students regardless of their gender or their sexual orientation. Research continues to document that schools differentiate between males and females, and between heterosexual and homosexual orientations to the disadvantage of all (Delamont, 1990; McCormick, 1994).

Gender and the Middle-School Years

Prospective middle- and junior high-school teachers need to be especially aware of the impact of early adolescence on many girls. Mary Pipher (1994), a clinical psychologist who specializes in the treatment of adolescent girls, calls junior high a "crucible" (p. 11):

> Something dramatic happens to girls in early adolescence. Just as planes and ships disappear mysteriously into the Bermuda Triangle, so do the selves of girls go down in droves. They crash and burn in a social and developmental Bermuda Triangle. In early adolescence studies show that girls' IQ scores drop and their math and science scores plummet. They lose their resiliency and optimism and become less curious and inclined to take risks. They lose their assertive, energetic, and 'tomboyish' personalities and become more deferential, self-critical and depressed. They report great unhappiness with their own bodies (p. 19).

Psychologist Carol Gilligan and her colleagues, who have been documenting women's psychological and moral development for many years, have produced a similiar description. In *Meeting at the Crossroads: Women's Psychology and Girls' Development* (1992), Brown and Gilligan published the findings of their long-term work with girls from preschool through high school in an all girls' school. They, too, identified early adolescence as a critical time in girls' development:

> Thus, while in one sense the girls we have studied are progressing steadily as they move from childhood through adolescence, in another sense adolescence precipitates a developmental crisis in girls' lives. . . . [T]he crossroads between girls and women is marked by a series of disconnections or dissociations which leave girls psychologically at risk and involved in a relational struggle . . . (p. 6).

Brown and Gilligan called "giving up . . . relationship for the sake of 'Relationships' " the "central paradox" faced by girls approaching adolescence (p. 7). While some girls successfully resist this social and cultural rite of passage, many succumb to self-silencing and self-doubt, going "underground" to conceal their true selves and to avoid hurting others (p. 184).

Schooling contributes to this process of "going underground" in subtle and not-so-subtle ways. But the school, as Pipher (1994) has pointed out, simply reflects the larger culture—a culture she calls "dangerous, sexualized, and media-saturated . . . " (p. 12). For early adolescent girls, this culture intersects in particularly toxic ways with the general developmental tasks of adolescence, e.g., moving toward independence from family while retaining enduring ties, moving toward adult sexuality, developing increasing autonomy in making personal decisions, and taking on intellectual challenges (Hamburg, 1994). Girls are pressured by schools, magazines, music, television, advertisements, movies, and peers to "split into false selves":

> Girls can be true to themselves and risk abandonment by their peers, or they can reject their true selves and be socially acceptable. Most girls choose to be socially acceptable and split into two selves, one that is authentic and one that is culturally scripted. In public they become who they are supposed to be (Pipher, 1994, p. 38).

Early adolescent boys undergo a similar though not so well publicized transformation. In *Failing at Fairness: How America's Schools Cheat Girls* (1994), Myra and David Sadker describe how society and schools cheat boys as well. When researchers interviewed boys from kindergarten through fourth grade in several Midwestern schools, they heard "voices that were sensitive and caring (p. 204)." These boys talked willingly about feelings of fear, vulnerability, and friendship. But boys, too, as they enter puberty, are forced to "go underground" by societal pressures to repress emotions, compete for and win honors and attention, and even use violence and force to solve problems. In fact, one could argue that while society and schools have expanded roles and opportunities for girls and women, boys and men remain locked in rigid, traditional roles. Boys who are pressured to be aggressive, self-reliant, and stoic may grow into men who are violent, driven, depressed, and unable to establish or enjoy intimacy with others (Brooks-Gunn, 1992; Thorne, 1994; Sadker & Sadker, 1994).

Gender and the Curriculum

In 1992, the American Association of University Women released a controversial report entitled *How Schools Shortchange Girls.* The study contained both good and bad news about girls' academic achievement and career aspirations. For example, the study found that gender differences in mathematics achievement are "small and declining" (p. 24). The same trend holds for girls' participation in math courses. In science, however, gender differences in achievement and course participation are "not decreasing and may be increasing" (p. 26). Overall, the study reported the disappointing finding that "[h]igh school girls, even those with exceptional academic preparation in math and science are choosing math/science careers in disproportionately low numbers" (p. 27).

When one looks at the overall performance of boys and girls in middle and high schools, however, the picture changes. For example, the Sadkers (1994) report that from elementary school through high school, boys receive lower report card grades than girls; that by middle school boys are far more likely than girls to be held back or to drop out; that boys make up the majority of students identified for special education programs, including seventy-one percent of those identified as learning disabled and eighty percent of those identified as emotionally disturbed (p. 221).

Teachers of all subjects must consider the role gender plays in their content area (Barbieri, 1995). For example, the AAUW report cites a 1989 survey that found that of the ten most frequently assigned books in English classes, only one was written by a woman and not one was written by a minority author (p. 64). In social studies, women are often depicted as "famous women" or as participants in protest movements (e.g., women's suffrage). Rarely are women's roles integrated into the main text of history, and their perspectives on events and issues are seldom presented. As one female high-school student commented: "It's so boring, just a bunch of kings and generals fighting each other. What were the women doing anyway?" (Pipher, 1994, p. 40).

Boys' curricular and extra curricular options may be limited by their fear of being labeled "sissies," "faggots," or "nerds" (Thorne, 1994). In fact, "[b]eing accused of being in any way like a woman is one of the worst insults a boy can receive" (AAUW, p. 73). We should be just as concerned about the small number of males who enter nurturing and service professions as we are about the small number of females who pursue careers in science and engineering. We should worry about the consequences of discouraging males from exploring the expressive, aesthetic, and creative aspects of themselves. In short, "there are a 'variety of ways of being male, many of them admirable' and . . . 'none need depend on being different from and superior to girls and women' " (Jordan, 1990 quoted in Thorne, 1994, p. 169).

For boys and girls alike, the cumulative impact of a curriculum biased in favor of White males is a skewed vision of how the world works and sends the message that the lives of women don't really matter:

> Students sit in classes that, day in and day out, deliver the message that women's lives count for less than men's. . . . There is no social science research to document cause and effect in this matter, but educators must take more responsibility for understanding that the curriculum is the central message-giving instrument of the school (AAUW, 1992, p. 67).

Gender and Social Interactions in School

Gender plays a role not just in the formal curriculum of schools, but in the lessons learned from patterns of interaction both inside and outside the classroom. Sadker and Sadker (1982), among others, have looked at patterns of interactions between teachers and students and between students and students. They found that boys get more attention of all sorts from teachers than do girls. This is hardly surprising, since, according to the Sadkers, boys arrive at schools as the "entitled gender." Here they report the reflections of an elementary school principal:

> Many boys come to school the center of attention, the pride and joy of their family. Then the shock hits: They're not the center anymore. As one of many, they must wait, learn to take their turn, and follow the rules. They come to school the Prince of Everything, and here they lose their royal standing (p. 199).

Thus, boys struggle to reclaim their "entitlement." They may capture teachers' attention in a variety of ways. Researchers who have observed gender interactions in the classroom have found that boys are more likely to receive the teacher's attention for disciplinary reasons; that teachers give more positive, active teaching attention to boys; that teachers direct more and higher-level questions to boys; and that teachers are more likely to praise boys for the intellectual quality of their work and more likely to praise girls' work for its neatness and compliance to rules of form (McCormick 1994; Sadker & Sadker, 1982). Out of school, boys are far more likely than girls to indulge in risk-taking behaviors, including alcohol and drug abuse and physical risks.

Gay, Lesbian, and Bisexual Students

During adolescence, if not before, most students become aware of their sexual orientation. Approximately ten percent of these young people will become aware that their sexual orientation is gay, lesbian, or bisexual (Grayson, 1992; Sears, 1991). If this estimate is true, then in your career as a middle- or high-school teacher, you will certainly teach students who are discovering that they are homosexual or bisexual in orientation (Jennings, 1998; Rubin, 1994). These students need supportive and accepting teachers as much as, if not more than, heterosexual students of any ethnic or socioeconomic group regardless of the difficulties they may face in society and in school. As Hetrick and Martin (1987) bluntly put it: "Blacks, Jews, and Hispanics are not thrown out of their families or religions at adolescence for being black, Jewish, or Hispanic; homosexual adolescents are" (p. 29).

In his study of thirty-six gay and lesbian adolescents growing up in South Carolina, James Sears (1991) found that most of them had performed poorly in school, with a distinct drop in achievement during the times of greatest personal conflict over sexual identity. Twenty-four of his respondents had repeatedly considered suicide; four had attempted it. Gay, lesbian, and bisexual adolescents contemplate, as well as attempt, suicide at much higher rates than heterosexual adolescents (Coleman & Ramefedi, 1989; Hetrick & Martin, 1987; Rofes, 1989). However, this is not to suggest that homosexuality invariably leads to unhappiness. Hetrick and Martin also emphasize that "studies have shown most homosexually oriented persons develop happy and productive lives" (p. 40). Unfortunately, for the most part they achieve this without the support of—perhaps even in spite of—schools.

Adolescents who are openly homosexual or are suspected by their non-gay peers of being homosexual are frequently subjected to verbal and physical abuse in schools. Many who have been abused are reluctant to report the abuser(s) for fear of reprisals. Worse, some teachers openly castigate, ridicule, and make jokes about homosexuals (Jennings, 1998; Sears, 1991). At a minimum, you have an obligation to educate yourself on issues of sexual identity so that you can be accurate and fair in your classroom presentation and so that you can recognize, avert, and avoid harm to gay, lesbian, and bisexual students.

▮ Reader Activity 3.3

IN THE FIELD
Observing Gender Interactions in the Classroom

Obtain permission from an experienced teacher to observe his or her interactions with students in the classroom. Determine whether the teacher's verbal interaction with males and females is roughly equal and identify any potentially biased teaching behaviors. Tally all the verbal interactions with each sex and divide by the number of males and females in the class. For example, if there are twelve boys and fifteen girls in a class and you tally forty-two interactions with boys and ten interactions with girls, you will find that there are 3.5 interactions per boy and .66 interactions per girl. Thus, this teacher is giving about five times more attention to boys than to girls. (McCormick, 1994) Discuss the results of your observation with others in your class. Does the subject area observed influence the type of interaction? Does the teacher's gender influence the type of interaction?

Race

Today, when you apply for a job or fill out almost any governmental form, you are asked to identify your race by selecting from the following choices: White, African American, Hispanic, Native American, Asian/Pacific Islander. Many of us can select one of these categories without hesitation, but the usefulness of "race" as a way to categorize human beings is called into question if we look at the increasing diversity of our society (Hodgkinson, 1997; Hollingshead, 1995). This became apparent to me while I taught for the Department of Defense Dependents Schools in Korea and the Philippines. What block would Floyd, whose father was Native American and whose mother was Korean, check? What about Tracy, whose father was Mexican American and whose mother was White? What about Barbara, whose father was African American and whose mother was Filipina?

"Despite the irrelevance of race as a concept for defining humanity, the United States is a race conscious society" (Bennett, 1998, p. 44). Just as we notice whether our students are male or female, whether they are short or tall, we notice the physical characteristics that imply race. It is neither honest nor helpful for teachers to claim to be "color-blind." Such a claim implies that difference in skin color is a disadvantage to be minimized. In other words, by saying that we don't notice skin color, what we may really be saying is that we don't notice that a student is not White. Furthermore, for many students race is an essential aspect of their identity that requires recognition and affirmation (e.g., Bennett, 1998; Nieto, 1996). As the following journal written by an Asian American male suggests, many students are proud of their racial heritage:

> Yes, I am a person of color and I'm damn proud of it! *Asian*-American, both from Chinese and Japanese ancestry. . . . Even though I'm a fifth-generation American, I have encountered numerous occasions of discrimination, accusations, etc. . . . I turned to the martial arts because of a lot of racial violence that happened to me and because I wanted something to boost my Asian pride. . . . (Rubin, 1994, pp. 168–169).

Particularly over the past twenty-five years, research—whether in the form of large-scale surveys, analysis of test scores, or in-depth studies of classrooms and schools—has documented the persistence of racism in our schools. Fortunately, research has also suggested many strategies for combating racism. The effective classroom teacher of today and tomorrow knows how to use a wide range of curricular materials representing the perspectives of people of color, to employ a variety of instructional strategies in order to reach all students, and to communicate in ways that are culturally appropriate.[2]

Ethnicity

Related to the concept of race is the concept of ethnicity. Banks (1994) defines an ethnic group as "a group that shares a common ancestry, culture, history, tradition, and sense of peoplehood" (p. 91). For example, the U.S. Census applies the racial category of "Hispanic" to people whose ethnic heritage may be Mexican, Salvadoran, Puerto Rican, Dominican, or Guatemalan. Similarly, there are countless "White" ethnic groups within our country: Jewish, Polish, Irish, Italian, German Americans, etc. Ethnicity, like race, is an important aspect of many students' identity.

In 1991, educational ethnographer Alan Peshkin published a study of a multiethnic high school in California, *The Color of Strangers, the Color of Friends: The Play of Ethnicity in School and Community.* Among other things, Peshkin wanted to discover how students at Riverview High School (a pseudonym) viewed ethnicity and what

---

2. A number of books on multicultural education contain extensive bibliographies of studies which have documented racism in schools. These books also contain in-depth discussions of teaching strategies, suggestions for curriculum content, and sources for obtaining further information. Among these books are: Bennett, C. I. (1998). *Comprehensive Multicultural Education*, Fourth Edition. Needham Heights, MA: Allyn & Bacon; Nieto, S. (1996). *Affirming Diversity: The Sociopolitical Context of Multicultural Education.* Second Edition. White Plains, NY: Longman; Banks, J. A. (1991). *Teaching Strategies for Ethnic Studies,* Fifth Edition. Needham Heights, MA: Allyn & Bacon.

role ethnicity played in their social interactions. Peshkin found that ethnicity was indeed a defining feature for many students at Riverview. As one male Puerto Rican student new to the school explained:

> Students want to know who you are. They do because they—when they first see me, they think I'm Mexican, but they just ask me to be sure. . . . I'm Puerto Rican. When you first meet students they don't really talk about it. But once you get to know them, they get to wonder, 'Are you. . . . ?' But we don't really talk about race (Peshkin, 1991, p. 172).

Peshkin found that Riverview students formed and maintained relationships based not on color but on actions: "To be sure, black students hung out with other black students, and Filipino boys bunched together over here and Mexican girls over there. . . . But, in addition, an ordinary, routine fact of life was the mingling: any type of interaction that could take place between students of the same ethnic background took place between students of different ethnic backgrounds" (p. 290). These interactions included friendships, dating, and, for some students, eventually marriage.

Peshkin's study highlights the boundless capacity of students to learn from one another and to shape their environments in positive and satisfying ways. Students achieved a state of ethnic peace largely on their own, since the curriculum at Riverview was not "ethnicized" and the majority of teachers claimed to be "color-blind" (p. 264). Peshkin suggests that Riverview teachers were only minimally aware of the amount or depth of cultural knowledge they were acquiring from their students. What if the teachers at Riverview had consciously tried to learn from their students? What if they had frequently and critically reflected on such cultural knowledge? Further, Peshkin points out that teachers rarely promoted ethnic consciousness in their classrooms. Realizing that such gestures might be dubbed "curricular tokenism," Peshkin nevertheless speculates that " . . . if such small curricular elements proliferate, they could communicate through the school's cognitive domain what is strongly apparent in its social domain: everyone counts" (p. 266).

Culture

Definitions of "culture" abound and are constantly being revised. One useful definition is Nieto's (1996): "The ever-changing values, traditions, social and political relationships, and worldview created and shared by a group of people bound together by a combination of factors (which can include a common history, geographic location, language, social class, and/or religion) and how these are transformed by those who share them" (p. 390). This definition is broad and rightly so. In fact, it is difficult to name any particular belief, behavior, or bit of knowledge that is not influenced by culture. Culture is such a deeply ingrained part of who we are that it is often invisible to us, leading us to believe that the way we think and behave is the "right" and "natural" way. In the United States, this taken-for-granted way of viewing ourselves and others has been called "the Anglo-Western European macroculture" (Bennett, 1998, p. 47). Schools are one manifestation of culture. Indeed, a major purpose of schooling has been and remains the transmission of culture. Not surprisingly, schools in the United States transmit and reflect the Anglo-Western European macroculture.

In our society, a variety of cultures co-exist (and quite frequently conflict with) the macroculture. When the culture in the home differs from the culture of the school, cultural conflicts can occur. These conflicts may spring from differences in verbal and nonverbal communication styles, the organization of time, the organization of space, and in a number of other ways. Cultural conflicts are often attributed to differences in race or ethnicity and the accompanying differences in world view.

In her book *Other People's Children: Cultural Conflict in the Classroom* (1995), Lisa Delpit recounts numerous episodes of cultural misunderstandings between teachers and students:

> In a recent research project, middle-school, inner-city students were interviewed about their attitudes toward their teachers and school. One young woman complained bitterly, 'Mrs. ——— always be interrupting to make you 'talk correct' and stuff. She be butting into your conversations when you not even talking to her! She need to mind her own business' (p. 51).

Obviously, neither Mrs. ——— nor the complaining student was sensitive to the unspoken rules of verbal communication employed by the other.

When teachers are informed about and sensitive to cultural issues, they are more effective in the classroom:

> Interviews with black teachers who have enjoyed long-term success teaching math to black-dialect-speaking students suggest that part of the solution also lies in the kind and quality of talk in the mathematics classroom. One teacher explained that her black students were much more likely to learn a new operation successfully when they understood to what use the operation might be put in daily life. . . . For example, she once brought in a part of a broken wheel, saying that it came from a toy that she wished to fix for her grandson. To do so, she had to reconstruct the wheel from this tiny part. After the students tried unsuccessfully to solve the problem, she introduced a theorem related to constructing a circle given any two points on an arc, which the students quickly assimilated (Delpit, 1995, p. 65).

Certainly, this kind of instruction is effective for all students. Few students of any culture would prefer a sterile introduction to a geometric theorem over the chance to solve a real world problem and help the teacher at the same time!

Language is a particularly salient manifestation of culture and a deeply ingrained aspect of one's identity. Today, more and more students whose first language is other than English or who speak a dialect other than Standard American English are enrolled in public schools. If you have ever traveled to a country where English was not the principal language of communication or even to a part of this country where a dialect of English other than your own was predominant, you can probably appreciate some of the challenges schools present to linguistically different students. While bilingual education programs and English as a Second Language programs support many English language learners, most attend middle and high school classes in which content area instruction is delivered in English and aimed at native speakers of English. While you probably cannot become fluent in several different languages in order to teach linguistically diverse students effectively, you can support their learning by showing an interest in and respect for their native languages and cultures and by considering linguistic differences among your students when planning for and implementing instruction. Speakers of dialects of English (e.g., some African American students, some students from rural Appalachia, speakers of Hawaiian Creole English) are infrequently served by special programs, but the linguistic identity of dialect speakers demands the same respect and consideration as that accorded to speakers of languages other than English.

If you listen to your students, they often reveal how you can best teach them.

Social Groups and Socioeconomic Status (SES)

Who were your friends in junior high and high school? Were you part of a group? Did your group eat lunch together in the cafeteria? Did you take classes together? Share lockers? In what kinds of extracurricular activities were you involved? Were certain styles and brands of clothing important to you and your friends? Did groups in your school have names—"Preppies," "Jocks," "Druggies," "Skaters," "Creekers"? Did a small number of students seem to "run" the school? Was there a particular area of your school where students always congregated to smoke? You can probably answer all of the above questions easily, since the answers are closely linked to the existence of student social groups in schools, an enduring and important feature of adolescent life (e.g., Brantlinger, 1993; Cusick, 1973; Eckert, 1989; French, 1993).

The purpose of this section is to reacquaint you with some features of adolescent society. That is, within the context of the larger society, middle- and high-school students form a sort of microcosmic society as they live and work within the institution of school. And, like the larger society, adolescent society can be said to have a culture. From a cultural perspective, student decisions about what to wear, with whom to socialize, where to spend the lunch period, and even what to eat at lunch are not whimsical or arbitrary. Such decisions are the very fabric of student culture. This section will focus on one feature of student culture and society—social groups and how they function in schools.

From a teacher's perspective, you may see school primarily as a setting for intellectual pursuits—a place for learning science, math, history, literature, and other subjects. No doubt you believe that students' academic endeavors will prepare them for future success and that academics are the rightful focus of schools. How quickly we forget our own experience as middle- and high-school students! Are your most vivid memories of those years centered around academic experiences? Probably not. Many students may see school primarily as a setting for social pursuits, such as finding acceptance, asserting independence, gaining status. While some students are certainly thinking of the future, many do not see any connection between academic endeavors and future success.

Jocks and Burnouts: A Case Study

In her study of social groups in a large Midwestern, suburban high school, Penelope Eckert (1989) claimed:

> One of the greatest errors in education is to assume that the larger social context of the school is irrelevant or even secondary to learning. . . . The social structure of school is not simply a context of learning, it is part of what is learned. What a student learns in the classroom is indeed a very small other part (p. 179).

Eckert, an educational ethnographer, spent two years "hanging out" in a high school. She observed student life outside the classroom and interviewed some two hundred high-school students. Eckert found two broad social categories among the students: "Jocks" and "Burnouts."

Eckert argues that the "Jock"/"Burnout" categories mirror "the split between the adult middle and working classes" (p. 4). "Jocks" embrace the values of the school (e.g., respect for authority, punctuality, orientation toward individual achievement) and participate enthusiastically in the activities it offers. Schools are structured around middle-class values, norms, and social relationships and reward "Jock" behavior. "Burnouts" are alienated from the school and generally decline to participate in either academic or extracurricular activities. School offers few incentives or rewards to "Burnouts," who expressed the feeling that the school could be, but was not, serving their needs. In Eckert's view, "Burnout" behavior is not deviant or delinquent; rather, it reflects working-class norms, values, and social relationships. Whether a student becomes a "Jock" or a "Burnout" is not entirely a matter of individual choice. Eckert sees the origin of the two categories in parents' socioeconomic status. This split between middle- and working-class culture is maintained by almost every aspect of junior high- and high-school structure.

Junior High School and the Emergence of "Jocks" and "Burnouts"   Entrance to junior high or middle school marks many adolescents' first experience with students from neighborhoods other than their own, with academic tracking, and with participation in school-sponsored extracurricular activities such as sports, clubs, and student government. One of the most immediate and urgent needs of students entering the large, impersonal, and often intimidating junior high is to develop a sense of identity through belonging.

Many "Burnouts" told Eckert that they had been introduced to "Burnout" culture during the summer before they entered junior high school. In the working-class neighborhoods where most "Burnouts" grew up, parents (because of long working hours or shift work) often relied on older children to look out for younger siblings. Thus, working-class children developed strong peer group networks that crossed age boundaries.

During evening neighborhood gatherings with older siblings and their friends, the soon-to-be junior-high students learned about smoking, marijuana, alcohol, and other illicit "adult" behaviors. The working-class students developed a sense of identity and belonging as "Burnouts" even before they set foot into junior high school. Although seventh-grade "Burnouts" participated in school social activities, they became alienated when they discovered that their precocious behaviors, such as smoking and drinking, disqualified them from sports and made them unwelcome at school social events.

"Jocks," on the other hand, experienced more adult supervision throughout childhood and less contact with adolescents outside their age group. From an early age, most future "Jocks" had experienced academic success. Because most foresaw a future that included four years or more of college, the middle-class youth had little need to assert themselves as adults early in life. When "Jocks" entered junior high, they were frequently placed in academic track classes. They formed friendships with similarly successful peers and began to emerge as school leaders. Their sense of identity and belonging was rooted in academic success and school-sanctioned extracurricular activities.

Social Class in High School   By the time students arrived in high school, the categories of "Jock" and "Burnout" were even more clearly distinguishable. In general, "Jocks" preferred to wear designer clothing, to eat lunch with other "Jocks" in the school cafeteria, to use and share lockers, to publicly oppose smoking, and to participate in school-sponsored sports as athletes or fans. "Burnouts" often wore dark-colored clothing and rock concert T-shirts, avoided the school cafeteria and any food offered there, generally refused to use lockers, smoked openly, and played sports for city or commercial leagues and in informal neighborhood games.

The values and norms of the "Jocks" were well-suited to the norms and values of the high school. "Jock" (middle-class) values encouraged competition, age-homogeneous friendships, task-oriented social contacts (e.g., working together on the school newspaper), and an implicit orientation toward higher education. For them, high school was a good setting in which to practice anticipated adult skills and roles. In fact, the high school played a direct role in helping "Jocks" procure college entrance.

The values and norms of the mostly working-class "Burnouts," however, often conflicted with those of the school. "Burnouts," most of whom did not anticipate attending college, generally pursued and developed interests outside the school. Often male "Burnout" interests, such as racing cars and motorcycles, were stigmatized by the school. In fact, it would have been difficult for "Burnouts" to participate in school-sponsored activities even if they had wanted to, since such activities generally required money and time the "Burnouts" did not have. Many "Burnouts" held after-school jobs that conflicted with after-school athletic practice. The school provided little help with job placement for vocational students.

The "Jock"/"Burnout" distinction directly affected what students learned—and didn't learn—in school. Since a "Jock" hallmark is acceptance of whatever roles the school has to offer, "Jocks" were predisposed to accept teachers as sources of authority and to perform as they were asked in academic classes. By rejecting any roles imposed on them by the school, "Burnouts"failed to acquire crucial knowledge and skills. Eckert concludes, "High school . . . is not simply a bad experience for these students—it teaches them lessons that threaten to limit them for the rest of their lives" (p. 181).

Eckert's work represents one researcher's analysis of how socioeconomic class functions in a single suburban high school; however, numerous other studies, conducted in this country and elsewhere, confirm the critical role socioeconomic class plays in students' attitudes toward school, teachers' attitudes toward students, and students' school success (Brantlinger, 1993; McLaren, 1986; Oakes, 1985). In any case, it is far too simplistic to assert that kids who sit in the back row wearing heavy-metal rock concert T-shirts, who put their heads down on their desks while you are giving assignments, who carry the tell-tale aroma of tobacco, and who rarely turn in their homework on time have had every opportunity to learn and they just don't care.

■■■ EXCEPTIONAL STUDENTS

Effective teachers know their students. They make it their business to appreciate their students as individuals; to discover the unique needs, talents, and interests of each; and to plan curriculum and instruction accordingly. In this view, all students have special needs that make them "exceptional;" however, in common educational parlance, the term "exceptionality" has come to refer to a growing array of student characteristics that qualify individual students to receive special services. Currently, these exceptionalities include: (1) mental retardation; (2) learning disabilities; (3) emotional and behavioral disorders; (4) communication disorders; (5) physical and health impairments; (6) hearing impairments; (7) visual impairments; (8) severe or multiple disabilities; and (9) giftedness (Culatta & Tompkins, 1999).

Traditionally, students with these characteristics have received special services in programs that removed them from the general education classroom. More recently, the trend has been toward inclusive schools that integrate students with exceptionalities into regular education programs. This means that you, as a prospective middle- or high-school teacher, will have exceptional students in your classroom. How will you respond?

As you spend more and more time in schools, you will be introduced to a whole vocabulary that is used to describe students served by special programs: LD (learning disabled), MR (mentally retarded), ADD (Attention Deficit Disorder), BD (behavior disordered), MSD (multiple and severe disabilities), TAG (talented and gifted). The list goes on, and the labels vary from place to place and change frequently. Some advocates of students with special needs urge educators to label the program—not the learner (Adelman, 1996; McDonnell, McLaughlin & Morison, 1997). Others question the need for labels at all, pointing to the stigma attached to such descriptors as "retarded" or "autistic" (Kliewer & Biklen, 1996). Once students have been labeled as "disabled" or needing "special services," the temptation exists to begin thinking of them only in terms of this characteristic. Mara Sapon-Shevin (1992), an advocate of full inclusion for all students, has written:

> We must think about the school community in terms of the many kinds of diversity that are represented. We must address children's economic, religious, cultural, ethnic, and family differences. We must consider responsiveness to children in foster care, children who do not celebrate major holidays, and children whose first language is not English. For example, adapting a lesson for Maria who requires a communication device is critical, but we must also address Maria's needs as a Hispanic child from a single-parent family. Our responsiveness to all children's differences is what creates inclusive schools—schools that model respect and appreciation for the full spectrum of human beings (p. 335).

The concept of inclusive schools becomes especially important when we consider that data from national surveys suggest that boys are identified for special education at higher rates than girls; that students of color are overrepresented in special education programs; and that students with disabilities are more socioeconomically disadvantaged than the rest of the population (McDonnell, McLaughlin & Morison, 1997). Perhaps as many as half of students with disabilities drop out before completing high school (Cantrell & Cantrell, 1995).

Although educators tend to think of special needs as "disabilities," giftedness also falls under the umbrella of exceptionalities. Proponents of gifted education argue that "the regular classroom as currently organized and implemented is largely not amenable to change, and many teachers and students are hostile to gifted students, thus necessitating the removal of gifted students to a 'safe haven' where they can be with other students like themselves" (Sapon-Shevin, 1995, p. 70). Proponents of inclusive schools would argue that the needs of gifted students should be accommodated in the regular classroom: when students with differences of any sort are removed from the classroom for whatever reason, the whole classroom community is diminished. In a longitudinal study of 200 talented high-school students, Csikszentmihalyi, Rathunde, and Whalen (1993) found that supportive, caring teachers who modeled enthusiastic involvement in their fields helped gifted teenagers maintain and develop their talents.

From the above discussion you can surmise why even the matter of informing general education teachers that students with exceptionalities have been assigned to their classes is controversial. On the one hand, if the general education teacher is aware that a student has a learning disability or a behavior disorder, he or she can plan more effectively to meet that student's individual needs. On the other hand, research suggests that when teachers are aware that students have been identified as having disabilities, they tend to have lower expectations of their performance and to interact with them less positively and less frequently than with students who have no diagnosed disabilities (Brantlinger, 1996; Vaughn & Schumm, 1996).

How will you know, then, whether students in your middle- or high-school classes have special needs? The disabilities of many students with special needs are diagnosed in the very first years of schooling. In fact, some children enter kindergarten already receiving special services (McDonnell, McLaughlin & Morison, 1997). As a middle- or high-school teacher, you will probably not have occasion to make many referrals for a disability diagnosis. Of course, especially in today's mobile society, it is possible that some students whose disabilities have not been diagnosed will enter your classroom. Any number of clues may lead you to refer a student for special needs assessment, including persistently poor academic performance (or, conversely, highly original and unusual academic work), difficulties with social interactions in the classroom, unusual physical behaviors such as squinting or straining to see (which might suggest an undiagnosed visual impairment), or noticeable patterns of significant errors in written expression (which might suggest a physical or cognitive disability).

The more common scenario is that you will be informed by a member of the school special education faculty that one or more of your students have been diagnosed with one or more disabilities. Special education faculty will share with you the goals that have been set for each student with special needs through collaboration among special education personnel, parents or other significant adults, and, to the extent possible, the student herself. In many cases, you will be informed of strategies you can use to adapt your instruction to accommodate students' special needs. Sometimes, a student may be assigned a personal aide to tend to his or her needs in the classroom setting. In some cases, a special education teacher may team teach with you in a collaborative classroom.

A number of educational innovations hold promise for helping schools better meet the needs of students with exceptionalities. Many of these practices will be discussed in detail in later chapters. These techniques include teaching higher-order thinking, teaching metacognitive skills, mastery learning, cooperative learning, activity-based learning, use of technology, and peer support and tutoring. Teacher use of knowledge about learning styles and multiple intelligences (discussed later) also enhances the learning environment for students with exceptionalities. Many middle and high schools have successfully become inclusive and report that all students benefit, both socially and academically, in an inclusive environment (e.g., Farlow, 1996; Hardin & McNelis, 1996; Sapon-Shevin, 1995; Staub & Peck, 1995).

▮ Reader Activity 3.4

CONSULTING OTHER SOURCES
Studying Implementation of Inclusion

The practice of full inclusion is controversial. Learn more about this issue by exploring the following sources or others given in this section: (1) Stainback, W. & Stainback, S., Eds. (1996). *Controversial issues confronting special education: Divergent perspectives.* **Second edition.** Needham Heights, MA (2) Fuchs, D. & Fuchs, L. S., Eds. (1995). Special Section on Special Education. *Phi Delta Kappan, 76* (**7**), 522–546.). Formulate a working definition of the term. Summarize arguments for and against inclusion. Are there exceptions to full inclusion? What are they? What are the characteristics of an inclusive classroom? An inclusive school?

If possible, arrange to spend a day or part of a day "shadowing" a special education teacher, either in a self-contained setting or in a collaborative classroom. Keep a log of her/his activities throughout the day. Arrange a follow-up time during which you can interview this teacher about the special needs of students in the school and how the school as a whole responds to such students. Next, solicit the opinions of some regular classroom teachers on this issue.

Finally, write a brief position paper based on your research, observations, and interviews describing your position on inclusion and how the philosophy of inclusion is translated into practice. Describe factors you discovered that appear to enhance or impede inclusion.

▮▮▮ LEARNING STYLES AND MULTIPLE INTELLIGENCES

Research on learning styles and multiple-intelligence theory has given educators a constructive way to view differences among students and how they learn. In the past, one style of teaching (e.g., lecture) was thought to "fit all," and teachers generally planned and implemented instruction aimed at the whole class. Students who were not successful with a single method of instruction were thought to be unskilled or perhaps incapable of learning. Learning-style research and multiple-intelligence theory suggest that all students can learn and learn well if given the opportunity to learn in ways that suit them best and to demonstrate learning in a variety of forms.

Learning Styles

Learning styles may be defined as "the unique ways whereby an individual gathers and processes information and are the means by which an individual prefers to learn"

(Davidson, 1990, p. 36). The key words here are *unique* and *prefers.* That is, not every person learns in the same way, and people have different preferences about how to learn best. Proponents of learning-style theory attempt to make teachers aware that: (1) students have different styles of learning; (2) teachers tend to teach according to their own preferred learning styles; (3) school success often hinges upon being able to learn in a single style; and (4) teachers need to vary their instructional styles to address the varied learning styles of their students.

Numerous learning-style inventories or profiles have been developed. For example, instruments have been developed to determine students' preferences in the areas of cognition, perception, learning environment, social interaction, and physiological factors (e.g., need for intake of food) (Dunn, Beaudry & Klavas, 1989). While each of these instruments yields somewhat different information, they do share some commonalities.

In general, school as we typically think of it seems to work best for learners who can deal in the abstract, who tend to think logically and sequentially, who learn well from listening and the written word, who are autonomous and/or easily motivated by authority figures (e.g., McCarthy, 1997; Shields, 1993; Schroeder, 1993). However, many students differ from this description. For example, some learners prefer the concrete and immediate to the abstract ("What does this have to do with real life?"); some learners think intuitively, imaginatively, or globally ("I found my own solution to this problem and it works. Why did you take points off?"); some students need to see, touch, move, manipulate in order to understand ("I don't want to read the directions! Just let me at that computer!"); some students learn best when they receive a lot of feedback from adults and/or can talk to their peers ("I wasn't cheating; I was just talking over the problem with Renee"). As the hypothetical student quotes in parentheses suggest, such traits as these sometimes land students in academic or disciplinary difficulty.

A number of researchers and scholars have looked for links between learning styles and culture, ethnicity, race, class, gender, students with special needs, and students whose first language is not English (e.g., Irvine & York, 1995; DeBello, 1990; Hilliard, 1989; Caldwell & Ginther, 1996; Reid, 1987). While looking at groups such as these through the lens of learning styles can lead to a better understanding of conditions that enhance the learning of students of diverse backgrounds, such an approach should be used with caution:

> One reason that the linkage between culture and learning styles is controversial is that generalizations about a *group* of people have often led to naive inferences about *individuals* within that group. Although people connected by culture do exhibit characteristic patterns of style preferences, it is a serious error to conclude that all members of the group have the same style traits as the group taken as a whole (Guild, 1994, p. 16).

In short, there is at least as much diversity within groups as among groups. The value of learning-style theory is that it gives teachers another tool for understanding students and determining what kinds of experiences may best help them learn. Learning-style theory allows teachers to view learners as "different,"—not necessarily as "slow", "bright", "motivated", or "unmotivated." If we accept the premise that students have different styles of learning, then we as teachers must accept responsibility for providing for these differences.

When I introduce preservice teachers to learning-style theory, they commonly make two mistaken assumptions. The first is that every lesson must be tailored to every student's individual learning style—an impossible task! The second is that if Wanda is, for example, a strong kinesthetic learner (e.g., learns best by hands-on activities), she should not be required to learn through reading or to demonstrate learning through writing. In response to the first concern, the most practical approach is to make sure that lessons and units include a variety of ways in which students can learn and demonstrate their mastery of content and skills. In response to the second concern, a student like Wanda needs to recognize and capitalize on her strengths, but she also needs to be a well-rounded learner. If you incorporate a variety of activities into your lessons and offer students choices, you will be well on your way to addressing students' diverse learning styles.

Multiple Intelligences

Do you recall ever taking an IQ (Intelligence Quotient) test? Do you know what numbers are considered to be in the high range of intelligence? The low range? Do you know your IQ? If so, how do you feel about it? If not, would you like to know your IQ? Why or why not? Have you ever thought about what it means to represent a person's intelligence by a single number, say 120? Who is more intelligent—Michael Jordan or Toni Morrison, Stephen Speilberg or Stevie Wonder, Nelson Mandela or Bill Gates? Of all of these individuals, who is the most intelligent? Why?

When we look at individuals who are gifted in very different ways, it becomes impossible to talk about a single concept termed *intelligence*. Toni Morrison is not likely to play professional basketball, nor Michael Jordan to win a Nobel Prize for literature. Yet, each has a unique genius and has made a lasting contribution to our society and culture.

The students you are preparing to teach may or may not become world leaders, world-class athletes, or world-renowned film-makers, but Howard Gardner's theory of multiple intelligences (e.g., Gardner, 1983, 1993a, 1993b) gives educators a soundly researched and scrupulously documented means to identify and describe the many ways in which people are intelligent. Prior to the publication of Gardner's theory, it was widely assumed that intelligence could be determined through a pen and pencil test which focused on students' verbal, mathematical, and logical skills, and that intelligence could then be translated into a single number that remained more or less constant throughout life. "IQ" was closely linked to school success, and this was not surprising because both instruction and assessment in schools generally focused on verbal, mathematical, and logical skills. Using rigorous criteria to define "an intelligence" and using examples of historical and contemporary "geniuses" from this culture and others, Gardner originally identified seven intelligences,[3] which are briefly described in Figure 3.1.

Obviously, the intelligences overlap and a person may be gifted in more than one intelligence (e.g., Michael Jordan appears to have intrapersonal and interpersonal gifts as well as bodily-kinesthetic intelligence). The theory of multiple intelligences, like learning styles, was not intended for use in simplistically labeling students. Rather, it offers teachers another important lens for viewing diversity in the classroom.

---

3. Gardner has recently identified an eighth intelligence—naturalist intelligence—the ability to use the materials and features of the natural environment to solve problems or create products (e.g., Charles Darwin). He is also looking at additional forms of intelligence, such as a spiritual or existential intelligence (see, for example Hatch, 1997; Gardner, 1995; and Gardner, 1999).

FIGURE 3.1   Gardner's Multiple Intelligences

Intelligence	Descriptors
Linguistic	Sensitivity to meaning, order, sounds or words, and to functions of language; capacity to use language effectively
Musical	Sensitivity to rhythm, melody, and timbre
Logical/Mathematical	Ability to see logical or numerical patterns, to carry through long chains of reasoning, to handle increasingly abstract levels of analysis
Spatial	Ability to perceive the visual-spatial world accurately, to manipulate or mentally transform objects and forms, to produce a graphic likeness of spatial information; sensitivity to the qualities that characterize a visual or spatial display
Bodily-Kinesthetic	Ability to handle objects skillfully, and to control one's own bodily movement for functional and expressive purposes
Intrapersonal	Ability to develop a reliable working model of oneself and to use that model as a means of understanding and guiding one's own behavior
Interpersonal	Ability to identify and understand the needs, motivations, and intentions of others and to act upon this knowledge

(Descriptions adapted from Willis, 1994 and Haggerty, 1995)

Learning-style and multiple-intelligence theory offer ways to appreciate the various strengths students bring to the classroom and provide frameworks to help teachers offer a variety of pathways to learning. Armstrong (1994), for example, has proposed that multiple-intelligence theory is particularly useful in teaching students with disabilities. A disability may affect only a small part of one intelligence, leaving vast areas of intelligences yet to be tapped. Armstrong recommends a strategy he calls "cognitive bypassing," which allows students to bypass their areas of disability and to use alternate modes in which their intelligences are more developed. In Chapter Nine, "Implementing Instruction: Strategies and Methods," we will examine some specific ways middle- and high-school teachers are incorporating learning-style research and multiple-intelligence theory into classroom instruction.

▌ Reader Activity 3.5

THEORY INTO PRACTICE
Experiencing Multiple Intelligences

One of the best ways to understand the potential of Gardner's theory of multiple intelligences for improving teaching and learning is to experience it for yourself. The purpose of this activity is to allow you to experience expressing yourself in various intelligences and to begin thinking about how you will apply multiple-intelligence theory in your teaching.

As a class, create learning centers or stations (see Chapter Nine, "Implementing Instruction: Strategies and Methods," for a fuller description of learning centers). Each will be devoted to a different intelligence. First, as a class agree on or ask your instructor to assign a topic (e.g., apples, rodents, insects) or theme (e.g., identity, time, friendship) for this experience.

Divide into seven groups and plan a learning center for each intelligence based on the agreed-upon theme (refer to Figure 3.1). Plan the materials you will provide and the tasks you will suggest. For example, at a linguistic intelligence center, you might provide a variety of writing implements and papers and suggest making a word game, or writing a poem or a story. For this exploratory activity, it is not necessary to get very specific about tasks. It is preferable to provide a few suggestions for using the materials, then let your peers' creativity flow.

Set up your learning centers in class. You will probably have time to experience three centers at the most. Visit one center that you know you'll enjoy and at which you'll feel comfortable; choose a second center that just looks interesting to you; and a third center that you would really rather avoid. As you move through and experience the centers you've chosen, keep track of what you're thinking and feeling at each one.

After everyone has had the chance to experience three centers, hold a debriefing discussion. Volunteers can share some of the products they've created at the centers (e.g., drawings, poems, graphs, music). Discuss the following questions.

1. What was your favorite center and how did it feel to work in this mode? How did it feel when it was time to move to a different center?
2. What was your least favorite center and how did it feel to work in this mode?
3. Within your class, were there any patterns of preference associated with specific subject areas? For example, did prospective English teachers prefer the verbal center? Did prospective physical education teachers prefer the bodily-kinesthetic center?
4. What are the implications of this activity for teaching in your subject area?

CREATING EQUITABLE AND INCLUSIVE LEARNING ENVIRONMENTS

Equity in education means "equal opportunities for all students to develop to their fullest potential" (Bennett, 1998, p. 16). Creating an equitable learning environment may require that you treat students differently according to relevant differences. Inclusive learning environments require that all students, regardless of any individual differences they might have, are fully included in the mainstream of school life. Nevertheless, a number of the studies cited in this chapter (e.g., Brantlinger, 1993; Eckert, 1989; Goodlad, 1984; Peshkin, 1991) suggest that many middle- and high-school teachers continue to treat all students the same because they believe this is the best assurance of being fair. In addition, when teachers are required to plan for several different courses each day and for a large number of students, it seems daunting to think of customizing or individualizing instruction. But when all are treated the same, not all are treated fairly and some are relegated to the periphery of classroom life. For these reasons and others, this chapter has focused on differences rather than similarities among students. We are well aware that adolescents (and all human beings) have more similarities than they do differences. Recognizing and building upon our similarities enable us to form communities in the classroom and in the world, sharing common values and goals. At the same time, we must respond to individual and group differences within communities in order to ensure that all members have equal opportunities to participate in the life of the community. One major purpose of this book is to help you learn to create an equitable learning environment in your classroom and to keep student diversity always in mind as you plan for and implement instruction.

In Chapter Two, "Understanding Multiculturalism," Richard introduced you to the concept of "culturally relevant teaching," gave you a glimpse of some middle- and high-school teachers who are successfully teaching diverse learners, and outlined some characteristics of effective teachers and their practice. The guidelines below build upon the material in Chapter Two and will enhance your ability to create equitable and inclusive learning environments. Stainback, Stainback, and Slavin (1989) have made recommendations for organizing classrooms to accommodate wide diversity among students. They explain that effective strategies focus on meeting the needs of all members of the classroom community. Their recommendations include:

- *Provide positive recognition for goal achievement* focused on competing against one's own achievement rather than achievements of others.
- *Foster student interdependence* through such strategies as buddy systems, cooperative learning, peer tutoring, and fostering informal friendships.
- *Foster student independence* through such practices as posting rules and schedules and organizing individual folders with activities and assignments in writing so that more students can function effectively without the personal attention of the teacher.
- *Collaborate within the school and within the school community* by working with other teachers in the school to learn more about students, to plan interdisciplinary units, and to model interdependence. Use the expertise of specialists available to you (e.g., special education teachers, reading specialists, language therapists, English as a Second Language teachers). Use aides and volunteers from within the school and within the community to support you and your students' learning in the classroom.
- *Use a wide variety of grouping practices* to give students experience working in a variety of group configurations including large, small, heterogeneous, and cooperative teams.
- *Physically organize the classroom for diversity* to ensure that your classroom decor and displays reflect the interests and accomplishments of all the students who spend time there. Attend to students' differing physical needs (e.g., students who are easily distracted may need a quiet area to work; students with visual impairments may need to sit close to the chalkboard or viewing screen) and make sure that the physical arrangement of the room accommodates all students (e.g., rearranging furniture so that students in wheelchairs feel included in the class).
- *Arrange for access to a variety of materials and equipment* that will appeal to a variety of learners and that can be adapted for a variety of learning activities. Make sure you know how to obtain specialized items such as large-print materials, materials in languages other than English, and adapted computer keyboards.
- *Take students' needs and abilities into account* when setting due dates for assignments, scheduling time for tests, and formulating a policy for late work.

❚ Reader Activity 3.6

WHAT WOULD YOU DO?
ROLE-PLAYING THE CASE OF J. T.

Role-playing the case of J. T. will give you the opportunity to apply what you have learned about students in this chapter. After reading the case below, role-play the various scenarios suggested. Don't worry about getting it "right." Just try to put yourself in the shoes of the characters based on the information given here.

The Case of J. T.

It is October and you are in your first year of teaching at Pine Grove High School, a mid-sized suburban/rural high school, which serves long-term residents of an established community as well as families stationed at a nearby U. S. Army base. Several years ago, Pine Grove eliminated tracking students into ability-level courses. You are teaching several classes of ninth-graders in your subject area. At mid-week, a new student appears in your classroom—J. T.

To date, things have been going well for you. You've established rapport with your classes, your management plan seems to be working, students are responding well to your teaching and several have given you compliments, such as, "Gee, Ms./Mr. _____ you're the best _____ teacher I've ever had!" Because you're busy setting up the day's activity, you hardly notice J. T. slipping into an empty desk at the back of the room. Once the rest of the class has started on the day's activity, you walk back to J. T.'s seat, assign him a textbook, put him into a group that's already engaged with the task, and assume he'll "get with the program." But he doesn't.

Soon the group to which you assigned J. T. is completely off-task, and you observe J. T. looking at you and then whispering comments to the group, while poking anyone within reach with his mechanical pencil. You're beginning to get very irritated with J. T., so you separate him from the group, tell him to work on the assignment alone, and ask him to stay after class so that you can review the class rules with him. J. T. gives you a stony look. When the bell rings, he walks out the door, avoiding eye contact with you.

In the days that follow, after correcting J. T. numerous times for not having materials, not being prepared for class, not participating in class activities, and bothering other students, you ask him to sit in a seat near the front of the classroom, thinking he will become more engaged in the class. Although J. T. moves to the seat when you ask him, the next day he is back at his post in the rear of the room. When you ask him to please take the seat you assigned, he tells you that the bright lights in the front of the room bother him. Exasperated and skeptical of J. T.'s excuse, you decide to concentrate your energies on the majority of students who **want** to learn your subject. Most of the time, you just ignore J. T. and, in fact, you're rather stunned to discover that you've actually begun to dislike this student for his sullenness, non-cooperativeness, and rather odd appearance, mannerisms, and behavior. For example, when J. T. actually does have his notebook open, he often draws pictures of weapons and Nazi insignia. When he occasionally raises his hand and you call on him, he usually offers a comment like, "Why are we doing this? This is stupid."

Soon, through "teacher talk" in the faculty lounge you learn that most of J. T.'s teachers— even the experienced ones—are having the same problems with him. You also discover that J. T. has been diagnosed with a behavior disorder and a learning disability, but the special education teacher has never discussed his case with you. Furthermore, you hear through the grapevine that J. T. behaves with particular disdain toward Ms. Henson, the special education teacher, and has even been known to hide in the library stacks rather than go to her classroom for special help. Suddenly you realize that this "silent treatment" by you and your colleagues is not fair to J.T. After all, you don't know much about him at all. Is it really right to label him as "hopeless"?

What little you do know has come via J.T.'s gregarious sister, Bernadette, who is in the twelfth grade. Unlike J.T., Bernadette is a "model" student who has quickly adapted to her new classes and teachers at Pine Grove. In conversations with teachers, Bernadette has disclosed that her father is a White, enlisted soldier in the U.S. Army. J.T.'s and her mother is a Filipina who is still strongly connected to her traditional culture. Bernadette says, for example, that their mother regularly consults "healers" rather than medical doctors when family members are ill.

You ask the school counselor to set up a meeting for all J.T.'s teachers to discuss his case before holding a full-scale conference that includes J.T. and his parents.

Role-Play Scenarios

Role-play as many of the following scenarios as time allows.

- The meeting of J.T.'s teachers during which you discuss what you know about J.T. and what you need to know. Brainstorm strategies you can use to get J.T. on the right track for learning.
- J.T. is staying after school to make up a test he refused to take earlier in the week. You decide to use this opportunity to try to connect with J.T. and to find out how you might help him connect to you and your class.
- The meeting of J.T.'s teachers, J.T.'s parents, J.T. himself, and the school counselor during which you try to bring J.T.'s school difficulties into the open and collaborate on a plan that can help him succeed.

Debriefing Issues for Discussion

1. What sociocultural issues surfaced during the role-plays? What issues did not surface, but in retrospect, might be relevant to J.T.'s case?
2. What happened when all J.T.'s teachers met to discuss his case? Did productive information emerge?
3. What happened in the interactions between the individual teacher and J.T.? Was any change in either the teacher's or J.T.'s attitude apparent?
4. What role did J.T.'s diagnosed disabilities play in the scenarios you enacted?
5. What information emerged in the family meeting that was previously unknown? How, if at all, did J.T.'s behavior differ in this context than in the classroom context?
6. Based on this case and the role-plays that followed, what happens when teachers and other concerned adults make a serious effort to understand "problem" students like J.T.?
7. How likely is it that you would actually have a student like J.T.? Do some students, like J.T., have such "bad attitudes" and lack of basic knowledge and skills that they are beyond hope in school?
8. What connections did you make between the content of this chapter and the case of J.T.?

▌▌SUMMARY

I began this chapter with an anecdote about how gender influenced my school performance. That story hinged upon my own, my peers', and society's perceptions of what it meant to be "feminine" when I attended high school. I can't point to a single school event or teacher that had a significant impact on how I defined my "feminine" role. Yet, in this chapter I have argued that schools and teachers can and should take an active role in fostering respect for differences and in using diversity as a resource for curriculum and instruction. Among the key points to remember are:

- Many adolescents experience societal problems that affect their school performance, but research shows that just one caring and effective teacher can help protect an adolescent from risk.
- Historically, schools have not been very responsive to adolescents' views and interests.
- Media reports often overlook "good news" about adolescents.
- Sociocultural characteristics of adolescents, such as gender, ethnicity, culture, language, and socioeconomic class, have a great deal to do with how they perceive schools and teachers, how teachers interact with them, and whether or not they will conclude that school success is a worthy goal.
- Exceptional students challenge teachers to break out of the old mold of "one-size-fits-all" instruction and to move toward creating equitable and inclusive learning environments.
- Research on learning styles and multiple intelligences can help teachers recognize differences in a non-judgmental way and design instruction that invites different kinds of learners to be successful.

We hope this chapter will encourage you to make observing, talking and listening to, and learning about your students a lifelong pursuit. A single teacher, a single class, or even a single learning experience can change the course of a student's life.

Finally, don't forget that students have a lot to teach you. If you show that you are interested in them, they will tell you where you can catch the biggest trout, where to get the best deals on tires for your car, what CDs are hot, and which movies to see. They will bring you books to read and funny-looking rocks to identify. Some will be gifted artists, poets, and musicians. Some will be skilled mechanics, computer whizzes, intrepid hunters, sports buffs, or environmentalists. Some will be parents. If you listen and learn from your students, they may unwittingly reveal how you can best teach them.

For many teachers, the most rewarding aspects of their profession are the relationships they develop with students and the moments when they realize that their students are actually learning.

▨▮ BUILDING YOUR BIOGRAPHY, YOUR PERSONAL PRACTICAL PHILOSOPHY, AND PORTFOLIO

Building Your Biography

What experiences in your life are relevant to knowing middle- and high-school students today? The following questions are intended to help you generate ideas for composing a chapter of your teaching biography. They are not intended to be answered sequentially or to limit your exploration.

- What kind of student were you?
- What experiences with gender, ethnicity, culture, language, or socioeconomic class shaped who you were as a student?

- What relations did you have with other students who differed from you?
- How was your own adolescence influenced by societal pressures and problems?
- What were the hallmarks of adolescent culture in your middle school and/or high school?
- What were your values when you were in middle or high school?
- How did you regard your school experiences?
- Does one experience stand out that crystallizes who you were as an adolescent?
- What experiences do you have with adolescents now? Siblings? Students? Friends?

Developing Your Personal Practical Philosophy

Draft a section of your personal educational philosophy that addresses adolescents, their characteristics, their differences and similarities and how you will respond to this knowledge as a teacher. Set the piece aside and return to it when you begin to write your final philosophy statement. You might respond to questions such as the following.

- What is meant by an "equitable" learning environment?
- What would that look like in your subject area?
- How can you help diverse students make connections to your subject area?
- What can middle-/high-school students expect from you as a teacher?
- What do you expect from adolescents?
- Are there groups or students with individual differences to which you feel a particular affinity?
- Are there groups or students with individual differences that you will need to make a special effort to reach?

Collecting Artifacts for Your Portfolio

Review the Reader Activities you have completed in this chapter. Identify any that you might eventually select for your portfolio. For each, jot down notes that will help you recall later what you were thinking at the time you completed the activity, what challenges you encountered while completing it, what you learned from doing it, and how this activity reveals something about who you will be as a teacher. Don't worry about style or correctness at this point. The purpose is to begin documenting your thinking as you move through this book and this class.

■■■■■■■ ▌▌ References

Adelman, H. S. (1996). Appreciating the classification dilemma. In W. Stainback & S. Stainback, Eds. *Controversial issues confronting special education: Divergent perspectives,* pp. 96–113. Second edition. Needham Heights, MA: Allyn & Bacon.

American Association of University Women. (1992). *How schools shortchange girls.* Commissioned by AAUW Educational Foundation. Researched by Wellesley College Center for Research on Women. Joint publication of AAUW & NEA.

Armstrong, T. (1994). *Multiple intelligences in the classroom.* Alexandria, VA: Association for Supervision and Curriculum Development.

Banks, J. A. (1991). *Teaching Strategies for Ethnic Studies,* Fifth Edition. Needham Heights, MA: Allyn & Bacon.

Banks, J. A. (1994). *Multiethnic education: Theory and practice* (3rd ed.). Boston: Allyn & Bacon.

Barbieri, M. (1995). *Sounds from the heart: Learning to listen to girls.* Portsmouth, NH: Heinemann.

Bennett, C. I. (1998). *Comprehensive multicultural education: Theory and practice* (4th ed.). Needham Heights, MA: Allyn & Bacon.

Brantlinger, E. A. (1993). *The politics of social class in secondary school: Views of affluent and impoverished youth.* New York: Teachers College Press.

Brooks-Gunn, J. (1992). The impact of puberty and sexual activity upon the health and education of adolescent girls and boys. In S. S. Klein (Ed.), *Sex Equity and Sexuality in Education* (pp. 97–126). Albany, NY: State University of New York Press.

Brown, L. M. and Gilligan, C. (1992). *Meeting at the crossroads: Women's psychology and girls' development.* Cambridge, MA: Harvard University Press.

Caldwell, G. P. & Ginther, D. W. (1996). Differences in learning styles of low socioeconomic status for low and high achievers. *Education, 117* (1), 141–147.

Cantrell, R. P. & Cantrell, M. L. (1995). Recapturing a generation: The future of secondary programs for students with disabilities. *Preventing school failure, 39* (3), 25–28.

Coleman, E. & Ramefedi, G. (1989). Gay, lesbian, and bisexual adolescents: A critical challenge to counselors. *Journal of Counseling and Development 68* (Sept.), 36–39.

Coontz, S. (1992). *The way we never were: American families and the nostalgia trap.* New York: Basic Books.

Csikszentmihalyi, M., Rathunde, K., & Whalen, S. (1993). *Talented teenagers: The roots of success and failure.* New York: Cambridge University Press.

Culatta, R. A. & Tompkins, J. R. (1999). *Fundamentals of special education: What every teacher needs to know.* Upper Saddle River, NJ: Merrill/Prentice Hall.

Cusick, P. A. (1973). *Inside high school: The students' world.* New York: Holt, Rhinehart & Winston, Inc.

Davidson, G. V. (1990). Matching learning styles with teaching styles: Is it a useful concept in instruction? *Performance and Instruction, 29* (4), 36–38.

DeBello, T. C. (1990). Comparison of eleven major learning styles models: Variables, appropriate populations, validity of instrumentation, and the research behind them. *Journal of reading, writing, and learning disabilities, 6* (3), 203–222.

Delamont, S. (1990). *Sex roles in the school* (2nd ed.). London: Routledge.

Delpit, L. (1995). *Other people's children: Cultural conflict in the classroom.* New York: The New Press.

Dunn, R., Beaudry, J. S., & Klavas, A. (1989). Survey of research on learning styles. *Educational Leadership, 46* (6), 50–58.

Eckert, P. (1989). *Jocks & Burnouts: Social categories and identity in the high school.* New York: Teachers College Press.

Farlow, L. (1996). A quartet of success stories: How to make inclusion work. *Educational Leadership, 53* (5), 51–55.

French, T. (1993). *South of heaven: Welcome to high school at the end of the twentieth century.* New York: Pocket Books.

Gardner, H. (1983). *Frames of mind.* New York: Basic Books.

Gardner, H. (1993a). *Creating minds: An anatomy of creativity seen through the lives of Freud, Picasso, Stravinsky, Eliot, Graham, and Gandhi.* New York: Basic Books.

Gardner, H. (1993b). *Multiple intelligences: The theory in practice.* New York: Basic Books.

Gardner, H. (1995). Reflections on multiple intelligences: Myths and messages. *Phi Delta Kappan, 77* (3), 200–203, 206–209.

Gardner, H. (1999). Are there additional intelligences? The case for naturalist, spiritual, and existential intelligences. In J. Kane (Ed.). *Education, information, and transformation.* Upper Saddle River, NJ: Merrill-Prentice Hall.

Goodlad, J. I. (1984). *A place called school: Prospects for the future.* New York: McGraw Hill.

Grayson, D. A. (1992). Emerging equity issues related to homosexuality in education. In S. S. Klein (Ed.), *Sex Equity and Sexuality in Education* (pp. 171–190). Albany, NY: State University of New York Press.

Guild, P. (1994). The culture/learning style connection. *Educational Leadership, 51* (8), 16–21.

Haggerty, B. A. (1995). *Nurturing intelligences: A guide to multiple intelligences theory and teaching.* Menlo Park, CA: Addison Wesley Publishing Company.

Hamburg, D. A. (1994). *Today's children: Creating a future for a generation in crisis.* New York: Times Books.

Hardin, D. E. & McNelis, S. J. (1996). The resource center: Hub of inclusive activities. *Educational Leadership, 53* (5), 41–43.

Hatch, T. (1997). Getting specific about multiple intelligences. *Educational Leadership, 54* (6), 26–29.

Hetrick, E. S. & Martin, A. D. (1987) Developmental issues and their resolution for gay and lesbian adolescents. *Journal of Homosexuality, 14* (1/2), 25–43.

Hilliard III, A. G. (1989). Teachers and cultural styles in a pluralistic society. *NEA Today, 7* (6), 65–69.

Hodgkinson, H. (1997). Diversity comes in all shapes and sizes. *School Business Affairs, 63*(4), 3–7.

Hollingshead, D. A. (1995). *Postethnic America: Beyond multiculturalism.* New York: Basic Books.

Irvine, J. J. & York, D. E. (1995). Learning styles and culturally diverse students: A literature review. In J. Banks (Ed.). *Handbook of research on multicultural education* (pp. 484–497). New York: MacMillan.

Jennings, K. (Ed.) (1998). *Telling tales out of school: Gays, lesbians, and bisexuals revisit their school days.* New York: Alyson Books.

Klein, S. S., Ortman, P. E. et al. (1994). Continuing the journey toward gender equity. *Educational Researcher, 23* (8), 13–21.

Kliewer, C. & Biklen, D. (1996). Labeling: Who wants to be called retarded? In W. Stainback & S. Stainback, Eds. *Controversial issues confronting special education: Divergent perspectives,* pp. 83–95. Second edition. Needham Heights, MA: Allyn & Bacon.

Knapp, M. S. & Wolverton, S. (1995). Social class and schooling. In J. A. Banks (Ed.), *Handbook of research in multicultural education,* pp. 548–569. New York: Macmillan.

McCarthy, B. (1997). A tale of four learners: 4MAT's learning styles. *Educational Leadership, 54* (6), 46–51.

McCormick, T. M. (1994). *Creating the nonsexist classroom: A multicultural approach.* New York: Teachers College Press.

McDonnell, L., McLaughlin, M. J., & Morison, P. (1997). *Educating one and all: Students with disabilities and standards-based reform.* Washington, DC: National Academy Press.

Meier, D. (1995). *The power of their ideas: Lessons for America from a small school in Harlem.* Boston, MA: Beacon Press.

Newmann, F. M., Ed., (1992). *Student engagement and achievement in American secondary schools.* New York: Teachers College Press.

Nieto, S. (1996). *Affirming diversity; The sociopolitical context of multicultural education.* Second Edition. New York: Longman.

Ogbu, J. U. (1995). Understanding cultural diversity and learning. In J. A. Banks (Ed.), *Handbook of research in multicultural education,* pp. 582–596. New York: Macmillan.

Peshkin, A. (1991). *The color of strangers, the color of friends: The play of ethnicity in school and community.* Chicago: University of Chicago Press.

Pipher, M. (1994). *Reviving Ophelia: Saving the selves of adolescent girls.* New York: Ballantine Books.

Powell, A. G., Farrar, E. & Cohen, D. K. (1985). *The shopping mall high school: Winners and losers in the educational marketplace.* Boston, MA: Houghton Mifflin.

Public Agenda. (1997). *Getting by: What American teenagers really think about their schools.* Press Release and Summary. http://www.publicagenda.org

Reid, J. M. (1987). The learning style preferences of ESL students. *TESOL Quarterly, 21* (1), pp. 87–111.

Resnick, M. D., Bearman, P. S., Blum, R. W., Bauman, K. E., Harris, K. M., Jones, J., Tabor, J., Beuhring, T., Sieving, R. E., Shew, M., Ireland, M., Bearinger, L. H., Udry, J. R. (1997). Protecting adolescents from harm: Findings from the National Longitudinal Study on Adolescent Health. *Journal of the American Medical Association, 278* (10), 823–832.

Rofes, E. (1989). Opening up the classroom closet: Responding to the educational needs of gay and lesbian youth. *Harvard Educational Review, 59* (4), 444–453.

Rose, M. (1995). *Possible lives: The promise of public education in America.* Boston, MA: Houghton Mifflin.

Rubin, N. (1994). *Ask me if I care: Voices from an American high school.* Berkeley, CA: Ten Speed Press.

Sadker, M. P. & Sadker, D. M. (1982). *Sex equity handbook for schools.* New York: Longman.

Sadker, M. P. & Sadker, D. M. (1993). *Failing at fairness: How America's schools cheat girls.* New York: Charles Scribner's Sons.

Sapon-Shevin, M. (1992). Inclusive thinking about inclusive schools, 335–346. In R. A. Villa, J. S. Thousand, W. Stainback, & S. Stainback (Eds.), *Restructuring for caring and effective education: An administrative guide to creating heterogeneous schools.* Baltimore, MD: Paul Brooks Publishing Company.

Sapon-Shevin, M. (1995). Why gifted students belong in inclusive schools. *Educational Leadership, 52*(4), 64–71.

Schroeder, C. C. (1993). New students—new learning styles. *Change, 25* (5), 21–26.

Sears, J. T. (1991). *Growing up gay in the South: Race, gender, and journeys of the spirit.* New York: Harrington Park Press.

Shields, C. J. (1993). Learning styles: Where Jung, the Beatles, and schools intersect. *Curriculum Review, 33* (2), 9–12.

Sizer, T. R. (1996). *Horace's hope: What works for the American high school.* Boston, MA: Houghton Mifflin.

Sizer, T. R. (1994). *Horace's school: Redesigning the American high school.* Boston, MA: Houghton Mifflin.

Sizer, T. R. (1984). *Horace's compromise: The dilemma of the American high school.* Boston, MA: Houghton Mifflin.

Sommerfeld, M. (1996, February 28). Amphibian inquiry. *Education Week,* p. 3.

Stainback, S. Stainback, W. & Slavin, R. (1989). Classroom organization for diversity among students. In S. Stainback, W. Stainback, & M. Forest (Eds.), *Educating all students in the mainstream of regular education* (pp. 131–142). Baltimore, MD: Paul Brooks Publishing Company.

Staub, D. & Peck, C. A. (1995). What are the outcomes for nondisabled students? *Educational Leadership, 52*(4), 36–41.

Steinberg, L. (1996). *Beyond the classroom: Why school reform has failed and what parents need to do.* New York: Simon & Schuster.

Thorne, B. (1994). *Gender play: Girls and boys in school.* New Brunswick, NJ: Rutgers University Press.

U. S. Department of Education. National Center for Education Statistics. (1998). *Digest of education statistics, 1998.* Washington, DC: Author.

Vaughn, S. & Schumm, J. S. (1996). Classroom ecologies: Classroom interactions and implications for inclusion of students with disabilities. In D. L. Speece & B. K. Keogh, Eds., pp. 107–124. *Research on classroom ecologies: Implications for inclusion of children with learning disabilities.* Mahwah, NJ: Lawrence Erlbaum Associates.

Viadero, D. (1995, September 20). Studies chart big boost in course-taking. *Education Week,* pp. 1, 16.

Willis, S. (1994). The well-rounded classroom: Applying the theory of multiple intelligences. *ASCD Update, 36* (8), 1, 5, 6–8.

Websites

http://www.aauw.org/home.html (American Association of University Women. Extensive site with information on research in gender issues and resources for gender equity.) Gender Equity

http://depts.washington.edu/cedren/ (Center for Educational Renewal. The Center for Educational Renewal (CER) was founded in 1985 by John Goodlad, Kenneth Sirotnik, and Roger Soder to advance the simultaneous renewal of P-12 schools and the education of educators within the larger context of education in a democracy. The Center is part of the Institute for the Study of Educational Policy within the College of Education. University of Washington, Seattle. Site contains links to portraits of schools participating in reform efforts and to works-in-progress of scholars of educational reform.)

http://www.educ.msu.edu/epfp/iel/welcome.html (The mission of the Institute for Educational Leadership is to improve individual lives and society by strengthening educational

opportunities for children and youth. IEL accomplishes its mission by connecting leaders from every sector of our increasingly multi-ethnic and multi-racial society and by reconnecting the public with our educational institutions. Among other links, the site contains links to publications describing increasing diversity of the student population.)
Education Reform and Diversity

http://www.edweek.org/ (Education Week is a weekly newspaper which chronicles educationals news and issues. Regular features about students. Good source for studying current events in education.)

http://www.publicagenda.org/ (Public Agenda authored the report *Getting By,* cited in this chapter. The organization regularly polls the public on issues of all sorts, including education.)
Education News

http://www.waf.org/ (We Are Family. Resources for supporting gay, lesbian, bisexual youth. Links to many other resources, many of them directed toward the gay, lesbian, and bisexual community.)
Gay, Lesbian, Bisexual Youth

http://falcon.jmu.edu/~ramseyil/learningstyles.htm (Site contains links to information on learning styles and multiple intelligences.)
Learning Styles and Multiple Intelligences

Classroom Contexts of Teaching

4

Rethinking Classroom Management

BUILDING ON BIOGRAPHY:
MANAGING MORE THAN MISCONDUCT

The day I began my student teaching, I (Richard) stepped into the classroom aware that my dream of becoming a teacher was turning into a reality. That thought was so unbelievably scary, and at the same time so incredibly exciting, that I wasn't sure if I could even get through the first day. I felt clumsy, shy, and unsure of myself as a teacher; my confidence was totally absent. But I did get through the day, and then many more days, with the days eventually turning into years.

Although I had spent much of my life in classrooms as a K-12 student, watched my teachers manage their classrooms, and completed the required number of courses in my teacher-preparation program, moving from the role of student to that of teacher was a monumental leap for me. Unlike many programs today that include classes taught in K-12 schools and close to 100 hours observing in K-12 classrooms, my professional courses were almost exclusively taught on the university campus. The lectures and discussions that comprised the bulk of my coursework were insightful and provided new perspectives on issues and problems associated with secondary education. The practical experiences included learning how to thread 16 mm films, developing overhead transparencies, constructing multiple-choice tests in science, and presenting a five-minute lesson to my peers, which was videotaped and critiqued by them and me. Prior to my student teaching assignment in high school biology, I had completed only ten hours of classroom observations— and those were spent in a middle school! These were all valuable experiences, but they weren't extensive enough to prepare me to teach fifty-five minute biology lessons to classrooms of sixteen-year-olds in secondary schools. The reality of high-school teaching seemed far removed from the artificial setting of the five-minute peer lesson I had taught safely and securely at the university.

I was fortunate, however, to have an excellent mentor teacher—Ms. Willis—during my student teaching. She guided me into the kind of practice she deemed valuable and that was personally meaningful for her. Had it not been for her patience and genuine interest in my well-being, I might not have completed student teaching.

Thanks to Ms. Willis, I received an on-the-job crash course in the many practical dimensions of classroom management. For the first two weeks of student teaching, Ms. Willis taught me how to *manage the information* I was expected to teach, which was mostly contained in the textbook. She illustrated strategies for developing lecture outlines and aligning these outlines with charts, posters, graphs, and other teaching aids. When she felt sufficiently confident I could manage the information, Ms. Willis allowed me to teach. She worked closely with me to appropriately *manage the time* I had for planning and teaching. She stayed with me in the classroom when I initially began teaching so that she could demonstrate strategies for *managing student behavior*. We agreed that at first she would handle student behavior and I would observe. Eventually Ms. Willis offered me full control of some classes so I could test my own ability to manage student behavior—unquestionably my biggest challenge and one of my biggest fears. During this time Ms. Willis also provided guidance in *managing student records* and *managing student learning*. She introduced me to the school's attendance and grading policies, shared her grading policies and grade book, and explained the classroom procedures permitting students to earn extra credit on selected assignments. When I assumed full control of all classes, we continued to have discussions about how best to set up the classroom for optimal student learning. Because Ms. Willis was responsible for five periods and 120 students, she introduced me to *managing student work,* efficient and proper methods of grading and returning student assignments.

Prior to student teaching, I had confused the idea of management with student discipline. I learned from Ms. Willis that student discipline is just one subset of the bigger and broader notion of classroom management. *Student discipline* is managing student behavior in effective, respectful, and trustful ways. *Classroom management* refers to the ways in which a teacher organizes the classroom environment so that he or she and the students can work together cooperatively on worthwhile academic activities. These activities are continuous, engaging, and culturally sensitive (Brophy, 1988). As my student teaching assignment concluded, I began to realize that the idea of management encompassed the quality of my instructional behavior, of my interactions with students, and of the interactions among my students.

Questions to Consider

1. How does Richard's story support or refute the claim of some classroom teachers that student teaching was the only valuable aspect of their teacher-education program?
2. Why was Richard so fearful? What, if anything, could Richard, the university, or the school have done to alleviate his fears?
3. Richard describes a complex set of management tasks he learned from Ms. Willis. How are these tasks similar to or different from the tasks performed by managers in other professions (e.g., sports, entertainment, business, industry)?

▓▐ PURPOSE

For every teacher there is a beginning, just as there was for me when I began teaching at the age of twenty-two. The idea of teaching starts when we say, perhaps all too glibly, "I'm going to become a teacher." Usually you make that decision based on some altruistic notion—for example, because you love kids, because you want to contribute to society in important ways, because you felt "called" to the teaching profession even though you knew that teacher salaries are comparably lower than for other professions (Hansen, 1995). Others enter teaching because they cannot seem to find their place in the world, and teaching, for the moment, seems like a good place to start a first career. Still others decide later in life to make a career change and move into teaching from another profession.

Regardless of why you embarked on a teaching career, all beginning teachers share one challenge: stepping into the classroom and facing the daunting responsibility of helping students become successful learners. Ask any teacher, and he or she will have stories to tell about those memorable beginning moments in the classroom.

The overall purpose of this chapter is to heighten your awareness of classroom management by helping you think about important aspects of organizing and managing classrooms in today's schools. Specifically, this chapter will help you:

- consider factors that influence classroom learning environments;
- explore factors that move you toward successful classroom management;
- reflect on management practices you experienced as a former student;
- think more broadly and critically about conventional classroom management approaches;
- explore alternative ways of thinking about classroom management;
- develop a personal plan for classroom management and student discipline.

Before moving into the next section of this chapter, we want to leave you with two important ideas. First, when teacher backgrounds and characteristics align with those of their students, management is less of an issue to the teacher and students. Second, when this alignment is less than optimal, classroom management may be more of a challenge. This means that:

- classroom management will always be an issue regardless of where you teach;
- understanding students' backgrounds and home lives is a prerequisite to understanding and implementing classroom management;
- increasing variety in classroom instruction minimizes student discipline problems;
- striving toward meaningful learning, which engages students culturally and personally, is one method of improving classroom management.

▪▪ TOWARD GREATER AWARENESS OF CLASSROOM MANAGEMENT

Today, most teacher-education programs introduce prospective teachers to the dynamics of classroom management well in advance of student teaching. Beginning with readings and followed by classroom observations or field-based research projects, you will have ample opportunities to explore the many facets of classroom management before you take your first steps into the classroom as a teacher (or as a student teacher). This does not mean, however, that your teacher-preparation program will teach you all you need to know about management or that you will be able to manage classrooms well from the first moment you step inside a school. No program could teach you all you need to know about classroom management, and very few persons manage classrooms well from the first instant they begin teaching; expertise in management improves with time, experience, and effective mentoring.

One way to begin thinking about classroom management is to view yourself as a relationship specialist (Zehm & Kottler, 1993). When you assume this role, you focus on the relationships you develop with students and you begin to notice how these relationships influence the tone and demeanor of your classroom. You will also explore your personal predispositions for interpersonal relationships and gauge how well they align with (or misalign with) those of your students. In this sense, managing a classroom is not about controlling or dominating students, nor is it owning students for the short time you have them in your classroom. Rather, managing becomes a process of negotiating space, listening to others, understanding needs, and affirming those needs.

■ ■ EASING YOUR CONCERNS ABOUT CLASSROOM MANAGEMENT

Imagine the following scenario. It is Monday morning, the second period, and students begin to arrive at your classroom. Maria, a student who always completes her homework on time, enters the classroom and immediately comes to your desk. She is all smiles as she tells you how glad she is to be in your class. Other students continue entering the classroom, and they immediately go to their seats and get out their class notebooks, eager and waiting to learn. John, another student who always seems happy to be in your classroom, yells "Hello" to you from the back of the room, waving wildly until he gets your attention. As the bell rings, all the students are in their seats and waiting for you to give the first assignment for the day, which is to write in their personal journals for ten minutes about the most important event or experience that occurred to them over the weekend. The tardy bell rings, the students settle down and wait for your instructions, and you give the writing assignment. The room becomes completely silent, and everyone begins writing. The students continue writing quietly until you ask them to stop.

This scenario is, of course, imaginary. In reality, not every one of your students will care about what you are teaching and not every one of your students will be intrinsically motivated to learn. Students may not always come into your classroom, obediently remain in their seats, and passively abide by the established classroom rules. As you anticipate organizing and implementing instruction for students who may not be intrinsically motivated to attend school nor to learn the content you teach, you begin to come to terms with the realities of classroom teaching. This realization might make you slightly nervous and weaken your self-confidence for becoming an effective teacher. Although you might have an extensive background in the subject you teach, you might feel indecisive and afraid that you will not be able to manage the behavior of your students.

Placing classroom management in proper perspective may help alleviate some of your concerns. Most of the challenges you will face relative to classroom management and student discipline will not be serious ones, although they might seem to be when you first interact with students. Experienced teachers will attest that the most common management challenges you will face will be minor ones and may resemble the following.

- Some of your students whisper to each other during a lesson. You respectfully ask them to stop, and, with harmless grumbling, they stop.
- You discover that one of your best students is daydreaming right in the middle of one of your better lessons. You walk by his desk and he immediately tunes back in to the lesson.
- Two students pass notes to each other. When one of the notes accidentally falls to the floor, you retrieve it and hand it to one of the students. They both become embarrassed.
- A whole class of students finishes an assignment twenty minutes earlier than you had expected despite your careful minute-by-minute planning.

As you can see, many classroom management issues are minor distractions, and because most teachers are innovators (and you will become one, too), you will quickly learn how to deal with these kinds of events without major disruptions to classroom instruction.

We would be naive, however, in saying that more serious classroom management and student misbehavior problems will not occur. Many veteran teachers believe that student behavior has changed dramatically since the mid-1980's (Jones, 1996). Many students bring the stress and violence they experience at home and in the community into the classroom. Some students seem unable to control their anger or to resolve conflicts peaceably. Some seem to abide by no linguistic or social taboos. Some students carry weapons to school, while others have drugs in their possession. These types of violent and destructive behaviors make managing in some classrooms more challenging than it has ever been. Nevertheless, most schools have regulations for these kinds of extreme student disruptions that are intended to safeguard you and your students. Moreover, while these more serious situations exist, they do not occur all the time. Believe it or not, in many schools they do not occur at all.

▪▪▪FACTORS THAT INFLUENCE YOUR CLASSROOM MANAGEMENT

The kind of classroom management you implement is influenced by factors which vary from school to school, district to district, and state to state. Classrooms in Miami, Florida, for example, vary in many ways from classrooms in Nogales, Arizona, and from classrooms in Boston, Massachusetts. They differ because the students in these classrooms very likely have differing personal, social, and cultural needs.

As an example of how students at varying locations have different needs, we draw again from a study we recently completed in Mark Keppel High School (MKHS) in Alhambra, California, Holibrook Elementary School (HES) in Houston, Texas, and Brown Barge Middle School (BBMS) in Pensacola, Florida (Powell, Zehm, & Garcia, 1996). As you may recall from Chapter Two, students at MKHS speak some thirty different first languages, with immigrant students from Asia and Central America—some with no English speaking skills—arriving daily. At HES, eighty-seven percent of the students are Hispanic, and like MKHS, HES is experiencing a daily influx of new immigrant students from Central America. The Spanish language is an important part of the HES learning environment. At BBMS, however, few students speak first languages other than English. Managing instruction at BBMS, with its mostly monolingual orientation, would be very different from managing classroom instruction at HES, with its bilingual orientation, or MKHS, with its multilingual orientation.

While schools in different locations have varying characteristics, as the examples above suggest, these same schools also share some commonalities (see Doyle, 1986). These factors are a function of how schools have been historically structured. Below are factors that will collectively shape your classroom and the kind of management plan you will ultimately develop. As you read about these factors consider how they might influence your own classroom.

Multidimensionality

The first factor shaping classroom management is *multidimensionality*—the many dimensions you facilitate almost every moment of the school day in your classroom. Think for a moment about what might happen in your classroom as you implement instruction. Whether it is a lecture, discussion, seat work, group work, or individual work, these activities involve learners representing various backgrounds and cultures.

Hence, because your students' needs on personal and academic levels are multidimensional, your classroom management should be flexible and multidimensional, accommodating the many phenomena occurring in your classroom every day.

As a former science teacher, I developed a variety of student activities. We performed laboratory exercises several times each week, took short field trips, became involved in group activities, and so on. When I reflect on my former classroom environment, I realize that there were many ways I could have improved my lessons. However, one strength of my classroom was the multidimensional features my students and I created together providing for instructional variety for the students and successful teaching experiences for me.

Simultaneity

The second factor is *simultaneity*—the many dimensions of your classroom occurring at the same time. As an effective classroom manager, you will become proficient in handling five or six different activities at once. I was able to observe this phenomenon with Joanie Phillips, the high school English/ESL teacher to whom you were introduced in Chapter Two, "Understanding Multiculturalism." Once, for example, I watched her monitor a whole class of students, provide individual assistance to some students who needed extra help, maintain the momentum of the lesson, and prod several students who were whispering in the back of the room into on-task behavior. On another occasion, she was managing an entire classroom of students working in small groups, each group with its own identity, momentum, and set of learning needs. All the student groups in this situation were working simultaneously, and one of Joanie's duties was to ensure that each functioned smoothly and properly.

Immediacy

A third factor influencing your management is *immediacy*—events happening in the classroom at a very rapid and continuous pace. Events in Joanie's classroom occurred at a rapid pace. Joanie was task-oriented, allowing herself and her students little time for experiences that were not related to instruction. Her classroom sessions were carefully planned and included meaningful and culturally relevant learning activities; her students were continuously on task, moving smoothly from one learning experience to another as she carefully monitored these activities. I never observed Joanie sitting behind her desk. Another aspect of immediacy is that classroom situations require immediate response. When a disruptive incident occurs, a teacher has little or no time to ponder a response. Action, for good or ill, is immediate.

Unpredictability

The fourth factor giving shape to your management plan is *unpredictability*—events that happen unexpectedly in your classroom and for which you cannot specifically plan. For example, students in different classes may react differently to the same lesson; normally quiet and courteous students may bellow forth, for no apparent reason, with an outburst of anger directed at you or another student; the fire alarm might sound while students are in the midst of an important and complex experiment.

During my student teaching, I experienced unpredictability firsthand. It was the seventh week of student teaching and I had assumed responsibility for all my classes. During one class, I was conducting a laboratory demonstration on frog anatomy. I thought the lab was running smoothly—most students were working co-operatively and rapidly, reflecting the quality of simultaneity described above. However, I noticed two students who were not focused on the activity: they were talking about other things and laughing aloud. Although the off-task behavior of the two students was not disrupting the whole class, these students were not working on the laboratory task, and I could see that they were not going to complete the assignment by the end of the period. I approached them and asked them in a respectful and courteous manner to focus on the laboratory activity and to talk about other things later, after class. One of the young men, Ray, who was several inches taller than I and physically very strong, said, "If you think you are big enough to make me do this lab work, then go ahead and try." Ray said this with firmness in his voice. I knew he wasn't joking. I also knew I wasn't "big enough" physically to make Ray do anything. Even if I were big enough, I knew that was not an appropriate course of action. I could not sit down and think over how I should react to Ray. I had to make a decision on the spot.

I had neither experienced nor observed such a confrontation thus far in my student teaching assignment. For a few, long moments, the entire classroom fell silent as students waited to see how this was going to end. I asked Ray to step outside the classroom and wait for Ms. Willis to return. Fortunately, Ray complied, the tension hanging in the classroom air dissipated, and the rest of the students returned busily to their assignment. When Ms. Willis returned a few minutes later, she had a conversation with Ray and me outside the classroom. When Ms. Willis asked Ray to explain his behavior, he said he was very angry about what had happened at his home the night before. His father, who was known for his violent outbursts, had physically abused his mother, and he had felt powerless to help her and his brothers and sisters. Ray apologized for his unpredictable behavior; he said that he must have been taking out his home problem on me. While you usually cannot anticipate specific behavioral incidents such as the one that I experienced, nonetheless, you can anticipate that such incidents will occur and outline general strategies to deal with them. Anticipation and flexibility are essential when addressing unpredictability.

Publicness

A fifth factor influencing management is *publicness*—the classroom viewed as a public place. At any moment of the day, many students are interacting in the presence of a teacher, and the teacher is interacting in the presence of many students. Whatever happens in your classroom will therefore be observed by many different people simultaneously. When Ray, in the story above, confronted me, the entire class became silent. This exemplifies how your management plan, particularly how you respond to unpredictable events, will be seen, felt, and experienced by your students. Consistencies and inconsistencies in your plan will be quickly noticed by the students. Consider again the story of Ray. What would students in that class expect to happen the next time a similar confrontation occurs between a student and me?

Classroom Historicity

A sixth factor is *historicity*—the routines, norms, habits, rules, and expectations that develop over time in a classroom. Because of historicity, your students learn what to expect from you, and you learn what to expect from them (e.g., the quality of the content you need to include in lessons to draw students' attention, student behavior in the classroom, study habits that meet the teacher's expectations).

Consider, as an the example of historicity the experiences of Mrs. Mitchell, a teacher I met while student teaching. Mrs. Mitchell was a seventh grade teacher who gave birth three months before the end of the school year. For the remaining three months of the school year, her long-term substitute was Mr. James. The historicity Mrs. Mitchell had developed with her students was interrupted by Mr. James, who had his own strategies for managing content, maintaining and negotiating student behavior, and establishing important relationships with the students. This presented Mr. James with some serious problems. Through their shared history, the students had come to respect and trust Mrs. Mitchell. They were uncomfortable, anxious, and even rebellious toward Mr. James. The management plan Mrs. Mitchell had used for much of the year—a plan embedded deeply within her understanding of teaching and learning—was suddenly jeopardized by Mr. James's way of understanding teaching and learning. The students' need for, comfort with, and predisposition toward Mrs. Mitchell's style of management remained with them until the end of the school year.

Diversity

A seventh factor is *diversity*—the influence of student characteristics on negotiations resulting in your classroom management plan. Most teachers view student diversity as an exciting professional challenge—a strategy meant to capture and put to use the many cultural strengths students bring to the classroom. Viewing diversity as a problem usually means blaming students for not aligning more with traditional, mainstream curriculum and instruction. Viewing diversity as a challenge, however, means that you, the classroom teacher, will seek out ways to align curriculum and instruction more with students, even if this means rethinking how you manage the content to be learned, student learning, student engagement in content, and assessment of student learning. Consider the implications of the following hypothetical situations on your classroom management.

- You teach in a suburban high school that has a large transient student population.
- You teach in a rural school. Many students are expected to assist with farm chores before coming to school.
- You teach in a community which has volunteered to support several families of immigrants from Kosovo. Because mathematics is a universal language, three students who speak little English are assigned to your algebra class.
- You've set the due date for culminating group presentations for Yom Kippur.
- You've just been informed that three students with behavioral disorders will be placed in your already overcrowded health class.
- Students in your class refuse to work in groups with a low ses student whose personal hygiene is poor.
- You touch a young woman who is off-task on the shoulder and she shouts, "Don't touch me, you lesbian!"

You cannot manage the student diversity in your classroom—that would be virtually impossible. But you *can* manage your classroom curriculum and instruction so that it more closely aligns with the backgrounds of your students. Effective teachers accept these assumptions and plan accordingly; you, too, should accept diversity as an inherent part of your practice and learn to work with it in productive and respectful ways. Your biggest challenge, therefore, is to recognize student diversity, accept its many forms, and incorporate this important classroom dimension into your planning process (Banks, 1993).

Personal Theories of Teaching

A final important influence on your classroom management is your *personal theories of teaching* (Connelly & Clandinin, 1988; Hunt, 1987). As a result of your experiences as a K-12 student, you have developed many personal theories regarding teaching and learning. Some of these theories relate to classroom management and student discipline. Research indicates that personal theories are not easily changed; what you have learned as a student will carry over as you prepare to become a middle- or high-school teacher (Hunt, 1987). This might pose a special challenge for you in today's classrooms, where alternative strategies for classroom management and student discipline are needed (Bullough, 1994). This is especially true if you attended schools that implemented conventional management and student discipline plans. Attending this kind of school gave you certain ways of believing how classrooms should be managed. These personal theories predispose you to certain strategies for classroom management and student discipline before you even step into the classroom.

You will find that some of your personal theories about classroom management might be very useful, while others might be less useful with today's students. This is why you must continuously reflect on the connections between classroom environment, management style, and curriculum and instruction, and how these elements engage students in—or perhaps disengage them from—positive and productive learning experiences (Winitzky, 1992). Two ways you can inform your own management practices and thus continuously improve and reconstruct your personal theories for managing classrooms of diverse learners are by reading about various approaches to classroom management and asking experienced colleagues, those who are known to be outstanding classroom managers, for their perspectives and expertise.

■ **Reader Activity 4.1**

IN THE FIELD
Observing Classroom Management

The purposes of this activity are to help you: (1) explore how the factors discussed above give shape to classroom environments and consequently to your management style; and (2) examine how these same factors might vary from middle to high school. Begin by making plans to observe several classrooms over time. Select one middle-school classroom and one high-school classroom. As you observe classroom teaching, find evidence for each of the factors which we have listed below, and as you make your observations record evidence for each in Figure 4.1.

FIGURE 4.1 A Framework for Recording Observations of Classroom Management

FACTORS	MIDDLE-SCHOOL CLASSROOM	HIGH-SCHOOL CLASSROOM
Multidimensionality		
Simultaneity		
Immediacy		
Unpredictability		
Publicness		
Historicity		
Cultural Diversity		
Personal Theories of Teaching		

Then ask an experienced teacher, preferably one you observed while doing this exercise, to provide her or his perspective about these factors. Compare and contrast the observations you made at each of the schools. Compare and contrast your observations with the reflections of the experienced teacher.

▮▮TOWARD SUCCESSFUL CLASSROOM MANAGEMENT

In this section we focus on the key elements needed for developing and implementing a successful management plan—one that engages students productively in the content they are expected to learn with you and their peers. We have organized them into four clusters: practical elements, cultural elements, metaphorical elements, and personal elements.

There are a number of perspectives to each cluster, but we have limited our descriptions to those that will help you most when you begin developing a management plan. What we discuss, obviously, is not exhaustive or complete; you may discover additional issues as you think and read more about a management plan for your classroom.

Practical Elements of Classroom Management and Student Discipline

Because *practical elements* of classroom management are among the foremost concerns of every prospective teacher, we shall consider these elements first. When teachers begin their careers, they face a similar set of questions: How do I set up my classroom instruction? How much time do I allow for specific activities? What materials should I use? How closely do I need to adhere to the district's prescribed curriculum? How much should the cultural backgrounds of my students influence what and how I teach? Should I put my desks in straight rows or in clusters? Under what circumstances should I send disruptive students to the principal's office and when should I deal with them myself?

Each of the above questions, like so many other questions about classroom teaching, can be answered with the same ambiguous response: "It depends." The "it depends" phenomenon becomes especially apparent when you speak with experienced teachers. For example, how you set up your classroom depends on the culture of the school where you teach, the content, and the needs of students. How much time you allow for an activity depends on the nature of the activity, what is to be learned, where it takes place, and the abilities of the students to engage in it. What materials you use depend on the instructional needs of your lesson and the expectations of the school for student learning. How close you stay to the district's prescribed curriculum depends on what kind of latitude the state, district, or school allows and your spirit of independence. Arranging your desks in a certain pattern depends on what you are teaching, your teaching style, school expectations with respect to classroom arrangement, and your relationships with students. Sending disruptive students to the office depends on school policy, the nature of the student misbehavior, and the views you hold of classroom management and student discipline.

As you can see from our brief treatment of each question, there are many variables to consider when you begin organizing a management plan, and there are even more to consider when you actually implement this plan. Recall the concepts of immediacy, spontaneity, unpredictability, and multidimensionality. When you implement your management plan, these factors give further shape to your classroom. To help you consider the practical dimensions of classroom management—similar to the dimensions that Ms. Willis helped me think about when I began student teaching—we provide you with descriptions of selected areas of classroom management.

Thinking About the Physical Classroom Environment and Tone

The physical environment of your classroom is the actual classroom setting: desk arrangement, placement of teacher's desk, storage room for teaching materials, and so on. When you set up your physical environment and express your own personality in this environment, another important dimension of the environment emerges—the *tone* of your classroom. *Tone* is how your classroom feels to your students as they interact with you, peers, and the prescribed curriculum. Does the tone help students feel comfortable, needed, and valued, or does it make them feel uncomfortable, undervalued, and unwanted? If you have a mutually respectful and trustful tone where all students feel comfortable, needed, and valued, then students will be more engaged in learning.

When you take a step back to appraise your physical classroom environment and attempt to gain a sense of the classroom tone you and your students have created, think about these questions: What does my classroom feel like for students? Are all students made to feel welcome regardless of their background, academic strengths and weaknesses, or cultural heritage? How much physical space do students have to move about? Do I need to make accommodations for students with special physical needs? What might be the best arrangement of the room for smooth and problem-free traffic patterns? Where is the best place to store equipment so it will be accessible when I need it, yet not in the way of classroom activities? Where should I place the overhead projector and/or other AV equipment so students can easily see what is being displayed? Where should I place the computers so students can have access to them? What should I do with my classroom walls? Should I hang posters, pictures, and work students have completed? How can I make the classroom comfortable and an engaging and challenging learning environment for my students?

Thinking About Time

The school day in most middle and high schools is divided into blocks of time. It usually begins and ends with ringing bells, and you become attuned to a life of seconds, minutes, and hours. How you use the time allotted for each class reflects your ability to plan effectively and carry out meaningful learning experiences. *Down time* in the classroom—when students are clearly off task and attending to almost anything but the lesson—represents lost instructional moments. Effective classroom managers know how to use every moment of classroom time for learning activities (Jones, 1996).

Central to managing time effectively is thinking about the amount of time you spend on instructional and non-instructional activities. Non-instructional activities include checking roll at the beginning of the class period, returning graded papers, dealing with interruptions, and transitioning from one instructional activity to another. In each of these instances, little or no instruction occurs unless you have planned in advance for it. Your goal should be to spend as little time as possible on non-instructional activities, thereby providing greater opportunities for meaningful learning experiences.

The following questions are intended to help you think more broadly about time management: How much time should I devote to administrative duties at the beginning of class? What should I have students do instructionally that engages them in the daily instruction when I am involved in administrative duties? How do I successfully end a class session? Should I give students free time at the end of a lesson or at the end of a class period? How can I move from one instructional activity to another and minimize off-task behavior? What kind of pace do I establish for the lesson? What should

I do when some students finish an assignment earlier than other students? How much time should I spend giving students individual assistance on specific assignments?

Thinking About Learning Experiences

As you plan instruction you should consider the kinds of learning experiences best suited for your students. *Learning experience* refers to an occasion when students are formally engaged in an instructional activity (or series of activities) for the purpose of acquiring or applying knowledge or skills. As you begin to think about learning experiences, you should consider diversity among your students and the content they are expected to learn. For example, if you are planning a field trip, what accommodations will you need to make for students with special physical needs? If you are having a guest speaker, what social skills will you need to review with students prior to the guest's arrival? How long can you reasonably expect thirteen-year-olds to work quietly and independently in their seats? (You will read more about learning experiences in Chapter Six, "Planning for Middle- and High-School Instruction," and Chapter Nine, "Implementing Instruction: Strategies and Methods.")

Thinking About Routines

An important way to help students acquire information in school and to engage them in useful learning experiences is to set up clear and predictable classroom routines. We believe that routines, which are central to the classroom historicity discussed earlier, are among the most important features of your classroom. This is because routines let students know what is expected—when they should perform certain tasks and how learning experiences are structured in your classroom.

Successful teachers learn how to connect routines, learning experiences, content to be taught, and classroom management so that the classroom runs smoothly, with clear expectations and direction. These teachers spend considerable time thinking carefully about maximizing productive instructional time and minimizing non-productive, off-task behavior. Figure 4.2 gives examples of routines you may need to consider in developing your management plan.

Thinking About Relationships With Students

The relationships you develop with your students are vitally important to their willingness to learn. Joanie Phillips, the high school English teacher described earlier in this chapter, believes she must first develop trusting, respectful, and caring relationships with her students before they will want to learn what she teaches, and consequently before they willingly engage in her instruction. Joanie works hard to build such relationships with students, and she does this by getting to know them personally, culturally, and academically (Powell, 1996a). Other experienced teachers in culturally diverse and inclusive classrooms demonstrate similar beliefs toward teaching and learning (Ladson-Billings, 1994; Ladson-Billings, 1995; Olson, Chalmers, & Hoover, 1997).

Reflect for a moment on three of your middle- and high-school teachers. The first teacher you think about should be one of your favorites, someone whose footsteps you would like to follow, a role model. The second teacher should be someone who has one or two qualities you admire and are considering incorporating into your teaching style. The third teacher should be someone who was not helpful to you and has few qualities you admire. Think about the relationships each of these teachers had with their stu-

---

FIGURE 4.2   Examples of Classroom Routines

It may not be necessary to develop routines for all the situations listed below. However, many beginning teachers are not aware of all the possibilities. You may want to develop routines for:

emergencies
entering the classroom
excusing oneself from the room
handling absences
handling make-up work
handling tardies
how to get a progress report
how to hand in work
how work is returned
leaving the classroom
moving into groups
procedures for written assignments (e.g., headings, spacing, ink)
straightening up the room after projects
what to do if you finish work early
when there is an interruption
when there is a substitute teacher
when to pay attention to the teacher
where and how to get supplies

(Adapted from Wong, H. K. & Wong, R. T., 1998). *The First Days of School: How To Be An Effective Teacher.* Mountain View, CA: Henry K. Wong Publications.

dents. How would you describe these relationships? Educational? Friendly? Warm? Close? Respectful? Distant? Cold? Professional? Helpful? Sensitive?

As you reflect on these teachers, consider how their relationships with students influenced the climates of their classrooms. Think also about their routines and reflect on the learning you experienced in their classrooms. Given the teachers' relationships with students and the routines and learning experiences they developed, how would you describe their classroom management? How did they address student discipline problems? How did their relationships with students compare to the relationships Joanie Phillips strives to develop with her students?

As your reflections might suggest, personal relationships have an important influence on how you manage student learning and on how students respond to the routines and experiences you establish. As you think about managing student learning and addressing discipline, what kinds of relationships are you capable of establishing with students? This is an important question you must address not only at the beginning of your teaching career, but throughout your career as well.

Thinking About Student Discipline

Few topics concern preservice and beginning teachers more than student discipline (Jones, 1996). In fact, student discipline is such an overpowering concern that many preservice teachers think it is synonymous with classroom management, as I did when I began student teaching. But as we have shown, discipline is only one subset of classroom management—the subset addressing student behavior. It is a subset, however, that challenges every educator on almost every day of his or her professional life.

We have organized ideas about classroom discipline into two broad categories. In the first category, which we call *academic theory,* are various theoretical and conceptual ideas about student discipline. In the second category, which we call *personal practical theory,* are the very personal ideas teachers have accrued over years of teaching (Connelly & Clandinin, 1988; Hunt, 1987).

Academic theory about student discipline consists of theoretical principles that can be quite helpful when considering generalizable approaches to student behavior. Generalizable approaches are presumed to work with most students in most classrooms most of the time, regardless of local variations in school, classroom, or student cultures. Books discussing the various academic theories of student discipline abound, and many present selected academic theories of student discipline in a single volume, making it convenient to compare and contrast various theories (e.g., Charles, 1992; Edwards, 1997; Tauber, 1995).

Figure 4.3 gives an overview of some of today's most widely used models and can give you an idea of the range of theories of student discipline. This figure places five academic theories of discipline on a continuum that ranges from student-centered to teacher-centered. Another way of arranging the theories might be from "influencing" student behavior to "controlling" student behavior (Tauber, 1995). If you read each column, you will understand in general terms each theorist's approach to changing student behavior. If you read across each row, you can identify the principles, goals, and strategies that most align with your current beliefs about discipline.

Not surprisingly, each theory has gathered a following of educators; some schools have even adopted a single model (e.g., Assertive Discipline) to be applied consistently by all teachers. More commonly, however, teachers use an eclectic approach to student discipline, taking bits and pieces of academic theories and mixing them with their own personal practical theories for student discipline.

Jones's (1987) work on discipline is not represented in Figure 4.3 but is a widely-used approach. Jones's theory falls somewhere to the right of Glasser on the student/teacher-centered continuum. His work appeals to many beginning and experienced teachers perhaps because his techniques are simple to use and time-saving. Jones's aim is to help classroom teachers eliminate wasted time when addressing student misbehavior. His discipline model is primarily concerned with the minor classroom transgressions of students, such as talking and moving about the room at inappropriate times. Transgressions of this type comprise ninety-nine percent of wasted time in the classroom. He recommends that teachers deal with minor transgressions by developing three sets of skills: (1) using effective body language, such as establishing eye contact with transgressors or physically moving near to them (*proximity control*); (2) employing effective incentive systems, or rewarding students for desired behaviors by allowing them to perform activities they enjoy, such as playing computer games, or by awarding points or tokens which can be redeemed for desirable items (e.g., gift certificates for pizzas) or activities; and (3) providing personal help efficiently, or responding quickly and briskly to individual students' requests for help so that neither the class as a whole nor the student waiting for help has the opportunity to become engaged in off-task behavior.

FIGURE 4.3 Five Discipline Models: Major Points

Student Centered Discipline Models →			Teacher Centered Discipline Models	
Thomas Gordon	Rudolf Dreikurs	William Glasser	Saul Axelrod and B. F. Skinner	Lee and Marilyn Canter
Teacher Effectiveness Training	**Positive Discipline**	**Reality Model**	**Behavior Modification**	**Assertive Discipline**
Principles Students strive for growth through the rational self; obstructing this pursuit causes misbehavior. Students cannot be directed, because they are unique.	Students strive to overcome a sense of inferiority by establishing a unique set of goals. Students primarily strive to belong. Students must experience the consequences of their behavior.	Students must learn to acknowledge irresponsible behavior and to accept the consequences. Students must take steps to behave logically and productively.	The inner rational self is a myth. Environmental stimuli determine behavior. Students work to avoid negative experiences and seek pleasant ones.	Students respond to conflict passively, hostilely, or assertively. Teachers have a right to teach and to meet their own basic needs. Teachers have a right to assert maximum control over student discipline.
Goals Build self-confidence to make decisions and solve problems. Support student's capacity for rational analysis.	Instruct students on how to belong. Help students develop a sense of compassion and community spirit. Help students understand the value of equal rights and human dignity.	Students will learn to make judgments about behavior and will commit to change based on rational analysis. Students will not avoid responsibility for behavior.	Teachers can control classroom environment and student behavior to achieve learning objectives. Student's behavior can be modified to acceptable standards.	Establish a classroom environment that provides an optimal learning environment. Meet teacher needs while encouraging social and educational development of the student.
Strategies Teacher pursues open communications. Students must identify and take ownership of problems. Students learn to actively listen. Students use Dewey's scientific method.	Teachers determine which goals are motivating students' behavior through observation or questions. Teachers use encouragement and natural and logical consequences.	Teachers demarcate parameters of acceptable behavior. Teachers must focus student's attention on undesirable behavior so they consider rationality of behavior. Teachers develop behavior contract/plan with students.	Teachers can evaluate and alter elements of classroom environment to affect a student's behavior. Teachers often use four intermittent reinforcement schedules. Teachers can use contingency contracting.	Teachers verbally limit student misbehavior. Teachers signal correct course of behavior. Teachers are assertive in their demands and never negotiate. Teachers use limit-setting consequences. Teachers develop a plan for discipline.
Problems Differences in student's growth and development make implementation difficult. Rationality and language abilities diminish the ability of student to deal with problems. Younger students have difficulty with complex reasoning operations.	It is very difficult to determine goal of student's behavior. Students often send false or mixed signals. Aggressive or violent students are difficult to deal with. It is difficult to differentiate between punishment and logical consequences.	This approach relies on an extraordinary degree of teacher patience. Student's physical or psychological difficulties may be beyond teachers' ability to use this approach effectively. Student may not be capable of devising a meaningful plan to improve their behavior.	Behaviorism is manipulative and treats students undemocratically. This system controls behavior without developing rational capacity. This system removes emotions and eliminates choice and the development of problem-solving strategies.	This approach establishes an authoritarian classroom environment. Students' rights are minimized. The responsibility of students to develop self-control is removed. The common discipline plan not useful within a group. This approach ignores individual differences.
Suggested Reading Gordon, 1974	Dreikurs, Grunwald & Pepper, 1982	Glasser, 1986, 1990	Axelrod, 1977 Skinner, 1968, 1982	Canter & Canter, 1992

Adapted from Queen, J. A., Blackwelder, B. B., & Mallen, L. P. (1997) *Responsible classroom management for students and teachers.* (pp. 16–17) Upper Saddle River, NJ: Merrill-Prentice Hall. Reprinted by permission of Prentice Hall.

While the academic theories of discipline described above can be implemented successfully with most classes, individualized methods may be called for in today's inclusive classrooms. For example, many teachers believe that techniques they have found tried and true are not effective with students who have emotional or behavioral disorders. Because sometimes students are not even aware of their own disruptive behaviors, self-management techniques teach them how to monitor and manage their own behaviors (Bradley & King-Sears, 1996; Carpenter & McKee-Higgins, 1996). Briefly, self-management consists of helping a student identify a problem behavior that can be defined and counted (e.g., talking out of turn), assisting the student in devising a means for charting this behavior, and reinforcing the student's appropriate use of self-management. While teaching students self-management techniques may initially be somewhat time-consuming, it is a time-saving technique in the long run with the added advantages of giving students ownership of their own behavior and teaching them valuable social skills.

Familiarizing yourself with a number of academic theories of student discipline, many of which have been developed by researchers with an extensive background in teaching and working in the schools, is an invaluable strategy for building a foundation to your discipline plan. It is also a good idea to talk to experienced, effective teachers. The personal practical theories of experienced teachers are very important sources of information about classroom student discipline. Listening to their comments and comparing and contrasting their personal theories can be quite helpful in developing your own personal practical theory.

▌Reader Activity 4.2

THEORY INTO PRACTICE
Applying Academic Theories of Discipline

The purpose of this activity is to give you the opportunity to familiarize yourself with and practice applying one or more of the academic theories of discipline. Working with a group of peers, select one of the academic theories for student discipline represented in Figure 4.3 and described earlier in the text. After completing background reading on the selected theory, determine how each of the situations below would be addressed, given the assumptions of the discipline model you explored. Compare the approach your theory suggests with other theoretical approaches and with your own personal practical ideas about discipline. What role might the "it depends" phenomenon play in each situation?

- In a sixth-grade language arts class, a small group of boys who sit near one another use hollowed out ball point pens to shoot spitballs at other students and you.
- In a tenth-grade social studies class, students have been poking fun good-naturedly at Akio's hair, which he has dyed green for Halloween. Akio, who is usually passive and even apathetic in class, suddenly jumps from his seat, knocking it over, and attacks his nearest tormentor.
- In a high school German I class, you have planned a game to review vocabulary that requires students to run quickly to the chalkboard and draw a picture of the word represented on a large index card you hold up. The game gets out of hand as some students begin to push one another playfully and others shout out answers violating the rules of the game. Students begin accusing one another of cheating and it looks as if the educational value of the game has been lost.

- In a middle school science lab, students must work in larger groups than normal because there are too few materials to go around for the day's experiment. One all-female group is working next to an all-male group. You hear the sound of breaking glass and look up from your work with one group to see a seventh-grade female struggling to retrieve a note she was passing from a seventh-grade boy who is holding it high in the air and laughing.
- For the third day in a row, Tonya comes in ten minutes late to your class. She slams the door behind her, bumps into her friends as she noisily makes her way to her seat. She plops down into a chair and demands loudly, "Hey, Mr. What's-Your-Name, what stupid #@#!*&@$! are we doing today?"
- Whenever you give the class fifteen minutes at the end of the class period to work on their math homework, Al puts his head down on his desk. When you walk over and stand by his desk, he lifts his head for as long as you are near. When you move on, he returns to his sleeping postion.
- Juan is a student in your family studies class. Two years ago a serious auto accident resulted in a traumatic brain injury. With support, Juan now participates fully in your class—perhaps too fully, as he eagerly blurts out comments, questions, and answers whenever there is a class discussion. His comments and questions are often quite funny; he is aware of this and enjoys the attention and laughs he can elicit from you and his peers. However, his antics can pull the whole class off-task.

Cultural Elements of Classroom Management

The second set of elements that are main components to a classroom management plan are *cultural elements.* In this section, we describe two cultural elements that influence your management practices: (1) multiple forms of diversity as expressed by the students in your classes and in their home communities and (2) early adolescent (middle school) and later adolescent (high school) cultures.

Thinking About Diversity Among Students

Over the past few decades, society has become more sensitive to all forms of diversity, a trend that increasingly manifests itself in schools and classrooms. This has occurred for several reasons. For one thing, America's shifting demographics are reshaping school populations everywhere. A second reason for the attention to diversity in schools is the growing movement toward educational egalitarianism. A continuation of the Civil Rights movement of the 1960s, educational egalitarianism aligns with the premise that all students should have an engaging and challenging school learning environment. Consistent with this movement is the reality that marginalized students who were once silenced in school, and who were pushed to the fringes of mainstream education, are no longer passive toward being silenced, nor are they complacent about curriculum and instruction that is seemingly misaligned with cultural and personal ways of knowing other than mainstream (Greene, 1993).

Diversity poses important challenges for teachers. Perhaps the most important is managing classroom learning environments in such a way that all students, not just those who comprise the mainstream culture, are engaged in meaningful learning experiences. When you reflect on the idea of *all students,* you may begin to appreciate why it may not be educationally sound or even possible to implement in its entirety any of the generalizable academic theories discussed earlier. That one academic theory of

The Middle School model of classroom management is responsive to the developmental needs of early adolescents.

management might not fit all students becomes more obvious when you consider the kinds of diversity possible in a single class of students, regardless of whether the classroom is located in an urban, suburban, or rural environment. Although diversity does not prevent you from using academic approaches, it does provide you with important reasons to pause and think more deeply about the alignment of your management strategies with the students you teach.

Thinking About Middle-School and High-School Cultures

Another kind of diversity relates to the developmental aspects of youth—namely early adolescent and later adolescent cultures. Each of these cultures has a unique set of traits and needs, and consequently each requires varying levels of flexibility in classroom management.

Several decades ago, the junior version of the traditional high school dominated education for early adolescents, ten- to fourteen-year-old students. The purpose of the junior high school is to prepare students for high school; that is, to provide students with the knowledge and skills to compete in high school. However, greater attention has been given recently to distinguishing between the developmental needs of ten- to fourteen- and fifteen- to eighteen-year-olds (Stevenson, 1992). Out of this concern has emerged the middle-school movement, an attempt to provide early adolescents with models of schooling meeting their developmental needs.

Consider the following description of the developmental tasks of adolescents:

1. Moving toward independence from parents, siblings, and childhood friends while retaining significant and enduring ties.
2. Developing increasing autonomy in making personal decisions.
3. Establishing new friendships.
4. Moving toward greater personal intimacy and adult sexuality.
5. Dealing with more complex intellectual challenges (Hamburg, 1994, p. 184).

While this is only one of a number of characterizations of adolescent needs (George, Lawrence, & Bushnell, 1998), this short list has many implications for managing middle-school classrooms. As students enter middle school, they may be only vaguely aware of these developmental needs. Some sixth-graders, for example, have difficulty just staying seated for an extended period of time. Some may look like children, while others exhibit all the physical characteristics of much older teens. How can you, as a prospective middle-school teacher, provide a classroom environment that helps early adolescents move toward independence and autonomy, but at the same time provide the structure and support they need as they learn to exercise these skills? What kind of a classroom environment will address students' needs to establish new friendships yet retain important ties with significant adults (including you)?

Developmentally responsive middle schools and middle-school teachers believe that the "imperatives of early adolescent development are too compelling to be denied" (Lipsitz, Mizell, Jackson, & Austin, 1997, p. 535). The behavior of most middle schoolers is not "immature;" it is developmentally on target. The culture of responsive middle schools and classrooms is warmer, happier, and more peaceful than that of the traditional junior high school. Students and adults treat each other with mutual respect. Time and space have been restructured to create small communities of learning where people know one another personally. Students in such middle schools report less fear and faculty report fewer disciplinary problems.

High-school students face the same tasks listed above, but by ninth grade many students are further along in development than they were even in eighth grade. However, perhaps because of the success of the middle-school movement and certainly out of concern for the number of students who fail or drop out after the ninth-grade year, some high schools are creating ninth-grade centers within the school in order to ease the transition to high school and to extend students' experience of being known and cared for by adults in the school. While high schoolers may resemble adults in many ways, compelling evidence suggests that older adolescents need the attention of caring adults no less than younger adolescents. Some schools and national networks are focusing on transforming competitive, impersonal, traditional high schools into personalized learning communities that acknowledge the imminence of students' transitions into the world beyond school as they know it.

▌ Reader Activity 4.3

In the Field
Revisiting Middle School/High School As a Student

Perhaps the best way to gain an understanding of how management styles differ between middle school and high school and from teacher to teacher is to experience these differences from a student's perspective. The purpose of this activity is to help you gain a sense of management styles by following a student or group of students during a typical school day.

For this activity, your instructor will identify a middle and a high school that will allow you to attend classes with student guides and will work with a school liaison to ensure that proper permissions are obtained. Optimally, for an entire school day you will attend classes and follow the schedule of an individual student. As you observe, note some of the factors described earlier in this chapter: multidimensionality, simultaneity, immediacy, and unpredictability. Afterward, share your experiences and observations in a whole-class discussion and compare and pinpoint differences in the management styles of middle- and high-school teachers. As a follow-up to this exercise, visit with a middle- and high-school teacher, asking each to comment on her/his management style and to explain how her/his management plans reflect the developmental characteristics of each age group.

Metaphorical Elements of Classroom Management

The third set of elements that underlie your classroom management is *metaphorical elements*. Think for a moment about some of the metaphors you might use for management: *controlling* behavior; *reaching* students; creating learning *environments*; *covering* content; being *ahead* and *behind* in learning content; getting *caught up*. These very powerful metaphors guide your thinking about classroom practice. Unless you consciously explore your metaphorical ways of thinking, you may be unable to understand how you presently view student discipline and whether alternative approaches to management and discipline may improve your classroom practice. Moreover, without considering alternative ways of thinking about management, you might remain inhibited for many years by the metaphorical perspectives handed down as truisms of practice from one generation of experienced teachers to the next generation of inexperienced teachers at a time when contemporary society has called into question traditional metaphors for management (Powell, Zehm, & Garcia, 1996).

Thinking About Traditional Metaphors

The traditional metaphors cited above are embedded in power relationships among teachers, students, administrators, parents, curriculum developers, and school district officials. These power relationships were borrowed by schools at the turn of the twentieth century from models utilized in America's factories (Bullough, 1994; McLaughlin, 1994).

The conventional management metaphor means operating schools where the majority of students can be "managed" with the least amount of unnecessary disturbance and the greatest amount of learning. Extending this metaphor, decisions about school climate, curriculum, pedagogy, and organization of the school day are driven by a "top down" decision-making process. Administrators make decisions, teachers are expected to comply with and carry out the decisions, and students are expected to comply with the teachers.

Two overarching themes of the factory model of schooling are obedience and control. As McLaughlin (1994) suggests, "a major purpose of authority—and the uses of power—in the obedience perspective is to maintain adult control over younger people" (p. 76). This is akin to high-level managers in a factory maintaining control over low-level workers who are expected to comply with existing norms and be obedient to these norms regardless of personal needs.

Thinking About Alternative Metaphors

We offer an alternative way of thinking about management and discipline. This alternative is not the only way of thinking about teaching in contemporary schools, but it is intended to pique your curiosity about your relationships with students and to offer you a pathway for thinking more carefully about how traditional factory-like metaphors may be less relevant in today's classrooms.

Rather than regarding yourself as the sole source of authority in the classroom, think about the classroom as a place where teachers share power. To assume this stance, you must be willing to give up the idea of having total *control* over students, and consider the idea of *sharing* power with them, viewing students as having a voice in classroom decision making. Remember, sharing power does not mean relinquishing all responsibility to the student for deciding what goes on in your classroom; it means bringing students into your classroom decision-making process more often.

Second, as you begin sharing power with students, you will also begin *negotiating* the learning environment with them. The idea of negotiation is not new, yet when it is applied to schools it has powerful implications for management and student discipline. This alternative metaphor raises an important question: What exactly do you negotiate with students? The answer is both simple and complex. You negotiate everything, including rules, curriculum, assessment strategies, classroom social interactions, and so on. Again, we are not advocating taking power away from the teacher and investing it in students. The metaphor of negotiation suggests that students are given greater *voice* in making decisions about curriculum and instruction and how they would like to approach their own learning. Because the practice of sharing power, negotiating, and giving students voice is relatively uncommon in today's middle and high schools, and because this alternative metaphor differs qualitatively from some of the more widely practiced academic theories of disciplines (e.g., Assertive Discipline), it is worth exploring in greater detail.

Alfie Kohn (1993), who writes and lectures extensively on education and human behavior, is an ardent advocate of sharing power with students. Kohn cites the following beneficial effects that accrue when students share power with the teacher rather than being controlled by the teacher.

- People who have the power to make choices experience a greater feeling of general well-being. For example, research has demonstrated that people are more likely to persist at constructive behaviors, such as quitting smoking or exercising, when they have some choice about the specifics of the program.
- Students learn to make decisions by making decisions. If we believe that one purpose of schooling is to prepare students for participation in a democratic society, then we must give them the opportunity to practice participatory skills.
- Academic achievement improves when students have choice. Numerous studies have shown that students of all ages are more likely to persist at a task and even to exceed normal expectations for performance when they have a sense of self-determination. Kohn reminds us that "students always have a choice about whether they will learn. We may be able to force them to complete an assignment, but we can't compel them to learn effectively or to care about what they are doing" (p. 12). This principle holds true for social behavior as well.
- Teachers who share power with students find their work more interesting. Relieved of the onus of constantly monitoring and controlling behavior, teachers are free to interact with students on issues that really matter.

- Students are not just "adults-in-the-making". They are people whose current needs and rights and experiences must be taken seriously (p. 12).

Many of the questions about management and discipline that teachers normally ask and answer themselves can be posed to students. What kind of environment do *we* want this classroom to be? How should *we* decorate our classroom walls? How should the furniture be arranged? What should people do when they finish a project early? How much noise is too much? When you think of a classroom as a community whose members have a stake in what goes on there, you can more easily imagine providing structured opportunities—regular and impromptu class meetings—for members to meet and make decisions. The decision-making process consists of talking, listening, and generating possible solutions to problems. Kohn argues that reaching consensus on general goals and guidelines is preferable to voting on specific rules and procedures, because it is in the *process* of decision-making that students learn and practice the skills of participatory democracy.

Sharing power does not mean abdicating power. You are still the responsible adult, but, as such, you can give guidance, ask questions, and offer suggestions rather than laying down laws. Ways to share power include taking turns at making decisions (e.g., you choose what to read on Friday afternoon one week; the students choose the next); limiting options available to ensure that students choose materials and activities that are appropriate and have educational value (e.g., sleeping on Friday afternoons is not an option); and setting parameters by specifying goals but letting students decide how to get there (e.g., how can we keep the noise level down when you are working in groups?). Negotiation is part of sharing power. That is, you are a member of the community as well. We are not suggesting here that "Students Rule."

The barriers to implementing an alternative management metaphor of shared power are formidable. You may work in a state, district, or school that makes negotiating some aspects of teaching and learning difficult. For example, rarely are students or teachers able to negotiate the content of standardized tests, when they are administered, scored, and how the results will be disseminated. Furthermore, many teachers are resistant to the idea of sharing power. After all, autocracy is a less time-consuming, simpler form of government. Many teachers are so steeped in the traditional metaphor of control that the only alternative they can imagine is chaos. Most discouragingly, students themselves may resist sharing power. Like teachers, they may have become so accustomed to traditional power roles that they may refuse to make decisions or simply parrot what they've learned from prior experience (e.g., "People who come in late should have to stay after school for fifteen minutes"). Students may also test a teacher's commitment to sharing power by proposing outrageous solutions (e.g., "Everyone gets As, no matter what"). Despite all these barriers, we nonetheless encourage you to consider negotiating some aspects of your classroom with students. If we are sincere when we say we want students to be problem-solvers, decision-makers, and risk-takers, then we must seriously question the assumptions about power and control in traditional approaches to management and discipline (Boomer, Lester, Onore, & Cook, 1992; McLaughlin, 1994).

Personal Elements of Classroom Management

The final set of elements contributing to your classroom management are *personal elements*. Teachers seem always to be pressured to reach instructional objectives, teach the required content, be efficient managers of school classrooms, and so on. In this pressured flurry of energy to *reach* and *teach* and *be,* you can easily overlook the influence that your personal biographical features—and those of your students—have on classroom life, particularly issues related to management and discipline. Yet personal factors have powerful and profound influences on your classroom learning environment and on your teaching self (Goodson & Walker, 1991; Bullough, Knowles & Crow, 1991; Bullough & Gitlin, 1995).

Thinking About Your Biographical Experiences

Think for a moment of the various kinds of classrooms you attended in elementary, middle, high school, and college. Did these classrooms align mostly with the conventional, factory model of management or with the idea of negotiation, where you were a part of the decision-making process? If you attended mostly public schools, then you probably became accustomed to conventional factory models of schooling. Because of the powerful influence of biographical experiences on your perspectives on teaching and on your classroom predispositions, you will likely implement similar kinds of classroom management practices. And chances are you will implement them automatically, without even thinking about it.

In addition to recalling earlier school experiences, think about your home and family life when you were younger. What kind of discipline did you receive from your parents or guardians? Were they strong disciplinarians, or did they give you freedom to "be yourself?" How do you think your experiences as a child living at home will influence your thinking about discipline in the classroom? Think about the kind of discipline you learned in school. Were you told what to do, thus giving you little freedom to be yourself or to interact with peers? Also think about your own behavior in and out of middle and high school. How do you think your own personal behavior will influence how you want students to behave in your classroom?

Thinking About Students' Biographical Experiences

Conventional approaches to management and discipline—those aligned with the factory metaphor of schooling—typically do not consider students' biographical and personal experiences. Alternative approaches such as negotiation, however, make students' biographical experiences central to decision-making. This means that when you begin thinking seriously about creating and implementing a management plan, you must also consider students' backgrounds: ethnicity, linguistic abilities, special physical and emotional needs, socioeconomic status (ses), and so on.

Students are no different from you in their humanness, and their biographical experience will vary widely. Some may live at home with a chronic alcoholic parent (Powell, Zehm, & Kottler, 1995). Some may have professional parents who are constantly telling them to earn high grades at any cost. Some may live in an urban or suburban community that is troubled by high crime rates, high drug usage, and lack of hope for economic gain and for greater quality of life. Some may live in a rural community that values academic achievement and high parent participation in school events. Like you, young persons bring their whole personal selves to the classroom along with their pencils, paper, and books.

Working in diverse classrooms with students like those we described gives you no option but to negotiate space. That is, you must be able and willing to create a caring, compassionate, and flexible learning environment. You must appreciate how your personal life and the personal lives of your students contribute to the tone and atmosphere of your learning environment. And you must also understand how your life and the lives of your students can contribute to cultural conflicts.

Thinking About Yourself As Manager, Disciplinarian and Negotiator

Given the personal complexities of classroom life (i.e., your personal predispositions and needs, your students' personal predispositions and needs), how do you envision yourself as a classroom manager? Disciplinarian? Negotiator? Can you be flexible with your beliefs and predispositions for interacting with students? Do you believe you can negotiate curriculum, instruction, and management with students? Are you willing to learn how the backgrounds of your students influence your classroom learning environment and management practices? That is, are you willing to learn how the student whose parent is a chronic alcoholic is affecting your classroom environment, or even more importantly, how your classroom environment is affecting that student? Thinking about yourself as manager, disciplinarian, and negotiator involves many personal and cultural factors.

▌Reader Activity 4.4

THEORY INTO PRACTICE
Creating an Initial Classroom Management Plan

While your student teaching experience may still be in the future, and you may not know the exact classroom or school in which you will work, you probably have acquired some experience observing and assisting in local classrooms. Draw upon this experience to target a grade level and subject that you expect to teach and identify as specifically as possible a school context. For this activity, you will create an initial classroom management and student discipline plan. This plan will surely change as you gain experience, but our intention is to help you feel confident from the outset of your career that you can be an effective classroom manager. The process of thinking through a plan honestly and methodically is valuable in itself, and will help you feel more prepared for the demands of teaching.

The Appendix following this chapter consists of a classroom management plan outlined in question form. Work through the questions listed under each of the four elements of the plan. Answer as many of them as seem important to you. Use your answers as the basis for writing an initial management and discipline plan. Be prepared to share your plan with your instructor and peers.

▌Reader Activity 4.5

IN THE FIELD
Exploring Experienced Teachers' Classroom Management Plans

Explore the classroom management and student discipline plans of two experienced teachers. Interview one middle- and one high-school teacher. Compare their management plans, using the questions you drew upon as you wrote your own initial classroom management plan in Reader Activity 4.4. How might you alter your own plan, given the personal practical theories of the experienced teachers on management and discipline?

▌▌SUMMARY

I began this chapter by describing how my understanding of classroom management was broadened by my student teaching experience. Equipped with little practical experience and few skills or strategies for managing classrooms, I began student teaching believing that managing a classroom was synonymous with managing student misconduct. Thanks to my mentor teacher, I learned that classroom management encompasses managing information, time, student behavior, student records, student learning, and student work. While today's teacher-education programs generally give more attention to classroom management issues than mine did, there is still no substitute for the actual experience of managing a classroom on a daily basis. Because it is unlikely that you have had this experience yet, classroom management and student discipline are probably two of your greatest concerns as you think about teaching. This is both normal and understandable. Yet, you will eventually discover that the vast majority of management and discipline challenges are minor and easily solved.

This chapter has emphasized the human dimension of classroom management and discipline. Knowing who your students are personally and culturally will help you to become an effective and a successful classroom manager, as will knowing who you are as a manager, disciplinarian, and negotiator. Among the key points to remember are:

- Regardless of the context in which you teach, your classroom management will be influenced by multidimensionality, simultaneity, immediacy, unpredictability, publicness, historicity, diversity, and your personal theories for teaching.
- Developing and implementing a successful management plan involves thinking through practical elements, cultural elements, metaphorical elements, and personal elements.
- Practical elements include thinking about physical classroom environment and tone, time, learning experiences, routines, relationships, and student discipline.
- Academic theories of discipline provide specific guidance for dealing with discipline problems, but are difficult to implement in their entirety. Most often, teachers use them eclectically, as the "one-size-fits-all" approach is appropriate for neither management nor instruction in today's diverse classrooms.
- Cultural elements of classroom management include ethnic, linguistic, religious, socioeconomic, and geographical differences among students, as well as the differences between middle- and high-school cultures.
- Traditional metaphors for classroom management are based on the model of a factory, with decisions emanating from the top down. Alternative metaphors for classroom management are more democratic and include sharing power, giving students a voice in decision-making, and negotiating the learning environment with them.
- Personal elements of classroom management include both teachers' and students' biographies.

In Chapter Five, you will read about creating classroom curriculum for middle- and high-school students. The kind of classroom curriculum you create—which should also be deeply rooted in the human dimension of teaching—is directly related to the kind of classroom management you establish with your students. As you read the next chapter and complete the Reader Activities, try to make connections between classroom management and your classroom curriculum.

▮▮ BUILDING YOUR BIOGRAPHY, YOUR PERSONAL PRACTICAL PHILOSOPHY, AND PORTFOLIO

Building Your Biography

What experiences in your life are relevant to your becoming a successful classroom manager? The following questions are intended to help you generate ideas for composing a chapter of your educational biography on this topic. They are not intended to be answered sequentially or to limit your exploration of the topic.

- What former teacher in your educational history provides the best role model for the kind of relationships you would like to develop and nurture with your students?
- What kind of relationship did you have with this teacher?
- What classroom management practices were used by the schools you attended?
- What student discipline practices were used by the schools you attended?
- How, if ever, were you disciplined as a student? What was the effect on you?
- Relative to classroom discipline, how do you think your home experiences as a child will influence you?

Developing Your Personal Practical Philosophy

Draft a section of your personal educational philosophy that addresses classroom management and student discipline. You might respond to questions such as the following.

- What are advantages and disadvantages of implementing the same kind of management you received as a precollege student?
- To what extent will your practice be guided by traditional, or "control," metaphors?
- To what extent are you capable of acting upon alternative metaphors, such as negotiating and sharing power?
- What do you see as the greatest barriers to acting upon the metaphors of negotiating and sharing power with students in schools as they are currently structured?

Collecting Artifacts for Your Portfolio

Review the Reader Activities you have completed in this chapter. Identify any that you might eventually select for your portfolio. For each, jot down notes that will help you recall later what you were thinking at the time you completed the activity, what challenges you encountered while completing it, what you learned from doing it, and how this activity reveals something about who you will be as a teacher. Don't worry about style or correctness at this point. The purpose is to document your thinking as you move through this book and this class.

▬▬▬ ▮▮ References

Axelrod, S. (1977). *Behavior modification for the classroom teacher.* New York: McGraw-Hill.

Banks, J. (1993). Approaches to multicultural curriculum reform. In J. Banks and C. Banks (Eds.), *Multicultural education: Issues and perspectives* (2nd ed.) (pp. 195-214). Boston: Allyn & Bacon.

Boomer, G., Lester, N., Onore, C., & Cook, J. (1992). *Negotiating the curriculum: Educating for the 21st century.* Philadelphia, PA: The Falmer Press.

Bradley, D. F. & King-Sears, M. E. (1996) *Teaching students in inclusive settings.* Boston: Allyn & Bacon.

Brophy, J. (1988). Educating teachers about managing classrooms and students. *Teaching and Teacher Education, 4*(1), 1–18.

Bullough, R. V. (1994). Digging at the roots: discipline, management, and metaphor. *Action in Teacher Education, 16*(1), 1–10.

Bullough, R. V., Knowles, G., and Crow, N. A. (1991). *Emerging As a Teacher.* London: Routledge.

Bullough, R. V. & Gitlin, A. (1995). *Becoming a student of teaching.* New York: Garland Publishers, Inc.

Canter, L., & Canter, M. (1992). *Assertive Discipline.* Santa Monica, CA: Canter and Associates.

Carpenter, S. L. & McKee-Higgins, E. (1996). Behavior management in inclusive classrooms. *Remedial and Special Education, 17*(4), 195–203.

Charles, C. (1992). *Building classroom discipline,* Fourth edition. White Plains, NY: Longman.

Connelly, F. M., & Clandinin, D. J. (1988). *Teachers as curriculum planners: Narratives of experience.* New York: Teachers College Press.

Doyle, W. (1986). Classroom organization and management. In M. C. Wittrock (Ed.), *Handbook of research on teaching, Third edition* (pp. 392–431). New York: Macmillan.

Dreikurs, R., Grunwald, B. B., & Pepper, F. C. (1982). *Maintaining sanity in the classroom: Classroom management techniques.* New York: Harper & Row.

Edwards, C. H. (1997). *Classroom discipline and management* 2d ed. Upper Saddle River, NJ: Merrill/Prentice Hall.

George, P., Lawrence, G., & Bushnell, D. (1998). *Handbook for middle school teaching.* Second edition. New York: Longman.

Glasser, W. (1986). *Control theory in the classroom.* New York: Perennial Library.

Glasser, W. (1990). *The quality school: Managing students without coercion.* New York: Harper & Row.

Gordon, T. (1974). *Teacher effectiveness training.* New York: Peter H. Wyden.

Goodson, I. F., & Walker, R. (1991). *Biography, identity and schooling: Episodes in educational research.* New York: Falmer Press.

Greene, M. (1993). The passions of pluralism: multiculturalism and the expanding community. *Educational Researcher, 22*(1), 13–18.

Hamburg, D. A. (1994). *Today's children: Creating a future for a generation in crisis.* New York: Times Books.

Hansen, D. (1995). *The call to teach.* New York: Teachers College Press.

Hunt, D. E. (1987). *Beginning with ourselves.* Cambridge, MA: Brookline Press.

Jones, J. (1987). *Positive classroom discipline.* New York: McGraw-Hill.

Jones, V. (1996). Classroom management. *Handbook of research in teacher education.* J. Sikula, T. J. Buttery, & E. Guyton (Eds.), Second Edition, (pp. 503–524). New York: Macmillan.

Kohn, A. (1993). Choices for children: Why and how to let students decide. *Phi Delta Kappan, 75*(1), 8–20.

Ladson-Billings, G. (1994). *The dreamkeepers: Successful teachers of African American children.* San Francisco: Jossey Bass.

Ladson-Billings, G. (1995). Toward a theory of culturally relevant pedagogy. *American Educational Research Journal, 32*(3), 465–491.

Lipsitz, J., Mizell, M. H., Jackson, A. W., & Austin, L. M. (1997). Speaking with one voice: A manifesto for middle grades reform. *Phi Delta Kappan, 78*(7), 533–550.

McLaughlin, H. J. (1994). From negation to negotiation: Moving away from the management metaphor. *Action in Teacher Education, 16*(4), 75–84.

Olson, M. R., Chalmers, L., & Hoover, J. H. (1997). Attitudes and attributes of general education teachers identified as effective inclusionists. *Remedial and Special Education, 18*(1), 28–35.

Powell, R. (1996a). The music is why I teach: Exploring the intuitive strategies of effective teachers in culturally diverse classrooms. *Teaching and Teacher Education. 12*(1), 49–61.

Powell, R., Zehm, S., & Garcia, J. (1996). *Field experience: Strategies for exploring diversity in schools.*Upper Saddle River, NJ: Merrill/Prentice-Hall.

Powell, R., Zehm, S., & Kottler, J. (1995). *Classrooms under the influence, addicted families/addicted students.* Thousand Oaks, CA: Corwin Press, Inc.

Queen, J. A., Blackwelder, B. B., & Mallen, L. p. (1997). *Responsible classroom management for teachers and students.* Upper Saddle River, NJ: Merrill/Prentice-Hall.

Skinner, B. F. (1968). *The technology of teaching.* New York: Appleton-Century-Crofts.

Skinner, B. F. (1982). *Skinner for the classroom.* Champaign, IL: Research Press.

Stevenson, C. (1992). *Teaching ten to fourteen year olds.* New York: Longman.

Tauber, R. (1995). *Classroom management: Theory and practice, Second edition.* New York: Harcourt Brace.

Winitzky, N. (1992). Structure and process in thinking about classroom management: An exploratory study of prospective teachers. *Teaching and Teacher Education, 8*(1), 1–14.

Wong, H. K. & Wong, R. T. (1998). *The first days of school: How to be an effective teacher.* Mountain View, CA: Harry K. Wong Publications.

Zehm, S., & Kottler, J. (1993). *On being a teacher: The human dimension.* Newbury Park, CA: Corwin.

Websites

http://www.wglasserinst.com/ (Commercial site of the William Glasser Institute. Describes Glasser's philosophy and has links to recent articles by Glasser on Control and Reality Therapy and Quality Schools.)

http://www.gordontraining.com/ (Commercial site of Gordon Training Institute. Gives additional insight into Teacher Effectiveness Training, Gordon's philosophy, and public's questions about Gordon's programs.)
Academic Theories of Discipline

http://www.nwrel.org
Northwest Regional Education Laboratory (Resources on Classroom Management and many other topics)

http://cis.georgefox.edu/sheadley/edpage/web/edmB/classmanage.html
Classroom Management and Discipline

APPENDIX

Key Elements of a Classroom Management and Student Discipline Plan

The outline that follows is designed to assist you in developing your classroom management plan. Develop your plan by reflecting on some or all of these questions, and then putting your responses together in a coherent written plan.

I. **Practical Elements of Your Management Plan**
   A. Physical classroom environment and tone
      1. What will be the tone of your classroom?
      2. How will students feel when they enter your classroom? How do you know they will feel this way?
      3. What will be the physical arrangement of your classroom?
      4. How will you decorate the walls of your classroom?
      5. How will you make all of your students feel like they belong in your classroom?

B. Time
   1. How will you begin your class sessions in an efficient, effective, and timely manner?
   2. How much "down time" will you allow in your classroom, if any?
   3. How will you insure a minimal amount of noninstructional time in each class session?
   4. What will you do when some students finish assignments earlier than other students?
   5. How will you move from one activity to another without losing instructional time?
   6. How will you end your lessons without wasting instructional time?
C. Learning experiences
   1. What is your definition of *learning experience?*
   2. What will be the best learning experiences for your students? How will you use students' cultural backgrounds in presenting content they are expected to learn?
   3. What part will seat work (e.g., worksheets) play in your students' learning?
   4. What part will hands-on experiences play in your students' learning?
   5. How will an outside observer know when your students are engaged in meaningful learning experiences?
D. Routines
   1. What routines will you establish in your classes?
   2. How will you know whether these routines reflect your students' backgrounds?
E. Relationships with students
   1. What kinds of academic and personal relationships are you capable of establishing with your students?
   2. Ten years from now, what kind of relationships do you think your former students will say they had with you?
   3. What personal/cultural features do you have that might foster positive relations with all students, and what personal/cultural features do you have that might hinder positive relations with some students?
F. Student discipline
   1. What part will academic theory on student discipline play in the development of your classroom management practices?
   2. What academic theory, among those described in Chapter Five, will be best suited to classrooms where you might teach? Are there other academic theories we have not described that might be better suited to your personal teaching style and to your students?
   3. How will you deal with minor student discipline problems?
   4. How will you deal with major student discipline problems?
   5. Many beginning teachers believe they must control their students. What are several advantages and disadvantages of the metaphor of control when applied to student discipline?
   6. Review the student discipline policy of a school district and of a school within the same district. How do the two policies differ? How are they alike? How will these policies help you as a classroom teacher?

II. Cultural Elements of Classroom Management

A. Cultural diversity of students

1. How will student diversity influence the kind of classroom management you implement?
2. What is the nature of the diversity of students in the school district where you will teach (i.e., socioeconomic status, ethnicity, religion)? What is the nature of the diversity of students in the school where you plan to teach?
3. How will you manage your classroom instruction so that all students, regardless of their backgrounds, are engaged in your lessons?
4. Is there an academic theory of student discipline that might be appropriate for the students you will teach, given their backgrounds and given the communities where they live?
5. In the school where you plan to teach, what are the values of the community toward education? How might these values influence student discipline in your classroom?

B. Middle- and high-school cultures

1. What kind of classroom management plan might be best suited to the developmental needs of middle-school students?
2. What kind of student discipline plan might be best suited to the developmental needs of middle-school students?
3. What kind of classroom management plan might be best suited to the developmental needs of high-school students?
4. What kind of student discipline plan might be best suited to the developmental needs of high-school students?
5. How should your classroom management and student discipline plans differ for middle- and high-school cultures?

III. Metaphorical Elements of Classroom Management

A. Traditional metaphors

1. What are several advantages of traditional metaphors of classroom management for contemporary classrooms? What are several disadvantages?
2. In what ways, if any, was your former schooling framed by the traditional metaphors described in this chapter?
3. If your former schooling was characterized by traditional metaphors, how might this influence the classroom management you implement in your classroom?
4. If you find that some of the traditional metaphors are inappropriate for managing the students you teach, how might you begin thinking in different ways about classroom management?
5. In what ways are traditional metaphors culturally sensitive? In what ways, if any, are they culturally insensitive?

B. Alternative metaphors

1. *Negotiate* is an alternative metaphor for classroom management. What dimensions of your classroom might you be able to negotiate with students? What dimensions would you not be able to negotiate? Why?
2. What process will you use to negotiate aspects of your classroom with students?

3. *Sharing,* as a classroom metaphor, is an alternative to the metaphor of *controlling.* What shape will your classroom management and student discipline take if you teach from a sharing perspective rather than a controlling perspective?

4. What will be the tone of your classroom if you adopt the sharing metaphor rather than the controlling metaphor?

5. In what ways are alternative metaphors culturally sensitive? In what ways, if any, are they culturally insensitive?

IV. **Personal Elements of Classroom Management**

A. Your biographical experiences (refer to end of chapter activity, "Developing Your Autobiography, Personal Practical Philosophy, and Portfolio," Part A.)

1. What experiences in your life are relevant to you becoming a successful classroom manager?

2. What distinction, if any, would you draw between classroom management and classroom discipline?

3. What field experiences have shaped your views on classroom environment and classroom management style?

B. Students' biographical experiences

1. How will students' biographical experiences influence what you decide about classroom management?

2. How will you accommodate differences between your biographical experiences and those of your students?

3. What strategies will you use to find out about students' biographical experiences?

C. Self as manager, disciplinarian, and negotiator

1. What image do you have of yourself as a classroom manager of students, specifically as a manager of their learning?

2. What image do you have of yourself as a classroom disciplinarian of student behavior?

3. What image do you have of yourself as a classroom negotiator with students?

4. Would you rather be primarily a classroom manager or primarily a classroom negotiator? Why?

5. How will the norms of the school district and the school where you teach influence the role you assume in the classroom (i.e., manager, negotiator)?

After writing responses to some of the questions above, compare your management plan to other preservice teachers' plans. In what ways is your plan similar to and different from your peers' plans?

5

Considering Curriculum for Middle- and High-School Students

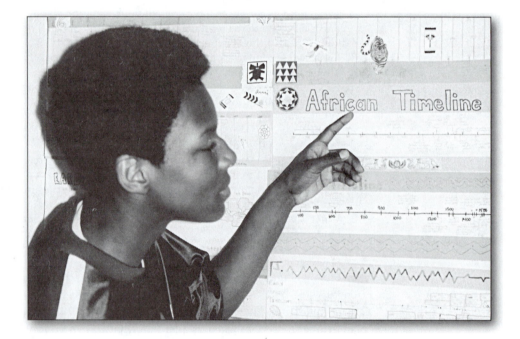

BUILDING ON BIOGRAPHY: LEARNING ABOUT CURRICULUM IN PLAINSVILLE, EDGETOWN, AND BEYOND

When I (Richard) began teaching, I understood the curriculum to be only one thing: the content I was expected to teach. Furthermore, this content was contained in textbooks. I had experienced this kind of instruction as a student myself and implemented it during my student teaching, when I taught five sections of Beginning Biology. Ms. Willis, my supervising teacher and a professional whom I greatly respected, wanted me to teach in a manner consistent with her own strategy, which was to help students walk through the textbook *Modern Biology* page by page and get to the last chapter by June.

The following August, I began my teaching career in the small, rural community of Plainsville (not the real name). Wheat farming and cattle ranching were central to the economic well-being of Plainsville and its schools. Like many other neighboring rural communities, Plainsville was proud of its schools and churches. The community of approximately one thousand persons was predominantly Protestant, White, and composed of middle- and working-class families.

Not surprisingly, in Plainsville I used the instructional practices I had learned from Ms. Willis. Admittedly, having a textbook my first years as a classroom teacher was a relief, since I taught three different classes each day: Earth Science to eighth-graders, Physical Science to ninth-graders, and Biology to tenth-graders. While I felt prepared to teach Biology, I felt under-prepared to teach Earth and Physical Sciences and, because of my limited knowledge, the adopted textbooks became my instructional "security blanket." Because I was preparing three different classes and had accepted various other extracurricular responsibilities (e.g., driving a school bus morning and evening, being a class sponsor, taking tickets at athletic events, helping student groups carry out fund raising events), I barely stayed one chapter ahead of the students.

As my self-confidence increased during my second year, I incorporated various hands-on laboratory activities suggested by the teacher's edition of the textbook. Nevertheless, because I adhered to the textbooks, I didn't offer my students non-traditional learning experiences that have now become the hallmark of excellence in science teaching. What I came to realize in Plainsville—which was politically conservative and strongly religious—was this: *what I did not teach* and *what I could not teach* were as much a part of my curriculum as *what I did teach*. Plainsville taught me that the *null curriculum*—the subject matter content that educators purposely do not teach in school—affects students as much as content that is taught.

I came face to face with the null curriculum in Plainsville. As a science teacher, I was told during the job interview that I would not be allowed to teach evolution and natural selection. In fact, school administrators told me exactly which pages in the book I was expected to skip. During my second year, this edict was further impressed upon me when I wanted to show a film to my biology students depicting human development during gestation. The final few seconds of the film showed the birth of a child. Wanting to do everything right during my first years as a teacher, I checked with the principal to gain his approval and informed him that I was going to show a film in my biology classes that included eight seconds of footage showing childbirth. The principal was surprised that I would even consider showing such footage. I was told to turn off the film projector during the last eight seconds of the movie, if I wanted to show the film at all.

Clearly, decisions about content were being made by individuals other than textbook publishers. The decision-making process, embodied in Plainsville's community values and guarded by its school administrators, was also central to the school's curriculum. After two years of teaching there, I no longer viewed the curriculum as simple information in a textbook.

The following year, I accepted an offer to teach Biology in Edgetown (not the real name), a larger community of approximately ten thousand persons. Like Plainsville, Edgetown's population was predominantly White, rural, middle class, and Protestant. Unlike Plainsville, however, Edgetown contained a state university, with an enrollment of approximately ten thousand students. Some of the more progressive ideas from the university influenced the community and thus Edgetown High School.

In Edgetown I taught about evolution and natural selection, and I was not questioned about showing films that depicted events related to biology. Although I was teaching only eighty miles from Plainsville, I was given freedom as a professional to make decisions about what information would be most appropriate for helping Edgetown students understand science structure and content. Preparing students for college was highly valued in Edgetown, and administrators wanted me to teach a science college preparatory curriculum. It was assumed that Edgetown graduates would ultimately enroll in college. In reality, many Edgetown graduates acquired jobs in the community that did not require a college degree.

I have fond memories of my Edgetown teaching days. The students were enjoyable, the classes were fun to teach, and the administration was supportive. I had the professional autonomy to develop the Biology and Anatomy and Physiology courses I was assigned to teach, and in my third year I was given an award by the Biology Club of the local university for my efforts at promoting collaborative research with high school biology students.

As a result of these two high-school teaching experiences, my view of curriculum expanded. By now, I had moved beyond the textbook for my Biology II and Anatomy and Physiology classes, and I was becoming more confident as I ventured into the world of scientific ideas. I was slowly developing my personal practical approach to science teaching. I had also learned that a school's curriculum and my own classroom curriculum could change from one community to another. Not only did the community have an influence on what was taught, but I, too, had an influence on what was taught and certainly on how it was taught. I became yet another decision-maker for my classroom and the school's curriculum. Not only did the community's values influence the school's curriculum, but my own values influenced and became part of the school's curriculum.

Although my perspectives on curriculum grew and matured during my years in Plainsville and Edgetown, they remained content-centered. My teaching was organized around the structure of content and laboratory activities that informed this structure. Content-centered, textbook-driven curriculum has been the mainstay of most middle- and high-school science programs, as well as programs in other subjects. This view of curriculum as content reflected widely held conceptions of learning in the early 1970s: students' minds are empty vessels waiting to be filled with content, and I—the knowing teacher—should fill these vessels to the brim.

Questions to Consider

1. Whose interests were served by Richard's decision to skip pages in the textbook on evolution and to censor the ending of the biology film?
2. If, as Richard suggests, curriculum is not content taken from a textbook, what is it?
3. Richard describes events that occurred in the 1970s. How have schools and society changed since then in regard to curriculum?

▌▌▐ PURPOSE

As a high school science teacher, I provided my students with a certain kind of classroom curriculum. I might have been able to connect more of them more meaningfully to the content and to help them reflect more directly on its value had I been more aware of the many factors that influence curriculum.

The overall purpose of this chapter is to help you understand the multiple dimensions of school and classroom curricula, thus helping you to broaden your perspective of curriculum. In the past few decades, an important body of research has surfaced in the areas of students' backgrounds, teachers' backgrounds, and student/teacher interactions. This information has significantly changed how educators view curriculum development and pedagogy.

Knowing how to design and implement a classroom curriculum that engages all students is fundamental to effective teaching and learning. If you begin your teaching career without knowing how students' backgrounds align (or misalign) with classroom curriculum and instruction, then you may, albeit unknowingly, distance some students from what you teach and from the learning environment you create. If the purposes of this chapter are attained, then you will enter the classroom aware of how to engage students with the curriculum. Specifically, this chapter will help you:

- define curriculum;
- consider how levels of curriculum—national, state, district, and school—give shape to classroom curriculum;
- examine the relationship between textbooks and school curriculum;
- identify the role culture plays in classroom curriculum, and the role of students' ages in creating developmentally appropriate curriculum.

In today's classrooms, you must have a firm grasp of the content you are teaching. But you must also know your students and help them to connect socially, personally, and culturally with what you teach and how you teach. From this perspective, your classroom curriculum reflects the interface between students' personal qualities and the content to be learned. This is significantly different from the perspective of curriculum that I accepted when I completed student teaching and during my first eight years of teaching. This expanded view of curriculum also raises questions about content. Should teachers, for example, focus on "core curriculum" and consequently on "the basics," or should teachers focus on larger themes and weave subject matter into these themes (Beane, 1993)?

▮▮ TOWARD A DEFINITION OF CURRICULUM

My initial definition of curriculum as content contained in a textbook was partly valid, but it was also limited. My definition took on new dimensions as I interfaced with the educational needs of the students in Plainsville and Edgetown. I began to understand that curriculum could change radically from one school district and from one community to another. Plainsville and Edgetown, two separate communities of different sizes in the same geographical region, had their own variations of curriculum policy. They defined their students' informational needs in biology differently, and a different kind of science content was taught to the students.

The complexity of attempting to define curriculum has been noted by Cuban (1996), who writes: "Over 1,100 curriculum books have been written since the turn of the century, each with different versions of what 'curriculum' means; many of the definitions conflict" (p. 221). You can envision the kind of heated debate that citizens of Plainsville and Edgetown might have had over what content should be included in the biology curriculum.

As you attempt to arrive at a definition of curriculum, you become aware of how it is shaped by myriad factors, how it gives shape to students' lives in and out of school, and how it may be more culturally suited and more engaging for some students than for others. When you relate questions about curriculum to specific communities (e.g., Plainsville, Edgetown), to specific minority groups (e.g., Hispanics, African and Asian Americans), to specific socioeconomic groups (e.g., working, middle, and upper classes), to gender issues, among other social and cultural factors, you can see how challenging these questions are.

▮▮ DIMENSIONS OF CURRICULUM

As complex as *curriculum* might be to define, and as debatable as any definition becomes as soon as it is written, you still must search for a working definition. As you search for and begin constructing a definition of curriculum, we encourage you to remain flexible. Just as soon as you believe you have a definition that is workable and generalizable to other schools, you will encounter some event or issue that will challenge your working definition. To help you formulate a definition, we introduce four dimensions of curriculum discussed by Cuban (1996): *intended, taught, learned,* and *historical.*

Intended Curriculum

An *intended curriculum* is a body of content that is usually contained in an official framework, such as a state curriculum guide, course syllabi, or a list of courses. The many recent standards documents developed by national organizations (National Science Teachers Association [NSTA], National Council of Teachers of English [NCTE], National Council of Teachers of Mathematics [NCTM], National Council for the Social Studies [NCSS]), states, and districts are other examples of intended curricula. These documents outline content, instruction, and assessment at various grade levels. The intended curriculum has usually been "adopted" by official policy-makers at the state or local level. Such policy-makers believe that the intended curriculum will convey core knowledge and values to students. Once adopted, the core knowledge then becomes official, even legalistic; some states have extensive accountability systems to ensure that teachers are teaching and students are learning the official knowledge of the intended curriculum. However, the idea of official knowledge has been criticized by such educators as Nieto (1996), Hollins (1996), Apple (1993), and Doll (1993). These educators argue that what becomes official for one group of students may be less relevant, less engaging, perhaps even fully inappropriate, for another group of students. We discuss the perceived relevance (or irrelevance) of official knowledge for some groups of students later in this chapter.

Taught Curriculum

The *taught curriculum* represents what is taught to students in classrooms and schools. Historically, the taught curriculum, a body of official knowledge (e.g., curriculum guides, standards) is provided by policy-makers to teachers. The responsibility of the teacher, who typically has played little or no role in its creation, is to help students acquire this body of knowledge. The taught curriculum is viewed as having two dimensions: *formal* and *informal*. The formal dimension is the transformation of official knowledge into classroom lessons; it is what teachers do and what they employ to teach targeted content, skills, concepts, ideas, and attitudes. The meeting and mingling of teachers, students, and official knowledge creates a dynamic for the informal dimension of the taught curriculum, a dimension that has also been called the *hidden curriculum*. The hidden curriculum consists of ideas, attitudes, and social values that are not explicitly part of the intended curriculum, but are implicitly—usually unconsciously— taught by individual teachers and the school. For example, according to Sadker and Sadker (1994), early adolescent girls in middle school and young women in high school are implicitly taught to participate less often in courses related to sciences and mathematics. African American students may learn that they must give up or at least conceal their own cultural systems and identities in order to be successful in school (Carter & Goodwin, 1994).

The formal dimension of the taught curriculum has recently been the subject of much criticism because such knowledge is viewed by some educators as being more representative of the "White middle-class community," the individuals and organizations who are seen by many as controlling schools and playing an influential role in shaping curriculum. Likewise, the informal curriculum would then be more culturally suited, although implicitly, to White middle-class students, thus creating a potential learning barrier for students whose cultures and world views, among other factors, do not align well with White middle-class culture.

For a final example of the taught curriculum at the school level we briefly return to the biology curricula of Plainsville and Edgetown. Because of community values, schools in general choose to teach certain topics in courses of study. Plainsville and Edgetown chose to focus differently on the topics of evolution and natural selection. Both communities were in the same state, and the state board of education adopted the same Science textbooks for both communities. Yet local values suggested that some topics should not be part of the taught curriculum, despite the fact that state policy-makers had sanctioned the same body of official knowledge for both communities. Local decision-making and local values are powerful parts of the taught curriculum.

Learned Curriculum

The *learned curriculum* represents what students learn in school. In the last few decades, this dimension has drawn considerable attention from educators and policy-makers. The concern has primarily focused on attempting to measure exactly what students learn. By employing the same kind of standardized tests, schools can compare their students' test scores, thus generalizing teaching and learning in one school to other schools in the district and to schools in the state and nation. This generalizable form of student assessment has become an overwhelming preoccupation in many schools across the country, giving rise to a multi-million-dollar testing industry. These efforts at comparing student achievement also take place internationally, as nations compete with regard to the effectiveness of the learned curriculum in such areas as math and science. For example, the 1998 release of scores from the Third International Mathematics and Science Study prompted a number of policy-makers and politicians to call for sweeping reforms to math and science education in the middle grades, in part because the average score for U. S. eighth-graders fell only slightly above the international mean (LeTendre & Baker, 1998).

Standardized testing has a powerful influence on school curricula, particularly in the areas of reading, social studies/history, and mathematics. You will also play a part in the assessment process because you will identify ways students can demonstrate having learned aspects of the formal, taught curriculum. Generally, students who demonstrate higher levels of learning the taught curriculum are placed in higher academic tracks; those who demonstrate lower levels of learning are placed in lower academic tracks.

Over the past few years, ethnographic studies in schools and classrooms have explored the relationship between unintended student learnings and student engagement in school and classroom events. Such studies include, for example, Wilson's (1991) examination of Native American students in mainstream schools. In this study, Native American tenth-graders experienced extreme cultural conflict when they attended mainstream schools away from their reservation; the students felt disconnected socially and academically from school and from mainstream students. Trueba, Kirton, and Jacobs (1990) studied the school experiences of Hmong children in school classrooms. They found that these new immigrants experienced extreme cultural conflict in school, thus predisposing them for disengagement from school and classroom curricula. Out of these and related studies has emerged the perceived need to develop and implement school and classroom curricula that are culturally relevant to all students, not just those who represent the mainstream culture.

Historical Curriculum

The *historical curriculum* touches the lives of every member of society. With respect to schools, this includes the individuals who enter schools as students; adults who enter schools as teachers, administrators, and support staff; and adults who enter schools as parents of students. These groups contend with and accommodate to past traditions of school curriculum. These traditions include "formal purposes of schooling, official content, buried assumptions about knowledge, [and] the organization and relationships within classrooms, schools, and districts" (Cuban, 1996, p. 223). The historical dimension of curriculum at least partially explains why fierce debates occur over such topics as the teaching of long division in mathematics or the teaching of reading by using phonics instruction: many adults use their own recollections of school experiences to gauge what is effective for today's students. Given that schools tend to be conservative institutions that have been remarkably resistant to widespread and lasting reform, you can begin to understand why changes in how schools are structured and how lessons are conducted are often slow to occur.

▌▌▌DEVELOPING A DEFINITION OF CURRICULUM

In the foregoing discussion, you learned about four dimensions of curriculum. These dimensions provide one approach to thinking about the curriculum you will teach in your classroom. Now that you have considered these dimensions, how might you develop a definition of curriculum? After thinking about your own definition, consider the one below.

> A curriculum of a classroom, school, district, state (or nation) is a series of planned events intended for students to learn particular knowledge, skills, and values and organized to be carried out by administrators and teachers. This concept of curriculum stresses purposes, content, organization, relationships, and outcomes for students (Cuban, 1996, p. 221).

As you consider this definition, address the following questions with peers.

- How does the definition reflect the four dimensions of curriculum?
- What parts of the definition, if any, align with the curricula of the elementary, middle, and high schools you attended?
- In what ways is the definition culturally sensitive?

After addressing these questions, consider minor editorial changes or major revisions to Cuban's definition. Working with peers, make the necessary changes to arrive at a new definition of curriculum. Explain the changes your group made and share your new definition with the class.

▌Reader Activity 5.1

CONSULTING OTHER SOURCES
Researching Differing Perspectives on Curriculum

Even if you agree with Cuban's definition of curriculum, many questions remain about the nature of the "planned events" that students should experience in school. Should the curriculum emphasize knowledge of facts, "big" ideas, or learning how to learn? Should the curriculum emerge from learners' interests or be delineated in advance by educators and scholars? Curriculum theorists have proposed different and often conflicting answers to these questions. The purpose of this activity is to help you become acquainted with a variety of perspectives held by prominent curriculum scholars.

Choose one of the authors listed in this activity or any other curriculum scholar suggested by your instructor. Read enough of his/her work so that you gain an overview of how this author defines curriculum, its content, and its processes. You might also attempt to answer several important questions. How does this author define the purpose of schooling? What is the author's position toward the disciplines? What is the student's role in the curriculum? What is the teacher's role? Where would you situate this writer on a continuum of content-centered/student-centered curriculum? On what points do you concur with this author? On what points do you disagree with this author? Write a two-to-three-page paper in which you summarize and react to the author's remarks. Share your work with the class.

Selected Curriculum Scholars

Mortimer Adler	Henry Giroux	Deborah Meier
Michael Apple	Carl Grant	Nel Noddings
Molefi K. Asante	Maxine Greene	William Pinar
John Dewey	Madeline Grumet	Theodore Sizer
Eliot Eisner	E. D. Hirsch, Jr.	Rudolph Steiner

(Note: See Eisner (1996) for a good summary of the ideologies of most of these authors.)

■■■ BUREAUCRATIC LEVELS OF CURRICULUM: NATIONAL, STATE, DISTRICT, SCHOOL, AND CLASSROOM

The process of developing and implementing curricula for classroom use is neither simple nor straightforward. Decisions about what content to teach are made on multiple levels, including national, state, district, school, and classroom (Armstrong 1989). In most instances, teachers are expected to guard, protect, and defend decisions made at every level. However, in some instances, teachers do not always agree with the curriculum decisions made for them, and some ignore these decisions or simply refuse to comply with them (Powell, in press). For example, when I began teaching in Plainsville, decisions about excluding specific content from the classroom science curriculum had already been made at the district level. As a new teacher in the district, I received these decisions and was expected to comply without question. I could make decisions about how to teach selected content, but not about what content to teach. My preference for teaching explicitly about natural selection was never part of the decision-making process. Not only did I inherit policymakers' decisions, but I also inherited community values that were embedded in these decisions, and that were embedded historically in the school's tradition for teaching and learning.

National Curriculum Initiatives: Standards

Curriculum initiatives at the national level can have an important influence on what you actually teach. In the 1990s, the major initiative was the standards movement. While its roots can be traced to the publication of *A Nation at Risk* (1983) and the adoption of Goals 2000 (1991), leadership in the standards movement has been provided by professional educational organizations. The publication of *Curriculum and Evaluation Standards for School Mathematics* (1989):

. . . ushered in a new era relative to the role of national organizations in the practice of schooling. Through the *Standards* document, NCTM helped to form a new perspective on how national subject-area groups can contribute to the improvement of education when it delineated . . . a consensus on what students should know and be able to do and how that might best be demonstrated in the classroom (Kendall & Marzano, 1996, p. 3).

Other subject-area groups soon followed suit. An overview of existing national standards documents is given in Figure 5.1.

These organizations are influential in making suggestions for curriculum and instruction in schools, but they hold no legal authority to mandate implementation of their curriculum preferences. However, because the membership of these national organizations is comprised of thousands of teachers across the nation, their decision-making is far-reaching.

Standards in the discipline areas are statements that "provide educators with guidelines for curriculum and teaching that will ensure that students have access to the knowledge believed to be necessary for their success" (Darling-Hammond & Falk, 1997, p. 190). These documents describe what knowledge students need to learn, at what grade level that knowledge should be presented, and, in many cases, provide examples of how that knowledge should be presented to students and their mastery assessed.

The national standards movement has been praised for "leveling the playing field"—informing all stakeholders of, for example, the definition of science, its purpose in the secondary curriculum, important science knowledge, and how best to teach science. However, many critics argue that the movement is leading the country closer to a national curriculum. If the trend continues, these critics charge, parents, students, and teachers will play a diminished role in influencing the development and implementation of local curricula (Noddings, 1997; Reigeluth, 1997).

The standards movement is not the first national curriculum reform initiative in this country. In 1958, the Soviet Union launched the Sputnik satellite, setting off a panic about the quality of American education and its ability to prepare future citizens to win the "space race." Consequently, policy-makers, experts in the disciplines, and educators embarked on a concerted effort to enhance instruction in public schools. Because this was a national effort, education organizations (e.g., NCTM, NCTE, NSTA, NCSS) were directly involved. In the area of science education, for example, national funding was made available for bringing together members of the science community (e.g., The Biological Science Curriculum Study) for the purpose of creating new science curriculum materials, including textbooks. Some of the project groups were headed by scholars who were not affiliated directly with public schools. While they were working toward the very important goal of enhancing science literacy of the general population, they inadvertently designed precollege curriculum materials more aligned with college science curricula. Some of the project materials were deemed "teacher-proof," meaning that any teacher in almost any teaching situation would be able to use the same materials and produce the same results with regard to student achievement.

The nation learned three important lessons—at great monetary expense—from the 1960s movement to improve curriculum. First, reform efforts initiated at the national level that do not involve teachers in the decision-making process have little chance of reaching the classroom. Second, "teacher-proof" curricular materials do not necessarily lead to higher achievement for all students. Third, new curricular material has little chance of being adopted when classroom teachers are not involved in its creation.

FIGURE 5.1 National Standards in Content Areas[1]

Content Area	Document Title	Organization
The Arts	Consortium of National Arts Education Associations. (1994). *National standards for arts education: What every young American should know and be able to do in the arts.* Reston, VA: Music Educators National Conference	Music Educators National Conference 1902 Association Drive Reston, VA 22091 703-860-4000 *http://www.menc.org/*
Business Education	National Business Education Association. (1995). *National standards for business education: What America's students should know and be able to do in business.* Reston, VA: Author.	National Business Education Association Reston, VA *http://www.nbea.org/partners/nbea/standard.html*
Civics and Government	Center for Civic Education. (1994). *National standards for civics and government.* Calabasas, CA: Author	Center for Civic Education 5146 Douglas Fir Road Calabasas, CA 91203 818-591-9321 *http://www.civiced.org/*
Economics	National Council on Economic Education. (1997). *Voluntary national content standards in economics.* New York: Author	National Council on Economic Education 1140 Avenue of the Americas New York, NY 10036 212-730-7007 *http://www.nationalcouncil.org/*
Foreign Languages	National Standards in Foreign Language Education Project. (1996). *Standards for foreign language learning: Preparing for the 21st century.* Lawrence, KS: Author	American Council on the Teaching of Foreign Languages Six Executive Plaza Yonkers, NY 10801-6801 914-963-8830 *http://www.actfl.org/*
Geography	Geography Education Standards Project. (1994). *Geography for life: National geography standards.* Washington, DC: National Geographic Research and Exploration.	National Council for Geographic Education 1600 M Street, NW, Suite 2500 Washington, DC 20036 202-775-7832 *http://multimedia2.freac.fsu.edu/ncge/*
Health Education	Joint Committee on National Health Education Standards. (1995). *National health education standards: Achieving health literacy.* Reston, VA: Association for the Advancement of Health Education.	Association for the Advancement of Health Education 1900 Association Drive Reston, VA: 22091 703-476-3437 *http://www.aahperd.org/cgi-bin/counter.pl/aahe.html*
History	National Center for History in the Schools. (1996). *National standards for history.* (Basic Ed.). Los Angeles, CA: Author	National Center for History in the Schools UCLA, Department of History 405 Hilgard Ave Los Angeles, CA 90024 310-825-4702 *http://www.sscnet.ucla.edu/nchs*

FIGURE 5.1 (continued)

Content Area	Document Title	Organization
Language Arts	National Council of Teachers of English and the International Reading Association (1996). *Standards for the English Language Arts.* Urbana, IL: National Council of Teachers of English.	National Council of Teachers of English 1111 W. Kenyon Road Urbana, IL 61801 217-328-3870 *http://www.ncte.org/*
Mathematics	National Council of Teachers of Mathematics. (1989). *Curriculum and evaluation standards for school mathematics.* Reston, VA: Author.	National Council of Teachers of Mathematics 1906 Association Drive Reston, VA 22091 703-620-9840 *http://www.nctm.org/*
Physical Education	National Association for Sport and Physical Education. (1995). *Moving into the future, national standards for physical education: A guide to content and assessment.* St. Louis: Mosby	National Association for Sport and Physical Education 1900 Association Drive Reston, VA 22091 703-476-3410 *http://aahperd.org/cgi-bin/counter.pl/naspe/naspe.html*
Science	National Research Council. (1996). *National science education standards.* Washington, DC: National Academy Press.	National Science Education Standards 2101 Constitution Ave., NW HA 486 Washington, DC 20418 202-334-1399 *http://www.nap.edu/readingroom/books/nses/*
Social Studies	National Council for the Social Studies. (1994). *Expectations of excellence: Curriculum standards for social studies.* Washington, DC: Author.	National Council for the Social Studies 3501 Newark St., NW Washington, DC 20016 202-966-7840 *http://www.ncss.org/*
Technology Education	International Technology Education Association. (1996). *Technology for all Americans: A rationale and structure for the study of technology.* Reston, VA: Author	International Technology Education Association 1914 Association Drive Reston, VA 20191-1539 703-860-2100 *http://www.iteawww.org/*
Vocational Education	Secretary's Commission on Achieving Necessary Skills. (1991). *What work requires of schools: A SCANS report for America 2000.* Washington, DC: U.S. Department of Labor.	National Center for Research in Vocational Education University of California, Berkeley 2150 Shattuck Avenue, Suite 1250 Berkeley, CA 94704 510-642-4004 *http://vocserve.berkeley.edu/*

(Mid-Continent Regional Education Laboratory, 1997)

[1] This figure is representative of national standards documents that have been developed by national professional organizations. In some content areas, standards may have been developed that are not represented here.

State Curriculum Initiatives: High-Stakes Testing

While national organizations and their participants hold no legal authority for mandating curriculum and instruction, state boards of education, state departments of education, and state educational agencies do. Consequently, these state entities make critical decisions about curriculum and instruction. Emerging from these decisions are guidelines for teaching in local schools. In some states, these guidelines are general in nature; however, in states like Texas and Kentucky, the guidelines have become more precise regarding what content must be taught in all schools throughout the state. Where guidelines have become more precise, state agencies are often charged with monitoring how well local schools comply with state regulations.

States that support strict and precise curriculum guidelines can have a strong influence on school and classroom curricula. For a number of years, Texas has had a list of central concepts and skills that must be taught in every subject in grades K-12. These concepts and skills are called *Essential Elements.* Every school in Texas must document when and how these elements are taught to students during the school year. More recently, however, the Essential Elements, while remaining an important dimension of state and local curriculum, have become secondary to the Texas Assessment of Academic Skills (TAAS), a state-mandated standardized test.

The TAAS is a "high-stakes" test: significant consequences are attached to student performance on the test. Low-performing schools, whose students demonstrate lower levels of achievement on the test, can be put on academic probation. On the other hand, when students at a particular school do exceptionally well, their teachers might receive pay bonuses, and students might be rewarded with special treats. Not surprisingly, the test has an important influence on school curriculum and instruction. Because the pressure to do well on the TAAS test is high, many Texas teachers have begun teaching to the test, a practice that has been widely criticized.

Although teaching to the TAAS may frustrate some Texas teachers who prefer to have more curricular autonomy, the test is nevertheless a state-mandated reality. Teachers who value their jobs and who have students' best interests in the forefront of their instruction believe they must prepare students for the test. This means that their classroom curriculum must, at least in part, reflect the content and skills required to do well on the TAAS.

To varying degrees, all states have curriculum guidelines, and most, like Texas, have state-mandated tests. Some states are more prescriptive and thus require greater accountability for compliance with state regulations, whereas others are less prescriptive. However, the trend has been for curriculum to be more closely and carefully defined at the state level, thus removing some of the decision-making about curriculum from local curriculum leaders and classroom teachers.

District, School, and Classroom Curriculum Initiatives

Much curriculum decision-making and certainly much curriculum development remain at the district level. Armstrong (1989) notes,

> . . . [C]urriculum development continues to occur locally, where curriculum leaders play very important roles. It is here that master plans guiding instructional programs are developed, and here that steps are initiated that will result in more specific building-level and individual-classroom-level plans. (p. 30)

The curriculum leaders Armstrong mentions are educators—often former classroom teachers—who have become specialists in the area of school curriculum. These professionals guide curriculum development efforts on the district, school, and classroom levels. Usually, the size of the district will determine the number and type of curriculum leaders. Large school districts might have an assistant superintendent for curriculum who oversees the activities of curriculum leaders in each subject area and for various grade levels. Small school districts, however, might have only one person who has responsibility for curriculum activities of the whole district.

District-level curriculum leaders often have the responsibility of ensuring that local classroom teaching aligns with state regulations for curriculum. They do this by helping classroom teachers, who are key players in local curriculum development activities, align their intended content with state regulations. In Texas, for example, district curriculum leaders must ensure that the Essential Elements and TAAS become explicit parts of local classroom teaching.

Although every level of curriculum development is important, the two most significant levels are the school and classroom. The school and the classroom are where curriculum is actually implemented, where the intended curriculum is transformed into daily lessons, and where teachers and students interface to create unique contexts for learning. The school, as a curriculum context, has the responsibility of linking state and district curriculum guidelines with classroom instruction. In an era of high-stakes testing, this linkage is often of paramount importance since schools are held accountable for meeting state curriculum goals.

When curriculum development reaches the level of the classroom, large numbers of teachers are directly involved. These teachers must ensure that state and district curriculum mandates are part of the instructional units they develop for daily teaching. Classroom-level curriculum work is very practical, and teacher wisdom is central to knowing how best to meet state and district requirements while providing students with meaningful, relevant, and useful lessons. The artistry of teaching becomes apparent when teachers become proficient at meeting the requirements of state legislators and district officials while simultaneously creating and implementing a classroom curriculum that is highly engaging for students.

▌ Reader Activity 5.2

CONSULTING OTHER SOURCES
Examining Curriculum Documents

The purpose of this activity is to enable you to get a firsthand look at curriculum documents written at the national, state, district, school, and classroom levels. For this activity, you will work in subject-area teams to examine documents in your teaching field. As a team select a broad topic in your subject area (e.g., geography in social studies, geometry in mathematics, writing in English language arts) and agree on a general grade range (e.g., middle school, ninth to tenth, eleventh to twelfth). Divide responsibility for locating a current curriculum document written at: (1) the national level (i.e., standards); (2) the state level (e.g., standards, curriculum framework, core content); (3) the district level; (4) the school level (e.g., scope and sequence); (5) the classroom level (e.g., a course syllabus).

As a team, examine the documents. Follow several statements through the various levels and note how the degree of specificity changes. Also note the extent to which the documents are interrelated and consistent with specific regard to the topic you selected. Design a graphic that displays selected statements and shows the relationships among the levels. In a class discussion, share your group's graphic and discuss the usefulness of the documents you examined.

▌▌▌DECIDING WHO REALLY MAKES THE CURRICULUM

As you reflect on the levels of curriculum development, also consider the question of who really establishes the curriculum. Who are the key stakeholders? What key factors influence the nature of curriculum being implemented in most local schools? In answering these questions, you might generate lists like those presented here.

Key Stakeholders

- teachers
- students
- administrators
- parents and community members
- local school board members
- state school board members
- curriculum leaders
- state legislators
- special interest group members

Key Factors

- selected content—subject matter—to be taught (or not to be taught)
- standardized tests (state and national)
- test agencies and services
- national-level and state-level educational organizations (i.e., NSTA, NCSS)
- community values
- political climate nationally and locally
- size of school district

Many stakeholders and various factors are at work—and often in tension—as school curricula are developed and implemented at the local level. Three additional factors, however, profoundly influence the nature of the classroom curriculum: textbooks, individual and shared characteristics of students and their communities, and developmental or age-level characteristics of students. Each of these factors is discussed below.

Understanding the Role of Textbooks in Your Classroom Curriculum

While textbooks have been the mainstay for middle- and high-school instruction, they have not been without criticism. For example, textbooks have been charged with narrowing the focus of instruction, determining the curriculum of schools and classrooms, and disempowering classroom teachers (Apple, 1993). Important questions surface from these criticisms. For example, what role should textbooks play in your classroom

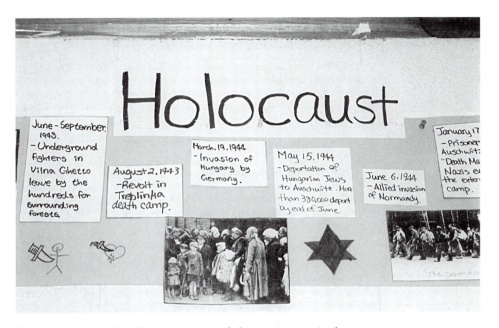

Textbooks provide only one source of classroom curriculum.

curriculum? Will your classroom curriculum be less engaging and less meaningful for students if you center your instruction on the textbook? How might textbooks enrich your classroom teaching? How might textbooks constrain your teaching? How might textbooks disempower you as a professional?

It is a widely held belief that textbooks and their publishers govern what is taught in school. Tanner and Tanner (1995) argue, however, that such exclusive governance of school content is a myth. The school textbook industry is a multi million-dollar enterprise, and textbook publishers, because of very large investments in producing even a single textbook, aggressively market their books to school districts. But publishers are not necessarily in control of the topics addressed in the texts. Tanner and Tanner (1995) explain:

> Authority for determining whether to buy the textbooks that publishers produce is vested in state and local education agencies. They decide whether the books contain what is most important to know and may either reject the books outright or make recommendations for changes, postponing acceptance until the changes are made. (p. 592)

Tanner and Tanner imply that textbook publishers are concerned with meeting market demands that translate into the informational needs of teachers and students. Typically, publishers provide written notice announcing textbook submissions for state adoption. The state receives copies of the texts and deposits them at key locations throughout the state for review by teachers, parents, and interest groups. When state agencies hold hearings for purposes of adopting new textbooks, stakeholders have an opportunity to examine closely and criticize openly the content of those textbooks. For example, in 1982, New York City rejected at least three biology textbooks being considered for adoption in the city's high schools. The reason for the rejection, according to local educators, was the inadequate treatment of Darwinian evolution (Tanner & Tanner, 1995). In reaching this decision , New York City was one of the first large school districts to take issue with national pressure to endorse the creationist perspective.

Textbook companies respond to issues like evolution and creationism in a manner that will be acceptable to as many educators and public citizens as possible without lowering sales and profits. However, when companies try to make their books be "all things to all people," the result can be textbook content that eliminates treatment of important, but sometimes volatile, social issues. For example:

> In 1985, the California Board of Education, on the recommendation of the State Curriculum Development and Supplemental Materials Commission, unanimously rejected every science textbook submitted for use in seventh- and eighth-grade classes stating that the textbooks are watered down so as to avoid controversy. The publishers were criticized by the board and the state superintendent for producing textbooks that fail to address adequately such controversial topics as evolution, human reproduction, and environmental problems. (Tanner & Tanner, 1995, p. 593)

Textbooks rejected by California and Texas cause very serious concerns for publishers who count on these states, the largest buyers of textbooks, to strongly influence content and adoptions across the country.

Other content area textbooks may also contain controversial content. For example, publishers and writers of social studies textbooks continuously struggle with how to appropriately and satisfactorily depict historical events and societal groups within the American experience. Can you give examples of controversial content in textbooks in areas such as English, health, family living or physical education?

Textbooks continue to be used extensively. However, in today's classrooms where both teachers and students can utilize new technologies to access information easily and instantaneously, there is a growing awareness that textbooks provide only one source of classroom content. The long-held perspective that textbooks are the sole source of information for student learning is no longer valid. Nevertheless, textbooks that are wisely and effectively used can help teachers and students alike, as the following narratives about Dan and Sarah suggest.

Textbooks As Curricular Tools: The Case of Dan and Sarah

Dan and Sarah began their careers in the same school district (Powell, in press). This district, which was the eleventh largest in the nation at the time, had prescribed courses of study for each subject taught in high school and had adopted textbooks approved by the state board of education.

Initially, Dan and Sarah taught the same course—Earth Science—but in different high schools. They each taught the course for five periods a day in schools with diverse student populations. Historically, the class was intended for students in the school district who had been placed in lower academic tracks. Neither teacher intended to make the adopted textbook central to classroom instruction. At the beginning of the school year, they both viewed the textbook as a secondary source of information. As the year unfolded, both Sarah and Dan encountered unexpected challenges.

Sarah had prepared to teach Biology and other Life Science courses, but was hired to teach Earth Science. Because she had completed only one university course in Geology, she was not looking forward to this teaching assignment. The school district granted her an emergency license in order to employ her, despite her lack of credentials for Earth Science.

Over the course of the school year, Sarah became less confident in her ability to teach Earth Science. She struggled continuously as she attempted to develop meaningful, engaging lesson plans, and searched for ways to enrich her classroom curriculum. Nevertheless, her lessons aligned closely with the textbook. Indeed, one of Sarah's class activities was to have students take turns reading aloud paragraphs from the textbook. When I asked Sarah to explain her reliance on the textbook, she said that she lacked confidence in her ability to teach the subject. She further noted that she did not have sufficient time to do extensive reading in Earth Science topics after school and in the evenings, and thus the textbook had become her most important instructional tool. Despite her intentions to make the textbook a secondary source of information in her Earth Science classes, by the end of the school year the textbook had become central to her classroom curriculum.

Unlike Sarah, whose background knowledge in Earth Science was limited, Dan possessed a master's degree in Hydrogeology and had worked as a field geologist for six years with an international science corporation. Dan possessed a strong background in the subject he was hired to teach and was fully licensed by the state to teach Earth Science and other geology-related courses as well as Chemistry and Physics.

Not surprisingly, Dan looked forward to teaching high-school Earth Science. Unfortunately, he had not given much thought to the students who would be in his classes and was unfamiliar with suitable approaches for teaching students who had been grouped into lower academic tracks. Dan relied on his extensive background to win over the students; he could deliver extemporaneous lectures on most earth science topics found in the district's syllabus and the textbook. However, such lectures, as Dan painfully learned early in the school year, were not suited to his students. During these first few months, he became increasingly frustrated with his unsuccessful attempts to share his extensive background knowledge with his students. Over time, Dan began turning more often to the textbook, and by the third month of school, his lessons focused on the textbook entirely. This focus was inconsistent with Dan's intention to make the textbook a secondary source of information.

When I asked Dan to explain his use of the textbook, he admitted his unfamiliarity with teaching strategies appropriate to his students' abilities in the earth sciences. He believed that the textbook provided both him and his students with a common basis for discussing key concepts and targeted content. Dan felt frustrated in using the textbook as a central organizer for his lessons, but he also felt relieved that he had the textbook to guide student learning. Interestingly, although Dan and Sarah had very different preparations, both viewed the textbook as a highly useful curriculum tool. And, by the end of their novice year, both had become dependent on the textbook.

The cases of Dan and Sarah demonstrate how textbooks, as tools for classroom curriculum, can be useful in organizing and delivering instruction. In fact, Sarah's situation was similar to my own in my first teaching position in Plainsville. Like Sarah, I was assigned to teach courses for which I lacked solid academic preparation and found the textbooks to be highly useful tools for organizing and implementing classroom curriculum. When teachers are not adequately prepared for teaching assignments, lack sufficient knowledge of pedagogy, and are unfamiliar with students' backgrounds, they may make textbooks the center of the classroom curriculum. Some schools, however, are proud of the fact that they use no textbooks in any of their classrooms. One such school is described here.

Non-Textbook-Centered Curriculum: The Case of Brown Barge Middle School

Brown Barge Middle School (BBMS) takes considerable pride in the fact that teachers and students there create their own curriculum. The school's decision not to use textbooks was based on curricular and social issues.

BBMS is a magnet school for technology. Students have ongoing opportunities to become proficient in accessing information through a multiplicity of new technologies. When students engage in various assignments, especially research projects, they access information from many sources and databases, but not from textbooks. One reason they do not use textbooks is that the school's curriculum is theme-based and not subject-based (Powell, Skoog, & Troutman, 1996). As a theme-based school, students complete twelve-week units of instruction on a variety of topics arising from the disciplines and from issues and problems BBMS and the community encounter on a daily basis. To complete each unit, teachers and students gather and synthesize information from multiple sources. Instead of relying on traditional units of study (e.g., the Colonial Period, Early American Literature) that are aligned with or dictated by textbook content, teachers and students at BBMS create their own theme-based units. These units are powerful because they represent the collaborative efforts of both teachers and students involved in the process of inquiry.

■ **Reader Activity 5.3**

Consulting Other Sources
Examining Curriculum at Brown Barge Middle School

Visit the home page of Brown Barge Middle School in Pensacola, Florida at: http://www.escambia.k12.fl.us/brobm/home.html. Explore this well-constructed site in order to answer the following questions:

1. What kinds of curriculum documents (e.g., national, state, local) can be accessed from this site?
2. Visit one of the streams that is described in detail (e.g., the environment, American Tapestry). Describe the role of your subject—if any—in the stream. What sources have been used to create the curricular streams?
3. Explore and describe some of the on-line resources for students, teachers, and parents.
4. Brown Barge Middle School is a technology magnet. Describe the role of technology in the school's curriculum.
5. From your exploration of the site, what can you infer about who makes the curriculum at this school?

▪▪CULTURALLY RELEVANT CURRICULUM

Throughout this chapter, various dimensions of school curricula have been examined. Still another essential facet of school curriculum is its *cultural dimension*. Over the past two decades, this dimension has received considerable attention from a variety of educators, particularly those concerned with providing every student with opportunities to be successful in school (e.g., Gay, 1988; Ladson-Billings, 1994; Hollins, 1996).

I introduced the concept of culturally relevant teaching in Chapter Two, "Understanding Multiculturalism." Here I review some of its key premises in order to explore the characteristics of culturally relevant curriculum. One premise is that teaching and learning are deeply embedded in cultural phenomena (Erickson & Shulz, 1992; Peshkin, 1992). Consistent with this premise is the idea that meaningful teaching is sensitive to cultural phenomena and to forces in communities surrounding the school and in students' lives as they are shaped by these communities (Powell, Zehm & Garcia, 1996). A second premise relates to student demographics. As the student population across the nation becomes more diverse, schools need to create curricula that are more sensitive to the diverse needs of students. The traditional approach to teaching that corresponds to the metaphor, "one size fits all," is being increasingly challenged by educators who are calling for school practices that are more sensitive to students' backgrounds.

Given the two premises above, a working definition of *culturally relevant curriculum* can be suggested. Culturally relevant curriculum extends and validates the learner's culture, not only through the intended curriculum, but also through the taught curriculum (Hollins, 1996). Such a curriculum focuses on four important questions integral to the teaching and learning process.

- How are students engaged with the content?
- How are students invited to learn by teachers?
- How are students invited and encouraged to interact with one another in the midst of school-related activities and events?
- How do teachers respond to students' personal backgrounds and to students' communities where these backgrounds are shaped?

A culturally relevant curriculum is student-centered, ensures that students' needs are addressed before, during, and after the presentation of the intended curriculum, and offers students multiple pathways to learning.

This working definition suggests that curriculum is a cultural product, as Hollins (1996) notes:

> School curriculum is itself a cultural product. A particular cultural or ethnic group existing as part of a larger society, and that has retained sufficient power, is likely to develop a school curriculum that promotes its own (a) cultural values, practices, and perceptions; (b) psychological, social, economic, and political needs, and (c) elevated status within the larger society. There is usually an observable relationship between the school curriculum and the pervading culture. (pp. 82–83)

Hollins argues, as do others (e.g., Delpit, 1988; Nieto, 1992), that the White, middle-class segment of our society continues to use its power to promote its own values, needs, and status despite the rise in diversity and shifting student demographics. As dropout rates for African Americans, Hispanics, Native Americans, poor Whites, and students with disabilities remain high, concern is increasing over the disparity between mainstream schooling and non-mainstream students.

Teachers who successfully implement a culturally relevant curriculum demonstrate certain characteristics, some of which are presented here as adapted from the work of Ladson-Billings (1994):

- The teacher creates a classroom curriculum that demonstrates a connectedness with all students.

- The teacher ensures that the classroom curriculum fosters a "community of learners."
- The teacher creates a curriculum that causes students to learn collaboratively.
- The teacher considers the extent to which the intended curriculum is appropriate for each "community of learners."
- The teacher ensures that students acquire the skills necessary to learn required content.
- The teacher views the curriculum as accessible to all students.

Developmentally Appropriate Curriculum

Another dimension of a culturally relevant curriculum is developmental appropriateness for students' cognitive, physical, social, and emotional needs. Most educators would readily agree that twelve-year-old Erin, for example, has different developmental needs from Sharon, a sixteen-year-old high school junior, and from Andi, a nineteen-year-old high school senior with Downs Syndrome. All three students share the same basic needs—food, shelter, clothing, a caring home environment. Yet all have needs that contrast. For example, Sharon might be preparing to attend college or vocational school, while Erin may not be thinking of these things yet. Andi's transition into the world of work is imminent. Because of their differing developmental needs, the three girls' educational needs differ as well. Sharon might be concerned about SAT scores or about completing a special high-school program that assures her entry into a related program at a local community college. Andi might be concerned about performing well in her community-based placement at a supermarket. Erin may still be wondering whether she should become an astronaut or an actress.

Middle-School Curriculum

For many decades, educators adhered to the belief that early adolescents had the same kind of learning needs as older adolescents. Consequently, a similar kind of content-centered curriculum was implemented for both groups. For ten- to fourteen-year-olds, this kind of curriculum arrangement was called the *junior high school* and, as the name implies, was designed as a preparation for high school. Traditional junior high schools are organized into subject departments and often place students in academic tracks. Students move from class-to-class and from teacher-to-teacher every fifty minutes or so.

Over the past several decades, however, increased attention has been given to the developmental characteristics and needs of early adolescents. A landmark paper commissioned by the Carnegie Corporation concluded that the high-school curriculum model was not well suited to early adolescents, and that an alternative curriculum and school structure were needed to better meet the developmental needs of these students (Carnegie Council on Adolescent Development, 1989). The resulting middle-school movement has caused educators everywhere to rethink the nature of schooling for ten- to fourteen-year-olds (Stevenson, 1992).

As the middle-school movement has grown, so has the range of alternative curriculum models for early adolescents. While some middle schools have changed in name only and still hold closely to the traditional junior high-school curriculum model, others have implemented an array of innovations. Two models are especially widespread at the middle school level: the integrative curriculum and the interdisciplinary curriculum.

Integrative curriculum is not subject-centered, but theme-based (Beane, 1993). Sometimes this curriculum is based on topics or questions generated by teachers; sometimes students themselves create the curriculum (Kenny, O'Donnell, & Smith, 1996). An integrative curriculum makes little distinction between planning and teaching because both occur simultaneously. Discipline boundaries are blurred, as teachers and students together identify topics they wish to explore, such as the self, the future, and the unknown. Brown Barge Middle School, described previously, uses this model.

Some middle schools have adopted an interdisciplinary curriculum model, thereby restructuring junior high notions about the nature of student and teacher interactions, content, instruction, and assessment. These schools group teachers in the core areas (i.e., Social Studies, English/language arts, Science, and Math) into teams and assign a designated number of students to each team. The teaching teams meet regularly to address the special needs of students and to discuss planning and instruction. To provide time for teachers to meet and to carry out instruction that is developmentally appropriate, schools have instituted block scheduling where traditional forty- to sixty-minute periods have given way to larger blocks of time. Middle-school educators believe the additional time provides for greater student involvement in and ownership of the learning process.

The Tort team, a group of four teachers in a middle school in the desert Southwest (the team's name comes from the desert tortoise, an endangered species), provides an example of interdisciplinary curriculum in the middle school (Powell, 1993). The four disciplines represented on this team were Mathematics, Science, Reading, and English/language arts. The teachers met daily during a team planning period, taught in adjacent classrooms, continuously provided each other with advice and support, and taught the same students over this time period. Tort students were heterogeneously grouped.

As an interdisciplinary middle-school team, the teachers did not view themselves as part of traditional subject-area departments. Instead, they viewed themselves as part of the Tort team. When Tort teachers met each day, they discussed student needs, addressed school-related issues, and planned instruction. Perhaps most significant were the units they created. Each teacher in the team developed subject-specific activities that related to the goals and objectives of the unit. The team's overall purpose was to help students make connections between diverse subject matter areas and to make school learning relevant.

The school tried to help students feel more secure by maintaining the same teams of students and teachers for both sixth and seventh grades. To promote responsibility, team unity, and school cohesiveness a student advisory period was instituted during which students and an assigned teacher discussed school governance and matters relating to creating safe learning environments. In addition, time was regularly provided for students to attend exploratory classes on topics teachers volunteered to teach (e.g., computer applications in science, badminton, guitar) and topics of interest to the students (e.g., karate, computer games, basketball).

As I spent time with the Tort team, I talked with students. These students communicated to me that, because of being on the same team for two years, they:

- viewed their team as an intra-group support network both in and out of school
- felt part of a team and the school
- were committed to the team
- had decreased levels of anxiety about learning and about coming to school

- were pleased with intra-team peer relationships
- liked team activities
- felt special and cared for by their teachers
- felt at ease with teaching styles and believed they knew what to expect as they began seventh grade
- appreciated teachers' familiarity with their learning styles
- had a better understanding of the teaching process and felt positive about the teaching-learning process (Powell, 1993, p. 56).

Middle schools attempt to reach two goals: to make curriculum more responsive to the needs of early adolescents, and to help ease the transition from self-contained elementary classroom environments to multi-period secondary classroom environments.

High-School Curriculum

The high-school curriculum model has remained relatively stable for years. Tour most high schools in the nation and you will find a similar kind of curriculum structure and a similar kind of schooling experience. Most high school days are segmented into six or seven fifty-minute periods. Bells or tones signify the beginning and end of these segments. School buildings are usually divided into areas, wings, or corridors where certain classes are taught: for example, all Science classes are taught in the Science corridor, and English classes are taught in the English corridor.

Students in many high schools are still put into some form of academically homogeneous track, even though tracking is of dubious benefit to students, particularly those placed in lower tracks (Oakes, 1985). Many high schools have extensive vocational programs and shop classes, while schools located outside metropolitan areas might offer agricultural education classes. High-school students tend to be known individually by their academic track, or by the nature of their selected educational program (e.g., college-bound, vocational, business education). To graduate from high school, students are generally required to have successfully earned a certain number of credits, which are called Carnegie Units. While these credits vary slightly from one state to another, most high-school students must complete credits in Mathematics, English, History, Science, and Physical Education.

Although the previous description applies to most high schools across the nation, many are restructuring time, resources, and the curriculum in order to be more responsive to the personal, social, and academic needs of older adolescents/young adults. In *Possible Lives: The Promise of Public Education in America,* Mike Rose (1995) reported on innovative educational programs and practices he observed while traveling across the country. Following are thumbnail sketches of some of the high schools he visited.

William Rainey Harper High School   Located in an impoverished and decaying west Chicago neighborhood, this school serves a student population that is virtually all African American. There, five teachers created a school-within-a-school called COMETS (Communication, Education, and Technology for Success) for some 130 students. Its purpose is to offer a comprehensive and integrated course of study to any sophomores who elect to participate. The curriculum is academically challenging. For example, students in COMETS are required to discuss, orally present, and write daily, and to conduct research, plan, and execute projects regularly. The teachers work to help students make connections across the disciplines. For example, the English and Social Studies teachers organize their curricula around common themes such as "Origins."

The *school-within-a-school* model is one way high schools are trying to combat the impersonal atmosphere of large institutions.

Bowen High School   Serving an impoverished neighborhood on Chicago's south side, the faculty at Bowen developed a ninth-grade academy. Its purpose is to prepare students to go to college and to pursue a career in teaching. The curriculum is designed to include an advisory period during which teachers work with individual students, and to incorporate a teacher-preparation program, Teachers for Chicago, into the daily life of the academy. One focus is on teaching students how to learn; another is on integrating instruction in English, Social Studies, and Math. *The ninth-grade academy* model addresses concerns about helping middle/junior high school students make a successful transition to high school.

The School for the Physical City   This is an alternative school in New York City. Its mission is "to prepare and empower city youth to take care of and take charge of the city" (p. 211). This combined middle and high school is sponsored by Cooper Union, an arts, architecture, and engineering college; Outward Bound, an expeditionary character-building program; and the New York City Mission Society, a charitable organization interested in increasing parent and community involvement in school. Students at the School for the Physical City acquire first-hand experience in public works projects, such as designing improvements for the city's water supply system, read poetry that connects to engineering, and take a wilderness trip in the Catskill Mountains to clarify their views of city life. *Alternative schools* provide curricular options that differ from those found in most traditional high schools. Although often associated with students who have had chronic attendance and disciplinary problems, alternative schools, like the School for the Physical City and others offer the personalization and focus that is generally lacking in the traditional high-school curriculum.

Wheelwright High School   Students in this eastern Kentucky school are benefiting from a number of innovative curriculum projects. Students take American Studies, which fuses Social Studies and English and which gives them numerous opportunities to think, write, and speak about social and historical issues. Building upon this foundation, the Telecommunications Project requires students to work in teams over the course of the year to develop and implement a community-based project. Students use electronic media to communicate with a variety of audiences and to locate and utilize resources across the state. Wheelwright students have developed a community recycling program, established a tutorial service at the elementary school, and surveyed the needs of local senior citizens. Through these projects, students acquire a sense of and appreciation for their own culture and dialect. They explore the history of the region and reflect upon its prospects for the future. From the writing they do in the American Studies course and in the Telecommunications Project, students collect and compile end-of-year portfolios in order to demonstrate their learning. Wheelwright students also publish an anthology, *Mantrip,* of oral histories preserving their local lore and customs. (For a full description, see Rose, pp. 256–281). The *integration of technology* into instruction helps to transcend disciplinary boundaries; to break down geographical, cultural, and generational barriers; and to give students authentic audiences for communication. Similarly, *community-based* or *service learning* projects give a real-life context to the practice and acquisition of academic skills and knowledge. *Oral history projects,* inspired by the work of Eliott Wigginton (Wigginton, 1985) with his students in Rabun Gap, Georgia, make curriculum culturally relevant and prepare students for responsible citizenship and stewardship.

Like all large and complex bureaucracies, high schools are slow to change. Curriculum restructuring initiatives such as those described earlier may never entirely supplant the traditional high-school curriculum model. Nevertheless, these programs prove that high schools can offer curricula that are academically challenging and culturally relevant, and that respond to the developmental, personal, and social needs of fifteen- to eighteen-year-olds.

▌ Reader Activity 5.4

WHAT WOULD YOU DO?
Examining a Curriculum Unit

The purpose of this activity is to help you apply what you have learned so far about curriculum by examining a curriculum unit developed by Traci O'Roark while she was a student teacher at the University of Kentucky. She developed this unit with her cooperating teacher, Rae Burgess. Traci completed her student teaching at the Scott County Ninth-Grade School in Georgetown, Kentucky. The Ninth-Grade School practices inclusion and heterogeneous grouping; teachers plan in interdisciplinary teams, and a special education teacher is assigned to each team and collaborates in the classrooms. Rae, Traci, and Lee Carter, a special education teacher, worked as a team throughout the semester. Traci and Rae developed this unit, "Self Discovery, Self Expression," for English language arts.

The ninth-graders in Traci's and Rae's English classes were a diverse group. Scott County is a suburban/rural community. Many students come from farming families, and the parents of many students work at a large Toyota manufacturing plant, both in labor and management. The Toyota plant has brought many changes to the community: increased prosperity, the promise of high-paying jobs for skilled workers, and an influx of Japanese visitors and residents. Ethnic diversity has increased as African Americans and Mexican Americans have moved into this historically White community to share in the prosperity. Traci, Rae, and Lee are all White, middle-class females. While many of their students are also middle-class Whites, some of their "different" students include:

- Mika, a shy Japanese teenager whose father is a Toyota executive. Her parents thought the American public school experience would be good for Mika. Mika seems to understand English much better than she speaks it.
- Lex and Al, working-class, white males who read and write at the third grade level. In order to mask their deficiencies, they often clown in class.
- Arlette, a physically well-developed and very attractive student whose designer jeans, cropped sweater, and name-brand shoes accentuate her charms. Arlette, who has been diagnosed with Attention Deficit Disorder (ADD), is often out of her seat for any number of reasons and usually manages to disturb others "accidentally" as she wanders about the room. Arlette responds quite theatrically to requests to sit quietly.

- Tim, Isaac, Reynaldo, and Kiki, four African-American students who usually sit together and rarely participate in class.
- Myrna, a gifted poet and artist who wears only black, including black lipstick and nail color. She has multiple, visible piercings. Her close-cropped hair is dyed burgundy. She is a "loner."

The following materials are included to help you understand the curriculum development process Traci and Rae adopted.

Exhibit A: Unit Overview
Exhibit B: Unit Calendar
Exhibit C: WebQuest Assignment
Exhibit D: National and State Documents Used

These materials should enable you to evaluate important aspects of the unit and to apply what you have learned about curriculum in this chapter and this text thus far. As you examine the exhibits, prepare answers to the following questions.

Bureaucratic Context of Curriculum

How did Traci and Rae make use of national and state documents in developing this unit?

Culturally Relevant Curriculum

What have Traci and Rae done to:

- create a classroom curriculum that demonstrates connectedness with all students?
- ensure that the classroom curriculum fosters a community of learners?
- create a curriculum that causes students to learn collaboratively?
- ensure that students acquire skills necessary to learn required content?
- ensure that the curriculum is accessible to all students?

Developmentally Appropriate Curriculum

What are some of the developmental needs of ninth-graders? How does this unit address them?

Addressing Student Differences

Based on the information given in the introduction, how might this unit meet the needs of Mika, Lex, Al, Arlette, Tim, Isaac, Reynaldo, Kiki, and Myrna?

Interdisciplinary Curriculum

What interdisciplinary content is reflected in this curriculum sample? How could other academic disciplines be incorporated into a "Self Discovery, Self Expression" unit?

Technology Integration

How is technology integrated into the unit?

EXHIBIT A   Unit Overview

Students received an abridged copy of this unit overview on the first day of the unit. Traci posted the "Essential Questions" on a bulletin board, and they remained prominently displayed throughout the unit.

Course: English I/9th Grade
Written by: Traci O'Roark, Rae Burgess
Implemented by: Traci O'Roark, Rae Burgess, and Lee Carter
Unit Title: Self Discovery, Self Expression
Organizer: Who Am I?
Projected Time: 21 days

Essential Questions

1. How have my past experiences sculpted my present sense of self?
2. How do I describe myself?
3. How can I most accurately express myself through the arts?
4. How can I most accurately express myself through writing?

Targeted Standards

- **Academic Expectations:** 1.1, 1.2, 1.11, 1.13, 1.16

- **Core Content**

Reading:
- Read and analyze personal pieces, responding critically by applying characteristics of the genre and by making connections to personal experience

Writing:
- Use writing-to-learn strategies (note-taking, freewriting) to generate ideas
- Use writing to demonstrate learning
- Write a personal narrative to communicate ideas
- Critique own and others' works by applying criteria for effective writing, including awareness of audience and purpose, organization, idea development, and standards of correctness

Inquiry/Technology As Communication
- Use WebQuest technology to complete individual research projects
- Option to use Powerpoint as mode of presentation of culminating project

Culminating Project

Students will create a poster that "sells" their art work to the O'Roark-Burgess Museum. Poster guidelines:

- Use a full-size poster board for display.
- Feature the abstract piece in a desirable and effective manner. Remember, the purpose is to "sell" your piece to the museum.
- On the poster, give rationales for the color and shape choices you made for your painting and explain why they are appropriate expressions of your personal narrative.
- Select lines from your personal narrative that reflect the mood and feeling of the painting and include on the poster.

EXHIBIT B Unit Calendar for "Self Discovery, Self Expression"

Monday	Tuesday	Wednesday	Thursday	Friday
Day 1 Students bring in family photos and share with classmates family stories and traditions. Students listen to Madonna's "This Used To Be My Playground," while mentally revisiting a place they used to frequent as children. After listening, students freewrite for ten minutes.	**Day 2** Students and teacher read aloud poems by Jewel. Students and teacher read aloud Walt Whitman's "Song of Myself." In-class writing: "Where Do I Stand?"	**Day 3** Teacher introduces 3-D autobiography project, "Identity Box." Teacher shows students her own "Identity Box." Students begin working on project.	**Day 4** Students complete and present "Identity Boxes." Boxes are displayed around room for duration of unit.	**Day 5** Teacher gives introduction to abstract art as means of self-representation. Students free-write in response to abstract painting. Exit slips: "What questions/comments do you have regarding abstraction?"
Day 6 Mini-lesson: Review design elements, color, and shape in abstraction. Introduction to WebQuest and Web Quest session #1 (see Unit Appendix) in computer lab.	**Day 7** Teacher reads aloud model student personal narratives (from previous years). Large group discussion: What constitutes a good personal narrative? Students review freewrites and project of past week and select topic for personal narrative.	**Day 8** Teacher reads aloud model student personal narrative. Large group discussion: Why is this an effective personal narrative? Students narrow personal narrative topics and list three reasons their topic will interest readers. Handouts: Drafting Tips, Personal Narrative Evaluation Sheet. Students are told they will be typing their first drafts on computer this week. Students who are uncomfortable composing on computer should write a first draft for homework.	**Day 9** Handout, transparency, and discussion: "Peer Response." Teacher assigns peer response groups. Students practice peer group response with student narrative, "Winning Big."	**Day 10** Mini-lesson: Writing Creative Leads. Students practice writing leads for narratives. Students use computer lab to type and print first draft.
Day 11 WebQuest Session #2 (see Unit Appendix)	**Day 12** Students review rules for Peer Response. Students practice on model student narrative. Students share personal narratives in Peer Response groups. Teacher conferences with individual students.	**Day 13** Students individually evaluate model student narrative, "You Are the Best." Peer Response groups continue. Teacher/student conferences continue.	**Day 14** Complete revision in Computer Lab.	**Day 15** Complete Web Quest #3 (see Unit Appendix)
Day 16 Review WebQuest activities in relation to essential questions, unit goals, writing activities. Students begin creating abstract paintings.	**Day 17** Mini-Lesson with handouts: Quotation Marks and Proofreading Symbols. Students share abstract paintings. Review Personal Narrative Evaluation and typing guidelines.	**Day 18** Students type and print final draft. Peers edit using proofreading symbols. Students correct errors, print final copy and hand in with Personal Narrative Evaluation and all drafts. Exit slip: Give at least three reasons why your personal narrative is an effective piece of writing.	**Day 19** Review culminating project guidelines and rubric. Work on culminating project. Students may choose between "hard" poster and Power Point demonstration.	**Days 20-21** Sharing of culminating projects. Students evaluate unit activities and teacher performance.

EXHIBIT C   WebQuest Handout to Students

Introduction

Who Am I?

In pondering this question during our "Self Discovery, Self Expression" unit, you have addressed issues of self-exploration, family history, and personal growth. In addition to these personal issues, you will address the question:

How can I accurately express myself through abstract art?

Like writers, artists use their talents and resources to embark on journeys of self-discovery. Through this WebQuest, you are going to look at art, discover what abstract art is, and then select appropriate colors and shapes to express your own sense of self. You will encounter websites that will help familiarize you with a number of contemporary artists who will serve as models for your own painting. You will also experience several roles, all of which will contribute to your understanding of art and how it can be an expression of self and a reflection of life.

The Task

Help! The O'Roark-Burgess Museum of Modern Art was robbed! Authorities are quickly closing in on two shifty looking suspects who they believe are masquerading as respectable teachers in our fair school. As we await the apprehension of these lawless (yet art-loving) criminals, museum curators O'Roark and Burgess need to build a new collection.

They need your help!

O'Roark wants to organize an exhibit of abstract art that reflects the personal nature of the artist. This exhibit will be titled "Self Discovery, Self Expression." You and your group will explore, discover, and create as you move through several roles.

1. Your journey will begin as Art Historians. Your group's task will be to research abstract art and specific artists.
2. Your group will then explore the role of Art Critic. Your task will be to learn to judge the art you previously encountered.
3. Finally, each member of your group will become an Artist. Your task will be to produce a piece of abstract art that reflects your personality and, specifically, your personal experiences shared in your narrative. You must give rationales for the choices you make when creating art. You will use the rationales when you design your final project.

The Process

As art historians, you must first complete the following activities.

1. As a group, choose one of these two web sites to visit. Each member of your group should then complete a handout that can be answered as you explore the site.

A. A. Pintura, Art Detective   http://eduweb.com/pintura
B. Inside Art: An Adventure in Art History   http://eduweb.com.insideart/index.html

2. Visit the National Museum of American Art.   http://www.nmaa.si.edu

A. Find and examine a number of abstract paintings.
B. As a group, select one piece to write about. Discuss this piece. What do you see? Shapes, color, mood, etc.? How does this piece relate to your personal experiences? What does it remind you of? What things do you recognize? What is the artist trying to say? How do you feel about this?

EXHIBIT C   Continued

As art critics, you must complete the following activities.

1. Visit Color Perception   http://www.insteam.com/LauraFunderburk
2. Fill out "Create Your Own Art—Part 1"
3. Visit How to Read a Painting   http://www.kcsd.k12.pa.us/~projects/critic/process.html
4. Fill out "Create Your Own Art—Part 2"

You will become an artist and produce a great piece of art! Your painting must reflect the mood and feeling of your personal narrative.

You will create a poster that "sells" your artwork to the O'Roark-Burgess Museum. Poster guidelines:

- You must use a full-size poster board for your display.
- You must feature your abstract piece in a desirable and effective manner.
- On the poster, you must give rationales for the color and shape choices you made for your painting and why they are appropriate expressions of your personal narrative.
- You must select lines from your personal narrative that reflect you and include on your poster.

Evaluation

You will be graded on the following for this portion of the unit.

1. Completion of WebQuest activities.
2. Completion of an abstract piece reflecting your personal narrative.
3. Completion of a poster presenting your piece along with appropriate rationales and narrative excerpts.
4. Completion of a two-page rationale explaining your poster.

Conclusion

The O'Roark-Burgess Museum of Modern Art has been saved and the "Self Discovery, Self Expression" Exhibit has become a huge success! All of this thanks to your efforts! The curators hope that this journey of self-exploration has been personally fulfilling and that you will continue to express your individuality through writing and art.

EXHIBIT D   Using National and State Documents to Guide Curriculum Planning

Traci and Rae examined the following documents as they planned this unit.

Standards for the English Language Arts
Of the twelve national standards for the English language arts, Traci and Rae targeted the following.

Standard Three: "Students apply a wide range of strategies to comprehend, interpret, evaluate and appreciate texts. . . ."

Standard Five: "Students employ a wider range of strategies as they write and use different writing process elements appropriately to communicate with a variety of audiences for a variety of purposes."

Standard Eight: "Students use a variety of technological and informational resources. . . to gather and synthesize information and to create and communicate knowledge" (National Council of Teachers of English and International Reading Association, 1996, p. 3).

Kentucky Learner Goals and Academic Expectations
The state of Kentucky has adopted seven learning goals for all students and connected those goals to specific academic expectations. Traci and Rae targeted the following.

1.1 Students use reference tools . . . and research tools . . . to find the information they need to meet specific demands, explore interests, or solve specific problems.

1.2 Students make sense of the variety of materials they read.

1.11 Students write using appropriate forms, conventions, and styles to communicate ideas and information to different audiences for different purposes.

1.13 Students make sense of ideas and communicate ideas with the visual arts.

1.16 Students use computers and other kinds of technology to collect, organize, and communicate information and ideas (Kentucky Department of Education, 1994).

Program of Studies for English I
The *Program of Studies* specifies the minimum content to be covered in subjects required for high school graduation. The *Program of Studies for English I* blends the strands of reading, writing, speaking, listening, observing, and using technology as a communication tool. In addition, academic expectations for the arts and humanities are incorporated into the reading and writing strands. Traci and Rae made sure the unit was firmly grounded in the *Program of Studies.* For example, specific skills and processes included in the unit and taken from this document include:

- Identifying writers' purposes and techniques used to communicate with different audiences
- Using writing-to-learn strategies
- Writing personal pieces
- Critiquing own and others' works
- Accessing appropriate print and nonprint resources for group, collaborative, and/or independent inquiry projects

Core Content for Assessment
Kentucky's *Core Content for Assessment* specifies the content for which all students will be held accountable on its statewide test. Kentucky high-school students are assessed in the eleventh grade for their mastery of core content in required school subjects. Twelfth-graders must complete a writing portfolio in order to graduate. Even though Traci and Rae teach at the ninth-grade level, they use the *Core Content* to ensure they are teaching the knowledge and skills students will need to succeed on the statewide assessments. Following are three examples of how they incorporated core content into this unit.

EXHIBIT D   Continued

1. The twelfth-grade writing portfolio must include a piece of personal expressive writing. In this unit, ninth-graders will gain experiences in writing personal narratives. As twelfth-graders, they might choose to revise these narratives and include them in their portfolios.
2. On the statewide assessment, student writing is evaluated according to the Kentucky Holistic Writing Scoring Rubric. Student writing is evaluated for awareness of audience and purpose, organization, idea development, and standards of correctness. Traci and Rae will evaluate the students' narratives using these criteria.
3. The Core Content for Arts and Humanities, on which students will be tested in the eleventh grade, specifies that students incorporate the elements of art and principles of design to generate several solutions to a variety of visual art problems.

Transformations: Curriculum Framework
This two-volume document provides direction to schools and districts as they develop curriculum. It offers further explanation of academic expectations, suggestions on teaching and learning strategies, and multiple resources to assist with the development of curriculum and units of study.

How to Develop a Standards-Based Unit of Study
This document, produced by the Kentucky Department of Education, is available in hard copy or electronically to all teachers in Kentucky. It helps teachers walk through the planning process step-by-step to ensure that the curriculum they develop is closely linked to state goals. Traci and Rae followed the steps described in this document as they planned their unit.

NOTE: (All Kentucky documents referenced here may be viewed at the web site of the Kentucky Department of Education >http://www.kde.state.ky.us<)

SUMMARY

At the beginning of this chapter, I described how my experiences as a new teacher contributed to my understanding of school curriculum. As you reflect on the contents of this chapter, and as you anticipate teaching in a specific school and community, begin thinking about which issues might influence your classroom curriculum. Think also about how your own perspectives, beliefs, and values in regard to teaching will influence your classroom curriculum and the curriculum of the school where you might teach.

Because curriculum is complex and multidimensional, you will likely broaden and deepen your understanding of it over time, just as I did. As you gain a better understanding of how personal, social, political, religious, academic, and cultural factors influence the curriculum you teach and the materials you use, you will be better prepared to meet the educational needs of your students. Among the key points to remember are:

- Many different definitions of curriculum exist. It is important to consider the following dimensions when attempting to define curriculum: the *intended* curriculum, the *taught* curriculum, the *learned* curriculum, and the *historical* curriculum.

- At the national level, the development of standards has dominated curriculum initiatives in the 1980s and 1990s. At the state level, high-stakes testing and accountability increasingly influence the classroom curriculum. Within these bureaucratic contexts, much curriculum development occurs at the district and school levels. Teachers have the ultimate responsibility for transforming the intended curriculum into daily instructional activities and interactions with students.
- Textbooks play an important role in the implementation of the classroom curriculum. They can be useful tools for organizing and implementing classroom curriculum. When they become central to delivering instruction, the needs of teachers may be met, but probably at the expense of students' needs.
- Culturally relevant curriculum is student-centered; ensures that students' needs are addressed before, during, and after the presentation of the intended curriculum; and offers students multiple pathways to learning skills, knowledge, and attitudes.
- Curriculum should be developmentally appropriate. For example, the growing middle-school movement emphasizes integrative and/or interdisciplinary curriculum geared toward the characteristics, interests, and needs of early adolescents.
- While many high schools still adhere to a subject-centered curriculum and to the "factory model" of school structure, an increasing number are successfully restructuring time, resources, and curriculum to better meet the needs of all students.

This chapter has focused on defining and describing the many dimensions of curriculum and the contexts that influence its implementation in the classroom. In Chapter Six, "Planning for Middle- and High-School Instruction," you will extend your understanding of curriculum by seeing how curricular decision-making is central to the planning process. You will see how experienced teachers identify instructional purposes, select and organize content and activities, propose learning outcomes, and reflect upon students' personal, social, and academic needs whether creating curriculum for a year, a semester, a unit of instruction, or from day to day.

▪▪ BUILDING YOUR BIOGRAPHY, YOUR PERSONAL PRACTICAL PHILOSOPHY, AND PORTFOLIO

Building Your Biography

What experiences in your life are relevant to creating curriculum for middle- and high-school students? The following questions are intended to help you generate ideas for composing a chapter of your educational biography. They are not intended to be answered sequentially or to limit your exploration of the topic.

Think about the curriculum you experienced as a student in kindergarten, early elementary, later elementary, middle/junior high school, high school, and college.

- How would you describe the curriculum at each of these levels?
- How did the curriculum change as you progressed through school?

- To what degree was the curriculum student-centered at the various levels? To what degree was it content-centered?
- What experiences do you have with curriculum outside the school setting? For example, did you study a sport, craft, or art as you were growing up? How was the curriculum like or unlike that of your formal schooling?
- How were the values of the community in which you grew up reflected in the school curriculum you experienced?
- Can you recall any instances of controversy over the curriculum?
- As you reflect on your schooling, can you point to one instance of the *null curriculum*—that which was deliberately not taught?
- Have you ever experienced the *hidden curriculum*—ideas, attitudes, and values that are implicitly taught (e.g., competition is natural and good)?

Developing Your Personal Practical Philosophy

Draft a section of your personal educational philosophy that addresses curriculum. You might respond to questions such as the following.

- How do you define curriculum?
- Where do you stand on the content-centered/student-centered continuum?
- What sources will you draw upon to create curriculum in your classroom?
- How important is content in your subject area?
- How can you make the curriculum in your subject area culturally relevant?
- How would curriculum in your classroom differ from middle- to high-school level?
- Where do you stand on national and state curriculum initiatives?

Collecting Artifacts for Your Portfolio

Review the Reader Activities you have completed in this chapter. Identify any that you might eventually select for your portfolio. For each, jot down notes that will help you recall later what you were thinking at the time you completed the activity, what challenges you encountered while completing it, what you learned from doing it, and how this activity reveals something about who you will be as a teacher. Don't worry about style or correctness at this point. The purpose is to begin documenting your thinking as you move through this book and this class.

References

Apple, M. (1993). *Official knowledge.* New York: Routledge.

Armstrong, D. (1989). *Developing and documenting the curriculum.* Needham Heights, MA: Allyn & Bacon.

Beane, J. (1993). *A middle school curriculum: From rhetoric to reality.* Columbus, OH: National Middle School Association.

Carnegie Council on Adolescent Development. (1989). *Turning points: Preparing American youth for the 21st century.* New York: Carnegie Corporation.

Carter, R. T., & Goodwin, A. L. (1994). Racial identity and education. *Review of Research in Education, 20,* 291–336.

Cuban, L. (1996). Curriculum stability and change. In P. W. Jackson (Ed.), *Handbook of research on curriculum* (pp. 216–247). New York: Macmillan.

Darling-Hammond, L. & Falk, B. (1997). Using standards and assessments to support student learning. *Kappan, 79,* 190–199.

Delpit, L. D. (1988). The silenced dialogue: Power and pedagogy in educating other people's children. *Harvard Educational Review,* 58(3), 280–298.

Doll, W. (1993). *A post-modern perspective on curriculum.* New York: Teachers College Press.

Eisner, E. W. (1996). Curriculum ideologies. In P. W. Jackson (Ed.), *Handbook of Research on Curriculum* (pp. 302–326). New York: Macmillan.

Erickson, F., & Shulz, J. (1996). Students' experience of the curriculum. In P. W. Jackson (Ed.), *Handbook of Research on Curriculum* (pp. 465–485). New York: Macmillan.

Gay, G. (1988). Designing relevant curricula for diverse learners. *Education and Urban Society,* 29(4), 327–340.

Hollins, E. R. (1996). *Culture in school learning: Revealing the Deep Meaning.* Mahwah, NJ: Lawrence Erlbaum.

Kendall, J. S. & Marzano, R. J. (1996). *Content knowledge: A compendium of standards and benchmarks for K-12 education.* Aurora, CO: Mid-Continent Educational Laboratory.

Kenny, M., O'Donnell, M. & Smith, C. (1996). Student-directed theme planning. In *Integrated thematic teaching,* (pp. 61–72). Washington, DC: National Education Association.

Kentucky Department of Education (1994). *Kentucky's learning goals and Academic Expectations: What Kentucky high school graduates should know and be able to do as they exit public schools.* Frankfort, KY: Author.

Ladson-Billings, G. (1994). *The dreamkeepers: Successful teachers of African American children.* San Francisco: Jossey Bass.

LeTendre, G. & Baker, D. (1998, June 17). International competitiveness in science. *Education Week,* pp. 46, 51.

Mid-Continent Regional Educational Laboratory. (1997). *Content knowledge home page.* Available at http://www.mcrel.org, September 26, 1997.

National Commission on Excellence in Education. (1983). *A nation at risk: The imperative for educational reform.* Washington, DC: United States Department of Education.

National Council of Teachers of Mathematics. (1989). *Curriculum and evaluation standards for school mathematics.* Reston, Virginia: Author.

Nieto, S. (1992). *Affirming diversity: The sociopolitical context of multicultural education.* New York: Longman.

Noddings, N. (1997). Thinking about standards. *Phi Delta Kappan, (79),* 184–189.

Oakes, J. (1985). *Keeping track: How schools structure inequality.* New Haven, CT: Yale University Press.

Peshkin, A. (1996). The relationship between culture and curriculum: A many fitting thing. In P. W. Jackson (Ed.), *Handbook of Research on Curriculum* (pp. 248–267). New York: Macmillan.

Powell, R. (In press). Teaching alike: A cross-case analysis of first-career and second-career beginning teachers' instructional convergence. *Teaching and Teacher Education.*

Powell, R. 1993. Seventh graders' perspectives of their interdisciplinary team. *Middle School Journal,* 24(3), 49–57.

Powell, R., Skoog, G., & Troutman, P. (1996). On streams and odysseys: Reflections on reform and research in middle level integrative learning environments. *Research in Middle Level Education Quarterly,* 19(4), 1–30.

Powell, R., Zehm, S., & Garcia, J. (1996). *Field experience: Strategies for exploring diversity in schools.* Upper Saddle River, NJ: Merrill/Prentice Hall.

Reigeluth, C. M. (1997). Educational standards: To standardize or to customize learning? *Phi Delta Kappan,* 79(3), 202–206.

Rose, M. (1995). *Possible lives: The promise of public education in America.* New York: Houghton Mifflin.

Sadker, M., & Sadker, D. (1994). *Failing at fairness: How America's schools cheat girls.* New York: Charles Scribner's Sons.

Stevenson, C., & Carr, J. F. (Eds.). (1992). *Integrated studies in the middle grades: "Dancing through walls."* New York: Teachers College Press.

Trueba, H., Jacobs, L., & Kirton, E. (1990). *Cultural conflict and adaptation: The case of Hmong children in American Society.* New York: Falmer Press.

Tanner, D., & Tanner, L. (1995). *Curriculum development: Theory into practice* (3rd ed). Upper Saddle River, NJ: Merrill/ Prentice Hall.

United States Department of Education. (1991). *America 2000: An education strategy.* Washington, DC: Author.

Wigginton, E. (1985). *Sometimes a shining moment: The Foxfire experience.* New York: Anchor Press/Doubleday.

Wilson, P. (1991). Trauma of Sioux Indian high school students. *Anthropology and Education Quarterly, 22,* 367–383.

Websites

http://www.nassp.org
(National Association of Secondary School Principals)

http://www.nmsa.org
(National Middle School Association—Middle school reform)

http://www.mcrel.org
(Mid-Continent Regional Education Laboratory—standards and many other resources)

http://www.coreknowledge.org
(E. D. Hirsch, Jr & Core Knowledge)

http://www.essentialschools.org
(Theodore Sizer and Essential Schools)

http://www.scott.k12.ky.us/9th/9th.html
(Scott County Ninth Grade School)

http://www.pbs.org/teachersource/
(Site for Public Broadcasting Service. Contains many useful resources for developing curriculum in most subject areas.)

6

Planning for Middle-and High-School Instruction

BUILDING ON BIOGRAPHY: TEACHING A PERSONAL INTERPRETATION OF HISTORY

I (Jesus) began teaching in the 1960s by appointing myself the expert in United States history. After all, I had earned a baccalaureate degree with a major in social studies and had read extensively in the general area of U.S. history with a specialization in the experiences of minorities (African, Mexican, Asian, and Native Americans) in the United States. I had grown up at a time when Americans were reflecting and raising questions about the nation's domestic and foreign policies. I had learned much from the popular press about America's treatment of its citizens and its policies toward Latin America, southeast Asia, and other parts of the world.

When I taught at the high-school level, I was responsible for sophomore and junior courses in U.S. and world history. My students were culturally diverse (i.e., White, Mexican and African American and working-and middle-class). Each year they entered my classroom with a variety of academic, social, and emotional strengths and weaknesses. Regardless of their characteristics, I was determined to integrate the historical experiences of Mexican Americans into my U.S. History classes. When I found the textbook wanting, I reviewed curriculum guides, history books, and other social studies materials describing the experiences of this group and attempted to include information I considered important into my instructional program. I was not going to lose the opportunity to highlight the exploitation Mexican Americans had experienced at the hands of Anglo Americans!

As I planned for instruction, it never occurred to me to ask myself whether my students needed my particular interpretation of U.S. history or how my interpretation of U.S. history fit into effective social studies education as described by leading scholars of the time. I did not question whether my approach to the teaching of U.S. history would help students learn about themselves and others and lead to responsible citizenship. I had not given much thought to the purpose of schools, a definition of social studies, or whether my interpretation of U.S. history complemented the interpretation held by the school district. My students learned U. S. history according to Jesus Garcia.

Questions to Consider

1. From what you have read of Jesus' biography so far, how did his school and life experiences influence who he became as a teacher?
2. Many teachers are experts on and feel passionate about topics, issues, and perspectives in their subject areas. What are the strengths and limitations of teaching one's "personal interpretation" of a subject?
3. What connections can you make between Jesus' story here and the topic of planning for instruction?

Purpose

Why do teachers plan for instruction? Planning allows teachers to organize what they wish to do for the year, semester, unit, and lesson. Second, good planning leads to meaningful instruction that facilitates student learning. Third, planning minimizes discipline problems. Students are less apt to involve themselves in off-task behavior when they know what is expected of them. Fourth, it allows for the articulation of subject matter, what Richard labeled in the previous chapter as "the intended curriculum." The art curriculum in a high school, for example, is planned as Art I, Art II, Art III, and so on. This means that Art II instructors expect students to have learned certain knowledge and skills in Art I, and that instructors for Art II will teach additional knowledge and skills that students should be familiar with when they enroll in Art III. Fifth, planning provides teachers with the opportunity to address individual needs. During the academic year, teachers conduct on-going dialogue with students to assess their strengths and weaknesses and gauge their interests. Finally, planning allows teachers to reflect on their ability to prepare for instruction and to evaluate their teaching. Teachers use this information to make changes in their teaching and to plan for the following year.

The purpose of this chapter is to introduce you to the many ways middle-and-high-school teachers plan for instruction. The chapter discusses the following: (1) major reasons teachers plan for instruction; (2) background information teachers bring to the planning process; (3) planning for the year, semester, unit, and individual lesson; (4) interdisciplinary planning; (5) standards-based planning; (6) major sections of a unit; and (7) examples of approaches to planning—subject-specific and student-based.

Specifically, this chapter will help you:

- understand why teachers plan for instruction
- gain insights into the background information teachers use when planning
- understand year, semester, lesson, interdisciplinary and standards-based planning
- understand two methods of planning for instruction - subject specific and student based
- follow the steps of two teachers using different approaches to planning and assess the strengths and weaknesses of each
- plan a unit and lesson in your subject area.

A special feature of this chapter is the "Planning Activities" that accompany the "Reader Activities." The "Planning Activities" enable you to go through the planning process step-by-step along with the teachers described in this chapter.

■■ WHAT DO TEACHERS BRING TO THE PLANNING TABLE?

Teachers employ an array of information when planning. For example, most teachers are familiar with documents describing the purposes of education, subject-area standards documents detailing what students should know (content) and be able to do (process and performance), and descriptions of specific planning approaches within subject areas. In this section we describe some of what teachers bring to the planning table.

■■ IDENTIFYING PURPOSES OF EDUCATION

What should be the purpose(s) of education? Many documents have attempted to answer this question, e.g., White House Conference on Education (1955); Educational Policies Commission (1935–1968); America 2000: An Education Strategy (1991). One document that has withstood the test of time (almost eight decades) is "*The Cardinal Principles of Secondary Education*" (1918), a document compiled by the National Education Association's

Commission on the Reorganization of Secondary Education. This document lists general purposes schools should pursue (i.e., health, command of fundamental processes [communication skills], worthy home-membership, vocational preparation, citizenship, worthy use of leisure time, and ethical character) followed by a brief description of each.

As we usher in the twenty-first century, many educators, politicians, students, and parents are calling for a greater focus on the aims and purpose of schools (Cheney, 1987; Finn & Ravitch, 1987; Hirsch, 1987). The command of fundamental processes (e.g., reading, writing, mathematics), for example, remains a high priority and has expanded to mean mastering the language of technology. The definition of citizenship also has changed. Today, educators and politicians speak about citizens living in a global village where political events occurring in one nation may affect others in a matter of seconds.

Today, standards documents exist for most major subject areas in the K-12 curriculum. (See Chapter Five, Figure 5.1) These documents help teachers align their personal definitions of a subject area and its purpose(s) with the views of many other educators in the discipline.

▪▪ CONCEPTUALIZING SUBJECT AREAS

Teachers know much about their subject areas. Because many are well grounded in subject-matter content, they are familiar with a variety of approaches to planning in their specific area. For example, teachers have conceptualized the definition and purpose of social studies—to promote citizenship—as (1) the transmission of the nation's history, traditions, and values; (2) an exploration and study of one or more of the social science disciplines; (3) an examination of contemporary issues and problems; and (4) providing for the well being of the individual (Allen & Stevens, 1994, p. 22–24). In the middle grades, approaches to reading in the language arts curriculum include basal reading programs, literature-based programs, Chapter 1/remedial programs, and reading-to-learn-in-the-content-areas classes. Similarly, several approaches are associated with science teaching: conceptual-change, activity-driven, discovery learning, and didactic learning (Muth & Alvermann, 1992, p. 98–109). Teachers adopt a particular conceptualization of their subject area based on a number of factors, including their personal experiences, preparation, and experiences in the classroom. But because they are eclectics, they also incorporate one or more of the other conceptualizations in their teaching.

In the following exercises, we provide you with an opportunity to gain background information that may help you understand why knowing different approaches to planning can help you become a more successful teacher. As you complete each exercise, reflect on what you learned that may be helpful as you become familiar with planning for instruction.

▪ **Reader Activity 6.1**

IN THE FIELD
Interviewing Students About Your Subject Area

Review the definition and purpose of your subject area as stated by its respective professional organization. Ask a group of middle-or high-school learners to define and describe the subject area. Try to determine their views in the following areas.

- How do students describe your subject area? As a collection and mastery of facts? As a process of becoming familiar with big ideas, and then using these ideas to address practical and intellectual problems and trends?
- What do students say they do to learn in the subject area?
- How do students describe assessment and evaluation? Do they believe they are being properly evaluated with respect to their learning in the subject area?
- What are the students' feelings about your subject area? Do they enjoy it?

Report your findings to the class.

As you listen to groups present the results of their interviews, determine if there are any differences between the responses of middle-and high-school learners. What do the student responses suggest about teaching your subject area in a middle school? High school?

▌Planning Activity 6.1

PURPOSE, DEFINITION, AND APPROACHES TO TEACHING IN YOUR SUBJECT AREA

Locate and examine a document that addresses the purpose(s) of education. (Several have been cited earlier in this chapter.) Based on this document, formulate a statement of the purpose(s) of education that seem most relevant to your subject area. Next, consult one of the professional documents in your subject area, such as the national standards, in order to formulate a definition of your subject area. Using this document (or others you discover or that are recommended to you by your instructor), identify common approaches to teaching in your subject area. As you complete this background work, begin thinking about a topic in your subject area that you would enjoy developing into a two-week instructional unit.

■■ TWO APPROACHES TO PLANNING

Articulation of subject matter and addressing student needs are two reasons teachers plan for instruction. In this section, we define these two planning approaches. Teachers who begin with subject matter we describe as *subject-specific*. These teachers first identify the essential content, skills, dispositions in a discipline or topic under study. They may review essential documents such as *"The Cardinal Principles of Education"* as they look to courses of study, textbooks, and other curricular material to guide their planning. Once the initial planning begins, they also reflect on student needs to build instruction.

The second group of teachers—those who focus on the needs of students—we describe as *student-based*. While these teachers are aware of the essential information of their subject area, they allow the informal and formal assessing they do in the classroom to guide their planning. They pay particular attention to student interests, academic strengths and weaknesses, and problems and issues when developing instruction. For example, after administering an initial fitness test, a physical education teacher might decide to spend more time on activities that build endurance in order to address a class weakness. In addition, the teacher has observed that the students enjoy working together and decides to build on this strength by placing students in teams to work on endurance.

Arends (1998) describes subject-specific teachers as "rational-linear" and student-based teachers as "nonlinear" to illustrate the models they employ when planning for instruction:

rational-linear (i.e., goals————->actions————->outcomes)
nonlinear (i.e., actions————->outcomes————->goals (p. 41).

The rational-linear model places the focus on goals and objectives as the first step in a sequential process. Modes of action and specific activities are then selected from available alternatives to accomplish "prespecified ends" (p. 41). The planning process employed by a subject-specific teacher follows this sequence.

1. Specify the desired outcomes (goals and objectives).
2. Identify students' strengths and weaknesses.
3. Outline and sequence learning activities.
4. Evaluate the outcomes of instruction.

Nonlinear planning, that utilized by student-based teachers, "start[s] with actions that in turn produce outcomes (some anticipated, some not), and finally [teachers] summarize and explain their actions by assigning goals to them" (Arends, p. 41). Teachers who follow this format are "spontaneous" planners. They are familiar with goals and purposes, but their planning is influenced by the daily realities of teaching. The planning process employed by a student-based teacher follows this sequence.

1. Identify students' strengths and weaknesses.
2. Outline and sequence learning activities.
3. Evaluate the outcomes of instruction.
4. Specify the desired outcomes (goals and objectives).

Teachers who are effective in the classroom employ both of these models on a daily basis. They are flexible; they know that a single approach to planning will not be adequate in today's classroom. Years of experience have made them sensitive to sequence; the unpredictable relations between teacher, students, and subject area; the porous boundaries among them; and how decision-making continuously shifts as the day-to-day happenings of school life influence what occurs in the classroom.

■■ PLANNING FOR INSTRUCTION

We begin this section by describing factors that influence planning. Time, for example, influences the level of specificity given to planning: yearly planning is usually sketchy and unit planning more detailed. School structure also plays a role in planning. Some schools, for example, encourage interdisciplinary approaches to planning. A third influential factor is school reform. As a result of factors such as school accountability and the standards movement, states, districts, and schools may require teachers to show that they are addressing reform measures in their planning.

Yearly Planning

As teachers begin to visualize the academic year, planning for instruction serves many purposes. One purpose is to acculturate students to the particular approach teachers use to carry out instruction. Teachers, for example, may use the first few weeks of the academic year to introduce students to rules, routines, and procedures; to plan and carry out instruction that emphasizes process (approaches to examining a subject area; ways of thinking) over content; to identify student interests, strengths, and weaknesses; and to build a sense of community.

As they begin to plan for the year, teachers may review the academic calendar and identify the beginning and ending dates of the semester, holidays, state-wide testing periods, and other days when instruction will not take place. During this initial planning, they may also check textbooks and other materials to make sure they have an adequate supply as well as review rosters to ascertain the size of their classes.

Yearly planning serves as the foundation for semester and unit planning. In this stage, teachers reflect on professional goals and objectives: what students should learn during the year. They identify information they would like to integrate in their classes and review courses of study and curriculum guides. They may review local and state mandates, examine course descriptions, and speak with previous instructors of the courses. They secure materials and gather information about their students' strengths and weaknesses as they speak formally and informally with department chairs, teams of teachers, individual teachers, and review student records. In this stage, as in other planning situations, teachers start at a point where they feel most comfortable.

Semester Planning

In the next stage, teachers plan for a semester, or whatever major divisions of the academic year the school has adopted. Semesters are approximately eighteen weeks long and broken into nine-week grading periods. For each grading period, teachers may plan three units of instruction. Planning for the semester is more detailed than yearly planning and includes the following:

- reviewing state and local mandates to identify the essential content, skills, dispositions to be included in the course
- inserting a personal perspective to content and instruction
- reviewing course syllabi of previous instructors (available from the department chair)
- focusing on the materials to be employed
- identifying specific student strengths and weaknesses
- outlining a tentative sequence of information (e.g., content, skills, and dispositions) to be presented during the semester.

This last stage represents an integration of all the steps and leads to the development of the course and units of instruction.

Figure 6.1 provides an example of semester planning in the area of the life sciences. The time frames given in this example are approximate. Teachers would undoubtedly include other learning as they plan their instruction in more detail, as their students acclimate to the culture of their classroom, and as they respond to school mandates (e.g., state wide testing).

Unit Planning

Unit planning is quite detailed. Teachers follow this general sequence in planning instructional units.

FIGURE 6.1 Course Title: "Learning About the Earth"

First Quarter
    Unit 1. Earth's Structure (two weeks)
    Unit 2. Earth's Resources (four weeks)
    Unit 3. Earth's History (three weeks)

Second Quarter
    Unit 4. Meteorology (three weeks)
    Unit 5. Oceanography (three weeks)
    Unit 6. Astronomy (three weeks)

---

1. Outline the concepts, concept clusters, or generalization(s) to be addressed.
2. Assess the level of difficulty of the content.
3. Establish instructional objectives.
4. Identify student strengths, weaknesses, and interests.
5. Establish performance objectives (what the student will need to know and do).
6. Sequence learning activities.
7. Synchronize student readings with teacher information.
8. Identify student activities (e.g., independent and group projects, writing assignments).
9. Map out teaching strategies.
10. Select formative and summative forms of assessment.

While subject-specific planners may begin by identifying content, student-based planners may begin by identifying student needs and interests.

There is no one preferred model of unit planning: a variety of models can be successfully implemented. The skeletal unit outline provided in Figure 6.2 represents one example of how to create a unit plan. As you become proficient in planning, you will develop a method that suits your purposes and instructional style.

FIGURE 6.2 Unit Outline

1. *Unit Topic Problem, or Theme* ("In Search of Gold," "How Can Acid Rain be Stopped?" "In Search of Self: Identity in the 21st Century")
2. *Background Information* (content, main ideas, key concepts)
3. *Teacher and Student Objectives* (knowledge, skills, attitudes/values/dispositions)
4. *Initiation* (suggestions for introducing the unit)
5. *Learning Activities* (a. introductory activities to focus attention on each main idea or problem to be investigated; b. developmental activities for intake, organization, application, and expression of content; c. concluding activities to state main idea, express idea creatively, and culminate the unit)
6. *Evaluation* (suggestions for assessment of learning during and at the end of the unit)
7. *Portfolio Options* (providing opportunities for student work to be included in portfolio)
8. *Bibliography* (references for teacher and students)

FIGURE 6.3A   Suggestions for Teaching in the Block Schedule

1. At the beginning of each semester, use "ice-breakers" and offer games and activities as a way of having students get to know one another and you.
2. Allow students to be creative. In various settings—alone, in pairs, small groups—encourage them to write poems, illustrate a short story, develop a game complete with rules, or a science experiment for others to complete.
3. Change the physical make-up of the class. Arrange desks differently, hold class at a different location (e.g., library, gym, outside), and redecorate your classroom on a regular basis.
4. Use cooperative grouping techniques such as jigsawing to complete lengthy tasks and place responsibility on the students to get tasks done.
5. Plan and use guest speakers and short field trips to connect students to their community.
6. Allow students to serve as teachers, and in a variety of settings, teach their peers. Probe and make use of student interests.
7. To provide breadth and depth, tie in and reinforce information being taught by other team members and in other disciplines.
8. Role play situations for better understanding and teaching. Have students pick a particular incident and alone or in a small group develop a skit.
9. Arrange for other teachers to come into your classroom and teach a mini-lesson.
10. Become friends with the school librarian/media specialist. Plan to have your students spend regular amounts of time researching and locating information and finding novel ways of presenting it.

Interdisciplinary Planning

In some middle and high schools, teachers may plan interdisciplinary units of instruction. One form of interdisciplinary planning refers to the integration of specific areas (e.g., human biology, genetics, ecology) within a general area of study (i.e., life sciences). In the physical sciences, meteorology, oceanography, and astronomy could be integrated into a unit of study entitled "The Earth's Resources." In the social studies, history, geography, economics, and government could be integrated to develop a unit on "The Rebuilding of Kosovo." This form of planning can be done by one teacher or a group of teachers.

A second form of interdisciplinary planning refers to the integration of content across the curriculum. Middle-school teachers frequently employ this form of planning. In the middle school, the focus is on personal development, skills for continued learning, and an introduction to the areas of organized knowledge. Instruction is active and varied, and students can progress at their own rates (George, Lawrence, Bushnell, 1998, p. 229). For example, a group of teachers could design an interdisciplinary unit of instruction entitled "The Beauty of Cities," drawing upon the curricula of several subject areas. Social studies students examine the historical and geographical descriptions of two or more cities; science students assess the scientific and technological advancements that have nurtured the growth of these cities; mathematics students graph the growth of the cities and display other data to help explain that growth; language arts students write descriptions highlighting the beauty of cities; and art and music students explore major works describing cities.

School structure also influences the planning process. One aspect of structure is the organization of teachers for instruction. In many middle schools, teachers form teams

FIGURE 6.3B   Examples of Block Planning

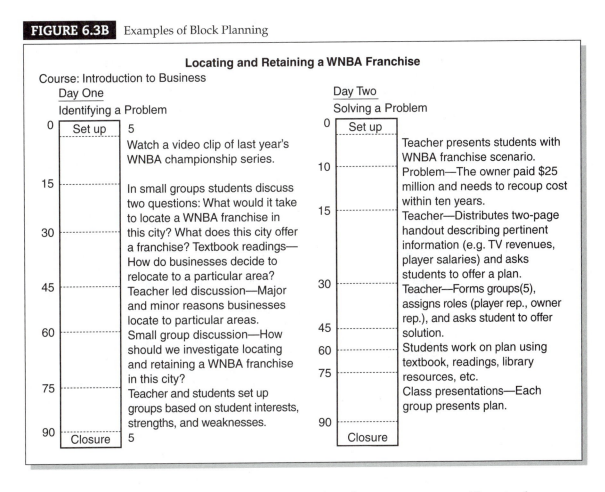

Locating and Retaining a WNBA Franchise

Course: Introduction to Business

Day One
Identifying a Problem

0 — Set up

5 — Watch a video clip of last year's WNBA championship series.

15 — In small groups students discuss two questions: What would it take to locate a WNBA franchise in this city? What does this city offer a franchise? Textbook readings— How do businesses decide to relocate to a particular area?

45 — Teacher led discussion—Major and minor reasons businesses locate to particular areas.

60 — Small group discussion—How should we investigate locating and retaining a WNBA franchise in this city?

75 — Teacher and students set up groups based on student interests, strengths, and weaknesses.

90 — Closure   5

Day Two
Solving a Problem

0 — Set up

Teacher presents students with WNBA franchise scenario.

10 — Problem—The owner paid $25 million and needs to recoup cost within ten years.

15 — Teacher—Distributes two-page handout describing pertinent information (e.g. TV revenues, player salaries) and asks students to offer a plan.

30 — Teacher—Forms groups(5), assigns roles (player rep., owner rep.), and asks student to offer solution.

45 —
60 — Students work on plan using textbook, readings, library

75 — resources, etc.
Class presentations—Each group presents plan.

90 — Closure

and are responsible for a group of students for one or more years. These teachers represent major subject areas (e.g., social studies, English/language arts, science, and math), and meet on a regular basis to plan interdisciplinary units reflective of their areas of expertise. Other teachers (e.g., art, music, physical education) and specialists (e.g., special education, vocational education, school counselor) serve as consultants to the teams.

Planning for Block Scheduling

In many middle and high schools, the fifty-minute class period has given way to block scheduling where classes may range from seventy to ninety minutes in length. With the increased flexibility that block scheduling allows, teams of teachers plan multiple activities (e.g., lecture, library time, group work, individual work, project), allowing students to experience subject areas in an integrated fashion at a pace more congruent to their needs.

Planning and teaching in "block" means planning for an extended period of time. It could also mean working with a team of teachers in structuring interdisciplinary lessons. Figure 6.3A provides suggestions for block planning and Figure 6.3B illustrates the first two day of a business unit employing block planning.

Standards-Based Planning

In Chapter Five, "Considering Curriculum for Middle-and High-School Students," you examined a curriculum unit developed collaboratively by Traci O'Roark and Rae Burgess. You discussed their unit as an example of culturally relevant, developmentally appropriate curriculum. They used a standards-based planning model to develop this unit. We will revisit the unit "Self Discovery, Self Expression" to gain an understanding of the standards-based planning process.

One purpose of the standards movement has been to articulate the knowledge and skills that all students should master by the time they graduate from high school. Standards identify broad outcomes of schooling. Unlike subject-specific planning, which begins with identification of content and activities, or student-based planning, which begins with reflection on student interest or factors influencing student learning, standards-based planning begins with the identification of desired outcomes: "What should students know and be able to do upon completion of this unit?" and "How will students show what they know and can do?" Standards-based planning does not disregard content, activities, or students' needs. Teachers consider all these factors when they engage in standards-based planning; but they use a different process, which is also referred to as "backwards planning." As you will see, "backwards planning" begins with the end in view and then builds the paths that students can take to reach that end (Wiggins & McTighe, 1993).

Traci and Rae began by brainstorming and agreeing on a unit *organizer*. Often written as a question, the organizer should set the context for learning and engage students in exploring an issue or problem. The organizer, or guiding question, should be open-ended yet focused, nonjudgmental, intellectually challenging, and succinct (Traver, 1998). Traci and Rae (Kentucky Department of Education, 1998; Traver, 1998) settled on the question "Who am I?" as their organizer. Other examples of subject-area guiding questions are:

What is a good proof?	Mathematics
How do waves originate?	Physics
What is health?	Health/Physical Education
When are laws fair?	Government
How would a new factory affect my community?	Business

Having selected an organizer, Traci and Rae turned to national, state, and local documents in order to target standards for the unit. They used the *National Standards for English Language Arts,* the *Kentucky Learner Goals and Academic Expectations,* the *Core Content for Assessment,* and the *Program of Studies for English I* to identify the most relevant standards.

Next, they generated several *essential questions*. Essential questions narrow the focus of the organizer. They, too, should be open-ended and encourage higher-order thinking and inquiry. These questions should be written in language students can understand because they will be shared with students to direct their learning. Traci and Rae generated four essential questions: (1) How have my past experiences sculpted my present sense of self? (2) How do I describe myself? (3) How can I most accurately express myself through the arts? (4) How can I most accurately express myself through writing? These questions flow naturally from the organizer "Who am I?" Questions they considered but discarded were: (1) Should teenagers have to abide by curfews? (too narrow; leading) (2) Why are the arts important? (too broad; leading) (3) Given the complexity of today's society in terms of the global economy, cultural diversity, and increasing technology, what might my life be like in the next millennium? (too confusing; too broad).

Traci and Rae used all their work up to this point to develop a culminating, authentic performance that would allow students to demonstrate that they could answer the unit's essential questions. They also wanted to give students a role, an authentic purpose, and an authentic audience beyond the teacher. They settled on this project: "Students will create a poster that 'sells' their art work to the O'Roark-Burgess Museum." The poster guidelines specified that, over the course of the unit, students would create a work of abstract art that expressed who they were. On the poster, students would need to explain their choices about color, shape, and line, and they would need to link their art work to the personal narratives they had written. Review Exhibit A and the Unit Overview presented in Chapter Five. How does this culminating project link to the essential questions?

Examples of possible roles, products, purposes, and audiences for culminating performances in other subject areas are:

Subject Area	Role	Product	Purpose	Audience
Science	Photographer	create a photo essay	to document environmental impact of waste disposal	for school open house
U.S. history	Historian	audiotape interviews with Vietnam veterans	to represent a variety of perspectives toward war	for local historical society's tribute to Veterans' Day
Health	Athlete	develop a fitness guide	to recommend healthful diet and exercise practices	for new junior and varsity athletes
Vocational Education	Mechanic	repair a small appliance and write a guide for small appliance repair	to help others decide whether to repair or discard small appliances	for small businesses in community

Once Traci and Rae had defined the culminating performance, they created a scoring guide of the critical attributes they would look for in the poster. These included the aesthetic qualities of the poster; the extent to which the art work reflected knowledge of art principles studied in the unit; the extent to which the student made insightful connections between her art work and her personal narrative; and the quality of the writing selected for inclusion on the poster.

At this juncture, Traci and Rae identified the skills, knowledge, instructional activities, and formative assessments that would lead students to be successful on their culminating performance. Lee Carter, the special education teacher, identified areas where she could provide help to individuals and instruction that could benefit the whole class but especially the students with learning difficulties. The three also identified the resources they would need to accomplish their goals. Traci and Rae had just completed

FIGURE 6.4   Day Five: Introduction to Abstract Art

Objectives
1. Students will identify how mood is expressed in the arts.
2. Students will explain how artistic elements are strategically manipulated in order to create mood and other effects.
3. Students will use art terminology to describe works of art.
4. Students will create mood in their own works of art.

Connections to *Kentucky Learner Goals and Academic Expectations*
Goal 1:3: Students will make sense of the various things they observe.
Goal 1.13: Students will make sense of and communicate ideas with visual arts.
Goal 1.14: Students will make sense of and communicate ideas with music.
Goal 2.23: Students will analyze their own and others' artistic products using accepted standards.
Goal 6.3: Students will expand their understanding of existing knowledge by making connections with new knowledge, skills, and experiences.

Materials

Overhead projector	CD player
Transparencies	Colored pencils/markers
Musical selections	

Procedure
1. While teacher performs administrative duties, students freewrite: "What do writers, musicians, and other artists have in common?" (5 minutes)
2. Large-group discussion of ideas generated in freewriting. Teacher will connect comments to previous days' activities and to today's objectives. (5 minutes)
3. Students already understand "mood" in popular music. The teacher will play selections from Mazzy Star, the Beach Boys, and Jimi Hendrix (all of which have distinct moods) while students express their understanding of each mood through the following steps.
   a. Write a word/phrase at the top of your paper that captures the mood of the musical excerpt.
   b. Create lines expressive of that mood.
   c. Create shapes/forms expressive of that mood.
   d. Use colors expressive of that mood.

Collaborating teachers circulate to give individual help and encouragement during this activity. Lead teacher creates abstract drawings along with students. (15 minutes)

4. Students share drawings with a partner. Volunteers share drawings with whole class. (5 minutes)
5. Teacher will project color transparencies of abstract works of art (e.g., *Red Canna*/Georgia O'Keeffe; *Le Vieux Guitarriste Aveugle*/Pablo Picasso). Teacher will use two transparencies to model analyzing how an artist manipulates line, color, and form in order to create a mood. Students will then independently write analyses of two paintings to share in large-group discussion. (15 minutes)
6. Teacher asks, "What did we learn today about how artists create mood?" Teacher asks students to complete exit slips: "What questions/comments do you have regarding abstract art?" Teacher explains that students will further explore mood in art next week when they begin WebQuest. (5 minutes)

Assessment
Teacher will assess participation, artistic responses to music, and written analyses of paintings to determine whether students have achieved the objectives.

Block scheduling allows students to engage in multiple activities at a pace more congruent to their needs.

training on WebQuest and were excited about integrating this technology into the unit. Refer to Exhibit B, the calendar for the "Self Discovery, Self-Expression" unit in the previous chapter, to see how the teachers sketched out each day.

Even at this point, the teachers' work was not complete. They would need to adjust their plan to accommodate unforeseen occurrences eventualities, such as computer problems and deadline extensions. And they would certainly learn much from students' culminating performances that would help them revise the unit for the next year.

Let's look now at one lesson plan from the "Self Discovery, Self Expression" Unit—Day Five: Introduction to Abstract Art (see Fig. 6.4). As you examine the plan, notice how the objectives, activities, and assessment link to the state standards, *The Kentucky Learner Goals and Academic Expectations* (1994).

■■ TWO APPROACHES TO UNIT PLANNING

Experienced teachers do not necessarily ponder the goals of education or the purpose(s) of a subject area each time they plan a unit. Rather, as a result of their experience, they have internalized this information, and it influences their planning as they focus on the needs of students, selecting curriculum, and pedagogy. We will now follow the process of two experienced teachers as they plan a unit of instruction. Sandy Eichhorst, a high school social studies teacher, takes a subject-specific approach to planning. Brian Kahn, a middle school social studies teacher, employs a student-based approach.

Subject-Specific Planning
Case Study: Sandy Eichhorst

Sandy Eichhorst is a U. S. history teacher at Centennial High School in Champaign, Illinois. We will observe her as she plans a two-week unit on "The Roaring Twenties." (Often, instructional units are restricted to one-, two-, three- or four-week time periods to maintain high student interest.) Sandy begins by concentrating on the first two steps of the planning process: specifying outcomes and identifying student needs. Sandy will identify content that will provide students with opportunities to study the topic in depth, to practice and extend skills, and to explore specific core civic values. She begins by drawing on her expertise in political science and her interest in the time period, reviewing the curriculum materials available, and assessing the needs of the students.

Sandy has the materials to explore the Twenties from a variety of perspectives. While the textbook is a major tool in her instructional approach, she also will use a variety of other resources, such as "Primary Source" folders she has compiled for particular events and issues in U.S. history. She will also consult with her colleagues about successful approaches to teaching the Twenties and identify community resources that might enhance the unit (for example, an historian who specializes in this decade and who teaches at the local community college). She thinks about incorporating the computer game *Decisions, Decisions* (Tom Snyder Productions) to discuss prejudice and, by extension, sexism in the Twenties. She is attracted to this program because it is designed to be used with the whole class and with one computer. She will also encourage her students to use Internet search engines to identify sites relevant to this time period. This year, she decides to focus on the following social studies themes: "power, authority, governance," "culture," "science, technology, and society," and "time, continuity, and change." (These themes are referred to as "standards" in National Council for the Social Studies [NCSS] documents.)

Mrs. Eichhorst is considering using "culture" to connect with the other themes and with the students. She reasons that, because of the diversity in her classroom and because some of her students are recent immigrants, they will have no difficulty exploring the diverse cultures of the Twenties, cultural borrowing, the forces that restricted and promoted cultural borrowing, and similarities between cultures then and now. Second, because students are sensitive to "style," Sandy will introduce the unit by inviting the historian from the community college to dress as a flapper and discuss why she has adopted this particular style of dress. This activity will become the introductory activity ("hook") to help students make the connection between culture and politics.

Teachers attempt to expand thematic learning by providing young adults with opportunities to move beyond the personal dimensions of knowledge to public understanding. As students gain a greater understanding of themes, they are able to engage in communication with an audience beyond their immediate environments. One of Sandy's goals is to have students gain a more comprehensive understanding of the theme "power, authority, and governance." Early in the unit, she will pose the question: What is more important to the individual—self-interest or the general welfare of society? In a culturally diverse classroom, this question becomes challenging and complex as students discuss their backgrounds, learn of the importance of the individual and society, and use this information to gain a rich understanding of "power, authority, and governance."

Sandy will use a *generalization* to guide the development of the unit (see Fig. 6.5). The themes she has selected will be embedded in the generalization. She reflects on the themes, her interests, the availability of resources, and the needs of her students, and then develops the following generalization:

> Sandwiched between two wars, the Twenties was a time of political change, a hands-off approach toward business, and a decade of social change and major scientific and technological advancements.

Mrs. Eichhorst is now at the "thinking-it-through" stage of the planning process: the outlining and sequencing of learning activities, and the evaluating of the outcomes of instruction.

Given the themes, she will consider four important questions:

1. In what order and at what level of intensity should I present these themes so that students gain a greater understanding of them?
2. How might I show interrelationships among the themes?
3. What content about the Twenties will provide students with an understanding of the themes, and the interrelationships among them, and create greater understanding of the Roaring Twenties?
4. What are appropriate methods of assessment? She has partially answered these questions by indicating how she would treat this decade and the role her students would play in shaping the unit.

Sandy is now ready to identify *core knowledge,* (see Fig. 6.6), content from the social studies that will provide for an examination of the themes.

After reflecting on her students and the identified generalization, Sandy selects the core knowledge she believes her students should possess about the Twenties. Note that she draws from several disciplines.

- The Harding administration (history and political science)
- President Coolidge's beliefs and policies (political science and economics)
- Factors such as technology, management methods, and credit that played a part in the prosperity of the time period (economics)

FIGURE 6.5   What Are Generalizations?

Generalizations are statements with wide applicability that are true or that can be verified on the basis of the evidence provided by the teacher and students. They are broad statements—summaries of information obtained from considerable evidence. They are powerful tools in the classroom because they provide students the opportunity—as a class, in a group, or independently—to explore, challenge, and offer evidence to support or alter statements thought to be true. The following are examples of generalizations from other subject areas.

- Problem-solving in mathematics involves using multiple approaches to computation, including estimation, mental mathematics, paper-and-pencil methods and technology.
- Elements with similar arrangements of outer shell electrons have similar properties.
- Geometry provides important methods for reasoning and solving problems in one, two, or three dimensions. Its applications are widespread in construction, mapping, architecture, and elsewhere.

FIGURE 6.6   What Is Core Knowledge? Why Is It Important?

Core knowledge refers to the knowledge, skills, and dispositions that will enable students to pursue independently their own intellectual interests in a discipline or across disciplines.

Core knowledge provides students with the opportunity to make choices. Without it, students are unlikely to possess the prerequisites to explore, identify, and examine issues, events, time periods, and personalities. When students are equipped with core knowledge, they are able to take responsibility for their own learning; they are free to let their intellectual curiosity drive their explorations of ideas and knowledge.

Certainly selecting core knowledge reflects subjective judgment, but teachers are professionals who attempt to minimize bias in planning. Sandy, for example, favors a political interpretation to historical issues and events, but is aware that student needs and interests also are important and will influence her planning. Once teachers identify the core knowledge, they believe is essential, they move from the role of directors to facilitators as they help students extend their knowledge, learn new skills, and gain a more complex understanding of events, topics, issues, and personalities.

- Influence of Henry Ford, a giant of the period (economics and social history)
- Changes in women's lives (sociology and social history)
- Societal reactions to Prohibition (sociology)
- Media, entertainment, and literature (social history, sociology, English/American literature)
- Examples of fear and intolerance that surfaced during the time period (sociology and social history)

Next, Sandy allocates days and amounts of time to the core knowledge, and assigns *instructional objectives* to each time period. Instructional objectives indicate the intentions of the teacher. Sandy also will develop skeletal lesson plans, including *performance objectives,* that is, statements describing what the students will do to show learning. This preliminary plan represents the "ideal" unit. In reality, she will continue to revise her plan over the next few months before the unit is implemented.

Mrs. Eichhorst teaches in a school and a department where instruction occurs in fifty-minute periods, a structure that influences the number and nature of the activities she plans for her students. Sandy will allocate instructional time to cover the core knowledge and conduct other student activities in the following way.

Instructional Objective: Review, overview, and a look at Harding and Coolidge (three class periods)
Instructional Objective: Explain why business prospered (two class periods)
Instructional Objective: Analyze scientific and technological advancements (two class periods)
Instructional Objective: Analyze changes in American lifestyles (one class period)
Instructional Objective: Describe the social tension created by the changes in American society (one class period)
Instructional Objective: Review and presentation of projects (one class period)

Sandy will next translate her instructional objectives into teacher objectives. *Teacher objective* refers to the specific content (i.e., core knowledge) the teacher will present to students. According to Armstrong and Savage (1998), teacher objectives are crucial in the planning process for two major reasons. First, they help sharpen the instructional focus by providing teachers with "guideposts" that influence subsequent steps in the planning process. Second, they contribute to organized and purposeful learning by providing direction to the teacher and students. Levine (1989) and others also argue that teacher objectives contribute to the sequencing and integration of learning.

To help her students gain an understanding of the themes and as an introduction to the Roaring Twenties, Sandy has decided on the following daily teacher objectives.

Instructional Objective: Review, provide an overview of the unit, and an examination of the Harding and Coolidge administrations

Day 1   *Teacher Objective:* The teacher will discuss previous learning, have a colleague discuss life as a flapper, provide an overview of the unit, and examine two of the political scandals that troubled the Harding administration.

Day 2   *Teacher Objective:* The teacher will examine President Coolidge's beliefs about government and at least two governmental policies he promoted.

Day 3   *Teacher Objective:* The teacher will identify specific government legislation that aided the business community and contributed to the prosperity of the decade.

Instructional Objective: Explain why business prospered

Day 4   *Teacher Objective:* The teacher will introduce business and consumer practices that led to the prosperity of the Twenties.

Day 5   *Teacher Objective:* The teacher will focus on Henry Ford as typical of the industrialists of the period to examine business practices.

Instructional Objective: Analyze scientific and technological advancements

Day 6   *Teacher Objective:* The teacher will present some of the scientific and technological advancements of the decade.

Day 7   *Teacher Objective:* The teacher will critically examine two or more of the advancements that heightened the prosperity of the Twenties.

Instructional Objective: Analyze changes in American lifestyles

Day 8   *Teacher Objective:* The teacher will survey changes to women's lives, discuss the American reaction to Prohibition, and describe the many changes that occurred in the media, entertainment, and literature.

Instructional Objective: Describe the social tension created by the changes in American society

Day 9   *Teacher Objective:* The teacher will introduce examples of fear and intolerance that surfaced in the Twenties.

Instructional Objective: Review and presentation of projects

Day 10   *Teacher Objective:* The teacher will provide an opportunity for students' presentation of projects and bring closure to the unit.

We know what content Sandy will teach (i.e., teacher objectives) but we do not know how she will present the core knowledge (i.e., methodology) or how students will demonstrate a mastery of the content (i.e., performance objectives). We will return to Sandy later to see how she develops performance objectives and selects methods of instruction.

Before illustrating these final steps, we introduce Brian Kahn, a middle-school teacher who employs a student-based approach to planning.

Student-Based Planning
Case Study: Brian Kahn

Mr. Kahn, a faculty member at Urbana Middle School for more than ten years, teaches U.S. history and is part of an interdisciplinary team. Each summer, Brian's team meets to outline the academic year, and throughout the year they meet regularly to plan and to discuss the needs, strengths, and weaknesses of their students. Mr. Kahn and his colleagues develop middle-school curriculum that: "(1) integrates content, thinking, feelings, and actions of young individuals; (2) recognizes that 'self' is a significant area of learning; and (3) develops the whole person within the school and society" (Allen, Splittgerber, Manning, 1993, p. 7).

Urbana Middle School uses block scheduling. Mr. Kahn enjoys the seventy-minute periods because they allow the team to develop interdisciplinary units, incorporate group activities, independent study, library assignments, and permit the team the time to get to know the students. As a result, Brian can understand and deal more effectively with the mood swings of adolescents while keeping them engaged in social studies instruction.

To illustrate the differences between subject-specific and student-based planning, we will describe how Mr. Kahn plans a unit of instruction on the Roaring Twenties. First, like Mrs. Eichhorst, he begins to "sketch out" the academic year. Unlike Sandy, he plans with an interdisciplinary team of teachers, including a reading and language arts teacher, a math teacher, and a science teacher. Brian will tentatively identify core knowledge that will provide opportunities for eighth-graders to learn about the Twenties as they learn about themselves, their peers, and gain a sense of place in school and society.

It is well into the fall semester, and Brian is about to introduce the unit. No sooner is he involved in the introductory activity—a colleague dressed as a flapper discussing her life style—than a fight breaks out in the back of the classroom between a Latino and an African American student. Two other students join the fray, resulting in a near riot and forcing cancellation of the introductory activity. Brian restores order and finds that the fight is the result of name-calling. After talking with the participants, with the class, and holding an emergency team meeting, the teachers identify the root of the problem. The school is experiencing a change in the student body. The number of Latino students attending the school has risen sharply over the last two years. As social groups interact, the students are experiencing difficulties with identity formation, self-concept, and friendship development (Allen, Splittgerber, & Manning, 1993, p. 60). Brian and his team concede that they have not paid sufficient attention to the social and emotional needs of their students when planning for instruction. They agree to act on the situation. At this juncture, Brian and the rest of the team become student-based planners.

Using input from students and colleagues, Mr. Kahn decides to change the unit by shifting the emphasis from political science to social history. He will focus on the experiences of African Americans and women and then turn to the experiences of Mexican Americans and Italian Americans. His intent is to explore individual and group identity and membership, clashes between and among groups, and group cooperation. While highlighting the groups' experiences, he will encourage student activities that demonstrate how the groups sustained themselves, combated the forces of racism and sexism, and worked with representatives of other groups to better their lives. His objective will be to have the students learn the value of group membership and the importance of group cooperation.

As a student-based planner and as a result of the classroom altercation, Brian will teach the unit in the following manner.

Instructional Objective: Review, provide an overview of the unit, and an examination of the Harding and Coolidge administrations

Day 1   *Teacher Objective:* The teacher will discuss previous learning, have a colleague discuss life as a flapper, provide an overview of the unit, and examine two of the political scandals that troubled the Harding administration.

Day 2   *Teacher Objective:* The teacher will examine briefly two governmental policies Coolidge promoted and illustrate how government legislation aided the business community and contributed to the prosperity of the decade.

Instructional Objective: Describe business practices

Day 3   *Teacher Objective:* The teacher will introduce business and consumer practices that led to the prosperity of the Twenties and introduce Henry Ford as typical of the industrialists of the period.

Instructional Objective: Analyze scientific and technological advancements

Day 4   *Teacher Objective:* The teacher will describe the many scientific and technological advancements of the Twenties.

Instructional Objective: Analyze changes in American lifestyles

Day 5   *Teacher Objective:* The teacher will survey changes to women's lives in the Twenties and American reaction to prohibition.

Day 6   *Teacher Objective:* The teacher will describe the many changes that occurred in the media, entertainment, and literature.

Instructional Objective: Describe how reactions to changes in culture led to social tension

Day 7   *Teacher Objective:* The teacher will introduce particular minority and ethnic groups and describe their participation in the prosperity of the period.

Day 8   *Teacher Objective:* The teacher will introduce examples of fear and intolerance in the Twenties and examples of individuals, groups, and public and private agencies that fought against these forces.

Day 9   *Teacher Objective:* The teacher will provide examples of how groups sustained themselves, fought racism and sexism, and worked to improve their place in society.

Instructional Objective: Unit review and presentation of group projects

Day 10   *Teacher Objectives:* The teacher will bring the unit to a close by asking the students to present their projects on the following question: "How did the government, business and labor, and societal groups in the Twenties work together so that more people shared in the country's prosperity?" In addition, the teacher will ask the students to discuss how they might work together to avoid conflicts such as the one that occurred in the classroom.

Although Mrs. Eichhorst and Mr. Kahn differ in many respects, they share a common trait: both are very effective in the classroom. Both place a premium on planning instruction, although each follows a different planning model.

▌Reader Activity 6.2

CONSULTING OTHER SOURCES
Reviewing a Teacher's Edition of a Textbook in Your Subject Area

The purpose of this activity is to examine unit planning in textbooks. A teacher's annotated edition (TAE) of a textbook contains a wealth of information aimed at helping teachers plan for instruction. Obtain a teacher's edition of a textbook in the academic discipline of your choice. Focusing on the introduction to a unit of instruction, identify what the authors have included to help the teacher. Make a list of the elements and features the unit includes. Which do you believe teachers would find most helpful?

From your review, what do you conclude about the usefulness of a teacher's edition textbook? Is it a help or hindrance in planning for instruction? What are some advantages in using a textbook when planning? What are some limitations? Report your findings to the class.

▌Planning Activity 6.2

IDENTIFYING THEMES, FORMULATING A GENERALIZATION, SELECTING CORE KNOWLEDGE, AND WRITING INSTRUCTIONAL AND TEACHER OBJECTIVES

For the topic and grade level you have selected, identify the themes you will incorporate into your unit. You can obtain examples of topics and themes from teacher's edition textbooks, course study guides, or by asking a classroom teacher. Write a generalization that includes the concepts you have identified (see Figure 6.5). List the core knowledge by which students will gain an understanding of the themes (see Figure 6.6). Sketch out the instructional objectives and time frame of your unit. Write teacher objectives for each day.

▌▌STUDENT PERFORMANCE OBJECTIVES

Performance objectives communicate the teacher's intent to the learner (Mager, 1975). They are translations of teacher objectives into student learning. Performance objectives state what students will do in the classroom, outside the classroom, and outside the school in order to demonstrate learning. They appear in unit and lesson plans as examples of learning outcomes and may be modified during instruction as teachers assess the availability of resources, student needs and interests, and other factors influencing instruction. Because there are multiple perspectives on the value of objectives and the degree of specificity with which they should be written, we suggest reviewing the literature, speaking with experienced teachers, and reflecting on your own educational philosophy in order to determine your position on performance objectives.

Objectives in Three Domains

Planning and teaching address various manifestations of thinking and knowing as they occur in the cognitive, psychomotor, and affective domains. The *cognitive domain* refers to the construction, retention, and assimilation of knowledge, that is, the learning of academic content. The *psychomotor domain* refers to the physical acts of movement, manipulation, communication, and creation (e.g., properly handling a microscope, writing and performing a speech, using a ruler, properly gripping a tennis racquet). The *affective domain* refers to students' values, feelings, and attitudes toward the content and learning activities as they matriculate through the unit.

Cognitive Objectives

The classification system of knowledge (cognitive) usually employed in the planning process is Bloom's Taxonomy of Educational Objectives, developed in the 1950s by Benjamin Bloom and his colleagues at the University of Chicago. The taxonomy illustrated in Figure 6.7 lists the cognitive (knowledge) levels of understanding followed by student processes suggesting understandings at each level.

FIGURE 6.7   Bloom's Taxonomy of Cognitive Objectives

LEVEL	STUDENT COGNITIVE PROCESSES
Level 1: Knowledge	The student can recall, define, recognize, or identify specific information presented during instruction. The information may be in the form of a fact, a rule, a diagram, a sound, and so on.
Level 2: Comprehension	The student can demonstrate understanding of information by translating it into a different form or by recognizing it in translated form. This can be through giving a definition in his or her own words, summarizing, giving an original example, recognizing an example, etc.
Level 3: Application	The student can apply the information in performing concrete actions. These actions may involve figuring, writing, reading, handling equipment, etc.
Level 4: Analysis	The student can recognize the organization and structure of a body of information, can break this information down into its constituent parts, and can specify relationships between these parts.
Level 5: Synthesis	The student can bring to bear information from various sources to create a product uniquely his or her own. The product can take a variety of forms—written, oral, pictorial, etc.
Level 6: Evaluation	The student can apply a standard in making a judgment on the worth of something, a concerto, an essay, an action, an architectural design, etc.

Adapted from Learning to Teach (4th Edition) by Richard Arends. Copyright 1998 by The McGraw-Hill Companies, Inc. Reprinted by permission of McGraw-Hill.

Psychomotor Objectives

In the psychomotor domain, we have constructed a four-level taxonomy that may be especially appropriate for middle-school learners who are practicing and extending general skills and skills specific to subject areas. Figure 6.8 illustrates this taxonomy.

FIGURE 6.8	Taxonomy of Psychomotor Objectives

	STUDENT PSYCHOMOTOR PROCESSES
Level 1: Introduce	The student observes the teacher introduce a skill in one or more contexts. Students may need to be reminded of one or more ways a skill can be performed effectively. (e.g., the science teacher will demonstrate the correct way of washing test tubes and other glassware).
Level 2: Imitate	The student imitates the teacher in the use of the skill in context. Teachers need to know whether students can perform a skill in the appropriate manner before asking them to employ the skill in learning activities. (e.g., after a demonstration on how to properly hold a tennis racquet for a backhand stroke, the student will demonstrate the skill to the satisfaction of the instructor).
Level 3: Practice	The student, in one or more settings, practices the skill in context. (e.g., the students, in groups of two, practice their dancing skills by performing the Charleston).
Level 4: Extend	The student is able to employ a skill and, with some direction from the teacher, extend its application to related and more sophisticated areas. (e.g., two students with learning disabilities will create and use a graphic organizer to illustrate growth in business as a result of technological advancements).

Affective Objectives

Krathwohl (1956) identified five categories of understanding in the affective domain. For the purpose of developing this unit of instruction, we focused on the first three categories, which are shown in Figure 6.9.

FIGURE 6.9	Partial Taxonomy of Affective Objectives

Receiving	The teacher is able to gain, hold, and direct the attention of the student. At this level, the focus is on the teacher developing units of instructional value and of interest to the student.
Responding	The student is willing to engage in the instructional program and is gaining some observed satisfaction from the interaction. That is, the student is enjoying the activities and is gaining knowledge and acquiring skills. (e.g., the students are actively involved in learning about lifestyle changes of the Twenties.)
Valuing	The student is committed to learning about the topic (e.g. the Roaring Twenties). The commitment is voluntary and observable (e.g., volunteering to attend a lecture on the Harlem Renaissance at the local museum.)

Writing Student Performance Objectives

Performance objectives, performance objectives usually possess the following elements: (1) performance (what the student will do), (2) condition (context or circumstances), and (3) criterion (the acceptable level of performance) (Mager, 1975). Armstrong and Savage (1998) suggest using the "ABCD" method: audience, behavior, condition, and degree of accuracy when writing performance objectives. We adhere to this format in our sample cognitive objectives, but use a variation of it in our sample objectives in the psychomotor and affective domains.

1. Audience (to whom the objective is directed)
   - The students will . . .
   - Mr. Kimura's class will . . .
   - All the students in Brian's U.S. history class will . . .
2. Behavior (the observable performance illustrating that learning has occurred)
   - dissect . . .
   - construct . . .
   - list . . .
   - compare and contrast . . .
   - write . . .
3. Condition (the manner in which the students will demonstrate learning)
   - an essay . . .
   - on a multiple choice test . . .
   - an oral argument . . .
   - a map . . .
   - a play . . .
4. Degree (minimal performance level illustrating mastery of the objective)
   - two arguments.
   - all items.
   - two of the three reasons.
   - at least 90% accuracy.

In implementing the "ABCD" method, you may find it helpful to refer to lists of verbs (behaviors) that are educationally meaningful. Figure 6.10 lists examples of verbs in all three domains.

We return to Sandy's unit outline (see p. 167–169) to develop a set of performance objectives in the three domains. We selected the fourth and fifth days of the unit, for which the instructional objective is to "Describe business practices." We begin by generating performance objectives that are applicable to the whole class, and in the next section add others to address the needs of individual students. Objectives in three domains are shown in Figure 6.11.

To summarize, teacher objectives state what knowledge, skills, and dispositions the teacher will present. Performance objectives state how students will demonstrate learning. Review Sandy's teacher objectives (p. 171) and Study Figure 6.12 to distinguish between teacher objectives and performance objectives.

FIGURE 6.10	Terms for Writing Student Performance Objectives in Three Domains

Cognitive	Affective	Psychomotor
Knowledge Define, describe, identify, label, list, locate, match, measure, name, select, state	**Receiving** Ask, attend, choose, describe, follow, listen, give, name, locate, select, reply	Introduce
Comprehension Alter, classify, convert, distinguish, estimate, explain, extrapolate, generalize, infer, predict, summarize, translate	**Responding** Answer, assist, discuss, do, help, perform, practice, read, recite, report, select, talk, watch, write	**Imitate**
Application Apply, calculate, compute, determine, predict, solve **Analysis** Analyze, differentiate, compare and contrast, relate	**Valuing** Accept, argue, complete, commit, do, follow, explain, initiate, join, propose, report, study, work, write, differentiate	**Practice**
Synthesis Arrange, compile, compose, construct, devise, design, reorganize, summarize, synthesize	**Organizing** Adhere, alter, argue, change, defend, modify, organize, relate, combine, explain, integrate	**Extend**
Evaluation Appraise, assess, conclude, evaluate, interpret, compare, criticize, explain, summarize, justify	**Characterizing** Act, confirm, display, propose, question, refute, solve, use, influence, perform, practice, verify, serve	

Based on Bloom, B.S., editor: *Taxonomy of educational objectives. Handbook I. Cognitive domain.* New York 1956. David McKay Co., Inc. and Krathwohl, D., Bloom, B.S., and Masia, B.B. *Taxonomy of educational objectives: Handbook II. Affective domain,* New York, 1965, David McKay Co., Inc.
From *Taxonomy of Educational Objectives Handbook I: Cognitive Domain* by B.S. Bloom, 1956, New York: David McKay Company, Inc. and *Taxonomy of Educational Objectives Handbook II: Affective Domain* by D. Krathwohl, B.S. Bloom, and B.B. Masia, 1965, New York: David McKay Company, Inc.

FIGURE 6.11 The Roaring Twenties: Objectives in Three Domains

COGNITIVE	
Comprehension	After reading "Business Practices of the 1920s," students will report, in their own words, on one such practice, indicating at least one way it contributed to the prosperity of the decade.
Application	Students will apply what they have learned about life in the Twenties by developing a skit illustrating four behaviors exhibited by the typical city dweller.
Analysis	Students will analyze a short biography of Henry Ford and, in a two-page essay, relate at least three business practices that led to his rise in the ranks of major industrialists of the period.
PSYCHOMOTOR	
Introduce	During the fifth lesson, two classmates who are experienced dancers will introduce students to the basic steps of the Charleston.
Imitate	Students will pantomime, as demonstrated by the dramatics teacher, a short skit of Charlie Chaplin ice skating.
Practice	Students will practice giving a "pep talk" speech by acting out the role of Henry Ford exhorting his workers to set new records in automobile production.
Extend	Students will extend the skill of constructing miniature sets by constructing a diorama depicting an assembly line in the production of the Model T.
AFFECTIVE	
Receiving	Students will attend to the lecture on "Henry Ford and the Model T" provided by the guest speaker.
Responding	Students are engaged in constructing a poster illustrating the advantages of buying products using the installment plan.
Valuing	Students exhibit interest in the Twenties by, for example, volunteering to provide the class with biographical sketches of other industrialists of the period.

FIGURE 6.12   Teacher Objectives and Performance Objectives in Various Disciplines

Subject Area: Science
Teacher Objective: The teacher will introduce the dating of rocks and fossils.

Performance Objectives
   Cognitive
   • After reading pp. 78-83 in their textbooks, students will write a short paragraph explaining a major difference between relative age and absolute age.
   • After visiting a local excavation site, students will develop a diagram showing how fossils are formed.
   Psychomotor
   • While on a field trip in search of fossils, students will practice the proper use of safety goggles and geology hammers.
   Affective
   • During the unit on Earth's Structure, the students will inquire about museums in the area noted for their geological exhibits.

Subject Area: Mathematics
Teacher Objective: The teacher will explain the structure and purpose of spreadsheets (i.e., to organize and analyze data) and illustrate their use when purchasing an automobile.

Performance Objectives
   Cognitive
   • After instruction, students will identify a practical use for spreadsheets.
   • Given a scenario for the purchase of a $15,000 automobile, with a 9.8% loan for three years, students will calculate monthly payments with a 5%, 10%, and 20% down payment and display the results in a spreadsheet.
   Psychomotor
   • After the teacher demonstrates the correct method of deleting cells and rows from a computer-based spreadsheet, students will delete cells and rows with 90% accuracy.
   Affective
   • During the lesson on spreadsheets, students assist one another in using the classified ads to identify cars they would like to purchase.

Subject Area: English/Language Arts
Teacher Objective: The teacher will identify and give examples of propaganda techniques used by the media and the animals in George Orwell's Animal Farm.

Performance Objectives
   Cognitive
   • Students will select three television commercials or magazine advertisements and write a brief analysis of the propaganda techniques used in each.
   • Students will debate whether *Animal Farm*, given the demise of communism, has relevance for today's youth.
   Psychomotor
   • Students will correctly operate a digital camera to photograph examples of persuasive messages in their homes and community.
   Affective
   • Students will volunteer to attend a Saturday matinée of *Babe: Pig in the City* and to meet afterward to discuss connections between this film and *Animal Farm*.

■■ PLANNING FOR INDIVIDUAL AND GROUP DIFFERENCES

Some students will need additional help or exposure to different instructional approaches in order to perform the tasks you outline for the whole class. Some of these students will be brought to your attention by school staff (i.e., special education and gifted and talented specialists) or you might identify them through on-going assessment, examining assignments, or simple observation. This semester, Sandy has identified four students in her U.S. history classes that will require special help. In her early morning class, two students—Sam and Justin—have learning disorders (i.e., difficulty organizing information). During the unit Sandy, will use a graphic organizer with her class when describing the many inventions that surfaced in the Twenties. While the students are in their seats using this tool to make sense of the information in their text, Mrs. Eichhorst will provide Sam and Justin with one-on-one instruction. If other students need her help, she will use the "buddy system" and assign peer tutors to them. In a writing lesson, she will have Sam and Justin use their graphic organizers to write a paper or create a poster on "Inventions of the Twenties."

In her third period class, Sandy will address the needs of Samantha, who has been diagnosed with attention deficit disorder. Samantha does not stay on task and attempts to carry on conversations with anyone seated by her. In an attempt to help Samantha connect with the unit, Sandy will have Samantha play a major role in the introductory lesson of the unit, assisting the historian who will dress as a flapper and talk about the Twenties. In lessons that make use of visuals and technology, Samantha will also serve as Mrs. Eichhorst's assistant.

In Sandy's last period class, Ron uses a wheelchair and has a visual impairment. Early in the semester, Sandy rearranged the furniture and offered Ron space toward the front of the class. She uses the copier machine to enlarge the text of quizzes and tests for him. In this unit, Sandy has decided to capitalize on Ron's interest in automobiles by encouraging him to lead a discussion of Henry Ford's contributions to the Twenties, and an examination of the Model T.

When Sandy taught the Twenties unit last year, a number of female students noted on their unit evaluations that instruction focused almost exclusively on males—except for the initial discussion with a "Flapper." Sandy realized the students had a point. This year, she will include more social history and more content depicting women's roles in:

- social causes—Margaret Sanger
- political activism—Mary McLeod Bethune
- the birth of the "beauty industry"—Madame C. J. Walker
- mass media—Aimee Semple McPherson
- professions, such as aviation, traditionally associated with males—Amelia Earhart, Elinor Smith Sullivan

Planning for instruction, as Sandy has demonstrated, is an on-going process that must be responsive to the needs of both individuals and groups.

■ Planning Activity 6.3

WRITING PERFORMANCE OBJECTIVES

Using the models we have presented in the preceding pages (Figures 6.7-6.12), develop student performance objectives as part of your unit plan. Include objectives in the affective and psychomotor domain if appropriate.

FIGURE 6.13 Sandy's Lesson Plan—Day Nine

Topic
The Roaring Twenties

Purpose
Describe how reactions to changes in American culture led to social tension.

Teacher Objective
Introduce examples of fear and intolerance that surfaced in the Twenties.

Performance Objectives
Cognitive: Students will *describe* one example of fear and intolerance in the Twenties, *analyze* how this example was a reaction to social change, and *relate* the situation to a contemporary example of fear and intolerance.

Relevant Content
- The Red Scare; Sacco and Vanzetti
- Resurgence of the Ku Klux Klan
- Prohibition
- Gangland Violence
- The Scopes Trial

Proposed Sequence
1. Students respond in writing to the prompt, "Have you ever been accused of doing something wrong that you did not do? What caused this to happen? How did you react?" (*5 minutes*)
2. Volunteers share responses as teacher writes key words/themes on board (e.g., anger, guilt, frustration, guilt by association, unfair). (*5 minutes*)
3. Teacher asks students to offer examples of unjust accusations, fear, intolerance from contemporary society (e.g., hate crimes, school shootings, KKK marches) and writes on board. (*5 minutes*)
4. Transition to Twenties: "Now, we will look at how similar events have happened historically." (*5 minutes*)
5. Teacher divides class into five groups according to five topics listed above as "Relevant Content," and assigns task. Students work in groups. (*30 minutes*)

GROUP TASK
Reporting on Fear and Intolerance in the Twenties

Roles: Facilitator, Recorder, Reporter, Materials Manager, Connections-Maker
Task: Prepare a brief presentation in which you teach the class about the topic assigned to your group.

- Read the pages from your textbook relevant to your assigned topic to gain an understanding of the facts.
- Pick up a Primary Source folder from teacher. Read, examine, and discuss the material in the folder.
- As a group, agree on an explanation for cultural/social changes that contributed to topic.
- Recorder prepares two overheads: (1) Five important facts to remember about this case (2) Cultural/social changes that contributed to this case.
- Select one memorable image, quotation from your Primary Source folder to share with the class and explain why you chose it.
- In your report to the class, make connections to at least one similar event in the recent past.
- Present your work to the class.
- Evaluate your own and your group's performance using attached forms.

FIGURE 6.13 Continued

6. Begin reports, if time. Allow time to collect and put away materials. (*5 minutes*)

Modifications for Special Needs
Teacher-assigns mixed ability groups to help with reading and writing
Enlarged textbook pages for student with visual impairment

Evaluation
Presentation will be evaluated for accuracy, clarity, analysis, and insightful connections.
Students assess their own and their group's performance using teacher-designed forms.

Resources
Textbook
Overhead transparencies and markers
Primary Source Folders containing photos, newspaper accounts, first person accounts, audio tape
5 sets of written directions
Self and group evaluation forms

Lesson Plan Formats

Lesson plans are detailed statements of teacher objectives, student performance objectives, and the procedures which will be followed to attain the stated objectives.

The following elements are commonly found in lesson plans.

Lesson topic
Lesson purpose
Teacher objective(s)
Performance objective(s)
Relevant content
Sequence of instruction
Modifications for meeting special needs
Assessment procedures
Needed learning resources

Figure 6.13 provides an example of one complete lesson plan from Sandy's unit. Figure 6.14 shows one lesson plan from Brian's unit. Following these figures is a detailed explanation of how these plans were developed.

DEVELOPING A LESSON PLAN

One of the first things Sandy did when building her unit was to use sequencing as she reflected on what to teach and when to introduce and examine the identified concepts. In sequencing, Sandy was influenced by Herbart's five-part sequence of instruction:

1. preparation,
2. presentation,

FIGURE 6.14   Brian's Lesson Plan

Topic
The Roaring Twenties

Purpose
Describe how reactions to changes in American culture led to social tensions.

Teacher Objective
Provide examples of how groups sustained themselves, fought racism, and worked to improve their place in society.

Performance Objectives
Working in pairs, students will research a group (e.g., women, African Americans, Mexican Americans, Italian Americans) and:
Cognitive: *describe* a brief history of the group; *select* one difficulty the group experienced and *explain* how it combated racism or sexism; and *summarize* an example of cooperation among the groups.
Psychomotor: Students will *extend* their art skills by constructing a poster that is informative and visually appealing.
Affective: Working in pairs the students will *assist* one another writing their group report and constructing their poster.

Relevant Content
- The Red Scare; Sacco and Vanzetti
- Rebirth of the KKK
- Chapter 28 "A More Diverse America"
- Library Resources

Proposed Sequence
Day One
1. Have students review sections of Chapter 26, "The Roaring Twenties," that connect with the lecture given by a local historian on fears and intolerance (e.g., lynching of African Americans, repatriation of Mexican Americans, lower wages for women) in the Twenties and during the Great Depression.
2. Guide the students through Chapter 27, "The Great Depression and the New Deal." Have them read for purpose the section entitled, "Life in the Depression Years" to identify information on the group they have selected to research.
3. Have the students "pair-up," select a group to research, identify a specific research topic and read together Chapter 28, "A More Diverse America" to collect information on their topic.

Day Two
1. Students will visit the library where the school librarian has on display a number of resources on the Twenties and the Great Depression and the societal groups of the period. The students review this material and other resources, including the Internet and digital libraries.
2. Students will return to the classroom where the language arts teacher, who is on Brian's team, will present appropriate literature (i.e., poems, short stories, newspaper articles, and other primary sources of the period, highlighting the groups' experiences.

FIGURE 6.14   Continued

Day Three
1. The art teacher will be in the classroom when the students arrive to help them review techniques for creating a poster that is informative and visually appealing.
2. Brian arranges for the students to look at the information collected and to plan what information will be included on a poster.
3. The students construct their poster.
4. Students will present their posters.

Modification for Special Needs
   • Pairing of students to help with reading and writing
   • Ancillary material—"Anti-Italian Prejudice in the 1920s" and chapter summaries written in Spanish
   • Textbook visual clues to engage students with the content

Evaluation
1. In pairs students will collect at least five "pieces" of information about their particular group. They will use at least two "pieces" of information in the poster they construct.
2. Observe students conduct library research, research in the classroom, construct a poster, work in groups, assist other groups, and practice their communication skills as they present information on a particular group using the poster they constructed.

Resources
America's Past and Promise, teacher input and teacher presentation, library resources, and on-line resources.

3. association,
4. generalization, and
5. application.

   Herbart, a nineteenth-century learning theorist was a strong believer in helping students make connections between previous and new learning and helping students retain new learning by application. Many of Herbart's ideas are an integral part of contemporary learning theories. (Van Til, 1971)
   We will take an in-depth look at how Sandy built the lesson plan for Day Nine. For this day, the instructional and teacher objectives are as follows:

Instructional Objective: Describe how reactions to changes in American culture led to social tension.
Teacher Objective: The teacher will introduce examples of fear and intolerance that surfaced in the Twenties.

   Examine the parts of the lesson displayed in Figures 6.15A , 6.15B, and 6.15C.
   The initial parts of Sandy's lesson (Figure 6.15A) are extrapolated from the unit. As she reflects on the teacher objective assigned to the lesson, Sandy develops performance objectives. The lesson plan may be slightly modified when she is involved in the day-to-day experiences of teaching.

FIGURE 6.15A   Parts of a Lesson Plan

	Definition	*Example from Sandy's Unit*
Lesson topic	Title with reference to the generalization	<u>The Roaring Twenties</u> Sandwiched between two wars, the Twenties saw political and social change, a hands-off approach toward business, and major scientific and technological advancements.
Lesson purpose	Core knowledge addressing the themes in the generalization; the instructional objectives	Describe how reactions to changes in American culture led to social tension.
Long-term objectives	Drawn from national, state and local goals or standards in the subject area	• understand the value of cultural diversity, as well as cohesion, within and across groups • explain and apply ideas, theories, and modes of inquiry drawn from political science to the examination of persistent issues and social problems • identify and analyze examples of tensions between expressions of individuality and efforts to promote social conformity between groups and institutions (NCSS Standards)
Performance objectives	What students will do in the course of or as a result of the lesson	**Cognitive** Students will: • describe one example of fear and intolerance in the Twenties (knowledge) • analyze how this example was a reaction to social change (analysis) • relate the situation to a contemporary example of fear and intolerance (analysis) • evaluate their own and their group's presentation (evaluation)

The body of the lesson plan is the development and sequencing of activities (Figure 6.15B). In this particular lesson, Sandy asks students to reflect on their own experience, read, write, and work collaboratively to explore a topic. Figure 6.15C illustrates how Sandy addresses student interests, strengths, and weaknesses. The assessment method she chooses directly corresponds to her teacher objective.

FIGURE 6.15B Sequence of Instruction

A. To insure that students possess core knowledge of the period, Sandy asks the students during day eight to review the section of their textbooks entitled "A Decade of Change" and read "Divisions in American Society" for general understanding.

B. To help students begin thinking of what is meant by the term social tension, Sandy will have students respond in writing to the prompt, "Have you ever been accused of doing something wrong that you did not do? What caused this to happen? How did you react?" Sandy will help students move from personal experience to general trends in society.

C. The students will read assigned textbook passages in order to gain a basic understanding of facts about each topic.

D. Students will extend their understanding of the facts by examining primary sources such as first-person accounts, photographs, and newspaper articles.

E. Students will work in groups to create a brief presentation for the whole class on the topic they have studied.

FIGURE 6.15C Lesson Modifications and Evaluation Procedures

Lesson Modifications (How the lesson meets the needs of diverse learners)	A. Relevant curriculum	Content is included that is of interest to students (e.g., photos of gangland violence, actions of the KKK)
	B. Addresses reading skills	Heterogeneous grouping allows students to help one another with comprehension and/or vocabulary.
	C. Addresses writing problems	Heterogeneous grouping allows students to help one another with note-taking.
	D. Addresses learning styles	Lesson incorporates aids for visual learners, (e. g., written instructions, variety of print and non-print materials).
Evaluation Procedures (How students will demonstrate what they have learned)	A. Cognitive	Students will create presentations in which they demonstrate comprehension, analysis, and ability to make connections between historical and current events.
	B. Affective	Students will evaluate their own and their group's performance.

■ **Planning Activity 6.4**

DEVELOPING A LESSON PLAN

Using the models we have provided or any other models your instructor recommends, develop a minimum of two detailed lesson plans for your unit.

Summary

Planning for middle-and high-school instruction is challenging, but becomes easier with experience. When teachers are knowledgeable about their students and their subject areas, planning becomes more meaningful and effective, and instruction becomes more enjoyable for both teacher and student. As you master the planning process and learn to plan in detail, we hope you will see the wisdom of the maxim "It's better to be over-prepared than under-prepared!" Among the key points to remember are:

- Effective planning begins with a consideration of purposes, definitions, and approaches to teaching a subject area.
- In general, teachers adopt a subject-specific or a student-based approach to planning. However, because they are eclectic, they may use both approaches.
- Planning units of instruction involves considering the "big ideas" in your subject area together with the characteristics, needs, and interests of students.
- Core knowledge consists of the knowledge, skills, and dispositions that will enable students to pursue independently their own intellectual interests.
- Instructional objectives give an overall structure to a unit. Teacher objectives provide daily guidance to the teacher.
- Performance objectives specify what students will do to demonstrate that they are learning. They can be classified into three domains: the cognitive, the psychomotor, and the affective. Objectives in all three domains may not be appropriate for every lesson.
- Teacher and performance objectives should be used to guide rather than dictate instruction. They help teachers stay focused on outcomes and help students know what is expected of them.
- Clear performance objectives specify audience (A), behavior (B), condition (C), and degree of mastery, (D).
- While there are many styles and formats for lesson plans, one test of an effective lesson plan is whether another teacher, with minimal preparation, could actually teach the lesson.
- Effective lesson plans include modifications for learners with special needs.

You may still have many questions about the planning process. In the chapters that follow, you will learn about selecting materials, implementing strategies, and designing activities and assessments that will bring your unit and lesson plans to life. Specifically, Chapter Seven focuses on identifying and selecting instructional materials from a variety of sources.

Building Your Biography, Your Personal Practical Philosophy, and Portfolio

Building Your Biography

What experiences in your life are relevant to becoming an effective planner? The following questions are intended to help you generate ideas for composing a chapter of your educational biography. They are not intended to be answered sequentially or to limit your exploration of the topic.

- As you reflect on your K-12 and college experiences, what teachers come to mind as either highly effective or ineffective planners?
- What criteria did you use to label someone highly effective or ineffective?
- What experiences or mental images do you have of teachers who were very well-prepared or not very well-prepared?
- How did you feel when you perceived the teacher to be well-prepared? Not very well-prepared?
- What have you learned about planning from your own life experiences?
- What life experiences do you associate with the maxim "It's better to be over-prepared than under-prepared"?

Developing Your Personal Practical Philosophy

Draft a section of your personal educational philosophy that addresses planning for middle-and high-school instruction. You might address questions such as the following.

- Why should you consider the purposes of education, definitions of your subject area, and approaches to teaching in your subject area when planning for instruction?
- What kind of planning process will you employ?
- What are your personal predispositions toward planning? Do you have characteristics or preferences that may predispose you to plan effectively? What characteristics or preferences may limit your ability to plan effectively?
- Are you more of a "team" planner or would you prefer to work alone?
- What are the benefits and limitations of detailed planning?
- What is your stance toward objectives?
- Is it always desirable or even possible to specify student behavior in advance?
- How, if at all, do you plan to balance negotiating the curriculum with planning for instruction?
- How will you account for student diversity and special needs in your planning?
- What features of the context in which you hope to teach might influence your planning (e.g., a middle school with instructional teams, a high school with block scheduling)?

Collecting Artifacts for Your Portfolio

Review the Reader Activities and Planning Activities you have completed in the course of this chapter. Identify any that you might eventually select for your portfolio. For each, jot down notes that will help you recall later what you were thinking at the time you completed the activity, what challenges you encountered while completing it, what you learned from doing it, and how this activity reveals something about who you will be as a teacher. Don't worry about style or correctness at this point. The purpose is to begin documenting your thinking as you move through this book and this class.

References

Allen, H. A., Splittgerber, F. L., & Manning, M. L. (1993). *Teaching and learning in the middle level school.* Upper Saddle River, NJ: Merrill/Prentice Hall.

Allen, M. G. & Stevens, R. L. (1994). *Middle grades social studies: Teaching and learning for active and responsible citizenship.* Boston: Allyn and Bacon.

America 2000. An education strategy. (1991). Washington, DC: U.S. Department of Education.

Arends, R. I. (1998). *Learning to teach.* New York: Random House.

Armstrong, D. G. & Savage, T. V. (1998). (Fourth Edition). *Teaching in the secondary school: An introduction.* Upper Saddle River, NJ: Merrill/Prentice Hall.

Cheney, L. V. (1987). *American memory.* Washington, DC: National Endowment for the Humanities.

Commission on the Reorganization of Secondary Education. (1918). *Cardinal principles of secondary education.* Washington, DC: U. S. Government Printing Office.

Committee for the White House Conference on Education. (1955). *A report to the president.* Washington. DC: U.S. Government Printing Office.

Educational Policies Commission. (1961). *The central purpose of American education.* Washington, DC: National Education Association.

Finn, C. E. Jr & Ravitich, D. (1987). *What do our 17-year-olds know? A report on the first national assessment of history and literature.* New York: Harper & Row.

George, P. Lawrence, G., & Bushnell D. (1998). *Handbook for middle school teaching.* (2nd. ed.). New York: Longman.

Hirsch, E. D. Jr. (1987). *Cultural literacy: What every American needs to know.* Boston: Houghton-Mifflin.

Kentucky Department of Education. (1994). *The Kentucky learner goals and academic expectations.* Frankfort, KY: Author.

Kentucky Department of Education (1998). *How to develop a standards-based unit of study.* Frankfort, KY: Author.

Krathwohl, D. R., Bloom, B. S., Masia, B. B. (1956). *Taxonomy of educational objectives. Handbook II: Affective domain.* New York: David McKay Company, Inc.

Levine, J. M. (1989). *Secondary instruction: A manual for classroom teaching.* Boston: Allyn and Bacon.

Mager, R. F. (1975). (Second Editon). *Preparing instructional objectives.* Belmont, CA: Fearon Publishers Inc.

Mason, L. C., Garcia, J., Powell, F., & Risinger, C. F. (1994). *America's past and promise.* Boston: Houghton Mifflin.

Muth, K. D. & Alvermann, D. E. (1992). *Teaching and learning in the middle grades.* Boston: Allyn and Bacon.

National Council for the Social Studies. (1994). *Curriculum standards for social studies: Expectations for excellence.* Washington, DC: National Council for the Social Studies.

Traver, R. (March 1998). What is a good guiding question? *Educational Leadership,* 70–73.

Wiggins, G., & McTighe, J. (1993). *Understanding by design.* Alexandria, VA: Association for Supervision and Curriculum Development.

Websites

http://school.discovery.com/schrockguide/
   A comprehensive site with links to most subject areas. (Resources for curriculum development, lesson planning, and assessment are included here.)

http://www.awesomelibrary.org/teacher.html
   Another comprehensive site with links to curriculum, planning, and assessment resources in most subject areas.

http://www.sonoma.edu/cthink/K12
   Site of the Center for Critical Thinking. Gives support for, instructions how to, and examples of integration of critical thinking into lesson plans in many subject areas.

http://www.pacificnet.net/~mandel/index.html
   Site of Teacher Helping Teachers. Contains numerous lesson plans in most subject areas.

chapter 7

Selecting Instructional Materials

BUILDING ON BIOGRAPHY: TEXTBOOKS AS TOOLS FOR BUILDING INSTRUCTION

When I (Jesus) was a junior high- and high-school student in the 1950s, textbooks played a major role in what my peers and I were asked to do in school. Certainly there were exceptions. For example, in an English class we read the paperback edition of Thornton Wilder's *The Bridge of San Luis Rey,* a stirring novel describing redemption through love and love giving meaning to life. In a U. S. History class, we examined primary sources such as Lincoln's *Emancipation Proclamation* and a series of speeches delivered from the Senate floor in the 1840s extolling the virtues of Manifest Destiny. In a woodshop class, textbook instruction was coupled with hands-on approaches to learning and student-centered projects. (I created a coffee table for my mom!) Beyond these examples, however, little else comes to mind in the area of non-textbook teaching and learning.

In the 1970s, when I was teaching at the fifth grade level, I had the opportunity to study in Mexico. The intent of the agency sponsoring the trip was to have U. S. teachers gain a sense of Mexican culture by touring museums, churches, and historical ruins, but we also visited secondary classrooms in Mexico City and in the states of Jalisco and Oaxaca. What I saw in Mexico's secondary classrooms was amazingly familiar. The students sat at their desks and the teacher lectured, or the students and teachers read from a textbook. While most of the students dutifully followed the teachers' instructions, many appeared disengaged or bored. When I spoke with teachers, their conversations focused on the importance of students mastering the curriculum as expressed in the textbook. They said little of the students who appeared to be disconnected from learning.

In the early 1990s, I was invited to visit Japan by the Keizai Koho Foundation to study Japanese culture, visit secondary schools, and observe the teaching of social studies in several schools in the Tokyo metropolitan area. Again, with few exceptions, I observed students sitting at their desks and instruction dominated by the teacher and the textbook. The teachers I spoke with stressed the importance of the curriculum, viewed the textbook as the embodiment of the curriculum, and saw themselves as assisting the students to understand the textbook. While they acknowledged that some students were not paying attention, sleeping, or doing other things, they attributed this behavior to students' unwillingness to commit themselves to learning.

Over the past twenty-five years, I have visited many classrooms in California, Texas, Indiana, and Illinois and observed teachers at all levels involved in instruction. While they use a variety of materials—primary sources, educational videos, speakers, realia, adolescent literature, the Internet—the textbook continues to dominate middle- and high-school classrooms.

While many of the teachers I have observed defended teacher- and textbook-dominated instruction, quite a few were not happy with their teaching and were becoming more and more disillusioned with schools. These teachers wanted to break away from the overreliance on one source, but felt society's perceptions of what constitutes "good education" discouraged change. When they reflected on their teacher-preparation programs, they remembered being encouraged to be creative when planning for instruction, but when they began their careers, they felt pressured not to do anything out of the ordinary. This feeling of having to conform has driven many teachers to the safe but predictable haven of the textbook and lectures and discussions that are primarily textbook-based.

Today, I like to think of textbooks and other instructional materials as "tools" because this metaphor implies a relationship among teachers, materials, and instructional goals. Take the example of the half-inch screwdriver your parents may have given you when you moved into your college apartment. While it did not come with a set of directions, one of your parents probably sat down with you and explained its use: to set, tighten, and loosen screws with half-inch heads. It is not effective and can be dangerous when used to set, tighten, and loosen smaller or larger screw heads, wedge a door, or pry open objects. A half-inch screwdriver is a tool designed for a particular purpose, and one must learn how to use it properly. In the hands of someone who knows how to use it, it can be quite effective. When used inappropriately, the tool ceases to be effective.

Like tools, instructional materials have both strengths and weaknesses; none is inherently good or bad. Effective use depends on one's purpose. Ultimately, it is the teacher—not the tool—who provides instruction. A tool is simply a means to an end.

Questions to Consider

1. What political, economic, social, institutional, and cultural factors might contribute to the seemingly universal dominance of textbooks that Jesus has observed?
2. How does your own experience support or refute Jesus' claim that textbooks continue to dominate instruction?
3. How would schools change if textbooks suddenly disappeared?

▮▮ PURPOSE

This chapter has three main purposes: (1) to introduce you to the major tools available for middle- and high-school instruction; (2) to introduce you to methods of evaluating whether materials are appropriate for particular subject areas, classrooms, and communities; and (3) to review standards and curriculum guides as instructional tools for teachers. Three sub-themes run throughout this chapter. First, curriculum resources are tools employed by teachers to promote student learning. Second, teachers should choose resources that reflect their educational philosophies and current research on teaching and learning. Third, when carefully selected and employed for their intended purpose, resources are effective in meeting the needs and interests of students and can provide for optimum learning. Specifically, this chapter will help you:

- identify and describe the use of the following classroom resources:

    teacher knowledge
    student textbook
    the teacher's edition textbook (TAE)
    ancillary materials provided by publishing companies
    other commercially prepared materials
    trade books and adolescent literature
    community resources
    realia
    media and technology

- use a professional decision-making process to select resources for instruction and to evaluate curriculum materials for appropriateness.
- see how standards and curriculum guides serve as instructional tools for teachers.

▮▮▮ USING MULTIPLE TOOLS FOR MULTIPLE PURPOSES

Do textbooks continue to dominate middle- and high-school instruction? As you visit middle and high schools, walk down the halls and look into the classrooms in order to identify what resources the teachers and students are using for instruction. While you will frequently see teacher- and textbook-dominated instruction, you will also see teachers who use the textbook as reference material, teachers who integrate other materials with the textbook, and teachers who do not use a textbook at all. These teachers have learned that a reliance on one tool will not usually pique students' curiosity, lead to in-depth understanding, or encourage students to think critically. Teachers who use a variety of resources are doing so to address student differences.

An example might help you see the importance of using multiple tools in the instructional process. Let's assume you are teaching a health education course at a suburban middle or high school and the topic you are covering is "Increased Smoking Among Adolescents." What would be an effective and creative way of providing knowledge and experiences that would engage students in learning more about this problem and reflecting on why they should not smoke or give up smoking? Reading passages in a textbook or listening to a lecture highlighting the illnesses related to smoking would probably have little impact on adolescents. If engagement is to take place and behavior is to change, a more complex approach is needed. If teachers wish students to make the decision not to smoke or to give up smoking, then they need to develop approaches to learning that will encourage students to reflect upon and take responsibility for changing their behavior. It is not difficult to have students respond in a particular way in test situations—the real challenge is engaging students in a decision-making process and encouraging them not to light up when they leave the school grounds.

Middle- and high-school teachers agree that the use of a variety of materials is a major key to effective instruction. First, the use of multiple resources places the responsibility for developing instruction on teachers. It is teachers—not a curriculum guide or textbook—who identify instruction (i.e., objectives of a unit or set of lessons, student needs and wants) and pool and manipulate resources to meet the envisioned instructional ends in the classroom. Second, the use of more than one resource encourages teachers to use their knowledge and skills to develop their personal approaches to planning for instruction. Teachers who develop their planning skills usually avoid becoming dependent on the textbook. Third, employing more than one resource allows teachers to use their knowledge and skills to plan creative instruction that reflects current trends in educational reform (e.g., cooperative groups, student involvement, authentic assessment) and attends to a variety of student needs. Fourth, as teachers become more successful planners, they become more effective risk-takers, assuming the role of facilitators and guides and giving students responsibility for their own learning. Last, as teachers see students involved in learning and pursuing their own interests, they become reassured, gain confidence, and begin to see the connection between creative instructional planning and productive student behavior.

Reflect on the examples provided in Chapter Five, "Considering Curriculum for Middle and High Schools" and Chapter Six, "Planning for Middle- and High-School Instruction" to gain a deeper understanding of the importance of using multiple tools in the instructional process. In Chapter Five, Sarah and Dan became textbook-centered teachers by the end of their first year, although each began with different intentions. In Chapter Six, Mrs. Eichhorst and Mr. Kahn used the textbook as only one of many tools in the instructional process. Sandy and Brian are experienced teachers who know their students. They know that effective teachers use a variety of tools, including the textbook, in order to create instruction that connects with students and promotes learning.

▍Reader Activity 7.1

IN THE FIELD
"Middle and High Schools Encourage Teachers to use a Variety of Materials"

Your instructor has identified a number of middle and high schools willing to invite you to their campuses. Your task is to observe whether schools purchase a variety of materials, provide incentives for teachers to purchase others, and encourage teachers to use a variety of resources in the classroom. Make arrangements with the principals of the schools you have selected for the purpose of identifying the many tools teachers use in the instructional process. Assure the principal you will not disturb teachers or students, and ask that an administrator or other school official accompany you as you observe instruction from the hallway. Next, visit the media center, teacher resource rooms, and technology labs to inventory the resources available and to ascertain who uses them. (Do not walk into classrooms or disturb teachers or students.)

1. For each visit record the grade level, subject taught, materials/resources used, and who (teachers, students, both) used them.
2. Inventory who used the teacher resource rooms and the technology classrooms, and for what purposes.
3. Reflect on what you saw and propose possible explanations for the results of your survey.
4. Report your findings to the class. (Do not reveal names of schools or teachers.) What tool, if any, dominates instruction in today's classrooms?

▉▉ TEACHER KNOWLEDGE AS AN INSTRUCTIONAL TOOL

Teachers enter the classroom with a wealth of information and experiences and add to this storehouse of knowledge as they establish themselves. The combination of a teacher's knowledge of a subject (content) and knowledge of how to teach the subject to students (pedagogy) is called *pedagogical content knowledge* (Grossman, 1990; Shulman, 1987). The case of John Foyle illustrates how pedagogical content knowledge becomes a powerful instructional tool in the classroom.

When John Foyle, a life-long resident of Lexington, was in high school, his favorite history teacher introduced him to the United Society of Believers in Christ's Second Appearance (the Shakers). This movement of the late eighteenth and early nineteenth centuries established a number of religious settlements, including one in Pleasant Hill, just twenty-seven miles southwest of Lexington. John became fascinated with the Shakers while he was a high-school student and visited the settlement at every opportunity. His fascination with the group and his interest in history and sociology convinced him he should pursue a career teaching secondary social studies.

In the middle 1990s, John enrolled at the University of Illinois because of its emphasis on interdisciplinary education, its strong history department, and a growing secondary teacher-education program. When he entered the university, John's dream was to return to his hometown and become a social studies teacher in one of Lexington's high schools. In 1997, after completing his program of study, he accepted a position teaching world cultures and U. S. history at the high school he had attended.

John's studies at the University of Illinois prepared him well for his teaching assignments. His major consisted of thirty-six semester hours of U. S. and world history with specializations in particular periods and topics. He minored in sociology and completed over twenty semester hours, many spent on gaining a more in-depth look at the Shakers and world-wide social movements. He also completed seventeen semester hours in the other social science disciplines where he focused on American and world heroes and heroines. John graduated from the university's teacher-education program with more than adequate content knowledge. Certainly, he knew more about most social studies topics than does the average middle- or high-school student.

Today, John is involved in what he likes most—teaching history, sociology, and world cultures—and doing what he did as a high school and university student: reading in the social sciences. Over the next few years, John will also gain a wealth of experience in pedagogy: how best to teach history, sociology, and world cultures. He will learn about himself, his strengths and weaknesses, the teaching strategies and activities he enjoys most, his preferences for particular social science interpretations, student characteristics, the strengths and weaknesses students bring to the classroom, and how to connect with students. Later in this chapter, we will return to John and turn to other middle- and high-school teachers to illustrate how teacher knowledge influences the selection and use of instructional tools.

Like John Foyle, you will graduate from your teacher-education program with a wealth of knowledge. Your academic preparation is no less demanding. You, too, are successfully completing a number of academic hours and you, too, will possess the necessary content knowledge to teach most of the basic courses in your discipline. However, to become an outstanding teacher, you will need additional knowledge in your discipline, expertise in pedagogy, and teaching experience.

■ ■ THE STUDENT TEXTBOOK AS AN INSTRUCTIONAL TOOL

The textbook is the most criticized of the instructional tools found in the classroom (McCarthy, 1993). Why is it so maligned? Is the student textbook a "bad" tool? We contend that the student textbook is neither "good" nor "bad." It is a tool—like the half-inch screwdriver mentioned earlier—that, when understood and properly employed, is appropriate and useful for planning and implementing instruction. In the next three sections, we describe the textbook and offer strategies on how best to employ it. We describe the student textbook, the teacher's annotated edition (TAE), and ancillary (supplementary) materials accompanying most textbooks and textbook series.

Student textbooks are instructional tools containing content students are required to learn about a particular discipline or area of study (e.g., mathematics, English, world cultures, Spanish, science, health) at a particular grade level. The content usually reflects district and state mandates, the standards for the disciplines, and information appearing on standardized tests. Because textbooks include content, some administrators and teachers see them as conveyors of the "official" content of an area of study. In their eagerness to market books, some publishing companies' representatives suggest to teachers that everything they need to teach in a particular discipline is contained in the textbook. However, textbook authors and editors readily acknowledge that a textbook is only as good as the person who is using it. In other words, textbooks do not teach; teachers do.

Student textbooks contain much more than content. They also are filled with a variety of features aimed at helping students master content and skills and gain a positive disposition toward the subject area. A typical chapter in a middle-school U. S. history textbook, for example, includes at least the following features: a clear explanation of the chapter main idea(s) and goals, a timeline, key terms, illustrations, reviews of chapter sections, maps and graphs, contextualized skills teaching, and a chapter summary. When properly used by the teacher and students, these features can be quite beneficial in helping students learn. At a minimum, as Callahan, Clark, and Kellough (1998) point out, textbooks can provide:

- a base for building higher-order thinking activities (e.g., inquiry discussions and student research) that help to develop critical thinking skills
- a basis for selecting subject matter that can be used for deciding content emphasis
- an organization of basic or important content for the students
- information about other readings and resources that can enhance the learning experiences of students
- previously tested activities and suggestions for learning experiences

Clark & Starr (1996) list a number of suggestions aimed at avoiding a textbook's limitations while integrating its use in instruction (see Fig. 7.1).

Katie Bridges, an Urbana Middle School teacher who has an extensive background in world history, will help us illustrate an effective use of the textbook, *America's Past and Promise* (Mason et al., 1995). Chapter Two, "Peoples of West Africa (Beginnings-1591)," introduces eighth-graders to the early civilizations of Africa, the development of West African empires, and their first contacts with Europeans. Katie has decided to whet her students' interests by selecting specific features that acquaint students with the main ideas in each chapter section. These include: (1) a timeline to introduce the students to the time period and to illustrate the spread of knowledge in Africa; (2) a photograph of a gold necklace and maps of West African empires to emphasize the idea that a profitable gold trade across the Sahara allowed prosperous states and empires to develop; and (3) a short biographical sketch of Alex Haley, the author of *Roots: The Saga of an American Family* (1976), to underscore the idea that the arrival of Portuguese ships and traders along the West African coast in the 1400s would have far-reaching consequences for the region and beyond. Katie will conclude the chapter introduction by mentioning to students that, while they are studying West Africa, they will plan a celebration of Kwanzaa, an American contemporary festival based on West African traditions during and after the time period under examination. At this point, she will turn to her pedagogical and subject-area expertise to select strategies to help her and her students delve more deeply into the early history of West Africa.

Textbooks include a variety of strategies aimed at addressing a problem that middle-and high-school teachers encounter on a daily basis—students who have difficulty reading the text. In social studies textbooks, for example, authors include an

---

FIGURE 7.1   Guidelines for Using Student Textbooks

1.   Become familiar with the textbook before you use it.
2.   Use the textbook in your planning as a source of structure if it seems desirable to do so, but do not let yourself become dependent on the book.
3.   Use the text as only one of many materials and activities. Additional readings, simulations, role playing, discussions, films, and visuals can enrich your instruction.
4.   Develop problem-solving activities for which the text is but one source of data.
5.   Use only those parts of the text that are relevant; rearrange the order of topics if necessary. Adapt the text to the needs and abilities of your students.
6.   Use additional or substitute readings to allow for learning differences. Provide taped versions of the text for students whose reading skills are markedly weak.
7.   Teach students how to use the major parts of the text, such as the table of contents, index, headings, charts, graphs, and illustrations.
8.   Build lessons around the illustrations, charts, graphs, and other aids included in the textbook.
9.   Encourage critical reading. Compare the text to other resources. Test the text for logic and bias.
10. Introduce new vocabulary in a systematic fashion.

(From Clark, L. H., & Starr, I. S. (1996). *Secondary and middle school teaching methods.* (7th edition). Upper Saddle River, NJ: Merrill Prentice Hall, p. 316).

array of clues aimed at developing students' abilities to read and learn information from visual sources. Specifically, clues that encourage students to: (1) make inferences regarding historical events and situations from visual sources, (2) improve students' ability to interpret data presented in visual form, (3) help students use visuals to improve their comprehension of written texts in print media and in textbooks, and (4) improve students' ability to think critically about historical and current events images in the mass media. Similar clues are found in most other student textbooks depicting the content areas (see Fig. 7.2).

▪▪▪ TEACHER'S ANNOTATED EDITION (TAE) AS AN INSTRUCTIONAL TOOL

The Teacher's Annotated Edition (TAE) of a student textbook is a rich source of information that, when properly used, can be quite helpful to the teacher. The TAE provides teachers with a wealth of ideas on how to introduce, reinforce, and extend knowledge and skills and suggests strategies for creating environments that lead students to positive dispositions toward a subject area. Recall the review of a TAE you completed in Chapter Six, "Planning for Middle-and High-School Instruction." This review should remind you that TAEs can be invaluable in planning. Teachers use the TAE because it provides a legitimate and accepted approach to organizing content and skills and suggestions on how to initiate, implement, and conclude instruction. Examine several TAEs in your discipline and become familiar with the ways authors and publishers package content for students and teachers.

FIGURE 7.2   Adapting Student Textbooks for Diverse Classrooms

1. Assess student reading levels in order to identify those who may not be able to comprehend textbooks written at grade level.
2. Have students articulate their purpose for reading prior to the act of reading.
3. Give students the option of hearing the text read aloud.
4. Provide xeroxed copies of readings so that students can highlight or otherwise mark text.
5. Allow students to read and work in pairs or cooperative groups.
6. Teach study strategies, such as SQ3R (Survey, Question, Read, Recite, Review).
7. Summarize or reduce textbook information.
8. Develop study guides to focus reading.
9. Teach students to use graphic organizers and other strategies to increase comprehension.
10. Use interactive notebooks that encourage students to record their personal understanding of what they read.
11. Give manageable reading assignments and reasonable times for completion.

From "Getting Ready for Inclusion: Is the Stage Set?" by J. S. Schumm and S. Vaughn, 1995, *Learning Disabilities Research and Practice,* 10(3), p. 169–179 and *Fundamentals of Special Education: What Every Teacher Needs to Know* by R. A. Culatta and J. R. Tompkins, 1999, Upper Saddle River, NJ: Merrill/Prentice Hall.

The fundamental features of a TAE can be beneficial to both novice and experienced teachers, providing an array of ideas and information on how to bring breadth and depth to ideas, issues, and personalities. For example, *Algebra 2: An Integrated Approach* (Carter, Molina, Sgroi, Hansen, & Westegaard, 1997), features introductory essays on team learning, learning styles, multicultural education, portfolios, manipulatives, technology, and a bibliography of suggested readings. Each chapter contains copious support for teachers. Some of the components of Chapter 1, "Modeling and Predicting," include

- a chapter theme (Cars and Business)
- a class project (build model race cars and hold a class car show)
- a lesson plan for each topic
- suggested assignments
- technology applications
- math journal prompts
- suggestions for addressing multiple intelligences
- vocabulary notes for English language learners
- interdisciplinary connections
- study skills tips
- suggestions for portfolio entries
- suggestions for a culminating performance assessment
- a cumulative review of the chapter (sample problems)
- problems commonly found on standardized tests

Even a cursory examination suggests that the teacher who made wise use of this TAE would be well on the way to addressing the needs of all learners.

CONSULTING OTHER SOURCES
"Examining TAEs"

Visit the university curriculum library to examine teacher-edition textbooks. Ask the librarian to direct you to the section of the library where textbooks published for use in K–12 schools are located. Scan the books, identify two in your subject area, and examine them carefully to identify the many features included to assist teachers. Use the questions listed below to select one of the textbooks to share with the class:

1. What features does the textbook include that you find to be quite helpful?
2. What features assist the teacher to teach content? to engage the students with the content? to assess learning?
3. What features do you find weak? Why?
4. Describe to the class how you would use the textbook to organize for instruction.
5. Would you recommend to your peers that they use a TAE to organize, facilitate, and assess teaching and learning?

■■■ ANCILLARY MATERIALS AS INSTRUCTIONAL TOOLS

Along with a TAE, publishers also develop and offer teachers ancillary (supplementary) materials that can be used with the student textbook. Ideas for these materials usually originate with teachers and curriculum experts in the schools. Four types of ancillary materials are generally available: (1) resources aimed at helping the teacher in the subject areas (e.g., study guides, lesson plans, and graphic organizers); (2) suggestions to address student differences (e.g., resources for Spanish-speaking students, skills practices and challenges, creative teaching strategies, reteaching resources); (3) ideas about interdisciplinary teaching (e.g., musical selections, multicultural resources); and (4) test generators.

While developing his unit on the "Roaring Twenties," Brian Kahn, the middle-school teacher introduced in Chapter Six, reviewed the ancillary materials and selected three sources to supplement the textbook's examples of prejudice toward immigrants during this period. Brian identified several resources to enrich the textbook's presentation of the Sacco and Vanzetti Case. He found one primary source, "Bartolomeo Vanzetti's Speech to the Jury," and a supplementary reading entitled "Anti-Italian Prejudice in the 1920s." Brian will provide his two Spanish-speaking students with a chapter summary written in Spanish (Spanish Language Resources). Next year, with a different group of students, Brian will use a different set of resources. The key, Brian has learned, is to identify specific needs and then look for the tools that will help address those needs.

WHAT WOULD YOU DO?
Your First Week of Teaching

You are teaching general mathematics at the high-school level. Your students are juniors, and this is the last required math course they must successfully complete to graduate in the following year. The students are a cross-section of the school population, but most are not highly motivated to study mathematics and few are thinking of pursuing post-secondary education.

As you arrive in the classroom on the fourth day of class, you sense that something is amiss. The bell rings, and before you can read the morning announcements, three students—Willie, Lana, and Lester—stand and ask to speak to the class. Willie has indicated to you that he would like to graduate from high school and begin a career in retail business; Lana just wants to pass the class and graduate; Lester, while showing very little interest in mathematics, possesses the academic skills to continue his education after high school. You wait anxiously to hear what the students have to say.

Willie: I don't speak for everyone, but I just want to tell you that, while I don't like mathematics, I know I need it if I am going to get a job at a department store. I don't mind starting as a sales associate, but I want to move up and join management. What I want to learn in this class is more than what is found in the textbook. I want you to show me the value of mathematics in the line of work I've chosen.

Lana: I've spoken to a few people in this class and we all agree that the textbook you are asking us to read is difficult, boring, and has no relevance to our lives. This book is about numbers, theories, and a lot of other mumble-jumble. We hate it! If this is mathematics, we don't need it!

Lester: When I'm with my friends, we talk about how boring school is. And I think this class and this textbook are boring. I don't think I'm going to pass this class.

What would you do if you were beginning your teaching career and a group of students in one or more of your classes blurted statements like those made by Willie, Lana, and Lester? Assume you agree somewhat with the students, and you announce to them that over the next few days you will revise the course so that the textbook is no longer the dominant tool of instruction. In groups or individually, develop a plan for changing your class to one where the needs of the students dictate what and how you will teach. Use the following questions to help you structure your plan.

1. With whom should I speak in my department and in the school if I wish to modify the role of the textbook in my classroom?
2. Who in the department or school can help me generate new plans for instruction?
3. What pedagogical questions should I ask as I plan for instruction?
4. What are effective ways of teaching mathematics to high-school students?
5. Is mathematics a textbook-bound discipline?
6. Is mathematics more theoretical than practical?
7. What should I know about the students to plan for instruction?
8. How do I connect the students with mathematics?
9. What resources other than the textbook are available to teach general mathematics?

   Share your unit with the class.

▮▮ COMMERCIALLY PREPARED MATERIALS AS INSTRUCTIONAL TOOLS

Many commercially prepared materials are designed to help teachers: (1) provide basic information in all subject areas; (2) enrich the curriculum; (3) address student differences; (4) highlight special topics; and (5) promote a particular view or interpretation.

Textbooks do not teach: teachers do.

These materials are produced and marketed by large publishing companies, such as Houghton Mifflin and Prentice Hall, and smaller publishing houses and clearing houses, such as Teacher's Video Company, Filmic Archives, and Scholastic Professional Books. Professional education organizations, such as the National Council for the Social Studies and the National Council of Teachers of Mathematics, also develop and market materials. A number of commercial enterprises and non-profit organizations, such as Greenhaven Press or the Anti-Defamation League of B'nai B'rith, market materials that promote alternative views on topics. While some commercially prepared materials can be dull, superficial, extremely biased, or of little value to either teachers or students, many are very well-prepared and can be quite useful.

John Foyle, whom you met earlier in this chapter, is looking forward to attending his first NCSS Annual Conference and strolling through the exhibit area where many publishing companies exhibit their wares. He discovers background information materials; books on tips and methods of teaching social studies; test banks in the areas of history, geography, and political science; materials aimed at addressing student diversity; materials to enrich the curriculum; posters; multicultural resources; computer software; trinkets and gadgets aimed at rewarding positive student behavior; and encyclopedias and news magazines.

John returned from the NCSS conference with a multitude of materials. To supplement his video library of biographies, John will order for preview and possible purchase two videos from Filmic Archives in Botsford, Connecticut: "General Douglas MacArthur: Return of a Legend" and "Attila: The Scourge of God." In addition, to sensitize his students to the accomplishments of the physically challenged in society, he will order for preview and possible purchase a set of books from Chelsea Curriculum

Publications in Broomall, Pennsylvania, describing the accomplishments of men and women "who have found the strength and courage to develop their special talents." Some of the individuals included in the list are Jim Abbott, a major league baseball player who was born without a right hand, and Stephen Hawking, a physicist who has Lou Gehrig's disease. Before making a decision to purchase any of these materials, John will reflect on his goals as a teacher, what he wishes his students to learn about military leaders and the physically challenged, and how he might integrate these materials into the curriculum. Last, he will use an evaluation instrument, like the one we describe later, to help him decide the value of these materials.

■■ COMMUNITY RESOURCES AS INSTRUCTIONAL TOOLS

All communities possess a wealth of resources, most of which are available to teachers. Community resources include field trip locations, resource people (including parents), resource materials, community organizations, and local businesses, industries, and agencies. Making use of community resources enriches the curriculum by bringing the classroom to the community or the community to the classroom. Often, districts or schools have documents listing approved community resources.

A field trip to the local university or college and a luncheon date with an English professor could provide students in a secondary English class with examples of the universality of themes and examples of their treatment in the college curriculum. A director of the Red Cross could provide a health class with examples of local strategies aimed at combating communicable diseases. A middle-school social studies class could use materials available through the local historical society to trace the beginnings of their community. A secondary science class could make use of the resources available through a weather bureau or storm center to study the impact of storm-related disasters on the community. A journalism class could visit the offices of the local newspaper and speak with a reporter to gain first-hand knowledge of the duties and responsibilities of reporters and the opportunities available to them. Foreign language classes could learn the advantages of being bilingual or multilingual by visiting a local self-help organization and observing the language skills of personnel responsible for helping recent immigrants become American citizens.

Community resources have the potential of helping students see the connection between classroom learning and their community. A strong bond emerges between school and community when students in the Florida Keys, for example, examine the topic "Weather and Climate" in a science class and then visit a near-by storm center or listen to a meteorologist discuss weather patterns in the southeast.

However, we must offer a word of caution here. Teachers should follow established procedures when contemplating the use of community resources and adhere to common-sense guidelines.

1. Be sure the community resources you wish to use appear on the school's or district's approved list. If the community resource is not on the approved list, check with your principal or department chair and obtain written approval.
2. Reflect on your educational goals and objectives and be sure the place you wish to visit, the materials you wish to use, or the speaker you wish to invite is the best source to help you address those objectives.
3. Personally preview the community resource before using it in your planning.

4. Brief speakers on your expectations so that they will be able to address your instructional goals.
5. Prepare students to get maximum benefit from the resource. For example, have students prepare questions in advance to address to a guest speaker.
6. Have students evaluate the importance of the community resource and contextualize the resource in the unit of study.

■■ TRADEBOOKS AS INSTRUCTIONAL TOOLS

While tradebooks are not found in every middle- and high-school classroom, they are a mainstay resource among teachers of social studies, English language arts, foreign language, and others who value a human dimension in their instructional programs. Tradebooks include works of adolescent and young adult literature, nonfiction, biographies and autobiographies, poetry, short stories, and historical fiction, among other genres. Teachers use tradebooks for a variety of reasons: to balance the narrow, fact-oriented stance of the textbook; to provide students with an open and interpretive stance on issues, events, and personalities; to engage students; and to promote critical thinking (Bean, Kile, and Readence, 1996).

Teachers engaged in collaborative and interdisciplinary teaching find tradebooks especially useful. At a middle school in suburban Chicago, for example, I observed a social studies teacher and an English language arts teacher agree that, along with the U. S. history textbook, the other major readings for a unit on the American Civil War should be the classroom classics *My Brother Sam is Dead* (1974) and *With Every Drop of Blood* (1994). Both novels are excellent tools for exploring themes related to race and ethnicity in American culture. At a high school in the Champaign-Urbana area, I spoke with a social studies and a science teacher who are using the novel *California Blue* (1994) to explore a common theme: issues related to citizenship in a changing community. An abundance of adolescent and young adult literature is available to middle- and high-school teachers. The themes, events, and personalities treated in this literature challenge the imagination. Biographical material describes countless individuals, including women, recent immigrants, and minorities. Fiction and nonfiction works treat topics across middle- and high-school curricula.

Teachers can stay abreast of tradebooks by attending state, regional, and national meetings in their subject area and visiting the exhibits area where publishers display their materials, by reviewing education catalogs sent to their schools, reading professional journals and browsing through the adolescent section of book stores.

■■ THE MEDIA AS INSTRUCTIONAL TOOLS

Media are the means through which messages are communicated. Whether teachers like it or not, young people today absorb more messages from commercial media than they do from textbooks or other school-related materials. Media include newspapers, television, radio, film, magazines, comics, music CD's, billboards, and other forms of advertising. Interactive media include CD-ROMs, video games, Internet sites, and virtual realities (Rosen, Quesada, & Summers, 1998). In the classroom, media materials can be easily integrated into almost any subject area. Film, television, and music clips can enhance motivation, enliven a lesson, reinforce content, and help students connect with the curriculum. Many schools subscribe to daily newspapers that are delivered right to classrooms. Newspapers, radio stations, and magazines around the country and the world have web sites where students can read and listen to the news as experienced from many perspectives. Both commercial and public television stations have web sites where students can access archives and pursue links to more information. Books-on-tape appeal to many students, especially auditory learners and students with reading difficulties. Students can produce their own instructional materials in the form of videotapes, audiotapes, and CDs.

Channel One, a commercial station developed exclusively for schools, is required viewing in those schools that subscribe. Channel One produces a daily twelve-minute news broadcast that includes two minutes of advertising, the most controversial feature of the programming. Schools that subscribe to Channel One—and in 1996 there were 12,000—receive televisions for each classroom, two VCR's, additional educational video material, a satellite link, and access to some educational programming (Hoynes, 1998). The system enables schools to produce their own programming, and many schools follow the national daily broadcast with a school news show produced by students. Supporters of Channel One believe it has the potential to "transform . . . school into places where learning can occur in all kinds of dynamic new ways" (Tiene & Whitmore, 1995, p. 42). Critics question the quality of its news coverage and its blatant marketing pitch to captive audiences (Hoynes, 1998).

It is important for teachers to use media as instructional materials and to use media as the subject of study. As media promise to become ever more sophisticated in their ability to reach and manipulate the public, it is critical that young people possess the media literacy needed to become critical producers and consumers. (Technology and methods for evaluating technological tools in the classroom will be discussed in depth in Chapter Eight, "Teaching with Technology.")

▌▌REALIA AS INSTRUCTIONAL TOOLS

Strictly speaking, realia are real objects or reproductions of real objects that are used most often in foreign language or social studies classrooms. For example, a Spanish teacher who travels to Costa Rica might bring back music, magazines, newspapers, menus, canned goods, fabrics, and many other items that can be used as instructional materials. Similarly, a social studies teacher who travels to Egypt can put together a trunk or suitcase of items that can become instructional materials in a world studies class.

By extension, realia can be any "stuff" you use in the classroom for instructional purposes. Classroom dramas and skits are enhanced by costumes and props. Everyday objects can serve to teach knowledge, concepts, and skills. Math students can examine patterns in traditional African fabrics, business students can work with tax forms and manuals, science students can closely observe flowers and leaves. Many creative teachers shop at flea markets, garage sales, and discount stores, seeking objects that might bring a lesson home in the classroom.

Figure 7.3 summarizes the strengths and weaknesses of all of the instructional tools described in this chapter.

FIGURE 7.3	Strengths and Weaknesses of Instructional Tools

Instructional Tool	Potential Strengths	Potential Weaknesses
teacher knowledge	• brings expertise and enthusiasm to the study of the discipline • brings depth of understanding to planning and instruction • models value of inquiry in discipline • builds on core knowledge in exploring new knowledge • promotes interdisciplinary learning	• may promote a particular view on topic or issue • may rely too heavily on personal expertise
student textbook	• provides organizational framework of content • has features aimed at connecting students to content • has features aimed at helping students master content (e.g., section reviews, activities) • has graphics and visuals aimed at engaging student interest	• may represent only one perspective of topic, issue, event • may be uninteresting • may not reflect students' interests and needs • may be viewed as representing a "lock-step" approach to learning
teacher's annotated edition (TAE)	• provides accepted method of organizing a subject area • provides accepted methods of organizing knowledge and skills • contains ideas on adding breadth and depth to study of discipline • contains suggestions for pedagogy, addressing special needs, making interdisciplinary connections, further reading and resources	• may present only one perspective • may encourage a "lock-step" approach to teaching
ancillary materials	• offer a wealth of ideas for teaching creatively • offer ideas for addressing student differences • offer ideas for addressing current topics in reform (e.g., portfolios, rubric development, teaching in the block schedule)	• may encourage reliance on one source • may discourage teacher creativity • may be used as "busy work" or means of controlling students
commercial materials	• provide alternative views on topics, issues, events • address student differences • enrich instruction with curriculum that aligns with students' interests	• may distort interpretations of topics, issues, events • may be inaccurate • may be expensive
trade books	• often of high interest to students • emphasize interdisciplinary connections • emphasize the human dimension of learning • strengthen students' literacy skills and reinforce value of reading	• if fiction, may be mistaken as factual • may provide distorted views of topics, issues, events • may not reflect community values

FIGURE 7.3   Continued

Instructional Tool	Potential Strengths	Potential Weaknesses
community resources	• help to build and enrich basic instruction • offer students opportunities to interact with adult experts and practitioners • offer students opportunities to see connections between school and community • help build partnerships between school and community	• may promote a particular view on a topic, issue, event • may be viewed by students as "fun" and not part of learning • may not connect to classroom curriculum
media	• capitalize on students interests and characteristics • bring "real world" to classroom • encourage critical analysis of multiple perspectives • appealing to many types of learners	• may present distorted views • may be used to "baby-sit" students • may be difficult to use if access to equipment is limited • may not reflect community values
realia	• engage student interest and imagination • appeal to hands-on learners • bring "real world" to classroom	• may be expensive or difficult to acquire • require teacher creativity
standards	• have been validated by cross-section of educational community • give guidance regarding content appropriate for all students • often include suggestions for teaching strategies, student performance • often include extensive lists of resources	• may be seen as mandates of what to teach • may be unnecessary because of material already contained in textbooks • may be viewed as initiatives aimed at creating national tests and curriculum
curriculum guides	• outline suggested content in subject areas • link to national and state standards and often assessments • often reflect community interests and needs • may suggest pedagogy appropriate for achieving goals	• may encourage a "lock-step" approach to teaching • may limit teacher creativity • may discourage teachers from sharpening their planning skills

▌Reader Activity 7.4

IN THE FIELD
Inventorying Instructional Materials in Your Subject Area

The purpose of this activity is to examine the resources used by practicing teachers in your subject area. You may work independently, in pairs, or in small groups. Select a middle or high school in your home community or in/near the city where your college is located. Focus on a single teacher (preferably one who uses a variety of resources) or an entire department. Make a list of the materials the teacher or department commonly uses in the course of a school year. Compare your list with lists your peers compile from other subject areas.

▌▌EVALUATING INSTRUCTIONAL TOOLS

It is important to be informed about how instructional tools are adopted by school districts and about the steps teachers follow when making decisions about what materials to bring into the classroom. Instructional materials can be expensive and school budgets are often restricted. Using evaluation procedures such as those described in this chapter can not only help you avoid needless controversy, but also guide you to use limited resources wisely.

Student textbooks, teacher annotated editions, and ancillary materials are reviewed by a variety of different groups before they are adopted at state and local levels. At the state level, board members, board staff, teachers, special interest groups, and others have many opportunities to comment on materials submitted for adoption. Once materials are adopted, local districts constitute their own committee structure to review textbooks and other materials and to recommend district adoption. This review process is exhaustive, but it effectively eliminates materials that do not meet state and local standards. District and teacher curriculum guides and state and local goals and standards are also reviewed, formally and informally. Documents produced by the educational community at national and state levels (e.g., national standards or recommendations of blue ribbon committees) are reviewed informally by other educators and may influence state and local policy and procedures. School officials usually avoid endorsing or adopting materials or documents that are viewed as controversial and that raise the ire of educators, politicians, and community members.

Commercially prepared materials and tradebooks usually are not reviewed at the state and local levels, and, while some community resources may appear on district lists, they may not have been stringently reviewed. If you are not sure about the appropriateness of materials you wish to bring into the classroom, ask yourself these questions.

1. Has the material been adopted by the district?
2. Has the material been reviewed by another teacher or group of teachers?
3. Has the material been employed by other teachers?
4. Have I checked with the department chair or the principal if I am unsure about the appropriateness of the material?

Becoming familiar with these general questions and the evaluation system in place in your school or district are the first steps in learning the importance of evaluating material you wish to employ in the classroom. The next step is using an evaluation instrument, such as the ones described below.

Because curriculum in the subject areas varies so widely, it is a good idea to explore the guidelines that have been established by your subject-area's professional organization. For example, the National Council of Teachers of English (NCTE) publishes a brochure entitled "Guidelines for Selection of Materials in English Language Arts Programs." This brochure poses two broad questions relevant to any subject area: (1) What is the connection between the resource and the stated educational objectives? and (2) How relevant is the resource to the educational needs of the students? Among other questions teachers need to consider are the following:

- What is the educational philosophy of the district?
- What are the goals of the subject-area program?
- Will this instructional tool be of use to other teachers in the school or department?
- What are the objectives to be met in the unit of study for which the material is intended?
- How will this tool help meet the developmental (e.g., intellectual, social, physical, and psychological) needs of students?
- How will this tool address ethnic, cultural, linguistic, religious, or other relevant characteristics of students?
- What is the need for multiple perspectives on a topic, issue, theme, or genre?

Another instrument, developed by the National Council for the Social Studies (NCSS) and entitled "Curriculum Guidelines for Multicultural Education," (NCSS Task Force on Ethnic Education, 1992), provides educators with guidance in evaluating instructional materials for their multicultural dimensions. The first part of this document includes a rationale for ethnic pluralism and multicultural education, background information on ethnic and cultural groups, principles of ethnic and cultural diversity, information on the nature of the learner, and goals for school reform. The second part of the instrument consists of twenty-three guidelines for multicultural education in a school. The third section is a materials-evaluation checklist with a rating system for use by the teacher. A middle-school math teacher, for example, might ask herself the following questions regarding a video series on women in mathematics she is considering purchasing.

- Does this material provide continuous opportunities for students to develop a better sense of self?
- Does this material help students to better understand themselves in light of their ethnic and cultural heritages?
- Does this material help students identify and understand the ever-present conflict between ideals and realities in human societies?
- Does this material help students identify and understand the value conflicts inherent in a multicultural society? (National Task Force on Ethnic Studies, 1992).

Using guidelines like these, an educator can gauge how well a school, a classroom, or an instructional resource promotes multicultural education. Both the NCTE brochure and the NCSS document could easily be adapted by teachers in other subject areas.

▌Reader Activity 7.5

CONSULTING OTHER SOURCES
Evaluating Resources for Classroom Use

Many of us have heard accounts of teachers bringing material into their classroom that students or parents found offensive. We have also heard reports of school administrators reprimanding or dismissing teachers for instructional practices that were considered unprofessional. Such events are more the exception than the rule. That is, teachers are professional and rarely are questioned by anyone about the material they bring into the classroom. It is more common to hear teachers being praised for their adept use of resources and innovative instructional practices.

In this exercise, you will work with a small group as you explore the question of evaluation. Should teachers be required to maintain some form of documentation in regard to the appropriateness of materials that are not adopted by the school district? You will address the following two questions: (1) What are the major arguments for requiring teachers to evaluate resources they wish to bring into the classroom? and (2) What are the major arguments for allowing teachers to make decisions relating to planning and implementing instruction with specific regard to materials selection?

Select and interview one or more representatives of the groups listed below.

- teachers
- students
- parents
- PTA/PTO officers
- school administrators
- librarians
- teacher's union officials and officials of other organizations representing teachers
- community organizations
- experts in the field

Pose a series of questions that will help you determine your interviewee's position on evaluating instructional materials and classroom teachers' rights and responsibilities in regard to selecting instructional tools. With your peers debate the issues associated with materials evaluation as derived from the views expressed in your interview.

▮▮ NATIONAL AND LOCAL STANDARDS AS INSTRUCTIONAL TOOLS

Standards documents can be viewed as instructional tools for teachers. As you recall from previous chapters, standards are general statements describing the major ideas of each of the subject areas in the K-12 curriculum. They define for teachers, students, parents, and other interested parties what teachers should be teaching and what students should be learning. If you are a high-school mathematics teacher responsible for second year algebra, for example, the standards document would indicate what knowledge and skills you should be teaching, examples of how you might teach algebra (e.g., lesson plans or case studies), and classroom scenarios of students exhibiting an understanding of this content.

The standards movement began in the 1980s, led by the National Council of Teachers of Mathematics, and gained momentum in the early 1990s when the National Council on Education Standards and Testing recommended the development of national standards in the core areas. It gathered even greater momentum with the passage of Goals 2000: Educate America Act. By the mid 1990s, most education organizations representing the subject areas in the K-12 curriculum had developed and published standards.

The educational community does not unanimously agree that standards are necessary to improve the quality of teaching and increase student performance. Critics have argued that standards will lead to the nationalization of the curriculum; that standards will lead to national testing and teachers teaching to tests; and that the movement is a "top-down" initiative originating with politicians and business leaders whose interests are not necessarily aligned with those of teachers and students (Noddings, 1997; Weinstein, 1996; Sabers & Sabers, 1996).

On the other hand, many educators view standards as an essential tool that belongs in teachers' "toolboxes." Proponents argue that standards provide teachers with guidance in the planning and teaching process. They further contend that standards are a valuable tool because they represent the best thinking of classroom teachers, personnel in curriculum, the disciplines, teacher education, and professional organizations. They point out that standards documents for each of the subject areas represent an integration of many perspectives on how to teach and how students can best learn, and that the statements are not mandates but guidelines and, when properly employed, can help bolster the role of teachers as classroom leaders.

The national standards are public documents, available to everyone. This availability "levels the playing field" by informing all parties of performance expectations with respect to each of the K-12 subject areas. Because they are national, standards are inclusive. Whether you are a teacher, student, or parent in rural, suburban, or urban America, the standards apply. As a result, they represent a step forward on the path toward equity. However, whether communities possess the will and resources to implement the standards is another issue.

▊▊CURRICULUM GUIDES AS INSTRUCTIONAL TOOLS

Most states and many districts have participated in the standards movement by creating their own standards for learning that are aligned with the national models. State, district, and school curriculum guides reflect this alignment. State and district curriculum guides vary in their level of detail, but they are usually formal documents approved by the school board and located in the offices of a district's curriculum director. School and teacher curriculum guides usually are not formally adopted and can generally be found in the offices of school administrators and department chairs or teachers' classrooms.

At all levels, curriculum guides are intended to help teachers stay on track in meeting national, state, or local goals. For example, one of the *Illinois Learning Standards* states, "As a result of their schooling, students will be able to locate, organize, and use information from various sources to answer questions, solve problems, and communicate ideas" (Illinois State Board of Education, 1997, p. 12). Local districts have responded to the state standards in a variety of ways. In Champaign, Illinois, for example, the Champaign Community Unit District #4 developed two parallel documents. First, curriculum handbooks provide the general community with descriptions of courses (or sets of experiences) offered in the middle and high schools. These handbooks further clarify and explicate the state goal given above. According to the curriculum handbook, in Champaign mathematics classrooms, students do the following:

- review and expand their knowledge of basic operations (addition, subtraction, multiplication, division)
- focus on decimals, fraction, numeration, and number theory
- learn about measurement, geometry, statistics, percent, integers, algebra, and probability
- complete activities involving math communications, math connections, critical thinking, math reasoning, and problem solving

- make use of technology, including calculators and computers, when appropriate (Champaign Community Unit District #4, 1998, p. 12).

A second document, entitled "State Goals for Learning and Local Learning Result Statements," contains state goals, district goals and student performance indicators. The following excerpts reveal how these interface.

Sample Illinois State Goal for mathematics: "As a result of their schooling, students will be able to use algebraic concepts and procedures to represent and solve problems" (Illinois State Board of Education, 1997, p. 22).

Sample Champaign district goal: "Students will be able to solve addition and subtraction problems involving ratios, proportions, interpret results and apply them to real life situations." (Champaign Community Unit District #4, 1998, p. 12).

Sample Champaign student performance indicator: "Students will be able to use correct terminology related to addition and subtraction" (Champaign Community Unit District #4, 1998, p. 12.

▍Reader Activity 7.6

WHAT WOULD YOU DO?
Eco-Graphics

The purpose of this activity is to give you the opportunity to apply what you have learned about instructional materials. Mary Micallef created a unit she entitled "EcoGraphics: Photographic Studies of Man's Impact on the Environment" as a project for approximately 100 students enrolled in the gifted program at Tapp Middle School in Powder Springs, Georgia. Ms. Micallef's goals were: (1) to make students aware of how destructive our society's "throw-away" ethic is to the environment; (2) to motivate students to discover solutions to environmental problems; and (3) to inspire students to commit themselves to bringing about change. Highlights of her project are presented here.

- Ms. Micallef launched the project by showing students the amount of trash that results from unwrapping all the items in one large bag of groceries. After discussing this problem and its extensions, she gave students a bibliography that included books, articles, resource people, poems, plays, records, films, and videotapes.
- Each student chose a topic to research in depth (e.g., pesticides, hazardous waste). Students reported their research to the whole group. In their presentations, they used pamphlets, handouts, graphs, displays, audiovisual aids, and guest speakers.
- Students worked in small groups to research problems in their communities, propose solutions, and then actually bring about improvements.
- To document their research, students used a variety of photographic techniques, including slide-tape presentations, photo essays, videotapes, collages, and photo displays.
- In the process of research, they interviewed community members, such as the manager of a solid waste disposal plant.
- During the action component of the project, students shared their findings with county officials, wrote letters to members of Congress, and contacted industries. Some cleaned up the sites they studied. Some conducted community surveys on attitudes toward recycling. Their projects attracted the attention of the media, which led to increased community awareness.

According to Ms. Micallef, the project helped students' self-confidence, sharpened their analytic and research skills, and enhanced their photographic/media skills. More importantly, students became personally invested in their projects and took pride in making a difference in their communities.

Questions to Consider

1. How many different instructional materials were used by Ms. Micallef and her students? Who created them and how were they used?
2. This project was designed for gifted middle-school students. Do you think it might be appropriate for other student populations? If so, how might it be adapted?
3. What are the strengths and limitations of this kind of project?
4. To what extent could such a project help students meet national and state standards?

▮▮▮ SUMMARY

I began this chapter by relating my experiences as a student, a teacher, and a teacher educator to highlight the popularity of textbooks in the United States and other countries. I also described the importance of using more than one tool when planning and implementing instruction. I concluded the first part of the chapter by challenging you to think beyond the textbook when planning and implementing instruction. A major component of the chapter was devoted to describing the many tools available to teachers when planning and implementing instruction. I concluded the chapter by describing two instruments that can be used to evaluate instructional materials. Among the key points to remember are:

- The use of a variety of instructional materials enhances student engagement and learning.
- Instructional materials may be viewed as tools. All tools are most effective when used for their intended purposes, and no single tool is most effective for all purposes.
- When teachers plan using a variety of instructional materials, they gain confidence in their skills and strengthen their roles as instructional leaders.
- One of the most important instructional tools available to a teacher is his or her own knowledge.
- All instructional tools have strengths and weaknesses.
- Teachers need to be informed of state and local procedures for adopting and approving instructional materials.
- Many instruments exist to help teachers evaluate the appropriateness of instructional materials and the effectiveness of the overall school and classroom curriculum.
- Standards and curriculum guides serve as instructional tools for teachers.

This chapter has focused on selecting, using, and evaluating instructional materials that have been available for many years. In the next chapter, "Teaching with Technology," you will be introduced to the ways in which technology is transforming our definition of instructional tools. You will learn how technology can be integrated into instruction in order to enhance student learning in ways that were simply unavailable in previous decades.

▌▌BUILDING YOUR BIOGRAPHY, YOUR PERSONAL PRACTICAL PHILOSOPHY, AND PORTFOLIO

Building Your Autobiography

As you recollect your school experiences, describe some of your teachers and the instructional tools they used. If your recollections focus on classes where teachers and/or textbooks dominated instruction, evaluate the effectiveness of these classes in your overall learning. If your recollections are about other classes, describe the value of that instruction and its influence on your overall learning.

Developing Your Personal Practical Philosophy

Draft a section of your personal educational philosophy that describes your views about tools for instruction in middle and high school. In your essay, draw a distinction between middle- and high-school teaching and explain why the use of instructional tools might be different at each level. Make reference to characteristics of students, learning styles, optimal learning environments, and methods of assessment.

Collecting Artifacts for Your Portfolio

Review the Reader Activities you have completed in this chapter. Identify any you might eventually select for your portfolio. For example, you might use the notes you collected to complete Reader Activity 7.1 "Middle- and High-Schools Encourage Teachers to Use a Variety of Materials" and write an extended essay on resources teachers use to organize, facilitate, and assess for teaching and learning. In the essay you might describe what you believe are the strengths and weaknesses of using a variety of resources in the classroom.

▌▌ References

Bean, T. W., Kile, R. S., & Readence, J. E. (1996). Using trade books to encourage critical thinking about citizenship in high school social studies. *Social Education, 60* (4), 227–230.

Callahan, J. F., Clark, L. H., & Kellough, R. D. (1998). *Teaching in the middle and secondary schools* (6th Edition). Upper Saddle River, NJ: Merrill/Prentice Hall.

Clark, L. H., & Starr, I. S. (1996). *Secondary and middle school teaching methods* (7th Edition). Upper Saddle River, NJ: Merrill/Prentice Hall.

Collier, J. L. & Collier, C. (1974). *My brother Sam is dead.* New York, Four Winds.

_____. (1994). *With every drop of blood.* New York: Delacorte Press.

Champaign Community Unit District #4. (ND). *State goals for learning and local learning result statements.* Champaign, IL: Author.

Champaign Community Unit District #4 (1998). *High school curriculum handbook.* Champaign, IL: Author.

Champaign Community Unit #4 (1998). *Middle school handbook.* Champaign, IL: Author.

Culatta, R. A. & Tompkins, J. R. (1999). *Fundamentals of special education: What every teacher needs to know.* Upper Saddle River, NJ: Merrill/Prentice Hall.

Gerver, R., Carter, C., Molina, D., Sgroi, R., Hansen, M., & Westergaard, S. (1997). *Algebra 2: An integrated approach.* Cincinnati, OH: Southwestern.

Grossman, P. (1990). *The making of a teacher: Teacher knowledge and teacher education.* New York: Teachers College Press.

Haley, A. (1976). *Roots: The saga of an American family.* New York: Doubleday.

Hoynes, W. (1998). News for a teen market: The lessons of Channel One. *Journal of Curriculum and Supervision, 13*(4), 339–356.

Illinois State Board of Education. (1997). *Illinois learning standards.* Springfield, IL: Author.

Mason, L., Garcia, J., Powell, F., & Risinger, C. F. (1995). *America's past and promise.* Evanston, IL: McDougal Littell.

McCarthy, M. M. (1993). Challenges to the public school curriculum: New targets and strategies. *Phi Delta Kappan 75,* (1), 55–60.

NCSS Task Force on Ethnic Studies Curriculum Guidelines. (1992). Curriculum guidelines for multicultural education. *Social Education, 56,* (5), 274–294.

National Council of Teachers of English. (ND). *Guidelines for selection of material in English language arts programs.* Urbana, IL: Author.

Noddings, N. (1997). Think about standards. *Phi Delta Kappan, 79*(3), 184–189.

Rosen, E. Y., Quesada, A. P., & Summers, S. L. (1998). *Changing the world through media education.* Golden, CO: Fulcrum Publishing.

Sabers, D. L. & Sabers, D. S. (1996). Conceptualizing, measuring, and implementing higher (high or hire) standards. *Educational Researcher, 25*(8), 19–21.

Shulman, L. (1987). Knowledge and teaching: Foundations of the new reform. *Harvard Educational Review, 57*(1), 1–22.

Schumm, J. S. & Vaughn, S. (1995). Getting ready for inclusion: Is the stage set? *Learning Disabilities Research and Practice,* 10 (3), 169–179.

Tiene, D. & Whitmore, E. (1995). Beyond "Channel One:" How schools are using their school-wide television networks. *Educational Technology, 35*(3), 38–42.

Weinstein, R. S. (1996). High standards in a tracked system of schooling: For which students and with what educational support. *Educational Researcher, 25*(8), 16–18.

Websites

http://www.about.com

At this extensive web site, chose "Education." The Education page has links to many sources of instructional materials, including a link called "Free Stuff."

http://www.ala.org/parentspage

This is part of the web site maintained by the American Library Association. The Parents Page has advice on books and reading materials, as well as links to worthwhile educational web sites.

http://www.ed.gov/

This is the home page of the U.S. Department of Education. The page contains links to free government publications, lesson plans, and instructional materials, as well as up-to-date information on educational issues.

http://www.edresources.com

This company sells hardware and software in a variety of subject areas at a variety of grade levels.

Educational Resources, 1550 Executive Drive, P.O. Box 1900, Elgin, IL 60121-1900, 1-800-624-2926

http://www.filmicarchives.com

This company specializes in films for many subjects and grade levels.

Filmic Archives, The Cinema Center, Botsford, CT 06404-0386, 1-800-366-1920

http://www.sundancepub.com

This company specializes in tradebooks for middle and high school teachers and students.

Sundance, 234 Taylor Street, P.O. Box 1326, Littleton, MA 01460

http://www.scholastic.com

This company maintains an extensive webstie of educational resources and publishes and sells a variety of instructional materials.

This company sells a wide variety of instructional materials for use in middle and high schools.

Teacher's Discovery, 2714 Paldan Dr., Auburn Hills, MI 48326, 1-800-543-4180

8

Teaching with Technology

BUILDING ON BIOGRAPHY: WRITERS' WORKSHOP IN THE COMPUTER LAB

My first job in public school teaching was in a large suburban high school in northern California, teaching ninth- and eleventh-grade English. During that time, I (Kevin) thought about technology in relatively straightforward, pragmatic ways. How would watching *Lord of the Flies* on video spark my students' interest in the story, especially those who seemed to avoid reading the book? How would putting a poem up on the overhead projector help to focus my students' attention? Should I use a computer grading program? I considered technology a practical tool that assisted me in achieving my teaching goals. Because I knew I needed a lot of help, I had a positive disposition toward teaching with technology.

My next teaching job took me to a very different context: an American school in northern Italy where I eventually taught both middle- and high-school English and French. The American school was small but had a large budget compared to the school in California. Additionally, a few teachers in the school were genuinely enthusiastic about technology in education. The material and human resources in this context made it relatively easy for me to explore uses of technology in teaching. At the heart of this exploration was a move toward developing technology-rich contexts of learning. That is, rather than simply considering my own use of technological tools, I became involved in developing technological environments that I believed could change the learning experiences of my students in important ways. These projects included a network-based French poetry project, a networked essay-exchange project, and the early development of a writing lab. I begin with a story from my second year of teaching in northern Italy.

Everything seemed to be running along fairly smoothly. Teaching junior-level English in an American school in northern Italy in 1990, I was in the middle of an eight-week writing workshop. One of the tricky things about teaching secondary English is that everything related to language manages to slip into the curriculum—drama, grammar, public speaking, literature, and "language appreciation." At this point, I was happy to have this time to focus on writing and to bring something else into the curriculum that I felt important for literacy: word-processing. I had managed to schedule my class into the computer lab every day but Fridays, and we had finally gotten into the flow of everyone understanding how the writing workshop ought to run.

I was pleased as I looked around the room. Jana, Tyrone, and Alicia were gathered in one corner, away from the terminals, reading Jana's argument against school dress codes and giving feedback using a response guide which they had retrieved from a color-coded folder on the side table. Jason, who had resisted writing all year long, was using a personal narrative assignment option to tell the story of the garage band that he had started with William, who was sitting next to him, occasionally pointing at Jason's writing on the monitor and laughing. With a frown and a groan, Michelle approached the table where I was sitting to turn in the fourth draft of a dialogue piece she had been working on for three weeks. I stamped the front of her paper packet with a date stamp: March 17. That was so we both knew when I got it.

From my perspective, the great thing about doing the entire writing workshop in the lab was that students could more readily revise their work as they moved from draft to draft. Their resistance to revision, which must be related to the onerous task of hand-scripting endless lines of text, could be decreased at least somewhat. Another advantage to me was that typed text is much easier to read than student handwriting. Furthermore, I could respond to student work quickly, on the fly. As I walked by, their writing was up on screen—not hidden in scraggly spiral notebooks.

By today's standards, the technology in use in the above scenario is unsophisticated. Why bother with this example at all in a textbook chapter on technology? Shouldn't we be talking about Java scripting and the Internet? I began with this vignette because despite the technical simplicity of the tools involved, the scenario raises a number of key questions about the use of technology in education.

Questions to Consider

1. Think broadly of technology as a tool. How many different tools are Kevin and his students using in the writers' workshop?
2. How does the technology in use support Kevin's purpose as a teacher and the students' purposes as learners?
3. How do you use technology in your own writing?

▮▮PURPOSE

After teaching in Italy for four years, I returned to the United States to work on a doctoral degree in education at the University of Illinois. One of my purposes was to further explore the potentials of technology in education, particularly with respect to written composition. During my years of graduate study, the Internet has been constructed as a medium for the masses, raising enthusiasm about technology in education to an all-time high while also bringing a number of important critiques to the fore. By listening as these debates unfold and by observing the uses of technology in a number of different research projects, I have been able to reconsider some of my earlier assumptions about technology. Initially a pragmatic technology-user, and then an enthusiastic technology-rich context developer, in the last several years I have reflected more broadly and critically about educational goals and contexts and their relationships to technology. The purpose of this chapter is to help you consider a number of important questions about technology-teaching-context relations, questions that in the end should extend your thinking from specific technologies to broader educational values.

▮▮TOWARD A RELATIONAL DEFINITION OF TECHNOLOGY: TOOLS, PRACTICES, AND PURPOSES

How many different tools did you identify in the preceding vignette? DOS machines? networked printers? the copies of Microsoft Word on the computer hard drives? the writing response guide used by Jana, Tyrone, and Alicia? the colored folder in which it was located? the final self-evaluation sheet Michelle stapled to her paper? the rubber stamp I used to inscribe the date? Are these technologies?

Beyond the tools involved, we should also consider the practices of individuals using these tools. Many writers have argued that practices themselves are technologies. The assembly-line production of automobiles is a ready example, and team-based management of such assembly work is a more up-to-date practice we can readily term a "technology." What about the specific activities of the teacher and students in the example above? Is the technology just the software itself, or is it a particular use of the software? For example, while Michelle completed a final spell-checking of her paper before printing it out, she could have used the program to outline it or consulted the thesaurus, yet she did not. Should we focus on the tool and its designers' intentions, or Michelle's use of it?

As we think about all of the individual and group practices with technology going on in the writers' workshop, what purposes do they appear to serve and from whose perspective? What about student purposes and perspectives? How might we infer their thoughts or possible responses to the learning context I've described? How does the technology in context support their common and individual purposes, their similar and diverse needs as learners?

Technologies cannot be understood as stand-alone entities that can be readily described and analyzed according to their technical characteristics, and simply placed "in" education once we understand them. They should also be understood with respect to their histories of development. An historical perspective asks us to inquire about the initial intentions of the developer. For example, an American Studies teacher who might shrink from the idea of creating an environment of "corporate America" within her classroom might have students using software that embeds not just the practices but the values of corporate America. Inquiring into the histories of our classroom technologies can help us understand their limitations and potentials for students.

Technological tools are not neutral, but come shrink-wrapped and boxed with tendencies to interact in predictable ways (Bush, 1983). We need to "be aware of what a technology brings with it into all situations . . . what norms built into it by its designers constrain its use; otherwise we risk seeing the artifact as a neutral tool amenable to any use at all" (Bromley, 1997, pp. 12–13). Some questions you might ask are: Who developed this technology and why? Who was the "modal user" the developer had in mind? How does this user compare with my students? What values about learning and society are implicit in this technology and in the context in which it was developed?

This consideration of technology in relation to tools, practices, purposes, and histories leads us to define technology as follows:

> Technologies in education are sets of relations between tools, practices, and purposes that shape student learning. Technologies are present in every learning situation. Thus, old and new technologies bear important relations to one another in practice and in historical development.

These relations are depicted in Figure 8.1. Reflect on these relations as you consider the use of technologies in education, in your subject areas, and at particular grade levels.

▌Reader Activity 8.1

CONSULTING OTHER SOURCES
Technology and Education in the Media

You can develop a more integrated view of technology by entering into and critiquing popular discussions. Evaluate an article from a general audience magazine or newspaper that discusses at some length reform efforts concerning technology and education. For example, the article might discuss funding for new computers in a local school district, or a national effort to make the web more accessible and the promises for learning this holds. Your article might be a success story, a story of obstacles and failures, or something in between. In writing or in an oral presentation to your class, discuss and critique this article with respect to the integrated perspective described earlier. In your critique, list the questions that you would want to raise concerning the technology reform effort at hand if you were evaluating it.

FIGURE 8.1   Considering Technologies

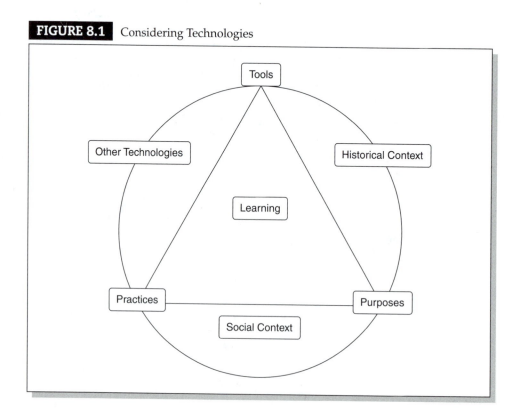

■■ A PURPOSE-BASED TAXONOMY OF EDUCATIONAL TECHNOLOGIES

Keep in mind the relational definition of technology in education as I return to and expand upon the issue of teachers' purposes in using educational technologies. A focus on purpose will help you, as a new teacher, bring together your practices with the specific tools that you select. In the following discussion, I have organized a range of educational technologies-in-use around valued purposes within education rather than around types of technologies (e.g., networked technologies, video, and word processing software).

As a framework for this section, I use a taxonomy that draws upon what Dewey (1943) described as our greatest educational resource: "the natural impulse to inquire or to find out things; to use language and thereby to enter into the social world; to build or make things; and to express one's feelings and ideas" (Bruce & Levin, 1997, p. 4). These four categories (inquiry, communication, construction, and expression) form the basic structure of the taxonomy and are an expression of both learner impulses and teacher purposes.

This purpose-based taxonomy of technology is grounded in a Dewey-inspired, inquiry-based approach to learning, an approach that is reflected in many other parts of this book. This taxonomy will help you consider how you can use the same technologies for multiple purposes and articulate your own purposes in teaching. In the four sections below, I discuss each of the media categories through extended stories drawn from my own or others' experiences. Many technological tools fit into more than one category of the taxonomy, and you may think of examples that do not fit any of the categories. Nevertheless, the taxonomy is a good starting place for considering the relationships of technologies to educational purposes (see Figure 8.2).

FIGURE 8.2   Media for Inquiry, Communication, Construction, and Expression

A. Media for Inquiry
   1. Theory building—technology as media for thinking
   2. Data access—connecting to the world of texts, video, data
   3. Data collection—using technology to extend the senses
   4. Data analysis
B. Media for Communication
   1. Document Preparation
   2. Communication—with other students, teachers, experts in various fields, and people around the world
   3. Collaborative media
   4. Teaching media
C. Media for Construction
D. Media for Expression

From "Educational Technology" by B. C. Bruce and J. A. Levin, 1997, *Journal of Educational Computing Research*, 17(1), pp. 79–102.

▪▪ MEDIA FOR INQUIRY

The current movement in education toward constructivist or inquiry-based teaching and learning is increasingly well-supported by developing technologies. The development of computer technologies is a good case in point. When I was in junior high and high school, computers were conceived of primarily as calculating machines, an image closely aligned with their history in big science. A few computer "geeks" would huddle in the back room and crank out their mystifying programs in BASIC, peering over one another's shoulders on the two clunky terminals.

Present developments and uses of computers and computer networks often redirect their raw calculating power to the presentation of media in many formats, to locating and retrieving vast amounts of information, and to sorting and analyzing this information in flexible ways. In sum, computer technologies are being used as tools that afford students access to a vast range of resources with which to work and about which to wonder. The first example discussed below, a project called ChickScope, is primarily related to data collection (extending the senses) aspects of inquiry. I then move on to discuss digital libraries (data access), and close with a discussion of SimCalc, as an example of both theory-building and data analysis.

ChickScope

Through a collaborative effort of several departments at the University of Illinois, students in grades two through twelve have become involved in Project Mayday/ChickScope. This collaborative project has permitted them to access interactively and manipulate a magnetic resonance imaging (MRI) microscope through the World Wide Web (WWW) in order to observe the development of a chick embryo inside an egg. This manipulation has been accompanied by other WWW information-gathering work by the students, such as reading written information and viewing video clips of embryonic development. In addition to having access to the MRI microscope, classrooms engaged in the project have hatched chick eggs in incubators and thus have been able to connect this low-tech direct experience with the high-tech scientific equipment accessed by the Web.

One might assume that many of the problems with such an effort could be linked to technical issues, e.g., classroom Web connections, or getting the MRI to interface with the Web. However, more questions have arisen related to how such a project fits into school structures, goals, and student knowledge. The chicks in the classroom have at times been reported by students and teachers to be more important than the chick on the Web, and the connections between the two have been uncertain. Even more interesting is the issue of student background knowledge. In an early round with the project, researchers found that classrooms were struggling to make sense of the MRI images. How does a student know that the dark region in the image is the heart? What is that blurry area, and why does it seem to shift? (Bruce et al., 1997). The problem is not student knowledge of technological tools, but student understanding of what technology makes available to them.

The ChickScope project demonstrates an important consideration: any technology should be thought of as only one resource in a well-developed curriculum. For example, one teacher made the following list of ideas for integrating ChickScope into her curriculum before the formal project was actually underway.

1. Egg dissection.
2. Have students search the Web for other related sites.
3. Read *Science World* article called: "From One-Cell to Full-Grown: Embryonic Development."
4. Relate to biology concepts like fertilization, gestation, and incubation.
5. Relate to vertebrate biology as far as the Ave (bird) phylum. Compare and contrast birds to other phyla of animals.
6. Relate MRI to what we have already learned about magnetism.
7. Investigate other real world applications for MRI. (Bruce et al., 1997, p. 8).

Even before using the new tools, this teacher is building up a conceptual basis for embryology as well as MRI imaging. The teacher is beginning to build a series of conceptual maps, or schemata, to which the new project can be related. Notice how she scaffolds the experience of the seventh-graders with both eggs and the Web so that their interactions with the MRI will be informed and constructive inquiries. Project researchers are finding that such thoughtful integration of ChickScope and other data-collection programs into a planned and broader range of curricular activities makes an important difference for the success of the project at the classroom level.

Digital Libraries

Digital libraries in their various forms—from stand-alone CD-ROM-based systems to the World Wide Web itself—can be wonderful resources for student inquiry. By their hypertextual nature, many digital libraries permit and even encourage open inquiry that expands student projects beyond predictable categories. However, it is critical to remember that the type of library to which students have access and the help they need with searching should be directly related to our purposes in the classroom.

While commercial searching programs and networks of databases such as Homework Helper are at least somewhat focused with respect to categories and resources valuable to students, the Internet is sometimes described in terms like "virtual Mardi-Gras." From the resource perspective, the Internet might be seen as a wonderful classroom and digital library of the twenty-first century, while from the perspective of searching and information retrieval, it may well be "the librarian's nightmare in terms of the lack of control over searching rules and expectations" (Jacobson & Ignacio, 1995, p. 21). The Internet is difficult to search not simply because it is large, but because of how it has become large through loosely related, flexible, self-organizing efforts distributed across the globe. Nilan's (1995) critique of the immense size and interconnectivity of digital libraries, that "even the systems no longer know what is in the collection" (p. 38), is especially true of the Internet, where at no single moment can one isolate the development of "a system."

Without training in digital searching, students can spend a great deal of time sifting through information of little relevance to their topic. Lacking any structure or guidance through large seas of data, both inquiry-based and more content-focused teachers risk being disappointed by student progress. While digital libraries, including the Internet, may reduce the need for teachers to go beyond the classroom or school library walls to find resources, at the same time they greatly increase the need for teachers to be educated about searching for and evaluating resources. In a very real sense, new information technologies, along with an emphasis upon inquiry, are influencing teachers to do more librarian work, and conversely, librarians appear to be doing more teaching than ever. In brief, your role as a teacher can shift depending upon the technologies with which your students interact. Most importantly, you must consider whether or not your students possess adequate background to use a tool you have selected as a means for inquiry. If not, then inquiry can quickly become unproductive meandering or mere frustration.

▌Reader Activity 8.2

THEORY INTO PRACTICE
Designing a Mini-Digital Library

Using the Internet, a CD-ROM Encyclopedia, or any other digital resource, design a mini-digital library that includes six to ten resources you would like students to use in order to explore information within a specific subject field or topic. You might consider selecting not only texts, but also media of different sorts from the same library (e.g., images, sound, film). In your design, make it clear why you have selected these particular resources. Additionally, reflect upon your own activity of locating and evaluating these resources. What problems and issues did you face? What problems and issues might your students face?

Visualizing Mathematics: SimCalc and the World Wide Web

In many cases, technologies are simply directed toward previous goals, to make familiar work faster, less arduous, or more convenient. SimCalc, however, is an intriguing example of how technologies can reshape educational goals. SimCalc is a collection of computer programs that permits students to learn basic calculus concepts in elementary or middle school, long before they would typically be introduced to them, thereby raising such questions as: What is the purpose and value of children learning calculus? What is the relationship between the possible and the valuable?

Through SimCalc MathWorlds, students can visualize problems and control the movements of animated characters. The characters move according to graphs, which can be edited with the computer mouse. Through visualizing and manipulating these relationships, students can experience the meanings of calculus more directly than as a set of symbolic abstractions. For example, students learn about the Mean Value Theorem (MVT) through a computer game of flying a UFO that picks up space rocks and drops them in a crusher. The students can adjust, on a graph, two different constant velocities that control the movement of the UFO. Thus, the game brings to life the relationships among rate of motion, distance, and time.

Educational theorists have been discussing for some time the ways in which visual representations and simulations mediate understanding. While we tend to believe that some subjects or problems are simply too difficult for students at a certain developmental stage, these difficulties might be more a matter of the ways in which complex issues are represented or taught than of the characteristics of either the individuals or the problems. Researchers have tested SimCalc in inner-city middle schools in Massachusetts. Their findings have been promising: "SimCalc students . . . were able to perform as well as—or better than—typical high school or college-age calculus students on problems involving graphical representations of motion or that require the interpretation of velocity-vs.-time graphs, or other calculus skills" (Viadero, 1997, p. 13). This testing of SimCalc was not simply the examination of a computer program, but was embedded into a range of practices (e.g., physical activities) and other educational tools (including pencil and paper) that the developers designed along with classroom teachers (Roschelle & Kaputt, 1996).

While multifunctional programs like SimCalc offer many advantages for constructing inquiry-based curricula, there are other options, often focusing upon a single problem, that are available from Web sites. With Web access, you (and your students) are not limited to the teachers, texts, or software down the hall. Rather, with patient searching, you will find that through the Web you are linked to a very large number of interactive technological tools and teaching materials. For example, a number of mathematics simulations have been developed for the World Wide Web using Java "applets." (Java is an operating system, and applets are small programs that are downloaded to your computer.) George Reese, a mathematics educator, has developed one such program called *Buffon's Needle*. This centuries-old problem entails dropping a needle on a lined sheet of paper and determining the probability of the needle crossing one of the lines on the page. The surprising result is that this probability is directly related to the value of pi. Reese's Web-based simulation permits students to virtually "drop" needles onto a lined background, either one, ten, or 100 at a time, and to observe

---

FIGURE 8.3   Resources: Media for Inquiry

General Media Types
CD ROM libraries, databases, library access and ordering, mathematical models, microcomputer-based science laboratories, multimedia, outline tools, semantic networks, simulation toolkits, spreadsheets, statistical analyses, survey makers, video recording, virtual reality environments, visualization software

Specific Media Examples
Cartopedia (CD-ROM based world atlas), Chem Viz (Visualization software), C-Video (Video and Sound Recording), Encarta (CD ROM encyclopedia), Mathematica (graphical mathematics environment), Intermedia (hypermedia environment), More (semantic network and outline software), SimEarth, Sim City, and Sampling Laboratory (Model Exploration), StarLogoT (programmable modeling environment), Where in the World is Carmen Sandiego? (problem-solving program).

Specific Media: Websites
ChickScope <http://vizlab.beckman.uiuc.edu/chickscope/homepage.html>
Connected Mathematics <http://www.tufts.edu/as/ccl/cm/connected>
Exploring Ancient World Cultures <http://eawc.evansville.edu/index.htm>
Science Learning Network <http://www.sln.org/index.html>
ScienceSpace <http://www.vetl.uh.edu/ScienceSpace/ScienceSpace.html>
WebMuseum <http://sunsite.unc.edu/wm>

Background Information
Pea, R. D. & Sheingold, K. (Eds.). (1987). *Mirrors of minds: Patterns of experience in educational computing.* Norwood, NJ: Ablex.

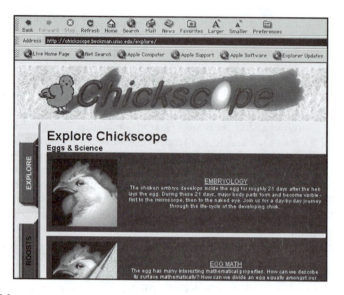

Illustration 8.1
Media for Inquiry: the Explore page from the ChickScope website
(http://chickscope.beckman.uiuc.edu/explore/) 1998.

changes in the estimated value of pi (calculated at the bottom of the Web page) as the number of drops accumulates. The Web site also offers an analysis of the problem, which reveals something of its brain-teasing quality, since the result is not a simple function (for example, where more drops would increase the estimation of pi).

A multitude of interactive simulations for secondary students are available through the Web, demonstrating the potential of the Web to distribute the work of curriculum-building among a very broad range of individuals and organizations. Thus, without being either an expert in educational technology or a major corporation, your efforts to develop curricula on the web can have important educational impact for distant classrooms and students. In this sense, your teaching is no longer bounded by the institutional context in which you find yourself. Figure 8.3 gives specific examples of the many types of media that can be used for the purpose of inquiry.

▪▪ MEDIA FOR COMMUNICATION

The development and use of new technologies have greatly influenced our students' desires to communicate with others and our desires to help them develop their communication skills. As more opportunities for various forms of communication (e.g., electronic text, graphic images, Web-based video-conferencing) with broad audiences are made possible for every level of teaching and learning, the very nature of what it means to communicate is shifting. Additionally, since the development of graphical computer interfaces and the consequent rapid growth of the Internet, much of the development of educational technologies has focused upon the ability to engage in synchronous (at the same time) and asynchronous (at different times) dialogue with experts, other students in more or less distant locations, or the general public. These combined tools afford exciting possibilities by opening up the classroom to include more distant participants in communication and learning.

Technology and Students with Special Needs: DragonDictate

That participation in communication has broadened through technologies is evidenced in the range of tools that have been developed to mediate for students with disabilities. One example of this type of valuable work is DragonDictate.

DragonDictate is a computer system developed to assist students for whom typing or writing assignments longhand is prohibitively slow or impossible. Students are able to speak their "texts" into a microphone that is mounted on their person and watch their words appear on screen. When the computer mistakes one word for another, the student can select the correct word from a list of choices the computer offers. Because many schools are moving toward full inclusion of students with special needs, technology holds great promise for allowing those students to function with unprecedented success. Debra Viadero writes:

> Technology has literally helped open the schoolhouse doors for disabled students and given impetus to the "full inclusion" movement, which calls for teaching disabled students in regular classrooms whenever possible (Viadero, 1997, p. 14).

We also need to ask how technologies that we currently use contribute to students' disabilities. Consider the student who is a very slow typist (not necessarily due to an identified disability) at work in a classroom context heavily dependent upon keyboarding skills. While the lesson you have designed may include interacting with NASA staff via e-mail and thus building students' science knowledge and language skills, the student who types three words per minute might be better served by pencil and paper, audio, or other technological tools. This example hints at the ways in which enabling technologies for some students might be disabling technologies for others. Of course, as a teacher you will not "hit it right" with every individual. At the same time, it is important to challenge our assumptions about given technologies improving the learning of all students, just as we seek ways to technologically mediate the learning of students with special needs.

E-Mail Communication Across Contexts and Cultures

Rich cultural learning (in addition to learning about communication skills and technologies) can take place through e-mail exchanges. The following case is illustrative. In 1987, Jeffrey Schwartz of the Schwickley Academy in Pennsylvania, Joanne Tulonen of Wilsall High School in Wilsall, Montana, and Bill Noll of Little Wound High School on the Pine Ridge Reservation in Kyle, South Dakota, began a collaboration that lasted several years and created a context in which students wrote over 500 e-mail messages to one another. At first, much of the project involved students getting acquainted with one another, a process that prompted teachers to realize the number of stereotypes with which students were operating. In response, the teachers added a unit on stereotypes. As the project moved into the second year, communications included self-portraits, essays on the local community, and oral histories. All projects were sent to students in the other schools as drafts. Student feedback became so valuable that the teachers decided that all writing projects should go through three exchanges so that all questions could be asked and all possibilities explored (Wresch, 1997).

Several years ago I was involved in a different type of "cross-cultural" exchange through e-mail. In this project, students in my French class communicated with other American high-school students, as well as with graduate students in French at Michigan State University. The French project in my classroom was fairly well-defined and short term, lasting approximately one semester. Its purpose was that upper level students in French would write poetry, get response from one another and especially from the graduate student leaders, and then publish one another's poetry in a collection. The students produced a very nice poetry collection in the end, featuring their work but also including the poems of other students from American schools abroad, which we mailed to the other schools and to the coordinators. Without the broader audience technology allowed and the quality of individual tutoring they received through e-mail, the students would have had little motivation to create this anthology.

Unfortunately, some of the other classrooms had failed to come through in various ways. Some classes initially became involved, and then dropped out after a few weeks. Of the remaining six classes, only three put together and distributed a final poetry collection. Since some students in my class had poetry selected for publication in these other collections, not receiving these final collections was very disappointing to them.

In most, if not all e-mail projects among classrooms, you are not merely crossing cultural boundaries among school communities and locations, you are also crossing the culture of the teaching and learning values embedded in different classrooms. Distance projects do not remove the difficulties inherent in collaborations among teachers; rather, in many ways they exacerbate them by placing new demands upon communication. Therefore, as you plan e-mail communication projects, remember that the success of any project is related to the strength of the relationships you develop and the values you share across the networks in which you are active.

An additional significant point about cross-cultural communication projects is that in many instances the very communities with whom we would like students to communicate (e.g., third-world countries, inner-city schools, minority populations) are currently inaccessible by Internet. The Internet is deceiving in this regard, for although we can access Web pages on nearly any language, people, group, or culture, in many cases this information does not come from indigenous peoples themselves, but is created by distant others with an interest or investment in representing them. Africa is a case in point, where getting even low-speed data links can be very difficult. Additionally, the groups with whom we communicate in any given culture may be more like us than unlike us for the very reason that they have access to modern technologies (Talbott, 1996). Figure 8.4 gives specific examples of the many types of media that can be used for the purpose of communication.

▌ Reader Activity 8.3

THEORY INTO PRACTICE
Distance Communication

Through e-mail, join a discussion group for several weeks to learn what it is like to participate in this form of virtual communication. Keep a brief journal of your experiences and reflections as a partic-

FIGURE 8.4   Resources: Media for Communication

General Media Categories
asynchronous and synchronous computer conferencing, collaborative data environments, collaborative writing environments, desktop publishing, drill and practice systems, instructional simulations, outlining and graphics aids, tutoring systems, student-created hypertexts, telementoring, word processing

Specific Media Examples
Common Knowledge (group editor), CommonSpace (collaborative writing software), DragonDictate, Eudora (e-mail software), FirstClass (asynchronous and synchronous communication), FrontPage (web page creation), Lotus Notes (integrated e-mail and discussion forums), Microsoft PowerPoint (presentation software), MUDs (Multiple User Dimension communication "worlds" of rooms and objects), MOOs (MUD, Object-Oriented), Netscape Navigator (Internet browser), UNIX Pine (e-mail program)

Specific Media: Websites
AskERIC Virtual Library <http://ericir.syr.edu/About/virtual.html>
CoVis <http://www.covis.nwu.edu/>
CyberProf <http://cyber.ccsr.uiuc.edu/cyberprof/general/homepage/>
Math Forum <http://forum.swarthmore.edu/>
News Web <http://www.nvnet.k12.nj.us/newsweb/index.html>
Science Teaching and Learning Project <http://www.si.umich.edu/UMDL/HomePage.html>

Background Information
Bruce, B. C., Peyton, J. K., & Batson, T. (Eds.) (1993). *Network-based classrooms: Promises and realities.* NY: Cambridge University Press.
Garner, R. & Gillingham, M. G. (1996). *Internet communication in six classrooms: Conversations across time, space, and culture.* Mahwah, N.J.: Lawrence Erlbaum.
Wresch, W. (1997). *A teacher's guide to the information highway.* Upper Saddle River, N.J.: Merrill-Prentice Hall.

ipant. How valuable is this as a learning experience for you? What issues or problems arise in this form of communication? What should you be aware of in using such communication with students?

▪▪▪ MEDIA FOR CONSTRUCTION

Media for construction help students learn through manipulation of and building with various materials. New technologies have supported knowledge construction activity and begun to redefine the meaning of "hands-on" by making various construction-oriented materials available virtually. Students can "build" many objects, models, and even robots without leaving their computer terminals. Other computer-based programs, such as Lego-logo, combine "hands-on" in the traditional sense with virtual forms of construction. In this section, I also discuss older educational tools—blackboards, whiteboards, and overhead projectors—and their potentials and problems for knowledge-construction. While these familiar tools are everyday channels of communication with students, they can also be powerful, low-cost means of learning when, as a teacher, you purposefully use them for knowledge construction.

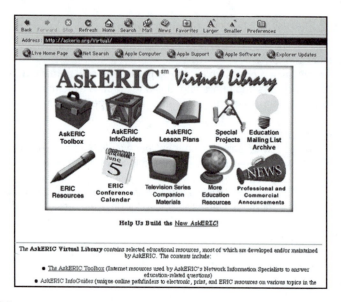

Illustration 8.2.
The AskEric Virtual Library (http://ericir.syr.edu/virtual/index.html) is a useful resource and also provides a forum for discussion of education-related topics.

Lego-logo

Lego-logo is a wonderful example of changing technologies that have incorporated old technologies within them. Lego has developed specialized bricks with sensors built into them (e.g. for temperature, light, or touch) that can be used, along with standard Lego bricks, in student engineering projects. These sensors are interfaced with a computer by way of a control box and LabView, a graphical programming language, which interprets the input and determines output to the student-made machine (for example, turning on a motor or light). While there are a number of different projects that can be made through the Lego "Dacta" kits, there is also a great deal of flexibility—students can develop their own work through various entrance points to the media: the computer program, the material bricks, or even the interface design.

In selecting knowledge-construction technologies, it is important to keep in mind student learning styles and their relation to the materials used. In many new technology-related projects, particularly projects related to the Internet, we tend to lose hands-on activity or exchange it for typing-mousing activity alone. We become excited about what students can do with their minds through these media, and rightfully so. Yet, there is also a risk in limiting students' opportunities to use their bodies and the material world to shape their thinking. This is an issue of both motivation and learning style: some students will be more oriented toward computers and keyboard activity, while others are highly kinesthetic and will learn best through manipulating actual materials.

Blackboards can become powerful technologies of knowledge construction for teachers and students working together.

Multiple Representations With FLiPS

FLiPS (Flexible Learning in the Periodic System) is a piece of software that could potentially be used in high school chemistry classes. Rather than just presenting the commonplace form of the periodic table, the software presents several different versions of the system, some of which are shaped in highly creative (e.g., a spiral) and colorful ways. A key idea behind the project is that through multiple representations of the table and through discussions of the varied relationships within and among these representations, students will develop a much deeper understanding of the periodic system and elements within it.

Consider, however, how the use of this tool challenges other commonplace goals. Many secondary chemistry teachers may have the relatively simple goal of having students recognize parts of the periodic table—be able to state where atomic weights are located, for instance. The teacher's purpose may not actually be an enriched understanding of the relations between the elements, let alone a disruption of the traditional tool used to understand them. On the other hand, FLiPS could advance the purposes of the chemistry teacher who is beginning to challenge the "page 320 by May or bust" approach, and is sacrificing broad coverage for the in-depth study of selected topics. Moreover, FLiPS could expand this teacher's conception of what an in-depth approach to chemistry might entail. New technologies can help us reflect upon, challenge, and reformulate our goals in education. While purposes can help us select tools, new tools can also challenge our purposes and help us discover new ones.

Blackboards, Whiteboards, and Overhead Projectors

While blackboards, whiteboards and overhead projectors are often used for one-directional communication of information *to* students, these tools can become powerful technologies of knowledge construction for teachers and students working together.

Blackboards are inexpensive large spaces that can be used for mapping out ideas-in-progress: graphs, proofs, and geometric shapes in mathematics; maps, charts, and timelines in history; apparatus and force diagrams in physics. One great advantage of blackboards is their sheer size. This space can be used to line up several students at one time working problems, as is the practice in some math classes. Teachers and students can use this space to map out ideas that are too complex for smaller spaces and that need a great deal of erasing in the process. For instance, I make use of concept mapping (also called "clustering" or "webbing") to think through complex issues with my English classes and to plan ideas for writing assignments. These maps can get very large with many convoluted arrows, dotted lines, and writing inside and outside of bubbles. The size and erasability of blackboards is amenable to such work. Also, there is an important kind of bodily interactivity with a blackboard (or whiteboard), where you can actually gesture through the space, words, and images you are creating. Interactions that bring individuals, gestures, images, and text together have been shown to be important in scientific knowledge construction (Lynch & Woolgar, 1990), and they are certainly important for student learning as well.

Many of the benefits of blackboards also apply to whiteboards. Whiteboards permit clear contrast between text or diagrams and a relatively pure background, and even enhance different kinds of constructions when colored markers are used purposefully. The only apparent disadvantage of whiteboards is that they are relatively expensive.

While limited in spatial breadth, overhead projectors permit depth that is an often-untapped potential for knowledge construction. By simply laying slides atop one another, a teacher or student can relate past information to new information in the form of maps, charts, and diagrammed text. This depth can allow for the sequential construction of ideas, and is highly flexible so that earlier and later versions can be compared. For example, I have used overhead projectors for discussing pieces of writing when teaching composition. Typically, I focus on a few paragraphs, perhaps marking the lines with simple notations for effective or problematic words and phrases. At times I work together with the students, as a large group, making such notations and building knowledge together about writing. On other occasions I pass out blank overhead transparencies to students in groups, which they overlay on a piece of common text and construct a group response around specific issues in writing. As a class we then compare these group responses, with students presenting at the front and comparing their interpretations and critiques of the common text with those of other groups.

Overhead projection seems to focus student attention more than many other media, including photocopies of the same text. Moreover, while facing the classroom, you can interact with students about a text. Therefore, overhead projection can be an effective tool for discussions that revolve around a focal point. This example highlights a convenience of overhead transparencies: they can be prepared ahead of time. For knowledge construction, overhead projection permits both a degree of advanced preparation (like the photocopied handout) and a degree of spontaneous on-the-spot development (like the blackboard).

To sum up, consider three qualities when making judgments about which media to use for knowledge construction purposes. These qualities or criteria are concerned

FIGURE 8.5	Resources: Media for Construction

General Media Categories
computer-aided design, construction of graphs and charts, control systems, robotics.

Specific Media Examples
AutoCAD (computer-aided design software), Datadesk (program to make tables and graphs), Geometers Sketchpad (geometry drawing and learning program), LabVIEW (graphical programming language), Lego DACTA (robotics kits), Microsoft Excel (spreadsheet program), whiteboards

Specific Media: Websites
Exploratorium Exploranet <http://www.exploratorium.edu/>
Lego Data Acquisition and Prototyping System <http://ldaps.ivv.nasa.gov/>
Odyssey Center for Education <http://www.students.uiuc.edu/~grosshan/odymain.htm>

Background Information
Gibilisco, S. (Ed.) (1994). *The McGraw-Hill illustrated encyclopedia of robotics and artificial intelligence.* New York: McGraw-Hill.
Macaulay, D. (1988). *The way things work.* Boston: Houghton Mifflin.
Pea, R. D. & Sheingold, K. (Eds.). (1987). *Mirrors of minds: Patterns of experience in educational computing.* Norwood, NJ: Ablex.

with the display capabilities of these media, but just as much with our purposes and practices in knowledge construction.

1. *Spatial dimensionality.* How does the space (breadth or depth) of the display media support the kind of interactivity of knowledge-making that you want to achieve with your students?
2. *Permanence.* How much do you want to continue to revise what you are shaping in the classroom? Do you want to save earlier versions or "drafts" of sketches, writings, or problems? Should the work continue to be present once class is over?
3. *Focus.* How important is it that students focus their attention on a particular item, and how does your medium support focus? Is the medium overly focused, not affording open exploration?

These qualities are a good starting place for thinking about not only the media discussed earlier, but also knowledge construction with other types of display media as well, including bulletin boards, butcher paper, chart boards, Web pages, and even photocopied handouts for students. Figure 8.5 gives specific examples of the many types of media that can be used for the purpose of knowledge construction.

▪▪▪ MEDIA FOR EXPRESSION

Dewey and many others have argued that people have a natural desire to express themselves. The educational purpose of expression is closely linked to communication. However, while communication often stresses the more practical side of interaction, ex-

Illustration 8.3
Lego blocks are a familiar low-tech media. The LDAPS provides technology-based ideas for using media for construction. (http://ldaps.ivv.nasa.gov/)

pression emphasizes the artistry and delight of producing something for its own sake. Expression is tied up with exercising the imagination, developing one's sense of self, and loosening constraints upon both media and content.

Elementary-school classrooms are typically full of media for expression, including puppet theaters, construction paper, musical instruments, and modeling clay. Unfortunately, secondary-school classrooms often contain few such materials. It is important to give students, especially adolescents, the opportunity to engage in different forms of expression.

While educational technology has emphasized developing media for inquiry and for communication, there is still a broad range of tools that allow student expression. Specific tools include advanced drawing and animation software, and a wide variety of new tools created for learning, writing, and producing music. Here, I focus on two general tools that are likely to be found in many schools and that can be purposefully used to weave student expression into the core curriculum: the Web as a creative multimedium and student-produced video.

The Web As Creative Multimedium

Using the Web as a tool of expression requires that we shift from all of the discourse about the Web as a "resource to be mined" and begin to imagine it as a "palette" and "painter's easel" on which students produce their work across many forms of media. The Web becomes a medium of expression when we see our students as producers of the Web, not simply consumers of it.

School and university homepages demonstrate the importance of this transformation toward student use of the Web. They also reflect our currently limited conceptions.

In general, from a pedagogical standpoint, school homepages are not very interesting. These home pages are often overburdened with marketing and public relations efforts, and the lived experiences of students and teachers get buried under a map of the school building or campus, a generalized mission statement, and a long list of courses or degree programs. But the media functionality of the Web is capable of providing much more, most importantly an outlet for a vast range of student expression. The Web can serve multiple functions: it can expand the audience of student work, preserve this work for future students as models in a virtual archive, and serve as an avenue of student expressive creativity through the multimedia it supports. For this latter purpose, learning basic Web authoring and design is not difficult. It may be that you have done some Web authoring yourself, either through html (hyper text markup language) coding or making use of one of the many authoring programs (e.g., Front Page, Navigator Gold) that are now available. If your school has some capability for students to develop Web pages, you could find this an excellent opportunity for student expression within the subject area you are teaching. In many schools, especially when students are taking an introductory technology course, they produce their own homepages. This work may be a good introduction to authoring, but students can also move far beyond it to explore and put together multimedia reports or "Web papers," which draw together multiple resources to maximize creative expression.

Student Video: Untapped Potentials

Video cameras first became common in public schools in the early 1970s, when I was in elementary school. At that time, video cameras were touted as the next wonderful technological tool in education. Somewhat surprisingly, the use of video cameras by teachers and students doesn't seem to have changed all that much in the past three decades. The technologies themselves have become more sophisticated, with 8 mm video cameras gradually replacing unwieldy camera-plus-deck units, and some schools even experimenting with video animation or on-line video. Yet, in terms of frequency of use, video cameras have just about as remote a connection to teaching as they seem to have had when they first appeared.

A number of technical and economic factors may explain the relative absence of video film production in schools. It is possible—even likely—that instruction historically has been too textbook-driven to accommodate video technologies. Although video production has played a supplemental role, it has never been well integrated into the curriculum. Video consumption, however, has been very well integrated. VCRs are standard equipment in most classrooms and are likely the items most frequently checked out from school media centers. Videotapes, which often only supplement classroom print material, seem to lend themselves to final classroom goals of written response and testing. But what do we do with student-produced videotapes? This situation reflects what often happens with new technologies: rather than becoming media with which students express themselves, these technologies become media for the expression of professional producers and educational companies, and students are merely consumers.

The capability of video production to expand the meaning of literacy to include oral, visual, and cultural practice has a great deal of potential for students with special needs, as well as for students who are simply waiting for schooling to offer an alternate medium of expression. Figure 8.6 gives specific examples of the many types of media that can be used for expression.

FIGURE 8.6   Resources: Media for Expression

General Media Categories
animation software, drawing and painting programs, interactive video and hypermedia, multimedia composition, music composing and editing, music making and accompaniment

Specific Media Examples
Art Rageous (CD-ROM, interactive worlds with masterpieces), Avid Xpress (video and multimedia editing), Fine Artist (virtual art studio), HyperStudio (multimedia authoring), Microsoft Creative Writer (multimedia authoring), Opcode's MusicShop (MIDI-based composition program), Quicktime (Mac-based sound and movie player)

Specific Media: Websites
ArtsEdNet (Getty Education Institute for the Arts)
<http://www.artsednet.getty.edu/>
Blackburn High School <http://www.ozemail.com.au/~bhs56/index.html>
Internet Resources for Music Teachers
<http://www.isd77.k12.mn.us/resources/staffpages/shirk/music.html>
Music Education Resource Links <http://www.cs.uop.edu/~cpiper/musiced.html>
Technology-Based Music Instruction
<http://camil40.music.uiuc.edu/Projects/tbmi/>
Vanna's Digital Video Information Site <http://www.ed.uiuc.edu/people/es/Vanna/video_site.html>
WebMuseum <http://sunsite.unc.edu/wm/>

Background Information
Csikszentmihalyi, M., & Robinson, R. E. (1990). *The art of seeing: an interpretation of the aesthetic encounter.* Los Angeles: Getty Center for Education in the Arts.
Eisner, E. W. (1988). *The role of discipline-based art education in America's schools.* Los Angeles: Getty Center for Education in the Arts.

▌ Reader Activity 8.4

IN THE FIELD
A Media Inventory

Visit at least two schools to see first-hand available technologies and technologies that are most often used in classrooms. Visit the library/media center to observe students using different media. If possible, observe the technologies in use in a number of classes. Make a simple chart of available technologies, typically used technologies, and reasons for use. Report your findings to your class. What technologies are most often used? What technologies ought to be made more available to these teachers? Why?

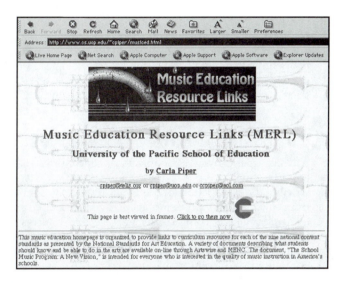

Illustration 8.4
Carla Piper's Music Education Resource Links page
(http://www.soundpiper.com/cpiper/merlmenu.htm) is a good starting place for finding
information about using media for musical expression.

■■■CHALLENGES TO EQUITABLE TECHNOLOGY USE

Thus far I have made reference to a number of challenges to effectively using technology in teaching. For example, I have emphasized the need to understand technologies as enabling for some while disabling for others, the need to carefully consider student diversities, and the importance of student background skills. These challenges and others have developed around the general issue of understanding technical tools in relation to educational purposes and practices.

Educational technology both poses challenges for diverse kinds of students and, at the same time, may offer paths to help students who have historically met with little school success. This section will address the interface between technology and the following types of student diversity: socioeconomic class, cultural and ethnic differences, gender differences, geographic diversity, and students with special needs.

Socioeconomic Class

For the most part, schools in affluent districts offer greater access to technology. Not only do such schools usually possess more and better tools, but often teachers and staff are trained in their use and implementation. Schools in less affluent districts usually have fewer and less powerful tools. Often, such schools are understaffed and teachers are poorly prepared to use technology effectively. Thus, the socioeconomic status of students plays a role in their access to and ability to learn from new technologies.

The influence of socioeconomic status does not stop at the school door. Clearly, students who have access to computers in the home have an advantage over students who do not. Although up to one-third of all U.S. students may have access to computers in their home, it is likely that these are the more affluent students (Forcier, 1999). As technology plays a greater and greater role in schooling and learning, students whose access to technology is limited both at school and in the home may be negatively affected. For example, poor students may fall so far behind technologically that they may lack the skills and knowledge to enter fields that are heavily influenced by technology, such as mathematics, science, engineering, and the entire technology industry (Roblyer & Edwards, 2000).

Cultural and Ethnic Differences

African American and Hispanic students continue to lag behind white students in access to technology both at home and at school (Roblyer & Edwards, 2000). It is unclear whether the explanation for this is purely socioeconomic. For example, how do students from cultures that value relationship over individual achievement perceive the value of technology? How comfortable with electronic forms of communication are students from cultures that value oral, face-to-face communication over written, impersonal communication? In what situations does technology disable students who are not fluent in English or comfortable in mainstream American culture? Thus, culture and ethnicity play a largely understudied role in students' access to and expertise in technology.

On the other hand, technology offers many avenues through which to increase cross-cultural and multicultural understanding. Web sites, electronic communication, and distance-learning technologies can help students communicate directly with others who differ from them, to gain more accurate information about cultural differences, and to interact with individuals and groups of diverse cultures. In addition, students who are learning English can benefit greatly from technology applications that address their linguistic needs and provide visual and spatial experiences to enhance their language learning.

Gender Equity

Gender raises questions of equity in access to and use of technology. First, males tend to be more involved with computers, both in and out of school, than females (Newby, Stepich, Lehman, & Russell, 2000). The findings of gender equity researchers cited in Chapter Three, "Knowing Middle- and High-School Students," seem to hold for technology use as well. That is, males tend to get more attention of every sort from teachers. In the case of technology, males seem to be steered toward more challenging uses of technology, while females are steered toward more clerical uses. Teachers tend to help males solve technological problems and to solve females' problems for them. And just as females, for a variety of reasons, come to believe they are not "good at" certain school subjects, such as math and science, so they may come to believe they are not "good at" computers (Forcier, 1999). Teachers must be as vigilant of gender equity in the computer lab as they are in the regular classroom.

Geographic Diversity

Just as affluence is usually associated with suburban areas, poverty is often associated with rural and urban areas. Issues of access and use raised by the unequal distribution of wealth are complicated by the geographical isolation of living in an inner-city or a rural area. Students who live in either setting may have to travel long distances to gain access to computers at a public library. Inner cities and rural areas are less likely to have an infrastructure that supports widespread technology use.

Technology holds great promise for breaking these barriers of geographic isolation. First, electronic communication transcends physical isolation and expands possibilities. Students who live in isolated areas can engage in electronic mentoring with role models whom they may never actually meet. Many states and districts are experimenting with on-line courses and "virtual" high schools that will open curricular opportunities for students who were previously denied them. For example, through technology Advanced Placement course offerings and upper levels of foreign language study may become accessible for all students regardless of where they live or go to school. Finally, technology may help to stop the "brain drain" of young people from inner-city and rural areas, as it is now possible to engage in many forms of communication and commerce without ever leaving home.

Students With Special Needs

Technology has great potential for creating inclusive learning environments. Many assistive devices exist to support the learning of students with disabilities. For example, "the Kurzweil Reading Machine scans printed documents and converts text to electronic speech. Speech synthesizers, speech recognition devices, image magnifiers, [and] specially designed keyboards . . . have made the computer useful to the physically impaired" (Forcier, 1999, p. 12). Much software is designed to enhance the learning of students with learning disabilities, with features such as interactivity, positive feedback, logical structure, and the ability to navigate freely within a learning activity. Furthermore, a student with a learning disability can practice and repeat as much as he or she needs to without fearing the computer's displeasure. Unfortunately, students with learning disabilities may have their computer use limited to drill-and-practice programs that do not require higher-order thinking (Roblyer & Edwards, 2000). This poses another challenge to equity.

▉▉ CHALLENGES TO EFFECTIVE TECHNOLOGY USE

The next section focuses more directly on your position as a teacher and the challenges you will face as you use technologies in school contexts. I consider below the limitations presented by the limited supply of tools, limited training, limited time, the limited application of tools to diverse students, multiple goals, and the unintended effects of technologies. I hope that considering these limitations will actually *encourage* you as you try out new technologies. This encouragement, I believe, will come primarily as you begin to consider and plan how you might cope with and move beyond the limitations of using technologies in school contexts.

Limited Supply of Tools

The most common critique of technology in education is that of supply and access: we simply do not have enough tools to go around. While I agree with this critique generally speaking, it is also important to recall that we have limited purposes and make limited use of the tools we already have. We have considered this issue previously in the discussion about blackboards, whiteboards, and overhead projectors as media for knowledge construction rather than simply using them for presentation. By developing new purposes for old tools, we "reinvent" these tools into new technologies.

Yet, tool limitations still exist and it is important to have a few strategies to address them. One common, yet underused, strategy is to break out of the one-computer-per-student model. A single computer (or two) in a classroom can become a collecting point for a great deal of activity, particularly if this computer is connected to the Internet. In planning classroom activities, look for ways in which inquiry, communication, or expression via a single computer are integral to the direction of the classroom. Have small groups or individuals use the computer and make it a "participant" within the flow of classroom activity. Avoid using the computer as a reward for students who are "caught up," and they will begin to see technology as integral to education rather than as a tool for gaming.

Another general strategy to address limitations in tool availability is to work on cross-disciplinary projects with other teachers. You will find that as you plan units across subject areas your ability to create projects or activities of larger scope and with more tools is increased dramatically. For example, when teaching middle-school English, I teamed with a social studies teacher and a math teacher on a unit about the voyages of Columbus. One of the student activities in this unit was constructing a life-sized paper layout of the floorplan of the Santa Maria. The tools used in this project—reams and reams of paper, markers, and the gymnasium itself—would have been very difficult for one teacher to manage. As a team, however, we were able to develop strategies to procure and use materials that went far beyond my individual abilities and time. You will find the same principle to be true when dealing with other tools, including computer networks, software, and laboratory equipment.

Limited Training

If you become involved in a technology-related reform effort in your school, you will probably experience the need for more training with the technology, but will lack the time and resources to get it (Zehr, 1997). It is likely that you will find it easier to obtain financial support for hardware and software than for ongoing training with new technologies, or for reflecting upon the meaning of technologies in relation to your curriculum and students. While this situation is in need of change, at the same time it provides an occasion to question some of your own assumptions about technologies before putting them to use in a classroom. To what extent do you need expertise with a new technology before trying it out in teaching?

If you approach your teaching from the perspective of having mastered knowledge and imparting it to your students, you will most likely not feel comfortable with using any technology that you have not yet mastered. And, because of the rate of change in technologies, such an approach will greatly limit the range of technologies you are willing to use. On the other hand, if you approach your classroom as an opportunity to learn with your students, then the thought of incomplete technological knowledge will not be so threatening. In fact, it could contribute to a valuable constructivist learning environment.

Several years ago I was put in charge of the newspaper for a model United Nations that our school was hosting. Several other international and American schools were participating, and my job was to facilitate a mixed group of students from these schools in order to put out a daily newspaper of high quality, with text, photos, comic strips, and other features. I was unfamiliar with the layout software, PageMaker. Fortunately, however, I had several students who were experienced in using PageMaker, and who kept the layout of the paper moving along. Together, we could look at the newspaper on the monitor as it developed and discuss layout decisions. I brought to these discussions my knowledge of English, journalism, and layout, and the students brought their technical knowledge of PageMaker. By the end of the week, we were developing a vision of what we wanted in our newspaper, how our technical tools could help us achieve it, and how all of us could become more knowledgeable in the process.

This experience and others have led me to believe in the potential of creating classroom environments that will permit both you and your students to learn about technologies as you use them together. In this vision, the classroom becomes less a delivery space and more a laboratory, where experimenting with the use of equipment is an important part of laboratory life. Especially at the secondary level, students' knowledge of certain technologies may well be ahead of the teacher's. You can conceive of this as a problem, where your own lack of training is an impairment to productive classroom activity, or you can accept these knowledge differences as a valuable resource for creating a learning community in your classroom. Such an approach can create important learning opportunities for the entire class, can shift power dynamics in favor of student participation, and can take some of the pressure off you to be the technology expert, which is a tremendous burden to bear in a realm that changes moment by moment.

Limited Time

There is an important distinction between learning technologies along with your students and simply being ill-prepared. Failure to understand the basics of technologies can be disastrous when the stakes are high. Once I observed a conference presentation by a professor who intended to open her discussion with a video that showed some data she had collected. Rather than fast-forwarding the video, she pushed the "flying erase" button, which meant that her entire tape was erasing at rapid speed as she stood in front of the group. She didn't seem to ever be able to recover from this opening disaster. You will likely have experiences like this as you use technologies: the video and monitor will arrive in your classroom from the library with a bizarre hook-up or channel settings, your new software will be incompatible with your computers, your school network server will require a new password on your big Internet Research Day. All of these experiences go along with the territory of using technologies. However, taking time to go over set-ups and making sure you have duplicate copies of irreplaceable materials will save a lot of heartache. As a new teacher, you may even feel most comfortable being overprepared.

And what if technologies break down? Should you have an alternate low-tech or "no-tech" plan? Perhaps. At the same time, it is unrealistic to think that you will go into every technology-mediated situation with an alternate plan in mind. In my view, more appropriate than squeezing double-planning into your already tight schedule is to have a good sense of your goals in using a particular technology in the first place. With a clear sense of initial goals for classroom activity, you'll learn to adapt to a range of means of pursuing those goals, both ahead of time and on-the-fly.

Besides advanced preparation and back-ups (which require more initial time but save eventual time), a second general point regarding time management and technology is simply to be patient and temper your expectations for immediate success. Realize that change takes a long time. While new technologies offer the potential of richer learning experiences, they may increase the time spent preparing to teach, especially at the outset (Wiske & Houde, 1988; Stearns et al., 1991). These time demands might run counter to your expectations; you may, in fact, expect new technologies to streamline your work, or at least "come out equal" with respect to time. Yet, consider the fact that along with a new tool that you are introducing into your teaching, you are trying to develop richer learning experiences for your students—that is, changing your purposes and practices. Such experiences will take more of your time, with or without technologies. Additionally, your third week of using a piece of software or Internet communication with your classroom will not be as chaotic for either you or your students as your first day. Rather than prematurely evaluating these efforts, give them time to play out. Pat yourself on the back for being courageous and innovative, and resist the temptation to call teaching experiments an absolute failure or success on first pass.

Limited Application

It is very tempting to consider a technology out of its relationship to a real student user, to trust statements that seem to prove technologies are generally effective for all students. However, technology always needs to be found more or less valuable with regard to real individuals or groups, the students we care about in our classes and not the imagined students of software and hardware producers. For example, Zorfass (1991) describes how the Carmen Sandiego program was a tremendous failure with a group of inner city students. The students were not fluent in English, nor did they know much about geography or how to use reference materials. Only after the teacher shifted the students' interactions with the software—having them work in small groups and teaching necessary background knowledge—were the students able to benefit from using it.

As in the case of limited time, look for and enjoy partial successes with new technologies as you use them in your teaching. Try to keep an informal record about what technologies seem to work with what students, given certain conditions and goals. Lastly, realize that the one-size-fits-all perspective is not restricted to educational technologies alone, but is the result of the incredibly challenging job of teaching a wide variety of students within an institutional setting. Being partially successful with more students, through a diverse program of contrasting technologies and plans, seems a reasonable, albeit challenging, goal.

Multiple Goals

Henry Levin, an education professor at Stanford University, writes:

> My concern is that the technology ought to basically be the servant of a very strong program that challenges students and gets them involved, as opposed to simply being an entity in itself which somehow is going to have an impact because it exists (quoted in Trotter, 1997, p. 7).

In using the term "servant," Levin is maintaining that technologies must build upon a range of other worthy curricular goals. In a national study of technologies and reform, Means et al. (1993) have also argued that, in order to be valuable and sustainable, reform efforts with technology must be linked to institutional goals as well as curricular goals and frameworks. As a teacher, it is sometimes difficult to be sure of just what different curricular and institutional goals are. Additionally, you may disagree with certain school, district, or state-wide goals. However, you will find that the kinds of support you will be able to garner for any technology-oriented reform will be significantly linked to your ability to connect these change efforts to broader curricular and institutional goals.

Yet, how does attention to multiple goals work out in practice? As you begin your teaching career, it is vitally important that you identify places in your teaching where you are doing what seems right and important to you. When you are doing these things, together with the technologies they employ, take the time to describe them to yourself through discussion with a colleague or by jotting notes on paper. Next, return again to district, state, or even national curricular goals that you recall seeing earlier, but set aside when faced with the task of making plans for Monday. Look for, and begin to document, connections between these documents and your current practices, including the technologies that you employ. You may be surprised to find that many of your ideas are validated and supported by a broader community. Secondly, be open to being challenged about your teaching by such documents. In this manner, multiple goals can become a dialogue, rather than a burden. Being in this dialogue will connect you to broader activity in educational reform and technology as you develop into a leader beyond your classroom.

Unintended Effects

Technology-in-education programs most often start out with some sort of expected gain for student learning. This was the case with a newly developed educational network, the AT&T Learning Network. However, when teachers in the program were surveyed about the benefits of this networking, most rated their own learning as primarily affected over that of their students (Riel, 1990). This change was unintended. A similar example of an unintended effect occurred in a science curriculum development program with which I helped some time ago. In that program, Internet technology was included only as a support for elementary school teachers to communicate with one another and gain access to resources. However, through the program, one teacher became so engaged with the Internet that she gave up her teaching position and went back to graduate school in library science! Naturally, the other project leaders and I had mixed feelings about this result—getting teachers to quit their jobs certainly wasn't part of our planning.

It's important to evaluate both intended and unintended effects that develop through the relationships of technology-oriented reform. You may find that the unintended effects are sometimes more powerful than the purposes you articulated early on. Should this be read as failure? Absolutely not. Rather, we need to realize that our frames for evaluating technologies in education are themselves limited. While we often approach such evaluation in a lock-step manner (e.g., hypothesis, results, conclusion), we need to be willing to be surprised by what the many relations of technology (e.g., tools-purpose-practice-context) will produce and to take some pleasure in these unexpected results. Moreover, if you are curious and open about intended and unintended results, you will find that your reflections on technology in practice will lead you toward new goals for its use.

■■ VALUABLE RELATIONAL QUESTIONS FOR TEACHING WITH TECHNOLOGY

There is a risk inherent in writing a "technology chapter" in a textbook on teaching methods. This risk is that the chapter will be written (and read) as just about technologies as technical tools, as about something separated from the larger activities and contexts of learning. As Jesus suggested in Chapter Seven, "Selecting Instructional Materials," this risk is similar to conceiving of textbooks in ways that are abstracted

FIGURE 8.7   Teaching with Technology: What Questions Should You Ask?

Technology-Teaching-Context Relations	Reflective Questions	Chapter Examples
Goals for Technology Use	• What general and specific educational purposes guide your choice of technological tools? • What purposes might motivate students in using them? • Is your educational goal to do something qualitatively different in education or to achieve a familiar goal through alternate means? • How might your initial goals change over time? • What other effects might using this technology have besides those planned or desired?	ChickScope, SimCalc, FLiPS
Practices with Technology	• What teaching and learning activity does this tool permit? • Would another tool permit similar activity? • What are the cost and access differences associated with these choices? • What forms of interaction are possible with this tool or material?	Digital libraries, SimCalc, Lego-logo, Blackboards, The Web
Student Understanding and Access	• What teaching and learning problems might be associated with using this tool in a given way? • What background knowledge is required for this use? • How might your purposeful use of a tool enable or disable certain students? • What teaching practices might encourage more enabling use? • What are the learning and sociocultural characteristics of the students for whom you are selecting technologies? • How do their backgrounds with this or similar technologies differ from schooling or home life?	Digital libraries, DragonDictate, Blackboards, Student video production

from classroom practices. A singular focus on the tools of education—whether they are textbooks, overhead projectors, computer networks, or file folders—can be called a *technocentric* approach, or *technological determinism.*

Technological determinism in contemporary culture is an overemphasis on specific tools, often in the form of positive or negative evaluations of them. In education, technological determinism asks questions like "How are word processors helping students learn to write?" or "What is the Internet doing to our children?" Accounts of how technology changes very little about learning within schools or how new technologies eventually get discarded or relocated to distant corners of classrooms are commonplace today (Cohen, 1988; Cuban, 1986; Piele, 1989). As a new teacher, it may be difficult to find your position between exaggerated claims about the "reforming power" of new technologies and critiques that there is nothing new under the sun in schooling after all, despite huge efforts and billion-dollar technology initiatives.

FIGURE 8.7 *continued*

Technology-Teaching-Context Relations	Reflective Questions	Chapter Examples
Technology Use and the Institutional Context	• How does the institution in which you work constrain or enable the use of technologies? • What is your relationship to this institution? • What other institutions does this technology put you in relationship with (e.g., through the Internet)?	Lego-logo, digital libraries
Technology and Culture	• Does this technology involve communication of your class(es) with distant individuals or groups? • What is the culture of these distant others, and why are they valuable interactants for your class, as well as you for them? • What are the cultural and educational values and practices of other educator(s) with whom you will be coordinating this activity?	E-mail, The Web
Evaluating Old and New Technologies	• How is this new tool like or unlike older technologies related to similar purposes? • For your goals, should the new and the old continue to be used alongside one another, or should one replace the other? • What "old tools" might be available but overlooked for your purposes?	Digital libraries, Lego-logo, Blackboards, Student video
Teacher Expertise and Planning	• How experienced and knowledgeable are you with this tool? • How much knowledge would you need to have before using it in a classroom? • What is the technological knowledge of the students in your classroom, and how can it be used as a resource? • What must be prepared, previewed, or preserved in advance, and what can be left for the classroom?	Digital libraries, Lego-logo

My hope in this chapter has been to provide an antidote to a technocentric perspective by helping you to think of technologies relationally. Understanding that technical tools are dynamically related to your own and your students' purposes and practices, as well as to school contexts, will help you to plan and implement technologies in meaningful ways, and to evaluate their effects on teaching and learning.

Figure 8.7 draws together many of the issues raised in this chapter and forms a framework for posing reflective questions about your practices with technology. These questions could also be used to evaluate technology reforms you will encounter in your professional career. The third column of Figure 8.7 refers you back to the most relevant sections from the major technology illustrations in the chapter.

▮▮SUMMARY

In this chapter, I have discussed four broad teacher and learner purposes—inquiry, communication, construction, and expression—and a broad array of practices, contexts, and technological media. My goal has been to expand your thinking about technology rather than present you with a menu of technologies and recipes for how to use them in your teaching. Among the key points to remember are:

- Technological determinism, or the overemphasis on specific tools in isolation, usually asks the wrong questions about technology (e.g., "Is it working?") because it fails to consider technologies in contexts of use.
- A relational perspective toward technology takes into account teachers' and students' purposes and practices, other tools at work in the classroom context, diverse student populations, and other complex dynamics of context.
- Media for inquiry support a constructivist view of teaching and learning and give students access to a vast range of resources with which to work and about which to wonder.
- Media for communication have opened up participation in communication for students with disabilities and have allowed students and teachers to engage in synchronous and asynchronous communication with experts, other students and teachers in other locations, and the general public.
- Media for construction allow students to manipulate and build with both virtual and real materials. Chalkboards, whiteboards, and overhead projectors are media for knowledge construction that are found in almost every classroom. When planning their use, you should consider spatial dimensionality, permanence, and focus.
- Media for expression give students the opportunity to engage in different forms of expression and to develop both personally and socially. Media for expression allow students to become producers rather than consumers of media.
- Many limitations to the use of technologies in teaching can present themselves as barriers. However, these limitations can also become opportunities for us to rethink and expand our ideas about educational technologies.

As the title of this book, *Contexts of Teaching,* suggests and as the authors have emphasized throughout, teaching is learned and practiced in multiple contexts—among them the personal, historical, institutional, classroom, and community. In this chapter, you have been introduced to technology in context. In Chapter Nine, "Implementing Instruction: Strategies and Methods," you will gain an overview of a variety of teaching strategies to add to your growing repertoire of knowledge and skills.

▮▮BUILDING YOUR BIOGRAPHY, YOUR PERSONAL PRACTICAL PHILOSOPHY, AND PORTFOLIO

Building Your Biography

What experiences in your life are relevant to teaching with technology? You are now ready to compose a chapter of your educational biography on this topic. The following questions are intended to help you generate ideas for writing. They are not intended to be answered sequentially or to limit your exploration of the topic.

- As you reflect on your K-12 and college experience, what experiences with technology do you recall?
- As a student, were you drawn to technologies? Uncomfortable with technology?
- Were any educational technologies "disabling" for you?
- How has the use of educational technology changed over the course of your school experiences?
- What learning experiences with technology have you had outside the arena of schooling? How technology-rich was the home environment in which you grew up?
- How has technology affected how you learn, what you learn, and how you demonstrate what you have learned?

Developing Your Personal Practical Philosophy

Draft a section of your personal educational philosophy that addresses teaching with technology. You might respond to questions such as the following.

- How can technology support your purposes as a teacher? With respect to the subject matter(s) you will be teaching, how will you use technology in your first year of teaching?
- Should teachers be willing to learn technologies along with their students?
- How can you as a teacher use technology to address equity issues?
- How can you respond to the equity issues raised by technology?

Collecting Artifacts for Your Portfolio

Review the Reader Activities you have completed for this chapter. Identify any that you might eventually select for your portfolio. For each, jot down notes that will help you recall later what you were thinking at the time you completed the activity, what challenges you encountered while completing it, what you learned from doing it, and how this activity reveals something about who you will be as a teacher. Don't worry about style or correctness at this point. The purpose is to document your thinking as you move through this book and this class.

References

Bromley, H. (in press). The social chicken and the technological egg: Educational computing and the technology/society divide. *Educational Theory.*

Bruce, B. C., Carragher, B. O., Damon, B. M., Dawson, M. J., Eurell, J. A., Gregory, C. D., Lauterbur, P. C., Marjanovic, M. M., Mason-Fossum, B., Morris, H. D., Potter, C. S., & Thakkar, U. (1997). Chickscope: An interactive MRI classroom curriculum innovation for K-12. *Computers and Education Journal, 29*(2), 73–87.

Bruce, B. C., & Levin, J. A. (1997). Educational technology: Media for inquiry, communication, construction, and expression. *Journal of Educational Computing Research, 17* (1), 79–102.

Bush, C. G. (1983). Women and the assessment of technology. In J. Rothschild (Ed.), *Machina ex dea: Feminist perspectives on technology* (pp. 154–55). New York: Pergamon Press.

Cohen, D. K. (1988). Educational technology and school organization. In R. S. Nickerson & P. P. Zodhiates (Eds.), *Technology in education: Looking toward 2020* (pp. 231–264). Hillsdale, NJ: Erlbaum.

Cuban, L. (1986). Teachers and machines: The classroom use of technology since 1920. New York: Teachers College Press.

Dewey, J. (1943). *The school and society (Rev. ed.).* Chicago: University of Chicago Press.

Forcier, R. C. (1999). *The computer as an educational tool: Productivity and problem solving.* Upper Saddle River, NJ: Merrill/Prentice-Hall.

Jacobson, F. F. & Ignacio, E. (1995). Evaluating digital libraries in the context of learning and teaching. *SIGOIS Bulletin 16* (2), 21–22.

Lynch, M. & Woolgar, S. (Eds.). (1990). *Representation in scientific practice.* Cambridge, MA: The MIT Press.

Means, B., Blando, J., Olson, K., Middleton, T., Morocco, C. C., Remz, A. R., & Zorfass, J. (1993). *Using technology to support educational reform.* Washington, DC: U.S. Government Printing Office.

Newby, T. J., Stepich, D. A., Lehman, J. D., Russell, J. D. (2000). *Instructional technology for teaching and learning: Designing instruction, integrating computers, and using media. Second edition.* Upper Saddle River, NJ: Merrill/Prentice-Hall.

Nilan, M. S. (1995). Ease of user navigation through digital information spaces. *SIGOIS Bulletin 16* (2), 38–39.

Piele, P. K. (1989). The politics of technology utilization. In D. E. Mitchell & M. E. Goertz (Eds.), *Education politics for the new century: The twentieth anniversary yearbook of the Politics of Education Association* (pp. 93–106). London: Falmer Press.

Riel, M. (1990). Cooperative learning across classrooms in electronic learning circles. *Instructional Science, 19,* 445–466.

Roblyer, M. D., & Edwards, J. (2000). *Integrating educational technology into teaching.* Second edition. Upper Saddle River, NJ: Merrill/Prentice-Hall.

Roschelle, J. & Kaput, J. (1996). SimCalc MathWorlds for the Mathematics of Change. *Communications of the ACM, 39* (8), 97–99.

Stearns, M. S., David, J. L., Hanson, S. G., Ringstaff, C., & Schneider, S. A. (1991, January). Cupertino-Fremont Model Technology Schools Project research findings: Executive summary. Menlo Park, CA: SRI International.

Talbot, S. (1996). Wired classrooms: What you're not hearing. *Northwest Educational Technology Consortium.* Portland, Oregon. ED402914.

Trotter, A. (1997, November). Taking technology's measure. *Education Week 17* (11), 6–11.

Viadero, D. (1997, November). A tool for learning. *Education Week, 17*(11), 12–18.

Wiske, M. S. & Houde, R. (1988). *From recitation to construction: Teachers change with new technologies* (Technical Report TR88-28). Cambridge, MA: Harvard Graduate School of Education, Educational Technology Center.

Zehr, M. A. (1997, November). Teaching the teachers. *Education Week 17* (11), 24–29.

Zorfass, J. M. (1991, April*). Promoting successful technology integration through active teaching practices.* Paper presented at the annual meeting of the American Educational Research Association, Chicago.

9

Implementing Instruction

BUILDING ON BIOGRAPHY: MY LEARNING STYLE ODYSSEY

When I (Liz) was teaching English and foreign languages to high-school and junior-high students during the 1970s and 1980s, I was not aware of research on learning styles or multiple intelligences, two theories you read about in Chapter Three, "Knowing Middle- and High-School Students." I was aware, however, that some methods I was using weren't particularly effective in helping students learn and that I didn't particularly enjoy teaching when my students didn't seem to be learning.

For example, during my first few years of English teaching, I usually devoted some portion of the school year to a grammar unit. I did this because the district, the department, and even the students expected it and because I, like many other English teachers at the time, thought that knowledge of the parts of speech, the parts of a sentence, and various rules of usage would help my students become better writers and speakers. I would block out a period of time—say, nine weeks—to teach this unit. With the aid of a textbook, worksheets, the chalkboard, and the overhead projector, I would explain a grammatical construction such as a prepositional phrase, review examples with the class, call on students to complete some exercises aloud, and then assign individual exercises to be begun in class and finished as homework. The next day, we would check and grade the exercises. At some point, students would take a quiz or test on the material covered. Predictably, students who did well on the exercises did well on the test—especially if the test closely resembled the exercises. Quite a few students did poorly on the exercises and on the test. Regardless of how students performed, I forged ahead to the next topic in the unit. Two weeks later, if I asked students to vary sentence beginnings by using prepositional phrases, most reacted with blank stares.

At the same time, I taught French in a very different way. For example, if we were studying prepositional phrases in French, I would have students physically respond to oral commands ("Put the pencil on the floor"); students would give oral commands using prepositions in a game of "Simon Says" ("Simon says, 'Walk toward the door'"); I would place familiar objects in unusual places around the classroom and have students tell me what was out of place ("The clock is on the floor"). As homework, students would write descriptions of their bedrooms in French, using at least five different prepositional phrases ("My jeans are under the bed"). The next day, they might read their descriptions to a partner who would sketch a picture of the bedroom based on the written description. My French students were having a lot more fun learning about and applying knowledge of prepositional phrases than my English students. And I was enjoying teaching French more than English because I could see and hear students' progress in using French. More importantly, my French students were learning more successfully than my English students.

One day, I realized that I wasn't really teaching my English students about prepositional phrases; I was simply assigning tasks and hoping that they would learn about prepositional phrases. My French students were more successful because they were using their knowledge for authentic communicative purposes and practicing it in a variety of different modes (i.e., seeing, hearing, speaking, doing). It took several years of teaching before I figured out that active involvement and application of knowledge to actual problems were key to learning across content areas—not just in foreign language classes. Furthermore, I realized that being on center stage at all times was not only exhausting but unnecessary, because students could often learn from and teach one another just as effectively as I could.

More and more, I selected methods for instruction with these principles in mind. For example, while reading *Wuthering Heights* each student selected a character to follow throughout the novel. Students kept journals about their characters and periodically wrote entries assuming that persona. I enlisted the help of the school counselor to administer and interpret the results of personality tests which each student completed as Heathcliff, Catherine, Edgar, Isabella or another of the unhappy individuals who populate the novel. As a final project, and again with the counselor's aid, students role-played family counseling sessions for the various relationship groups in the book.

The real light dawned, however, as a result of career counseling that I experienced while on a leave of absence from classroom teaching. As part of the counseling, I completed inventories that revealed my preferred learning style and my personality type. Among other things, I was surprised to discover that I learned best from "hands-on" activities. I was surprised because I had always been an excellent listener and note-taker in lecture-style classes. But as I reflected upon this finding, I realized that I had learned to be an effective listener because it was necessary to my academic survival. My scrupulous note-taking was actually the manifestation of my need for active involvement while learning. When I reflected upon my teaching style, I realized that I was most comfortable when my students were role-playing characters in literature, working in groups to create visual representations of people and places, or ordering from a menu in my classroom French cafe.

I also discovered that I prefer unstructured learning situations in which I have some freedom to choose what to learn, how to learn, and how to show what I've learned. Because I had rarely been given such freedom in my own school experience, I had assumed this quality was just a quirk. I also realized that this preference was reflected in my teaching. For years, I had simply assumed that, like me, my students would relish the freedom to be creative and to demonstrate originality. Therefore, when I gave assignments in English class—which I usually did orally—I was inevitably irritated by students who wanted the instructions repeated (endlessly, it seemed), who wanted to know the exact number of pages required, and who expressed great concern about whether a paper needed to be double-spaced, typed, written in ink, and on and on. In retrospect, I realized that my students were simply exhibiting their own learning styles and personality types. Because I (as a learner) didn't need to see written guidelines myself, I (as a teacher) assumed no one did. Because I (as a learner) didn't need clear parameters for projects, I (as a teacher) assumed no one did. I (as a teacher) was wrong.

Because I did not return to public school teaching after my leave of absence, I was unable to apply these insights to teaching in middle or high school. But learning styles and multiple intelligences are important topics in the courses I teach for both prospective and experienced teachers. My students discover their own learning styles and discuss the implications for their teaching. I encourage them to discover the learning styles of the middle- and high-school students with whom they work. I strive to model and use instructional strategies that will engage the variety of learners in my courses and to provide the structure (although it's a struggle) that so many of my students prefer.

Questions to Consider

1. What does Liz's story suggest about how teachers select instructional strategies?
2. What does Liz's story suggest about how high-school teachers view subject areas?
3. Have you observed or experienced the teaching of grammar (or another topic) as Liz described it in the first part of her story? How can you account for the persistence of this model of instruction?

▌▊▍PURPOSE

When asked to recall a teacher who greatly influenced them, many people—the authors of this book included—describe a teacher who was an inspiring and charismatic lecturer. Reflect on your own educational experiences. Is there a teacher whose lectures particularly inspired you and whom you hope one day to emulate? If you are a person who learns well by listening, you will probably answer yes. Lecture is one instructional strategy that will be discussed in this chapter, but you will also be introduced to other methods that are even more effective with the diverse learners in today's middle- and high-school classrooms.

The main purposes of this chapter are to introduce you to a variety of instructional methods you can implement in the classroom and to help you select the ones best suited to your instructional goals and your students' learning. Specifically, this chapter will help you:

- devise ways to begin and end lessons effectively;
- choose instructional strategies that meet standards for *authentic pedagogy* and that foster students' *authentic intellectual achievement;*
- choose instructional strategies that are appropriate for the content you are teaching and your instructional goals;
- become familiar with a variety of teaching/learning strategies including methods for large group, small group, and individualized instruction;
- consider the implications of individual differences, such as learning styles and multiple intelligences, sociocultural differences, and special needs among students when selecting instructional strategies.

The strategies to which you will be introduced in this chapter are organized around a set of standards that have recently been proposed for *authentic pedagogy,* a concept explained in detail later (Newmann, Marks & Gamoran, 1996). These standards provide a framework for examining a number of instructional strategies that help students engage in higher order thinking, hold substantive conversations with teachers and peers about subject matter, develop depth of knowledge, and make connections to the world beyond the classroom. As you read on, keep in mind that these categories are not distinct; no single strategy serves only one purpose or is always effective.

Good teachers possess a wide repertoire of techniques and choose instructional strategies based on many criteria, including their own familiarity and comfort with particular techniques; the academic, social, and personal goals they set for their students; the effectiveness of certain strategies with specific groups and individuals; the changing learning needs of students; and the availability of resources such as time, space, and materials.

▌▌CHOOSING INSTRUCTIONAL STRATEGIES

Today, most educators agree that students learn best when they are "actively constructing meaning grounded in their own experience rather than simply absorbing and reproducing knowledge transmitted from subject-matter fields" (Newmann, Marks & Gamoran, 1996, p. 281). Active learning can take many forms: class discussions, cooperative learning tasks, independent research projects, role-playing, peer teaching, the use of manipulatives and realia, and, as you read in the preceding chapter, the application of educational technologies. However, activity alone does not guarantee learning. For example, students might work diligently in small groups to complete a vocabulary worksheet that requires only factual knowledge. Furthermore, one student in a group might be doing all the work while the others merely copy her answers. How can you choose instructional strategies that promote authentic intellectual achievement, not just the appearance of learning?

Standards for Authentic Pedagogy

Newmann, Marks & Gamoran (1996) have proposed three criteria for authentic intellectual achievement for students. The term *authentic* refers to something that is "genuine rather than artificial or misleading" (p. 282). For example, determining the optimum location for a compost pile on school grounds is an authentic activity for a high-school science class (National Center on Education and the Economy, 1995); labeling a diagram of a compost pile is not. While labeling the parts of a compost pile might be a valuable first step in acquiring the core knowledge and skills needed to carry out the complex project of determining the actual site, it does not meet the standards for authentic intellectual achievement.

An authentic intellectual achievement demonstrates *construction of knowledge.* Such activities as labeling body parts, defining terms, or matching authors to works require students to *reproduce* knowledge. Students construct knowledge when they use words or symbols to write or speak about their learning, make things such as machines or movies, and perform for audiences.

The second standard for authentic intellectual achievement is *disciplined inquiry.* Disciplined inquiry requires individuals to build on a prior knowledge base from one or more fields. The knowledge base may include "facts, vocabularies, concepts, theories, algorithms, and conventions for the conduct and expression for inquiry" (p. 283). Disciplined inquiry aims to develop in-depth understanding, which requires more than knowing lots of details about a topic. Disciplined inquiry requires elaborated communication, not brief answers, such as true/false, fill-in-the-blank, or the memorization of short sentences. Traditionally, much school activity has been devoted to helping students build a knowledge base, but rarely have students had the opportunity to put it to use.

Finally, authentic intellectual achievement has *value beyond school.* Activities have value beyond school when they satisfy "aesthetic, utilitarian, or personal" purposes, such as speaking a foreign language, creating a painting, or writing a letter to the editor (p. 284). Unfortunately, students continue to spend the majority of their time in school demonstrating academic competency: taking spelling quizzes, writing essay exams restating the causes of the Great Depression, or conducting laboratory exercises with pre-specified outcomes.

Newmann, Marks and Gamoran (1996) have proposed four standards for authentic pedagogy that fosters authentic intellectual achievement. These standards should apply to most of the strategies you use in the classroom.

1. *Higher-order thinking.* Instruction should involve students in manipulating information and ideas by synthesizing, generalizing, explaining, hypothesizing, or arriving at conclusions that produce new meanings and understandings for them. In this chapter, strategies grouped under this standard include techniques for presenting information effectively and for questioning.

2. *Substantive conversations.* Students should engage in extended conversations about subject matter with the teacher and/or their peers in a way that builds an improved and shared understanding of ideas or topics. In this chapter, strategies grouped under this standard include large-group discussions, small-group work and peer tutoring.

3. *Depth of knowledge.* Instruction should address central ideas of a topic or discipline with enough thoroughness to explore connections and relationships and to produce relatively complex understandings. In this chapter, strategies grouped under this standard include mastery learning, learning centers, activity packets, learning contracts, independent study, and writing to learn.

4. *Connections to the world beyond the classroom.* Students should learn to make connections between academic knowledge and either public problems or personal experience. In this chapter, strategies grouped under this standard include role-playing, drama in the classroom, and problem-based learning.

Figure 9.1 shows how the strategies presented in this chapter relate to standards for authentic intellectual achievement and for authentic pedagogy.

These standards do not preclude the use of drill, lecture, repetition, or memorization. However, the standards do suggest that such activities have value principally as means to an end: "The point is not to abandon all traditional forms of schoolwork but to keep authentic achievement clearly in view as a valued end" (Newmann, Marks & Gamoran, 1996, p. 288).

It is appropriate to expect authentic intellectual achievement and to use authentic pedagogy with both middle- and high-school students. Students of diverse backgrounds and abilities benefit from active learning (e.g., Newmann, Marks & Gamoran, 1996). A number of the topics discussed in this chapter—attention to lesson structure, advance organizers, small group work, peer tutoring, teaching learning and study skills, using learning styles and multiple intelligences to design instruction—have great promise for students with learning disabilities and other special needs in inclusive classrooms (King-Sears & Cummings, 1996; Mercer, Lane, Jordan, Allsopp & Eisele, 1996; Summey & Strahan, 1997). In fact, students who have been the least successful in school may stand to gain the most when they are engaged in challenging and exciting school projects (Braddock & McPartland, 1993).

Authentic Pedagogy and the Nature of Middle- and High-School Students

One look around a middle-school classroom should convince you that one size of instruction doesn't fit all. The different rates at which early adolescents develop physically, cognitively, and psychosocially are reason enough to vary instructional strategies.

FIGURE 9.1   Instructional Strategies Organized Under Standards for Authentic Pedagogy

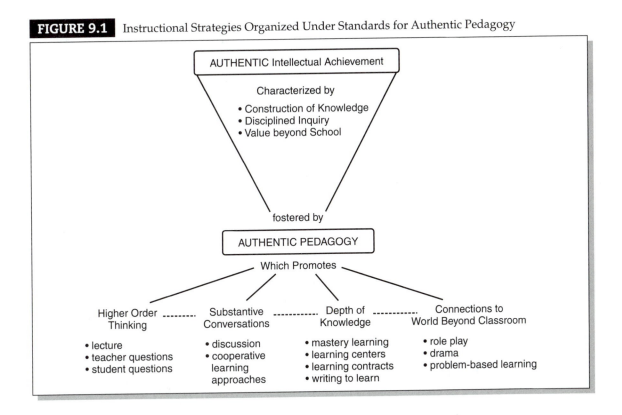

Among the developmental characteristics of early adolescents that make authentic pedagogy especially appropriate for this age group are the need for peer interaction and for opportunities to practice independence from adults, the need to deal with more complex intellectual tasks, and the need to earn respect and build self-esteem through experiencing school success (Hamburg, 1994).

Because middle schoolers can be challenging, especially when not engaged in the type of instruction they are receiving, some teachers claim that middle-school students "can't do group work" or need to be "kept busy" with worksheets and drills. However, strategies such as the following have been identified as particularly ineffective with early adolescents: (1) more teacher control of classroom assignment and whole-group instruction; (2) fewer opportunities for student choice and self-management; (3) less variety in tasks and learning materials; (4) more competition for grades; and (5) more emphasis on memorization and recall of teacher-assigned material (Braddock & Mc-Partland, 1993).

While high-school students, particularly juniors and seniors, may have passed through the most tempestuous period of adolescence, their need for active engagement in learning is no less. At least as much as younger students, high-school students need to be known, to experience positive relationships with adults and peers, to see a purpose in their academic work, to develop attitudes of inquiry, and to pursue individual interests in depth (e.g., Perrone, 1991; Lee, Bryk & Smith, 1993; Sizer, 1994; Meier, 1995).

■ ■ GETTING STARTED AND BRINGING CLOSURE

The best-planned and most exciting lesson in the world can turn into a disaster if you haven't thought through how you will help students get ready to learn and how you will help them consolidate their learning. Good lessons can be compared to good workouts: they begin with a warm-up, phase into the aerobic work, and end with a cool-down. If you exercise regularly, you know that it can be tempting to skip the warm-up and cool-down periods—especially if you're pressed for time—but sooner or later your body will let you know it needs both phases to get the maximum bene-fit from your workout. You should plan lesson openings and closings as carefully as you plan the body of a lesson. Otherwise, your students' "workout" may be less effective.

As Richard pointed out in Chapter Four, "Rethinking Classroom Management," often the first few minutes of a class period must be spent on "bookkeeping" chores, such as taking attendance or distributing materials. For student teachers and beginning teachers, these moments can be among the most problematic—a time when manage-ment problems are likely to occur. Many teachers establish a routine that students can expect when they enter the classroom. Math teachers may have a problem written on the board that relates to the previous day's work or that previews the topic for the day (e.g., "Look around the room and list as many obtuse angles as you can."). English teachers may play soothing music during a five-minute journal writing period, while students write silently on the topic of their choice or to a planned prompt. Known by a variety of names such as "sponges" or "bell-ringers," these initial activities get students thinking and signal to them that learning has begun.

Once you're ready to begin the body of the lesson, you need to decide how to cap-ture students' attention and interest and prepare them for learning. The simple com-mand, "Open your books to page 635," isn't a very effective motivator. If students have completed a silent writing or problem-solving activity, you will probably want to elicit some of their responses as an entree into the lesson. In addition, previewing the day's agenda helps many students—especially those who need structure—focus on the tasks at hand. Many teachers post the day's agenda in a prominent location and use it as a lesson outline, returning to it periodically during the class period to help students consolidate or summarize their understandings. Again, establishing this as a routine in your classroom is good practice both for management and instructional purposes. On the other hand, there's nothing wrong with deviating from routine sometimes by springing the occasional surprise or introducing an element of antici-pation or suspense!

Only your imagination limits the number of techniques you can employ to capture students' attention. It may take you some time, as a beginning teacher, to discover the difference between an effective attention-getter and an invitation to chaos. Much de-pends on your personality and the "personality" of your class. For example, Clayton's tenth-grade English students, frustrated with the difficult prose and abstract themes of Hawthorne's *The Scarlet Letter*, loved it when he appeared in class garbed in black, climbed upon a chair, began declaiming Dimmesdale's final speech, then dramatically ripped open his shirt to reveal a blood-red "A" painted on his chest. On the other hand, when Pete, a student teacher in science, stood before a class of ninth-graders holding a terra cotta pot filled with a plant and soil, nonchalantly scooped up a handful of "dirt" from the pot and ate it, his students were horrified. Although Pete intended to capture their interest by his bravado (the dirt was actually crushed chocolate cookies), he almost started a riot.

Many teachers use *advance organizers* to introduce content to be studied. An advance organizer is introductory material presented ahead of the learning task. It "helps students become active learners in situations where they receive information through lectures and written assignments. They learn to strive for conceptual structures of the content, which will enable them to organize information and make it their own" (Joyce & Calhoun, 1996, p. 25). Developed by David Ausubel (1963), the concept of advance organizers is based on the assumption that students will learn more effectively when they know what to expect and how what they are learning relates to what they already know. Advance organizers help students link new or unfamiliar ideas or concepts to existing knowledge, thus strengthening understanding. Joyce & Calhoun (1996) emphasize that an advance organizer is not simply an introductory overview or brief statement, such as "Today we will learn about the caste system in India." Rather, the advance organizer is an idea that must be explored intellectually. An appropriate advance organizer for the topic of the caste system in India might be the concept of social stratification. The teacher might elicit from the students what they already know about social stratification in the community or in the school and perhaps hypothesize about the social status of people from various cultures depicted in photographs. The advance organizer need not be lengthy, but it should be based on a major concept or generalization in your discipline. Advance organizers are particularly helpful tools for encouraging students to think at higher levels.

The ending of a lesson is as important as its beginning. Most new teachers are still learning how to manage time—whether in the block or traditional scheduling—and, consequently, overplan or underplan. If you overplan, you may not be able to bring appropriate closure to the lesson as you had intended. You need to monitor time so that the bell doesn't ring while you and your students are immersed in an activity, and you find yourself shouting a homework assignment to an empty room strewn with art supplies and a pile of student papers tossed haphazardly on your desk. If you underplan, you may find yourself with dreaded "dead time" on your hands—another management challenge for beginning teachers. This is one good reason to start now collecting brief but engaging activities that can be used to begin or end a lesson.

The most important reason for bringing closure to a lesson is instructional: you want students to remember and continue thinking about what they have learned. This is also an opportunity for you to assess how successful instruction has been and on what points students still have questions or misunderstandings. Just as "Open your books" is an ineffective lesson starter, asking "Any questions?" is not sufficient as closure. You can review by questioning or asking students to summarize the day's lesson. Some teachers have students use notebooks or journals to record what they have learned and what they still have questions about. Many teachers pass out index cards to be used as exit slips on which students summarize what has occurred in class (Gere, 1985). By quickly reading through the day's exit slips, you can easily monitor students' learning and find out whether your instruction was in the "target zone."

▌Reader Activity 9.1

WHAT WOULD YOU DO?
Middle/High School Volleyball

The purpose of this activity is to enable you to apply what you have learned thus far about the overall structure of a lesson. As you read the description of this physical education class, focus on how the instructor has structured the lesson for optimum learning by all students.

1. *Volleyball Warm-up* (5 minutes). Instructor has volleyballs out and ready to go. Instructions for the warm-up activity are posted prominently on the wall. Students are to practice bumping the ball off the wall to see how many consecutive bumps they can hit in the same spot. Students can join one or two other people to go for a record by bumping back and forth. While students warm up, instructor takes roll and performs other administrative tasks.

2. *Instant Activity* (3 minutes). Students quickly sit down with a partner, clasp wrists, and see if they can pull each other up at the same time. Try the same activity with four people, eight people, etc.

3. *Capturing Students' Attention*. To introduce the day's activities, instructor asks students to recall the most exciting points scored in recent Olympic volleyball games. Students will probably respond with "spiking." This is the skill to be learned today.

4. *Lesson Focus* (10 minutes). Instructor teaches skills sequence for spiking. Because some students will successfully complete the entire sequence quickly, the instructor posts challenges and refinements. (How many times can you toss and hit the ball in a row?)

5. *Application: Spiking Dodge Ball* (10 minutes). Instructor has already set up equipment for the game throughout the gym. Students form teams of three or four. They play with light-weight foam balls. The object is to spike the ball over a slanty rope and hit a member of the opposing team.

6. *Assessment*. Instructor observes and records students' progress in mastering the skills of spiking. In addition, to demonstrate their understanding, students will form into teams of news analysts, create commentary on spiking in Olympic volleyball, and videotape their commentary.

7. *Closure* (5 minutes). Instructor tells students to stop what they're doing, put equipment into bins, and gather in a large group. Instructor reviews what students learned about spiking and reminds students that their commentaries are another chance to show what they know. Instructor tells students that the first group assembled in the gym tomorrow will be the first group to videotape their commentary.

This plan was created by Ken Bell and is described in greater detail at:
http://pe.central.vt.edu/lessonideas/middlehigh/kenslessonguide.html

1. What are the advantages to students and teacher of the warm-up and instant activity?
2. How does the instructor capture the students' attention?
3. How do the standards for authentic pedagogy apply to this lesson in physical education?
4. In what respects does this lesson maximize opportunities for all students to succeed?
5. What are the advantages to students and teacher of the assessment and closure portion?

▌▌STANDARD ONE: STRATEGIES FOR DEVELOPING HIGHER-ORDER THINKING

Brad March, a high-school social studies teacher, enjoys lecturing. In fact, lecture is the predominant instructional strategy Brad employs. His knowledge of his subject area is impressive; he spends many hours preparing his lectures and synthesizing information from a variety of sources. His classroom is filled with costumes and props that he often uses to enliven his talks. He puts lecture notes on the overhead so that students can follow the course of the lesson. He is a dynamic speaker and obviously enthusiastic about his subject. His students enter his classroom, sit down, open their notebooks, and begin writing as soon as he begins speaking. They write furiously, sometimes asking him to slow down or to leave an overhead up a few minutes longer so that they can copy the information. He tells students what information will likely appear on the test, and some students use colored highlighting pens to target these items for future study. Brad's students seem to be learning a great deal about U.S. History.

Steven, a preservice teacher, admired Brad's style so much that he chose Brad as his mentor during his field experience at Brad's high school. After he had observed Brad teaching for a number of weeks, Steven felt ready to conduct his own lesson on weaponry and battle tactics in World War I. Just as they did for Brad, the students wrote furiously as Steven lectured. They attentively watched a video clip from a recent popular film depicting the soldiers' terror, confusion, and suffering. They waited for Steven to tell them what they needed to know for the test. Instead, Steven said, "Now, I want you to put yourself in the place of one of those soldiers and write a letter home about what you're feeling." At this point, the lesson began to fall apart. The students became agitated and declared that Mr. March never made them write "stupid letters." Steven switched gears and instructed the students to write the letter for homework. He went on to the next activity he had planned. He distributed three primary source documents concerning proposals to put an end to the war. He asked students to work in groups to compare these documents and evaluate them in light of what they knew about the actual terms of peace in World War I. Again, chaos threatened. To everyone's relief, the bell rang and the students filed out, no doubt hoping that tomorrow Mr. March would be back at his post as usual with all the important facts.

This was a critical incident in Steven's development as a teacher, for it helped him realize that he wanted students to think and have opinions about history. Facts were still important to Steven, but he knew then that facts were not enough. When asked to apply the facts they were learning, Mr. March's students stumbled. Steven is now working on developing his own teaching style in which he combines interactive lectures with activities to promote higher-order thinking about history and to develop students' empathy for the human dimensions of history. The story of Brad and Steven highlights the strengths and weaknesses of lecture as an instructional technique.

Helping Students Get the Most Out of Lecture

Students often do need a framework of facts and information upon which to build deeper understandings. In Steven's case, for example, it is not likely that the students could analyze primary source documents accurately without knowing something about the authors, the circumstances, and the dates of the documents. Lecture remains

Whenever you lecture or explain, stay tuned in to the classroom atmosphere and the actions of your students.

a widely used strategy for presenting and explaining information to students and is especially appropriate in the following situations identified by Good and Brophy (1997):

1. When the objective is to present information that is not readily available from another source, is original, or must be integrated from different sources.
2. When the material must be organized and presented in a particular way.
3. When it is necessary to arouse interest in the subject.
4. When it is necessary to introduce a topic before students read about it on their own or to provide instructions about a task.
5. When the information needs to be summarized or synthesized (following discussion or inquiry).
6. When curriculum materials need updating or elaborating.
7. When the teacher wants to present alternate points of view or to clarify issues in preparation for discussion.
8. When the teacher wants to provide supplementary explanations of material that students may have difficulty learning on their own (pp. 364–365).

As an instructional strategy, lecture does not recognize diversity among students and is based on the assumption that all students learn equally well by listening. In addition, because lecture places the teacher at center stage, students can easily become disengaged or mindlessly copy facts without processing them at higher levels. However, lecture is still widely regarded as the most efficient means of conveying information to large numbers of people at one time. What can you do then, to ensure that stu-

FIGURE 9.2   Effective and Succinct Explanatory Techniques

Technique	Example
Identify goals for the students.	"We want to understand the meaning of an *ecological niche*, so we can use the concept to describe the plants and animals in ecologies and compare ecologies with one another."
Monitor and signal progress toward the goals.	"Francis, when you said that sharks are predators in the sea, you made a smart connection: We hadn't talked about sea creatures at all. But sure, sharks are predators. What other sea predators can we identify?"
Give abundant examples of the concepts treated.	"Let's compare the animals in our local forests with those in Australia, Alaska, and Madagascar."
Use demonstration, including offering complementary representations, highlighting links among them, and identifying conditions for use and nonuse of the concepts.	"As we watch this film about African animals, we'll stop it and talk about the niches we see. And we'll ask whether different animals are always in different niches or sometimes the same niche and why."
Link new concepts to old through identification of familiar, expanded, and new elements.	"*Niche* is an odd word. Who knows what a niche in the ordinary sense is?"
Connect a new concept or procedure to principles that students already know.	"Is the niche concept really such a useful way of talking about ecologies? Well, let's explore that. Let's think about other situations where we talk about roles in a system; for instance, the roles of people in a business or a school."

From *Smart Schools: From Training Memories to Educating Minds* (p. 16–17) by D. N. Perkins, 1992, New York: The Free Press.

dents get the most out of a lecture? In short, your lecture presentations need to be succinct, clear, and interactive.

Making Presentations Succinct

In *Smart Schools: From Training Memories to Educating Minds* (1992), David Perkins has presented some characteristics of effective and succinct lecture techniques. These characteristics are illustrated in Figure 9.2. The example shows how a middle-school science teacher might explain the concept of "ecological niche." The lecture is succinct because it is focused on a single concept and each segment is a necessary step in leading students to understanding.

Making Presentations Clear

If you've ever been the captive audience of a rambling, mumbling lecturer, you know that clarity is essential to effective presentations. Figure 9.3 depicts aspects of clarity identified by McCaleb and White (1980) and summarized by Good and Brophy (1997, pp. 365–366).

FIGURE 9.3   Clarity in Presentations

Aspect of Clarity	Definition	Guidelines for Teachers
Understanding	*Determining how the information to be learned links to students' current knowledge*	• *Determine students' familiarity with information to be presented* • *Use terms that are unambiguous and within students' experience* • *Clarify and explain terms that are potentially confusing*
Structuring	*Organizing the materials to promote student understanding*	• *Establish a purpose for the lesson* • *Preview the organization of the lesson* • *Provide internal summaries and a final review*
Sequencing	*Arranging the information in an order conducive to learning, e.g., by gradually increasing the difficulty or complexity of the material*	• *Order the lesson in a logical way, appropriate to content and learners*
Explaining	*Explaining principles and relating them to facts through examples, illustrations, or analogies*	• *Define major concepts* • *Give examples to illustrate concepts* • *Use examples that are accurate and concrete as well as abstract*
Presenting	*Volume, pacing, articulation, and other speech mechanics*	• *Articulate words clearly and project speech loudly enough* • *Pace presentation at a rate appropriate to learners* • *Support the verbal content with appropriate nonverbal communication and visual aids*

Adapted from Chapter 9 "Active teaching" in Looking In Classrooms by T. L. Good and J. E. Brophy. Copyright 1997 by Addison-Wesley Educational Publishers, Inc. Reprinted by permission of Addison Wesley Longman, Inc.

Making Presentations Interactive

Merrill Harmin (1994) has compiled a number of strategies for keeping students involved in lecture presentations. Figure 9.4 shows a sequence of steps for making a presentation of information interactive. This sequence can be adapted to various subjects and grade levels (pp. 18–19).

In addition to building teacher-student and student-student interaction into your lectures, you can keep students engaged by weaving audio, visual, or electronic resources into your presentations. As Kevin pointed out in Chapter Eight, "Teaching With Technology," presentation programs such as Power Point allow you to combine text with images to create interesting audio and visual effects. However, the more common classroom technologies of chalkboard, whiteboard, and overhead projector can also enhance presentations when thoughtfully and purposefully used.

Remember that your students are an involuntary audience. Unlike church-, movie-, or play-goers, they cannot walk out if they are bored or frustrated. Whenever you lecture or explain, stay tuned in to the classroom atmosphere and the actions of your students. They will surely send you signals, both subtle and overt, about the effectiveness of your presentation.

FIGURE 9.4   Lecture-Share-Learn Sequence

Speak-Write (whole class; 2-5 minutes)	Lecture until reaching a natural break in the material, but not more than 5 minutes. Say, "Take a moment and write the key ideas you've heard so far or any questions you have."
Working Alone (1-2 minutes)	Students write. When three or four students have finished writing, say, "One more moment please."
Speak-Write (whole class; 3-5 minutes)	Continue lecture to next natural break point. Then say, "Now I want you to make some notes again about what you heard or questions you have about what I just said." Continue this sequence as appropriate.
Sharing Pairs (2-8 minutes)	Ask students to form pairs and share a summary of what they heard, what they think are important points, or questions that occurred to them.
Lecture Summary (whole class; 2-5 minutes)	"Let me summarize what I would most like you to understand, what I see as the main points."
Attentive Discussion (whole class; as appropriate)	"Who would be willing to share ideas, reactions, or questions?"
Outcome Sentences (independent; 2-4 minutes)	Ask students to review lesson, make note of key things they learned, rediscovered, or perhaps are now wondering about.
Whip Around, Pass Option (whole class; as appropriate)	"Starting at this wall, let's whip around part of the class. When it comes your turn, read one of your 'I learned' statements or, if you prefer, say 'I pass.'"

From *Inspiring Active Learning* (p. 18–19) by M. Harmin, 1994, Alexandria, VA: Association for Supervision and Curriculum Development.

Learning Through Lectures: Organizing and Understanding Information

If you expect students to take notes from a lecture (or a reading assignment), you need to provide guidance about what and how they need to record. Some teachers provide students with note-taking guides to accompany lecture or reading in the form of skeletal outlines or partially completed webs or concept maps, which students fill in as the lecture proceeds.

Graphic organizers can also help students comprehend and interpret information that is delivered via lecture or text. Graphic organizers have been extensively studied and found to be effective aids to learning for a variety of students in a variety of settings (Robinson, 1998). They provide ways to represent and organize one's thoughts and knowledge visually. Graphic organizers may be especially helpful for students with learning disabilities and for students who are not yet fluent in English. Figure 9.5 illustrates some common graphic organizers and their uses. The concept map is probably the

FIGURE 9.5   Four Common Graphic Organizers

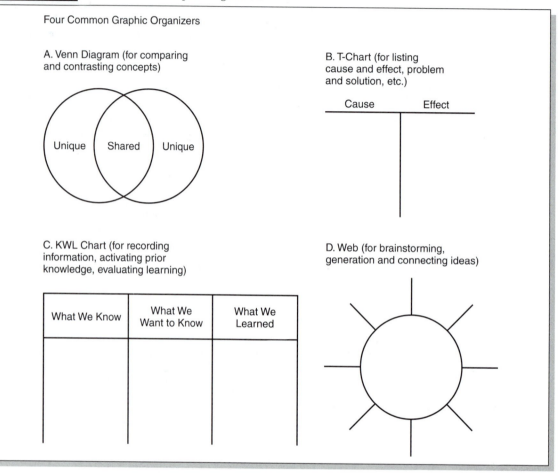

Four Common Graphic Organizers

A. Venn Diagram (for comparing and contrasting concepts)

Unique   Shared   Unique

B. T-Chart (for listing cause and effect, problem and solution, etc.)

Cause   Effect

C. KWL Chart (for recording information, activating prior knowledge, evaluating learning)

What We Know	What We Want to Know	What We Learned

D. Web (for brainstorming, generation and connecting ideas)

most commonly used graphic organizer. It allows students to show the relationship among numerous concepts and sub-concepts in relation to one another and to a single, overarching concept, topic, or theme (e.g., culture, the Middle Ages, patterns). Teachers can create graphic organizers for students or students can create their own. Access to drawing software and on-line clip art makes graphic organizers more attractive and easier to create than ever before (Ekhaml, 1998; Hyerle, 1995/1996). At the same time, much can be accomplished with plain paper and markers.

Some teachers employ *dialectic journals* to help students understand and organize information (Gere, 1985). To create dialectic journals, students divide a notebook page horizontally. On the right side, they record important facts and ideas from lecture or reading; on the left, they list comments and questions about the material. (Of course, if you use this technique while lecturing, you must pause to allow students time to write.) Depending on the topic, students might quickly sketch a scene, process, or timeline. You will be doing your students a valuable service if you teach them not only content in your subject area, but skills that they will use for a lifelong learning.

▌Reader Activity 9.2

THEORY INTO PRACTICE
Planning a Presentation of Information

Choose a topic in your subject area that would require you to present information to students in lecture format (e.g., Elizabethan theater, French Impressionism, the periodic table). You might leaf through a textbook in your subject area to get an idea of a manageable topic for this activity or build upon the skeletal unit plan you began developing in Chapter Six, "Planning for Middle- and High-School Instruction." Plan a lesson in which you incorporate some of the strategies and ideas presented in the preceding section. Write a one-day lesson plan that includes these components:

- an introduction of the topic via an advance organizer or other strategy
- a detailed content outline following the principles for effective and clear explanations (Figures 9.2 and 9.3)
- interactive portions similar to Harmin's "Lecture-Share-Learn" strategy (Figure 9.4)
- a summary or closure activity and preview of the next day's learning

Write a one-page introduction to the plan in which you explain how your plan will help students get the most out of this lecture. In class, share your plan in a small, interdisciplinary group and ask for feedback from peers who are not familiar with the content you intend to teach. Use their suggestions to revise your plan before submitting it to your instructor.

Encouraging Higher-Order Thinking Through Questions

Just as lecture has been overused as an instructional strategy, so has teacher questioning. Some research has shown that teachers may ask as many as 300-400 questions per day (Wilen, 1991). It is doubtful that such a large number of questions could be intended to stimulate higher-order thinking in students. In fact, stimulating higher-order and creative thinking is only one of the reasons teachers ask questions. The two most common purposes for which teachers use questions are to determine whether students remember and understand what has been taught, and to have students apply what they have learned. Other common purposes include to stimulate student participation, to assess student progress, to personalize subject matter, and to support student contributions to the class (Wilen, 1991). In this section, we will concentrate on posing thought-provoking questions. As you plan for and implement instruction, you need to consider the purposes of your questions and whether those questions are achieving your intended purposes.

Kinds of Questions

On the television game show *Jeopardy*, contestants are given answers and win money by offering the correct question. All *Jeopardy* questions are factual and have only one correct answer—contestants are never asked to explain, speculate, evaluate, or analyze. *Jeopardy* contestants display an impressive amount of factual knowledge, but viewers have no way of knowing whether these individuals can actually use this factual knowledge to solve problems, analyze issues, or construct arguments. A lot of classroom questions resemble *Jeopardy* items—in fact, many teachers use the *Jeopardy* format as an entertaining way to review facts before a test. Factual knowledge is important, but being able to put facts to use is more important. Effective teachers know how to ask questions that probe beyond sheer recall.

In Chapter Six, "Planning for Middle- and High-School Instruction," you read about Bloom's taxonomy of educational objectives (Bloom et al., 1956) and how it has been used to guide the development of student objectives in the cognitive domain. Bloom's taxonomy identified six levels of objectives in the cognitive domain ranging from simple to complex intellectual operations: knowledge, comprehension, application, analysis, synthesis, and evaluation. This taxonomy has also been used as a basis for classifying the questions teachers ask.

William Wilen (1991) combined Bloom's work with that of several other researchers and produced a relatively simple system for classifying teacher questions. He divided questions into two broad categories: *convergent* and *divergent*. The purpose of convergent questions is to determine basic knowledge. That is, such questions require responses to converge upon a single or simple answer. The purpose of divergent questions is to engage students in "critical thinking as they process information" (Wilen, 1991, p. 13). That is, such questions encourage responses to diverge in various directions. He then subdivided each of these categories into "low order" (knowledge, comprehension) and "high order" (application, analysis, synthesis, evaluation) based on Bloom's taxonomy. Figure 9.6 shows Wilen's classification of questions.

Models of questioning such as Wilen's are not intended to be used as rigid templates; rather they provide useful frameworks for planning and analyzing the questions you might ask in the classroom. You might wish to explore other models for planning questions (e.g., Christenbury & Kelly, 1983; Latham, 1997; Penick, Crow & Bonnstetter, 1996). Skilled teachers possess a repertoire of techniques for generating thought-provoking and challenging questions that will engage the minds of diverse learners.

Questioning Techniques

Planning good questions is one aspect of effective teaching. Knowing how and when to ask them is another. The first time you use questions in teaching, you will discover a whole array of questions about questioning: Should you insist that students raise their hands before speaking? Should you call only on volunteers? What do you say when a student gives a wrong answer? What do you do if no one answers? How do you get a discussion back on topic? How can you increase participation in a discussion? What do you do if one student monopolizes the discussion?

Some of these questions can only be answered through experience and getting to know your students. By watching your students as they interact in discussion, by listening to their responses, and by being mindful of your own actions, you will develop insight into the best ways to respond to the variety of situations that arise in the course of discussions. Following are some guidelines that can help you be a better questioner in most classroom settings.

Wait time   The time that elapses between the moment you finish asking a question and the moment a student volunteers an answer may seem like an eternity. But, in fact, researchers have shown that many teachers wait less than one second after asking a question before reacting in some way, e.g., answering the question, restating it, asking

FIGURE 9.6 Levels of Questioning

Question Type	Definition	Teacher's Intention	Student Responses	Example
Level I Low-Order Convergent	Questions requiring students to reproduce others' thinking	Students recall or recognize information	Students' responses can be easily anticipated	1. Who invented the sewing machine 2. What is the definition of *photosynthesis?*
Level II High-Order Convergent	Questions requiring students to engage in first levels of productive thinking	Students go beyond recall and demonstrate understanding of information	Students' responses can usually be anticipated	1. What is the meaning of this political cartoon? 2. According to our definition of revolution, which of the following conflicts would be considered revolutions?
Level III Low-Order Divergent	Questions requiring students to think critically about information	Students analyze information to discover reasons or causes, to draw conclusions or make generalizations, or to support opinions	Because higher-level productive thinking is involved, students' responses may not be anticipated	1. Why do you think the girl ran away from home? 2. Now that you have finished the experiment, what is your conclusion as to why the substance became denser?
Level IV High-Order Divergent	Questions requiring students to perform original and evaluative thinking	Students make predictions, solve problems, produce original communications, and judge ideas, information, actions, and aesthetic expressions based on internal and external criteria	Because this level represents the highest level of productive thinking, students' responses generally cannot be anticipated	1. Suppose that England had won the American War for Independence, how might pioneers' movement to the West have been affected? 2. How would you rate the effectiveness of the Environmental Protection Agency?

Adapted from *Questions, Questioning Techniques, and Effective Teaching* (p. 3–24) by W. W. Wilen (Ed.), 1987, Washington, D.C.: National Education Association.

another question (Wilen, 1991). Rowe (1986) found that when teachers increase "wait time 1" to three seconds or longer, both the quality and quantity of students' responses improve. "Wait time 2" occurs after a student responds. Again, Rowe found that when teachers increased "wait time 2" to three seconds or longer, students were more likely to elaborate and produce higher quality responses. Swift, Gooding & Swift (1988) have identified "wait time 3" as" . . . the pause that occurs between student-to-student dialogue" (p. 192). Teaching yourself and your students to wait just a few seconds before speaking can enhance the quality of talk in your classroom.

Responding to student responses   Costa (1990) has categorized types of teachers' responses to students during questioning and discussion into those that close down discussion and those that promote it. Teacher responses that close down discussion are criticism, put-downs, and praise. You may be surprised to learn that Costa and other researchers have found that indiscriminate and excessive use of praise encourages students to be dependent on others for their ideas; when praise is reduced, students tend to experiment and speculate more in their responses. In fact, Costa reports that "the one person in the classroom for whom praise has the most beneficial effect is the teacher" (Brophy, 1981 quoted in Costa, 1990. p. 60).

Costa recommends using wait time, and *accepting responses* to promote discussion. Accepting responses are those that acknowledge but do not place a value judgment on students' contributions. *Passive acceptance* includes nodding the head, recording the student's response on a chart, or uttering a neutral response such as "Um-hmm" or "That's one possibility." *Active acceptance* includes paraphrasing, summarizing, or building upon a student's response. *Empathic acceptance* accepts the feelings as well as the ideas behind a response. An example of an empathic response is, "I understand why you feel strongly about this, especially since you say your father served in Vietnam."

Often, *probing* or asking a *follow-up* question ("You said you thought the character's decision was stupid. Could you tell us a little bit more about why you think so?") can help clarify and extend a student's thinking. Sometimes, you may want to *redirect* a question that you have asked ("Mike has told us what he thinks of the character's decision. Claire, what do you think?"). If you ask a factual question that has a right or wrong answer and a student answers incorrectly, you will need to use your professional judgment about whether to help the student answer your question correctly or acknowledge the error and redirect the question.

Because students are different, it is not possible to offer a "sure-fire" set of strategies for questioning. Like so many aspects of teaching, questions about strategies must often be answered with "It depends." Your best option is to listen to your students.

Using questions to control student behavior   Conventional wisdom and quite a few education texts advocate using questions to reclaim the attention of students who appear to be off-task or daydreaming. Certainly, it is tempting to use this technique, which often appears to be successful. However, classroom management is one thing; learning is another. We send a faulty message to students if our purpose in asking questions is not to stimulate their thinking but to control their behavior.

Employing equitable patterns of questioning   As you observe and teach in classrooms, you will soon discover that frequently only a small number of students consistently volunteer to answer questions and tend to dominate discussion. Furthermore, teachers, albeit unconsciously, tend to call on some students consistently and to overlook others. In addition to becoming aware of your own questioning patterns and to getting feedback from an observer who is monitoring your questioning patterns, there are several strategies you can employ to distribute questions more equitably.

Freiberg & Driscoll (1996) describe the "Go-Around System," in which the teacher goes around the room, calling on each student in turn, and asking for one contribution, e.g., "Tell me one idea you learned from yesterday or from today's class without repeating another student's answer" (p. 207). Students who cannot respond when called upon may "Pass," but must give a response before the activity is over. Another strategy is to pose a question, have all students write down the answer, and then call for responses or have students share responses with a partner. Some teachers write students' names on index cards and pull randomly from the deck to call on students. Good teachers vary their questioning strategies systematically to ensure all students have the opportunity to participate.

Sociocultural Differences and Teacher Questioning

Although teacher/question—student/answer continues to be the dominant type of classroom interaction, it is by no means the only or the best way to organize classroom talk. In fact, it is a pattern rarely seen in other social settings or in the work place. We need to work at creating classroom environments that enable students to engage in more natural conversations and discussions.

Furthermore, as recent research has focused on the sociocultural features of classroom talk, more and more teachers are realizing that no model of questioning fits all contexts. Heath (1983) found, for example, that young black students in a southeastern town were reluctant to respond to "known answer" questions of the kind teachers often ask. When teachers formulated questions that were more like questions the children were normally asked in their home settings, the students responded avidly and thoughtfully. Styles of verbal and non-verbal communication are influenced and shaped by language, culture, ethnicity, gender, and social class. In order to ask good questions and understand students' responses, teachers need to take into account and build upon the patterns of verbal interaction found in students' home communities (White, 1990).

Encouraging Students to Generate Questions

How would you characterize a "good learner"? With words like "curious" and "inquisitive"? Most people would probably agree that good learners, regardless of their age, wonder and ask "Why?" Thus, while it is important that you, as a teacher, possess good questioning skills, it is even more important that you create a classroom environment in which students can pose their own questions and seek answers to them.

Students have much more experience at answering questions than asking them, so it is not surprising that they are often reluctant to ask substantive, thought-provoking questions. Think about the last time you heard a classroom teacher ask, "Are there any questions?" This inquiry is usually met either with utter silence or a barrage of procedural questions ("Will this be on the test/quiz?" "Do we have to write it in ink?"). One major focus of current efforts to improve teaching and learning is on helping students ask the questions that will lead them to deeper understandings of concepts and issues (e.g., Cohen, McLaughlin & Talbert, 1993; Sizer, 1994; Sizer, 1996).

At Central Park East Secondary School (CPESS) in New York City, teachers are committed to helping students develop the intellectual habit of inquiry. To that end, teachers developed a set of essential questions that guide their work and that of their students:

(1) How do you know that? (2) Who said it and why? (3) What led to it? What else happened? (4) What if . . .? Supposing that . . .? (5) Who cares? (Meier, 1995; Darling-Hammond & Ancess, 1994). CPESS is only one example of how students and teachers can learn from one another's questions. If you want your students to be curious, then you need to model this quality yourself in the questions you ask of them and of the subject under study. And while it is often appropriate that you, as a teacher, pose questions, it is also essential that students have frequent opportunities to be inquirers themselves.

▌ Reader Activity 9.3

THEORY INTO PRACTICE
Planning for Questioning

For this activity, you may use the topic you selected for Reader Activity 9.2 or choose a different topic. Generate a set of questions for that topic using Wilen's taxonomy as a guide (Figure 9.6). Imagine asking these questions over some period of time—they need not be asked in rapid-fire succession. Envision an activity (e.g., looking at a reconstruction of the Globe Theater) that would accompany your questions. Identify each question by type (e.g., low-order divergent). Focus on writing questions at various levels—not on fine-tuning definitions of levels. Share your questions with others in your subject area to get feedback on your work. If time allows, share the questions in interdisciplinary groups to get the perspective of others unfamiliar with your subject area.

▪▪ STANDARD TWO: STRATEGIES FOR ENGAGING STUDENTS IN SUBSTANTIVE CONVERSATIONS

Students need many opportunities to engage in substantive conversations about subject matter both with you as the teacher and with their peers. Your job is to provide the opportunities and create the atmosphere in which such conversations can happen. Large-group discussion, when structured and facilitated effectively, can accomplish this goal. Small-group work offers students more opportunity to talk, interact, practice new skills, and test out ideas in a relatively risk-free setting. In small groups, students have greater access to help if they need it and more opportunities to enhance their understanding of material by teaching it to others.

Recommendations for middle- and high-school reform are united in their call for creating small, personalized communities for learning (e.g., Task Force on Education of Young Adolescents, 1989; National Association of Secondary School Principals, 1997). While you may not be able to influence the size of your school or even the size of your classes, you can create a sense of community within your classroom by encouraging substantive conversations among all its members.

Discussion

When I ask beginning English teachers to share with me their vision of an ideal classroom, they most often describe a room where students are sitting in a circle enthusiastically discussing a novel or poem while the teacher occasionally and sagely remarks upon their insightful comments. Many later become frustrated and even angry when they are unable to figure out how to make this vision a reality: some students are sleeping, some are chatting, some shouting out strong opinions, some shushing others, and the lone student who actually raises her hand before speaking wants to know when yearbook pictures are being taken. This scenario points to an important maxim: The keys to leading successful discussions are planning and practice.

Wilen (1990) defines *discussion* as "an educative, reflective, and structured group conversation with students" (p. 3). These qualities distinguish discussion from *recitation*, which is a style of questioning characterized by a pattern of teacher question-student response-teacher reaction (p. 9). Recitation is generally used to determine students' command of factual knowledge, a prerequisite for and often a prelude to discussion. The same qualities distinguish discussion from what Roby (1988) has called "bull sessions," in which students and teachers alike articulate unsupported opinions and every position is as valid as every other position.

Among the situations in which discussion is an appropriate instructional strategy, Hyman & Whitford (1990) have suggested the following:

- When students need to go beyond acquiring information.
- When students need to learn and practice interpersonal skills.
- When students need motivation to master problem-solving skills.
- When students need to apply knowledge, skills, and values associated with the subject field.

According to these authors, the teacher's role in discussion is "to lead, to enable, to orchestrate so that students can engage themselves with the content of their subject matter in a meaningful, deliberative matter" (p. 143). Thus, discussion can be an effective method of teaching and learning in any subject area.

Structuring Discussion

As noted above, good discussions are structured. They begin with what Wilen (1990) has called an "entry phase." The purpose of this phase is to focus students' attention on a topic. This phase might consist of a question that invites divergent responses and serves as a springboard into the topic. For example, an art teacher might show students a painting and pose the question, "Why do you think Monet painted this landscape as he did?" Hyman & Whitford (1990) call this phase of discussion "priming the pump" (p. 129). They describe a discussion in an English class in which the teacher asks the students to write down one idea about a poem they have just read and to share that idea with one or two peers. This technique gets ideas flowing, helps to create an atmosphere of acceptance for the ensuing discussion, and can be successfully implemented in any subject area. Wilen calls the next phase "clarification," which has two purposes: to clarify the roles and rules for the discussion and to clarify key terms, concepts, and ideas necessary to the discussion.

Leading the body of the discussion requires a teacher to keep one eye on the substance of the discussion and the other on the classroom interactions that are occurring. On the one hand, you as the teacher will have planned the questions that you hope will lead students to the desired outcomes. On the other hand, if you have created an atmosphere conducive to discussion, opinions and views for which you have not planned will most likely emerge in the course of the discussion. With practice and experience, you will learn to distinguish between "teachable moments" and students' attempts to turn a discussion about civil disobedience into a "bull session" about the fight at last night's football game. Hyman & Whitford (1990) describe a technique called "regrouping," which is useful when the discussion bogs down and seems to be headed off topic. "Regrouping" is actually a repetition of "priming the pump:" students return to their pairs or trios, discuss a specific question, record their ideas, and then return to the large group. Finally, you must plan for how you will bring closure to the discussion and help students pull it all together. One way to accomplish this is by asking students themselves to summarize and by suggesting how they will apply their learnings from the day's discussion to future learnings.

Types of Discussion

Five types of discussion are useful for teaching content in any subject area (Hyman & Whitford, 1990).

1. The *debriefing discussion* encourages students to reflect on the facts and meaning of a shared activity, such as a field trip, experiment, film, or poem.
2. The *problem-solving discussion* is especially suited for science, math, and social studies. Students identify a problem, generate alternative solutions, consider consequences for each solution, and discuss ways to implement the solution.
3. The *explanation discussion* helps students understand "why" a situation, phenomenon, rule, or policy exists. Students first recognize and describe the situation, analyze it, come to understand it, and consider the situation as it relates to their own lives.
4. The *predicting discussion* asks students to consider "What if . . .?"
5. The *policy discussion* asks students to answer the question "Should . . . ?" In an effective policy discussion, students consider the pros and cons of a situation, reflect on their values, and take a stand. The policy discussion requires students to apply knowledge and skills previously learned (pp. 138–142).

The questioning techniques described earlier—wait time, acknowledging, probing, redirecting—are all applicable to managing a discussion. In addition, Costa (1990) emphasizes the importance of teachers modeling behaviors that are consistent with the goals and values of the discussion technique: "The powerful teacher is constantly searching for ways to bring his/her own words and actions into harmony with the beliefs, values, and goals they [sic] hold for students" (p. 73). Among the behaviors teachers need to model are listening, problem-solving, acceptance of multiple perspectives, empathy, enthusiasm, and sharing their own metacognitive processes.

Metacognition and Discussion

Costa (1990) defines *metacognition* as:

> . . . the ability to know what we know and don't know . . . . to plan a strategy for producing what information is needed, to be conscious of our own steps and strategies during the act of problem-solving, and to reflect on and evaluate the productiveness of our own thinking (p. 66).

Costa describes a number of strategies for helping students use, monitor, reflect on, and improve their discussion skills. One technique he suggests is "strategy planning:" taking time before a discussion to establish with students criteria for effective participation and taking time afterward to debrief as a class on the discussion process. An observer can be appointed and can use a checklist, similar to the one depicted in Figure 9.7, to evaluate the performance of the class.

FIGURE 9.7   Group Process Observer Checklist

Criteria for Good Discussions	Often	Sometimes	Not Yet
1. We are critical of ideas, not people.			
2. Our purpose is making the best decision, not winning.			
3. Everyone involved participates.			
4. We ask questions to gather and try to understand as much relevant information as possible.			
5. We listen to everyone's ideas even if we do not agree with them.			
6. We restate (paraphrase) what someone has said to demonstrate we understand his or her idea.			
7. We clarify what someone has said if we do not understand his or her idea.			
8. We bring out all the ideas and information supporting both sides, then try to put them together in a way that makes sense to everyone involved.			
9. We try to understand all sides of the issue.			
10. We change our mind when the evidence indicates that we should do so.			
11. We explore the consequences of plans and actions before we adopt one.			
12. We are willing to give up an idea or hold it in abeyance in order to experiment with another's idea.			
13. We summarize what we have said and decided.			
14. We make sure that everyone understands the conclusions we've reached.			
15. We evaluate how well we used these discussion skills.			

From "Teacher Behaviors that Promote Discussion" by A. L. Costa, 1990, in *Teaching and Learning Through Discussion* (p. 68) by W. W. Wilen (Ed.), Springfield, IL: Charles C. Thomas.

Other techniques Costa suggests for helping students improve their metacognitive skills through discussion include (1) having students use journals to record their thoughts and questions during discussion and keep track of their changing ideas over time; (2) having students volunteer to map for the class on chart paper or overhead the concepts and sub-concepts that emerge during the discussion; and (3) having students use a set of predetermined questions to monitor their thinking during discussion (e.g., Does this discussion make sense? How does this relate to what I already know? What are this person's basic assumptions?) (pp. 66–72).

Rules and Roles in Discussion

When you're having a conversation with a small group of friends or family, it is not necessary to establish rules or assign roles. In the classroom, however, most teachers find discussion rules and roles indispensable. Figures 9.8 and 9.9 show samples of each.

FIGURE 9.8   Roles for Large- and Small-Group Discussions

1. RECORDER: to serve as group memory. The recorder is an influential person in every group. Emphasize the significance of this role.

2. TIMEKEEPER: to keep everyone on schedule.

3. PERIODIC SUMMARIZER: two or four times during a long discussion but at least one time during a brief discussion.

4. LOGICIAN: to help the discussion leader note flaws in reasoning.

5. RECAPITULATOR: to verbalize the essence or the highlights of the total discussion.

6. DESIGNATED FIRST SPEAKER: to break the ice when discussion is to begin (after seeing a film, for example).

7. LAUNCHER: to suggest to the discussion leader how to connect the discussion points with future activities.

8. CONTENT EXPERT/RESOURCE PERSON: to consult textbook, or other reference material as necessary.

From "Strategic Discussion for Content-Area Teaching" by R. T. Hyman and E. V. Whitford, 1990, in *Teaching and Learning Through Discussion* (p. 143) by W. W. Wilen (Ed.), Springfield, IL: Charles C. Thomas.

FIGURE 9.9   Rules for Large- or Small-Group Discussion

1. Each person is responsible for contributing to the task set for the group.

2. Be reasonable with other people; avoid arguing just to advance your own individual position.

3. As you listen to others, try to understand what they are saying; support points which you can agree with; accept differences among you as helpful to making a decision.

4. Stick to the topic as you comment on what others have said; be relevant.

5. Help in summarizing the main ideas discussed.

6. Be courteous and sensitive to your classmates.

From "Strategic Discussion for Content-Area Teaching" by R. T. Hyman and E. V. Whitford, 1990, in *Teaching and Learning Through Discussion* (p. 142) by W. W. Wilen (Ed.), Springfield, IL: Charles C. Thomas.

▌ Reader Activity 9.4A

WHAT WOULD YOU DO?
Role-Playing a Large-Group Discussion

The purpose of this activity adapted from Costa (1990) is to help you experience, in a risk-free environment, what a discussion in a middle- or high-school classroom might be like. Part of your class will be active participants; others will serve as observers. Depending on time available, your instructor may then ask you to switch roles for a second simulation.

1. Agree on a topic that your class can easily discuss within a designated time period (e.g., fifteen minutes). The topic might be a controversial educational issue or one selected from national, international, or local news.
2. The role of *discussion leader* may be assigned to a volunteer. The remaining roles should be assigned covertly. They are:
   - *devil's advocate* (espouses position in opposition to emerging group consensus)
   - *negative responder* (has a fixed opinion and does not listen to others; disagrees with any ideas not his or her own)
   - *non-responder* (does not participate or participates monosyllabically)
   - *distracter* (consistently attempts to pull the discussion off topic)
   - *supporter* (listens to everyone's ideas; encourages and invites participation by others; supports weaker members)
   - *clarifier* (seeks clarification of terms, examples, ideas; raises questions to reveal multiple perspectives on issues)
   - *positive responder* (supports discussion goals; listens to others and often agrees with them; sincerely seeks to learn from discussion)
3. Observers should watch the discussion interactions closely, making note of leader and participant behaviors that enhance and impede discussion.
4. In a whole-group debriefing, identify the roles played, describe the effects of each on the group's discussion, and the effects on individuals in the group. Participants and observers should also discuss how they would behave in a classroom situation if they encountered students who displayed these attributes.

▌ Reader Activity 9.4B

THEORY INTO PRACTICE
Planning a Strategic Discussion

The description in the preceding section of the various types of discussion is taken from Hyman & Whitford's (1990) chapter entitled "Strategic Discussion for Content Area Teaching." These authors emphasize the importance of planning and writing out questions and strategies for discussion. Choose a topic in your content area that lends itself to discussion and formulate a specific goal for the discussion. Plan a "strategic discussion," choosing one of the five types of discussion described earlier. Outline the phases of the discussion and list the specific questions you intend to pose. In a one-page introduction to the outline, explain what kinds of responses you hope to elicit with each question by making reference to Wilen's Levels of Questions (Figure 9.6).

Cooperative Learning Strategies

In cooperative learning approaches, students work in groups of four to six to complete a task such as solving algebraic equations, listing pros and cons of protecting endangered species, or constructing an interpretation of a poem. Some group tasks are competitive, such as contests or games that encourage groups to compete against one another. Other group tasks are cooperative, such as working together to apply a formula, prepare a report, or dramatize a scene from literature.

The benefits to students of cooperative learning approaches are numerous. First, studies have consistently documented the positive effects of cooperative learning approaches on achievement. These effects are positive for all types of students (e.g., Slavin 1990). Furthermore, cooperative learning arrangements can promote positive social interactions among students and enhance positive feelings about self, peers, and school (Good & Brophy, 1997). Business leaders would add that the problem-solving and social skills students learn and practice while working in groups are sorely needed in the workforce of today and tomorrow.

Cooperative learning, however, is not simply a matter of having students "count off by fours" and "get into groups." Blumenfield, Marx, Soloway, and Krajik (1996) have identified several factors that teachers must consider in order for group work to succeed. These include:

- *Attention to group norms.* Putting students into groups doesn't guarantee that they will actually cooperate. Some students may dominate, while others are excluded. Some students may not do their fair share of the work, while others feel unfairly burdened to accomplish the task. Some students may simply refuse to work with other students. You need to establish norms for positive interaction and to teach students the skills they need to function successfully as a group.
- *Attention to tasks.* Design tasks that lend themselves to group work. Completing a worksheet, for example, does not require cooperation so much as division of labor. ("You do the first three problems, I'll do the next three.") A well-designed group task should be complex enough that it cannot be completed satisfactorily by any single member. It challenges students' thinking and allows for a variety of solutions to a problem. The parameters of the task and the criteria for the group product must be clearly communicated to students.
- *Giving and seeking help.* One of the central purposes of using small groups for instruction is to encourage students to seek help from and give help to one another. Students may need instruction on how to give help effectively (e.g., helping someone arrive at a solution as opposed to giving someone a solution). In addition, students may not be aware of when they need help, what kind of help they need, or how to ask for help without "looking stupid."
- *Accountability.* Unless individual accountability is built in to group assignments, some students may be content to reap the rewards of others' work. One way some advocates of cooperative learning build in individual accountability is through assignment of specific roles and responsibilities to each group member, such as facilitator, time-keeper, recorder, and reporter. In addition, students can evaluate their own contributions to the group and the group's success as a whole. As you think through how you will evaluate the products of group work, you will need to decide how individual contributions and group processes will be assessed. (Strategies for assessing group processes and products are discussed in Chapter Ten, "Assessing Student Learning.")

- *Group composition.* Consider many factors when arranging students in small groups. Although you may sometimes decide to allow students to work in self-selected groups, you should be aware that students often choose to work with others most like themselves. In order to achieve the positive academic and social outcomes mentioned earlier, it makes sense to compose groups that are mixed in ability, ethnicity, and gender. However, this is more complicated than it sounds and some research suggests that status hierarchies within groups can be detrimental to the learning of individuals:

  > Those seen as "smart" are expected to be good at all school tasks. Those seen as "not smart" are expected to be incompetent at all school tasks. We are not just talking about expectations of teachers, but expectations for competence that students hold for each other and for themselves. . . . Once general expectations for competence and incompetence have been formed, the stage is set for self-fulfilling prophecies (Cohen, Kepner, & Swanson, 1995, p. 18).

As you get to know your students, you will develop a sense for how best to organize groups. You will gain a lot of information about how well groups are functioning simply by circulating around the classroom and observing students closely.

Managing small group work is a complex task (Cohen, 1994). To do it well, you must think through each of the factors mentioned earlier. In addition, you will need to attend to procedural issues, such as how students will physically move into groups, how the furniture in the classroom is arranged, how you will distribute and collect materials, and how and when you will give instructions to the groups. If you are thoughtful in your planning and reflective about your practice, you will become more comfortable with acting as a facilitator of learning rather than a fountainhead of knowledge.

▌ Reader Activity 9.5

CONSULTING OTHER SOURCES
Evaluating a Group Task in Your Subject Area

The purpose of this activity is to give you the opportunity to examine a cooperative learning lesson plan and apply what you have learned so far about this technique.

Use the Web, a teacher's annotated edition of a textbook, a subject-specific methods book, or any other appropriate source to locate a lesson plan that incorporates cooperative learning. Evaluate the task using the following questions:

1. Is this a well-designed task according to the criteria given in the preceding section?
2. Is individual accountability a component of this task?
3. What are some things students learned about subject matter and about group processes in this activity?
4. Does this task maximize opportunities for all students to experience success?

Share your plan and your evaluations in small, interdisciplinary groups.

Several specific approaches to cooperative learning have been developed. Because this chapter serves only as a general introduction to teaching strategies, five common approaches are summarized in Figure 9.10. We encourage you to explore these further.

| **FIGURE 9.10** | Five Main Cooperative Learning Strategies |

STAD	*Student Teams-Achievement Divisions* (Slavin, 1978, 1983, 1995): The teacher presents a lesson. Students meet in four- to five-member teams, helping one another to master a set of worksheets on the lesson. Each student takes a quiz on the material. The individual scores, based on the degree of individual improvement over previous scores, contribute to a team score. Teams with high scores are recognized in a weekly class newsletter.
TGT	*Teams-Games-Tournament* (DeVries and Slavin, 1978): Instruction is similar to STAD, with students trying to help one another learn the material. But instead of taking individual quizzes, students compete with classmates of similar achievement from other teams. Based on their relative success against competitors from other teams, students earn points for their own team and teams with high scores are publicly recognized.
JIG	*Jigsaw* (Aronson, Blaney, Stephan, Sikes, & Snapp, 1978): Each student in a five- to six-member group is given unique information on a topic that the whole group is studying. After reading their material, the students meet in "expert groups" with their counterparts from other teams to discuss and master information. Next they return to their teams to teach it to their teammates. In a variation called "Jigsaw II" (Slavin, 1986), all students are first given common information. Then the "experts" teach more specific topics to the group. Finally, students take tests individually, and team scores are publicized in a class newsletter.
LT	*Learning Together* (Johnson and Johnson, 1987): Students work in small groups on assignments to produce a single project. Teachers use various methods for nurturing a philosophy of cooperation based on five elements: positive interdependence, face-to-face interaction, individual accountability, social skills, and group processing. Students are instructed to seek help from one another before asking for teacher assistance. Students are usually rewarded based on a combination of individual performance and the overall performance of the group. Rewards include teacher praise, tokens, and privileges, but neither individuals nor groups compete against one another.
GI	*Group Investigation* (Sharan and Sharan, 1976): Students work in small groups, but each group takes on a different task or project, and within groups, students decide what information to gather, how to organize it, and how to present what they have learned as a group project to classmates. In evaluation, higher level learning is emphasized.

From Newman, F. & Thompson, J. A. (1987). Effects of Cooperative Learning on Achievement in Secondary Schools: A Summary of Research. Madison, WI: National Center on Effective Secondary Schools, Wisconsin Center for Education Research ED 288 853.

Peer-Tutoring Strategies

As you move into classroom teaching, you will find that, regardless of the grade level or subject you teach, some students need a lot more help than others in mastering the content or skills being taught. For example, students who do not speak or are not yet fluent in English will undoubtedly have difficulty following the rapid pace of talk in the classroom. Likewise, students with mental or physical disabilities may, for a variety of reasons, lack certain skills needed to succeed in your class. Peer tutoring can be effective in both homogeneous (tracked) and heterogeneous (untracked) classrooms.

With proper training, students can effectively learn from and teach one another. Within the classroom, you might set up peer study groups in which higher achieving students help lower achieving students apply skills or concepts you have introduced. For such an arrangement to be successful, however, you must be sensitive to the needs of both the tutors (who may feel they are being "used") and the tutees (who may feel stigmatized). For this reason, some peer-tutoring advocates propose randomly assigning pairs who must alternate roles of tutor and tutee. In this arrangement (classwide peer tutoring), everyone gets the chance to learn and to teach. King-Sears and Cummings (1996) point out that classwide peer tutoring is especially effective in inclusive classrooms, benefiting both general and special education students academically and socially.

Cross-age tutoring is more challenging to arrange but may be more beneficial to both tutors and tutees. For example, eighth-graders who are having difficulty with reading can be trained to help younger students (e.g., fourth- or sixth-graders) who are also having difficulty with reading. Studies have shown that, when properly implemented, cross-age tutoring has benefits for both parties: "If anything, the potential benefits of assuming the tutor role are greatest for low achievers, who rarely get the opportunity to act as the competent expert giving instruction rather than receiving it" (Good & Brophy, 1997, p. 296).

Reciprocal teaching is another form peer tutoring can take. Reciprocal teaching emphasizes reading comprehension, which is often the source of students' difficulties in their academic classes. In reciprocal teaching, students can be taught to help other students use the strategies of effective readers and to monitor their own reading processes (Carter, 1997).

▌Reader Activity 9.6

In the Field
Observing Small-Group Learning

Visit a middle- or high-school classroom in which small-group work is being done. If possible, arrange to sit in with and observe the interactions of a group at work. Take notes and write a report that addresses the following concerns.

- physical arrangement of the classroom
- how procedural issues are handled
- how a group interacts
- how the group task is structured
- whether and how students give and seek help from one another
- how individual and group accountability are built into the task
- how the groups are composed

If time allows, arrange to interview the teacher about his/her philosophy of small-group work and/or interview a student about his/her attitude toward small-group work. Report your findings to your class.

▮▮ STANDARD THREE: STRATEGIES FOR HELPING STUDENTS DEVELOP DEPTH OF KNOWLEDGE

Historically, teachers have felt compelled—perhaps by district or departmental guidelines—to sacrifice depth of understanding for breadth of coverage of content. In our haste to cover content, not only are students who learn at different paces and in different styles often left behind, but those who do keep up may lack true understanding. Howard Gardner, researcher of multiple intelligences and author of *The Unschooled Mind* (1991), summed up the problem this way:

> Most schools have fallen into a pattern of giving kids exercises and drills that result in their getting answers on tests that look like understanding. It's what I call the'correct answer compromise'. . . . But the findings of cognitive research over the past 20-30 years are really quite compelling: students do not *understand*, in the most basic sense of that term. That is, they lack the capacity to take knowledge learned in one setting and apply it appropriately in a different setting (Brandt, 1993, p. 4).

Many teachers are now asking themselves, "What are the essential learnings I want students to take away from this class and retain long after they have forgotten the details?" The strategies presented in this section will give more students the opportunity to develop depth of knowledge by giving them some control over the pace, content, mode, and processes of learning.

Mastery Learning

First proposed by Benjamin Bloom and later adapted by others, mastery learning assumes that "the major difference between learners is the time it takes them to learn" (Good & Brophy, 1997, p. 312–313). This is a powerful idea because it proposes that all students can learn, given time and resources. Generally, a teacher who uses mastery learning specifies student objectives, teaches the concepts or skills, and assesses student attainment of the objectives. At this point in most classrooms, students receive their scores on the test or assessment and the class moves on to the next concept or skill, regardless of whether the concept or skill was mastered by all or most of the students.

Mastery learning interrupts this traditional progression. After students receive feedback on their performance, the teacher provides additional time or resources for the students who have not yet demonstrated mastery, often stated as a particular level of mastery (e.g., eighty percent). Students who have attained this level move on to the next unit or complete enrichment activities, while the students who need more time get it. After reteaching, the teacher retests. Theoretically, this cycle goes on until all students have achieved mastery. In practice, the cycle usually stops after the second test. While this may not match Bloom's original vision of mastery learning, it still offers more opportunity for students to succeed than the traditional sequence described earlier.

Implementing mastery learning requires in-depth knowledge of content, students, and resources, as well as excellent classroom management skills. As a beginning teacher, you might find it impossible to implement a complete mastery learning program. You can, however, be guided in your practice by the premise of mastery learning: that given time and resources, all students can learn.

Learning Centers and Learning Activity Packets

Learning centers offer a way to tailor instruction to student needs and interests, to give students choice and responsibility for their own learning, and to offer meaningful learning experiences to students who are working at different paces. A learning center is usually a physical space in the classroom where individual or small groups of students can work independently on an activity or series of activities. Learning centers can be set up to provide for varying learning styles or multiple intelligences. A foreign language teacher, for example, might maintain learning centers at which students can study and acquire vocabulary through their preferred learning style (e.g., by listening to tapes, writing the words, matching words to images, playing word games). A middle-school science teacher might teach photosynthesis by having students read about the concept (linguistic), use diagrams or pictures (spatial), analyze the sequence of the process (logical-mathematical), dramatize the process (bodily-kinesthetic), create a song about it (musical), work in groups (interpersonal), and do a reflective activity, such as comparing photosynthesis to a change in their own lives (intrapersonal) (Willis, 1994, p. 5). Learning centers can also be organized thematically. For example, if a social studies class is studying a unit on Africa, learning centers might offer students the chance to explore areas of interest such as music, art, literature, food, youth culture, or entertainment (Tiedt & Tiedt, 1998).

Learning centers need not be elaborate or permanent installations. They can be set up simply by rearranging furniture and labeling areas with signs or posters. For example, Sarah, a student teacher in English, wanted to give students a variety of points of entry into a unit on the Holocaust. She devised five different stations at which students might look at and react to photographs, read and respond to poetry, listen to an interview with a Holocaust survivor, read and react to first-hand accounts, and construct a contribution to a class collage. Sarah had thought through how the students would move through the centers, how many students could experience a center at one time, and how long students could spend at each center; nevertheless, she was very apprehensive about losing control of the class once they were out of their seats and moving around the room. To her relief, the experience went smoothly and afterwards students thanked her for the active involvement and choice the centers offered.

Learning activity packets can be likened to learning centers in envelopes. Learning activity packets are self-guided units of instruction or activities that students can work through with minimal, if any, teacher guidance. Learning activity packets can be used as enrichment for students who complete required assignments early or as review and reinforcement for students who need extra practice. They can even be used as the foundation for entire self-directed units of study (Tiedt & Tiedt, 1998).

Jan Collins, an English teacher, and Barbara Swenson, a special education teacher, collaboratively made learning activity packets the centerpiece of the ninth-grade English curriculum as Westerly High School in Westerly, Rhode Island moved toward inclusive classrooms. They developed packets for *Romeo and Juliet, The Odyssey,* and themes, such as "Who Am I?" and "Mysteries." Usually, Jan created reading and writing activities, while Barbara created graphic organizers and other learning aids for the packets. All units included whole class activities, but students had much time to work individually on vocabulary, reading comprehension, and writing skills. With the packets, students progressed at their own pace and could easily catch up following absences (Logan & Hawk, 1994).

In addition to the benefits described above, learning centers and learning activity packets allow teachers to include content that might not be covered in the classroom curriculum or traditional textbook (e.g., arts and literature related to a particular period of U.S. history; biographies of female mathematicians; career explorations in physical science). Although learning centers and activity packets require a large investment of out-of-class time in planning and constructing them, the investment pays off in the extra time a teacher gains in the classroom. When students are working independently, you will have more opportunity to observe their learning and to help those students who most need help.

Learning Contracts and Independent Study

Some teachers have found learning contracts effective for giving students both freedom and responsibility. Learning contracts allow students to make choices about the content, pace, and structure of their learning. Some learning contracts allow students to select the grade they wish to receive (usually "A" or "B") and clearly state the criteria students must meet to receive that grade. Most often, learning contracts are drawn up for independent study that enriches the classroom curriculum. For example, if students are studying a thematic unit on "Rites of Passage" in an English class, individuals or small groups of students might sign contracts to research rites of passage as depicted in the arts, in other cultures, in the natural world, or in history. Contracts are signed by both the student and the teacher as a gesture of mutual respect and a formal agreement to fulfill the terms of the contract. When the parameters of the project and performance criteria are clearly stated, learning contracts can be quite effective in individualizing instruction (see Figure 9.11).

Writing to Learn

For many years, we thought of school as a place where students learn to write. We now know that school is also a place where students should write to learn. Writing is no longer thought of solely as a form of communication; it is an expression of thinking and a way of making thinking visible (National Council of Teachers of English, 1996). Through writing (and drawing or sketching) students can express their personal understandings of concepts, practice newly acquired skills, and make connections between the content and their own experience (Murray, 1990).

Brainstorming is a commonly used writing-to-learn technique. Its purpose is to generate as many ideas as possible in a short period of time. During brainstorming, there is no discussion or evaluation of ideas—all ideas are equally valid. Brainstorming can be used with large groups, small groups, or as an individual activity. It can be used to introduce a unit of study to find out what students already know, what they are interested in learning, and to generate possible topics for individual or small group study. In a brainstorming session, all ideas are recorded for future reference.

Sometimes, teachers follow brainstorming with *concept mapping, clustering,* or *webbing,* forms of graphic organizers discussed earlier. After as many ideas as possible on a topic are generated, students organize these ideas into conceptual categories. This activity allows students to explore relationships among ideas. In the course of the unit of study, students might periodically revisit and revise their maps or webs based on new understandings.

FIGURE 9.11   A Sample Learning Contract

CONTRACT

John Jones   To be completed by May 1.
During the period of April 10 to May 1, I will

1. Read Chapters X–XII of book A.
2. Do problems and exercises # 1, 2, 4, 7, 8, 9, 11 of the study guide.
3. Participate on the map committee with Mike Smith, John Walsh, and Ted Burke.
4. Prepare a report on the topography of the area.
5. XXXX
   (Remaining activities omitted to save space)

Signed _____
                                          Student
Approved _____
                                          Teacher

To pass with a D you must complete activities 1–12 and pass the posttest.

To receive a C you must complete activities 1–12, receive at least a C on the posttest, and do two (2) of the optional activities satisfactorily.

To receive a grade of B, you must complete activities 1–12, receive at least a grade of B on the posttest, and satisfactorily complete at least four of the optional activities very well.

To receive a grade of A you must complete activities 1–12, do four of the optional activities excellently, complete at least one major optional activity very well, and receive at least a B+ on the posttest.

From *Secondary and Middle School Teaching Methods* (7th ed.) (p. 143–144) by L. H. Clark and I. S. Starr, 1996, Upper Saddle River, N.J.: Merrill/Prentice Hall.

Many teachers use learning logs, journals, or diaries to encourage students to record their understandings of the content. For example, Tishman, Perkins and Jay (1994) describe a physics teacher who has his students keep "inquiry diaries" in which they connect physics concepts to personal experience. A sample entry appears below:

> "I noticed how hard it is to open the post office doors. . . . You really have to lean into them to push them open. This is because of inertia. The doors have a high mass, so it is hard to accelerate them. When I push on them, this tries to accelerate them" (p. 171).

Admit slips are brief written responses that are turned in to the teacher at the beginning of class. An admit slip might request a personal response to a reading assignment, a homework problem, or a question for discussion. The teacher may simply collect the slips and read them aloud anonymously to generate discussion.

Similarly, *exit slips* are completed and turned in to the teacher at the end of class. An exit slip might require students to summarize what they have learned that day, write down questions they still have, or evaluate the day's activities. Both admit and exit slips help students learn in greater depth while giving the teacher important information about their on-going progress (Gere, 1985).

Writing to learn can take many other forms. For example, math students can write their own problems or write explanations of problem-solving strategies for an audience of younger students. Science students can sketch the night sky and record their reactions to its beauty in poetry or prose. Steven, the aspiring U.S. history teacher described earlier in this chapter, was using a writing-to-learn strategy when he asked students to adopt the persona of a World War I soldier and write a letter home.

You don't have to be an English teacher to use writing-to-learn strategies. When students write to learn, neither you nor they should worry about their grammar, style, or usage. Writing to learn is exploration: "The more you write, the more you discover about your subject, your world, yourself" (Murray, 1990, p. 264).

▌▌STANDARD FOUR: STRATEGIES FOR HELPING STUDENTS MAKE CONNECTIONS BEYOND THE CLASSROOM

Each May, students in the secondary teacher-education program at the University of Kentucky where I teach demonstrate their ability to meet Kentucky's New Teacher Standards. All soon-to-be teachers select one standard and choose evidence from their portfolios that they present to a group of peers, faculty, and public school teachers involved with the program. Here are some of the projects students presented recently to demonstrate their ability to plan and implement instruction.

- Leah, a prospective math teacher, shared parts of a graphing unit she had developed for ninth-graders. After students were introduced to various types of graphs, Leah distributed graphs that had no labels or identifying information. Students worked in teams to determine what the graphs represented and then defended their decisions.
- Joe, a prospective science teacher, passed out yardsticks, strings, and balloons. He then posed the question, "What do you think we could learn about the respiratory system by using these objects?"
- Doug, a future business teacher, distributed laminated game boards, paper money, and tokens for a Monopoly game designed to teach budgeting. Each square on the boards named a well-known business or location in or near Lexington, Kentucky, where the university is located.
- Sarah, a future German teacher, used maps and information gleaned from the World Wide Web to introduce a unit on the impact of Turks, an ethnic minority, on German culture.

What impressed me most about these presentations was how Leah, Joe, Doug, and Sarah—all in different ways—were able to connect important subject matter to students' lives beyond the classroom. For many years, teachers did not see a need to help students make connections between school learning and their own lives. Either teachers assumed students were making such connections on their own, or they responded to the perennial question "Why do we have to do this stuff?" with "Because you'll need it in high school . . . college . . . later on." As one high-school science teacher put it after abandoning her tried-and-true lecture approach to teaching about DNA in favor of presenting students with a DNA "mystery" to solve:

> "Students need to see the links between the material they're studying and the real world, and to make connections to their own experiences. Therefore, the tasks we ask students to carry out should, to the extent possible, be connected to the world of work, academe, the arts, and the local community" (Geocaris, 1996/1997).

In this section, you will be introduced to strategies such as role-playing, simulations, and drama that help students make connections between content and their own lives. You will also learn about problem-based learning approaches that can extend beyond classroom walls and into the community.

Role-Playing, Simulations, and Drama in the Classroom

Role-playing, simulation, and the use of drama in the classroom are strategies that offer students the opportunity not only to personally connect with content but to improve their interpersonal, presentational, and reflective skills, and to develop a better understanding of multiple perspectives on issues. Furthermore, students gain experience in problem-solving and decision-making (Freiberg & Driscoll, 1996; Joyce & Calhoun, 1996). Implementing these techniques effectively in your classroom will undoubtedly require extra preparation time. In addition, because outcomes are not always predictable or controllable, you will need to be willing to take risks, act as a facilitator, learn from your mistakes, and be flexible. Not every teacher—nor every student—is comfortable with such open-ended learning experiences. It is important to establish a classroom climate of trust and respect if students are to benefit from participating in dramatizations.

Role-play "enables participants to think, feel and act as another person . . . [It is] an enactment or rehearsal of behavior with some reality and a safe environment for trying out new ideas and making mistakes" (Freiberg & Driscoll, 1996, p. 324). For role-plays to be successful, students must act out their roles with believability and the roles or situation must have a real-life quality. Role-plays may be used to address actual social issues in the classroom or school. For example, Joyce & Calhoun (1996) describe how a seventh-grade teacher used role-play to resolve conflicts over the use of sports equipment. Role-play is an effective strategy for addressing interpersonal conflicts, intergroup relations, individual dilemmas, and historical or contemporary problems.

Joyce and Weil (1980) have identified nine phases of role-playing.

1. *Warm up.* The teacher first introduces students to a problem and creates a climate of acceptance in which students are assured that their views, feelings, and behaviors can be safely explored. Secondly, the teacher presents a problem vividly through story, film, or other medium. In the third part of the warm up, the teacher poses questions that help students explore the relevant issues.
2. *Selecting participants.* After describing and analyzing the roles with the class, the teacher asks for volunteers to play those roles. Students must want to play a particular role.
3. *Setting the stage.* The teacher has the players outline the scene or ask questions about the general setting so that participants have enough direction to begin to act.
4. *Preparing the observers.* The teacher helps observers determine what to look for and assigns observational tasks, such as watching one particular character.

5. *Enacting.* The teacher directs players to begin, maintain, and break off dramatization. The enactment should be only long enough to highlight the main ideas.
6. *Discussing and evaluating the role-play.* The teacher focuses discussion on the motivations of the actors and the consequences of their actions. Alternative interpretations will probably arise in the course of the discussion, which can then be explored in the next phase.
7. *Reenacting.* The teacher determines if the role-play should be re-enacted to explore alternative interpretations, other possibilities for cause and effect, and the effects of change on the outcome. Reenactment can be repeated as often as it is fruitful.
8. *Discussing and evaluating.* The teacher repeats Step 6.
9. *Sharing experience and generalizing.* The teacher helps participants and observers relate the role-play to their experience and to the issues on which the activity focused.

Elaborate props are not necessary for role-playing, although many teachers haunt garage sales and flea markets collecting odds and ends that enhance classroom dramas. You may, however, want to create "briefing sheets" for characters and forms for observers to use.

Simulations are somewhat more extensive than role-plays in that they may require students to assume roles for extended periods of time or to do research in preparation for their task or role. Simulations are generally more structured than role-plays and the outcomes more predictable. For example, students might enact the roles of a space flight crew facing an emergency, act as advisors to the United States government, or learn the rules and assume the roles of a different culture. Simulations may be teacher-developed, but are also commercially available. *Bafa Bafa* (Shirts, 1977), for example, is a popular, commercially-developed, cross-cultural simulation that can be used in a number of subject areas to achieve a variety of educational goals. Technology, too, is helping to create ever more sophisticated simulations. *InvestSmart Market Simulation* (http://library.advanced.org/10326) helps students learn about investing by giving them 100,000 fantasy dollars to invest in stocks.

An effective simulation is structured with four essential components: (1) an *orientation,* giving an overview of goals, tasks, and roles as appropriate; (2) *participant training,* which includes a practice session; (3) *simulation operations,* including stopping periodically for feedback and clarification; and (4) *participant debriefing* during which both the content and process of the simulation are analyzed and connections to the real world made explicit (Joyce & Weil, 1980).

Drama in the classroom can be as elaborate or simple, as prepared or spontaneous as you prefer. Long-overlooked in secondary classes—except, of course, drama classes—dramatic techniques are especially appropriate for engaging students who learn best through movement and physical involvement. Students can dramatize texts in print or write and tell their own stories. Students can form tableaux, or still-lifes, of critical moments in a literary text, an historical event, or a chemical reaction. Pantomime can be used to show scientific, economic, legal, or interpersonal processes. Students can prepare and deliver monologues by literary, scientific, or historical characters, or even by entities that do not have the power of speech, such as objects, places, or animals. Students can write, rehearse, direct, and produce skits and plays in all subjects. It is not necessary to be a drama teacher in order to use dramatic techniques in your classroom, since the focus is on providing opportunities for students to make connections to the world beyond the classroom (Heathcote, 1992; Heathcote & Bolton, 1994).

Problem-Based Learning

Problem-based learning is founded upon the educational and social philosophy of John Dewey. Inquiry-based and issues-centered education share the same problem-solving, democratic orientation (Evans & Saxe, 1996; Joyce & Calhoun, 1996). In problem-based learning approaches, students are first presented with a genuine problem, a truly puzzling situation, a mystery, or a strange phenomenon. In problem-based learning, minimal time is spent on lecture. The teacher serves primarily as a resource and facilitator. Students serve as resources for one another and perform their work both independently and in small groups.

Savoie and Hughes (1994) generated the following guidelines while planning a problem-based learning experience for a ninth-grade global studies class.

1. Begin with a problem.
2. Ensure that the problem connects with the students' world.
3. Organize subject matter around the problem, not around the disciplines.
4. Give students the major responsibility for shaping and directing their own learning.
5. Use small teams as the context for most learning.
6. Require students to demonstrate what they have learned through a product or performance (p. 54).

These teachers used a case study of a two-career couple with a troubled marriage as the problem around which students focused their study of tradition and change as they affect families. They taught students a three-step problem-solving process to apply to the case: (1) What do we know? (2) What do we need to know? and (3) What are we going to do? Students studied such concepts as equity, sharing, and responsibility, and looked at statistics on dual-earner families in order to understand the couple's problems. Over the course of the unit, a psychologist and a counselor came to the classroom to discuss their jobs and to share their perspectives on the fictional couple's situation. Eventually students demonstrated their learning in the unit by either writing a letter to the couple or participating in a role-play of a counseling session.

Technology provides important tools for problem-based learning. Bolt, Beraneck, & Newman, Inc. (1993) have described the Cooperative Networked Educational Community of Tomorrow (Co-NECT). Schools design their own plans for participating in the network. One school divides the year into four nine-week cycles, each with a different global theme. Students and teachers collaboratively develop projects for each cycle. Other schools participate in EARTHWATCH'S Mystery of the Pipe Wreck Project in the Caribbean. Students can download and analyze data from project sites and communicate electronically with past and present project participants and staff.

Problem-based learning is democratic in its orientation because students work together toward a common goal. The solution of complex problems requires everyone, regardless of ability or disability, to contribute. Jones, Rasmussen, & Moffitt (1997) have summarized how problem-based learning aligns with constructivism, multiple intelligences, and brain-based research. Students are motivated to engage in it because it is authentic, contextualized, allows them to interact with a variety of individuals, and involves them in processes (problem formulation, self-assessment, decisions about representation of work) that give them ownership of the projects. In addition to being an effective strategy for teaching academic knowledge, problem-based learning also teaches social processes, respect for negotiated rules and policies, respect for the dignity of others, and independence in learning.

Wraga (1996) has suggested a number of issues that can be formulated as problems in the various subject areas:

English language arts	use and abuse of language by public officials
Fine and performing arts	arts funding and the First Amendment
Foreign languages	English First/English Only controversy
Health and physical education	racism and sexism in sports
Home economics	world hunger
Vocational education	consumer rights

Implementing problem-based learning in the classroom is not simple. For one thing, problem-based learning lends itself to an interdisciplinary curriculum, in which a complex problem, such as acid rain, is examined through the lenses of various subject areas. Secondly, it requires teachers to give up, to some degree, control of content and the processes students use to learn. Many teachers probably share this science teacher's reservations about embarking upon problem-based learning: "I wasn't at all certain that the students would be capable of grasping such complex material without direct instruction" (Geocaris, 1996/1997, p. 73). However, after comparing the results of her traditional approach to teaching DNA to a problem-based approach, the same teacher concluded: "I learned that carefully planned, inquiry-based teaching strategies that call upon students to make sense of concepts and data can be every bit as effective as more traditional approaches" (Geocaris, 1996/1997, p. 75).

Figure 9.12 gives an overview of the instructional strategies discussed in this chapter. Refer to it as you analyze one teacher's methodologies.

▌ Reader Activity 9.7

WHAT WOULD YOU DO?
The Case of Abby

In this chapter, you have been introduced to a variety of instructional strategies. However, you may still be wondering how a teacher puts all this together in the classroom. We will now look at how one teacher—Abby Bright, an English teacher in her fourth year of teaching—conducts a tenth-grade English lesson using a variety of instructional strategies (Spalding, 1997).

As you read this vignette, think about how Abby exhibits the qualities of an effective teacher and how she applies the various strategies presented in this and other chapters. Questions follow the case to help you focus your analysis.

Vignette of Abby's Classroom

Abby did not have her own classroom—she "traveled." This period she shared a classroom with a foreign language teacher, but had managed to secure the use of one bulletin board for English. On it was a neatly arranged display of landscape photographs and poems by Carl Sandburg. Abby's desk, in the back corner of the room, reflected her preference for order and logic. Reference books lined the front of her desk; student papers were stacked tidily by class. Behind her desk were large tote bags of books and other reading materials that she could easily access in case of sudden inspiration.

FIGURE 9.12 Summary of Instructional Strategies

Choose	When the goal is for students to	Potential strengths	Potential limitations	Learning style/Multiple intelligences connection	Enhance or adapt for individual differences	Technology connections
Lecture	• learn new information	• efficient • can be motivating • learn and practice listening skills	• can be boring • appeals to limited learning styles • teacher as "expert"	• effective for auditory learners, logical/ mathematical intelligence	• build in interaction • use audio and visual aids • be clear, succinct • use graphic organizers and teach note-taking skills • uerbal cues for note-taking	• multimedia presentations • video, TV, music clips • slides • Internet • overhead • chalkboard, whiteboard • distance learning
Questioning	• recall information • apply learning • think critically	• interactive • elicits multiple perspectives • learn and practice speaking, listening, and interpersonal skills	• can be intimidating • some students may dominate • may require only lower-level thinking • teacher as "quiz show host"	• effective for verbal learners, linguistic and interpersonal intelligences	• use wait time • use accepting responses • encourage student/student interaction • employ equitable patterns of questioning	• drill-and-practice software • instructional games software • interactive Web sites • on-line tutorials
Discussion	• apply learning • think critically • analyze, evaluate, synthesize information • practice interpersonal skills	• interactive • elicits multiple perspectives • improves speaking, and interpersonal skills • encourages reflection on learning	• can be intimidating • some students may dominate; others may "hide" • can get off-track • can be teacher-dominated	• effective for verbal learners, linguistic and interpersonal intelligences	• structure discussion • plan questions in advance • be open to "teachable moments" • teach discussion skills • assign roles and formulate rules • model and teach metacognitive skills	• e-mail • listservs • newsgroups • on-line conferencing • multimedia presentations • desktop publishing software • collaborative project software • WWW research • digital library research • Web page authoring

FIGURE 9.12   *Continued*

Choose	When the goal is for students to	Potential strengths	Potential limitations	Learning style/Multiple intelligences connection	Enhance or adapt for individual differences	Technology connections
Cooperative/ small-group learning	• learn new information • practice and apply skills • learn by teaching • assume social responsibility	• everyone contributes • students teach one another • enhances positive social interactions and self-esteem • student-directed	• may reinforce classroom status hierarchies • students may get "off task" • students may not participate fully • requires planning and presents logistical challenges	• depending on task, appeals to variety of learning styles and intelligences	• create complex, challenging tasks • teach group process skills • assign roles • build in positive inter-dependence • build in individual accountability • limit time	• multimedia presentations • desktop publishing software • collaborative project software • WWW research • digital library research • Web page authoring
Peer tutoring	• learn new information and skills • apply knowledge and skills	• students may learn better from peers • students-as-experts • one-on-one interaction • beneficial for both tutor and tutee	• tutees may feel stigmatized; tutors may feel used • students may lack tutoring skills • presents logistical challenges	• appeals to variety of learning styles and intelligences, especially interpersonal and intrapersonal	• ensure everyone plays roles of tutors and tutees • use cross-age tutoring • teach tutoring skills • set clear expectations for outcomes	• on-line tutorials • e-mail • listservs • Web sites for students • tutoring software
Mastery learning	• learn new information • apply knowledge and skills • think critically • experience multiple perspectives • choose own mode for learning	• individuals work at own pace • maximizes opportunities for success for all • students in control of own learning	• some students may grow discouraged before achieving mastery • teachers need to manage information, time, and routines well	• appeals to students who prefer structure; may not appeal to students who prefer freedom and choice	• reteach using a variety of strategies • provide enrichment activities • ensure opportunities for social interaction	• drill-and-practice software • integrated learning systems software

FIGURE 9.12 *Continued*

Choose	When the goal is for students to	Potential strengths	Potential limitations	Learning style/Multiple intelligences connection	Enhance or adapt for individual differences	Technology connections
Learning centers/ learning activity packets	• learn new information • apply knowledge and skills • think critically • experience multiple perspectives • choose own mode for learning	• students have choice • usually high-interest • packets allow students to work at own pace • frees teacher to observe and help individuals	• time-consuming to prepare and implement • may be seen as "teacher-owned" • time and space constraints	• appeal to variety of learning styles and intelligences	• engage students in center and packet design • provide choices within structure • organize centers by intelligences	• include at least one computer learning station • integrate Internet activities in learning packets
Learning contracts/ independent study	• learn new information • apply knowledge and skills • analyze, evaluate, and synthesize information • take ownership for learning	• students have choice about learning • students accept responsibility for learning • encourages self-assessment • many opportunities for "real world" connections	• students may not fulfill contracts • students my lack skills to persist in independent study • constraints of school structure	• appeal to variety of learning styles and intelligences	• state clear expectations for performance in contract • teach research skills • have students document process • build in checkpoints	• numerous connections depending on topic, including programming, authoring, software design
Writing to learn	• interpret and apply knowledge and skills • make personal connections	• students construct understanding • connects to "real world" • provides information for formative assessment • encourages reflection on learning	• teachers may feel uncomfortable incorporating writing • teachers may worry about "grading" writing • increased paper load	• appeals to linguistic, visual, intrapersonal intelligences	• teacher writes with students • assess for content, not "correctness" • provide prompts for journals	• e-mail • listservs • word processing software

FIGURE 9.12 *Continued*

Choose	When the goal is for students to	Potential strengths	Potential limitations	Learning style/Multiple intelligences connection	Enhance or adapt for individual differences	Technology connections
Role-play/ simulation/ drama	• experience and value multiple perspectives • synthesize knowledge • make personal connections • experience a process • personalize learning	• usually high-interest, highly motivating • encourages self-expression • learn and practice speaking, listening, and interpersonal skills	• outcomes may be unpredictable • open-ended • some teachers and students may be uncomfortable • may involve controversial issues	• appeals to kinesthetic, intrapersonal, interpersonal intelligences	• provide clear ground rules and expectations • create climate of acceptance and trust in classroom • debrief	• simulation software • virtual experiences • WWW research • Multi-User Dimensions (MUDs)
Problem-based learning	• analyze, synthesize, and evaluate information • practice problem-solving • experience multiple perspectives • practice social and interpersonal skills • practice social action skills	• interdisciplinary • complex tasks • students take ownership of learning • teaches democratic processes • students realize they can make a difference in "real" world	• may not be well-suited to schools as currently structured • present logistical challenges • outcomes may be unpredictable • may involve controversial issues	• appeals to variety of learning styles and intelligences	• collaborate with colleagues • accept uncertainty • provide students with resources • help students find real audiences for their work • involve community	• spreadsheet software • database software • multimedia presentations • Web page authoring

Seated in rows, twenty-two tenth-grade English students awaited Abby's arrival. As the bell sounded, Abby, wheeling an overhead projector, propped open the door and entered. Stationing the projector at the front of the room, she strode to the back and deposited a stack of materials on her desk. She briskly took roll and donned a lavaliere microphone, which allowed a hearing-impaired student in the class to participate.

"All right, everybody! Just please stand and concentrate. Can you concentrate? Chris, Chris, focus! You know how it's played—it's Simon Says. Simon says, 'Raise your right hand'. . ."

The astonished students stood up and raised their right hands. Abby quickly called out commands, "Simon says, 'Touch your left hand to your head.' Simon says, 'Hop up and down.'"

"Stop."

Students who "stopped" looked around at their classmates still hopping, giggled in embarrassment at their error, and sat down. At the end of three minutes, only a few students were still standing.

"Why is it you have to sit down in Simon Says?" Abby asked.

"If you didn't say 'Simon says'," several students responded.

"That's right," said Abby. "If you messed up, you're out. And this is the same concept as quoting in your papers. Now we're going to practice with another game. It's called The Article Says. I need three volunteers."

Two males and a female came forward. On the chalkboard, Abby drew two large squares. In one, she wrote "Direct Quote"; in the other she wrote "Paraphrase." She positioned Chrissy under the "Direct Quote" heading and Mark under the "Paraphrase" heading. Bill stood to one side. His job was to read aloud the highlighted sentences of the xeroxed articles Abby handed him. Chrissy received two cards, each containing a set of quotation marks. Her job was to repeat what Bill read: "The article says (she held up one set of quotation marks), 'School uniforms are good (she held up the other set of quotation marks).'" Mark's job was to paraphrase: "The article says that school uniforms are . . . (long pause) . . . nice."

Abby instructed the rest of the class, "Please concentrate and follow along. The quizzes were pretty dismal and I don't want this to happen in your research papers."

As the game progressed, the sentences became more complex and difficult to restate. "To show solidarity with the students, the teachers will wear similar clothes twice a month," read Bill.

"To show solidarity with the students, the teachers will wear clothes twice a month," quoted Chrissy to the amusement of the other students. Mark was having trouble rewording the statements, but ended on a triumphant paraphrase of the sentence, "A slob is still a slob in a uniform." "The article says . . . (long pause) . . . . that a messy person is still a messy person in a uniform," Mark blurted out with relief.

"Good paraphrase! Let's all clap for Mark! Thank you all very much. You can sit down now," Abby said and began handing back the "dismal" quizzes.

The students were midway through a unit on writing research papers. Abby had spent several days teaching a method of making note cards. On the previous day's quiz, students had created mock note cards for an article Abby had distributed. But the students had not performed well and clearly did not understand the difference between direct quotes and paraphrases. During the next five minutes, Abby briefly discussed each quiz item, asked volunteers to share their correct responses, and answered questions. Satisfied that most students appeared to have "gotten it," she moved on to the main activity of the day.

"What are we supposed to be doing today?"

Students began leafing through their notebooks.

"What are we doing? Does anyone know?"

"Outline," someone suggested.

"Right," responded Abby, handing out worksheets. The worksheet was a duplicate of a visual designed to help students remember the structure of a five (or more) paragraph theme. Abby flicked off the lights and flicked on the overhead, revealing a drawing of a saw-toothed dinosaur with a segmented body, a tapering tail, and a large horn on its head.

"If you remember this monster guy, you'll know where everything goes. It works this way for this paper and it'll work this way for other papers during the year. This is less an exercise in creativity than it is an exercise in logic and thinking," Abby explained.

As Abby labeled each part of the monster, the students filled in the information on their own sheets: the teeth represented grabbing the reader in the first sentence; the horn represented hooking the reader with the thesis statement; the body was filled out with facts and information; the tail represented the conclusion because "it comes to a point at the end and drags over the same ground." On the bottom half of the visual was a block for each paragraph of the research paper, so that students could write in sample sentences. Abby announced that, as a class, they would practice outlining someone's paper.

"I think this would be good thing to write down in your notebooks," she hinted.

A young woman volunteered her topic: "Should we continue to tear down the rain forest?"

"Okay, Maria, you're the judge. You're the expert. You've done the research. You know both sides of the argument. What's it going to be—yes or no?"

"No," Maria said tentatively.

Over the next twenty minutes, Abby questioned and coached Maria through the outline. Other students joined in to suggest rewordings and reasons to support her position. Abby wrote each sentence on the overhead while the students copied them in their notes. She read aloud the completed outline, which now sounded authoritative and clear.

"Okay. Basically we have written Maria's paper for her. How do you feel, Maria?"

"Good," Maria answered softly.

Realizing how Maria had benefited from volunteering, other students began proposing their topics for outlining: Should minors be allowed to have abortions without their parents' consent? Should female reporters be allowed in male locker rooms? Should rock music lyrics be censored?

Time was short, however, and Abby announced, "Tomorrow—outlining. I'll show you my outline for my research paper on school uniforms." Several students clustered around Abby with questions about their papers. She was still conferencing quietly with them as the bell signaled the end of class.

Questions for Analyzing the Case of Abby

1. What instructional strategies did Abby use in this lesson?
2. How did the instructional strategies Abby used accommodate the varying learning needs, interests, and characteristics of her tenth-grade students?
3. Does Abby know her students? Give evidence to support your answer.
4. Why did Abby teach this lesson in a large group? Would other configurations have been as appropriate? More appropriate?
5. Identify how, if at all, the strategies Abby used reflect the standards for authentic pedagogy presented in this chapter: (1) promoting higher order thinking; (2) encouraging substantive conversations; (3) developing depth of knowledge; (4) helping students make connections beyond the classroom.

6. Suppose you are Abby reflecting on the lesson you have just taught. What would you identify as the lesson's strengths? What didn't work so well? What might you do differently next time?

7. Imagine that, upon reflection, Abby has decided that next year she wants to use small-group instruction to teach some of the research skills addressed in this lesson. Which skills might be taught with small-group strategies? What kind of task(s) might Abby design?

▮▮ SUMMARY

I began this chapter by describing my learning-style odyssey, the long process by which I learned through experience and reflection that teachers need to use a variety of instructional strategies if they are to address the personal, social, and academic needs of students and engage them in learning. However, engagement alone does not constitute authentic intellectual achievement, which is characterized by construction of knowledge, disciplined inquiry, and value beyond school. This chapter presented a sampling of strategies that help to foster authentic intellectual achievement. These strategies were organized according to four standards for authentic pedagogy: (1) encouraging higher order thinking; (2) holding substantive conversations; (3) developing depth of knowledge; and (4) connecting to the world beyond the classroom. As a teacher, you should use these standards to monitor the quality of the instructional strategies you choose.

The strategies introduced here were clustered under particular standards, but this was primarily an organizational device: good strategies meet more than one standard, and no strategy meets any of the standards if it is poorly planned and implemented. For example, it would be wrong to infer that discussion only helps students and teachers hold substantive conversations; good discussions clearly meet all four standards. Likewise, a lecture that lacks clarity does not promote higher-order thinking. Among the key points to remember are:

- Planning lesson beginnings and endings is critical to implementing instruction successfully.
- Lecture can be an effective instructional strategy when used for appropriate purposes and planned with student learning needs and characteristics in mind.
- Preparing good questions and using good questioning techniques are skills that can be learned and refined. However, the success of any question or questioning technique depends on the context in which it is asked or used.
- Students need the opportunity to pose questions, not just answer them. By learning to pose significant questions, students acquire the habits of lifelong learners.
- Good discussions usually require planning and structure. The teacher's role in discussion is to lead, empower, and orchestrate so that students can engage themselves in substantive conversations about the subject matter.

- Cooperative learning approaches can promote academic achievement as well as positive social interactions among students and positive feelings about self, peers, and school.
- In schools, breadth of coverage has historically been emphasized at the expense of depth of knowledge. Using strategies that encourage students to develop depth of knowledge will probably require that less content be "covered."
- Dramatic experiences and problem-based learning approaches can help students connect content to their own experiences and to the world beyond the classroom.
- When selecting instructional strategies, you should consider your own teaching style, the characteristics of your students (e.g., learning styles, sociocultural characteristics, special needs), educational goals, and the appropriateness of the strategy for the content or processes you are teaching. No strategy is always effective for all students.

Ideally, you have now formulated tentative answers to such questions as: "How do teachers select content that students should learn?" "How do teachers plan for instruction?" "How do I select materials and strategies that will foster student learning?" A critical question remains, however: "How do I know what students are learning or have learned?" Assessment, the process of gathering information about student learning, is the subject of Chapter Ten, "Assessing Student Learning."

▌▌BUILDING YOUR BIOGRAPHY, YOUR PERSONAL PRACTICAL PHILOSOPHY, AND PORTFOLIO

Building Your Biography

What experiences in your life are relevant to becoming a teacher who uses a variety of instructional strategies to foster students' authentic intellectual achievement? Compose a chapter of your educational autobiography on this topic. The following questions are intended to help you generate ideas for writing. They are not intended to be answered sequentially or to limit your exploration of the topic.

- To what extent do you believe your K-12 and college experiences promoted authentic intellectual achievement?
- What opportunities did you have to construct knowledge, conduct disciplined inquiry, or see the value beyond school of academic activities?
- What teachers do you recall who were particularly effective lecturers? Ineffective lecturers?
- As a student, how did you respond to lecture, questioning, discussion, group learning, dramatic techniques, and problem-based learning?
- To what extent did your educational experiences emphasize breadth of knowledge? Depth of knowledge?
- What opportunities did you have, in or out of school, for substantive conversations about subject matter with your peers? With other adults?
- Have you ever taught someone something? If so, what strategies did you use? Were they effective?

Developing Your Personal Practical Philosophy

Draft a section of your personal educational philosophy that addresses authentic pedagogy. You might respond to questions such as the following.

- What is your evaluation of the standards for authentic pedagogy presented in this chapter?
- Of what value are these standards to you as a prospective teacher in your subject area?
- What institutional barriers could you foresee to using any or all of the strategies described in this chapter? How, if at all, can these barriers be overcome?
- Where do you stand on the issue of "breadth vs. depth" in the curriculum?
- What role, if any, should students play in selecting instructional strategies?
- What are your personal characteristics that might predispose you to implement some strategies described in this chapter and not others?

▪▪ COLLECTING ARTIFACTS FOR YOUR PORTFOLIO

Review the Reader Activities you have completed in this chapter. Identify any that you might eventually select for your portfolio. For each, jot down notes that will help you recall later what you were thinking at the time you completed the activity, what challenges you encountered while completing it, what you learned from doing it, and how this activity reveals something about who you will be as a teacher. Don't worry about style or correctness at this point. The purpose is to document your thinking as you move through this book and this class.

References

Ausubel, D. (1963). *The psychology of meaningful verbal learning: An introduction to school learning.* New York: Grune & Stratton.

Bloom, B. S. (Ed.). (1956) *Taxonomy of educational objectives: The classification of education goals. Handbook I: Cognitive domain.* New York: Longmans, Green & Co.

Blumenfield, P. C., Marx, R. W., Soloway, E., Krajik, J. (1996). Learning with peers: From small group cooperation to collaborative communities. *Educational Researcher, 25* (8), 37–40.

Braddock II, J. H. & McPartland, J. M. (1993). Education of early adolescents. In L. Darling-Hammond (ed.), *Review of Research in Education 19,* pp. 135–170. Washington, DC: American Educational Research Association.

Brandt, R. S. (1993). On teaching for understanding: A conversation with Howard Gardner. *Educational Leadership, 50* (7), 4–7.

Brophy, J. E. (1981). *Teacher praise: A functional analysis.* (Occasional Paper No. 28.). East Lansing, MI: Michigan State University for Research on Teaching.

Carter, C. J. (1997). Why reciprocal teaching? *Educational Leadership, 54* (6), 64–68.

Christenbury, L. and Kelly, P. (1983). *Questioning: A path to critical thinking.* Urbana, IL: National Council of Teachers of English.

Clark, L. H. & Starr, I. S. (1996). *Secondary and middle-school teaching methods.* Seventh edition. Upper Saddle River, NJ: Merrill/Prentice-Hall.

Cohen, D. K., McLaughlin, M. W., & Talbert, J. E. (Eds.). (1993). *Teaching for understanding: Challenges for policy and practice.* San Francisco, CA: Jossey-Bass.

Cohen, E. G., Kepner, D. & Swanson, P. (1995). Dismantling status hierarchies in heterogeneous classrooms. In J. Oakes & K. H. Quartz (Eds.), *Creating New Educational Communities, Ninety-fourth Yearbook of the National Society for the Study of Education, Part I* (pp. 16–31). Chicago, IL: National Society for the Study of Education.

Cohen, E. G. (1994). *Designing groupwork: Strategies for the heterogeneous classroom* (2nd. ed.). New York: Teacher College Press.

Costa, A. L. (1990). Teacher behaviors that promote discussion. In W. W. Wilen (Ed.), *Teaching and learning through discussion*, pp. 45–78. Springfield, IL: Charles C. Thomas.

Darling-Hammond, L. & Ancess, J. (1994). *Graduation by portfolio at Central Park East Secondary School.* New York, NY: National Center for Restructuring Education, Schools, and Teaching.

Delpit, L. (1995). *Other people's children: Cultural conflict in the classroom.* New York: New Press.

Ekhaml. L. (1998). Graphic organizers: Outlets for your thoughts. *School Library Media Activities Monthly*, 14(5), 29–33.

Evans, R. W. & Saxe, D. W. (Eds.). (1996). *Handbook on teaching social issues.* (NCSS Bulletin 93). Washington, DC: National Council for the Social Studies.

Freiberg, J. H. & Driscoll, A. (1996). *Universal teaching strategies* (2nd ed.). Needham Heights, MA: Allyn & Bacon.

Geocaris, C. (1996/1997). Increasing student engagement: A mystery solved. *Educational Leadership, 54* (4), 72–73.

Gere, A. R. (1985). *Roots in the sawdust: Writing to learn across the disciplines.* Urbana, IL: National Council of Teachers of English.

Good, T. L. & Brophy, J. E. (1997). *Looking in classrooms* (7th ed.). New York: Longman.

Hamburg, D. A. (1994). *Today's children: Creating a future for a generation in crisis.* New York: Times Books.

Harmin, M. (1994). *Inspiring active learning.* Alexandria, VA: Association for Supervision and Curriculum Development.

Heath, S. B. (1983). *Ways with words: Language, life and work in communities and classrooms.* New York: Cambridge University Press.

Heathcote, D. (1992). Excellence in teaching: What it takes to do it well. *Teaching Theatre, 4* (1), 3–6.

Heathcote, D. & Bolton, G. (1994).*Drama for learning: Dorothy Heathcote's mantle of the expert approach to education.* (Dimensions of Drama Series.) Portsmouth, NH: Heineman Publishers.

Hyerle, D. (1995/1996). Thinking maps: Seeing is understanding. *Educational Leadership, 53*(4), 85–89.

Hyman, R. T. & Whitford, E. V. (1990). Strategic discussion for content area teaching. In W. W. Wilen (Ed.), *Teaching and learning through discussion*, pp. 127–146. Springfield, IL: Charles C. Thomas.

Jones, B. F., Rasmussen, C. M., & Moffitt, M. C. (1997). *Real-life problem solving: A collaborative approach to interdisciplinary learning.* Washington, DC: American Psychological Association.

Joyce, B. R. & Calhoun, E. E. (1996). *The role of instructional theory and research.* Alexandria, VA: Association for Supervision and Curriculum Development.

Joyce, B. R. & Weil, M. (1978). *Models of teaching* (2nd ed.) Englewood Cliffs, NJ: Prentice-Hall.

King-Sears, M. E., & Cummings, C. S. (1996). Inclusive practices of classroom teachers. *Remedial and Special Education, 17*(4), 217–225.

Latham, A. (1997). Asking students the right questions. *Educational Leadership, 54* (6), 84–85.

Lee, V. E., Bryk, A. S. & Smith, J. B. (1993). The organization of effective secondary schools. In L. Darling-Hammond (Ed.), *Review of Research in Education 19*, pp. 171–268. Washington, DC: American Educational Research Association.

McCaleb, J., & White, J. (1980). Critical dimensions in evaluating teacher clarity. *Journal of Classroom Interaction, 15*, 27–30.

Meier, D. (1995). *The power of their ideas: Lessons for America from a small school in Harlem*. Boston, MA: Beacon Press.

Mercer, C. D., Lane, H. B., Jordan, L., Allsopp, D. H., & Eisele, M. R. (1996). Empowering teachers and students with instructional choices in inclusive settings. *Remedial and Special Education, 17*(4), 226–236.

Murray, D. M. (1990). *Writing to learn* (3rd ed.). Fort Worth, TX: Holt, Rinehart & Winston.

National Association of Secondary School Principals (1997). Breaking ranks: Changing the inservice institution. *NASSP-Bulletin, 82* (585), January, 9–12.

National Center on Education and the Economy (1995). *Performance Standards, Volume 3, High School*. Washington, DC: Author.

National Council of Teachers of English (1996). *Standards for English Language Arts*. Urbana, IL: National Council of Teachers of English.

Newmann, F. M., Marks, H. M., Gamoran, A. (1996). Authentic pedagogy and student performance. *American Journal of Education, 104* (4), 280–312.

Penick, J. F., L. W. Crow, and R. J. Bonnstetter (1996). Questions are the answers. *Science Teacher, 63* (1), 26–29.

Perkins, D. N. (1992). *Smart schools: From training memories to educating minds*. New York, NY: The Free Press.

Perrone, V. (1991). *A letter to teachers: Reflections on schooling and the art of teaching*. San Francisco: Jossey-Bass.

Robinson , D. H. (1998). Graphic organizers as aids to text learning. *Reading Research and Instruction, 37*(2), 85–105.

Roby, T. W. (1988). Models of discussion. In J. T. Dillon (Ed.), *Questioning and discussion: A multidisciplinary study*, pp. 163–191. Norwood, NJ: Ablex.

Rowe, M. B. (1986). Wait time: Slowing down may be a way of speeding up! *Journal of Teacher Education, 37* (1), 43–50.

Savoie, J. M. & Hughes, A. S. (1994). Problem-based learning as classroom solution. *Educational Leadership, 52*(3), 54–57.

Sizer, T. R. (1996). *Horace's hope: What works for the American high school*. Boston, MA: Houghton Mifflin.

Sizer, T. R. (1994). *Horace's school: Redesigning the American high school*. Boston, MA: Houghton Mifflin.

Slavin, R. E. (1990). *Cooperative learning: Theory, research and practice*. Englewood Cliffs, NJ: Prentice-Hall.

Spalding, E. (1997).'Swallowing an elephant': The subject perspectives of selected novice English teachers. In D. M. Byrd & D. J. McIntyre (Eds.), *Research on the education of our nation's teachers*, pp. 172–188. Thousand Oaks, CA: Corwin Press.

Summey, H. K. & Strahan, D. B. (1997). An exploratory study of mainstreamed seventh graders' perceptions of an inclusive approach to instruction. *Remedial and Special Education, 18*(1), 36–45.

Swift, J., Gooding, C., & Swift, P. (1988). Questions and wait time. In J. Dillon (Ed.), *Questioning and discussion: A multidisciplinary study* (pp. 192–212). Norwood, NJ: Ablex.

Task Force on Education of Young Adolescents (1989). *Turning points: Preparing American youth for the 21st century*. New York: Carnegie Council on Adolescent Development.

Tiedt, P. L. & Tiedt, I. M. (1998). *Multicultural teaching: A handbook of activities, information and resources* (5th ed.). Needham Heights, MA: Allyn & Bacon.

Tishman, S., Perkins, D. & Jay, E. (1994). *The thinking classroom: Learning and teaching in a culture of thinking*. Needham Heights, MA: Allyn & Bacon.

Vermette, P. J. (1998). *Making cooperative learning work: Student teams in K-12 classrooms*. Upper Saddle River, NJ: Merrill/Prentice-Hall.

White, J. J. (1990). Involving different social and cultural groups in discussion. In W. W. Wilen (Ed.), *Teaching and learning through discussion,* pp. 147–17. Springfield, IL: Charles C. Thomas.

Wilen, W. W. (1991). *Questioning skills for teachers.* (3rd ed.). Washington, DC: National Education Association.

Wilen, W. W. (1990). Forms and phases of discussion. In W. W. Wilen (Ed.), *Teaching and learning through discussion,* pp. 3–24. Springfield, IL: Charles C. Thomas.

Wilen, W. W. (Ed.) (1987). *Questions, questioning techniques, and effective teaching.* Washington, DC: National Education Association.

Willis, S. (1994). The well-rounded classroom: Applying the theory of multiple intelligences. *ASCD Update, 36* (8), 1, 5, 6–8.

▮▮▮▮▮ ▮▮ Websites

http://www.atozteacherstuff.com/
> An extensive site of resources for K-12 educators. Click on "Cooperative Learning" for tips and links to other sites.

http://snow.utoronto.ca/Learn2/introll.html
> Learning to Learn is for learners. teachers, and researchers. It teaches the value of self-awareness as a critical part of learning. Learning to Learn is a course, a resource, and a source of knowledge about learning, how it can be developed in children and adults, and how it differs among learners. Includes extensive resources on metacognition.

http://www.graphic.org/
> This site offers many examples of graphic organizers and how to use them in the classroom. Contains examples of student work.

http://metalab.unc.edu/cisco/schoolhouse/
> A comprehensive site for educators in all subject at all levels. Set up as a virtual schoolhouse, you can access many teaching ideas and resources.

http://www.accesseric.org/
> Home page of the Educational Resources Information Center. From here you can go to one of many specialized ERIC Clearinghouses and search for subject-area resources. Includes many other educational resources as well.

http://www.education-world.com/
> A comprehensive site with links to many educational resources in all subject areas at all grade levels.

Assessing Student Learning

BUILDING ON BIOGRAPHY: FROM POINT COLLECTOR TO THOUGHTFUL ASSESSOR

As a student, I (Liz) was generally a "good" test-taker. This meant that I had acquired the skill of figuring out what the teacher thought was important and remembering it long enough to fill in the blanks, choose the right answer, or list and define key terms. Essay tests, although not the norm, were not a problem for me, since I could write fairly fluently and express in paragraph form the content I had learned. I rarely experienced test anxiety: the agony of feeling my mind go blank even though I knew I knew the answer, of watching the minutes tick away as I struggled to recall a fact. My test-taking skills enabled me to earn high grades in most of my school subjects, since tests and quizzes like those I described earlier were the principal means by which grades were assigned. High grades affirmed that I was "good" at these subjects, and so I worked to ensure that I would continue to receive high grades. Math, however, was a different story.

I gave up on math in third grade when I first encountered word problems. Once simple computation was contextualized into a situation, I was lost: "How much change will Sally get back if she uses the five dollar bill she received for her birthday to buy three candy bars costing fifteen cents each and a magazine costing fifty cents?" My unspoken response was, "Who knows? Who cares?" As time went on, word problems became more frequent and more complicated features of tests in math. In high school, algebra was a complete mystery. I had no idea what "X" or "Y" stood for, why I would ever want to find the slope of a line or solve a quadratic equation. On tests, I could work problems that resembled homework I had done, but I didn't even attempt anything that looked unfamiliar. I earned Cs and sometimes Ds on tests, but I didn't really care as long as I passed. After all, my test-taking history had already taught me that I was not "good" at math.

My facility with the kinds of tests I became familiar with in high school served me well in college, since the most common forms of testing remained the objective and essay tests. In the course of my K-12 and college education, I memorized a prodigious quantity of information, some of which remains with me. No doubt I have forgotten the vast majority of facts I memorized for tests. In retrospect, I wish my education had focused more on the understanding of "big ideas" and less on the memorization of isolated facts. For example, I recall memorizing the symbols for and placement of the elements on the periodic table for high-school chemistry, and today I can recognize the names of most elements from their symbols—but I have only a vague idea of the purpose of the periodic table.

Eventually, when I began teaching, I found myself in the position of "test-maker" rather than "test-taker." As a test-maker, I was guided by my own experiences as a student, what other teachers around me were doing, by what students seemed to expect, and by prepackaged tests that accompanied the textbooks I used. In my English classes, the cycle went something like this. On Monday, assign spelling or vocabulary words. On Tuesday, assign a short story to be read as homework. On Wednesday, give a quiz to determine whether students had read and understood the story. Discuss the story. Assign essay questions about the story as homework. On Thursday, collect the homework and assign another story. On Friday, give a spelling or vocabulary quiz. Repeat for several weeks, then give a test on short stories and spelling or vocabulary. At some point in the cycle, assign an essay about some aspect of the short story, such as conflict, symbolism, or character.

This pattern generated enough grades to fill in many squares in my grade book, so that at the end of each nine weeks I could sit down with a calculator, compute the number of points possible, and determine what percentage of this number each student had earned. I allotted some number of points for participation, so that I could reward students for their "effort" or "progress" (and penalize students who were "lazy" or "disruptive"). In short, I was not a thoughtful assessor; I was a point collector.

Contrary to what I thought I had been taught in education courses—that grades would reflect a bell-shaped curve—my grade profile looked more like a two-humped camel. There were lots of As, several Bs, one or two Cs, several Ds, and quite a few F's. This distribution remained fairly constant over the school year, even though most Ds and Fs resulted from empty squares rather than low numbers in the grade book. Some students, it seemed, simply didn't care whether they passed English or not—even though passing English was prerequisite to high school graduation. I did not make the connection between my own experiences in math and the experiences of some students in my English classes. That is, low test scores and grades did not motivate my poorly performing students to work harder; on the contrary, low grades and test scores helped convince them they weren't "good" at English—so why bother?

My methods of assessment and evaluation improved over the years. I developed more systematic ways to assign value to student work so that a single low test score, for example, would not have a devastating impact on a student's overall grade. I devised projects that allowed students to demonstrate their understanding of content in ways other than paper-and-pencil tests, e.g., through art work, dramatization, or creative writing. I conscientiously recorded students' contributions to class discussions, so that I would have concrete evidence upon which to assign participation points. Students had multiple opportunities to revise their writing before submitting it for a grade. Nevertheless, grading remained a painful issue for me. Isn't the fact that Chris wrote a wonderful short story this nine weeks, even though he did very little else, enough to assign him a passing grade? Carolyn has an average of 89.3% this nine weeks and she will surely be upset (and her parents will surely demand an explanation) if she receives a B. Kwang is still struggling with English and his earned grade of C doesn't begin to reflect the progress he has made this semester. Like many other teachers, I wondered, "Is it possible to design an assessment system that fairly reflects what students know and can do, that makes criteria for success clear to all stakeholders, and that encourages students to take responsibility for assessing their own learning and determining what they need to learn next?"

Questions to Consider

1. You have probably heard about the "gender gap" in mathematics performance. What role might gender have played in Liz's experience with mathematics?
2. How did Liz's experiences as a "test-taker" influence who she became as a "test-maker"?
3. If grading is such a painful issue for both students and teachers, as this story suggests, why do we still require students to earn grades?

▮▮ PURPOSE

Tests and grades play a critical role in students' lives. As a teacher, you must make sure that the methods of assessment and evaluation you employ accurately reflect the learnings you value and that you want your students to value. Assessment and evaluation become even more complex when you consider the many ways in which students differ, including differences in learning styles and varieties of intelligences. Throughout this book, we have stressed the theme that one kind of instruction does not fit all; neither does one type of assessment fit all. The reality of student diversity challenges teachers to design assessments that allow all students to demonstrate learning in ways that are both personally meaningful and academically appropriate.

The purposes of this chapter are to introduce you to some of the issues and factors involved in assessing and evaluating student learning and to help you begin thinking about how you will approach assessment and evaluation in the classroom. One of the greatest challenges beginning teachers face is determining how to collect, interpret, record, and report evidence of student learning in equitable, defensible, and understandable ways. In addition to the assessments and evaluation you conduct in your classroom, you will also encounter some form of standardized testing at the school, district, state (and perhaps national) levels. You need to be able to interpret the significance of the information yielded by such tests and to help your students interpret this information. Ultimately, your job is to use the information gathered from assessment and evaluation to help students judge their success in learning and to help you improve instruction. Specifically, this chapter will help you:

- become familiar with the terminology of assessment, such as *performance assessment* and *formative assessment*;
- identify criteria for fair assessment;
- design appropriate assessments of student learning;
- consider issues involved in assigning and reporting grades;
- understand the role of district, state, and national tests in monitoring student learning.

▮▮ BARBECUING RIBS: A METAPHORICAL APPROACH TO UNDERSTANDING THE LANGUAGE OF ASSESSMENT

Perhaps no other area of education uses as much specialized terminology as the area of assessment and evaluation. It is important that you become familiar with some of this terminology in order to make and justify your own decisions about assessment and in order to understand and participate in debates that occur locally, nationally, and even internationally over test scores and their interpretation. Because discussion of this terminology can become abstract and even daunting, I'd like to step outside the field of education and use my recent experiences at a barbecuing competition in Louisville, Kentucky as a metaphor to guide this discussion.

At this event, about fifteen teams of cooks—from first-time competitors to seasoned champions—were competing for awards. Imagine you are one of the contestants. As you prepare the spices to rub on the ribs and the sauce to baste them in, you may taste the sauce and decide more mustard is needed—so you add it. Or you may observe that the spice blend is too bland—so you add another dash of cayenne pepper.

These actions may be likened to *assessment,* the process of gathering information in a valid, timely, and efficient manner in order to make decisions (As a teacher you will be making *instructional* rather than culinary decisions.).

Usually, assessment is seen as having two categories. One is *formative assessment:* the process of gathering information while work is still in progress in order to influence the final outcome, as in the example above. Once the ribs are done and you sample a slice, you may decide "Perfect!" or "Too tough!" This is *summative assessment* or evaluation: the process of using and interpreting the information collected during the formative stage to make decisions (Neill, Bursh, Shaeffer, Thall, Yohe, Zappardino, N. D.). At this point, you can't go back and change the ingredients or the technique. But the next time you barbecue ribs, you can incorporate what you learned from this experience.

In school, as students are working toward a goal, they need lots of feedback (formative assessment) along the way to help them achieve a desired outcome. Once their work is evaluated (summative assessment), they need feedback that will help them progress toward the next learning goal. In addition, the teacher should use the information gained from formative and summative assessment to make decisions about what students still need to learn and how they might go about learning it.

To return to the barbecuing example, suppose that instead of actually barbecuing ribs you were required to take a multiple-choice test on the subject: "The correct temperature inside the grill for barbecuing ribs is: (A) 250 degrees (B) 375 degrees (C) 425 degrees (D) None of these."

Such a test could tell us whether you possessed a certain amount of knowledge about barbecuing, but it would not tell us whether you could, in fact, barbecue edible ribs. Suppose, for example, that you can barbecue excellent ribs but that you learned the techniques from your uncle who never used a thermometer or a recipe. You would not score very well on such a test! From this example, you can see where the terms *alternative assessment, performance assessment,* and *authentic assessment* originated. *Alternative* means "alternative to traditional, multiple choice, objective tests." If you want to determine whether someone knows how to barbecue ribs, then ask that person to barbecue. This is *performance* assessment. It is also *authentic* assessment in the sense that there is little or no difference between the skill being tested and the way it is tested.

The problem with giving someone a multiple-choice test on barbecuing is that we still won't know whether the person can actually barbecue or not. A *valid* test is one that accurately assesses the skills or knowledge in question. Barbecuing ribs is a highly valid test of barbecuing ability. A multiple-choice test can be a highly valid measure of a person's knowledge about barbecuing. A *reliable* test is one that consistently measures what it claims to measure. A multiple-choice test on barbecuing might be extremely reliable—that is, it could be administered year after year to many different groups of test-takers with fairly predictable results. In addition, it can be scored reliably because all questions have one right answer. On the other hand, while actually barbecuing ribs may be an extremely valid test, it may not always be reliable: cuts of meat vary in quality, climate may affect how well coals in the grill burn, various brands of charcoal may heat up more quickly than others. More importantly, judges, unless they have undergone a common training for judging, may disagree about the qualities of good barbecued ribs. At a national level, debates rage over the validity and reliability of multiple-choice tests versus alternative forms of assessment. But even in the classroom, you will need to consider the validity and reliability of the assessments you design.

Now, let's suppose you, along with many other aspiring cooks, have barbecued a slab of ribs to demonstrate your mastery of barbecuing and you have submitted your ribs for judging. One approach a judge might take is to assume before even taking a bite that only a small percentage of the ribs will actually be excellent and that another small percentage will be inedible. Most of the ribs will rank somewhere in the middle. Your ribs will be judged in comparison to other groups of ribs that have already been judged and be ranked accordingly. (E.g., Your ribs are better than 80% of ribs produced by beginning cooks.) This illustrates the concept of *norm-referenced* testing: a few will excel, a few will fail, but most will perform in the middle range. (Neill, Bursh, Shaeffer, Thall, Yohe, Zappardino, N.D.) On the other hand, a judge could have before her a sample of an excellent barbecued rib. As the judge tastes the entries, she will decide how close each of the entries comes to the exemplary rib. This illustrates the concept of *criterion-referenced* testing: a standard of mastery is set and everyone works toward that standard. It is possible that all ribs might meet the standard. Again, there is a national level to the debate over norm-referenced and criterion-referenced testing. As a classroom teacher, you will need to decide whether you want your evaluations to rank and sort student performance according to a predetermined distribution or whether every student should have the opportunity to demonstrate mastery.

You may agree that having students barbecue ribs to demonstrate their knowledge and skill in barbecuing is educationally sound. But you may question whether rib -judging might not be a very subjective process—and you want to be fair to everyone. One way to make judging fair and consistent is to use methods of *holistic scoring.* In holistic scoring, judges sample a broad range of performances (in this example, ribs) and agree on a set of criteria for the characteristics of excellent, good, fair, or poor work. For barbecued ribs, the characteristics might include taste, texture, and appearance. The judges thoroughly discuss these characteristics and practice applying the criteria to a number of ribs before they sample yours. The criteria they ultimately use to judge your ribs form a *rubric:* "A series of narrative statements describing the levels of quality of a product or performance" (Educators in Connecticut's Pomperaug Regional School District 15, 1996, p. 279). You can also imagine that if you had this rubric in front of you as you barbecued your ribs, you would know very clearly what the judges were seeking. You would know even more about their expectations if you tasted several ribs, *exemplars,* that had already been judged. Because many teachers want to maximize their students' opportunities for success, they are creating rubrics, collecting exemplary work, and applying holistic scoring methods in their classrooms.

Finally, if you really wanted to show that you could barbecue, you would barbecue more than one slab of ribs. You might want to show judges your creativity by making up your own marinades or sauce. Or you might want to highlight your versatility by barbecuing some chicken, salmon, or beef. You might want to prepare barbecued ribs in several different ways in order to show your mastery of this particular form. You might want to write a statement articulating what you've learned about barbecuing as you've become more experienced. In the end, the judges would have a very good idea of the breadth and depth of your barbecuing knowledge and skill. This is one illustration of why portfolios have become so popular as an assessment tool. A *portfolio* is "a systematic or purposeful collection of selected student work and student self-assessments developed over time, gathered to demonstrate and evaluate progress and achievement in learning" (Educators in Connecticut's Pomperaug Regional School District 15, 1996, p. 278). Portfolios allow students to show many aspects of themselves as learners and to show their learning over time. Such important information cannot be obtained from a single test or performance.

Let's take a look at some of the entrants into the Louisville competition. Bob and Sandra are veterans of hundreds of competitions. Furthermore, they live in an area of the country where beef and pork are raised and renowned for their quality. When Bob and Sandra fly to competitions, they bring their raw materials, and their custom-built grill along with them. After being introduced to the hobby through a course at a local college, Tim and Lisa are barbecuing competitively for the first time. Their grill is an off-the-shelf model, and they purchased their ribs at the local grocery store. A third team, Matt and Mike, had seen the ad for the event in the previous night's paper, thought it sounded like fun, loaded their supplies into their truck, and showed up ready to cook. Matt and Mike had never grilled anything more sophisticated than hot dogs and hamburgers. Of the three teams, which is most likely to win the competition? Why? These three teams have widely differing backgrounds, experience, and access to resources, yet all will be judged by the same standards. Is this fair? It is around similar issues in education that debates occur over *opportunity-to-learn*. That is, should all students be held to the same standards regardless of their different experiences? And, if they are to be held to the same standards, is it possible to make the testing situation more equitable for students who, like Matt and Mike, are not starting at the same level as students like Bob and Sandra?

For the teams described above and for most people, a barbecuing competition is a low-stakes event. Entrants barbecue as a hobby, and, although it is pleasant to win and disappointing not to be awarded a ribbon, no significant consequences are attached to the results. At the competition in Louisville, contestants strolled around sampling other teams' entries, sharing tips on recipes and timing, and chatting about mutual acquaintances and travel plans. What if significant consequences had been attached to this competition—for example, large monetary rewards for the winners or banishment from future grill-offs for those who did not place in the top five? This would have made the competition a *high-stakes* event. Do you think that under these circumstances the atmosphere would have remained casual and convivial? Probably not. In schools, similar tensions surround high-stakes assessment, particularly in statewide testing programs that reward or sanction schools and teachers based on students' test scores. Other instances of high-stakes testing in schools include tests that determine placement into special education programs, gifted and talented programs, admission into advanced-level courses, or higher education. When life-changing decisions are made on the basis of a single test score or even several sets of test scores, you can see why opportunity-to-learn is a critical factor in assessment policy and practices.

This example of a barbecuing competition is intended to provide a concrete way of thinking about some rather abstract terms. As a metaphor, it works well to illuminate some aspects of assessment while it obscures others. For example, you may be thinking, "Okay. I get it. But no one barbecues a history rib or a math rib. Sometimes, a multiple-choice test is the best way to find out who knows the important facts—and who has time to judge a hundred 'history ribs' anyway?" Given the reality of high-school teaching, this is a valid point. As a teacher, you will probably work toward creating an assessment system that includes a judicious amount of time-efficient information gathering with a greater emphasis on formative assessments and authentic performances.

EQUITY IN ASSESSMENT

A great deal of evidence points to the fact that assessment and evaluation practices in this country—from the classroom quiz to large-scale standardized tests of achievement or IQ—have been unfair to a large number of students, especially those with linguistic, cultural, and ethnic differences, students with disabilities, and those from low-income families (Farr & Trumbull, 1997; Carroll, 1995; Hanson, 1993; Hilliard, 1990). In the traditional view of teaching and testing, teachers have been dispensers and examiners of knowledge, while students have been expected to receive and replicate this knowledge. In such a view, it makes sense, for example, to test students' knowledge of the Civil War by giving everyone the same multiple-choice test to be completed independently, without reference to books or notes, and under time constraints. The assumption is that everyone received the same knowledge from the teacher and therefore has an equal chance at scoring well on the test.

As research has given us more insight about the diverse ways in which students learn and know and the contexts in which they learn and demonstrate their learning, educators have realized that methods of assessment and the roles of students and teachers in assessment and evaluation must also change: "Variations in culture, ethnic and language background, economic and social status, and learning opportunities all contribute to the larger context in which students are assessed" (Farr & Trumbull, 1997, p. 254).

Equity in assessment means giving all students opportunities to demonstrate what they actually know in a given subject area. Imagine the frustration of English language learners who may know a great deal about the subject in question but cannot yet fluently express what they know in English. Students with reading difficulties may not be able to demonstrate what they know under the same time limits imposed on others who read quickly. Students from cultures where collaboration is valued more highly than competition may be penalized for cheating on a test when, in fact, giving the answer to a friend is simply the "right thing" to do. Test items that rely on cultural knowledge, such as computing a bill in a restaurant or planning a skiing vacation, may disadvantage students who have never eaten in any restaurant but McDonald's or vacationed anywhere at all. Students with disabilities need the same accommodations during assessments as they receive during instruction, e.g., listening to material on tape or making use of a scribe (Shriner, Ysseldyke, Thurlow & Honetschlager, 1994).

Grant Wiggins (1993), an ardent advocate of alternative assessment, has proposed a students' "Assessment Bill of Rights." These principles, reprinted in Figure 10.1, provide an ideal toward which to work and are worth keeping in mind as you read this chapter and as you move into teaching and assume responsibility for assessing student performance.

■■ ASSESSMENT AND EVALUATION IN THE CLASSROOM

Recall the distinction made earlier between assessment (the process of gathering information in order to make instructional decisions) and evaluation (the process of making judgments about the quality of students' progress toward instructional goals). For example, regular recording of class participation is a form of assessment. Evaluation occurs when you review a student's participation over the course of a grading period and assign some numerical or letter-grade value to it. As the above "Bill of Rights" suggests, you will want to gather information for purposes of assessment and evaluation from a variety of sources. Although tests and quizzes are usually the first forms of assessment and evaluation that come to mind, there are many other sources of information you can use to obtain information about student progress, including projects, performances, observations, conferences, journals, notebooks, and homework.

Planning for assessment and evaluation is an integral part of the planning process; as you identify instructional goals and objectives you must also determine how you

FIGURE 10.1   Assessment Bill of Rights

All students are entitled to the following:

1. Worthwhile . . . intellectual problems that are validated against worthy 'real world' intellectual problems, roles, and situations.

2. Clear, apt, published, and consistently applied teacher criteria in grading work and published models of excellent work that exemplifies standards.

3. Minimal secrecy in testing and grading.

4. Ample opportunities to produce work that they can be proud of . . .

5. Assessment, not just tests: multiple and varied opportunities to display and document their achievement; and options in tests that allow them to play to their strengths.

6. The freedom, climate, and oversight policies necessary to question grades and test practices without fear of retribution.

7. Forms of testing that allow timely opportunities for students to explain or justify answers marked as wrong but that they believe to be apt or correct.

8. Genuine feedback: usable information on their strengths and weaknesses and an accurate assessment of their long-term progress toward a set of exit-level standards framed in terms of essential tasks.

9. Scoring/grading policies that provide incentives and opportunities for improving performance and seeing progress against exit-level and real-world standards.

From *Assessing Student Performance: Exploring the Purpose and Limits of Testing* (p. 28) by G. P. Wiggins, 1993, San Francisco, CA: Jossey-Bass.

will know whether students are progressing toward those goals and whether they have achieved them.

Sometimes assessment can be as simple as asking questions, observing students' behavior, or scanning their homework. As you plan for instruction, you should always ask yourself, "How will I know whether they are learning what I am teaching?" and "What will I do with this information?" If the whole class fails to master an algebra homework assignment, you need to use this information to reteach the material—perhaps using different techniques if you conclude that your first presentation was not effective. If only a few students fail to master the homework assignment, you need to use this information as well and to provide additional opportunities for those students to learn the material. If you observe that students are not working well in groups, you need to use this information to make instructional decisions: Do students need a lesson on communication skills? Is the task clear? Is group work the best structure for helping students learn this material, skill, or concept? Should the groups be reconfigured? These are only a few examples of the instructional decisions teachers make based on classroom assessment.

Planning "Backwards" for Assessment

Identifying the outcomes or targets of instruction should be the first step in planning for assessment. This holds true for planning a course, a semester, a unit, or a lesson. Once you have identified the target, you can then plan "backwards" to ensure that students learn the skills that will enable them to reach your goals. For example, a team of math and science teachers at Central Park East Secondary School (CPESS) in New York City decided to focus their curriculum on the "big ideas" of forces, motion, and the conservation of energy. They designed a final assessment in which students would use what they knew about these ideas to design scary but safe amusement park rides. With this final goal in mind, they then identified the knowledge and skills students would need to be successful in the culminating task and planned the curriculum "backwards" to include such scientific concepts as mass, volume, density, gravity, acceleration, and velocity. Mathematical skills and concepts needed to complete the task included area vs. volume, linear vs. non-linear equations, probability, trigonometry, the Pythagorean theorem, and basic arithmetic skills (National Center for Restructuring Schools and Teaching, 1993). Undoubtedly, these teachers gathered much information about student progress along the way, but formulating the final assessment in advance gave focus and purpose to their instruction throughout the course. The students, too, were well aware of the expectations for their learning.

While this is an example of an end-of-course assessment, the same principles can be applied to smaller units of instruction. For example, look at the mathematics task (see Figure 10.2) designed by teachers in Connecticut. This task, used at the culmination of an algebra unit on graphing, lines, and slopes, provides a clear map of the instruction that needs to occur in order for students to be successful.

Assigning Value to Habits We Value

Often the behaviors and habits of mind we value most in students—inquisitiveness, persistence, attention to detail, the asking of important questions, and a willingness to help others—are inadequately reflected in the assessments they complete and the grades they are assigned (Wiggins, 1996). One reason for this is that teachers see judgments about such qualities as subjective. Yet if you value these qualities, and if you plan effectively, it is possible to design defensible and fair ways to incorporate their value into your classroom assessment system. For example, in designing group projects, many teachers have developed techniques to assess group process as well as final product and require students to submit written reflections concerning their contributions to the group and the group's success as a team. Figures 10.3A and 10.3B illustrate one way teachers can record observations and incorporate student self-evaluation into assessment of group projects.

Figure 10.4 shows a scale that students can use to evaluate their own participation in class discussions. The teacher has each student fill out this form after each major discussion and the teacher completes a simplified version of the form weekly for each student.

More and more teachers are developing systematic methods of observation as an assessment technique. For example, during a science lab, a teacher may circulate around the room observing and taking notes on the processes used by individual students. Interviews and conferences can also be valuable sources of information about student learning (Hill & Ruptic, 1994; National Center for Restructuring Schools and Teaching, 1993; Paris & Ayres, 1994).

FIGURE 10.2   Performance Task Cookbook Algebra

Background
Have you ever cooked a potato in a microwave oven and wondered how long it should cook? How about that ham or turkey for Thanksgiving? You have been hired by a cookbook publisher to create a set of graphs for a new cookbook.

Task
Your task is to review cookbooks and find recipes that describe different lengths of cooking time for different amounts of food such as cooking beef, roasts, or turkeys in the conventional oven or cooking vegetables in the microwave oven. Make a graph that shows the amount of time required to cook different amounts of food. Write an algebraic formula and a word formula for the slope of the line on each graph.

Audience
The audience for your graph is mathematicians who cook.

Purpose
The purpose of your graphs and algebraic formulas is to show mathematically how long to cook various amount of food.

Procedure

1. Review the assessment list for cookbook algebra.
2. Find six examples of food that takes different amounts of time to cook based on the amount of that food to cook.
3. Make a graph for each type of food that shows the amount of time required to cook different amounts of that food.
4. Write an algebraic formula for the slope of the line on each graph.
5. Write a word formula for each algebraic formula.
6. Study all the graphs you have made and their formulas. Describe what patterns you see in the relationship between the amount of time and the amount of food to be cooked.

From *A Teacher's Guide to Performance-Based Learning and Assessment* (p. 74) by Educators in Connecticut's Pomperaug Regional School District 15, 1996, Alexandria, VA: Association for Supervision and Curriculum Development.

Learning logs and journals are additional sources of information about whether students are developing habits of mind we value and deepening their understanding of subject matter. For example, math and science teachers can have students summarize their understanding of the day's material, express how they feel about it, or respond to a subject-related prompt. In English, students can keep records of their reading and record their responses to literature. As students complete research projects, they may keep logs in which they record their activities, summarize their growing understanding of the topic, and note sources that remain to be consulted (Murray, 1990).

Surveys of students' interests and attitudes, administered at strategic points throughout the year, provide information that can help teachers plan instruction and assessments as well as monitor student engagement with and learning in the subject area. An example of a survey that can be given in middle- and high-school math classes appears in Figure 10.5. How might a math teacher use the information gained from this survey to make instructional decisions?

| FIGURE 10.3A | Teacher Observation Chart for Team Projects |

Observation Category	Student	Student	Student	Student	Student
Assumes leadership role					
Demonstrates effective leadership style (specify)					
Contributes ideas					
Contributes work such as drawing, filming					
Contributes to the class presentation					
Demonstrates comprehension					
Demonstrates grasp of details					
Demonstrates facility in working as team member					
Demonstrates particular talent (specify)					
Demonstrates ability to articulate ideas					
Demonstrates ability to synthesize ideas					

From *A Measure of Success: From Assignment to Assessment in English Language Arts* (p. 107) by M. F. Claggett, 1996, Portsmouth, NH: Heinemann.

Helping Students Become Self-Assessors

We know that, outside the arena of school, successful people—athletes, actors and actresses, trial lawyers, and surgeons, to name a few—constantly monitor their own performance and modify what they do on the basis of this information (Gladwell, 1999). How can you, as a teacher, create the conditions that will help students become skilled self-assessors, true independent, lifelong learners?

Most of the assessment techniques described earlier (e.g., learning logs, conferences, reflections on group process) are intended to promote student self-assessment. In addition, self-assessment is an important feature of performance assessment and portfolios, which will be described later in this chapter. Because most students are not accustomed to assessing their own performance, their first attempts at self-assessment may be disappointingly vague or brief. You may need to provide students with scaffolding—prompts and structured questionnaires that enable students to understand and complete an unfamiliar task. These can gradually be removed as students develop skills in this area and see that their opinions are valued.

These are only a few of the ways that you can ensure that students know that learning is as much a process as a product. Using a variety of sources of information for assessment and evaluation will not only give you more insight into the effectiveness of your own teaching, but will help you form a more accurate picture of student learning.

FIGURE 10.3B Student Project Evaluation

Name _____ Period _____ Date _____

Project Title: _____

List members of team and indicate their degree of participation in the project as well as their contributions in terms of leadership, willingness to work, creativity, or other special area (such as expertise in filming). Rank contributions in range of 5 (high) to 1 (low).

Team Members	Degree of Participation	Leadership	Willingness to Work	Creativity	Other Contributions (Specify)
Self					

On a separate page, describe the process that your team went through in completing this project. Include how you made your decisions about the subject of your project, research needed, talents needed to carry out your ideas, and anything else that affected the way you worked. What did you do when things didn't turn out as expected, for instance? The focus here is on how you worked together as a team. Be sure to include your part in the process.

Name _____ Period _____ Date _____

Project Title: _____

Evaluate your project in terms of the following: (5=high; 1=low). In the column at the right, explain your evaluation.

Project Qualities	Evaluation	Explanation
Information presented		
Creativity in presentation		
Overall effectiveness of presentation (written)		
Overall effectiveness of presentation (visual)		
Overall effectiveness of presentation (oral)		

From *A Measure of Success: From Assignment to Assessment in English Language Arts* (pp. 108–109) by M. F. Claggett, 1996, Portsmouth, NH: Heinemann.

FIGURE 10.4   Discussion Rating Scales.

How did you feel about today's discussion?

Class's treatment of issues
superficial   1   2   3   4   5   thorough and deep

Helpfulness of discussion to your understanding
low   1   2   3   4   5   high

Your own level of engagement
low   1   2   3   4   5   high

The class's overall level of engagement
low   1   2   3   4   5   high

Quality of your own participation
poor   1   2   3   4   5   excellent

Quantity of your spoken remarks relative to your normal performance
low   1   2   3   4   5   high

Degree of your own understanding of material
limited   1   2   3   4   5   full

Facilitator's Success
too much input   1   2   3   4   5   too little input

too much control   1   2   3   4   5   too little control

great respect for others   1   2   3   4   5   too little respect for others

Comments:

From *Assessing Student Performance: Exploring the Purpose and Limits of Testing* (p. 66) by G. P. Wiggins, 1993, San Francisco, CA: Jossey-Bass.

▌ Reader Activity 10.1

IN THE FIELD
Interviewing Teachers About Assessment and Evaluation

Arrange to interview a middle- or high-school teacher about assessment and evaluation. You may wish to ask questions like the following.

1. How do you go about planning for assessment and evaluation?
2. From what sources do you gather information for assessment and evaluation (e.g., observation, interviews, homework, tests, projects)?
3. How do you use the information you gather?
4. How, if at all, do you involve students in assessment and evaluation?
5. How do you record the information you gather for assessment and evaluation?

FIGURE 10.5   Math Survey

Name _____ Date _____

1. Do you enjoy math? Why or why not?

   _____

   _____

   _____

2. What helps someone become good at math?

   _____

   _____

   _____

3. Describe some ways in which people use math in "real life."

   _____

   _____

   _____

4. What types of math topics and activities do you most enjoy?

   _____

   _____

   _____

5. How have you used math outside of school?

   _____

   _____

   _____

6. Any other comments about math (feelings you have about math, types of math activities or topics you find difficult, etc.).

   _____

   _____

   _____

From *Practical Aspects of Authentic Assessment: Putting the Pieces Together* (p. 190) by B. C. Hill and C. A. Ruptic, 1994, Norwood, MA: Christopher-Gordon Publishers.

6. How do you report the information you gather for assessment and evaluation?
7. How do you assign grades for a learning period, such as a nine-week period, a semester, or a year?
8. What, if anything, troubles you about grading?
9. How does state or district testing influence your teaching?

Share the results of your interview with the whole class or in small groups. What differences and similarities do you find between middle- and high-school teachers? What differences and similarities do you find within and across subject areas? What assessment and evaluation techniques described thus far in this chapter are commonly used? Rarely used? Not used at all? How do you account for this? What are the implications of your findings for you as a beginning teacher?

■■ TRADITIONAL FORMS OF CLASSROOM ASSESSMENT

Most middle- and high-school teachers regularly use quizzes and tests to assess and evaluate student learning. Objective quizzes and tests—those containing items that are designed to have only one correct answer—are an efficient way to gather information. Many schools have their own scoring machines, which make this form of assessment even more attractive to busy teachers. In addition, many textbooks come with prepackaged tests and quizzes, as well as item banks from which you can construct your own customized tests. Like microwaveable frozen dinners, these ready-made tools can make your life easier. But a steady diet of such foods soon becomes monotonous. Both you and your students will probably find quizzes and tests more engaging if they are most often homemade.

When you sit down to design an objective quiz or test, you have several forms from which to choose, including multiple choice, true/false, and matching. Because objective items have only one right answer, it is difficult to write good items that elicit higher levels of thinking from students—a serious limitation of this type of test. Research suggests that traditional, teacher-made, objective tests generally call for knowledge of facts, even when teachers claim to value higher-order thinking (Madaus & Kellaghan, 1996).

One of the cardinal rules of writing objective test items is to avoid ambiguity. The right answer should be evident to the student who has prepared for the test. Convoluted wording can be confusing even to fluent readers, let alone students who have reading difficulties or who are still learning English. Likewise, a good objective item tests students' knowledge of the material—not their test-taking skills. For example, many high school students have learned that a true/false item containing the word *always* or *never* is most likely false.

Figure 10.6 presents guidelines for constructing common types of traditional test items.

Essay Questions

Essay questions and tests have the advantage of allowing students to demonstrate more fully what they know and can do, but they are more time-consuming to evaluate and teachers and students alike may see the grading of essay items as "subjective" (Aker, 1995). Well-written essay questions are more likely than objective items to elicit higher-order thinking (i.e., analysis, synthesis, evaluation) from students. However, an essay question that simply requires students to recall facts (e.g., "List the life stages of a cell and explain the function of each") does not serve the purpose of essay items. A well-written essay item clearly states the expectations for the response. Consider the following examples of essay items.

> *What is the contribution of art to our culture?*
> This question is so vague and broad that it is difficult to imagine how students might respond, much less how a teacher might grade it.
> *What was Paul Klee's contribution to the art of the first half of this century?*
> This question is more specific than the first, but it still doesn't communicate to students what is expected of them.
> *In a one-page essay (approximately 150 words) describe the single most identifiable characteristic of Paul Klee's painting in the 1920s and 1930s, and give an example of how his work influenced other artists of his time.*

| **FIGURE 10.6** | Guidelines for Constructing Traditional Test Items |

Multiple Choice	True/False	Matching	Fill-in-the-Blank	Essay
• Structure the stem and choices so that they are succinct. • Avoid repetition of phrases and terms. • Minimize use of negative terms (*no, none, never*) and absolutes (*all always, very*). • Limit the use of *all of the above* and *none of the above* as choices. • Proofread to ensure that only one correct answer is offered for each item. • Proofread for grammatical correctness. • Work through the items yourself to check for feasibility.	• Use precise language. Avoid indefinite terms such as *more, few, large*. • Be sure the statement is entirely true or entirely false. • Challenge students, but do not "trick" them. • Instruct students to write out response (*true, false*) in order to avoid confusion between *t* and *f* when scoring. • Consider asking students to correct false statements. This avoids "guessing." • Work through the items yourself to check for feasibility.	• Construct homogeneous categories for matching. For example, don't mix dates, people, and events in one set of items. • Keep the list of matching items brief (5–10). • Include a few "distracters"— items that do not match any other item. • Specify whether an item can be used more than once in your directions. • Work through the items yourself to check for feasibility.	• The desired response should be definite and brief. • Be sure that response blanks are of equal length. • Avoid grammatical clues (e.g., is/are, she/he) preceding the blank. • Avoid excessive use of blanks within one question. • Make sure the item includes sufficient context for the desired response. • Complete the items yourself to check for feasibility.	• Be sure the question is clear and directs the student to the desired response. • Suggest time to be spent on and point value of each question or portion of question. • Avoid using essays to test for recall (e.g., list, how many). • Be open to acceptable, alternative responses. • Avoid offering choice in essays, as it is difficult to construct comparable but different essay questions. • Give students as much information as you can about requirements of a correct response. • Respond to the essay yourself to determine clarity of item and feasibility of expectations.

This item requires students to synthesize what they know about Klee's painting, to make an evaluative judgment, and to apply what they know. Expectations for the nature of the response as well as its length are clear (Kindsvatter, Wilen & Isher, 1988, p. 310).

Refer to Figure 10.6 for guidelines for constructing *essay questions*.

Remember that, when formulating an essay response, students should have some time to organize their thoughts before beginning writing. Encourage students to spend some time planning (e.g., making notes, outlining, mapping) before they begin writing. Because essays are written under time constraints and students rarely have time to access reference tools or proofread carefully, it is not entirely fair to hold them accountable for written mechanics.

Once you begin teaching, collect examples of student responses to essays. You can share these responses with students, together with a scoring rubric (rubric development will be discussed later), and have them evaluate the essays. Techniques like this help to make your expectations clear to all students.

■ **Reader Activity 10.2**

THEORY INTO PRACTICE
Analyzing Test Items

The purpose of this activity is to enable you to apply the guidelines given earlier to several samples of traditional test items and item sets. For each sample, discuss the extent to which the guidelines apply and any other concerns you may have about the representative items.

Sample A: Multiple Choice Items—Earth Science
1. Rocks that contain dinosaur fossils most likely formed
   a. several days ago
   b. several years ago
   c. on land
   d. several million years ago
2. As a hurricane approaches, people are usually asked to evacuate
   a. immediately
   b. low-lying coastal areas
   c. urban areas
   d. all of the above
3. Which of the following is *not* a reason why oceanography is often carried out by a team of many different kinds of scientists and professionals?
   a. Oceanographers are loners and unable to work together.
   b. Oceanography is a very complex science.
   c. Oceanographers need help from other branches of science.
   d. None of the above.

Answers: (1) c (2) b (3) b
NOTE: These sample items have been altered from original test items that appear in Fronk, R. H. & Knight, L. B. (1994). *Earth Science. Annotated Teacher's Edition.* Austin, TX: Holt, Rinehart & Winston.

Sample B: True/False Items—Life Science
Directions: If the statement is true, write "True." If it is false, change the italicized word or words to make the statement true.

1. *Carnivore* means "flesh-eater." (True)
2. The *pituary* produces adrenaline. (False; should be *adrenals*)

3. A method of selective breeding that is the opposite of hybridization (the process in which two species that are genetically different are crossed) is called *inbreeding*. (True)

NOTE: These sample items have been altered from original test items that appear in Maton, A., Hopkins, J., Johnson, J., LaHart, D., Warner, M. Q., Wright, J. D. (1994). *Exploring Life Science. Teacher's Edition.* Englewood Cliffs, NJ: Prentice Hall.

Sample C: Matching—Algebra II
Directions: Match the terms with the correct definitions.

1. a rectangular arrangement of numbers enclosed in brackets	a. linear equation
2. the most commonly occurring item in a data set	b. mode
3. the middle item is a data set	c. median
4. place where data is stored	d. matrix
5. the average of the sum of a data set	e. mean
	f. cell
	g. spreadsheet

Answers: (1) a (2) b (3) c (4) f (5) e
NOTE: These items have been altered from the original test items which appear in Gerver, R., Cater, C., Molina, D., Sgroi, R., Hansen, M., Westgaard, S. (1997). *Algebra 2: An Integrated Approach. Teacher's Annotated Edition.* Cincinnati, OH: Southwestern Educational Publishing.

Formatting and Logistical Issues

Every test or quiz should be legible with plenty of white space, so that the act of reading the test is not a test in itself and so that all styles of student handwriting are accommodated. This is especially important for students with visual impairments or some learning disabilities. You should edit, proofread, and work through every test or quiz you create to catch errors before they create confusion among your students and to get some idea of how long it might take students to complete the test. When estimating time, you should also build in time for students to check their work. Many teachers arrange test items in order of increasing difficulty, so that students are not discouraged at the outset. Students may benefit from your suggestions about how to organize their test-taking time. (e.g., "You should spend about twenty minutes on the final essay.")

Quizzes and tests should be graded and returned promptly. When appropriate, students should be given opportunity and credit for revising work. Students should also have the chance to explain their thinking if they believe an answer marked wrong is correct. Think carefully about how you will present test results to the class. Some teachers habitually return tests in descending order of performance (i.e., A - F). Students soon catch on to this pattern and can identify who received the highest and lowest grades. If, for some reason, you think it necessary to post grades, you should identify students by number rather than name. Some teachers post grade distributions (e.g., A=5, B=10, C=8, D=2, F=1). Imagine how you would feel if you were F=1!

Teaching Study and Test-Taking Skills

Many students perform poorly on tests because they lack study skills and knowledge of test-taking strategies. You can teach these skills yourself or collaborate with a special

Performance assessment requires students to apply knowledge and skills to situations as close to "real life" as possible.

education teacher on teaching these skills, as special education teachers are usually quite knowledgeable in this area. Later in this chapter you will see how one special education teacher prepared her students to succeed on a statewide test.

Because many tests require recall of information, you can teach students strategies for remembering facts. Repetition, visualization, rhymes, graphic organizers, abbreviations, and acronymic sentences are some of the strategies students can use (Strichart, Mangrum & Iannuzzi, 1998). You can help students prepare for tests by presenting a plan for studying and by teaching test-taking skills. For example, you can teach an overall strategy for approaching a test and specific strategies for particular item types, such as multiple-choice, true/false, and matching. DETER is an acronym for a five-step approach to test-taking. The letters stand for (1) read the DIRECTIONS; (2) EXAMINE the entire test to see what is required; (3) decide how much TIME to allot to items and parts; (4) begin with the EASIEST parts; (5) REVIEW your answers when you have finished. QUOTE is a strategy for approaching an essay test. The letters stand for (1) determine what the QUESTION calls for (e.g., describe, compare, explain); (2) UNDERLINE the most important words in the question; (3) ORGANIZE the facts and write; (4) monitor TIME; (5) EVALUATE the content and mechanics of your response (Strichart, Mangrum & Iannuzzi, 1998).

ALTERNATIVE FORMS OF CLASSROOM ASSESSMENT

As you can conclude, constructing fair tests and quizzes is not as simple a matter as it may appear to be. Often, teachers are left with the nagging feeling that some students have not performed up to their potential simply because of the testing situation. And, as you may discover from reflecting on your own testing history, even a perfect score on a multiple-choice test may not be an indicator of real understanding or the ability to apply knowledge. For these and many other reasons, more and more teachers are turning to alternative forms of assessment. In this section, we will look at two broad categories of alternative assessment: performance tasks and portfolios. We will also look at how these complex demonstrations of student learning can be scored.

Designing Performance Assessments

Performance assessment is not a new idea. Teachers in some subjects have been doing it for years. For example, when students drive in a driver education course, or type in a business education course, or carry on a conversation in a foreign language class, they are demonstrating their mastery by performing. However, in many other school subjects, assessment has tended to be more pencil-and-paper oriented. This is understandable in part because of the many constraints on teachers' work: large classes, many different preparations, and little time for preparation. But teachers' reliance on traditional forms of testing, especially in core subjects like English, math, social studies, and science, has widened the gap between students' perception of "school knowledge" and the knowledge they need for "real life." How many times have you wondered yourself or heard students ask, "What are we ever gonna use this for anyway?" Performance assessment helps to answer this question because it requires students to apply knowledge and skills to situations as close to "real life" as possible.

Figure 10.7 suggests many ideas for designing performance assessments in various subject areas.

In designing performance assessment tasks, you must attend to at least three critical features: (1) the task must be linked to meaningful learner outcomes and students must see these links; (2) the task must be clearly structured so that all students can understand what is expected of them; and (3) students should be well aware of the criteria by which their response will be scored. If you fail to attend to these elements, you have made no improvement over traditional assessment and have quite possibly set some students up for failure. If done well, performance assessment is more intellectually demanding than traditional forms of assessment. Unless you design the task with attention to learner outcomes, structure, and scoring criteria, you may get some entertaining performances, but they won't be of much use for assessment or evaluation purposes. Figure 10.8 shows a performance task developed by English teachers in Connecticut. Note how these teachers have specified important learner outcomes, structured the task, and made scoring criteria clear.

Designing Rubrics and Scoring Performance Assessments

As the example in Figure 10.8 shows, one way to score performance assessments is to state your expectations for a quality performance, allot a number of points to that feature, and assign some portion of that number to the performance. (Note that in this example, the student is required to assess his or her own performance.) Assigning a numerical grade, then, is simply a matter of adding up the points earned and negotiating any differences between your assessment as the teacher and the student's self-assessment.

| FIGURE 10.7 | Performance Task Formats |

Analysis Map of a Leader
Autobiography
Bulletin Board Display
Business Letter
Cartoon or Comic
Cause and Effect Essay
Children's Book
Cinquaine Poem
Collage
Composing and Performing a Song
Consumer Decision Making
Data Table or Chart
Display
Drawing or Illustration, Creative
Drawing or Illustration, Technical
Editorial
Ethnic Food
Event Chain Graphic Organizer
Experiment, Designing and Troubleshooting
Expository Essay
Fairy Tale
Folk Tale
Friendly Letter
Geographic Game
Grant Application Simulation
Graph, Bar or Line

Graph, Bar Using Algebra
Graph, Pie or Circle
Graph, Picto-
Graphic Design
Group Work
History Book Chapter
Hyperlearning Stack
Idea Web Graphic Organizer
Information Problem Solving
Interview
Invention
Issue Controversy
Journal, Geographic
Lab Report
Land Use Survey
Letter Asking for Information
Letter to the Editor
Management Plan for a Group Project
Management Plan for an Individual Project
Map
Math Problem Solving with Algebra
Math Problem Solving with Arithmetic
Math Problem Solving with Geometry

Math Problem Solving with Statistics
Models
Newspaper Article
Observing
Oral Report with Visuals
Pamphlet
Peer Editing
Persuasive Writing
Geographic Portfolio
Poster
Reading Journal for a Novel
Research Report
Science Fair Display
Scrap Book
Skit
Slide Show or Photo Essay
Song with Music and Lyrics
Story Problem, Creating
Survey
Time Line Graphic Organizer
Travel Brochure
Tribute or Eulogy
Venn Diagram
Video
Weather Map
Writing Fiction
Writing Nonfiction

From *A Teacher's Guide to Performance-Based Learning and Assessment* (p. 45) by Educators in Connecticut's Pomperaug School District 15, 1996, Alexandria, VA: Association for Supervision and Curriculum Development.

A *rubric* describes the various levels of performance. Like performance assessment, rubrics are not entirely new. If you've ever used a AAA® or Michelin guide to lodgings and restaurants, you have seen a rubric: clear, concise statements that detail the qualities that distinguish a two-star establishment from a four-star one. In education, rubrics are usually formatted as tables, with performance criteria running along one dimension (e.g., horizontally) and descriptions of the quality of the performance on each criterion running along the other dimension (e.g., vertically).

Figure 10.9 shows a rubric used by English language arts teachers in one California middle school to score their students' portfolios for reading. These teachers used traditional letter grades to identify levels of performance. In Kentucky, where students take statewide performance assessments, many teachers use descriptors taken from the rubric developed by the state: "Distinguished," "Proficient," "Apprentice," "Novice." Still other teachers

FIGURE 10.8   Performance Task/Assessment List

Responding to Literature—Creative Writing
The Adventures of Huckleberry Finn: High School

The Task: Creative Writing

Background: You have just completed the novel *The Adventures of Huckleberry Finn.*

Task: Create an additional chapter "Huck to Finn." This chapter may be an incident that occurs between two incidents already depicted in Huck's river journey or may be one that takes place after Twain's story closes. The choice is yours. Adhere to the parameters of the following assessment list to ensure that you will do your very best writing and not make Twain spin miserably in his grave!

Performance Task Assessment List. Creative Writing: *The Adventures of Huckleberry Finn*

| | ASSESSMENT POINTS | | |
| | Points | Earned Assessment | |
Element	Possible	Self	Teacher
Initial Understanding:			
1. Chapter shows accurate portrayal of character.	_____	_____	_____
Developing an Interpretation:			
2. Flows well stylistically and thematically with the existing text.	_____	_____	_____
3. Thorough and natural use of dialect and character voice.	_____	_____	_____
Critical Stance:			
4. Use of satirical elements: i.e., exaggeration, understatement, humor, caricature, irony, parody, etc.	_____	_____	_____
Connections:			
5. Chapter revolves around a key dramatic incident (humor, of course, may be used).	_____	_____	_____
6. Dramatic incident makes a statement about human nature.	_____	_____	_____
7. Proofread and polished. **MUST BE TYPED.**	_____	_____	_____
Total	_____	_____	_____

From *A Teacher's Guide to Performance-Based Learning and Assessment* (p. 159) by Educators in Connecticut's Pomperaug School District 15, 1996, Alexandria, VA: Association for Supervision and Curriculum Development.

FIGURE 10.9 Portfolio Grading Rubric: Reading

	Consistency and Challenge	Control of Processes	Self-Assessment and Reflection	Knowledge and Work Products
A	Reading done habitually almost every day, often for long periods of an hour or so. Readings not only entertain, but also challenge and stretch capabilities. Reads widely; experiments with new authors and forms.	Rereads and revises interpretations. Supports views with references to text. Uses a variety of strategies and response types. Shows persistence.	Sets complex goals for reading and achieves them. Applies personal/public criteria and supports judgments. Analyzes own processes thoughtfully.	Reads like a writer. Creates organized, complete, and effective work products. Learns new vocabulary regularly. Pays attention to literary and stylistic features of texts. Interprets shared readings personally and deeply.
B	Reading done habitually almost every day, often for shorter periods of time. Readings entertain, not so much challenge and stretch capabilities. Less experimentation with new forms, though perhaps tries new authors.	Tends to stick with one interpretation. Supports views but may need to explain more thoroughly. Uses less variety of strategies and response types. Sometimes shows persistence; sometimes satisfied when understanding could be improved.	Sets complex goals for reading and works to achieve them. Applies criteria to texts but with less clear support. Analyzes own processes superficially.	Creates organized and complete work products. Shows some attention to learning new vocabulary. Pays less attention to literary and stylistic features of texts. Understands shared readings thoroughly.
C	Reading done at least once or twice a week, often for brief periods of ten to thirty minutes. Readings mainly for entertainment. Little evidence of concern for experimenting with new authors or forms.	Interprets readings superficially. Only occasional support for own views. Relies on one or two strategies and response types. May give up easily or quickly when bored or challenged.	Sets simple goals for reading and achieves them. Applies criteria to texts mechanically. Analyzes own processes with clichés; may use reflective-type terms with little understanding.	Creates only superficially polished products. Occasionally shows interest in learning new vocabulary. Rarely pays attention to style and literary features. Understands shared readings superficially.
D	Reading done quite sporadically. Resists even readings that entertain. May not finish books.	Sketchy interpretations. Little, if any, support for views. Relies on one strategy or response type.	Sets simple goals and works to achieve them. Seems uninterested in own learning and processes.	Work products may be put together haphazardly. Little interest in vocabulary development. Evidence of exposure to shared readings.
F	Little or no evidence of reading.	Little evidence that the student interprets reading. Little evidence of views.	May set simple or no goals with little work. No evidence of interest in own learning	Few, if any, work products.

From *Middle School Portfolio Tool Kit* by the National Council of Teachers of English, 1996, Urbana, IL: Author.

have developed quality descriptors in more student-friendly language (e.g., "Awesome," "Getting There") or images (e.g., a lit electric bulb, a question mark). When developing rubrics, it is important to consider the effect of category names and descriptors on students. Reflect, for example, on the difference between receiving a designation of "Novice" (suggests someone who is still learning) and receiving a score of "Very Poor." Similarly, some rubrics begin with a glowing description of a top performance (thoughtful, insightful, perceptive, original) and work their way down the scale to a poor one (lacks insight, not original, carelessly done.) If the rubric is to be of any use to the student, the student must clearly understand what the various descriptors mean. That is, if a student is informed that her writing "lacks insight," what exactly is she supposed to do in order to improve?

Rubrics can be used to assign a holistic—or single—score, such as a letter grade or a category. Rubrics can also be used to assign analytic scores along several major dimensions of the performance. In writing, for example, a student might receive a score for purpose, organization, idea development, and mechanics. Rubrics are most useful for students and teachers when they are accompanied by student work samples, or *exemplars,* which illustrate each level of performance. This allows students themselves to place their work on a continuum of quality and to identify how they might improve their work.

Since rubrics are supposed to be tools to enhance student learning and self-assessment, whenever feasible students themselves should be involved in creating them. Goodrich (1996/1997) has recommended the following guidelines for developing and using rubrics with students:

1. Look at models. Show students examples of good and poor work and discuss the qualities that distinguish a good performance from a poor one.
2. List criteria. Use the discussion to generate a list of the distinguishing features of quality work.
3. Describe gradations of quality. Describe the top and the bottom levels first, then fill in the middle levels.
4. Practice on models. Have students practice applying the rubric to the models used in Step One.
5. Use peer- and self-assessment. As students work on a task, have them periodically apply the rubric to their emerging work or have it assessed by a peer.
6. Revise. Students should revise based on the information gained in Step Five.
7. Use the same rubric students used when you assess their work (pp. 16–17).

When teachers in a department or school collaborate on developing tasks, rubrics, and exemplars, then scoring becomes less subjective, time-consuming, and isolated. The conversations teachers have about what constitutes a task worth doing, what distinguishes quality work from work that is mediocre, and how one knows quality work when one sees it can lead to important insights about improving teaching and learning (Allen, 1998; Stiggins, 1995).

▌Reader Activity 10.3

THEORY INTO PRACTICE
Designing an Assessment

For this activity, you can continue to flesh out the skeletal unit plan you developed in Chapter Six or you may wish to choose a new topic. Choose a topic from your unit or from some other source in your subject area and create several samples of assessment that you might administer. The purpose of this activity is to give you experience with creating alternative assessments. At this point, the samples you create should be considered drafts; it is not necessary to perfect each one. The focus is on simply trying your hand at a number of different tasks. You may work alone or in small groups in your subject area. Choose one of these options:

- A performance assessment task to be administered at the end of an instructional unit.
- An end-of-course performance assessment.

Portfolios

Every experienced teacher knows that a student may perform well on one day and not on another. Similarly, a student may excel at one type of task (e.g., writing editorials) and not at another (e.g., writing poetry). Some students may excel at any task they undertake; others excel only in their specific areas of interest. Some students make amazing progress in the course of a school year; others progress only slightly. These are only a few of the reasons why *portfolios,* samples of a student's work collected over some period of time, have become a widely used tool for classroom assessment and are also being used in some states and school districts for large-scale assessment. Although interest in portfolio assessment in education has grown intense over the past decade, models, artists, and architects—to name only a few professions—have long used portfolios of their work to demonstrate what they know and can do. Professional portfolios are not static; portfolio keepers select from the whole body of their work and arrange selections to fit a particular purpose. In the classroom, students can use portfolios to show different facets of themselves as learners.

Teachers have differing philosophies about and approaches to portfolios, but many agree that using portfolios for classroom assessment purposes has at least the following benefits.

- Portfolios offer "the opportunity to observe students in a broader context: taking risks, developing creative solutions, and learning to make judgments about their own performances."
- Portfolios allow a student to be "a participant in, rather than the object of, assessment."
- Portfolios encourage "students to develop the abilities needed to become independent, self-directed learners" (Paulson, Paulson, & Meyer, 1991, p. 63).

If you believe these are valuable outcomes, then you may be interested in using portfolios in your own classroom.

The process of using portfolios for assessment sounds deceptively simple. Students *collect* their work in folders or other containers in your classroom. Periodically, students *select* work from their folders to be revised, adapted, or polished for inclusion in their portfolios. Students regularly *reflect* on the work completed or in progress and, ultimately, on the whole body of work in the portfolio in order to assess their own learning, accomplishments, strengths, weaknesses, and to set future goals (Paulson & Paulson, 1992). I call this process "deceptively simple" because logistical and instructional problems can arise at every step. For example, *collecting* work requires space (often at a premium), containers (cost money), and a system for keeping track of the work in the portfolio (extra time for teacher). *Selecting* work requires that there be enough pieces, both finished and unfinished, from which to make selections. For many teachers this requires completely rethinking their curriculum. For example, if a math portfolio requires evidence of problem-solving, then students need many opportunities to solve many different kinds of problems. Helping students to *reflect* on their work is probably the greatest challenge of all in portfolio assessment and the step that is most crucial in achieving the benefits suggested earlier.

Reflection in Portfolios

Reflection is the process of looking back on a learning experience and articulating what one has learned from it (Camp, 1992; Paris & Ayres, 1994). Most middle- and high-school students are not accustomed to thinking about their own thinking, much less putting those thoughts into words. Paulson and Paulson (1992) have described a "continuum of reflectivity" along which students move as they practice reflection: (1) "What I did"—the ability to state what is contained in the portfolio; (2) "What I learned"—the ability to make claims to specific learnings and to substantiate those claims by making reference to changing behaviors, attitudes, and practices; and (3) "What's next"—the ability to formulate, implement, and monitor "necessary next steps for professional and personal growth" (pp. 12–13). Figure 10.10 illustrates one tenth-grader's reflection on her learning in English.

Where would you place this student on the "continuum of reflectivity"? What did you learn about this student as a reader, writer, and learner that you might not have learned from looking at a page in a gradebook? What specific knowledge and skills does this student demonstrate here? How could a teacher use this information to make instructional decisions?

Teachers can model reflection and help students learn to reflect by providing questions which stimulate reflective thinking. Some sample questions appear in Figure 10.11.

School-wide Portfolio Assessment: Tucson Magnet High School

A motto of Tucson Magnet High School is "Anyone can work anytime, anywhere, on anything." Tucson Magnet High School has five buildings, over 2600 students, and 200 faculty and staff—all connected by a powerful computer network. Students maintain dedicated folders on the school file server and save their work as they progress through school. These dedicated folders enhance curriculum integration across the subject areas and over time. By senior year, students have essays, term papers, reports, pictures, movies, and web pages from which they can select to create an integrated portfolio of their high school experience. Upon graduation, each student is presented with a custom CD-ROM containing the contents of his or her folder to take into the world of work or higher education (Volpe, 1998). Technology holds great promise for many of the logistical problems (e.g., storage, transportability) associated with portfolio assessment.

Scoring Portfolios

Portfolios are usually scored or graded at the end of a semester or a course by means of rubrics that describe the varying levels of quality of the work in them. Most teachers allot some portion of the semester or course grade to the portfolio. Even though various pieces of work may have been graded along the way, teachers look at the pieces in the portfolio with fresh eyes. For example, a student may have revised a piece of earlier work so that it is now much improved. Some teachers ask students to select pieces of work that show their growth or progress over the course of the semester or year and to explain why they have selected these pieces. The role the portfolio plays in a student's

FIGURE 10.10   Excerpts of Reflective Letter from High School English Language Arts Portfolio

Before I begin, it is important that you, the reader, understand a few things about me. In the past English classes, the curriculum has included a unit of Shakespeare study. I never truly appreciated the language until this year. Comprehension of the language happened gradually. I became frustrated because I'd never given Shakespeare half a chance. This year, when we read *Hamlet*, I kept an open mind and worked hard to stay focused. The more we read, the easier it became to understand. . . .

In the future, I wish to continue reading a wide variety of literature as I've done throughout the school year. In the past, my parents and teachers have always encouraged me to read and I have done so with sincere ardor. Losing myself in the pages of a book and blocking out hassles of daily life is an important part of my weekly routine.

Until this year, I was still reading silly mystery books by R. L. Stine and Christopher Pike. This was partially because I'd never really been introduced to any other mystery authors. My teacher suggested I read a Mary Higgins Clark book and I did just that . . . all in the same night. I fell in love with these stories and whenever I pick one up, the book usually doesn't get put down until it is finished.

At the beginning of the year, I never thought I would ever actually read a classic novel in my free time. For class, we were required to read a classic and do a text reaction. Later on, I found myself reading another classic, and then another . . . all during my free time. One novel I especially enjoyed was *The Moonstone* by Wilkie Collins. It was a complicated mystery with a twisted ending . . . one I never would've guessed in a million years. That's what made it so great. The author kept my attention throughout the text. Inside and outside of class this year, I managed to read about thirty books . . . everyone of them appealed to me in one way or another. Recently, I became interested in poetry and have been reading selections by Robert Frost. . . .

One of my strengths in writing is selecting a theme from a book and expanding on it. This is done by using effective quotes to prove a point or solve a problem I've discovered. I get very involved when doing research for such projects and lose all sense of time, but not direction. I possess the ability to stay focused on the assigned task and it comes in handy when I have a lot of work to do. . . .

One weakness I plan to work on is the development of many types of moods. Usually, when I write the mood is peaceful and calm, but life doesn't always work that way. I need to learn to create a setting where the reader can feel the tension mounting or the fear running through the victim's body. Choosing to compose a wider genre of writings should help me accomplish this goal.

The portfolio I've assembled is one which represents me very well as reader, writer, learner. The goals I set for myself at the beginning of the year have been attained. My main obstacle I wanted to conquer was to write in a more mature manner . . . I feel I've accomplished this goal. I am very proud of myself for all the hours of hard work and dedication I have put into this representation of me. I have heeded Polonius' and Frost's words . . . above all I have been true to myself and taken the road less traveled by. I have celebrated learning and that has made all the difference. I hope you enjoy living the experience of my portfolio.

From *Assessing Student Performance, Grades 9–12* (pp. 48–50) by M. Myers and E. Spalding, Eds., 1997, Urbana, IL: National Council of Teachers of English.

FIGURE 10.11   Sample Questions for Student Reflection

Reflections on Single Pieces of Work
- What do you see as the strengths of this work?
- What was important to you as you were working on this piece?
- Is there a particular idea, topic, or technique you would like to investigate further as a result of your work on this piece?
- If you could go on working on this piece, what would you do?
- Is there anything about this piece that is still puzzling or intriguing to you?
- How did working with others help you better understand the concepts presented here?
- How did you know when this piece was finished?
- What do you need to do next?

Reflections on a Body of Work (Portfolio)
- What do these pieces show about you as a (writer, mathematician, historian, etc.)?
- What do you notice when you look at your earlier work?
- Are there any pieces here that you've changed your mind about (e.g., didn't like before but like now)?
- At what points did you discover something new about (writing, science, art)?
- How does this collection show your growth or mastery?
- In what ways has putting this portfolio together been a learning experience in itself?
- What kinds of (projects, problems, pieces) are still difficult for you?
- What is most important to you about each of these pieces?

Compiled from Claggett, 1996; Murphy & Smith, 1992; Stenmark, 1993.

grade depends upon "what portion of the course goals the portfolio is expected to represent" (Herman, Gearhart & Aschbacher, 1997, p. 41).

The most common advice for any teacher who is interested in exploring portfolios in the classroom is "Start small." Begin with only one class and take incremental steps toward building a portfolio program. Many teachers in various subjects and at all grade levels are successfully using portfolios. If you are active in your professional organization and read its publications, you will find many pointers and ideas for getting started with portfolios.

Pros and Cons of Performance Assessments and Portfolios

Alternative forms of assessment, such as performance tasks and portfolios, have both advantages and disadvantages. Some pros and cons of alternative assessment techniques are identified in Figure 10.12.

As stated in the introduction to this chapter, no single assessment technique is best for all purposes at all times. Your responsibility as a classroom teacher is to be informed of all the assessment options that are available and to select the ones most appropriate for your purposes.

▌ Reader Activity 10.4

CONSULTING OTHER SOURCES
Examining a Test You Have Taken

You will need to select, bring to class, and share with your classmates a college test you have taken. The purpose of this activity is to apply your emerging understanding of assessment and evaluation by analyzing an actual test critically and dispassionately. As you go through your archives, make note of the selection criteria you use to choose the test you will share. For example, you may decide to select a test on which you performed very well, on which you performed poorly, a test you considered "fun," a challenging final examination, a unique approach to assessment. This activity will be most interesting if, as a class, you bring together a variety of kinds of assessments and an array of levels of performance.

Apply the criteria for the various forms of assessment that have been introduced in this chapter to the test you have selected. For example, if you have selected an essay test, do the questions require higher-order thinking? Are expectations clear? Consider other issues surrounding the test you selected. Does this test raise any equity issues? To what extent does this test reflect Wiggins's *Assessment Bill of Rights,* Figure 10.1? How was the test graded? How was the information used? How was the score reported?

In small groups, share your tests and analyses. Compile your observations within the small group (e.g., types of assessments, grade ranges, clarity of items, degree to which the assessment elicited higher-order thinking, opportunity to revise, etc.). Then, debrief as a whole class and attempt to create a composite of the information that surfaced in this analysis.

Discuss the implications of this activity for teaching and learning at the college level and at the middle- and high-school level. For example, many high-school teachers say they continue to give multiple-choice tests because this is the form of testing that dominates at the college level. What did your class analysis reveal? There is also a common belief that one purpose of testing at the undergraduate level is to "weed out" those who lack aptitude for the subject. Were any of your findings relevant to this belief? To what degree did the tests you analyzed as a class assess the ability to demonstrate learning in context? To what degree were assessments "authentic"?

▌▌▌ RECORDING AND REPORTING RESULTS

Despite the quantity and quality of information teachers gather about student learning, most of it boils down to a single letter in a grade book or on a report card. At this point, you may be beginning to feel uncomfortable with the notion of condensing what you as a teacher know about student learning and progress into an A, B, C, D, or F. And you would not be alone. Many teachers, students, parents, and school administrators are frustrated with traditional forms of recording and reporting grades, yet—particularly at the high school level—little progress has been made in devising alternatives. Elementary schools have been much more successful in moving away from traditional grading practices by substituting narratives for letter grades, using scales to describe students' progress along a continuum, and using portfolios to illustrate student learning and progress to parents. One reason for this is that elementary teachers generally work with one, relatively small group of students throughout a school year. As long as middle- and high-school teachers must record and report on the learning of over one

FIGURE 10.12   Advantages and Disadvantages of Performance Assessments and Portfolios

ADVANTAGES	DISADVANTAGES
They evaluate both products and processes of learning.	The judging of process may be seen as subjective.
They allow the integration of learning and assessment.	They may require teachers to change their teaching style.
Evaluation is not limited to a single score.	Evaluation can be subjective and inequitable if standards are not set and shared by students and teachers.
They provide more information about a student's progress.	They may require more individualized instruction and less whole-class instruction.
They encourage students to take charge of their own learning.	Teachers need to spend time explaining, modeling, and practicing personal, social, and communication skills required to successfully complete performance tasks and portfolios.
Students feel that they are part of the assessment process.	Students who are accustomed to producing "the one right answer" may resist new forms of assessment.
They help develop skills necessary for lifelong learning.	They require a level of self-discipline that not all students have.
They may actually reduce the daily burden of grading papers.	They require a reorganization of classroom time and space to allow for conferencing, observing, and other assessment-related activities.
Information gained from portfolios and performance assessments is meaningful and substantial.	Interpreting and using the information gained from performance assessments and portfolios can be complicated and time-consuming.
They provide a continuous example of a student's work in a context that is relevant and understandable.	The student's work may not be understandable to those unfamiliar with the context unless explanations are provided.
They assess global understanding and thinking skills.	Teachers will probably need to give up some breadth of "coverage" in order for students to do work in depth.
Parents tend to understand and approve of this form of evaluation because it is personalized.	Parents may be more familiar with traditional assessment practices and question the value of the information gained from portfolios and performance assessments.

Adapted from "Making Assessment a Meaningful Part of Instruction" by D. A. Gilman, R. Andrew, and C. D. Rafferty, 1995, *NASSP Bulletin, 79*, pp. 20–24.

hundred students per grading period, it is unlikely that much will change in this area. How can you ensure that the grades you assign reflect as fairly as possible what a student knows and can do? How can you ensure that students and parents understand the meaning of the grades you assign?

Accurate Recording of Assessment and Evaluation Information

While most teachers use commercially produced grade books, Aker (1995) points out that these

> ". . . make it difficult to group and organize the information a teacher collects about students. For example, scores on unit tests and examinations are often recorded next to scores on quizzes and assignments, so it is difficult for a teacher to make a distinction between the various types of work the students are doing. As well, commercial plan books foster the assumption that student performance must always be reduced to a number which can be recorded in a block in a column" (p. 29).

Aker's solution was to create his own customized binders. He enters his class lists on computer (so that he can add or delete students as the year progresses), and runs off several copies of the lists for each class that he teaches. He uses one set of lists to record attendance, another to record homework and classwork, another for projects, another for tests. Keeping forms of assessment separate allows him to see patterns of progress or lack of progress. The binder format also allows him to create forms for recording his observations of students and for summarizing the results of conferences.

Computer gradebook programs help teachers organize and calculate grades more quickly and accurately than ever before. Most such programs allow users to combine letter and number grades, weight categories of grades, keep attendance, and add comments to students' records (Newby, Stepich, Lehman, & Russell, 2000). One great advantage to this technology is that keeping yourself, your students, and their parents or guardians informed of students progress is now very simple. However, you should remember that electronic gradebooks have the same limitations as commercial gradebooks: you must reduce performances to numbers and it is difficult to keep different forms of assessment separate. As you move into teaching, you will need to think critically and creatively about how you will record assessment information.

Reporting Assessment and Evaluation Information

Because we are collecting all this information for the benefit of students and their learning, students should always be aware of their standing in your class. If you allow papers and projects to pile up and do not grade and give feedback promptly, students (and their parents) may be justifiably upset when grades are assigned at the end of a reporting period. This is another reason why planning for assessment and evaluation is critical to effective teaching.

Guskey (1996) has provided three general guidelines that can help you ensure that your grading and reporting practices are "fair, equitable, and useful to students, parents, and teachers" (p. 20).

1. *Begin with a clear statement of purpose.* This statement should address "why grading and reporting is done, for whom the information is intended, and what the desired results are" (p. 20).
2. *Provide accurate and understandable descriptions of student learning.* Even if this description is reduced to a single letter, students and parents must understand what that letter represents. For example, does a B represent level of achievement

only or were other factors, such as attendance or progress, involved in calculating the grade?

3. *Use grading and reporting methods to enhance, not hinder, teaching and learning.* The common practice of averaging, Guskey points out, can lead to an inaccurate picture of student learning: "If students demonstrate that past assessment information no longer accurately reflects their learning, that information must be dropped and replaced by the new information" (p. 21). Similarly, the practice of assigning zeros for late or missing work can have a devastating effect on students' grades, especially when averaging is used.

Of all the important decisions you will make as a teacher, decisions about grades can be the most difficult for you and the most significant for your students. If you take this responsibility seriously, you will continue to educate yourself in this area and to reflect often and critically about the grading and reporting practices you employ in your teaching.

▌▊ THE ROLE OF EXTERNAL ASSESSMENT AND EVALUATION

External assessments originate outside your classroom. Most often, external assessments are standardized, multiple-choice tests designed and marketed by large testing companies and required by districts and states. The stated purpose of such tests is accountability. *Accountability* may be defined as "responsibility for general school processes and student achievement, including confirming that resources were effectively used and using assessment results to provide information to the public about what children have learned" (Educators in Connecticut's Pomperaug Regional School District 15, p. 273). When important consequences to teachers and/or students are linked to external assessments, they are known as *high-stakes assessments.* Over the past two decades, the trend in external assessment has been toward greater accountability and higher stakes for schools, teachers, and students. In Chapter Five, "Considering Curriculum for Middle- and High-School Students," Richard showed how the classroom curriculum of teachers in Texas has been affected by the Texas Assessment of Academic Skills. Kentucky provides another example of a comprehensive, high-stakes accountability system, which relies partially on performance assessment and portfolios for information about student learning.

▌▊ HIGH-STAKES TESTING AND ACCOUNTABILITY: THE CASE OF KENTUCKY

In 1990, the Kentucky legislature passed the Kentucky Education Reform Act (KERA), an ambitious, multifaceted plan "to see that all children learn and that they learn at a high level of academic knowledge and skill" (Prichard Committee for Academic Excellence, 1995, p. xiii). Soon after, the Kentucky Instructional Results Information System (KIRIS) was designed to inform the public of the progress of Kentucky schools toward this goal. Student achievement is tested annually at key grade levels and in a variety of subject areas. At its inception, KIRIS testing was performance-based; that is, the assessment included open-ended items, on-demand writing, and, for some grade levels and subjects, portfolios and performance events. In 1999, KIRIS was replaced by the Commonwealth Accountability and Testing System (CATS), which includes a multiple-choice component and no performance events. Students' scores on CATS form a major part of an accountability index, which is calculated for each school in the state. Each school is evaluated on its progress toward meeting a level of performance that is calculated and set by the state. CATS scores are reported (and highly publicized) annually, but every two years high-stakes consequences occur. Successful schools receive monetary rewards; schools that do not show progress are designated "in decline" or "in crisis." A school "in decline" is assigned a "Highly Skilled Educator," whose role is to help the school develop an improvement plan. If a school is designated "in crisis," all certified staff are placed on probation and parents will be able to transfer their children to a successful school (Petrosko, 1996). This sanction has yet to be invoked.

What have been the effects of KIRIS and CATS on students and teachers? For one thing, test scores have been steadily, and in some cases dramatically, improving (Blackford, 1997). In some respects, the idea of "creating tests worth teaching to" seems to be working. For example, students are reading and writing more because the tests require students to read and write as opposed to selecting a correct answer. Teachers focus their instruction on core content that they know will be tested and participate in professional development activities that enhance their understanding of the tests and of how to link instruction to assessment. Many teachers regularly use the scoring rubrics developed by the state to assess student work, and many Kentucky students can accurately describe the quality of their work using the language of the rubrics.

On the other hand, there have been bitter feuds within school faculties over the distribution of reward money and accusations against teachers for attempting to cheat on the tests, for example, by correcting errors in students' writing portfolios. Prior to the spring testing period, many schools stage pep assemblies to urge students to do their best. During testing, students are offered meals, snacks, and free time as incentives. After testing, some schools reward students with picnics, parties, and field trips. Such practices may cultivate cynicism and the belief that "bribes" have a place in education.

While no other state has enacted accountability measures as stringent as Kentucky's, you will undoubtedly encounter some form of high-stakes testing as a teacher. You will have to make decisions about the extent to which this testing will influence teaching and learning in your classroom. You will need to know how to interpret and use the information yielded by large-scale testing. Finally, you must make sure that you and your students fully understand the purpose, limits, and consequences of external assessments.

▌Reader Activity 10.5

WHAT WOULD YOU DO?
Teaching to the Test

Laura Barnum, a special education teacher with fifteen years experience, teaches at East Jessamine Middle School, a suburban/rural school in central Kentucky. Laura serves as a resource teacher at her school, which is moving closer to full inclusion. Laura's goals are not just to help her students succeed in school and in life but to educate other teachers about how they can integrate students with various types of disabilities into the regular classroom and the life of the school. Laura is especially enthusiastic about tapping in to her students' multiple intelligences and believes her students would be more successful in regular classrooms if more teachers used this approach.

Two years ago, Laura noticed that none of her special education students had been targeted to participate in an eighth-grade trip to Washington, D. C. She knew that two of her students, Tom and Jarrod, were history buffs—even though both were far below grade level in their reading and writing skills. When she approached the teacher in charge of the trip to see why no special education students had been included, she was told that chaperones were concerned about possible behavior problems with special education students. She assured them that Tom and Jarrod would present no problems. Then, she learned that students would be required to keep a journal of their experiences and that, since Tom and Jarrod could not write well enough to record their observations, they weren't eligible to go along. Laura suggested that the boys might keep visual rather than written journals. The teacher in charge of the trip was open to this alternative. Tom and Jarrod, armed with their sketchbooks, happily boarded the bus for Washington with the rest of their class. According to their current teacher, the boys still refer to this trip as a high point in their lives to date.

Kentucky's statewide testing system is noteworthy in at least two ways. First, all students—except those with the most serious disabilities—participate in the assessment. Secondly, much of the assessment requires constructed response, although multiple choice items comprise a portion of the test. As Laura talked with her students during and after the tests in March, she realized that her students knew much more than they were able to show on the test. Ella, for example, could talk knowledgeably about events in ancient history, but her written response to a test question on the Pelopponesian War was practically incomprehensible. Laura went home and thought through the steps her students would need to take to be successful on the statewide test. And, thus, GO cards were born.

Laura knew her students had the knowledge to succeed on the tests, but they needed help with organizing and expressing that knowledge. Laura studied the list of verbs, disseminated by the Department of Education, which commonly appear in test questions. She selected ten to use with her students. She paired each verb with a graphic (G) organizer (O). For example, she paired the verb "compare" with the Venn diagram. Each student received a jumbo index card. On the top of each card, students wrote the verb in large letters, defined it, and drew the graphic organizer. Along the bottom, students wrote key words to use in responding to this kind of item. As a class, the students identified topics and developed Venn diagrams. Laura then modeled how to write a paragraph based on the diagram. Students practiced by writing group paragraphs, and, finally by writing individual paragraphs. Laura followed this procedure with nine more key verbs. She stressed—and eventually her students agreed, "If you fill out the organizer first, then writing the paragraph is no big deal." By the time state testing was due to begin, each of Laura's students had a set of GO cards, punched and put on a ring. Since the state allows special education students to use resources such as scribes and reference books as indicated on Individualized Education Plans (IEP), Laura's students were able to use their GO cards to help structure their responses to open-ended questions in the content areas.

In addition, the students made up a "Silly Sentence" to help them remember how to approach the testing situation: "Really fat ostriches waddle sideways." This sentence reminded them to *Read* the question carefully, to *Focus* on key words by underlining and circling them, to *Organize* their thoughts using their GO cards, to *Write* their responses, and to *Stretch* their responses by concluding with a personal evaluation of the topic or issue.

At the conclusion of annual testing, students hung their GO cards on hooks in Laura's classroom and now use them whenever they are called upon to construct responses to tasks in their academic subjects.

Questions for Reflection

1. Many people criticize teachers for "teaching to the test." Was Laura's use of class time to teach test-taking strategies justified?
2. How, if at all, could regular education students benefit from instruction such as Laura devised?
3. On the basis of this vignette, what seem to be key points to remember in modifying instruction and assessment to accommodate students with special needs?

▌▌▌SUMMARY

At the beginning of this chapter, I shared with you some of my own history as a "test-taker" and "test-maker" and how I gradually evolved from a "point collector" to a more "thoughtful assessor." Writing that history helped me to see with greater clarity the awesome responsibility that comes with the power to evaluate others. When I look back on the assessment and evaluation practices I employed in my first years of teaching, I am struck by my naive arrogance in believing that the As, Bs, Cs, Ds, and Fs I doled out represented some absolute truth about my students' learning. As you move into teaching, I urge you to approach the assessment process with thoughtfulness and humility. Carelessly designed assessments and hastily assigned grades may have little effect on students who always perform well academically, but may very well curtail the educational opportunities, occupation, and future income of students who are less adept at "doing school." Among the key points to remember are:

- Both assessment and evaluation involve gathering information about student learning in order to make relevant instructional decisions. Because these decisions have weighty consequences, it is important to understand the terminology of assessment and assumptions underlying the use of assessment.
- Students' cultural, ethnic, linguistic, socioeconomic, individual backgrounds, as well as the opportunities they have had to learn and practice skills being tested, contribute to their performance on assessments. Teachers must design equitable assessments.
- Assessment requires planning. Planning "backwards" is one approach to assessment.
- Well-designed, traditional forms of classroom assessment can be efficient means of gathering information about student learning.
- Alternative forms of classroom assessment are more time-consuming, but have the potential to yield greater insight into students' knowledge, learning, and understanding.
- When rubrics are developed by students and teachers and used regularly to assess performance, students have greater opportunity to become skilled self-assessors.
- Recording and reporting methods should enhance, not hinder, teaching and learning.
- Helping students become self-assessors should be the ultimate goal of assessment.

This chapter concludes Part Two of this book, "Classroom Contexts of Teaching." The chapters in this section—managing classrooms, creating curriculum, planning for instruction, using technology, selecting instructional materials, implementing instruction, and assessing student learning—were intended to give you a solid introduction to the central instructional tasks of middle- and high-school teachers. In Part Three, you will be introduced to the professional contexts of teaching. In addition to being an effective teacher in the classroom, you no doubt hope to have a long and rewarding career in education. The chapters in Part Three examine many of the factors that play a role in teachers' careers.

▪▪ BUILDING YOUR BIOGRAPHY, YOUR PERSONAL PRACTICAL PHILOSOPHY, AND PORTFOLIO

Building Your Biography

What experiences in your life are relevant to becoming a thoughtful assessor of student work? The following questions are intended to help you compose a chapter of your educational autobiography on this topic. They are not intended to be answered sequentially or to limit your exploration of the topic.

- How many tests do you think you have taken in all your years of schooling?
- How many grades have you been assigned?
- Do you recall tests or grades that had a significant impact on your life?
- Have you ever questioned the results of a test or the fairness of a grade?
- What kind of "test-taker" are you?
- Do you recall a particularly good experience with testing? A particularly bad experience?
- How do you know when you have done quality work?
- What experiences do you have with tests outside of school, e.g., earning a driver's license, merit badges in scouting, lifeguard certification? How, if at all, do such experiences differ from academic tests?
- What influence might your own experience with tests have on how you test as a teacher?

Developing Your Personal Practical Philosophy

Draft a section of your personal educational philosophy that addresses issues of assessment and evaluation. You might respond to questions such as the following.

- In your subject area, what would an assessment system look like that fairly reflects what all students know and can do?
- Are some of the assessment strategies described in this chapter more or less relevant for teaching and learning in your subject area?
- How can you create equitable assessment conditions in your own classroom?
- To what extent should individual, sociocultural, linguistic, and other differences be accommodated in assessment and evaluation?
- What are the purposes of assessment and evaluation?
- To what extent are the students you expect to teach capable of self-assessment?
- What is the value of self-assessment?
- What are the purposes of grades?

- Is it possible/desirable for all students in a class to earn high grades?
- What factors will you consider when assigning grades?
- What is the role of accountability in public education?
- Who should be held accountable—Students? Teachers? Schools? Superintendents?
- How will you as a teacher react to large-scale, high-stakes testing?
- What are your personal characteristics that might predispose you to implement some of the assessment strategies described in this chapter and not others?

Collecting Artifacts for Your Portfolio

Review the Reader Activities you have completed in this chapter. Identify any that you might eventually select for your portfolio. For each, jot down notes that will help you recall later what you were thinking at the time you completed the activity, what challenges you encountered while completing it, what you learned from doing it, and how this activity reveals something about who you will be as a teacher. Don't worry about style or correctness at this point. The purpose is to document your thinking as you move through this book and this class.

References

Aker, D. (1995). *Hitting the mark: Assessment tools for teachers.* Markham, Ontario: Pembroke Publishers Limited.

Allen, D., Ed., (1998). *Assessing student learning: From grading to understanding.* New York: Teachers College Press.

Blackford, L. B. (1997). Improved scores found in majority of state schools. *Lexington Herald-Leader,* Friday, December 5, pp. A1 & A8.

Camp, R. (1992). Portfolio reflections in middle and secondary classrooms. In K. B. Yancey, (Ed.), *Portfolios in the writing classroom,* pp. 61–79. Urbana, IL: National Council of Teachers of English.

Carroll, J. B. (1995). Reflections on Stephen Jay Gould's the mismeasure of man: A retrospective review. (Book Review.) *Intelligence, 21* (1), 121–34.

Claggett, M. F. (1996). *A measure of success: From assignment to assessment in English language arts.* Portsmouth, NH: Heinemann.

Educators in Connecticut's Pomperaug Regional School District 15. (1996). *A teacher's guide to performance-based learning and assessment.* Alexandria, VA: Association for Supervision and Curriculum Development.

Farr, B. P. & Trumbull, E. (1997). *Assessment alternatives for diverse classrooms.* Norwood, MA: Christopher-Gordon Publishers, Inc..

Fronk, R. H. & Knight, L. B. (1994). *Earth Science. Annotated Teacher's Edition.* Austin, TX: Holt, Rinehart & Winston.

Gerver, R., Cater, C., Molina, D., Sgroi, R., Hansen, M., Westgaard, S. (1997). *Algebra 2: An Integrated Approach. Teacher's Annotated Edition.* Cincinnati, OH: Southwestern Educational Publishing.

Gilman, D. A., Andrew, R. & Rafferty, C. (1995). Making assessment a meaningful part of instruction. *NASSP Bulletin, 79* (573), 20–24.

Gladwell, M. (1999). The physical genius. *The New Yorker,* August 2, pp. 56–65.

Goodrich, H. (1996/1997). Understanding rubrics. *Educational Leadership, 54* (4), 14–17.

Guskey, T. R. (1996). Reporting on student learning: Lessons from the past—prescriptions for the future. In T. R. Guskey, Ed., *Communicating student learning,* pp. 13–24. Alexandria, VA: Association for Supervision and Curriculum Development.

Hanson, F. A. (1993) *Testing, testing: social consequences of the examined life.* Berkeley, CA: University of California Press.

Herman, J. L., Gearhart, M., & Aschbacher, P. R. (1996). Portfolios for classroom assessment: Design and implementation issues. In R. C. Calfee and P. Perfumo, Eds., *Writing portfolios in the classroom: Policy and practice, promise and peril,* pp. 27–62. Mahwah, NJ: Lawrence Erlbaum.

Hill, B. C. & Ruptic, C. A. (1994). *Practical aspects of authentic assessment: Putting the pieces together.* Norwood, MA: Christopher-Gordon Publishers.

Hilliard, A. G. III. (1990). Misunderstanding and testing intelligence. In J. I. Goodlad & P. Keating (Eds.), *Access to knowledge* (pp. 145–158). New York: College Board.

Kindsvatter, R., Wilen, W. W., Ishler, M. F. (1988). *Dynamics of effective teaching.* White Plains, NY: Longman.

Madaus, G. F. & Kellaghan, T. (1996). Curriculum evaluation and assessment. In P. W. Jackson, (Ed.), *Handbook of research on curriculum,* pp. 119–156. New York: Macmillan.

Maton, A., Hopkins, J., Johnson, J., LaHart, D., Warner, M. Q., Wright, J. D. (1994). *Exploring Life Science. Teacher's Edition.* Englewood Cliffs, NJ: Prentice Hall.

Murray, D. M. (1990*). Write to learn.* (3rd ed.). Orlando, FL: Holt, Rinehart and Winston.

Murphy, S. & Smith, M. A. (1992). *Writing portfolios: A bridge from teaching to assessment.* Markham, Ontario: Pippin Publishing.

Myers, M. & Spalding, E., Eds. (1997). *Assessing student performance, Grades 9-12.* Urbana, IL: National Council of Teachers of English.

National Center for Restructuring Education, Schools, and Teaching. (1993). *Authentic assessment in practice: A collection of portfolios, performance tasks, exhibitions, and documentation.* New York: Author.

National Council of Teachers of English (N. D.). *Middle school portfolio tool kit.* Urbana, IL: Author.

Neill, M., Bursh, P., Shaeffer, B., Thall, C., Yohe, M., & Zappardino, P. (N. D.). *Implementing performance assessments: A guide to classroom, school, and system reform.* Cambridge, MA: FairTest.

Newby, T. J., Stepich, D. A., Lehman, J. D., Russell, J. D. (2000). *Instructional technology for teaching and learning: Designing instruction, integrating computers, and using media.* Second edition. Upper Saddle River, NJ: Merrill/Prentice Hall.

Paris, S. G. & Ayres, L. R. (1994). *Becoming reflective students and teachers with portfolios and authentic assessment.* Washington, DC: American Psychological Association.

Paulson, F. L. & Paulson, P. R. (1992). The varieties of self-reflection. *Portfolio News 4* (1), 1 & 10–14.

Paulson, F. L., Paulson, P. R., & Meyer (1991). What makes a portfolio a portfolio? *Educational Leadership, 51* (5), 38–42.

Petrosko, J. M. (1996). Assessment and accountability. In *A Review of Research on the Kentucky Education Reform Act 1995.,* pp. 57–98. Prepared by the University of Kentucky/University of Louisville Joint Center for the Study of Educational Policy. Frankfort, KY: Kentucky Institute for Education Research.

Shriner, J. G., Ysseldyke, J. E., Thurlow, M. L. & Honetschlager, D. (1994). "All" means "All"— Including students with disabilities. *Educational Leadership, 51*(6).

Stenmark, J. K. (1993). Assessment alternatives in mathematics. In L. Darling-Hammond, L. Einbender, F. Frelow, & J. Ley-King (Eds.). *Authentic assessment in practice: A collection of portfolios, performance tasks, exhibitions, and documentation,* pp. 45–60. New York, NY: National Center for Restructuring Education, Schools, and Teaching.

Stiggins, R. J. (1997). *Student-centered classroom assessment.* (2nd ed.). Upper Saddle River, NJ: Merrill-Prentice Hall.

Strichart, S. S., Mangrum, C. T., Iannuzzi, P. (1998). *Teaching study skills and strategies to students with learning disabilities, attention deficit disorders, or special needs.* Second edition. Boston, MA: Allyn and Bacon.

The Prichard Committee for Academic Excellence (1995). *Keepin' on: Five years down the road to better schools.* Lexington, KY: Author.

Volpe, M. (1998). *Cultural artifacts of literacy at a Southwestern magnet high school.* Paper presented at "Inside Portfolios," a conference sponsored by the National Council of Teachers of English, San Jose, CA, January 15–17, 1998.

Wiggins, G. P. (1993). *Assessing student performance: Exploring the purpose and limits of testing.* San Francisco: Jossey-Bass.

Wiggins, G. P. (1996). Honesty and fairness: Toward better grading and reporting. In T. R. Guskey, Ed., *Communicating student learning.* (pp. 141–177). Alexandria VA: Association for Supervision and Curriculum Development.

Websites

http://www.fairtest.org/

The National Center for Fair & Open Testing (FairTest) is an advocacy organization working to end the abuses, misuses and flaws of standardized testing and ensure that evaluation of students and workers is fair, open, and educationally sound.

http://www.kde.state.ky.us/

The home page of the Kentucky Department of Education. To learn more about the assessment and accountability system described in this chapter. select "Assessment and Accountability" and explore the site. You can even take a sample test online.

http://www.cse.ucla.edu/

Funded by the U.S. Department of Educational and the Office of Educational Research and Improvement, the National Center for Research on Evaluation, Standards, and Student Testing (CRESST) conducts research on important topics related to K-12 educational testing.

http://stone.web.brevard.k12.fl.us/html/comprubric.html

Contains tips on rubric construction and using technology to improve assessment.

http://score.rims.k2.ca.us/index.html

This is the site of the Schools of California Online Resources for Education. Click on the various subject areas to see examples of standards-based units and assessments.

part

Professional Contexts
of Teaching

11

Understanding the Role of Community

BUILDING ON BIOGRAPHY: A STORMY START TO THE FIRST YEAR OF TEACHING

On a late August morning in 1974, I (Liz) arose after a nearly sleepless night and shakily prepared to set off in my red Volkswagen Beetle for my very first day as a teacher. As I drove the ten or so miles to Valley High School, my fears of being a total and immediate failure in the eyes of my adolescent students abated somewhat. In fact, my jitters about controlling a classroom full of unruly teenagers turned out to be unnecessary. Although I was handed class rosters listing some thirty names for each class, the halls were noticeably uncrowded, and when the bell sounded the beginning of first period, only five or six students sat scattered about the room. As the day progressed, the pattern held. In no class were more than ten students present. The Kanawha County Textbook Protest was underway in Charleston, West Virginia.

During the summer months preceding the start of the school year, I had been aware that trouble was brewing over the language arts textbook adoptions in my school district. When I had gone to the Board of Education building to sign my contract and fill out other personnel forms, a crowd of protesters were brandishing homemade placards proclaiming "No Dirty Books" and shouting at people (like me) entering and leaving the building. I had no idea how these people and the many others involved in the protest would influence my first year as a teacher.

The rural/suburban high school where I was hired to teach served a mostly blue-collar community. The largest employers were the chemical and coal industries. Many families lived "up the creek" or "up the hollow." The few African American families lived in a neighborhood that most whites and some blacks referred to as "L.A."—"Little Africa." The community was predominantly Protestant, and many of the churches could be described as fundamentalist in their beliefs. It had never occurred to me that this community would be one of the hot spots of the Textbook Protest and that, as a result, parents would keep their children out of school in droves. Even though I had grown up only a few miles away, I was as unfamiliar with Valley High's culture as if I had grown up several states away.

Soon after that first day of school, protesters began picketing the school parking lot. They didn't stop teachers, staff, and students from entering, but they certainly made us uncomfortable. When area coal miners went on strike—some ostensibly in sympathy with the textbook protesters—and joined the picket lines, we teachers grew even more uncomfortable. One hot afternoon during the first month of school, the principal's voice blared over the intercom: "Teachers! I want you to shut your windows and lock your doors. Do not leave your rooms or let any students leave your room. Do not panic. There's nothing to worry about." We were later informed that angry, striking miners with shotguns were roaming around the school grounds. Although no violence happened that day or any day in my school, violent incidents did occur elsewhere in the county, and a nearby elementary school—empty at the time—was bombed. How could textbooks cause such turmoil?

In *Storm in the Mountains* (1988), James Moffett, the author of one of the most vilified textbook series in the adoption, has provided a thorough account of events and an insightful analysis of issues surrounding the protest. Among other charges, the textbooks were accused of promoting "relativism in language usage," which Moffett calls "an oblique conservative strategy that makes it possible, while upholding proper grammar, to discriminate against minority dialects in literature selections" (p. 14). Mrs. Alice Moore, a member of the school board and a leader of the protest called the books "filthy, trashy, disgusting, one-sidedly in favor of blacks, and unpatriotic" (p. 15). Widely distributed fliers mixed textbook excerpts, taken out of context, with text and graphics of a sexual nature taken from books that were not even part of the language arts adoption. In full-page newspaper ads paid for and written by the protesters, I recognized excerpts from many works of literature that had been anthologized and read by high-school students for years. The writers of the ads had combed the literature selections for every expletive or slang word they could find, and these words and phrases were reprinted out of context as a great catalog of obscenities with the warning, "This is what your children are studying in English class!"

Eventually the textbook protest faded from the front page, the pickets disbanded, the miners went back to work, and schools negotiated with parents about what books could and could not be read by their children. Students began trickling back to school, and the second semester of my first year of teaching began normally. I, like many young and inexperienced teachers, had been wary of parents from the outset. The textbook protest made me even more reluctant to communicate with parents and certainly contributed to the general feeling that the school and the community were adversaries, not partners, in a common enterprise of educating youth.

Over the next five years, I learned a great deal about the community that Valley High School served. I helped organize homecoming parades, which were as widely anticipated and as enthusiastically attended as any Macy's Thanksgiving Day Parade. The Latin Club, which I sponsored, met monthly, each time in a different student's home—although we never met in the home of an African American student, and my African American students informed me that they simply could not attend parties "up the creek," as they feared for their safety. When my Latin students begged me to take them to Rome, we held car washes and bake sales to raise money. Parents—most of whom were working class and few of whom had traveled outside West Virginia, let alone the United States—paid the bulk of the expenses and were grateful for the opportunity to give their sons and daughters the gift of a European tour. Parents volunteered to chaperone and transport students to statewide Junior Classical League (a national organization for Latin students) events. They donated pet food and supplies to our club's service project for the local humane society.

I eventually discovered that parents were not the enemy, but my greatest allies in building a flourishing Latin program at Valley High School. I now realize that those who attacked the textbooks in Kanawha County were as sincere and passionate in their opposition as those who defended them. The view many other teachers and I held at the time—that the educational establishment was "enlightened" and "right" and the protesters were "ignorant" and "wrong"—is simplistic and biased.

Questions to Consider

1. From this brief account what cultural values do you believe were contested in the Kanawha County Textbook protest?
2. To what extent are teachers obligated to respect and preserve community values, especially when they may conflict with teachers' personal values?
3. The Kanawha County Textbook Protest occurred in 1974. How have schools and society changed since that time, regarding censorship issues?

▉▉PURPOSE

Tensions are inherent in public education. Sometimes these tensions erupt into open conflicts, as in Kanawha County, West Virginia. Moffett (1988) summarized the complexity of the issues that continue to challenge public education in America:

> Public schools not only mirror society but also provide a theater for enacting society's conflicts. In the school district come together all the factions of a community that otherwise might not have to deal with each other. For business, religion, recreation, and social life a populace can go different ways, but unless families opt out of public schools at their own expense, education remains the exception. As the central meeting place where differences are smoked out, the classroom becomes an arena for contending over divergent ways of life and modes of thought (p. 209).

How will you as a teacher manage the differences within and factions of the school and classroom community to which Moffett refers? To what communities will you belong as a teacher and how will you participate constructively in them? Often beginning teachers are so overwhelmed by planning and implementing instruction, evaluating student work, maintaining an orderly learning environment, and supervising extracurricular activities that they neglect cultivating relationships with other members of the school community. This is understandable but unfortunate because school administrators, other teachers, community agencies, local businesses, and most importantly, parents and guardians all play a role in helping you become a successful teacher. The main purposes of this chapter are to introduce you to some of the principal players in school communities and to help you think about how you will interact with them as you enter the classroom. Specifically, this chapter will help you:

- define "community" and identify individuals and groups that compose a school's community;
- understand your role as a member of communities within the school, e.g., as a member of a faculty, a subject-matter department, an interdisciplinary team, or a collaborative classroom;
- understand the origins and functions of school-based councils;
- plan to have productive relationships with parents and guardians;
- become aware of the many ways in which schools and communities collaborate to improve education for all students, including school-to-work programs, service learning projects, and the growing trend toward schools that offer comprehensive services.

▉▉WHAT IS COMMUNITY?

In his essay "Building a Responsive Community," John Gardner (1995) contrasts traditional with contemporary communities and identifies six ingredients of today's and tomorrow's successful communities. In the past, traditional communities—schools, congregations, neighborhoods, towns—were relatively homogeneous. They changed little from year to year. They were often suspicious of outsiders and demanded conformity from insiders. Members of traditional communities shared generations of history and continuity.

This description no longer fits many contemporary communities. Recall, for example, the description in Chapter Two, "Understanding Multiculturalism," of Monterey Park, California and Mark Keppel High School; of Garden City, Kansas; of Pensacola, Florida and Brown Barge Middle School. Gardner (1995) offers us a new vision of community. First, successful contemporary communities are characterized by "wholeness incorporating diversity":

> To prevent the wholeness from smothering diversity, there must be a philosophy of pluralism, an open climate for dissent, and an opportunity for subcommunities to retain their identity and share in the setting of larger group goals. . . . To prevent diversity from destroying the wholeness, there must be institutional arrangements for diminishing polarization, for teaching diverse groups to know one another, for coalition-building, dispute resolution, negotiation and mediation" (p. 169).

Reflect upon some of the successful schools and programs described in previous chapters. How did these schools and programs illustrate "wholeness incorporating diversity"?

Second, successful contemporary communities are characterized by "a reasonable base of shared values" (p. 170). This does not mean that all values must be shared, but a "reasonable" number must. As diversity increases in this country, Gardner argues, we must identify shared secular values such as liberty, justice, and tolerance, all of which transcend religious differences. In Kentucky, where I work, incidents are periodically reported of middle-and high-school students wearing or displaying the Confederate flag, a symbol that many whites and African Americans view as racist. Many schools regard the display of the Confederate flag as an offense worthy of suspension or expulsion. Sometimes students, backed by their parents, defend their behavior by claiming "freedom of speech and expression." How could a "reasonable base of shared values" mediate such situations? For example, would it be possible for educators, students, parents, and other adults in the community to reach consensus on a core set of values upon which school dress and behavior codes might be built?

Third, Gardner avers that caring, trust, and teamwork are essential to successful communities.

> The members of a good community deal with one another humanely, respect individual differences, and value the integrity of each person. A good community fosters an atmosphere of cooperation and connectedness. There is recognition and thanks for hard work, and the members are aware that they need one another. There is a sense of belonging and identity, a spirit of mutual responsibility . . . . altruism . . . . trust . . . . tolerance . . . . loyalty. Everyone is included. There is room for mavericks, nonconformists, and dissenters; there are no outcasts (p. 171).

Reflect upon how the above statement applies to your own experiences of schools and communities. Also, consider how this description might apply to some of the students described in Chapter Three, "Knowing Middle- and High-School Students," for example, "Jocks" and "Burnouts."

Fourth, participation, ". . . a two-way flow of influence and communication . . ." (p. 173), characterizes successful communities. This means that many individuals are willing to share leadership tasks and to speak out on issues of concern. As you reflect on your own past and present school experiences, how and to what extent do parents participate in the school community? Students? Teachers? Who carries out leadership tasks?

Fifth, successful communities reaffirm themselves and build their own morale. They celebrate their history, traditions, and shared values. Recall, for example, the efforts of Garden City, Kansas to celebrate and affirm new traditions. Are time-honored high-school traditions, such as homecoming, proms, and pep assemblies examples of affirmations that all members of the community are valued?

Finally, according to Gardner, successful communities have "institutional arrangements for community maintenance" (p. 176). That is, the maintenance of community is not left to chance; rather, mechanisms are in place to pass on shared values and leadership to the next generation, to maintain participation, and to resolve conflicts. Many educational reforms fail to survive changes of leadership and personnel because provisions have not been made to maintain a supportive school community. In *Horace's Hope: What Works for the American High School* (1996), Theodore Sizer describes the reforms that have been taking place at Thayer Junior-Senior High School in Winchester, New Hampshire since 1981. Sizer attributes much of the school's current success to the visionary and stable leadership of principal Dennis Littky. Littky established routines, such as encouraging teachers to write him weekly letters to which he responded individually, in an effort to build and maintain a coherent school community. Although Littky moved on in 1994, his successor, Jed Butterfield, shares his values and vision for Thayer, which, according to Sizer, continues to flourish. As you read in the pages that follow about the various participants in school communities, keep Gardner's attributes in mind and reflect upon how they apply to groups and individuals who comprise a school's community.

▌Reader Activity 11.1

CONSULTING OTHER SOURCES
The Many Facets of School Communities

For this exercise, draw upon your experiences in the school community in which you grew up and/or the school community in which you are currently involved. Brainstorm and list as many members of a school's community as you can. Then work with a partner to create a web that illustrates the relationships among the many individuals and groups that might compose a school community. Share your webs in small groups. Expand or revise your web based on small-group sharing. Then, select a group or individual depicted in the web. Locate, read, and bring to class an article from an educational journal or periodical that addresses how classroom teachers can work with this group or individual in a positive way. Prepare to explain why you selected this topic and article; summarize its contents; identify how Gardner's six attributes apply to the article; and suggest its value to prospective teachers. After sharing in small or large groups, as a class discuss the extent to which Gardner's six attributes are useful for discussing successful contemporary school communities.

▌▌CONNECTING WITH COMMUNITIES WITHIN A SCHOOL

Although teaching has long been viewed as an isolated profession (Lortie, 1975), more and more educators are realizing the benefits of collegiality. Seymour Sarason (1993) has described the personal satisfaction that can be derived from one's peers: "There are many things money can't buy, and one of them is the sense that you are continuing to experience the sense of growth with and from children and with and from colleagues. Over the long run, it is these two senses that keep you willingly engaged in your work" (p. 67). In this section, you will be introduced to several ways teachers work collegially: communities of inquiry, high-school subject departments, middle-school teams, and collaborative classrooms.

In addition to the personal rewards of working with like-minded colleagues are the professional payoffs in improving the school experience for both students and teachers. When teachers come together to focus on identifying ways to improve teaching and learning, the results can be powerful (Allen, Cary & Delgado, 1995). Brubacher, Case, and Reagan (1994) describe what happened when teachers at Center Park High School decided to look closely at the school's high ninth-grade dropout rate. The teachers read and discussed literature about students who drop out, listed the assumptions they had been making about such students, and then divided into task groups to test the validity of their assumptions. The teachers studied attendance records, grades, and test scores. They gathered information from other teachers and interviewed successful tenth-graders, dropouts, and the parents of both groups of students. While their research confirmed some of their assumptions, it also revealed a number of surprises. For example, although the teachers had assumed that drug abuse played a role in students' dropping out, they discovered that it was more commonly a consequence of having dropped out. Overall, the teachers gained a greater understanding of the situation, finding it much more complex than they had originally predicted. Equipped with a more accurate picture of students who drop out and their reasons for doing so, the teachers were ready to begin solving the problem. Many classroom teachers are engaged in individual inquiries about student learning, but inquiry conducted with colleagues can ultimately lead to personal growth and transformation of school culture (Cochran-Smith & Lytle, 1996).

Another level of community within the school is subject departments. Research on secondary school teaching reveals that the colleagues who matter most are the members of one's subject department. Even when schools restructure into "houses" or interdisciplinary teams, teachers tend to retain their identity as subject specialists and to see the subject department as their professional home (Siskin & Little, 1995). Not all subject departments, however, are cohesive and collegial. In her study of academic departments in secondary schools, Siskin (1994) described several departmental configurations ranging from "bonded" in which "members all work collaboratively with a high degree of commitment toward departmental goals" to "fragmented" in which teachers simply "do their own thing" (p. 99).

Siskin found that department norms can differ even within a school, and she describes a single high school in which one department is fragmented, while another is bonded. The first did little "to promote or organize . . . [friendships], or to foster rituals of inclusion or a sense of commitment to collective endeavor" (p. 103). Teachers in the second department, on the other hand, regularly shared materials and plans, visited one another's classrooms, and shared responsibility for leading the department. According to Siskin, "Even a new teacher was quickly brought into the group discussions of school and district problems—and demonstrated his loyalty by taking on the extra duties of union representative despite the countervailing demands of a new job and a new baby" (p. 103). As you begin to work in schools and eventually seek employment in one, it is important to pay attention to how subject departments function in school settings.

While subject departments remain the dominant form of community at the high-school level, many middle schools organize students and teachers into interdisciplinary teams. Middle school teams share the same group of students, the same part of a building, and the same schedule and planning time. These are the foundations of teamwork. The actual work of a team falls into four categories. First, teams share common methods of organization. They collaboratively develop and enforce team rules and procedures. They share a common approach to communicating with parents and to using school time. Second, they actively work on community-building. They accomplish this through developing team names, mottoes, and symbols. They plan and implement units as a team, produce team publications, and stage a variety of group activities. Third, they teach as a team. They plan together and implement interdisciplinary instruction either along parallel courses or in integrated blocks. Finally, a team has some form of self-governance and is represented in the governance of the school (George, Lawrence, & Bushnell, 1998).

Many schools use the designation *collaborative* for classrooms in which general education and special education teachers work together to meet the needs of all students. This is perhaps the most challenging collegial relationship of all, as teachers have historically been soloists. They have not been required to negotiate teaching tasks, procedures, or rules. Collaborative classrooms, on the other hand, include at least two certified teachers and often at least one paraprofessional. Two teachers (Kimbrell-Lee & Wood, 1994) who have become adept at this form of collaboration share this advice for beginners.

1. *Double-up and teach.* For example, one teacher might lead discussion while the other records on the whiteboard.
2. *Double your space.* The special education teacher probably has his/her own classroom, which may be empty during the collaborative period(s). Use this space to provide a quiet setting for those who need it or to conduct conferences with individuals.
3. *Capitalize on each other's strengths.* For example one member of the team may have strong technology skills, while another has subject-area expertise.
4. *Be positive role models.* When disagreements arise, as they certainly will, demonstrate to students how conflict can be handled respectfully and constructively.
5. *Stand together on discipline.* Not surprisingly, students may try to pit one teacher against the other, much as they do their parents. Collaborating teachers need to agree on and consistently apply classroom policies and procedures.
6. *Plan together.* Collaborating teachers need a minimum of one planning period per week together. Collaborating for inclusion is not easy, but teachers who have done it successfully extol its benefits for themselves and for their students.

■■ SCHOOL-BASED COUNCILS AS FORMS OF COMMUNITY

Historically, individual schools have had little control over such areas as textbook adoption, staffing, budgeting, or allocation of time and space within a school. These decisions have usually been made at the state or district level, with schools and teachers expected to comply and enforce policy. Recall, for example, that the Kanawha County Textbook Protest I described at the beginning of this chapter was sparked by a district-level decision on textbook adoption. However, one trend in current educational reform is to place decision-making power in the hands of school-based councils. In fact, between 1986 and 1990, one-third of all school districts had some form of school-based management, and since 1990, at least five states have mandated this form of governance (David, 1995/1996).

School-based councils are undergirded by the belief that "school improvement is best achieved by giving the people closest to the student the authority to make important decisions . . ." (David, 1994, p. 704). Because school-based councils are composed of a variety of representatives of the school community, they can also help to build the kind of successful contemporary community described by Gardner earlier in this chapter. The powers of councils vary, but their responsibilities may include decisions about school personnel, curriculum and textbooks, extracurricular activities, discipline policies, and allocation of physical and financial resources. While the composition of councils varies, they usually include the school principal, teachers, parents, and sometimes students and other members of the community. In Kentucky, Texas, Chicago, and Dade County, Florida, school-based councils are required by law, but many schools are instituting school-based management and participatory decision-making as part of a comprehensive reform plan (Sandidge, Russo, Harris & Ford, 1996).

Why should you, as a prospective teacher, be concerned about school-based councils? From a pragmatic perspective, you may be interviewed by council members before you are offered a teaching position, as school councils often play a role in hiring personnel. Therefore, you need to have some knowledge of school-based councils' powers and responsibilities, and you need to be prepared to respond to questions and concerns of the various representatives. While you may have no interest in serving on a school-based council during your first years of teaching, you do need to know who serves on your school council and how you can participate in the decision-making process. As a member and citizen of your school community, you may eventually be called to serve on your school council.

The implementation of school-based councils challenges teachers to acquire and use skills and knowledge that were not needed when all important decisions were made by district and state personnel. Teachers who serve on school-based councils need ". . . skills in setting agendas, soliciting input from their larger constituencies, holding efficient meetings, delegating authority, and feeding back information to others" (David, 1994, p. 709). Participation in school-based councils and on the various committees connected to them is an additional responsibility for teachers, who are already charged with the primary responsibility of educating students. Some teachers question whether the time spent on school-level committee work might be better spent on planning for instruction. Whether school-based decision-making does indeed improve student learning outcomes remains to be seen; however, ". . . to the extent to which SBDM [school-based decision-making] has brought parents and educators together to work for the common good of students, it is off to a promising start" (Sandidge, Russo, Harris, & Ford, 1996, p. 327).

▌ Reader Activity 11.2

In the Field
Observing School Communities at Work

The purpose of this activity is to give you a first-hand look at how school communities function. Following is a list of meetings of various types you might attend. (Obtain permission from the proper authorities to attend the meeting(s) you select.) Attend alone or with a partner, observe and take notes, and then report back to the class.

Possible meetings to attend:

1. A subject-department meeting
2. A middle-school team meeting

3. A site-based council meeting
4. A school committee meeting
5. A meeting to establish a program for or assess the progress of a student with special needs

---

▪▪ PLANNING FOR PRODUCTIVE RELATIONSHIPS WITH PARENTS AND GUARDIANS

In 1994, Public Agenda, a nonpartisan, nonprofit public opinion research and education organization, published the results of its national telephone survey of 1,100 adult Americans, half of whom were parents of children in public schools at the time. According to Public Agenda, their report, entitled *First Things First: What Americans Expect From the Public Schools,* explained "why support for education reform by the public is languishing" and highlighted ten findings that suggested that what the public says it wants from public schools and what educators think the public wants are out of sync (Public Agenda, 1997). The ten findings are summarized in Figure 11.1.

How should you as a beginning teacher respond to this report? In considering the implications of these findings, you should keep in mind that only one-half of the respondents actually had children in public schools at the time of the survey. Those without children in public schools may have based their responses primarily on popular media reports, which tend to sensationalize "bad news," such as violence, falling test scores, and cases of inappropriate and unprofessional behavior by educators. On the other hand, the findings—especially the apparently contradictory ones—indicate that schools may not be doing a very good job of communicating with the community about their work. For example, most respondents stated that schools should teach tolerance and equality; at the same time, respondents had little concern about multicultural content in the curriculum and some were opposed to tolerance of homosexuality. While most respondents agreed that students should not be bored or fearful in school and that learning should be interesting and fun, they also were skeptical about teaching strategies designed to engage and challenge students, to provide more equitable learning opportunities, and to teach tolerance and equality through social interaction.

The Public Agenda Report captured educators' attention. Since its publication, many professional organizations and journals have issued guidelines for enhancing the public's and parents'/guardians' involvement with schools. For example, the Education Commission of the States recommends that schools and school personnel: (1) listen to people first and talk later; (2) be clear about what it means to set high standards for all students and what it will take to meet them; (3) show how new ideas enhance, rather than replace, old ones; (4) make involving parents and the community a top priority; and (5) help parents and other community members understand how students are assessed and what the results mean (Brandt, 1998).

While elementary schools have historically been more attuned to involving parents as partners in their children's education, middle and high schools are now seeking to promote parental engagement and support as well. One example is D. R. Hill Middle School in Duncan, South Carolina. The school sponsors family nights twice a year and offers incentives for parents and students to attend. In family night sessions, teachers and school personnel explain and demonstrate why the school is implementing certain practices and methodologies, such as writing across the curriculum. The school dis-

FIGURE 11.1 Public Agenda's Ten Findings

1. Americans want schools to provide a safe, orderly environment and effective teaching of "the basics."
2. The public supports raising academic standards, but does not believe this can be accomplished unless or until finding #1 is in place.
3. The majority of those surveyed were uncomfortable with new teaching methods that often accompany school reform, e.g., focus on understanding concepts rather than rote learning in mathematics; focus on writing processes rather than grammar and spelling in composition; focus on performance assessments rather than standardized, multiple choice tests.
4. The public rejects schools which promote boredom and fear. They want learning to be interesting and enjoyable for their children. They want school to help children become more confident and self-assured.
5. Concerns about sex education and multiculturalism are not at the top of the public's list of concerns with public schools.
6. People want schools to teach tolerance and equality.
7. Parents want the help of public schools in educating their children about sex. However, parents are divided about whether and how schools should address specific topics in the area of sex education, e.g., abortion, homosexuality, sex outside of marriage.
8. Traditional Christian parents share most of the same concerns about public schools as the majority of those surveyed. However, they have special concerns about sex education, the content of assigned reading, and the inclusion of Christian religious materials in the curriculum.
9. African American parents share most of the same concerns about public schools as the majority of those surveyed. However, they are more dissatisfied with their local schools. They want more candid sex education and are concerned about negative stereotypes in curricular materials.
10. While Americans still trust educators to make decisions about running schools, "some specific findings about teachers and principals suggest that substantial numbers of Americans are not completely confident about their performance and judgment."

From *First Things First: What Americans Expect from the Public Schools* (p. 3–6) by Public Agenda, 1994, New York, NY: Author.

seminates and analyzes parent satisfaction surveys, invites parents to attend school with their children for a day, and sponsors an early morning reading program for students whose parents must get to work (Rasmussen, 1998). Such work with the community can be critical to the success of innovation.

What Parents and Guardians Want from Teachers

As a beginning teacher, you may feel some anxiety about communicating with parents and guardians. If you are in your early twenties, you may feel intimidated because most parents of adolescents may be at least a decade older than you. Furthermore, both novice and experienced colleagues may be eager to share stories of unpleasant encounters with students' parents and guardians. At the high-school level, communications between educators and parents have historically been minimal, confined to phone calls reporting misbehavior or conferences concerning academic underachievement. Conventional wisdom has it that parents of adolescents just don't want to be involved.

This wisdom is supported by anecdotes of sparsely attended parent-teacher conferences and evening open houses. Yet, according to the president of the National Parent Teacher Association, "We know from three decades of research that children with involved parents do better in school and are more successful in life" (National PTA, 1997).

How can you as a beginning middle- or high-school teacher increase the involvement of the significant adults in students' lives? When asked, parents consistently voice three broad concerns: (1) How much does a teacher *know and care* about teaching? (2) How much does a teacher *know and care* about my child? (3) How much does a teacher *know and care* about communicating with me? (Rich, 1998). Generated from these three major concerns, the following guidelines can help you communicate effectively with parents and guardians.

1. *Communicate your knowledge of and enthusiasm for teaching and students.* You can do this every day in the classroom and in your interactions with parents/guardians inside and outside school.
2. *Show that you know your students, understand how they learn, and value them as individuals.* When you talk with parents/guardians, be prepared to mention positive attributes about students.
3. *Put yourself in the shoes of the parent and empathize that parents have a tough job.* A comment such as, "I know you're working hard to help Ernest get to school on time and I really appreciate that" can go a long way toward setting a pleasant tone for a conference.
4. *Use plain language.* Teachers are familiar with educational terminology, such as "criterion-referenced" or "stanine." Most parents are not. Be conscious of your audience.
5. *Demonstrate that your expectations for behavior are fair, consistent, and respectful.* It helps to have a written management plan. Some teachers distribute classroom rules in the first days of school and require students to take them home for adult signatures. However, in communicating your policies, adhere to the guidelines listed above.
6. *Demonstrate that your academic expectations are high, yet attainable.* It's a good idea to distribute an abbreviated syllabus to parents via a letter home or during "Back-to-School" night. Display examples of student work that meets your expectations and keep examples in your files to share with parents.
7. *Show interest in parents' views of and goals for the student.* Parents are usually eager to share this information with you if you ask and then listen.
8. *Be accessible and responsive to parents.* Although such information is always available in the central office of a school, many teachers ask students to complete index cards with adult contact information during the first days of school. Return all calls from parents promptly—preferably the same day. In a letter home to parents, suggest best times and ways to contact you.
9. *Contact parents promptly with any behavioral and/or academic concerns and persist in trying to build partnerships.* If your discipline policy requires a call to the home after a certain number of infractions, don't procrastinate. Also, do not procrastinate on academic problems, hoping a student will improve without intervention. Even if parents do not return your call promptly, do not give up after one attempt at contact.
10. *Be the bearer of good news as well as bad.* Many teachers set aside a regular time to call parents/guardians. Sometimes they call simply to pass on a compliment: "I want to let you know how much I appreciate Silvia's leadership skills. She is an

asset to whatever group she is working in." Some teachers create standardized forms that they fill out right away when a student has accomplished something noteworthy. Students are usually eager to take such notes home and share with parents (Davern, 1996; Giannett & Sagarese, 1998; Rich, 1998).

Programs to involve middle-and high-school parents and guardians as school volunteers are becoming more widespread. Even if parents cannot demonstrate their engagement by coming to the school, their engagement at home remains important. Research has documented that two broad categories of parental engagement at home are associated with school performance: holding high expectations for a student's school success; and providing a supportive home environment (Thorkildsen & Scott Stein, 1998). You can encourage parental engagement at home by communicating your academic expectations, by suggesting how parents can help students achieve course goals, by encouraging them to talk with their children about school, by inviting them to review and comment on student work, and even by involving them in projects and assignments (Finn, 1998).

Technology is enhancing school/home communications. Many schools have Web pages containing important information about the school. Student work of all sorts can be posted to the Web page (after student and parent permission is obtained), and those outside the school can get a clear idea of what's going on inside. Some teachers create personal Web pages conveying essential information about themselves and their teaching. While many teachers still do not have telephones in their classrooms, voice-mail systems and e-mail are making it much easier to communicate with parents. Many schools have "homework hotlines" from which students and parents can obtain information on assignments. As mentioned earlier in this book, computerized gradebooks and attendance data are more accurate, up-to-date, and easy to read than traditional forms of recording and are more "parent-friendly." The "mail merge" feature of word-processing programs allows teachers to personalize written communications in ways that were not possible before.

When Parents/Guardians Disagree

Despite your knowledge, training, and best efforts to communicate, parents and guardians may disagree with your classroom practices or selection of instructional materials. What should you do when you receive complaints? First, you should be familiar with district or school policies on this issue. These policies should be shared with parents and can be used to resolve conflicts. Willis (1995) suggests the following guidelines to help you avoid or minimize conflicts.

- Seek community input before selecting books and other texts. If you know a topic is controversial, consider forming an advisory committee that represents a range of perspectives.
- Have a written policy and procedures for dealing with complaints.
- If a protest should occur, focus on how the community was involved in the selection process, the content of the book, and how it is used in your classroom.
- Remember that curriculum must reflect the knowledge of experts and scholars as well as the culture of the community.
- Acknowledge that context doesn't necessarily legitimize all offenses. For example, parents or guardians may be offended by the use of the word *nigger* in *The Adventures of Huckleberry Finn,* regardless of the fact that the novel is a classic work of American literature.

▌Reader Activity 11.3A

THEORY INTO PRACTICE
Written Communications

Using the guidelines offered earlier, design the following kinds of written communication: (1) a beginning-of-school letter introducing yourself and informing parents/guardians what they can expect their children to learn in your class; (2) a personal note home informing parents/guardians of something good their child has done in class; (3) a personal note home requesting a conference concerning a student who is not performing well in your class. Make sure your communications give parents/guardians enough information so that they know the purpose of the conference.

Consider the fact that not all parents/guardians speak or read English. Draw upon the language resources in your class and ask volunteers to produce written communications in languages other than English that you are likely to encounter in the classroom (e.g., Spanish, Japanese, Korean).

Bring your drafts to class and share them with a small group of peers for feedback.

▌Reader Activity 11.3B

THEORY INTO PRACTICE
Verbal Communications

Using the guidelines offered earlier, work with a partner to role-play the following telephone communications.

1. Earl is a twelfth-grade honors student intent on gaining admission to a prestigious university. Nevertheless, in your class for this grading period, Earl earned a "B" because he did mediocre work on a major project. His mother, a prominent citizen in the community, has called and left a message that she would like to discuss Earl's grade with you. Return the phone call.
2. Shannon sleeps in class. You know she is the single parent of an infant and that she lives with her parents. Make the call to her home and discuss Shannon's behavior with a parent. Try to come up with a plan that will help her stay awake in class.
3. Cal is failing your class. He is the star of the school baseball team. If he fails, he will be ineligible to play at the beginning of the season, and his chances of receiving an athletic scholarship will be jeopardized. Cal's father has left a message that he would like to discuss Cal's future with you. Return the call.
4. For the third time in three weeks, Sasha has stormed out of your class in tears after being asked to change her seat because of her incessant chatting. She has told the school counselor that you don't like her and that you do not discipline other students who talk just as much as she does. The current infraction calls for in-school suspension. You have already had an unpleasant encounter with Sasha's grandmother—her guardian, who believes Sasha can do no wrong. Now, you must call Sasha's grandmother to inform her of this disciplinary action.

Full-service schools offer activities, enrichment, sports, and workshops for students and members of the community.

■■ CONNECTING WITH COMMUNITIES THROUGH SERVICE AND WORK

As more and more middle and high schools seek ways to engage communities as partners in education and to improve student learning, many have expanded the services they offer, embedded service to the community in the school curriculum, and enlisted the help of business and industry in preparing students for employment and careers. In this section, we will briefly examine these three avenues for reconnecting with communities.

Full-service schools aspire to be "one-stop centers where the educational, physical, psychological, and social requirements of students and their families are addressed in a rational, holistic fashion" (Dryfoos, 1996). As society has grown increasingly bureaucratic, services have become more difficult to access. Those who advocate full-service schools reason that, because most children pass through the public schools, the school is the logical site to offer comprehensive services to the community. Intermediate School 218 in New York City is an example of a full service school. It opens at 7:00 a.m. to offer breakfast and activities to students and remains open until 10:00 p.m. to offer enrichment, sports, and workshops for students and members of the community. The school also offers weekend and summer programs. A Family Resource Center offers social services, and there is a health and dental clinic on site (Dryfoos, 1996). Expanding school services requires additional funds, personnel, and space, but the investment may pay off in students who are physically and psychologically ready to learn and families who can support them in their learning.

While full-service schools may be a trend for the future, many schools and individual teachers are implementing service learning as an immediate way to reconnect schools and communities. Service learning seeks to "promote students' self-esteem, to develop higher order thinking skills, to make use of multiple abilities, and to provide authentic learning experiences—all goals of current curriculum reform efforts" (Kahne & Westheimer, 1996). In addition, service learning projects offer students the opportunity to practice citizenship while meeting community needs. Service learning projects may involve students in analyzing environmental issues, compiling and publishing an oral history of the community, tutoring younger students, or working with the homeless. When service learning is integrated into the curriculum, both academic and social goals can be met. For example, art students at Spring Harbor Middle School in Madison, Wisconsin became interested in supporting Habitat for Humanity. As a class, they decided to raise money for Habitat by collecting, restoring, and decorating old chairs for resale. The chairs symbolized the comforts of home. The classroom teacher provided lessons in color, design, and painting techniques, while the students also practiced interpersonal and written communication skills in organizing and conducting a silent auction of the completed chairs at a local mall (Petto, 1998). Service learning can be integrated into any subject, and students of all ages are capable of contributing to the welfare of their community.

A third major avenue through which schools are attempting to reconnect with communities is through school-to-work or career exploration programs. In contrast to traditional, job-specific vocational education, school-to-work programs seek to meet the academic and occupational aspirations of a broad range of students. Many high schools now offer career "academies" through which students explore employment opportunities in health care, travel and tourism, public safety, or technical fields. While studying academic subjects, students in school-to-work programs also complete paid or unpaid internships and assume job responsibilities under the guidance of a worksite mentor. The goal is for students to leave high school with authentic, problem-solving skills in a given field; a realistic idea of the opportunities and constraints offered by a particular career path; an appreciation of the link between academic and workplace learning; and connections to adult practitioners and, eventually, to employment (Goldberger & Kazis, 1996).

Community-based instruction and community-based employment programs allow students with mental and physical disabilities to gain social and vocational skills that will enable them to make a successful transition to independent living (Culatta & Tompkins, 1999). For example, instructional programs may use nondisabled peer tutors to model and teach appropriate behaviors in such settings as restaurants, theaters, and shopping malls. Employment programs offer training and experience at a job site and, ideally, culminate in job placement. (Hardman, Drew, & Egan, 1999).

The initiatives described above are indicative of educators' growing consciousness that schools and communities must work in partnership to address the changing intellectual, social, emotional, and physical needs of today's middle-and high-school students. Just as the image of the teacher as an isolated expert dispensing knowledge to passive learners is changing, so too is the image of the middle or high school as an efficient and impersonal factory. Today, many businesses are adopting policies and implementing practices that address the complex human needs of their employees. Schools, perhaps more than any other institution, have the potential for creating caring communities in which all members can acquire and practice the skills needed to sustain our sense of common humanity in a rapidly changing world.

■■ SUMMARY

I began this chapter by describing my experiences with the school community of Valley High School as a beginning teacher. Many members of this community were leaders and supporters of the Kanawha Valley Textbook Protest. Like many new teachers, I was wary of parents at the outset. The Kanawha County protest reinforced my perception that parents and guardians were my adversaries, not my allies. Over the next several years, however, I learned I was wrong. I owe my proudest achievements and fondest memories of Valley High School to the support and trust of parents and guardians who were deeply committed to their children's education.

Most of the preservice teachers with whom I work today are just as reluctant as I was in 1974 to initiate dialogue with parents and other concerned adults. They are confident and competent before a class of sixteen-year-olds, but they shrink at the thought of parent-teacher conferences. While this chapter is no substitute for actual experience, it should at least have stimulated you to reflect upon the strategies you will use to draw parents into partnership with you.

Likewise, when I began teaching I did not see myself as a member of a teaching/learning community nor do I think other teachers at Valley High School saw themselves in this role. The other teachers in my department were friendly enough, but we rarely discussed teaching or learning. Department meetings focused on bureaucratic or clerical matters. When you begin teaching, you may be tempted to shut your classroom door and keep your problems and your questions to yourself. I hope this chapter has convinced you to do otherwise.

Among the key points to remember are:

- Successful contemporary communities balance wholeness and diversity, share core values, practice participatory democracy, and continually reaffirm and renew themselves.
- While teaching has historically been an isolated profession, collaboration and teamwork increasingly characterize teaching today.
- Collaboration is essential to successful departments, teams, and inclusive classrooms.
- School-based councils have made school governance more democratic and participatory.
- Teachers must plan for and invite parent/guardian involvement.
- Most parental conflicts can be resolved through listening and negotiation.
- More and more schools are making an effort to reconnect with the community.

It is not too early to begin thinking of yourself as a member of a school community, and we hope that as you begin your work in schools you will contribute to the creation and maintenance of a vital and thriving community of teachers and learners. In Chapter Twelve, "Making a Difference in Today's Classrooms," Richard will introduce you to teachers who are making a difference by functioning as members of teams, of the school community, and of the larger community.

BUILDING YOUR BIOGRAPHY, YOUR PERSONAL PRACTICAL PHILOSOPHY, AND PORTFOLIO

Building Your Biography

You are now ready to compose a "chapter" of your educational biography on the topic of community. The following questions are intended to help you generate ideas for writing. They are not intended to be answered sequentially or to limit your exploration of the topic.

- To what extent do you believe your K-12 and college experiences promoted a sense of community?
- How was wholeness achieved and diversity accommodated?
- What values were shared by your school and your community? What values were contested?
- To what extent were your own parents or guardians involved in your school and your education?
- What do you recall about interactions between your parents or guardians and your teachers?
- What, if anything, do you recall about the interactions among the teachers in the schools you attended? How did the schools you attended celebrate their history, traditions, and shared values?
- What services did the schools you attended offer the community?
- Did you ever participate in a service learning project—even though it might not have been called that—or a school-to-work program? What did you learn from the experience?

Developing Your Personal Practical Philosophy

Draft a section of your personal educational philosophy that addresses your position on "community." You might respond to questions such as the following.

- Why should you, as a beginning teacher, be concerned with the idea of community?
- What is the relationship between community and student learning?
- How can you create effective communication with parents and guardians and encourage their involvement in their children's education?
- What barriers can you foresee to inviting parents to be partners in education? How, if at all, can these barriers be overcome?
- How can you, as a beginning teacher, participate constructively as a member of a team or subject department?
- What are your personal characteristics that might predispose you to building community or to isolating yourself?

Collecting Artifacts for Your Portfolio

Review the Reader Activities you have completed for this chapter. Identify any that you might eventually select for your portfolio. For each, jot down notes that will help you recall later what you were thinking at the time you completed the activity, what challenges you encountered while completing it, what you learned from doing it, and how this activity reveals something about who you will be as a teacher. Don't worry about style or correctness at this point. The purpose is to document your thinking as you move through this book and this class.

References

Allen, J., Cary, M., & Delgado, L. (1995). *Exploring blue highways: Literacy reform, school change, and the creation of learning communities.* New York: Teachers College Press.

Brandt, R. (1998). Listen first. *Educational Leadership 55*(8), pp. 25–30.

Brubacher, J. W., Case, C. W., & Reagan, T. G. (1994). *Becoming a reflective educator: How to build a culture of inquiry in the schools.* Thousand Oaks, CA: Corwin Press.

Cochran-Smith, M., & Lytle, S. L. (1996). Communities for teacher research: Fringe or forefront? In M. W. McLaughlin & I. Oberman, Eds., *Teacher learning: New policies and practices,* pp. 92–114. New York: Teachers College Press.

Culatta, R. A., & Tompkins, J. R. (1999). *Fundamentals of special education: What every teacher needs to know.* Upper Saddle River, NJ: Merrill/Prentice Hall.

Davern, L. (1996). Listening to parents of children with disabilities. *Educational Leadership, 53*(7), 61–63.

David, J. L. (1994). School-based decision making: Kentucky's test of decentralization. *Phi Delta Kappan, 75*(9), 706–712.

David, J. L. (1995/1996). The who, what, and why of site-based management. *Educational Leadership 53*(4), pp. 4–9.

Dryfoos, J. G. (1996). Full service schools. *Educational Leadership 53*(7), 18–23.

Finn, J. D. (1998). Parental engagement that makes a difference. *Educational Leadership 55*(8), pp. 20–24.

Gardner, J. (1995). Building a responsive community. In A. Etzioni (Ed.), *Rights and the common good: The communitarian perspective,* pp. 167–178. New York: St. Martin's Press.

George, P., Lawrence, G., & Bushnell, D. (1998). *Handbook for middle school teaching.* 2nd edition. New York: Longman.

Giannett, C. C. & Sagarese, M. M. (1998). Turning parents from critics to allies. *Educational Leadership 55*(8), pp. 40–42.

Goldberger, S. & Kazis, R. (1996). Revitalizing high schools: What the school-to-career movement can contribute. *Phi Delta Kappan 77*(8), 547–554.

Hardman, M. L., Drew, C. J., & Egan, M. W. (1999). *Human exceptionality: Society, school, and family.* 6th edition. Boston, MA: Allyn & Bacon.

Kahne, J. & Westheimer, J. (1996). In the service of what? The politics of service learning. *Phi Delta Kappan 77*(9), 592–599.

Kimbrell-Lee, J. & Wood, T. (1994). The inclusive writing workshop. In M. Dalheim, (Ed.), *Toward inclusive classrooms,* pp. 39–52. Washington, DC: National Education Association.

Lortie, D. C. (1975). *Schoolteacher: A sociological study.* Chicago: University of Chicago Press.

Moffett, J. (1988). *Storm in the mountains: A case study of censorship, conflict, and consciousness.* Carbondale, IL: Southern Illinois University Press.

National Parent Teacher Association (1997). New standards to bolster parent involvement in education. Press Release. Washington, DC: Author.

Petto, S. G. (1998). Art and service learning: Connection within a community of shared experience. *Network 7*(2), 1–3.

Public Agenda. (1994). *First things first: What Americans expect from the public schools.* Press Release and Summary. New York: Author.

Rasmussen, K. (1998). Making parent involvement meaningful. *Education Update 40*(1), pp. 1, 6–7.

Rich, D. (1998). What parents want from teachers. *Educational Leadership 55*(8), pp. 37–39.

Sandidge, R., Russo, C. J., Harris, J. J., & Ford, H. H. (1996). School-based decision making, American style: Perspectives and practices throughout the United States. *Interchange, 27*(3 & 4), 313–329.

Sarason, S. B. (1993). *You are thinking of teaching? Opportunities, problems, realities.* San Francisco: Jossey-Bass.

Siskin, L. S. & Little, J. W., (Eds.) (1995). *The subjects in question: Departmental organization and the high school.* New York: Teachers College Press.

Siskin, L. S. (1994). *Realms of knowledge: Academic departments in secondary schools.* London: Falmer Press.

Sizer, T. R. (1996). *Horace's hope: What works for the American high school.* New York: Houghton Mifflin.

Thorkildsen, R. & Scott Stein, M. R. (1998). Is parent involvement related to student achievement? Exploring the evidence. *Research Bulletin No. 22.* Center for Evaluation, Development, and Research. Bloomington, IN: Phi Delta Kappa.

Willis, S. (1995). When parents object to classroom practice: Resolving conflicts over techniques, materials. *Education Update, 37*(1), 1, 6–8.

Websites

http://www.getinvolved.net

This site of the Community Action Network provides individuals with volunteer opportunities and helps link community agencies with volunteers, advocates, and donors.

http://www.bgca.org

This is the home page of the Boys' and Girls' Club of America. This organization's mission is: To inspire and enable all yoiung people, especially those from disadvantaged circumstances, to realize their full potential as productive, responsible and caring citizens.

http://www.pta.org

The mission of the National Parent Teacher Association is three-fold: 1) To support and speak on behalf of children and youth in the schools, in the community and before governmental bodies and other organizations that make decisions affecting children; 2) To assist parents in developing the skills they need to raise and protect their children; 3) To encourage parent and public involvement in the public schools of this nation.

http://www.fiu.edu/~time4chg/Library/index.library.html

This site operated by Florida International University contains extensive information about service learning and service learning curricula.

http://www.publicagenda.org

Public Agenda is a nonpartisan, nonprofit public opinion research and citizen education organization based in New York City. Its mission is two-fold: 1) To help leaders better understand the public's point of view on major policy issues; 2) To help citizens better understand critical policy issues so they can make their own more informed and thoughtful decisions. Public Agenda has addressed a wide range of issues through its research and citizen education work including school and health care reform, national security, AIDS, crime, economic competitiveness and environment.

http://www.libertynet.org/nol/natl.html

National Neighborhoods Online was created in 1995 by the Institute for the Study of Civic Values and Philadelphia's LibertyNet—now hosted by RegionOnline—as an online resource center for people working to build strong communities throughout the United states. The site has links to many community, government, and information agencies.

12

Making a Difference in Today's Classrooms

BUILDING ON BIOGRAPHY: VOICES FROM THE PAST

In the eight years I taught life sciences in public schools, I (Richard) attempted to make a difference in the classroom by committing myself to helping students learn about the natural world around them. To me, making a difference meant helping students understand, appreciate, and respect the world in which they lived. I didn't necessarily want all of them to become scientists, but I did want my students to know how science influenced their lives and the perspectives they held of the world as a living ecosystem. Because I usually saw my students for only one class period each school day, I wasn't always sure I was reaching this idealistic goal.

As a high-school teacher, my responsibilities included teaching Advanced Biology and Anatomy and Physiology. For these courses, students completed original research projects. They would select topics, brainstorm research strategies, and pursue their initiatives within the course parameters. Students chose their own topics, and I would offer guidance and assistance in carrying out their plans. Through this project, I hoped students would better understand how science influenced their lives. One young woman who was enrolled in both of my courses used her artistic talents in drawing the complete musculature of the human body and in producing a series of sketches highlighting the anatomical make-up of a beetle, wasp, and mosquito. In both projects, she used her talents to master some of the course content while acquiring a positive attitude toward science as a subject area. Her talents also served as a bridge between my teaching and the pragmatic value she found in science.

The environment I created in my classroom provided this student the opportunity to develop her artistic talents, and allowed me to become better acquainted with her and some of the other students. The more time I spent with these students, the more I saw them as individuals and became sensitive to the strengths and weaknesses they brought to the classroom. I knew when to challenge them, when to listen, and what motivational techniques would be successful with one and not the others. Not surprisingly, they became better acquainted with me as we learned to work together. Nevertheless, I was still uncertain whether the difference I tried to make with students in the classroom extended into their lives outside of school. I was, after all, only one of the many teachers they interacted with each year. Years would pass before I would learn how I had influenced one of these students' lives.

After entering a doctoral program at Indiana University, I received a phone call from the student I referred to earlier. She began by telling me about her unsuccessful attempts to reach me over the past few years, about giving up, and then deciding to mount one last effort. She had called a number of my former teaching associates and eventually located me in Indiana. I was elated to hear from one of my former students, although I wasn't sure why she was contacting me. Her phone call not only surprised but intrigued me. She described how she had earned a degree in chemistry and now worked as a chemist for a large corporation. Then she told me something that I shall never forget: that she had decided to leave her present position to pursue a career in teaching science. I was pleased, but unprepared for her next comment: "I want to become a science teacher because of my experiences years ago in your classroom. It was what I accomplished interacting with you and my peers that inspired me to want to be a teacher."

I wondered, after speaking with this former student, how many other lives I might have influenced in similar positive ways. I also wondered, with concern, how many lives my teaching may have influenced in other, perhaps negative, ways. Something became personally and vividly clear to me: teachers can and do make a difference in students' lives.

Questions to Consider

1. What specific features of Richard's teaching seem to have made a positive difference in his student's life?
2. His student's call stimulated Richard to wonder whether he might also have influenced students' lives in negative ways. How could this happen?
3. How do you define "making a difference"?

▌▌PURPOSE

The purpose of this chapter is to help you explore ways of making a difference in today's classrooms. After completing this chapter, you should know that, by making a difference in your classroom, you can also make a difference in the lives of students. These differences may occur while students are in your classroom or in later years. The chapter also describes how you might create healthy classroom environments in the face of today's societal challenges. Like experienced teachers who are still making a difference, you, too, will discover ways of dealing with challenges in positive ways. Specifically, this chapter will help you:

- realize the importance of making a difference in today's classrooms;
- identify challenges you face in making a difference in today's classrooms;
- explain the relationship between making a difference in today's classrooms and making a difference in students' lives;
- examine cases of teachers who create classroom environments that make differences in the lives of students;
- understand how the concepts of *equality, equity* and *excellence* are central to making a difference in classrooms.

▌▌REALIZING THE IMPORTANCE OF MAKING A DIFFERENCE

People enter the teaching profession for a variety of reasons. When asked why they want to teach, prospective teachers almost universally respond that they want to make a difference in the lives of students—however such a difference might be defined and interpreted (Veenam, 1984). This is especially true for persons who enter teaching as a second career (Powell, 1992). Yet, when these prospective teachers strive to make a difference and confront the challenges of daily classroom teaching, they realize that some factors can and do interfere with their heartfelt goal.

Because making a difference can be such a powerful motivational factor for entering the teaching profession, we devote an entire chapter to this idea. We believe you can derive professional and personal satisfaction from teaching if you understand the relationship between making a difference and the realities of teaching. At times, you may wonder whether you are making a difference or not. Sometimes years pass before you discover you have made a difference. Most successful teachers, however, soon learn to recognize the signals that they are making a positive difference and savor this most rewarding aspect of their profession.

Identifying Challenges

For many teachers, knowing they are making a difference in today's classrooms means experiencing positive feedback such as comments on your teaching from students, parents, and administrators, noteworthy samples of classroom work that show you have contributed to students' understanding of your subject area, and even better school attendance by students as a result of your teaching. However, with the many social problems besetting today's schools, you might be wondering whether you are being realistic in thinking you can help students overcome obstacles to learning and success.

Most teachers like to think that confronting social problems in the classroom is one way they are making a difference in the lives of students. But when facing such problems as teenage pregnancy, drug and alcohol abuse, individual and group violence, inner city decay, inequitable school conditions, student apathy, and parental indifference, how can teachers influence students and gain a sense of accomplishment as professionals? Finding an answer to this question can be crucial to your feelings of professional and personal accomplishment and satisfaction (Bullough, Knowles, & Crow, 1991; Zehm & Kottler, 1993).

Other challenges you will face include special interest groups attempting to control the school curriculum. State and local requirements may conflict with your ideas about the content you would like to teach and that, in your professional judgment, should be taught. Because schools' reputations and futures may depend on the results of standardized tests, administrators and teachers sometimes lose sight of students' interests and emphasize test-taking skills and subject matter found in these tests at the expense of authentic learning. Reflecting on these forces may cause you to think that in today's classrooms, autonomy—a key ingredient in making a difference as a teacher—is being undermined.

Another challenge you face pertains to transforming your teacher education experiences into successful practice. Many preservice teachers hear comments such as the following from experienced teachers: "Now that you are in the classroom, you can really learn what teaching is about." "What they teach you at the university is fine and good, but what really is worth knowing happens right here in the classroom." Hearing these comments can be confusing, causing you to lose sight of the value of university learning. If you can keep these challenges in perspective, you can develop and maintain an optimistic and wholesome approach to teaching and the institution of schooling. The key is gaining an understanding of the relationship between making a difference in students' lives and teaching in the twenty-first century.

■■ TEACHERS WHO MAKE A DIFFERENCE

Teachers who make a difference are those who are effective at meeting students' personal, academic, social, and cultural needs. Of course, most students have multiple needs that intertwine and vary in intensity. However, teachers often have what Borich (2000) calls *patterns of effective teaching:* a teacher who helps one student with a set of needs is likely, because of this pattern, to be sensitive to the same needs in other students. In the next sections, we will see examples of teachers who effectively meet students' varying needs.

Making a Difference with Team Teaching: The Case of Jimmie

Many educators consider teaming, an innovation especially popular in today's middle schools, to be an effective strategy for meeting students' needs. A team is usually composed of a group of teachers primarily responsible for the core subject areas working together with a group of approximately one hundred students for one or more academic years. Because such interdisciplinary teams are responsible for the same students for an extended period of time, they become quite familiar with student strengths and weaknesses. I recently reported how one team of middle-school teachers made a difference in the life of Jimmie, one of their students (Powell, 1997a). Jimmie's needs were many, but in this case we focus on his personal needs.

Four teachers—Mrs. Birdman (language arts/reading), Mr. Whitley (mathematics), Mrs. Rollins (social studies), and Ms. Wiley (science)—made up an interdisciplinary team responsible for sixth and seventh grades and were a fully functioning unit (Irvin, 1992). They collaborated in all school functions and spent a great deal of school time together. During regularly scheduled class time, they flowed in and out of one another's classrooms. At other times, they met regularly—formally and informally—to plan for instruction. While close-knit, they also allowed themselves the freedom to enjoy the privacy needed when working in such an intense environment. Whether they were alone or in their classrooms, together in team meetings, monitoring the hallways together between classes, or chatting at lunch, their focus was on helping students be successful at school. If they felt one of their students was "falling between the cracks," they would discuss ways to bring the student more into the team and school culture. Consequently, much of their effort was spent on appraising student growth, monitoring progress, and meeting the daily challenges students brought to the classroom. The team's commitment to educating the whole student resulted in successes, such as the case of Jimmie.

When Jimmie enrolled in sixth grade, Mrs. Birdman, the team leader, observed that he possessed a poor self-concept and expressed little commitment to academic learning. He continuously spoke about dropping out of school. Because the team viewed middle-school learning as a total school experience, it emphasized group learning and involvement in school-related activities such as clubs, student government, and sports. Because Jimmie avoided this level of school involvement and wanted to be left alone, he was quickly identified; the team did not allow him to lose himself in a crowd of students and quickly looked for ways of reaching out to him.

The team identified two approaches aimed at addressing Jimmie's low self-concept and lack of interest in school work: academics and an extra curricular activity, a tumbling organization maintained by Mr. Whitley called Knight Flight. Mrs. Birdman explained the team's strategies over two academic years:

> We first started helping Jimmie in small ways. We didn't start with, "We want all A's and we want you involved in this and that." We started with attendance, with the request, "Just come to school." From attendance we went to academics and to involvement in Knight Flight and performing in school and on special occasions out in the community. We also worked on helping Jimmie have a more influential voice in our team. We kept trying different avenues with Jimmie until we found some that worked.

Teachers who make a difference are those who are effective at meeting students' personal, academic, and social needs.

By the end of the second year, the teachers had gradually brought Jimmie into school in important ways. Perhaps one of the most important ways was keeping him from dropping out, a behavior he was seriously contemplating when he entered middle school. In seventh grade Jimmie's presence in school became more pronounced. He was involved in Knight Flight, and his grades improved. Jimmie said:

> About half way through the sixth grade something just snapped. All I can remember is that I was coming to school and doing my work. In the seventh grade I really got to like the teachers, especially Mr. Whitley. I'm now involved with Knight Flight. I don't know, I might try other things, like a judo class, before I leave this school.

Conversing with some of the teachers on the team, I learned that nothing had really changed in Jimmie's home life from one year to the next. He still lived with his brother and mother, although she was gone much of this time. What seems to have changed for Jimmie is the determined work of the teachers. Today, Jimmie is still in school and on his way to becoming a successful high school graduate.

Making a Difference Through Personal Transformation: The Case of Lee Colsant

The teachers who made a difference for Jimmie were members of a team, but educators who work in traditional settings—self-contained classrooms—also can make a difference in students' lives. These teachers develop curriculum that addresses students' personal, academic, social, and cultural needs and create environments in which students feel free to express themselves. Some teachers must critically examine and make changes in their beliefs about schools and students in order to start making a difference. Such is the case of Mr. Lee Colsant (1995), a French teacher in Chicago, who after seventeen years of experience underwent a personal transformation that has enabled him to better meet students' many needs.

Mr. Colsant began questioning his practice a few years ago, when he noticed that he was distancing himself from his students as they became less responsive to his teaching. Once he accepted the proposition that he could be losing his effectiveness in the classroom, he reached out to his students for feedback by initiating a series of honest discussions aimed at gaining insight into what was occurring in the classroom. Out of these discussions came a renewed vision for making a difference in his classroom and a promise from his students that they, too, would commit themselves to learning. Mr. Colsant's goal was to regain the level of effectiveness that had provided him with professional self-fulfillment and to create a classroom environment in which students enjoyed learning language and appreciated how knowledge of another language and culture enriched their lives.

For most of his career, Mr. Colsant had considered himself to be a good teacher. He enjoyed working with adolescents and was an effective classroom manager. He was involved in a variety of school activities. His students had won medals in Chicago's Academic Olympics, and some spent summers in Europe practicing their language skills and immersing themselves in French culture. He regularly received positive reinforcement from students, parents, teachers, and administrators. His professional teaching portfolio consistently received excellent ratings.

But several years ago, the demographics in the school neighborhood began to change. His French classes were no longer primarily populated with white, middle-class adolescents, but with African Americans, Latinos, and first generation Vietnamese. His teaching and his relationships with students began to change. Mr. Colsant was not happy with himself or his ability to connect with this changing student population. Although his teaching methodology—a traditional, grammar-oriented approach—had been quite effective during the first fifteen years of his teaching career, it was not effective with many of the students currently enrolled in his classes.

Mr. Colsant's transformation was facilitated by the reading he was doing for a graduate course in education at a nearby university. One of the required readings was *Contradictions of Control: School Structure and School Knowledge* (McNeil, 1986), a discussion about the relationships among students, control, and knowledge in school classrooms. Specifically, McNeil argues that the purpose of controlling school knowledge is to control students. Mr. Colsant initially rejected McNeil's argument because he found it contradictory to his life-long professional goals. Upon reflection, however, he realized that his methods of instruction did not truly engage students.

Through reading and reflection, Mr. Colsant took a most important first step. After continued reflection and classroom discussion with students, he began moving toward a group-oriented, student-centered approach. Acknowledging that the students he was teaching today were different from those who populated his classroom years earlier, he expanded his notion of culture to include Francophone regions from Southeast Asia, West Africa, Latin America, and the United States. He accepted the proposition that learning French would include hearing the language as it is spoken around the world, and took measures to ensure that his classroom and curriculum would reflect this broader notion of French language and culture. Mr. Colsant compromised, but did not give up completely on grammar-oriented, textbook-centered instruction. He continued with this approach and incorporated group projects and activities reflecting student interest in Francophone culture. He developed small-group tasks and individualized activities that provided students the opportunity to acquire and demonstrate competency in French in ways that were meaningful and comfortable for them.

Mr. Colsant became an observer in his own classroom. As he invited students to talk more openly about the French language and how French could influence their personal lives, a trusting relationship emerged between teacher and students. He became a quiet listener, accepted student voice, and acknowledged that he might need to change. Earlier in his career, Mr. Colsant had been preoccupied with teaching the subject matter of French. His transformation as a teacher helped him understand that he could better meet students' academic needs if he would first hear their concerns, issues, hopes, and personal agendas. Today Mr. Colsant once again believes he is making a difference.

▮ Reader Activity 12.1

IN THE FIELD
Interviewing a Teacher Who Made a Difference

Reflect on the middle- and high-school teachers who made a difference in your life. Interview one of these teachers in person, by telephone, in writing, or via e-mail. Tell the teacher that he or she made a difference in your life and ask him or her a series of questions that will allow you to construct a biographical sketch. The sketch should include information about students, curriculum, and making connections with students. Some of the questions to ask could include:

1. Why did you choose teaching as a profession?
2. What do you see are your responsibilities as a middle- or high-school teacher?
3. How do you view adolescents? Why are you successful at connecting with students?
4. Why are you successful at engaging students in learning?
5. What role, if any, does professionalism play in your success as a teacher.

In a class session focusing on outstanding teachers, share your biographical sketch with the class. Be sure to include a short description of why this teacher made a difference in your life.

Making a Difference Through Culturally Sensitive Teaching: The Case of Amy Whitlow

Amy Whitlow, a teacher of American literature and English as a Second Language (ESL), is making a difference by being sensitive to the social and cultural needs of her students. (Powell, 1997b). For over ten years, Ms. Whitlow was a successful floral designer in a large Southwestern city. She enjoyed the personal autonomy and creativity allowed in this career, as well as the freedom to change and improve the environment in which she worked. When she decided to make a career change, she carried these qualities over into the classroom. An openly caring and compassionate person, Ms. Whitlow wanted to create a learning environment in which students felt needed and wanted. She accepted a high school position in American literature and ESL because she wanted to introduce young adults to many of America's classic and contemporary writers and to help them become proficient in the English language. She envisioned a classroom reflective of her students' cultural backgrounds, one in which students would have opportunities to use their own language, culture, and experience as rich resources for learning.

Unfortunately, Ms. Whitlow ran into two obstacles. First, she knew very little about the Mexican American students who walked into her classroom. She had grown up in a predominantly white, upper-middle-class suburb of Dallas and, except for a few experiences in her teacher education program, had little knowledge of Mexican Americans, the major sub-group of Hispanics who attended her school. Her second obstacle was the district. Her principal was sympathetic to the academic difficulties many of the Mexican American students were experiencing, but he was more interested in test scores and graduation rates. He made it clear that he expected her to devote her time and energy to helping Spanish-speaking students master basic skills in English. He acknowledged the importance of knowing and relating to the students, but stressed cognitive issues and test-taking skills. He wanted the students to have opportunities at entry level jobs upon graduation.

Ms. Whitlow did not openly disagree with the principal, but she personally believed that the basic skills curriculum did not align with students' backgrounds and interests. She suspected that the curriculum itself was disconnecting students from learning. She knew she was obligated to teach the curriculum, but her principal had not prescribed a specific pedagogical approach. So Amy applied her creativity to learning about her students and using this information to develop a curriculum that connected the students to the required knowledge as outlined in the district's curriculum.

Over the summer prior to the beginning of the school year, Amy read everything she could about the history of Mexico and Mexican Americans, particularly in the state where she was teaching. She toured school neighborhoods, stopping to visit with individuals who might provide insights into the educational history of Mexican Americans in the community and who could offer suggestions on what she could do in her classroom to help students master basic skills in English while acquiring a love of reading. Next, she contacted key people in the district responsible for providing services to non-English speaking Hispanics. She would use these individuals and agencies as resources to help her meet her students' many and varying needs.

Amy used what she had learned from her readings and excursions to decorate her classroom with artifacts reflecting students' backgrounds and celebrating literacy in both English and Spanish. To supplement the textbooks and other instructional material purchased by the district, she submitted a long book order to the school library for the purchase of works written by Hispanic authors. She used her own money to purchase books for her students focusing on the Mexican American experience, books written by Mexicans, Mexican Americans, and other Latino/a writers.

During the first weeks of the academic year, she conducted classroom activities that enabled her to learn about the students as individuals. For example, she often asked them to write about their personal lives, encouraged them to collate their experiences into autobiographies, and to place their stories in a booklet for the class to read. The students were at first reluctant to write in English, but once they felt Ms. Whitlow was sincerely interested, they told their stories eagerly.

As Ms. Whitlow completed her first year of teaching, she remained compassionate and caring but had not lost sight of her responsibilities. In the area of American literature, she learned how to balance her student-oriented curriculum with the prescribed one. She did this by employing her creative energy to fuse various ethnic perspectives within a broader framework of American literature. She also understood and supported mastery of the standardized curriculum. Like her principal, she, too, wanted students to be successful in school, and, upon graduation, have the opportunity to enroll in college or gain an entry-level job that would place them on the road to realizing some of their personal, social, and financial goals.

The difference Amy made in her classroom occurred over time and deliberately. The metaphor of *inviting students to learn* might best represent Amy's classroom and her teaching. She acknowledged and affirmed their language and culture, accepted them as individuals, and incorporated Hispanic insights into the curriculum. Amy made a difference in her classroom and in her students' lives by creating a learning environment in which students had continuous opportunities to approach their studies from many perspectives, including the perspectives of their own cultural backgrounds.

■ **Reader Activity 12.2**

WHAT WOULD YOU DO?
Diversity in the Classroom

You are about to graduate from a small university in the Midwest and, at a job fair, you accept a high-school teaching position in one of St. Louis's western suburbs. Responsibilities will include teaching your subject and coaching women's soccer. The district administrator who interviewed you described the student population as "predominantly white and middle-class." You learned that ninety-five percent of the students graduate and pursue post-secondary education or accept an entry-level job in the area's growing computer industry.

Shortly before graduation, you receive a letter from your future principal, Ms. Lourdes, introducing herself and Walter Perry High School. You learn that WPHS is a "newcomers' magnet" school, charged with developing instructional programs that meet the needs of recent immigrants who are entering the district. Although your interviewer's description of the student population as "predominantly white and middle-class" is true for the district as a whole, it appears that Walter Perry High School has quite a diverse student body. Ms. Lourdes's letter lists the following groups of students who will be enrolled at WPHS this fall:

- Poor Afghan Muslim families, with few skills, displaced by the country's civil war, and brought to the St. Louis area by Christian organizations.
- Middle-class Chinese from Hong Kong who refused to be governed by the Peoples Republic of China, immigrated to Seattle, and migrated to the St. Louis area in search of skilled work and entrepreneurial opportunities.
- Working class Russians who are in St. Louis looking for entry-level positions.
- Jewish and Muslim Palestinians who were dislocated as a result of the latest breakdown in Arab/Israeli negotiations.

Together, these groups comprise about twenty percent of the student body of 1000. The school continues to enroll a majority of students from white, African American, and Hispanic families.

Two major challenges face you: (1) What approach(es) will you use to become acquainted with your school community and the students it serves? and (2) What modifications, if any, will you need to make in planning and teaching business and general math and in coaching soccer?

Brainstorm in small groups and lay out an action plan aimed at addressing these questions. Your action plan should include specific steps you need to take before the start of the school year, some ideas for curriculum modification to reflect student diversity, ideas about how student diversity might impact the women's soccer program, and a list of resources (including people) that can help you get off to a good start at Walter Perry High School. Share your plan with the class.

▪▪▮ REFLECTION ON THE CASES: EQUALITY, EQUITY, AND EXCELLENCE

The previous discussion highlighted teachers who made a difference: the team of middle-school teachers who focused on Jimmie's personal needs; Mr. Lee Colsant, who focused on the academic needs of his French students; and Ms. Amy Whitlow, who focused on the social and cultural needs of her Mexican American students. The cases show teachers at various grade levels, in different parts of the country, and in a variety of subjects. The teachers ranged from novice to experienced. What these teachers shared was the disposition to take action in their own classrooms so that their students could be more successful. Helping all students be more successful in school-based learning is a goal that has become increasingly challenging and will continue to challenge teachers everywhere in the decades to come.

You can meet this challenge by understanding three key elements of curriculum and instruction: *equality, equity,* and *excellence.* The relationship among these terms has been described by Geneva Gay (1988), who wrote:

> The challenge, one of both equity and excellence, is to provide *all* students with an equal opportunity to learn to the highest possible level of their ability, regardless of where they live, their family structure, gender, economic background, ethnic identity, or home-based cultural orientation (p. 327).

The teachers described in this chapter wanted to offer all students equal opportunities to maximize their potential. Jimmie's teachers, for example, refused to let him "slip through the cracks" and drop out. Lee Colsant wanted his working-class, African American students to have the same opportunities to learn and appreciate the French language as his mostly white, upper-middle-class students previously had. Amy Whitlow wanted her Mexican American students to acquire skills in English that would give them the same chances for success in school and society as native speakers of English have.

At the same time, these teachers were committed to equity and modified their instruction according to relevant differences among their learners. Jimmie's teachers knew he needed more encouragement than the average student and went a bit out of their way to make him feel a part of school life. Lee Colsant realized that his traditional teaching methods were out of sync with the communicative styles of his students. Amy Whitlow provided literature written by Latino/a authors in order to hook her Hispanic students on reading.

Finally, all these teachers were committed to excellence. They did not lower their expectations for academic performance or offer a "watered-down" curriculum to their diverse learners. Rather, they offered alternative experiences and pathways that would help their students reach the same level of success as other, more privileged students. Furthermore, each teacher strove for professional excellence. They achieved success with students because they were willing to commit extra time and energy to hard work and hard thinking about their classroom practices.

FIGURE 12.1   Focus on Equality, Equity, and Excellence

The following questions focus in various ways on issues related to equity and excellence in the classroom and school. You can use them as a guide to developing curriculum in your own classroom as well as for evaluating how well a course, department, or school is working to make a difference in the lives of diverse learners.

- Does diversity permeate the curriculum, especially the content and activities?
- Will students from different ethnic and cultural backgrounds and students with exceptionalities find the proposed instructional materials personally meaningful?
- Has a variety of diverse (e.g., culture, gender, ableness) examples, situations, scenarios, and anecdotes been used throughout the curriculum design to illustrate major intellectual concepts and principles?
- Are the diverse content, examples and experiences included comparable in kind, significance, magnitude, and function to those selected from mainstream culture?
- Are the performance expectations (goals and objectives) for diverse learners similar to those for mainstream students?
- Do evaluation techniques allow different ways for students to demonstrate their achievement? Are these sensitive to cultural, ethnic, and other forms of diversity?
- Will the proposed learning activities stimulate and interest different kinds of students?
- How do the content and learning activities affirm the culture of diverse students?

Adapted from "Designing Relevant Curricula for Diverse Learners" by G. Gay, 1988, in *Education and Urban Society 29* (4), pp. 338–339.

Becoming a teacher who makes a difference is a lifelong process and usually involves overcoming formidable challenges. Figure 12.1 provides a set of questions you can ask yourself in order to evaluate how well you and/or the school in which you teach addresses issues of equality, equity, and excellence—three key elements in making a difference in today's classrooms.

▌Reader Activity 12.3

IN THE FIELD
Community Perspectives on Students' Needs

This activity will help you discover what other service providers perceive as the needs of today's young people. Work in groups to identify community agencies (e.g., Boys' and Girls' Clubs, YMCA or YWCA, church or synagogue, social services offices) that serve middle- and high-school students. Make an appointment to interview staff who might offer perspectives on youth that augment those we have presented in this chapter. The following questions can help you focus your interview:

1. What are the characteristics of the population you serve (gender, ethnicity, special needs, socioeconomic status, religion, family patterns, employment)?
2. What are the personal, academic, social, and cultural needs of the population you serve?

3. How does your agency address students' needs?
4. In your view, how well are schools addressing the needs of students you serve?
5. What are schools already doing and what might they do differently in order to address the needs of the students you serve?
6. Do you know of any cases in which teachers have made a difference (positive or negative) in the lives of the students you serve?

Present your findings to the class. Identify what each organization believes needs to be done to help adolescents. Compile a list of needs and then discuss as a class how social agencies and schools can work more closely to meet the academic, social, and cultural needs of adolescents.

▌▐▐ MAKING A DIFFERENCE WITH STUDENTS AT RISK

Adolescents are experiencing increasing risk of dropping out of school, of perpetrating or becoming victims of violence, and of engaging in health and/or life-threatening behaviors. The risks to poor adolescents and adolescents with disabilities are greater than average. Cantrell & Cantrell (1995) have summarized three measures that can help both regular and special education teachers make a difference in the lives of students at risk.

First, "Learning experiences must relate to the youth's real life; we must teach youth rather than curriculum" (p. 25). Specifically, students need help in learning how to solve [both academic and social] problems, such as anger management and conflict resolution. Students also need to learn how to interact positively with others. Many have few role models and little experience with prosocial group interaction.

The second theme the Cantrells have identified is "Youth need experiences that both allow and prepare them to enter adulthood" (p. 26). This is true for both middle- and high-school learners, who need to learn and practice the academic and social skills required for success in the workplace. Adults function independently, and adolescents need many opportunities to practice and acquire skills for adult living.

Finally, the Cantrells assert, "Youth need adults who genuinely care, and who care enough to act on their behalf" (p. 27). Young people need to learn how to accept help from a caring adult and how to care for others. Service learning projects, described in the preceding chapter, can help students learn and practice caring.

▌▐▐ SUMMARY

At the beginning of this chapter, I described how I influenced the life of one of my former students. One of the most powerful lessons I learned from this experience was that teachers can and do make a difference in students' lives, differences that might not be evident for several years. The majority of teachers entering the profession aspire to influence students' lives in positive, meaningful, and lasting ways. In order to remain focused on this goal, teachers need assurances that they are making a difference in the classroom. They also need to maintain a balanced view of factors influencing their classrooms and the realities of teaching. Influencing students in positive ways becomes increasingly possible when the concepts of equality, equity, and excellence guide instruction. Some key points to remember are:

- Making a positive difference often requires you to demonstrate initiative, creativity, and innovation.
- Making a positive difference in the lives of your students requires you to know them well enough so that you can create a classroom environment that will connect them more fully to what you are teaching.
- At least three sets of student needs are addressed when you make a difference in your classroom: personal, academic, and social/cultural.
- Working in a team of teachers can provide you with professional support for making a difference in students' lives.
- Transformation of your personal perspectives on teaching might be needed before you can actually make changes in your classroom environment.
- Concepts of equality, equity, and excellence are directly related to making a difference in the classroom.
- All students, but especially those at risk, need help in seeing connections between the curriculum and "real life," in preparing to assume adult roles, and in accepting and offering care.

This chapter has focused on how teachers can make a difference in the lives of students by modifying curriculum and instruction to meet students' needs. In the next and final chapter, "Reflecting for Professional Renewal," you will learn about ways to insure that your desire to make a difference remains alive for many years. You will learn about strategies that will keep your professional and intellectual life vital. Finally, you will reflect upon all you have read and learned in this course, compose your teaching autobiography and educational philosophy, and compile a portfolio that demonstrates who you are and may become as a teacher.

■■ BUILDING YOUR BIOGRAPHY, YOUR PERSONAL PRACTICAL PHILOSOPHY, AND PORTFOLIO

Building Your Biography

Write a chapter of your educational biography dealing with the idea of making a difference in today's classrooms. The following questions can help you develop this chapter. They are not intended to be answered sequentially or to limit your exploration of the topic.

- What experiences in your life have provided you with initiative, creativity, and responsiveness to the needs of others? How did you develop these attributes?
- In what ways can you be responsive to student cultural heritages, socioeconomic status, exceptionalities, family histories, and learning styles?
- Which of your former teachers made a difference in your life? What was the nature of this difference? To which set of needs—academic, personal, social and cultural—did these teachers seem most responsive? How did this teacher (or these teachers) actually make a difference in your life? Was the difference short-lived or lifelong?

Developing Your Personal Practical Philosophy

Write a section of your personal educational philosophy that addresses making a difference in today's classrooms. You might respond to questions such as the following.

- How do you define *making a difference* in today's classrooms?
- Which of your personal beliefs represent the idea of *making a positive difference for all students?*
- What kinds of differences should teachers be making in their classrooms today?
- What part do equity and excellence play in making a difference in today's classrooms?

Collecting Artifacts for Your Portfolio

Review the Reader Activities you have completed in this chapter. Identify any that you might eventually select for your portfolio. For each, jot down notes that will help you recall later what you were thinking at the time you completed the activity, what challenges you encountered while completing it, what you learned from doing it, and whether this activity reveals something about who you will be as a teacher. Don't worry about style or correctness at this point. The purpose is to document your thinking as you move through this book and this class.

References

Borich, G. D. (2000). *Effective teaching methods* (4th ed). Upper Saddle River, NJ: Merrill-Prentice Hall.

Bullough, R. V., Knowles, J. G., & Crow, N. A. (1991). *Emerging as a teacher.* New York: Routledge.

Cantrell R. P. & Cantrell, M. L. (1995). The future of secondary programs for students with disabilities. *Preventing School Failure, 39* (3), 25–28.

Colsant, L. C. (1995). "Hey, man, why do we gotta take this?" Learning to listen to students. In J. G. Nicholls & T. A. Thorkildsen (Eds.). *Reasons for learning: Expanding the conversation on student-teacher collaboration* (pp. 62–89). New York: Teachers College Press.

Gay, G. (1988). Designing relevant curricula for diverse learners. *Education and Urban Society, 29* (4), 327–340.

Irvin, J. (Ed). (1992). *Transforming middle level education: Perspectives and possibilities.* Boston: Allyn and Bacon.

McNeil, L. (1986). *Contradictions of control: School structure and school knowledge.* New York: Routledge and Kegan Paul.

Powell, R. R. (1992). The influence of prior experiences on pedagogical constructs of traditional and nontraditional preservice teachers. *Teaching and Teacher Education, 8* (3), 225–238.

Powell, R. R. (1997a). Teams and the affirmation of middle level students' voices: The case of Jimmie. In T. S. Dickinson & T. O. Erb (Eds.). *We gain more than we give: Teaming in middle schools* (pp. 271–297). Columbus, OH: National Middle School Association.

Powell, R. R. (1997b). Then the beauty emerges: A longitudinal case study of culturally relevant teaching. *Teaching and Teacher Education, 13* (5), 467–484.

Veenam, S. (1984). Perceived problems of beginning teachers. *Review of Educational Research, 54* (2), 143–178.

Zehm, S. J. & Kottler, J. A. (1993). *On being a teacher: The human dimension.* Newbury Park: Corwin Press.

▪▪▪ Websites

http://www.ceousa.org

The Center for Equal Opportunity is a think tank devoted exclusively to the promotion of colorblind equal opportunity and racial harmony. CEO focuses on three areas in particular: racial preferences, immigration and assimilation, and multicultural education.

http://www.nmci.org

The National MultiCultural Institute (NMCI) was founded in 1983 in response to the nation's growing need for new services, knowledge, and skills in diversity. NMCI's mission is to increase communication, understanding and respect among people of different racial, ethnic and cultural backgrounds, and to provide a forum for discussion of the critical issues of multiculturalism. The organization sponsors Spring and Fall conferences and offers individualized training and consulting programs.

http://projects.aclin.org/diversity/

This site, constructed by Access Colorado Library and Information Network, features a Diversity Tool Kit with printable bookmarks for each month, a calendar of events, and a bibliography of diversity resources.

http://dir.yahoo.com/Society_and_Culture/Cultures_and_Groups/Teenagers/Organizations/

An extensive listing of organizations for adolescents.

http://ymca.net

The nation's 2,283 YMCAs are the largest not-for-profit community service organizations in America, working to meet the health and social service needs of 16.9 million men, women and children in 10,000 communities. YMCAs are for people of all faiths, races, abilities, ages, and incomes. No one is turned away for inability to pay. YMCAs' strength is in the people they bring together.

13

Reflecting for Professional Renewal

BUILDING ON BIOGRAPHY: A SUCCESSFUL START TO THE FIRST YEAR OF TEACHING

Preservice teachers often ask me (Jesus) whether I really enjoyed teaching at the elementary and secondary levels. My response has remained the same over the years. Yes, I enjoyed teaching because I like young people. When teaching at the secondary level, for example, I found that class discussion—a teaching strategy I favored—offered me the opportunity to gain greater insights into students' views on academic learning and what they considered important. I believe I was effective in the classroom because I was able to form close relationships with my students, and I was challenged intellectually by the subject areas and pedagogy. I also enjoyed the camaraderie with fellow teachers, department chairs, and administrators.

Despite a shaky start, I recall my classroom experiences as positive. When I completed my teacher preparation programs, I was reasonably well-prepared to teach at the elementary and secondary levels. I possessed some background knowledge on the characteristics of children and adolescents, an understanding of the elementary and secondary social studies curriculum, and sufficient pedagogical skills to do more than teach the textbook. My colleagues were helpful and encouraged me to grow professionally. The parents I met while teaching at the elementary level cared about their children, wanted them to do well in school, and were cooperative when I asked for assistance. Although I met fewer parents at the secondary level, colleagues filled the void by mentoring my growth in the profession.

Occasionally I did consider leaving teaching, but when such thoughts surfaced, a colleague, administrator, student, or parent would stop me in the hallway or call to tell me what a great job I was doing, or relate a specific instance in which I was making a difference in a student's life. These conversations helped to reassure me that I was becoming a good teacher and that I was making a difference in students' lives. To this day, a verbal comment, an e-mail, or a letter—particularly from a student—goes far in reinforcing my perception of myself as a good educator.

However, there is another side to this biography. I must confess that I still think about those students I was unable to reach. Each year I taught, there were students who did not do well in school despite my best efforts. I remember Johnny, Blaine, Belinda, and Hector, whom I met during my first years of teaching. They were fine children, but some of the problems they brought to the classroom were so deep-seated and complex that I did not possess the expertise to help them. While I had learned that students bring problems into the classroom, I had not learned how to address many of them. Today, specialists of all sorts—special educators, school psychologists, social workers—are available to help identify and treat such problems. However, when I began teaching I lacked knowledge of how to get help and was somewhat reluctant to ask for it lest I be seen as incompetent.

Johnny lived with foster parents. He would come to school unwashed, sometimes wearing the same clothes several days in a row. He spent his time in the classroom daydreaming and looking for companionship from anyone, particularly adults. His academic performance was poor, but neither Johnny nor his foster parents seemed to care. (Today, Johnny would probably be identified as a possible victim of child abuse. At that time, however, I had no training in recognizing the symptoms). Blaine was an introvert, lacked a healthy self-concept, and was picked on by the other boys in the class. He disliked school and was chronically absent. As a fifth-grader, Belinda read at the third-grade level and none of the techniques I employed helped to raise her reading ability. Hector was a student in one of the U.S. history classes I taught during my first year of secondary teaching. He was so involved in gang activity that I was powerless to help him see the value of doing well in my class and staying in school. I don't know what happened to these four individuals, but I suspect they were unable to reach their potential.

Was I a failure at teaching? Was I just not "cut out" to be a teacher? When these questions have popped in my mind, I have responded with, "I don't think so." Frankly, as I matriculated through my teacher preparation program and throughout my first few years of teaching, I rarely reflected upon my views of teaching, the content of my teacher education courses, and the complexity of solving problems in the classroom. Neither I, my university professors, nor my colleagues in the schools challenged my initial perceptions of teaching and schools. As a result, I think I lacked the predisposition to use analytical methods in order to identify and solve classroom problems. I did not leave college with the predispositions or habits of mind that would help me grow professionally. That is, I entered *and* exited teacher education with flawed perceptions. I believed that, because I selected teaching as a profession, I must possess some well-founded views on teaching and learning, and that my program would give me the skills I needed to teach as I saw fit. I believed that, when I graduated, I would be prepared to teach. I believed there was little I would need to do to improve on that preparation, and that I knew what there was to know about student characteristics, content, and pedagogy.

Because my initial views on teaching and schools went unchallenged, I tended to blame the students or my teacher education program when I was unable to identify, address, or solve a problem. Today, I don't do that quite so often.

Questions to Consider

1. If Jesus had reflected on the problems of Johnny, Blaine, Belinda, and Hector, what insights might he have gained?
2. Blaming students for classroom problems, as Jesus did as a beginning teacher, has been referred to as "blaming the victim." How do you interpret this phrase?
3. Do schools and teachers today do a better job of meeting the needs of students like Johnny, Blaine, Belinda, and Hector?

▮▮ PURPOSE

When you graduate from your teacher preparation program and step into your own classroom, you will quickly learn that a great deal of responsibility rests on your shoulders. Assistance will be available, but you will be expected to take the initiative in becoming a professional. You have the "core knowledge:" learning from your education classes, observations, student teaching experiences, and interactions with teachers and teacher educators. Now, you will need to do the rest.

This chapter describes an approach to achieving success while you are student teaching and during your first few years in the profession. We begin by suggesting an approach that might reduce any feelings of ambivalence and apprehension you may have about teaching: adopting a proactive predisposition toward teaching and acquiring habits of mind that will allow you to grow professionally. A proactive predisposition means accepting the notion that becoming a teacher is a lifelong process, begun but not completed during a teacher education program. It also means cultivating the habits of mind that encourage an analytical approach to solving classroom problems. Another major goal of this chapter is to introduce several avenues you can follow toward professional growth and career development. Throughout this course, you have been developing the documents that will lead to the development of your teaching biography, personal practical philosophy, and portfolio. In the last part of this chapter, we provide guidelines for completing these three tasks. Specifically, this chapter will help you:

- use introspection, including the identification of metaphors and/or similes for teaching, as a tool for professional growth;
- explore the benefits of becoming an action researcher in your own classroom;
- become aware of the many opportunities for lifelong learning through participation in professional education associations;
- make use of networks and support groups, including mentors and the National Board for Professional Teaching Standards;
- compile an initial teaching portfolio consisting of your teaching autobiography, your personal practical philosophy, and other artifacts that reveal who you are and may become as a teacher.

▗▖ PRELUDE TO BECOMING A TEACHER

Predisposition refers to the mind-set you use to understand self, colleagues, incidents affecting your life, and the like. As you prepare for a teaching career, we believe you should view a teacher education program as providing you with core knowledge for becoming a professional teacher. This predisposition of *becoming* rather than *being* means that you view a teacher education program as providing building blocks: knowledge that needs further reconstruction as you attempt to understand self, subject area, pedagogy, students, and schools. When you enter the classroom, you add to this core knowledge with insights you gain from your teaching experiences and knowledge you acquire from professional activities, such as exploring the literature in your teaching field, conversing with colleagues, and learning more about your personal and teaching selves. As you gain confidence and mature, you add to this reservoir of knowledge. Throughout this process, you are reconstructing knowledge to give meaning to what you are experiencing. The end, while in sight, remains a goal you are continually pursuing: becoming a professional.

We encourage you to adopt habits of mind that allow you to be analytical in classroom decision-making—the processes you use to identify an issue or problem and the approaches you use to solve it. For example, suppose you are observing a secondary history teacher delivering a lecture to a group of high school juniors on the persecution of Christians living in the Roman Empire in the second century. As you observe, you notice that more than a few students are sleeping, doodling, or gazing out the windows. As the teacher concludes the lecture and prepares to dismiss the class, she walks by you and remarks, "Well, back to the drawing board. That lecture really bombed." If you adopt a view of teaching as *becoming* rather than *being,* then you would be predisposed not to blame the students or the teacher, but to be analytical and look for possible explanations for students not being engaged in the lecture. Predisposition, in the context of becoming a teacher, refers to "surveying the land" and including for possible examination self, preparation, experiences, students, school policy and practice, societal expectations, and the like.

Habits of mind refer to the mental strategies individuals regularly use to understand, interpret, and act upon the world around them. The habits of mind of teachers who are reflective practitioners include (1) tolerance for the ambiguity of complex problems; (2) the ability to identify problems of practice and to generate tentative solutions; (3) a willingness to examine one's own knowledge and actions; (4) the ability to draw upon intuitive knowledge to solve problems; and (5) the inclination to implement and evaluate new procedures (Schon, 1987; Vacca, Vacca, & Bruneau, 1997).

Let's see how the history teacher you observed might identify the problem areas in her unsuccessful lecture and hypothesize possible solutions through reflection. She might ask herself a series of probing questions. What were the possible sources of students' apparent disengagement? Was the lecture too long? Too abstract? Did it lack ways to engage the variety of learners in the classroom? Did students possess adequate background knowledge? Did the lecture enable students to make meaningful connections between history and their own experiences? Was the room too hot or too cold? Did the off-task students have particular learning needs that were not being met? If she concludes that the lecture's failure was a combination of many factors, she might, for example, resolve to begin any subsequent lectures by questioning for students' prior knowledge, stating her purpose clearly, including visuals, and providing students with note-taking guides.

As a reflective practitioner, this teacher may conclude that modifying her lecture technique in order to address a variety of learning styles, building more interaction into the lecture, and setting aside adequate time each day for preparation are the answers to her problems. What if these actions do not solve the problem of student disengagement? She will continue the reflective process and generate other possible explanations and solutions. (Perhaps the assigned background readings are too difficult for students; perhaps she needs to work on her delivery; perhaps some students are repeating the class and are simply resentful). Reflective professionals know that there are many ways to look at problems and issues and that explanations and solutions are just as numerous. They also have learned that, to increase success in the classroom and to grow professionally, they must be willing to look at themselves and at other variables that may affect what they do in the classroom. Let's now turn to a few practices you may wish to adopt that can lead to greater success in the classroom.

▮▮ INTROSPECTION

In Chapter One, "Exploring Biographies and Teaching Perspectives: Personal Narratives," we introduced several forms of introspection: (1) using biography to better understand self, students, classrooms, and schools; (2) developing a practical teaching philosophy that articulates your motivations for teaching and your views of students, curriculum, and issues related to teaching; and (3) developing a portfolio of activities you have completed throughout this course, selecting those most meaningful to you, reflecting upon how they reveal you as an individual and a professional, and composing a portfolio for a specific audience. In each subsequent chapter, reader activities and writing prompts were provided to help you develop and complete these three tasks.

Introspection is a first step to becoming a professional. The assignments in the preceding chapters were intended not only to enable you to look critically at the predispositions you bring to teaching, but to foster habits of mind that will enable you to become a reflective and effective decision-maker in the classroom.

Exploring Your Metaphor for Teaching

Much of human thinking is metaphorical (Lakoff & Johnson, 1980). That is, we tend to give meaning to experience by using comparisons, whether implied (metaphor) or explicit (simile). For example, the simile "Life is like a box of chocolates" reveals much about the speaker's optimistic approach to the vicissitudes of life. Teachers, too, use comparisons to explain their conceptions of themselves, the subjects they teach, and their students. Often, however, these guiding images remain tacit (Bullough, Knowles, & Crow, 1992). Identifying and exploring the metaphors or similes you use to think about teaching may lead you to greater self-understanding.

Undoubtedly you entered this teacher education program with particular views about teaching and about your subject area, but perhaps your coursework and experiences have caused you to modify those views. Review the prompts and exercises you have completed. Have you repeatedly used words or images that may suggest your teaching metaphor or simile? Do you see your teaching self as facilitator? Scholar? Parent? If you envision yourself as a scholar, for example, what role will you play in your classroom? What role will your students play? What will be the role of curriculum?

Consider the following metaphors and similes suggested by middle school teachers of English/language arts (Spalding, 1997).

- Jack (eighth-grade teacher)—"Teaching English is like swallowing an elephant."
- Celia (seventh-grade teacher)—"Teaching English is like conducting an orchestra of kazoo players."
- Claire (sixth-grade teacher)—"I feel like a Mom here—a teaching Mom."

What does Jack's metaphor say about the English language arts curriculum? What role does it suggest for the teacher? What role does it suggest for the students? What does Celia's metaphor suggest about her level of satisfaction with teaching? What problems might Claire, who views herself as a "teaching Mom," encounter in the classroom?

By putting your teaching metaphor into words and exploring its implications for yourself as a teacher, you may gain insight into the special attributes you will bring to teaching and the special challenges you may face in the classroom. In the next section, we present strategies for addressing such challenges.

▌▌BECOMING AN ACTION RESEARCHER

Student teachers often tell me, "I am really enjoying myself in the classroom. Will I continue to have this much fun when I have my own classroom?" I usually respond with an emphatic "Yes! Oh, you'll experience some difficulties, but if you follow up on what you are saying to your cooperating teachers and to me, you will continue to have fun in the classroom." What sorts of behaviors are these novices exhibiting?

These student teachers show an inclination to take ownership of their classroom and act on the problems and issues that stymie their efforts at teaching and students' efforts at learning. They are gaining confidence as they gain experience, and they are learning that they possess the intellectual prowess to address the many problems they encounter in the classroom. They are beginning to assume the role of action researchers.

Action research is defined as "the application of social science methods to practical problems with the goals of contributing to theory and knowledge in education and improving teaching practice" (Sprinthall, Reiman, & Thies-Sprinthall, 1996, p. 694). Action research is not new; it has its roots in the work of Dewey and others who argued for teacher preparation programs that integrate knowledge and action and encourage preservice teachers to become inquirers who use rational methods for exploring problems of practice. Unfortunately, educational research has historically been viewed as the province of university professors, while teachers have been relegated to the level of unskilled workers who must be trained to put researchers' theories into practice (Goodlad, Soder, & Sirotnik, 1990).

Today the action research movement has strong supporters among teacher educators and K-12 classroom teachers who believe they possess the intellectual ability and the experience to identify and solve their own problems. Action research encourages teachers to see themselves as autonomous professionals who are able to uncover new knowledge that can challenge current perceptions and offer fresh perspectives on learning in contemporary classrooms.

Cochran-Smith and Lytle (1993) divide the area of action research (also called *teacher research*) into two general categories: empirical and theoretical. Empirical research originates from observable classroom phenomena and entails collecting, analyzing, and interpreting data. In Chapter Eleven, "Understanding the Role of Community," Liz described the empirical research of a group of teachers at Center Park High School who collected, analyzed and interpreted data from a variety of sources in an attempt to understand why so many ninth-graders dropped out of school (Brubacher, Case & Regan, 1994). Conceptual research, while grounded in experience, refers to the exploration and analysis of ideas. Richard made use of Mr. Lee Colsant's conceptual exploration of his own teaching in Chapter Twelve, "Making a Difference in Today's Classrooms" (Colsant, 1995). Figure 13.1 depicts a five-phase model for conducting action research (Powell, Zehm, & Garcia, 1996).

Using this model, let's see how one teacher used action research to solve a problem in her Algebra I class. An experienced teacher, she was hired for a part-time mathematics position at an urban high school with a large enrollment of African Americans and students from a lower socioeconomic status. Having previously taught in a suburban, predominantly white, middle-class high school, she was having trouble adjusting to her new position. She enrolled in a graduate course at a nearby university in order to update her teaching credentials. Conducting an action research project was one of the course requirements.

In the *description/speculation phase* of her research, the teacher decided to focus on discipline in a particular class that was giving her difficulties. During the *exploration phase* of her research—about a month—she kept a journal, noting the daily events in each class and especially the class on which she was focused. She studied student records in order to construct profiles of the students in each of her algebra classes. She asked a colleague to observe her teaching, to note patterns of disruption, and to record how she handled disruptions. She administered a survey to her students in order to get their input on what was causing discipline problems in the class. During the on-going *discovery phase* of her research, she discovered that the problem was not really discipline at all. Yes, a few troublemakers were clearly identified in her colleague's observation,

| FIGURE 13.1 | A Five-Phase Model for Doing Action Research (Powell, Zehm, & Garcia, 1996) |

Phase	Description
Description and Speculation	Begin this phase by asking questions about some dimension of your teaching. Examples of questions you might pose for your selected topic include: What is happening here? What are the dimensions of this topic? Which dimension seems to be the most pressing or critical? What might happen if I changed something?
Exploration	Ask yourself additional questions about your topic. For example: What is already known about this problem? What have others done? Locate readings, jot down notes, and develop a plan for carrying out the project.
Discovery	Discovery actually occurs throughout the research project as you attain new insights from your reading, observations, and data collection.
Reflection and Modification	Begin developing a report of your research. Reflect upon your personal beliefs, your teaching practice, and your classroom or school environment. Modify them in light of your findings.
Description and Speculation	Consider what you have learned from your research project and pose questions that lead to additional research.

From *Field Experience: Strategies for Exploring Diversity in Schools* by R. R. Powell, S. Zehm, and J. Garcia, 1996, Englewood Cliffs, NJ: Merrill/Prentice Hall.

but the real problem was student learning. She discovered that many of the students in this class were repeating algebra. Thus, students differed greatly in motivation, skill, and maturity, and even age. From the student surveys and subsequent class discussions, the teacher found that many of the students did not learn well from her style of teaching. While she preferred to work numerous illustrative problems on the board, a number of students said they could not concentrate when she did this. They preferred to work problems quietly at their seats. Having examined all the data, the teacher changed her classroom instruction—the *reflection and modification phase* of her research. She began using heterogeneous cooperative groups, mixing students with different levels of motivation and maturity. She gave students choices for solving problems: those who wished could cluster around her when she worked problems at the board; others could work independently at their seats. Her discipline problems almost disappeared as a result of these changes. Furthermore, her research project affected her own attitude toward the class. She stepped back and took an analytical approach, viewing the situation as a problem to be solved, not a struggle for control. In the final phase of her project, *description and speculation,* the teacher decided that she would make journal-keeping and regular feedback from students a permanent part of her teaching. She grew curious about gender differences in students' learning of mathematics and about the performance of minority students in her classes. Today this teacher continues to study her classroom practices, illustrating how even a small-scale action research project can improve conditions for teaching and learning.

Action research offers an effective and rewarding way for teachers to address difficulties they experience in the school and classroom. First, it modifies the strategy schools have traditionally followed—administrators and consultants telling teachers what to do—by placing teachers in control of their classrooms. By accepting the notion that they control the success they have in the classroom, teachers are more inclined to act on what occurs about them and to assume the role of researchers when they experience a classroom problem. They use their preparation and experience to conceptualize a problem, offer a means of addressing it, and embark on a solution. If you find this strategy attractive and it increases your success in the classroom, adopt it as one of many available to you when addressing classroom challenges.

▌▌▌ PROFESSIONAL ASSOCIATIONS

As a preservice teacher, you can observe and experience firsthand the advantages of joining and becoming an active member of professional education organizations. In this section, we will discuss both general professional organizations with a broad base of membership and subject-area professional organizations whose membership consists primarily of teachers in a specific field (see Figure 13.2).

The American Federation of Teachers (AFT) and the National Education Association (NEA) are organizations concerned with the status of teaching, learning, and education in general. These organizations keep abreast of national and state initiatives, pending legislation, and other matters relating to education. Because they are teacher organizations, they concern themselves with teacher working conditions and salaries. At the local level, they may be involved in teacher salary negotiations, contract disputes, and other related issues. These organizations monitor and play a role in issues relating to initiatives and legislation related to curriculum, certification, teacher and student evaluation, and other related matters (e.g., Shanker, 1996). Many colleges and universities have local chapters of these organizations that provide services to preservice teachers. For example, at the University of Illinois the local chapter of the NEA, the Illini Education Association, is quite active. Among the services offered by the Illini Education Association are: an introduction to teacher education and specific information on individual programs; advice on transitioning from the College of Liberal Arts to the College of Education; programs that describe contemporary issues of interest (e.g., certification, state legislation, state and local initiatives); speakers versed on the challenges and problems encountered in today's classrooms; suggestions on preparing to assume a teaching position.

Kappa Delta Pi is an education honor society with 60,000 active members across the country. Selection to Kappa Delta Pi is based on high academic achievement, a commitment to education, and a professional attitude that assures steady growth in the profession. The organization sponsors recognition programs, such as the National State Teachers of the Year, the National Teachers Hall of Fame, the National Student Teacher of the Year, and a host of community service projects.

Subject-specific professional organizations, such as the National Council for the Social Studies (NCSS), National Council of Teachers of Mathematics (NCTM), and the National Council of Teachers of English (NCTE), offer many benefits to preservice teachers. Among them are: access to journals and books published by the organization; opportunity to attend state and national conferences at discounted rates; opportunity to network with other professionals in your field; access to forums, such as electronic discussion groups, on current and enduring issues in the teaching of your subject.

FIGURE 13.2   Selected Professional and Subject Area Organizations

The Arts
Music Teachers National
Association
The Carew Tower
441 Vine Street, Suite 505
Cincinnati, OH 45202-2814
513-421-1420
http://www.mtna.org

Civics and Government
The Center for Civic Education
5146 Douglas Fir Road
Calabasas, CA 91302
818-591-9321
http://www.civiced.org

Economics
The National Council on
Economic Education
1140 Avenue of the Americas
New York, NY 10036
212-730-7007
http://www.nationalcouncil.org

Foreign Language
American Council on the
Teaching of Foreign
Languages
Six Executive Plaza
Yonkers, NY 10701-6801
914-963-8830
http://www.actfl.org

Geography
National Council for
Geographic Education
Indiana University of PA
16A Leonard Hall
Indiana, PA 15705-1087
724-357-6290
http://www.ncge.org

**Health/Physical Education,
Recreation and Dance**
American Alliance for Health,
Physical Education, Recreation
and Dance
1900 Association Drive
Reston, VA 20191
703-476-3400
http://www.aahperd.org

History
The National Center for History in
the Schools
Department of History
University of California,
Los Angeles
6339 Bunche Hall
405 Hilgard Avenue
Los Angeles, California 90095-1473
310-825-4702
http://www.sscnet.ucla.edu/nchs

Language Arts
The International Reading
Association
800 Barksdale Road
P.O. Box 8139
Newark, DE 19714-8139
302-731-1600
http://www.reading.org

The National Council of Teachers
of English
1111 W. Kenyon Road
Urbana, Illinois 61801-1096
217-328-3870
http://www.ncte.org

Mathematics
National Council of Teachers of
Mathematics
1906 Association Drive
Reston, VA 22091-9988
703-620-9840
http://www.nctm.org

Science
National Science Teachers
Association
1840 Wilson Boulevard
Arlington, Virginia 22201-3000
703-243-7100
http://www.nsta.org

Social Studies
National Council for
the Social Studies
3501 Newark St. NW
Washington, DC 20016
202-966-7840
http://www.ncss.org

Technology Education
International Technology
Education Association
1914 Association Drive,
Suite 201
Reston, Virginia 20191-1539
703-860-2100
http://www.iteawww.org

Business
National Business Education
Association
1914 Association Drive
Reston, VA 20191-1596
703-860-8300
http://www.nbea.org

Subject area and general professional organizations actively recruit preservice teachers. University and college sponsors of these organizations encourage preservice teachers to begin their careers by joining an organization and becoming involved in professional activities. Preservice teachers attend workshops, and local, state, and national meetings and learn first-hand about their subject area and education as a profes-

The National Education Association (NEA) holds local, state, national and international meetings to discuss problems and challenges, such as professional standards, academic freedom, and testing and evaluation.

sion. School district recruiters who visit colleges and universities to attend job fairs view positively the professional activities of new teachers.

▍▐ MENTORS, NETWORKS, AND SUPPORT GROUPS

Many of the student teachers with whom I have worked over the years who have become highly successful professionals were individuals who developed a mentoring relationship with experienced teachers. What is a mentor? What does it mean to become involved in a mentoring relationship?

The concept of mentor is as ancient as the Greeks, perhaps older. Homer describes Mentor "as the 'wise and trusted counselor' whom Odysseus left in charge of his household during his travels. Athena, in the guise of Mentor, became the guardian and teacher of Odysseus' son Telemachus" (National Academy of Sciences, 1997, p. 1). In its broadest sense, a mentor is "someone who takes special interest in helping another person develop into a successful professional" (p. 1–2).

Mentors provide guidance and support as they bring out the best in an individual. They can be teachers, friends, family members, peers, or others who have knowledge and experience in a particular area. Mentors know and respect you, wish to see you grow professionally, and are willing to commit the time to nurture a relationship with you. There are as many ways to select a mentor as there are individuals searching for mentors. Because mentoring is about bringing out the best in an individual, it is a learning relationship. Mentors do not rubber-stamp the actions and behaviors of a preservice teacher; nor does a preservice teacher become a mentor's clone.

Novice teachers can learn much from mentors: how to organize units, develop lesson plans, employ a variety of teaching strategies, and other skills related to sound pedogogy. In addition, a mentor can help one develop positive habits of mind: introspection, a willingness to admit mistakes and seek help, acceptance of constructive criticism, adoption of an analytical approach to classroom problems, and recognition that becoming an excellent teacher is a lifelong process.

When seeking a mentor, we advise you to select a teacher who is respected by his or her peers, whose ideas about teaching and subject matter are similar to yours, and who respects you and shows interest in helping you enter the profession. It is also important to choose someone who is honest, who will not hesitate to offer you positive reinforcement and constructive criticism about your professional behavior in and outside the classroom. The best mentors are those who model the thinking and behavior that you need to understand in order to become an effective and reflective teacher (Tatum & McWhorter, 1999).

A number of states have implemented formal mentoring programs to ease the difficulties associated with the first year of teaching. For example, the California Formative Assessment and Support System (CFASST) pairs beginning teachers with experienced teachers in order to reflect on student achievement. Through a series of inquiries and observations, beginning teachers learn a process for improving their own teaching. Mentors benefit as well by gaining new skills in observation, assessing teaching, and applying standards to practice (Olebe, Jackson, & Danielson, 1999). Similarly, the Kentucky Teacher Internship Program aims to "nurture and retain good teachers by providing *all* beginning teachers with meaningful mentoring to help them develop the necessary skills to become more effective" (Brennan, Thames, & Roberts, 1999, p. 49). Beginning teachers (interns) in Kentucky work with a committee of individuals—a resource teacher, the school principal, and a teacher educator—throughout the first year of teaching. Interns demonstrate through practice, portfolios, and conferences with their committee members that they are progressing toward meeting the Kentucky New Teacher Standards.

Recently, the National Council of Teachers of English (NCTE) launched an on-line mentoring initiative, TEACH2000. TEACH2000, designed to benefit both new and experienced teachers, provides e-mailed "cyber-briefs" (resources of special interest to new teachers), an on-line "teachers' lounge," teaching ideas, interactive discussions, and "cyber-mentors" (McCullough, 1999). A number of other listservs and Web sites are geared to beginning teachers.

Finally, new teacher support groups can "offer a safe place where beginning teachers can voice their concerns, share their joys and frustrations, and help one another deal with problems" (Rogers & Babinski, 1999 p. 38). New Teacher Groups, a project for novice teachers in central North Carolina, convene biweekly to engage in group problem-solving. An outside facilitator helps participants work through the problems they bring to the table. The New Teacher Group project suggests that peers can play an important role in supporting one another through the beginning years of teaching.

■ ■ NATIONAL BOARD FOR PROFESSIONAL TEACHING STANDARDS

Historically, teachers have had few opportunities or incentives to hone their craft while staying in the classroom. Many have found that the only career ladder available led them out of the classroom and into administration. Financial rewards for teaching have been based primarily upon longevity and/or acquiring graduate credit hours in education. As plans for educational reform have been formulated over the years, little thought has been given to improving education by recognizing outstanding teachers for their work or encouraging teachers to improve their teaching.

In the late 1980s, however, government, university, business and foundation leaders, and concerned citizens came together to find ways of improving America's schools. The group formed the non-partisan National Board for Professional Teaching Standards (NBPTS). The Board, composed mostly of teachers committed to improving schools by strengthening teaching as a profession, has a three-part mission: (1) to establish high and rigorous standards for what accomplished teachers should know and be able to do; (2) to develop and operate a national voluntary system to assess and certify teachers who meet these standards; and (3) to advance related education reforms for the purpose of improving student learning in American schools (NBPTS, p. 1).

Over the last decade, the NBPTS turned to educational leaders to develop standards in each of the major subject areas and in the major student developmental levels (i.e., early childhood, middle childhood, early adolescence, and adolescence and young adulthood). Assessments and a scoring system have been developed in order to identify teachers' proficiency at meeting the standards. Teachers who meet the Board's standards are recognized as accomplished teachers and awarded advanced certification. Today, many states, districts, and education organizations are encouraging teachers at all grade levels and in all subject areas for which advanced certification has been developed to take on this challenge. In many cases, teachers receive guidance on how best to prepare for the rigorous assessments and financial support to pay the costs of the process. Teachers who are awarded advanced certification often receive financial rewards as well as community and national recognition for their achievement (Buday & Kelly, 1996; Roth, 1996).

■ ■ PUTTING TOGETHER YOUR BIOGRAPHY, YOUR PERSONAL PRACTICAL PHILOSOPHY, AND PORTFOLIO

You should now be able to complete your educational biography, your personal practical philosophy, and portfolio. If your instructor has provided you with a rubric to follow when completing these three tasks, you may wish to disregard the suggestions provided below. However, if you are looking for guidance, you may want to read on. We suggest you begin by reviewing the activities and end-of-chapter exercises that highlighted key ideas that should be part of a biography, educational philosophy, and portfolio. In addition, you may have other ideas about what you would like to include in these documents.

An autobiography is a portrayal of self. It describes your past and present experiences and tells how these experiences have influenced your process of becoming a teacher (Clandinin & Connelly, 1995). It should also relate some of your interactions with adults and adolescents and reveal your perceptions about education and schooling. You may wish to include summaries of and reflections on your experiences with diversity and education, curriculum and the use of the textbook in the classroom, technology in schools, test-taking experiences, and communities and community building.

An educational philosophy represents your views on education and schooling, adolescents, learning, knowledge, and evaluation. It also describes your role in the classroom and definition and purpose of your subject area. In your personal, practical philosophy about education and the role of the teacher, include reflections on the following: teaching in a pluralistic society; the past, present, and future of multicultural education; definitions of curriculum; educational tools for middle- and high-school instruction; assessment, and evaluation; and building community in culturally diverse settings.

A working portfolio should include documents that represent you (i.e., autobiography and educational philosophy) and that highlight your accomplishments as you progress through your teacher education program. Moreover, it should include some of your attempts to address important issues related to instructional planning, implementation, and assessment. Some of the components of your portfolio might include your thoughts on multicultural education; your reflections on your strengths and weaknesses in the area of diversity; an outline of your experiences examining curriculum documents; an evaluation of curriculum resources; your mini-digital library; your examination of different methods of assessing your subject area; and an explanation of the methods you would use to build community in your classroom.

▮▮ SUMMARY

In this chapter we focused on methods and strategies to help you experience success in the classroom throughout your professional career. We began by suggesting introspection as a means of better understanding self and self in a classroom (e.g., autobiography and personal practical philosophy). We then suggested strategies aimed at empowering teachers to "become" rather than to "be." We concluded by encouraging you to complete an autobiography, a personal practical philosophy, and a portfolio. These three tasks offer you the opportunity to synthesize your learning at this point in your teacher education program.

References

Brennan, S., Thames, W., & Roberts, R. (1999). Mentoring with a mission. *Educational Leadership, 56* (8), 49–52.

Brubacher, J. W., Case, C. W., & Reagan, T. G. (1994). *Becoming a reflective educator: How to build a culture of inquiry in schools.* Thousand Oaks, CA: Corwin Press.

Buday, M. C., & Kelly, J. A. (1996). National Board Certification and the teaching profession's commitment to quality assurance. *Phi Delta Kappan, 78* (3), 215–219.

Bullough Jr., R. V., Knowles, J. G. & Crow, N. A. (1992). *Emerging as a teacher.* New York: Routledge.

Clandinin, D. J. & Connelly, F. M. (1995). *Teachers' professional knowledge landscapes.* New York, NY: Teachers College Press.

Cochran-Smith, M. and Lytle, S. L. (1993). *Inside outside: Teacher research and knowledge.* New York: Teachers College Press.

Colsant, L. C. (1995). "Hey, man, why do we gotta take this?" Learning to listen to students. In J. G. Nicholls & T. A. Thorkildsen (Eds.), *Reasons for learning: Expanding the conversation on student-teacher collaboration* (pp. 62–89). New York: Teachers College Press.

Goodlad, J. I., Soder, R., & Sirotnik, K., (Eds.) (1990). *Places where teachers are taught.* San Francisco, CA: Jossey-Bass.

Hubbard, R. S., & Power, B. M. (1993). *The art of classroom inquiry: A handbook for teacher-researchers.* Portsmouth, NH: Heinemann.

Lakoff, G. & Johnson, M. (1980). *Metaphors we live by.* Chicago, IL: University of Chicago Press.

McCullough, K. (1999). New teachers enthusiastic about TEACH2000. *The Council Chronicle, 9* (2), pp. 1 & 7.

National Academy of Sciences. (1997). *Advisor, teacher, role model, friend: On being a mentor to students in science and engineering.* Washington, DC: National Academy Press.

National Board for Professional Teaching Standards. (1996). *Social Studies-History: Standards for National Board Cerrtification.* Washington, DC: Author.

Olebe, M., Jackson, A., & Danielson, C. (1999). Investing in beginning teachers—the California model. *Educational Leadership, 56* (8), 41–44.

Powell, R. R., Zehm, S., & Garcia, J. (1996). *Field experience: Strategies for exploring diversity in schools.* Upper Saddle River, NJ: Merrill/Prentice-Hall.

Rogers, D. L., & Babinski, L. (1999). Breaking through isolation with New Teacher Groups. *Educational Leadership, 56* (8), 38–40.

Roth, R. A. (1996). Standards for certification, licensure, and accreditation. In J. Sikula, T. Buttery, & E. Guyton, (Eds.), *Handbook of research on teacher education,* 2nd ed., pp. 242–278. New York: Macmillan.

Schon, D. A. (1987). *Educating the reflective practitioner: Toward a new design for teaching and learning in the professions.* San Francisco, CA: Jossey-Bass.

Shanker, A. (1996). Quality assurance: What must be done to strengthen the teaching profession. *Phi Delta Kappan, 78* (3), 220–224.

Spalding, E. (1997). "Swallowing an elephant:" The subject perspectives of selected novice English teachers. In D. M. Byrd & D. J. McIntyre, (Eds.), *Research on the education of our nation's teachers,* (pp. 172–188). Thousand Oaks, CA: Corwin Press.

Sprinthall, N. A., Reiman, A. J., & Thies-Sprinthall, L. (1996). Teacher professional development. In J. Sikula, T. Buttery, & E. Guyton, (Eds.), *Handbook of research on teacher education,* 2nd ed., pp. 666–703. New York: Macmillan.

Tatum, B. & McWhorter, P. (1999). Maybe not everything, but a whole lot you always wanted to know about mentoring. In P. Graham, S. Hudson-Ross, C. Adkins, P. McWhorter, & J. McDuffie Stewart, (Eds.), *Teacher/Mentor: A dialogue for collaborative learning,* pp. 21–33. New York: Teacher College Press.

Vacca, R. T., Vacca, J. L., & Bruneau, B. (1997). Teachers reflecting on practice. In J. Flood, S. B. Heath, & D. Lapp, (Eds.), *Handbook of research on teaching literacy through the communicative and visual arts,* pp. 445–450. New York: Macmillan.

Websites

http://teachnet.org

TeachNet.org is the WorldWide Web site for IMPACT II—The Teachers Network, a national nonprofit organization that supports classroom teachers in teh United States. The site contains links to many teaching resources, especially professional development resources such as mentors and teaching portfolios.

http://www.teachermentors.com
> This commercial site features over 1100 links and 100's of Web pages with resources, articles, research reports, tips and advice, events and other information on mentoring, induction, peer coaching, school improvement, staff development, and assessment.

http://www.aftky.org
> This is an example of a Web site of a state affiliate (Kentucky) of the American Federation of Teachers.

http://www.aacte.org
> This is the Web site of the American Association of Colleges for Teacher Education. Of interest to preservice teachers is information on professional development schools, mentoring, and teaching protfolios.

http://wwwnbpts.org
> The National Board for Professional Teaching Standards works to strengthen the teaching profession and to improve student learning. The Web site contains information of the Board's system of advanced, voluntary certification for teachers.

http://www.gowrie.k12.ia.us/highsch/latta/lattapag.shtml
> This site has links to many educational resources in both general education and specific subject areas.

INDEX